Abstracts of Montgomery County Pennsylvania

Wills and Administrations

1784-1823

Ellwood Roberts

HERITAGE BOOKS
2007

HERITAGE BOOKS
AN IMPRINT OF HERITAGE BOOKS, INC.

Books, CDs, and more—Worldwide

For our listing of thousands of titles see our website at
www.HeritageBooks.com

Published 2007 by
HERITAGE BOOKS, INC.
Publishing Division
65 East Main Street
Westminster, Maryland 21157-5026

Copyright © 1998 Ellwood Roberts

Other books by the author:

Biographical Annals of Montgomery County, Pennsylvania, Containing Genealogical Records of Representative Families, Including Many of the Early Settlers, and Biographical Sketches of Prominent Citizens

CD: Biographical Annals of Montgomery County, Pennsylvania, Containing Genealogical Records of Representative Families, Including Many of the Early Settlers, and Biographical Sketches of Prominent Citizens

All rights reserved. No part of this book may be reproduced or transmitted in any form or by any means, electronic or mechanical, including photocopying, recording or by any information storage and retrieval system without written permission from the author, except for the inclusion of brief quotations in a review.

International Standard Book Number: 978-1-58549-455-2

INTRODUCTION

These wills were abstracted under the direction of Ellwood Roberts, Norristown, Pennsylvania, and completed in 1911. This and the abstracts of wills and administrations of other Pennsylvania counties are part of the collection of the Genealogical Society of Pennsylvania which is housed at the Historical Society of Pennsylvania. Copies of these abstracts were made available to various libraries in Pennsylvania and microfilm copies made by the Genealogical Society of Utah (LDS). Recently bound photostat copies of the original abstracts were offered for sale by the Genealogical Society of Pennsylvania.

In making these abstracts of Montgomery County wills and administrations, Ellwood Roberts dictated to a stenographer as he read the wills and administrations at the Register's Office. Later she reproduced her notes in the manner as re-copied here.

We extend our appreciation to the Genealogical Society of Pennsylvania and encourage membership in the Society (1305 Locust Street, Philadelphia, PA 19107-5699), whose collections are mainly housed at the Library of the Historical Society of Pennsylvania (1300 Locust Street, Philadelphia, PA 19107). We encourage use of its holdings and facilities which are available at a modest fee.

F. Edward Wright
Westminster, Maryland
1998

REES, HANNAH. Upper Merion. Widow.
Sept 28, 1784. Oct 20, 1784. 1.1
To brother Hugh Richards 5 pounds. Rem. to Elizabeth Rees, daughter.
Execs: Isaac Richards, Joseph Roberts. Joseph Roberts to be daughter's guardian. Wit: Lindsay Coats, John Jones, Hugh DeHaven.

RICHARDS, JOHN. Upper Merion. Formerly of Radnor, Chester County, but at death residing with his brother in law, John Rees, Upper Merion.
Sept 23, 1784. Oct 20, 1784. 1.1
To sister Susanna, wife of John Rees, 20 pounds (exclusive of charge for care in my illness). Rem. to brothers and sisters: Susanna Rees, Hugh Richards, Richard Richards, Isaac Richards, Hannah Rees, Rachel Black in equal sharing. If plantation in Radnor is not the property of testator in fee simple, then Isaac Richards in the event of holding it, is to take nothing under the will.
Exec: John Rees. Wit: Lindsay Coats, John Evans, James Burk.

MEYER, JOHN. Douglass.
Sept 20, 1784. Oct 21, 1784. 1.2
To wife Anna Barbara. "Besides what I got with her by marriage" one third of personal estate during life, to live in house where I now reside, if she choose, along with my grandson Anthony Fuchs. Otherwise, he to repair the smith-shop for her to live in, to find her fire-wood ready cut, she to have 1/3 of the garden, 1/4 of an acre for Indian corn and potatoes, the apples of two trees in each orchard yearly her choice, a cow kept on the place, summer and winter. Said Anthony Fuchs to give her every year 5 bushels wheat, 5 of rye, 5 of buckwheat and to sow every year 1/4 of an acre with flaxseed for her use, but she to find the seed. To grandson Anthony, plantation in Douglass, 70 acres and 30 perches, subject to privileges of wife and subject to the payment of 400 pounds as hereinafter directed. To daughter Anna Mary, widow of Matthias Fuchs, 100 pds. To daughter Margaret, wife of Anthony Spees, 100 pds. To daughter Anna Margaret, wife of Peter Diener, 100 pds. To daughter Anna Catherine, wife of Andrew Young, 100 pds.
Execs: Bernard Gilbert, George Dengler. Wit: Peter Richards, Henry Engel, Bernard Gilbert.

BERNHARD, JACOB. Limerick.
Sept 28, 1784. Oct 21, 1784. 1.3
To son Jacob, 20 pds. To wife Christiana during her life the new back room in the house, her bed and her choice of utensils, chest, sermon book and flax. Sons Henry and Philip to find for her 3 bushels wheat and 3 of rye each, fifty lbs. of pork each every year, to keep a cow for her; to my wife also 1/3 part of all personal estate and my teacups and saucers. To son Philip, weaver's loom and my Bible. Residue equally divided amongst seven children: Jacob, Henry, Philip, Elizabeth, Charlotte, Susanna and Betty, as directed at length.

Execs: Wife Christiana Bernhard, son Henry Bernhard. Wit: Gottfried Longdein, Jacob Crous.

VOGELI, GEORGE. Douglass.
Aug 31, 1784. Nov 3, 1784. 1.4
To wife Philippina, my plantation, with grain sowed, "to rent out or have it tilled as she pleases", kitchen furniture, bed, cow, horse, mare saddle and bridle during widowhood. To son George and Conrad, the farm at her death. To son Nicholas, 5 pds. and the remaining part an equal sharing. To daughter Anna Maria, the housekeeping articles.
Execs: Sons Nicholas and John. Wit: Bernhard Gilbert, George Gilbert.

SCHNEIDER, GEORGE. Douglass.
Sept 23, 1784. Nov 4, 1784. 1.5
To wife Susanna, bed, bedstead and curtains, chest and her clothing, kitchen dresser, half personal estate and free living with fire-wood in room in upper story of my house. Execs. to sell farm if they see proper and Philip Christman or one of his exrs. or adms. to deliver Deed for same containing 128 acres, 1/3 the purchase money for farm sold to wife. The other 2/3 to children of my 4 sisters: Christiana, Elizabeth, Juliana and Margretha in four equal shares, one share to each sister's children.
Execs: Wife Susanna Schneider and Philip Christman. Wit: George Mock, Benjamin Meyer.

EVANS, JOHN. Whippen.
Sept 9, 1784. Nov 16, 1784. 1.6
To brother Josiah, wearing apparel. To niece Elizabeth Griffiths, wife of Hugh Griffiths, all cash money and out standing debts.
Exec: Hugh Griffiths. Wit: Resolve Smith, John Harry, William Custer.

GEORGE, GEORGE. Moorland.
June 22, 1784. Nov 17, 1784. 1.7
To granddaughter Catherine Hatterbachen, 50 pds. at the age of 21 years. Rest to two children George George and Magdalene. Exrs. to make Deed to son George for farm which he holds under agreement. N. B. granddaughter Catherine Hatterbachen, to have bed, bedclothes and chest.
Execs: Son George George, David Cumming, Geo. Rax. Wit: Edward Farmer, Rhoda Heart.

MARPLE, ELIZABETH. Moorland.
Oct 9, 1784. Nov 19, 1784. 1.8
To sons Benjamin, Enoch and Able Marple, one shilling each. To son Jacob, 5 pds. To grandson Nathan Marple, son of Jacob, 10 pds. when 21 years old. To daughter Pheby, riding carriage. To daughter Elizabeth, cow, featherbed, one-half bedclothes and half my lining cloth. To 3 daughters Pheby, Elizabeth and Amy, my wearing apparel. To son Nathan

his indebtedness, 160 pds., two cows, riding mare and rem. of household goods, all sums of money, but to pay debts and funeral expenses and the legacies to other sons and grandson.
Exec: Son Nathan Marple. Wit: Samuel Erwin, Elizabeth Yerkes.

SHEERMAN, JOHN. Moorland.
Sept 24, 1784. Nov 19, 1784. 1.8
To wife personal estate, house and lot in Phila. to be sold and lands in back parts of Pennsylvania. From the proceeds 10 pds. to William Morrison. Interest on balance to wife. At her death to brother Robert Sheerman's children, share and share alike.
Execs: Margerat Sheerman, John Mann, Samuel Erwin. Wit: Rebekah Yerkes, Daniel Howell, Jacob Craft.

WAGENER, MELCHIOR. Worcester.
Feb 7, 1784. Nov 29, 1784. 1.9
To Rosina Weegener 6 pds. To Ann Weegener, Christopher Weegener's widow, 6 pds. Forty pds. for the Poor of Schwenkfelders. To wife Gertraut, bedstead, bedding, furniture, clothes-press, walnut drawers, spinning-wheel, armchair and 3 other chairs. To son David, Berlegurger Bible. To daughter Anna Reumost, 50 pds., bedstead, bedding, furniture, best spinning-wheel and best new saddle. To son David Wagener, 179 1/2 acres in Worcester at 1200 pds., 450 pds. in his hands for maintenance for wife; at her death, divided among children and rem. of estate sold at public sale. To daughter Susanna, wife of Philip Clumberg, 25 pds. Rem. of estate 1/3 to son David, 1/3 to son Jacob in trust. One share to youngest daughter Anna. Son David to pay 100 pds. yearly to his brother Jacob and sister Anna until all is paid. "Divide in peace, live in peace, that you may die in peace is my last wish and desire".
Execs: Son David Wagener, Abraham Kreeble Sr. Wit: Owen Thomas, Henry Urmy.

EDGE, JACOB. Whitemarsh.
Nov 4, 1784. Dec 7, 1784. 1.11
To Abington Preparative Meeting of Friends 10 pds. to keep up burying ground fence. To Gwynedd Preparative Meeting 10 pds. toward finishing their meeting house. To 4 daughters: Ann, Mary, Susanna and Rachel after their mother's death 103 acres of land each an equal share thereof as tenants in common. To wife Margaret and 4 daughters rem. of estate to be equally divided among them.
Execs: Wife Margaret Edge, brother in law Jacob Paul and friend Jonathan Thomas. Wit: John Roberts, John Evans.

MEYER, GEORGE. Upper Salford.
Aug 23, 1784. Dec 8, 1784. 1.12
To sons George and Jacob farm of 53 3/4 acres and 20 acres in Rock Hill, Bucks County, with grist, saw and oil mills. They to pay 100 pds. each

year for 16 years, 200 pds. to remain in their hands, income to my daughters Margaret and Barbara in equal shares. To wife Catherine use of farm of 62 acres during widowhood. In case of marriage to have a third part. To daughters Mary and Sarah, who had portions, 5 shillings each. Rem. of 1600 pds. to be equally divided between my sons: George, Jacob, Henry, Samuel and Abraham and my daughters Margaret and Barbara.
Execs: Michael Scholl, Michael Hertzel. Wit: John Philip Wentz, Abraham Stout.

FRY, JACOB, SR. Towamensin.
Feb 28, 1782. Jan 7, 1785. 1.14
To wife Margaret, bed, bedstead, bedding, cow, mare, teatable and 40 pds. in household goods. Personal estate to be sold and wife given 50 pds. and the interest of 250 pds. If she marries, 150 pds. At her death to be divided among sons: Jacob, Joseph, George, William and Henry. If she choose, to live in my house and if not sons Jacob and Joseph to build her a house with four acres of land and pasture for her cow and mare. Jacob to use the mare when my wife has no use for her. Farm in Towamensin 220 acres, to be divided into 2 parts, that part on the side next to Skippack to be again divided into two parts. One-half of farm with the buildings on to son Jacob at the rate of 600 pds. To son Joseph 1/2 of the other half part. To son George, the other remaining half part. Joseph and George to pay 600 pds. for their part, but Joseph must make up to George what his part lacks in value. Sons to pay 50 pds. a year after becoming of age until all is paid. Rem. of estate including 1200 pds. for lands paid by sons to be equally divided among all my children. Younger children to be schooled out of estate sufficient to read and write.
Execs: Sons Jacob and Joseph Fry. Wit: Melchior Wagener, Gerred Godshalks.

LOT, HENRY. Moorland.
Dec 1, 1784. Jan 10, 1785. 1.16
Five shillings to each of son Peter's children and daughter Mary's children. Rem. to be equally divided among the rest of children: Stephen, Henry, Zepheniah and Leonard Lot and Latatia Carter. Daughter Latatia's share in trust. She to receive the interest. After her death the share to be paid to her daughter Prudey, wife of Daniel Coursen.
Execs: Zepheniah Lot, Stephen Lot, Daniel Coursen. Wit: John Hogeland, John Hogeland, Jr., Derick Hogeland.

HUGHES, MARTHA. Norriton.
Sept 1, 1784. Jan 10, 1785. 1.17
To nephew Evan Hughes, 5 pds. To sister Susanna, best featherbed, high post bedstead and sacken bottom, sheets, pillow-cases, looking-glass, silver buckles, pin cusion, hoop and chain, tablecloth and clothes, 3 napkins and one half of wearing apparel. To mother, feather-bed, bedstead, sacken bottom &c. and other half of wearing apparel. Rem. of estate to be equally

divided to brothers Michael and John and sister Susanna.
Execs: Michael Hughes and John Hughes. Wit: Miles Evans, John Supplee, Nathan Potts.

SHOEMAKER, ELLIN. Gwynedd.
Sept 24, 1784. Jan 19, 1785. 1.18
To husband Joseph, all land in Gwynedd, but to pay to little son, not yet named, when he is 21 years old, 350 pds.
Exec: Husband Joseph Shoemaker. Wit: Jacob Wismer, Evan Jones, John Gwiner.

MARKLY, JACOB. Skippack.
June 19, 1779. Jan 24, 1785. 1.19
To wife Barbara, bed, bedstead and bedding, pewter and earthen ware as she shall judge necessary, table, two chairs, two iron pots, teakettle and teatackling, towel, our present lodging room and kitchen for her use and the yearly interest of 150 pds. Son in law Jacob Brutzman to farm plantation as now for the third bushel. At death of wife plantation to be sold. To my daughter Eleanor, wife of Tobias Boganer, 5 shillings. All money to be divided into 11 equal shares. One share each to sons: Abraham, Philip and Isaac. One to 5 children of my daughter Zornica. One to daughter Christiana, wife of William Anits. One to daughter Elizabeth Benner. One to daughter Barbarah, wife of John Smith. One to daughter Rebekah, wife of Frederick Isaac. One to daughter Hanah, wife of Jacob Brutzman. One to daughter Caterine, and one to my two sons Abraham and Isaac for the use of ny daughter Eleanor.
Execs: Sons Abraham and Isaac. Wit: William Penevacer, Jacob Markley (cord wainer).

MORGAN, ENOCH. Gwynedd.
Dec 29, 1784. Jan 25, 1785. 1.20
To wife Sarah the use of dwelling with 90 acres during her life, at her death to son Enoch. To son Daniel, 50 acres with buildings. To son Edward, 33 acres of land. To daughters Mary and Meriam, 50 pds. worth of household goods equally divided. To wife all rem. of estate, at her death equally divided among 5 daughters: Christiana, Sarah, Hannah, Mary and Meriam.
Execs: Sons Edward, Enoch, Daniel Morgan. Wit: Job Spencer, John Evans.

GEYER, HENRY. Douglass.
March 27, 1784. Jan 28, 1785. 1.22
To son Henry, farm, money in loan offices and the money he owes. To daughter Caterine Wartman, utensils. Henry's portion I appraise at 700 pds., 250 pds. to be his, 50 pds. he has paid heirs of Matthias Richard. To daughter 20 pds. and rem. 380 pds. divided into 3 equal shares and Henry to pay one year after my death 33 pds. to Elizabeth Klein, second year 33

pds. to my daughter Caterine and the following year 33 pds. to daughter Margareth Betz and yearly 3 pds. until all be paid.
No exrs. being named in will, son Henry become administrator with will annexed. Wit: Conrad Smith, John Schmidt.

BALTY, JOHN. Pottstown.
Jan 13, 1785. Feb 29, 1785. 1.23
To wife Maria, house, furniture &c. To son Jacob, bible. To daughter of first wife Catherine, 12 pds. Rem. of personal estate to be sold and money divided thus: One-fourth to wife, the other 3/4 to three children: Jacob, Hannah, and Maria. Son Jacob to pay 30 pds. to his sisters Hannah and Maria when he becomes 21 years of age. Wife to receive income until son Jacob is 21. In case she marries, children to receive profits.
Exec: Vallentin Krauz. Wit: Jacob Bechtelle, Henry Warley, William Thomason.

LEVERING, WICKARD. Plymouth.
Feb 21, 1785. March 1, 1785. 1.24
To brothers Joseph and Benjamin all real and personal estate, except to nephew Able 10 shillings.
Execs: Brothers Joseph and Benjamin Levering. Wit: Jacob Peterson, Levi Bartleson.

STADELMAN, WILLIAM. Lower Merion.
March 15, 1785. March 21, 1785. 1.25
To wife Mary, 1/2 personal estate. To son Thomas, the other half. Wife to receive all income until son is 21. If son and wife die, to sister Elizabeth Paul and brother in law William Broades.
Execs: Uncles Wm. Staddleman, Hugh Jones. Wit: Hugh Jones, Thos. Johnston, George Horn.

PHIPPS, JOSEPH. Abington.
March 1, 1785. March 25, 1785. 1.25
To son in law George Fisher, 100 pds. To daughter Susanna, 150 pds. To son in law Stephen Mershon, 100 pds. To son Joseph, wearing apparel. To grandson William Coats, 20 pds. at 21 years. To sons John and Joseph, real estate, 33 acres to be equally divided.
Execs: Son John Phipps, son in law George Fisher. Wit: John Child, David Lockart, Thos. Levizey.

DAGER, PETER. Whitemarsh.
March 8, 1785. March 29, 1785. 1.28
To wife Catherine, stock, household goods and grain during widowhood. If she marries, to have 2/3. Rem. divided equally among children: Jacob, Peter, John, Barbara, Elizabeth, Christiana, Margaret, Mary, Sarah and Rachel.
Execs: Wife Catherine and son Jacob Dager. Wit: John Rynear, Daniel

Rynear.

ROYER, ELIZABETH. Providence.
March 3, 1785. April 5, 1785. 1.29
To son Michael, 1 shilling. To John, Elizabeth and Hannah Kepeler children of daughter 1 shilling each. To son John Royer and Elizabeth Catherine Royer, bed, featherbeds &c. Rem. to son John Royer.
Execs: John Royer, Benjamin Dismant. Wit: Thos. Ashenfelter, Michael Bowers, Benjamin Dismant.

COBLANZ, JACOB. Cheltenham.
Jan 17, 1781. April 5, 1785. 1.30
To wife Elizabeth all estate. Should she die without children to be equally divided among 3 relations: Peter Coblanz, David and Philip Coblanz.
Execs: Elizabeth Coblanz, widow, Bartholomew Mather. Wit: Isaac Cleever, Anthony Siddons.

HOLTZHOUSEN, CASPER. Upper Hanover.
Aug 12, 1784. May 17, 1784. 1.32
To son Jacob, farm in Upper Milford, North Hampton County and 3 shillings and the equal 5th part of rem. And 1/5 part of same each to sons Andrew and Michael Holtzhousen and daughters Anna Margaret wife of Hartman Dills, and Catharine, wife of Nicholas Shupping all of North Carolina.
Execs: Christopher Zigler, Jr., Wendal Weyant. Wit: Joseph Siegfried, Ludwick Gerber.

BARTLESON, SAMUEL. Norriton.
Dec 21, 1784. May 13, 1785. 1.33
To sister in law Jane Bartleson pair of blankets and swarm of bees. To nephew Samuel Bartleson all Continental money and spotted suit of clothes. Should he die in his minority his legacy to be given to his 3 brothers: Abner, Bartle and James Bartleson. To brother Henry all rem.
Execs: Brother Henry Bartleson and Henry Potts. Wit: Isaac Ellis, Isaac Shoemaker.

JONES, HANNAH. Gwynedd.
March 16, 1785. May 21, 1785. 1.34
To mother and sister Elizabeth and Mary all rem. of personal estate coming to me by father to be equally divided. To mother the side saddle. To sisters Elizabeth and Mary all land coming by father, the teatable, pewter, earthen ware and wearing apparel. To sister Mary a bond worth 5 pds., chest &c.
Exec: Jacob Histler. Wit: John Evans, William Maris.

CLEAVER, EZEKIEL. Gwynedd.
April 7, 1785. May 25, 1785. 1.35

To son Ezekiel, 200 acres in Virginia with buildings. To son Ellis and daughter Sarah 15 pds. each. To daughters Mary and Elizabeth 10 pds. each. Rem. of estate to 7 children: Ezekiel, Sarah, Ellis, Mary, Elizabeth, Peter and Martha Cleaver, equally divided.
Execs: Daughter Sarah, sons Ezekiel and Ellis Cleaver. Wit: John Cleaver, John Evans, Jr., Nathan Cleaver.

NORTH, ROGER. Providence.
Aug 27, 1784. June 22, 1785. 1.37
To wife Anna, 3 bonds, to the amount of 150 pds. and all household goods, except what is given to son George. The middle room in dwelling, to live with son Thomas. If she cannot, he to pay 15 pds. yearly to her. To son Samuel, 1 shilling. To 2 sons William and George, 20 pds. each. To 4 sons: John, Jossua, Roger and Caleb, 15 pds. each. To 4 daughters: Sophia, Sarah, Elizabeth and Ann 15 pds. each. To granddaughter Sarah Jordan, 10 pds. To son Thos. 70 acres with buildings and stock.
Execs: Sons Caleb and Thomas North. Wit: Elizabeth Dismant, John Dismant, Benjamin Dismant.

GRIESINGER, JACOB. Hanover.
Sept 27, 1784. June 11, 1785. 1.38
To wife Anna Catherine a maintenance or 10 pds. yearly. If she marries to have nothing. Son in law Christian Betz, who married my daughter Christiana, is not to inherit anything except his share and shall be divided among his children. To son George Leonard that sum which I gave him for Nicholas Young.
Execs: Son George and Leonard Griesinger and son in law Lawrence Siesholtz. Wit: Peter Munner, Nicholas Young.

EHMAN, GEORGE. Whitemarsh.
June 30, 1785. July 22, 1785. 1.40
To wife Agnes, 12 pds. and yearly income from farm, 14 acres and interest during her life from the sum of 150 pds. Henry Scheetz to become guardian of my wife. Exrs. to sell personal estate and 1/3 rem. to son George Ehman, 1/3 to daughter Catherine Calender's children, and 1/3 part to John Ehman. Exrs. to sell farm after wife's death the money together with 150 pds. to be equally divided into 3 parts. To son George 1/3 part. To son John 1/3 part and to daughter Catherine Calender's children 1/3 part; except 43 pds. to my sons George and John.
Execs: Sons George and John Ehman. Wit: Abraham Houser, Henry Doul, John Stanert.

BOULTON, EDWARD. Limerick.
July 10, 1785. July 30, 1785. 1.43
To wife Mary all things necessary. To son John Boulton, 50 acres of land. He to pay his sisters: Lydia Staut, Elizabeth Sower, Anna Rambo and Pheby Boulton the sum of 100 pds. equally divided. Rem. to my 3 sons:

Aaron Boulton, Levy and Nathan Boulton equally divided. They to pay their 4 sisters the sum of 220 pds.
Execs: John and Aaron Boulton, son in law Aaron Rambo. Wit: Gunne Rambo, Abraham Updegraff, Francis Hobson.

COULSTON, SAMUEL. Whitpain.
July 7, 1784. Aug 20, 1785. 1.44
To wife Elizabeth, use of estate. At her death to sons William and Israel. To daughter Priscilla White, 10 shillings, and to John White deed for 12 acres where he now lives. To daughters Abigail and Bulah 50 pds. each. To granddaughter Mary White, 3 pds.
Execs: Wife Elizabeth, son William Coulston. Wit: Mathias Shoemaker, Nathan Potts.

KINDIG, MARTIN. Franconia.
July 18, 1785. Aug 27, 1785. 1.46
To wife Susanna all things necessary. Farm of 80 acres to be let by exrs. until son is of age. Rem. to be sold. Exrs. to pay wife her maintenance. My 6 children to be under exrs. care. Rem. to 4 children in equal shares.
Execs: Henry Rossenberger, George Sholl. Wit: Jacob Oberholser, Andrew Hentz, John Barkey.

HOLSTEN, PETER. Upper Merion.
Sept 2, 1785. Sept 27, 1785. 1.48
To daughter Mary all estate real and personal. If she dies before she is 21, estate to be divided among 3 sisters.
Execs: Saml. Holston, Benj. Eastborn, Richard Miles. Wit: Jesse Roberts, M. Bower, Levi Priest.

JONES, JEHU. Lower Merion.
Sept 1, 1785. Sept 27, 1785. 1.49
Widow Catharine to convey to brother John half-interest in grist mill in accordance with prior agreement. Rem. divided equally between 3 daughters Margareth, Rebecca and Catharine. To nephew John Jones, 15 pds. at 21 years. Trustees, brothers Norris Jones, James Jones to "assist wife".
Exec: Widow Catharine Holsten. Wit: Lindsay Coats, Benjn. Brooke, Peter Rambo.

SYFRET, MICHAEL. Whitpain.
Dec 13, 1784. Sept 27, 1785. 1.50
To son Boltser, lot of 5 acres with buildings. To wife, Margaret, free recorse in house; in case of disagreement, son to find her meat, vegetables and grain. To son Bolster yougest mare. To wife Margaret two hogs, young cow, best bed, utensils, spinning-wheel. Rem. of estate to be sold, proceeds equally divided betwen wife and 4 children: George, Catharine, Michael and Bolster.

Execs: George Kreeger, Job Roberts. Wit: John Roberts, Michl. Gerret, Baltzer Yetter.

DUBRE, JACOB. Moreland.
April 26, 1785. Oct 18, 1785. 1.51
To wife Rebekah income of estate during widowhood. She to school 4 children: Jacob, Thos., Margaret and Rebekah. In case of decease or marriage of widow, estate to be divided among 4 children, except large silver spoon to son Jacob and 5 shillings to granddaughter Linda Palmer. Execs: Wife, Rebekah Dubre, David Parry. Wit: Thos. Hollowell, Will Penington, Jacob Penington.

HENDRICKS, PETER. Towamencin.
Oct 15, 1785. Nov 12, 1785. 1.52
To wife, Anna, household goods, value of 20 pds. To son Joseph, farm of 88 acres, he to pay 100 pds. within 5 years of testator's death and 100 pds. after wife's death. He to find her house room, fire-wood &c. To daughter Maria, 20 pds. To daughter Catharina, 20 pds. To daughter Margaret, 20 pds. To daughter Dorothe, 20 pds. To son Joseph, 20 pds and implements. Movable estate to be divided equally among 5 children. Execs: Sons in law Henry Climer, Daniel Shambach, son Joseph. Wit: Jacob Kolb, Henry Cassel, Benjn. Hendricks.

WENTZ, MAGDALENA. Upper Salford.
July 1, 1783. Nov 11, 1785. 1.54
Estate to be divided into 5 equal shares: one to deceased son Valentin's children; one to deceased son Jacob's daughter. Three other shares to living sons: Wendel, Peter and Philip.
Execs: Sons Wendel and Philip. Wit: Jacob Fillman, Christian May.

LONG, MARY CATHARINE. Widow of Elias Long. Marlborough.
Oct 2, 1773. Nov 11, 1785. 1.55
To daughter Anne Catharine, 33 pds. to be placed on interest and bed linen. Rem. to 5 children: Anne Catharine, John George, John Jacob, Joseph, and John Peter, each an equal fifth part.
Execs: Conrad Zimerman, Henry Bachman. Wit: Fridrick (X his mark) Miller, George Phil. (X his mark) Long.

LATCH, RUDOLPH. Lower Merion.
Sept 20, 1785. Nov 12, 1785. 1.57
To sons John and David all estate, they to maintain their grandmother, Dorothy Barlort and their mother, Mary Latch, during widowhood; if she marries, only legal dower. Two children Anna and George to be brought up. To daughter Ann Snider, 10 pds. To daughter Mary James, 10 pds. To son Jacob, 30 pds. To daughter Elizabeth Roberts, 20 pds. To daughter Hannah Latch, 20 pds. To son George, 30 pds. To granddaughter Mary Nosses, 5 pds. To grandson Wm. Nase, 5 pds.

Execs: Wife Mary Latch, sons John and David Latch. Wit: Phineas Roberts, John Jones, Isaac Roberts, Algernon Roberts.

EVANS, GEORGE. Limerick.
Aug 10, 1784. Nov 12, 1785. 1.58
To sons William and Amos. farm of 200 acres. To daughter Phebe, out of farm 400 pds. To son William 15 pds., loom and Sorrel mare. To son Amos, 75 pds., implements, 2 mares and horse. To daughter Phebe, 65 pds., wearing apparel, bedding, household goods. Rem. to be divided equally among 3 children.
Execs: Sons William and Amos and daughter Phebe Evans. Wit: Adna Evans, Mary Evans and Francis Hobson.

EMERSON, CHRISTIANI. Gwynedd.
May 13, 1785. Nov 14, 1785. 1.59
To sister Eve Weaver, house and garden for life. To John Dilcart and Eve, his wife (niece of testator) farm of 18 3/4 acres where testator lived.
Exec: John Dilcart. Wit: Jno. Martin, Geo. Heist.

MACKLEIN, JOHN. New Hanover.
June 23, 1781. Nov 14, 1785. 1.60
To wife Anna Margareth, necessary support according to agreement. To son Jacob, tools. Rem. to be divided equally amongst children.
Exec: Son Jacob Macklein. Wit: Leonh Griesinger, Marin Sensenderfer.

TREAT, REBECCA. Moreland.
May 7, 1785. Nov 14, 1785. 1.61
To son Joseph Leech all that he is indebted to me by first husband's will. To son Thomas Leech, all he is indebted to me, Bible, two silver spoons, and best chair. To son Samuel Leech, al lhe is indebted to me and gold buttons. To granddaughter Rebecca Leech (daughter of Samuel Leech) 6 silver spoons. To granddaughter Margaret Leech, pinchusion. Rem. of estate to son Isaac or his heirs. Money from Corporation in Phila. 1/2 to daughter Rebecca Erwin, the other part to two granddaughters the children of my daughter Mary, deceased.
Exec: Daughter Rebecca Erwin. Wit: William Bradford, Hugh Rea.

LEVERING, WILLIAM. Springfield.
Aug 8, 1785. Nov 16, 1785. 1.62
To wife Margaret, all personal estate and use of rents from house and lots. After her death to brothers and children of brothers and sisters. To Mary Marewine, 10 pds. To Methodist Society, 10 pds. for poor. To poor of Springfield, 10 pds. To brother Abraham Levering, 5 shillings, together with equal share.
Execs: Wife Margaret and brother Anthony Levering. Wit: Leonard Streeper, John Streeper, John Huston.

ROBERTS, LEVI. Norriton.
June 9, 1785. Nov 18, 1785. 1.63
To son Jesse all real estate. He to pay sisters Mary and Ruth Roberts 25 pds.; 10 pds. to Mary in one year and 15 pds. to Ruth at 18 yrs. To daughter Mary, case of drawers. To daughter Ruth, one dining table, and pewter. Rem. equally divided between two daughters.
Execs: Son Jesse Roberts, brother in law Roberts Evans. Wit: Joseph Roberts, Joseph Evans, Anthony Potts.

DENGLER, JACOB. Douglass.
July 7, 1785. Nov 28, 1785. 1.64
To wife Catharine, farm of 23 acres in Douglass with grain, household goods and farming tools for life. At her death to be sold; also bond of 17 pds. due from Peter Egner and 300 pds. Half 6 months after death of testator. The other half 4 years after his death. To son John Dengler, 230 pds. subject to deduction of 227 pds. 17 s. which he already received. To son George, 230 pds. with 22 pds. 14 s. deduction received. To sons Jacob and Henry similiar legacies with similiar deductions. To daughter Elizabeth, wife of John Schnell and daughter Catharine 225 pds. each. Rem. equally divided among 6 children.
Execs: Sons John and George Dengler. Wit: Frederick Beitenman, Peter Richards, John Richards.

SLINGLOOF, JOHN. Springfield.
Sept 22, 1785. Nov 29, 1785. 1.67
Estate to be sold and money equally divided among children: Joseph, Hannah, John, Samuel, Henry and Jesse Slingloof.
Execs: Son John and son in law Peter Stem. Wit: Christopher Ottinger, Alexander Loller.

SMITH, JACOB. Gwynedd.
Dec 7, 1782. Dec 13, 1785. 1.68
To son Jacob dwelling place, 101 1/2 acres. He to pay 100 pds. Not to be sold till after death of wife Elizabeth. She to live there and to be provided for by son Jacob. To wife Elizabeth, a cow and choice of beds and bedding &c. Rem. to be sold. One half of money to wife Elizabeth. The other half to son Jacob. To daughter Elizabeth, wife of David Marsh, 50 pds. and bond of 28 pds. To daughter Elizabeth's children: Jacob, Catharine, Elizabeth and Daniel, and her youngest 50 pds. equally divided.
Execs: Son Jacob and friend, George Heist. Wit: Daniel Bloom, Melchior Wagener.

COLFLISH (KALBFLEISH), HENRY. Upper Merion.
Dec 18, 1785. Dec 28, 1785. 1.71
To wife Barbara, household goods named and privilege in house during life, in care of sons: Mattis, John and William. To son Mattis, farm of 19 acres and 5 1/2 acres of woodland. He to pay son Henry 80 pds. To Mary

Saintman, daughter 26 pds., 13 s. 4 d. To son John, house where he lives and 41 1/2 cares of land and 5 1/2 acres of woodland. To son William 46 3/4 acres. He to pay to daughter Catharine 80 pds. To son Jacob 80 pds. to be paid by son John. To daughter Mary Saintman, 80 pds. to be paid by sons. To daughter Catharine, 80 pds. to be paid by son William.
Execs: wife Barbara, son Mattis Kalbfleish. Wit: John Jones, Peter Matson, John Johnston.

KROB, JACOB. Lower Salford.
Feb 25, 1785. Jan 13, 1786. 1.75
To wife Mary, household articles, she to live in house by garden during widowhood under care of sons. She to receive interest of 200 pds. during life. To sons Andrew and Samuel farm of 134 acres, stock &c. they to pay 600 pds. To son Abraham, 10 pds. Rem. to my 10 children in equal shares: Jacob, Abraham, Isaac, Andrew, Samuel, Catharine, Mary, Susannah, Elizabeth and Sarah, advances already made to be deducted from each share.
Execs: Sons Andrew Krob, Samuel Krob. Wit: Anthony Miller, Samuel Oberholtzer, John Barkey.

HENDRICKS, JOHN. Worcester.
Jan 28, 1781. Feb 28, 1786. 1.76
To wife Elizabeth, dwelling place until son John is 21. Then she to live in upper room. Wife to school 3 children. To son John, dwelling place, 60 acres, 40 acres in Worcester and 20 acres in Towamencin. John to have from farm 25 pds. Rem. divided among children: Mary, Margaret, Hannah, Elizabeth, Catharine, John and Susanna. Rem. to be sold. Wife to have 1/3 part, 2/3 to children.
Execs: Jacob Kolb, Herbert Cassel. Wit: Anthony Miller, Samuel Oberholtzer, John Barkey.

RIDERPOGH, BARBARA. Moreland.
Jan 27, 1786. March 20, 1786. 1.78
To daughter Sophia Road, new brass kettle. To daughter Rosina, large brass kettle, cupboard &c. To daughter Elizabeth, cotton coverlet. To granddaughter Elizabeth Road, the largest of 2 teakettles. To grandson, Michael Bekly, shoe buckles. To granddaughter Barbara Havner, shoe buckles and small teakettle. To daughters Sophia Road, Rosina Havner and Elizabeth Bekley rem. of wearing apparel, beds, bedclothes equally divided. Rem. to 3 daughters and sons in law equally divided.
Execs: Son in law John Havner, brother Lavance Sentman and Samuel Erwin.

WOMBOLT, CASPER. Whitemarsh.
March 16, 1785. March 28, 1786. 1.79
To wife Hannah, all real and personal estate during widowhood. If she marries 1/3 estate. Then estate to be divided among 4 children: Margaret,

Magdalena, Frederick and Elisabeth Wombolt as follows: to son Frederick, plantation I now live on; to daughter Margaret, 50 pds.; to daughter Magdalena, 50 pds.; to daughter Elisabeth, 50 pds.
Execs: Wife Hannah, brother in law Frederick Meller. Wit: Geo. Geiger, Philip Culp.

STIRKE, GEORGE. Abington.
March 22, 1785. March 28, 1786. 1.80
To wife Rebeckah residue of personal estate and plantation of 50 acres. After wife's death to Rebeckah Jones, wife of Ebenezer Jones to have farm. They to pay to son Henry Stirke, 20 shillings. To son James, 30 pds. To son Henry, 80 acres in Buckingham. To son James 40 acres in Buckingham.
Execs: Stephen John Wright and his son Joseph Wright. Wit: John Child, Jr., John Craft, Sarah Craft.

WAGER, JACOB. Plymouth.
Dec 13, 1785. March 31, 1786. 1.81
To wife Cartry [Gartry?], real and personal estate during widowhood. If she marries lawful dower. After wife's death movable estate to be sold and divided as follows: 1/3 to daughter Elizabeth Cooper, 1/3 to daughter Dillilah (otherwise Mary Miller), after her death to son Jesse's children. The other 1/3 part together with interest to daughter Hannah. After her death 20 pds. to be given to granddaughter Amy Cooper and rem. as follows: 1/2 to son Benjamin and other half between Jesse's children. To son Jesse farm next to Colley's after wife's death. He to pay to daughter Hannah 30 shillings a year during life. Rem. of land to son Benjamin after wife's death. He to pay daughter Hannah 30 shillings a year.
Execs: Wife Cartry [Gartry] and Jacob Evans. Wit: Atkinson Hugh, Nathan Potts.

BARKER, PETER. Providence.
Dec 15, 1785. April 10, 1786. 1.83
To wife Elizabeth, bed and bedstead. To heirs of son George, 1 crown. To son Peter, 1 crown. To son Philip, 1 crown. To Philip Barker's son, Peter, 5 pds. To son Frederick, 1 crown. To daughter Christina, 1 crown. To daughter Mary, 1 crown and to her daughter Betsey, 5 pds. To son Barker, farm of 55 acres and implements. Rem. to children: Elizabeth, Anna, Mary Sophia, Susanna, Catharine, Jacob and Dorothy equally.
Execs: Wife Elizabeth and son John. Wit: George Essig, Benedict Garber.

FREDERICK, GEORGE MICHAEL. Douglass.
June 22, 1783. May 10, 1786. 1.84
To son Peter, farm where he lives, in Northampton County, 129 acres. He to pay 25 pds. in two years. To son John, 3 tracts of land, one 29 acres 130 perches, the other two, 100 acres each. He to pay 188 pds. in two years. To son Michael Frederick, farm 100 acres 10 perches in Douglass.

He to pay 437 pds., 3 s. 3 d. to daughter Anna Mary, wife of Ludwick Schick; Rosina, wife of Yost Winchinger; Esther Frederick; and Barbara, wife of Moses Bower 162 pds. 16 s. and 9 d. each. Rem. to be divided amongst children: Peter, John, Michael, Anna Mary, Rosina, Esther and Barbara.
Execs: Sons John and Michael Frederick. Wit: Abraham Bob, Frederick Shienlin.

KRAUSS, VALENTINE. New Hanover.
April 2, 1786. May 18, 1786. 1.87
To wife Elizabeth, furniture, beds &c. with use of house and her maintenance during widowhood. Farm to be sold. One hundred pds. to wife provided Martin Bechtell, her father or his heirs shall not demand the sum of money owing me. Rem. to be equally divided among wife and 4 children: John, Henry, Daniel and Jacob.
Execs: Brothers in law John Swenk, Jacob Shanz. Wit: Jacob Bechtell, Adam Brant, Leonhard Hartranft.

HUGHES, SUSANNA. Norriton.
March 27, 1786. May 22, 1786. 1.89
To mother, featherbed &c. To nephew Evan Hughes, 5 pds. when 21. to brother Michael double coverlet, 3 silver spoons. To brother John, 3 teaspoons, &c. House and lot to be sold and interest given to mother. After her death rem. divided between two brothers Michael and John.
Execs: Brothers Michael and John Hughes. Wit: John Meredith, Nathan Potts.

CRESSMAN, JOHN. Franconia.
April 16, 1785. May 26, 1786. 1.90
To son Anthony, 250 pds. To John Cressman, 209 pds. To daughter Elisabeth, wife of Henry Hartman, 200 pds. To daughter Mary, wife of George Wissel, 200 pds. To daughter Catharine, her son William Mellinger, 100 pds. To daughter Hannah, wife of Cunrad Siple, 200 pds. To son Anthony, deed for plantation in Rockhill. Rem. to be divided among children. Farm and movable goods in Franconia to be sold.
Execs: Son Anthony and son's son Jacob Cressman. Wit: Daniel Wambold, David Wambold.

SMITH, CHRISTIAN. Abington.
July 7, 1781. June 28, 1786. 1.91
To wife Mary Susannah, all estate during widowhood. If she marries 1/3 part, rem. to her children Philip Seam and Elizabeth Seam.
Execs: Henry Sheetz, Andrew Redheffer. Wit: Wm. Wright, John Jacob Knoedler.

PETERS, JONATHAN. Abington.
March 8, 1786. Aug 3, 1786. 1.91

To mother Margaret Peters, 1 cwt. of wheat flour and 60 cwt. pork. If she remains a widow, her brother to support her. To Edith Peters, daughter of William and Jane Peters, 15 pds. To brother William, testators part of 60 acres of land and rem.
Exec: Brother William Peters. Wit: Phineas Waterman, Henry Butler.

BACHTEL, MARTIN. New Hanover.
July 18, 1786. Aug 28, 1786. 1.92
To son Jacob, farm, 100 acres and he to pay 330 pds. To son Daniel, home farm 200 acres and to pay 470 pds. To son Joseph, farm 73 acres and he to pay 140 pds. To daughter Anna, 70 pds. Rem. to 10 children, Jacob, deceased son Martin's children, Christian, David, Joseph, Mary, Samuel, Elisabeth and Anna.
Execs: Christian Bliem, Isaac Bechtel, John Barkley Sr.

DOTTERER, MICHAEL. Frederick.
Oct 10, 1783. Sept 29, 1786. 1.95
Children to have shares, except daughter Suffia Troxel. To daughter Suffia, 5 shillings. Rem. divided among 3 children: Mary Hefners, Margaret Dotterer and Mary Rife.
Exec: Conrad Dotterer. Wit: Thos. Fisher, Henry Worsheler, Adam Winteroth.

CUNNARD, JOSEPH. Whitpain.
Sept 17, 1786. Nov 20, 1786. 1.96
To wife Rebekah, use and profit of estate and money until youngest child is of age and then estate divided among 3 children and wife, children: Joseph, John and Rachel Cunnard.

SHEETZ, CATHARINE. Lower Merion.
Oct 22, 1786. Dec 4, 1786. 1.96
To children of son Benjamin Sheetz, Henry, Francis, Ann and Catharine 25 pds. to be divided. To Hester and Elisabeth Sheetz daughters of son William 5 pds. to be equally divided. To son Ellis, 5 pds. Rem. to sons Frederick and Conrad and daughters Catharine Kemmerer, Mary Stedgoon and Elisabeth Hembold.
Execs: Thos. Cochran, son in law George Helmbold. Wit: Anthony Righter, Jonthan Robeson.

DETWILER JOSEPH. Upper Dublin.
Oct 18, 1786. Dec 5, 1786. 1.98
To wife Elisabeth, 800 pds. to be paid her 3 years after son Joseph is 21, they to live on farm with stock and implements, until he is 21. To son Joseph farm and grist mill, 110 acres. He to pay 800 pds. and interest to his mother and 100 pds. to exrs. To daughter Mary 700 pds. on May 27, 1790, and profits of testators half of another grist mill and farm. Rem. to 5 children: John, Jacob, Susanna, Mary and Joseph.

Execs: Wife Elisabeth, son in law Jacob Reif. Wit: Morris Taylor, Thos. Potts.

CUNNARD, HENRY. Whitpain.
Sept 9, 1786. Dec 28, 1786. 1.100
To wife Elisabeth, room, furniture &c., use and profits of estate until second son is 21. After that 24 pds. yearly during widowhood. If she marries 12 pds. a year. To 3 sons: David, Jonathan and Streeper, real estate equally divided. To daughter Rebekah, 1/4 part of real estate with interest when 18. To son David, 10 pds. for 5 years for caring for mother. Rem. equally divided among 4 children.
Execs: Wife Elisabeth, son David, brother in law, Isaac Shoemaker. Wit: Daniel Yost, David DeHaven, Nathan Potts.

PENROSE, BENJAMIN. Whitpain.
Jan 24, 1779. Dec 29, 1786. 1.101
To mother Mary Penrose, horse, riding chair and harness. To Richland Monthly Meeting of Friends, all money due testator on book accounts, interest for schooling of poor Friend's children. To brothers: Jonathan, Joseph, John, William, Robert, Samuel, Jesse and sister Mary Fell, 10 acres in Whitpain. Rem. equally divided among 7 brothers and 1 sister.
Execs: Brother Robert and friend Owen Morris. Wit: Joseph Roberts, John Evans.

LUKENS, RYNEAR. Upper Dublin.
June 9, 1786. Dec 29, 1786. 1.102
To son Jacob, home farm, 116 acres. He to pay exrs. 100 pds. To daughter Elizabeth, 100 pds. To daughters Hannah, Sarah, Rebeckah, Mary and Elizabeth, aforesaid 100 pds. from son Jacob and all other money, bonds, furniture equally divided. Rem. equally divided among children.
Execs: Son Jacob and daughter Sarah. Wit: John Child, Joseph Lukens.

KUGLER, MATTHIAS. Limerick.
Nov 4, 1786. June 2, 1787. 1.103
To wife Elizabeth estate during widowhood. If she marries, to have 1/3 of profits of land which shall then be sold as well as personalty and equally divided among children.
Execs: Wife Elizabeth, Benjamin Dismant. Wit: Frederick Saur, Joseph Frey, Benjamin Dismant.

MAYBURRY, CHARLES. Montg. Co.
Nov 25, 1785. Feb 19, 1787. 1.104
To friends, Peter Aston and Charles Jolly, farm 121 acres in Bucks County in trust, for mother Ann Tea. Land in Berks County to be sold, to pay following legacies: Elizabeth Prockden, wife of Charles Prockden, Dorothy McKensie, widow of Robert McKensie, Elizabeth Johns, widow of Richard Johns, and Mary England, 100 pds. each. To Elizabeth, wife of

Peter Aston, Margaret Boon, wife of George Boon and John Jolly and Charles Jolly, 100 pds. each. To Samuel Langdale and Margaret Langdale, his wife, 100 pds. Rem. to brother Thomas Mayburry.
Execs: Brother in law Peter Aston, nephew Charles Jolly. Wit: Samuel Jago, William Moore Smith, James Willson.

TYSON, JOSEPH. Abington.
Nov 17, 1785. Feb 28, 1787. 1.105
To daughter Sarah Tyson, 12 acres of land and 50 pds. To son John Tyson, farm of 145 acres. Rem. equally divided between widow Agness, son John and daughters Rebecca and Sarah. In case of children's death without issue, real estate to brother Rynear Tyson's sons: Joseph, William, Rynear, Abraham; and John Tyson's sons Thomas and Isaac Tyson.
Execs: Rynear Tyson, brother in law, Thos. Hallowell, Thos. Leech. Wit: Benjamin Hallowell Sr., Wm. Tyson, Rynear Tyson, Siles Watts.

KELLER, MARTIN. Limerick.
Nov 13, 1786. April 16, 1787. 1.107
Estate sold and money divided. To daughter Anna, 20 pds. To daughters Susanna and Catharine, 60 pds. each. to daughters Bally and Packey, 70 pds. each. Rem. to 3 sons, John, Martin and Reinhard, equally.
Execs: Sons John and Martin Keller. Wit: John Herstein, Christian Berky Jr., John Berky Sr.

JONES, MARY. North Wales.
Feb 28, 1787. April 19, 1787. 1.108
To daughter Mary, featherbed &c. To daughters Elizabeth and Mary, 85 pds, due from Samuel Cunard equally and wearing apparel. To son Evan, 1/2 rem. To daughters Elizabeth and Mary, other half, equally.
Exec: Cousin James Hammer. Wit: Evan Jones, Anos Griffiths, Joseph Bates.

SPENCER, SARAH. Upper Dublin.
Feb 3, 1786. April 25, 1787. 1.108
To husband, James Spencer, land bequeathed by mother, Elizabeth Walton, in little Borough of Billet.
Execs: Husband James Spencer, George Richards, Enos Spencer.

ENGART, JOHN. Upper Dublin.
Feb 15, 1787. April 26, 1787. 1.109
To wife Mary, estate except sums mentioned to 4 children, as they come of age. To wife during life, should she marry, estate to be sold and dower given her only. To son Adam, 5 pds. To daughter Mary, 5 pds. To daughter Catharine, 5 pds. To daughter Anne, 5 pds. If widow marry, estate to be divided among 4 children.
Execs: Wife Mary Engart, John Jarret. Wit: Jacob Gilbert, John Stanert,

Jacob Houp.

GLUCK, PETER. Franconia.
March 9, 1786. April 28, 1787. 1.110
Farm of 115 acres in Franconia to Ludowig Pilger and Magdalena his wife, daughter of testator's deceased wife Mary. To son John Albrecht, 1 s. To son John Ludowig, previously provided for, 1 s. To Michael Kensert, stepson of deceased wife, 1 s. To Valentine Kensert, 1 s., and Andrew Kensert, 1 s. To stepdaughter, Elizabeth, 1 s. To daughter Mary Barbara, 1 s. To daughter Catharine, wife of Henry Keyser, 1 s. To stepdaughter Margareth, wife of Cunrad Hefentrager, 1 s. Rem. of estate to stepdaughter Magdalena Pilger.
Exec: Ludowig Pilger. Wit: Frederick Rudy, John Barnd, Adam Sharer.

AMAN, AGNES. Whitemarsh.
April 22, 1787. May 2, 1787. 1.112
To grandson George, son of John Aman, 6 pds., with interest when of age. Rem. with money from husband, George Aman's estate to brother Jacob Rush.
Exec: Henry Sheetz. Wit: Isaac Cleaver, John Stanert.

TOMKINS, JOHN. Moreland.
Oct 7, 1784. May 7, 1787. 1.112
To wife Elizabeth, home farm, furniture and farm purchased from Elizabeth Ferguson in Horsham. After wife's death to Sarah Johnston, wife of William Johnston and Hannah Waterman, wife of Humphrey Waterman and Mary Young, wife of William Young and Elizabeth Gilbert, spinster, children of former wife Abigail, estate equally divided.
Exec: wife Elizabeth Tomkins. Wit: Abel Wells, William Moland, Henry Puff.

DRUMBORE, ANDREW. Franconia.
Feb 7, 1787. May 31, 1787. 1.113
To wife Louisa, cow, furniture &c. To daughter Sophia Drollinger, wife of Peter Drollinger, 5 acres, during life, to be sold and money equally divided among her children at her death. To daughter Catharine Mock, 60 pds. Rem. to be sold. Income of 300 pds. to be for wife's maintenance. To son John, 50 pds. of rem. Rem. to be divided among sons: John, Jacob, George, Andrew and Henry, except 10 pds. to be paid to daughter Sophia.
Execs: Sons John and George Drumbore. Wit: Christian Leidich, Abraham Stout.

MAYER, CHRISTIAN. Franconia.
April 26, 1782. May 31, 1787. 1.114
To wife Magdalena, 125 pds. &c. To Congregation to which testator belonged, 10 pds. for poor and needy. To Philip Lauterbach, 5 pds. To son Samuel Mayer, farm of 170 acres. He to pay 800 pds., 75 pds. yearly until

all is paid. Rem. to children equal shares, sums already received to be deducted. One seventh part to son Christian, 1/7 part to greatgranddaughter. Margaret Mayer, 1/7 part to son Samuel, to sons in law John Krotz, Abraham Krotz and Martin Detwiler, 1/7 part each, to daughter Esther Gehman's children 1/7 part.
Execs: Son Samuel Mayer, son in law Abraham Krotz. Wit: Isaac Dorstone, Abraham Stout.

PHILLIPS, JOSHUA. Upper Merion.
March 14, 1787. June 2, 1787. 1.116
To wife Sarah all estate, also negro wench "Nan". If she marries again, the furniture she brought with her and aforesaid "Nan" in lieu of Dower. To son Phineas, home farm, 100 acres. He to maintain daughter Jemima. To son Samuel, farm on Schuylkill, 124 acres. He to provide for son John. to daughter Mary 100 pds. from sons Samuel and Phineas.
Execs: Wife Sarah, son Samuel and brother Jonathan. Wit: Samuel Phillips, James Davis.

DERRINGER, THOMAS. Providence.
Feb 1, 1785. June 12, 1787. 1.117
To nephew John Derringer, 2/3 of land after wife's death, other 1/3 at wife's disposal. To wife Catharine rem. of plantation and land in Providence. To Jacob Buckwalter, deed for rem. of land. To brother Adam Derringer, 1 s. To sister Anna Elisabeth, 1 s. To Jacob Commins, sons of Catharine Commins, 25 pds. when of age. To wife rem. of all movable estate.
Execs: Wife Catharine, Daniel Longacre. Wit: Jacob Longacre, Jacob Good, Charles Couf.

PUGH, RACHEL. Montgomery.
March 9, 1784. July 28, 1787. 1.117
To sister, Sarah Hamer, real estate, wearing apparel &c. To niece, Martha Hamer, daughter of James Hamer, bed, bedstead and furniture. Rem. of movable goods to husband, John Pugh. Wit: Israel Jacobs, Sarah Hamer, James White.

DAVIES, EVAN. Gwynedd.
Dec 13, 1783. Aug 4, 1787. 1.118
To wife Hannah, use of estate until daughter Margaret is 18, then land 16 acres to be sold. to daughter Margaret, 100 pds. when 18. Rem. to wife Hannah. After her death to daughter Margaret. At her death to brother John's children.
Exec: Wife Hannah Davies. Trustees, Owen Hughes, Isaac Lewis. Wit: Johannes Delgard, John Evans.

PENNEBACKER, ADOLPH. Limerick.
Feb 14, 1760. Aug 11, 1787. 1.119

To 8 children: Henry Pennebacker, Mary Boyer, wife of Philip Boyer, John Pennebacker, Catharine Seypel, wife of Valentine Seypel, Eve, Elizabeth, Ledia and Martha Pennebacker, estate equally divided.
Execs: Sons Henry and John. Wit: John Pennebacker, Conrad Beidler, Nicholas Bunn.

BROOKE, JAMES. Limerick.
June 2, 1787. Aug 25, 1787. 1.120
To son Jonathan, 13 acres and saw mill in Hanover. To son Barnabas, 1/2 carpenter tools. Rem. to wife Mary during widowhood. If she marry to take under intestate laws; balance equally among children. If wife die unmarried, moneys equally among children: Owen, Mary, Elizabeth, Benjamin, Barnabas, Jonathan, James, Hannah, Ann, Ruth and Rachel. Each to be charged with sum already received.
Execs: Wife Mary and sons Benjamin and James. Wit: Jacob Brant, Matthew Brook, James Fennell.

EVANS, ELIZABETH. Limerick.
May 8, 1775. Sept 1, 1787. 1.121
To daughter Mary, wife of Enoch Evans, 5 s. To sons James and Samuel Evans, 40 pds. and half household goods and wearing apparel in trust. Other half use of daughter Mary for her children. To son William Evans, 20 s. To Sarah Hoven, daughter of John Hoven, 20 s. To Hannah, wife of Robert Shannon, 40 pds. and 1/2 household goods and wearing apparel. To son James, 7 pds. to son Samuel, rem.
Execs: Cousin James Evans, Samuel Evans. Trusteees, cousin James Brooke and Francis Hobson. Wit: Susanna Hobson, Francis Hobson.

YOCUM, MOSES. Upper Merion.
Sept 25, 1787. Sept 29, 1787. 1.121
To wife Martha, 1/2 profits of farm during widowhood, room and firewood. Farm to son William. To son Thomas, 10 pds. To Ann Ramsey, bed. To sister Margaret Supplee, 10 pds.
Execs: Peter Matson, Benjamin Ramsey. Wit: Lindsay Coats, Joseph Williams, John Roberts.

EIDEMILLER, NICHOLAS. Marlborough.
April 1, 1787. Sept 29, 1787. 1.122
To wife Catharine, estate during widowhood. If she marry 1/3. To son Jacob, goods brought by wife at her death. Rem. to daughter Catharine, wife of John Shuler, sons Jacob and Philip and heirs of son Michael Eidemiller. To son Michael, who has been undutiful, 1 s.
Execs: Jacob Karver, Henry Snyder. Wit: Christian Sheid, Michael Croll.

MUHLENBERG, REV. HENRY MELCHIOR. Providence.
June 12, 1782. Oct 16, 1787. 1.123
To wife Ann Mary during widowhood, estate including 7 acres in

Providence, 10 acres between George Diehl's and Andrew Miller's and lot near German Lutheran Church, 3 acres, 1/2 draw well between Mr. Badman's lot and whatever wife has from her deceased father Conrad Weiser. To daughter Solome, wife of Matthias Richards, 100 pds. Rem. at wife's death to 3 sons and 4 daughters.
Execs: Wife Ann Mary, sons Frederick A. and Ernest Henry Muhlenberg. Wit: Francis Swaine, Christian Streight, Matthias Richards.

MAUS, DOCTOR MATTHEW. Pottstown.
Aug 8, 1787. Oct 25, 1787. 1.124
To wife Charlotte, widow's legal share and household furniture &c. Rem. to children: Louisa, John Nicholas, Frederick Gustavus equally. To son John Nicholas, watch. To daughter Louisa, silver buckles. To son Gustavus, gold sleeve buttons. Wife to have above until children are 21.
Execs: Wife Charlotte, brother Frederick. Wit: James Thomason, George Beekley, Jacob Witz.

WYANT, WENDEL. Upper Hanover.
Dec 1, 1781. Nov 2, 1787. 1.125
To wife Magdalena, furniture and household goods &c. Rem. to children. Wife to live in house during widowhood. To son Yost Wyant, farm 168 acres. He to support wife during widowhood. She to receive yearly interest of 100 pds. Tract of land in North Carolina, 350 acres to be sold by exrs. and equally divided among testator's heirs. To son Jacob, 1 s. Son Jacob's children to have 1/7 part of estate. To eldest child of daughter Philippina, wife of Andrew Boyer, dec. and now wife of Henry Frick, 1/7 part. To young child 1/7 part. To son Wendel, 1/7 part. To son Yost, 1/7 part. To daughter Sophia, wife of Jacob Klotz, 1/7 part. To daughter Christiana, 1/7 part. Memorandum. As daughter Philippina has lost her dower from first husband to her 1/7 part.
Execs: Sons Wendel and Yost. Wit: Abraham Shultz, Joseph Siegfried.

BULL, WILLIAM. Norriton.
Feb 10, 1783. Nov 8, 1787. 1.127
To daughter Mary, house, cow &c. and negro girl "Philles". To daughter Elisabeth, wife of Christopher Stuart, farm occupied by Robert Archibald and negro girl. To daughter Rebecca, wife of Henry Pawling Jr. negro girl, Susannah. Rem. to be sold by exrs. and money equally divided among 3 daughters: Rebecca, Elisabeth and Mary.
Execs: Daughter Mary and son in law Henry Pawling Jr. Wit: Robert Curry, John Baker, Jacob Auld.

HOFFMAN, MICHAEL. North Wales.
April 24, 1787. Nov 9, 1787. 1.128
To wife Katharine, 50 pds., cow &c. income of 100 pds. To son William, 50 pds. Exrs. to sell land, 200 acres, and personal estate and money from same to 6 children: Peter, William, John, Daniel, Abraham and Mary

equally.
Execs: Thomas Shoemaker, Evan Jones. Wit: George Gossinger, Henry Hollman.

UPDEGRAVE, EDWARD. Perkiomen and Skippack.
March 11, 1775. Nov 24, 1787. 1.129
To wife Ann income of estate until son Joseph is 21. Afterward he to pay to wife yearly 7 pds. and maintenance. To son Joseph, 1 s. To son in law, Jacob Clemens, 1 s. To daughter Ann Clemens, 1 s.
Exec: Wife Ann Updegrave. Wit: John Lukens, John Edwards, Gottshalk Gottshalk.

BECHTELL, MAGDALENA. Hanover.
Dec 8, 1786. Nov 24, 1787. 1.130
Testator was widow of George Bechtell. Household goods &c. to be sold and money divided as follows: 10 pds. to son George Bechtell's son George when 21. Rem. to son Martin's and daughter Mary's (both deceased) children, to sons: George, Jacob, Abraham and daughter Magdalena's children.
Exec: Son George Bechtell. Wit: Jacob Bechtell, Daniel Bechtell.

RESE, HARRY. Hatfield.
Dec 4, 1787. Jan 9, 1788. 1.131
To wife Christiana a maintenance. She to keep bonds and notes during widowhood and receive interest from same. After her death to be equally divided among son Jacob and daughter Magdalena. To son Jacob, farm. He to pay to daughter Elisabeth's children, 200 pds. To daughter Magdalena, 200 pds. to be paid by son Jacob.
Execs: Wife Christiana and son Jacob. Wit: Jacob Reed, Conrad Leidy.

MILLER, JACOB. Upper Hanover.
March 6, 1786. Feb 26, 1788. 1.133
To son Leonhard, 5 pds. To wife Anne Margareth, farm in Upper Hanover, 3 tracts of land 240 acres &c until youngest child is 15 years. Children to sell farm and give wife 6 pds. yearly, otherwise she to live on farm and have a maintenance. If farm be sold, widow to have income of 300 pds. Rem. to 11 children in equal shares: Leonhard, John, Jacob, George, and William and daughters Margareth, wife of George Ultzfesser, Catharine, wife of George Miller, Christiana, Anna Elizabeth, Eva Elizabeth, and Elizabeth. To mother Anna Elizabeth, a maintenance from wife and children.
Exec: Wife Anne Margareth. Wit: Jacob Wistler, John Heis.

HARRY, REES. Gwynedd.
Dec 20, 1787. March 11, 1788. 1.134
To daughters Jane and Ann, 100 acres in equal shares, also moneys owing, room furniture and maintenance in charge of son Benjamin. To

daughter Lydia, house and lot where she lived. Rem. of land to son Benjamin. To daughter Sarah, 10 pds. to be paid by daughters Jane and Ann and son Benjamin. To son John, 20 s. to be paid by daughter Sarah. To son David and Benjamin, rights in disputed lots, daughters Jane and Ann to share with them. To son Benjamin, live stock, furniture &c.
Execs: Son Benjamin and daughters Jane and Ann. Wit: Owen Thomas, James Morris, Joseph Lewis.

SHUT, GEORGE. Perkiomen and Skippack.
Jan 19, 1788. March 20, 1788. 1.135
To wife Barbara, bed, furniture, plates, &c. and 5 pds. yearly during widowhood. To children: Magdalena, John and Rebeckah, each 9 pds. Rem. equally divided among children: Henry, Margaret, Elizabeth, Magdalena, John and Rebeckah.
Execs: Peter Kuster, Henry Pennebacker. Wit: Isaac Hunsicker, Henry Hunsicker.

WIREMAN, MICHAEL. Hatfield.
Jan 9, 1783. March 29, 1788. 1.137
To wife Sophia, maintenance, bed, furniture &c. during widowhood also 200 pds. If she marry said 200 pds. to be in lieu of dower. To son John, 10 pds. To son Henry, 100 pds. and remaining furniture. To sons: John, Henry, Martin, daughters Barbara, Mary and Catharine and Hester, each 100 pds. which each owes testator. To daughter Marharet [Margaret?], 100 pds. Rem. after sale of estate equally divided among said 8 children.
Execs: Wife Sophia and son John. Wit: Peter King, Abraham Ruth, John Funck.

LUKENS, JOHN. Horsham.
March 9, 1788. March 25, 1788. 1.138
To wife Dorothy, 25 pds. yearly. To grandson Azor, farm of 150 acres. He to pay 25 pds. yearly to wife. For repairing walls of burying grounds on Fitzwater land in Upper Dublin, 10 pds. in care of daughter in law Hannah. To Ann Davis, brought up by testator, 10 pds. To granddaughter Susanna, 1/3 rem. To granddaughter Deborah, 1/3 rem. To daughter in law Hannah, income of remaining 1/3. At her death to be divided among her 3 children: Azor, Susannah and Deborah.
Execs: Daughter in law Hannah Lukens, and grandson, Azor Lukens. Wit: James Spencer, Abraham Lukens.

LEVERING, ANTHONY. Lower Merion.
Feb 25, 1787. March 26, 1788. 1.139
To wife Agness, house and lot of 3 acres, during widowhood, also bed, bedding &c. and 10 pds. and 10 pds. yearly. To each of 5 daughters: Hannah, Elisabeth, Margrate, Abigial and Sarah, 140 pds. each paid, one, two, three, and four and five years after testators dec. To daughter Abigial, case of drawers, &c. To daughter Sarah, bed, case of drawers, &c.

To son Anthony, clock. Rem. of household goods, equally divided among son Anthony and 5 daughters. Rem. of estate including lot left to wife, to son Anthony, he paying legacies above.
Execs: Wife Agness, son Anthony. Wit: Paul Jones, Algernon Roberts.
Wife renounced in favor of son Anthony.

RICHARDS, CALEB. Norriton.
March 5, 1788. March 26, 1788. 1.140
To wife Rachel, whole estate. To brothers Hosiah and John Richards, wearing apparel equally.
Execs: Wife Rachel, Isaac Shoemaker. Wit: John Chican, Robert Shannon, Samuel Vanpelt.

JACOBS, BARBARA. Perkiomen and Skippack.
Dec 8, 1786. March 31, 1788. 1.141
To 4 sons: Richard, John, Anthony and Samuel, 20 s. each. To son John, warming pan. To daughter Christiana Cadwallader, spinning-wheel. All testator's diapers to 3 daughters: Rebeckah, Christiana and Mary for use of granddaughters and all linen to them equally divided. To grandson, Daniel Henry, 1 s. To grandson, Joseph Cadwallader, 10 pds. To daughters wearing apparel and silver. To granddaughter Barbara, silver spoons. Rem. equally to daughter Rebeckah Cadwallader's 3 children, daughter Christiana Cadwallader's 3 daughters and daughter Mary Rees's 3 daughters. Testatrix was widow of Richard Jacobs.
Execs: Sons John and Samuel Jacobs. Wit: Christian Gross, Israel Jacobs.

DAVIS, THOMAS. Upper Merion.
March 2, 1787. March 25, 1788. 1.143
One hundred acres and personal estate to be sold. To wife Margaret, goods, household furniture, she brought and liberty to build house on land unsold, and have interest of 100 pds. to be paid yearly during life and 25 pds. in cash. To daughter Catharine, 5 pds. To daughter Hannah, 10 pds. To daughter Sarah, 5 s. To daughter Susannah, 5 pds. To daughter Jane, 5 pds. To daughter Rachel and Mary 5 pds. each. To son Thomas, 10 pds. besides what he had. To grandson Rees Davis, son of Moses Davis, land used by wife. to Baptist Church, Tredyffrin, 10 pds.
Exec: Moses Davis. Wit: George George, James Davis.

ELLIS, ISAAC. Whitpain.
March 24, 1788. April 7, 1788. 1.143
Personal estate to be sold and money to be paid to 3 sons: William, Amos and Humphrey. To daughter in law, Rachel Ellis, privilege of living in house during widowhood. To daughter Elizabeth, 3 pds. yearly. To son Humphrey, featherbed. All real estate to 3 sons aforesaid. Amos to receive 100 pds. worth more land than 1/3 part. To son Isaac's children 25 pds. each.
Execs: Sons Amos, William and Humphrey. Wit: David Norman, Isaac

Shoemaker, Nathan Potts.

WEIS, FREDERICK. Douglass.
Feb 21, 1788. April 16, 1788. 1.144
To wife Christina, bed, furniture &c. and 6 pds. yearly, privilege of house and meadow. To sons John and Christopher, 300 acres in North Hampton [Northumberland] County. To son John, grist mill and 140 acres, and rem. to son Christopher. Fifty acres and 50 perches in Douglass to be sold. Eight acres and house for father to live in. To son Frederick, house and lot of 14 3/4 acres. To daughter Hannah and Elizabeth, bed, spinning-wheel and 200 pds. each. To son John, wagon &c. Rem. equally divided among sons John and Christopher. To son Frederick, 25 pds.
Execs: Sons John and Christopher. Wit: Jacob Beltz, Jacob Crous.

DICKENSHEED, CHRISTOPHER. Lower Salford.
March 12, 1787. April 28, 1788. 1.147
To wife Margaret, 100 pds. and 1/3 of personal estate. Farm of 107 acres and personal estate to be sold. To son Dillman, 1 s. To grandson Christopher (son of Dillman) 30 pds. Rem. equally divided to son William 1/4 part, to daughter Susanna, wife part and 3 grandchildren of son Valentine dec. 1/4 part.
Execs: Son in law John Wentz, John Shuler. Wit: Henry Sweitzer, Gabriel Shuler.

JACOBS, THOMAS. Philadelphia.
May 11, 1787. May 6, 1788. 1.148
To daughter Hannah, 20 pds.. To son Thomas, 20 pds. Land 330 acres in West Moreland, sold. To wife Lydia, part of personal estate, rem. to be sold. To wife, wearing apparel and rem. of personal estate after raising and schooling children.
Execs: Wife Lydia and brother John. Wit: Matthew Pratt, Benjamin Yarnall, Israel Jacobs.

BAKER, ELISABETH. Whitemarsh.
June 19, 1785. May 9, 1788. 1.149
To daughter Philipbeana Elisabeth Walteren, 5 pds. To daughter Mary Magdalena Shimer, 5 pds. Rem of estate to daughter Philipbeana's children and daughter Mary's children.
Exec: David Shoemaker. Wit: Barent Jacob, John Howell.

LEDYERT, JOHN. Moreland.
June 19, 1787. May 9, 1788. 1.150
To son Thomas, 5 s. To grandson John Ledyert, 30 acres. To wife Elisabeth all real and 1/2 personal estate. Rem. of personalty to be sold and money from same to granddaughters. Real estate to be divided among grandsons Moses and George, after wife's death.
Execs: Wife Elisabeth and Benjamin Cotman. Wit: Thomas Austin,

Benjamin Austin.

HORN, ANDREW. Merion.
March 6, 1788. June 24, 1788. 1.151
To wife Margaret, farm of 75 acres, stock &c. during widowhood. In case of marriage or death to son John. Son John to pay 2 brothers George William and Frederick, 30 pds. each and to sisters Mary Trayxler, Susannah Horn and Elisabeth Trayxler, 30 pds. each.
Execs: Wife Margaret and brother George Horn. Wit: Benjamin Cochran, George Mitchell.

STROUD, JAMES. Plymouth.
May 16, 1788. July 18, 1788. 1.152
To son Edward's 3 children, 100 pds. when of age. To daughter Mary, 5 pds. To daughter Mary's children, James and Isaiah Bell, 100 pds. when of age. To daughter Elisabeth income of 100 pds., if she survive her husband, money to be at her disposal, otherwise at her death to be divided among her children when of age. Rem. to 4 sons: Joshua Josiah [Joshua], James, Samuel and Thomas equally. Wit: Ezra Comfort, Jesse Rex, Nathan Potts.

HUNSICKER, ELIZABETH. Skippack and Perkiomen.
Feb 2, 1787. July 29, 1788. 1.153
Sum of 200 pds. left by testatrix's husband, Valentine Hunsicker, bequeathed in 7 equal shares as follows: to son Jacob, 1 share. To son Isaac, 1 share. To son Henry, 1 share. To daughter Sarah Gotshalk, 1 share. To daughter Catharine Clemens, 1 share. To heirs of stepdaughter Elizabeth Roht, 1 share divided as follows: to her daughter Mary Funck, 1/3 part, 1/3 part equally between 2 granddaughters Elisabeth Tintshman and Magdalena Lederman; 1/3 part equally between her grandsons Henry Roht and Jacob Roht. To stepson Samuel Hunsicker, income of 7th share; at her death divided among other legatees. To 2 daughters Sarah and Catharine, wearing apparel equally.
Execs: Sons Isaac and Henry Hunsicker. Wit: Henry Sweitzer, Israel Jacob.

MOWRER, HENRY. Upper Hanover.
July 2, 1788. Aug 5, 1788. 1.154
To wife Philipbina, 2 beds, furniture, cows and farm of 30 acres in Douglass, during widowhood, she to retain farm of 108 acres in Upper Hanover, subject to annuities to parents. Other movables to be sold. Both farms to be sold when son Michael comes of age, proceeds divided as follows: income of 150 pds. to wife Philipbina; rem. equally divided among children.
Execs: Wife Philipbina, brother in law Michael Dotterer. Wit: Michael Dotterer, Mosi Kehl, John Richards.

LEWIS, ENOS. Gwynedd.
Feb 22, 1787. Aug 30, 1788. 1.156
To grandson, Enos Roberts, 80 acres. Appraisers to lay out lands to best advantage, Enos to pay his mother 15 pds. yearly and at her death, grandson Enos to pay half value to his brothers Nathan and Amos and sister Edith equally from said tract. To son Isaac rem. of lands. To daughter Ellin, stoves, dresser, pan &c. To son Isaac, half rem. of personal estate; income of other half to daughter Ellin, at her death principal to go to her children equally.
This will was executed but after death of testator was lost by accident, while in possession of son Isaac. But the original writer of it, John Evans reproduces it.
Execs: Son Isaac Lewis, grandson Enos Roberts. Trustees, Azariah Lewis, Job Roberts, to assist exrs.

BARTLESON, HENRY. Montgomery.
April 7, 1788. Aug 7, 1788. 1.158
To son Enos, mare and desk. To daughter Katharine, featherbed, case of drawers, dining table, teatable, 6 chairs &c. Farm of 30 acres to be sold. To daughter Katharine, 200 pds. therefrom to release unto son Enos any right in farm inherited from her grandfather, Theophilus Williams. Gray mare and 3 cows and 3 sheep for 3 years for use of mother in law and her 2 children. Rem. to be equally divided between son Enos and daughter Katharine.
Exec: Thomas Shoemaker. Trustees, Evan Jones to assist exr. Wit: David Bruner, Jacob Bruner, Evan Jones.

DETWEILER, JACOB. Frederick.
July 9, 1788. Sept 16, 1788. 1.159
To wife Mary value of 50 pds. in movables, she to have house and keep house with children. Mill &c. to be rented. Rem. farm and mill and other property to be divided when eldest son Joseph comes of age; widow to have a double child's share, during widowhood.
Execs: Wife Mary, brother John Detweiler. Wit: Wm. Pennebacker, Samuel Pennebacker, Henry Sweizer.

PRACHTHISER, HENRY. Perkiomen and Skippack.
Aug 22, 1788. Sept 26, 1788. 1.160
To wife Elizabeth certain furniture, bedding &c. and income of real estate during widowhood, she to raise children if she marry before eldest daughter is 18, then to have 40 s. a year. Rem. to be equally divided among children.
Execs: Wife Elizabeth, father in law Godshalk Godshalk, Henry Hunsicker. Wit: Henry Pennebacker, David Allebach.

JONES, JOHN. Chettenham.
Aug 15, 1787. Sept 24, 1788. 1.161

To son Jonathan, 100 pds. To daughter Sarah Comly, 125 pds. and case of drawers. To daughter Hannah Janney, 150 pds. To son Thomas, 5 s. To son John, 5 s. To son Isaac, 10 pds. To son Amos household goods. To granddaughter Rebecca Jones (daughter of son Amos 20 pds. To granddaughter Rebecca Jones (daughter of son Isaac) 5 pds. Rem. of money divided among 7 children. Exrs. to make deed for plantation to son Jonathan.
Execs: Sons John and Amos. Wit: Deborah Lloyd, Jeshua Morris.

BUCHER, GEORGE D. New Hanover.
Aug 6, 1788. Nov 14, 1788. 1.168
To wife Helena, farm during life, beds, cows and stock. Farm of 280 acres and woodland of 13 acres to be rented and children for 6 years to give wife maintenance. In 6 years farm to be divided as follows: to son George, 175 acres, he to pay for it. Rem. of land to son who pays most for it. To son George, 150 pds. To son Dieter, 100 pds. To son Matthias, 100 pds. To daughters Mary, Albertine and Solomy, 40 pds. Rem. divided among children.
Execs: Son George Bucher, son in law Philip Leitig. Wit: John Richards, Berni Dodder, Jacob Snider.

FISHER, CONRAD. Douglass
March 29, 1777. Oct 13, 1788. 1.164
To wife Anne Margaretha, 88 acres, house, household goods and all estate during widowhood. If she does not live with son in law or daughter to rent place during widowhood. If she marry, to have 1/3 part personal estate. Daughter to give wife yearly 12 pds.
Execs: Wife Anne Margaretha, George Bechtel. Wit: Herman Bunn, Michael Newman.

ROYER, JOHN. Providence.
Oct 14, 1786. Nov 7, 1788. 1.165
To wife Catharine, use of 30 acres and personalty during widowhood. If she marry or in case of death, farm to be sold. Money to be divided among children, except son Joseph to have 75 pds. more than his share. Personal estate to be divided among children. Exrs. to give mother a pair of grave stones.
Execs: Wife Catharine, Benjamin Dismant. Wit: Valentine Sharer, Michael Royer, Rebecca Isaac.

SHULER, ELISABETH. Lower Salford.
Sept 17, 1788. Dec 1, 1788. 1.166
To son Gabriel, 2 bonds of 40 pds. in care of son in law Nicholas Rial. To son John, 5 pds. Farm of 7 acres to be sold, 120 pds. to son Henry. Personal estate to be divided among son Henry and 2 daughters Catharine, wife of Frederick Antes, and Margaret, wife of Nicholas Rial. Son in law Nicholas Rial, bond of 50 pds. and bond of 20 pds.

Execs: John Lukins, Abraham Alderfer and son Henry. Wit: George Heydrick, Balzer Haydrick, Henry Switzer.

HALLOWELL, THOMAS. Moreland.
Aug 1, 1788. Dec 24, 1788. 1.167
To wife Margaret, use of two rooms, furniture and maintenance during widowhood, 10 pds. yearly to daughter Elizabeth, 60 pds. and maintenance. To son Jesse, 35 acres. He to pay to 3 other sons: Thomas, John and Joseph, 12 pds. 10 s. each. Rem. of realty to son Joseph, about 31 acres, 7 perches. He to pay to 3 sons aforesaid, 62 pds. 10 s. each and 25 pds. each to 3 daughters: Mary, Elisabeth and Priscilla. To 4 sons wearing apparel equally.
Execs: Sons Thomas, Jesse and Joseph. Wit: Benjamin Hallowell Jr., Thomas Walton, Edward Edwards.

MOYER, ABRAHAM, SR. Upper Hanover.
Jan 17, 1786. Jan 16, 1789. 1.168
To wife Catharine, kitchen furniture &c. and interest of 300 pds. Farm 325 1/2 acres for wife and children to live on for 1 year. Then to be sold together with personalty and divided among heirs. After wife's death children to have her share, 3 sons: John, Jacob and Abraham and 4 daughters: Barbara, Elisabeth, wife of Jacob Kreter, and Catharine, wife of Peter Kugler, Mary, wife of Abraham Friet.
Execs: Christopher Ziegler Sr. and son in law Abraham Friet. Wit: John Shleisser, Balzer Shultz.

CRAWFORD, ANDREW. Plymouth.
Dec 22, 1788. Jan 23, 1789. 1.170
To son William state notes for 680 pds. 14 s. 7 d. To son Joseph state notes for 643 pds. 3 s. 10 d. To wife Sarah, income of 100 pds. the money being in the hands of Rev. Nathaniel Irwin also bed, furniture &c. riding mare, cow and maintenance during widowhood, and in lieu of dower, also state notes for 712 pds. 10 s. and other notes and bonds not otherwise bequeathed. To son Joseph, 20 pds. in trust for care of grandson, Andrew Crawford. To grandson Andrew Torbit, state notes, 24 pds. 16 s. 9 d. To granddaughter Anne Dowillan state notes 18 pds. 12 s. 1 d. To grandson Samuel Torbit, state notes, 60 pds. 18 s. 9 d. in event of death divided between Andrew Torbit and Ann Dowillan. To son Alexander for support of daughter Elizabeth and her children 20 pds. and half the money on John Rambo's bond; other half to Andrew Crawford, son of William. To son Alexander, bond for 60 pds. with certain provisos; also farm in Plymouth, 180 acres.
Execs: Robert McDowell, son William Crawford. Wit: John McDowell, William McDowell, Nathaniel Irwin.

KUSER, EVA. Douglass.
Jan 8, 1789. Feb 14, 1789. 1.172

To son John Freind, all personal estate and everything willed by testator's father Michael Kuser. In event of sons death estate to be divided among brothers and sisters: Michael, Jacob, John and Peter Kuser and Catharine, wife of Samuel Boyer, Christina, wife of Jacob Fronheuser and Mira, wife of John Witman and Elizabeth Kuser, equally.
Exec John Witman. Wit: Elizabeth Kuser, Maria Witman, Mths. Richards.

McGLATHERY, JOHN. Whitpain.
Feb 7, 1789. March 9, 1789. 1.173
To son John, cloth for cloak. To son William's children: John, Mary and Charles each 20 s. when of age. To son Matthew, 20 s. To granddaughter Jane Hunter, 20 pds. also her mother's and grandmother's furniture and room in dwelling. To son Isaac rem. He to pay legacies out of same.
Exec: Son Isaac. Wit: Daniel Yost, William Knox, Jacob Yost.

UNDERKOFFLER, JACOB. Frederick.
Sept 10, 1788. March 10, 1789. 1.174
To wife Mary Eva, free living in house &c. and 8 pds. yearly during widowhood. To son Jacob, blacksmiths tools. Rem. to be sold and equally divided among children. To 2 sons Jacob and David, farm of 418 acres in Frederick to be equally divided. To son Jacob, 50 pds. Each son to pay 15 pds. yearly until 100 pds. is paid to each of following: to daughter Eva Mary, wife of Peter Lock, and daughter Elizabeth, wife of John Danehauer; to 3 children of dec. daughter Regina, wife of George Weidman, 100 pds.; in equal share, 3 bonds given by their father to be deducted. To daughter Anna Mary, wife of George Weidman, 100 pds. after his dec.
Execs: Sons Jacob and David. Wit: George Michael, Jacob Pennybacker, John Barkey.

MOORE, WILLIAM. Providence.
Dec 8, 1788. March 13, 1789. 1.175
Estate to be sold and rem. after payments of debts and other legacies to wife Elizabeth, who is to educate children.
Execs: Wife Elizabeth, brother in law Jesse Trump. Wit: John Cauffman, Derick Casselberry.

TYSON, SAMUEL. Abington.
Aug 18, 1785. March 25, 1789. 1.176
To mother, Mary Tyson, a living. To nephew Samuel Tyson, watch. To brother Abraham farm, household goods, utensils, mortgages &c.
Exec: Abraham Tyson. Wit: Rynear Tyson, Benjamin Hallowell Sr., William Tyson.

WEBER, MARY. Montgomery.
Feb 2, 1789. March 25, 1789. 1.177
To daughter Hannah Crisman, 100 pds. To daughter Sarah Cope, 10 pds.

To daughter Mary Chew, 10 pds. yearly interest of 200 pds. To son John, 20 pds. To daughter in law Ann Weber, 5 pds. To grandson Jacob, 15 pds. To granddaughter Mary, 10 pds. To son George, 50 pds. Rem. of household goods and wearing apparel to 4 children: George, Hannah, Sarah and Mary equally. Rem. to 3 children: George, Hannah and Sarah equally.
Exec: Son George Weber. Wit: John Drake, Matthias Hines Jr., Evan Jones.

ROBERTS, ELDAD. Montgomery.
Jan 29, 1789. March 26, 1789. 1.178
To wife Jane, household goods and 20 pds. yearly. To son Mordecai, 250 pds. To daughter Elizabeth, 120 pds. To daughter Mary, 150 pds. To son John, farm of 200 acres, also personal estate except legacies.
Exec: Son John Roberts. Wit: John Roberts Jr., Joseph Roberts, Evan Jones.

DETWEILER, JACOB. Upper Hanover.
Jan 7, 1788. March 28, 1789. 1.179
To wife Margareth, furniture, maintenance and income of 200 pds. To 5 children of dec. son Jacob, 200 pds.; 80 pds. payment due for 2 farms previously sold to son Jacob, to be deducted. Rem. to 3 youngest children: John, daughter Margareth dec. wife of Benjamin Sell and Barbara, wife of Nicholas Steyer.
Execs: Son John and son in law Nicholas Steyer. Wit: Frederick Bannebacker, Henry Bornaman.

KEYSER, PETER. Worcester.
Feb 4, 1789., March 30, 1789. 1.181
To wife Regina, 50 pds. furniture, living and 3 acres; on which a dwellling is to be erected. To son Derick, John and Benjamin, carpenter tools. To 2 sons, John and Benjamin, pump maker tools. To son Jacob, blacksmith tools. To daughter Susannah, pewter, chest, &c. To sons John, Paul and Andrew, 5 pds. each. Rem. to be sold and wife to have 1/3 income of money arising therefrom; at her death said 1/3 to be divided among living children. The other 2/3 to children: Derick, John, Jacob, Benjamin, Susannah, Joseph, Paul and Andrew equally.
Execs: Sons Derick and John Keyser. Wit: Melchior Shultz, Henry Kolb.

NYER, DANIEL. Douglass
April 1, 1789. May 2, 1789. 1.183
To heirs of dec. brother Godfrey and sister Rosina what is coming to testator from father's estate. To dec. wife's brother Benedict's daughter Mary Barbara, 300 pds. To Evangalical Lutheran Congregation, 30 pds. To widow Mary Zerley, 80 pds. Rem. to brothers and sisters of dec. wife and to children of those dec. Henry Moll, Michael Moll, the heirs of Benedict Moll, except Mary Barbara, who has her share, Christopher

Moll, heirs of Barbara Sechlar, Appollo Wean and George Moll, equally. Execs: Brother in law, John Wean, Bernhard Gilbert. Wit: Jacob Hoover, Abraham Sechlar, Mary Zerley.

NEWBERRY, HENRY. Skippack and Periomen.
Oct 15, 1788. May 13, 1789. 1.184
To son Israel, 130 pds. To 3 daughters: Rebeccah, wife of Abraham Skeen, Elizabeth, wife of David Thomas and Jemima, wife of Samuel Skeen, 80 pds. each. To 2 daughters Mary and Ann, 80 pds. each, featherbed &c. To son Henry, farm in Worcester, 118 acres. To sons Thomas and John, farm of 231 acres, Thomas taking upper half. Sons Henry, Thomas and John to pay 100 pds. to daughters. To wife Ann, 1/3 personalty and maintenance, 1/3 real estate profits. Rem. equally divided among children. Execs: Wife Ann and son Henry and Henry Pennebacker. Wit: Isaac Casel, Abraham Cracker, Israel Jacobs.

YEAKLE, BALTZER. Towamencin.
Feb 14, 1789. May 18, 1789. 1.186
To wife Rosina, bed, furiture, linen &c. 12 pds. yearly. At her death said principal 200 pds. for use of school in Lower Salford. To son Abraham, 50 pds. and one horse. To daughter Catharine, 50 pds. in household goods or money. Rem. equally divided among 3 children: Abraham, Hester and Catharine.
Execs: Abraham Creeble, Melchior Shultz. Wit: Christopher Hoffman, Jacob Kolb, Abraham Kreble.

WHITE, ROBERT. Providence.
Dec 14, 1788. June 1, 1789. 1.187
To granddaughter Martha, 20 s. To daughter Isabella Knox, wife of Andrew Knox, 10 pds. to son Thomas, 10 pds. To grandson Robert White, 10 pds. to grandson Robert Knox, 10 pds. to daughter Mary, 10 pds. to be paid at the birth of first child to herself and husband, Wm. Knox. To 2 sons William and Abner, farm of 150 acres. If William does not care to farm, then Abner to have the whole and pay his brother William 1/2 the value thereof. To grandson Robert White, 10 pds. to son William, bed, bedding. To son Abner, walnut desk. Rem. equally divided among children.
Execs: Sons William and Abner White. Wit: Jacob Longacre, Israel Jacobs.

ROEDER, MICHAEL. Upper Hanover.
April 18, 1789. June 10, 1789. 1.189
To wife Catharine, 60 pds. bed, bedstead, furniture, stock, kitchen utensils, maintenance on 119 acres &c. during widowhood, at her death or marriage to be sold and equally divided among children. to son Michael, 3 pds. to Michael Nuss and Catharine Nuss and Catharine Nuss, children of daughter Ann Mary and Jacob Nuss, 15 pds. each. Rem. equally divided among children: Michael, John, Susannah, wife of Jacob Dankel,

Margaret, wife of Conrad Nuss, George Ladack, husband of dec. daughter Anna Margareth, Barbara, wife of Yost Wyant, daughter Hannah, wife of Martin Kieler, son Adam Roeder's children, daughter Catharine, daughter Eva, wife of Peter Trump; sons Peter and Henry Roeder and daughter Magdalena Roeder. To daughter Magdalena in addition enough to make her marriage portion equal to her sister's.
Execs: Son John Roeder, Yost Wyant. Wit: John Schliver, Christopher Niwman.

DANEHOWER, ABRAHAM. Gwynedd.
---. June 13, 1789. 1.191
To wife Catharine, key and chest, 1/4 part of fruit, maintenance from son Henry during life. to son George, maintenance. To son Henry, farm, he paying to his brothers and sisters, 450pds. To church in Whitpain, income of 5 pds. If a school house be erected by church in Gwynedd, income of 5 pds.
Execs: Wife Catharine, son Abraham, John Swenk. Wit: Stephen Bloom, Jacob Swenk.

LOBER, PETER. Douglass.
May 27, 1789. June 17, 1789. 1.192
To wife Dorothy, rooms, furniture, maintenance and 30 pds. To son in law Joseph Brendlinger, 25 pds. To trustees of Evangelical Lutheran Congregation, 5 pds. Rem. to children, equally as follows: 1/4 part to George Folk, husband of daughter Barbara, 1/4 part to John Brendlinger, husband of daughter Rosina, 1/4 part to Anthony Bender, husband of daughter Catharine, and 1/4 part to George Seyfreed, husband of daughter Anna Maria.
Execs: Sons in law George Folk and Joseph Brendlinger. Wit: Ludowig Lindel, Rowland Young, John Richards.

WEBSTER, SARAH. Abington.
Oct 16, 1784. June 19, 1789. 1.193
To son Richard Leedom, bond due to testatrix and bible. To son Joseph, bond with 2/3 interest on it and clock. To son George, bond with 2/3 interest and 2 featherbeds. To daughter Hannah Combs, bed, furniture and bond due from her husband. David Combs, and all wearin apparel and 1/3 interest due on 2 notes against sons Joseph and George. Rem. equally divided among 3 children: Joseph, George and Hannah Combs.
Execs: Sons Richard Leedom and Joseph Webster. Wit: John Fenton, William Leedom.

BOWMAN, CASPER. Douglass.
Dec 1, 1785. July 27, 1789. 1.194
To son Jacob, farm 168 acres, he to pay 840 pds. To sons and daughters equally; Susannah Stouffer, Abraham and Esther, Maria Miller, John, Jacob, Isaac and Martin Bowman. Money due from any children to be

deducted from their share.
Execs: Son Jacob, son in law Abraham Stouffer. Wit: John Beghtell, Christopher Shultz.

KIRKBRIDE, STACY. Plymouth.
Oct 6, 1786. Sept 3, 1789. 1.196
To son Joseph, wearing apparel, bookcase. To daughter Mary Potts, 20 pds. to daughter Sarah Buckman, 1/2 of land in Morris County, N.J., 230 acres and 1/2 mine bank and 1/6 part of all mines which testator divided with partners, Jonathan Dickenson and Minor Lefever. to son Joseph, and son in law Joseph Potts, 1/2 said land and share in mine as aforesaid in trust for benefit of daughter Prudence. They to sell same if they think proper and place money on interest; after her dec. to go to her children, in equal shares. Rem. to son Joseph and daughters Prudence and Sarah equally.
Execs: Son Joseph and sons in law Joseph Potts, Jonathan Buckman. Wit: John Stall, John Yetter, Thomas Stroud.

COLEMAN, JACOB. Lower Merion.
Oct 1, 1785. Sept 3, 1789. 1.194
To wife Catharine, household goods, 20 pds. &c. Farm to be sold and 350 pds. put to interest and the income of that and 50 pds. placed in the Continental Loan Office to wife. Rem. to 6 children: Nicholas, William, John, Mary, wife of George Zeller, Catharine, Elizabeth, wife of William Wentz. To daughter Catharine, silver cream pot. To son Nicholas, 2 silver spoons. To son John, 2 silver spoons. To 3 sons: Nicholas, William and John, wearing apparel. To grandson Jacob, son of William, silver spoons. To daughter Mary Zeller, after her mother's death, 50 pds. To daughter Catharine, 50 pds. To daughter Elizabeth Wentz, 50 pds. Rem. after death of wife to 3 sons equally.
Execs: Wife Catharine, son William. Wit: Peter Thomson, Conrad Gearherd, Peter Thomson Jr.

PHILIPS, ABRAHAM. Whitpain.
July 23, 1787. Sept 30, 1789. 1.198
To son Abraham, farm, he paying sisters, Rebekah, Elizabeth and Hannah, 40 pds. each. They to have room and firewood. To son Abraham wagon, grain, furniture, clock &c. and 1/3 rem. of personal estate. Rem. to be equally divided among 3 daughters.
Execs: Son Abner, Nathan Potts. Wit: Daniel Yost, Isaac McGlathery, Abraham Yost.

DELP, GEORGE. Franconia.
Dec 11, 1788. Oct 12, 1789. 1.199
To Mennonite Congregation to which testator belonged, 5 pds. for poor. To son Samuel, 5 pds. To son Abraham, farm in Franconia, 146 acres. He to pay 700 pds. at the rate of 50 pds. monthly. To son Abraham, crops. To

son Isaac, farm in Lower Salford, 150 acres. He to pay 600 pds. Personal estate to be sold and equally divided among sons: Samuel, George, John, Abraham and Isaac and daughters Catharine, and Elizabeth, 300 pds. which George owes to be deducted.
Execs: Sons George and Abraham and son in law Isaac Dirstine. Wit: Jacob Oberholtzer, Christian Meyer, Abraham Stout.

LONG, JOHN JACOB. Marlborough.
March 17, 1789. Nov 4, 1789. 1.201
Farm and personal estate to be sold. To wife Margaret Barbara, 50 pds. small house and 10 acres, cow, bedstead, furniture &c. during widowhood. To son Elias, 5 pds. Rem. equally divided among children.
Execs: Jacob Reier, son Jacob Long. Wit: George Brey, Andrew Bossert.

WENTZ, ELIZABETH. Worcester.
Dec 8, 1784. Nov 23, 1789. 1.202
To grandson Jacob, watch. Rem. to grandchildren of daughter Catharine, equally.
Exec: Michael Croll. Wit: John Barkey Jr., John Barkey Sr.

TAYLOR, ISAAC. Whitpain.
May 24, 1789. Nov 28, 1789. 1.203
To wife Hannah personal estate, farm containing 50 acres during widowhood. If she marry to be sold and 1/2 given wife and other half to niece Mary Williams.
Execs: Wife Hannah, Job Roberts. Wit: John Roberts Jr., Job Roberts.

PARRY, JOHN. Moreland.
Dec 29, 1786. Nov 30, 1789. 1.204
To wife Margaret, 1/2 income of estate during widowhood; she to educate children: David and Daniel. If she marry, to have 10 pds. yearly. Other half of income of estate to be divided among 5 children. After wife's death or marriage, estate to be divided among sons: Benjamin, Thomas, David and Daniel, daughter Phebe Walton and 2 grandsons, John and Charles Parry.
Execs: Wife Margaret, sons Thomas and Benjamin. Wit: Samuel Gummere, Samuel Gourley, Susanna Lukens.

HOUF, PETER. Providence.
May 6, 1784. Dec 4, 1789. 1.205
To wife Anna Mary, income of estate during widowhood. If she marry to have 1/3 of income. Rem. of estate after wife's death to son Andrew.
Execs: Wife Anna Mary, Joseph Dubois. Wit: Israel Jacobs, Jesse Jacobs, John Jacobs.

SHILLIGH, MICHAEL. Frederick.
March 16, 1789. Dec 4, 1789. 1.206

To wife Susanna, household goods and 20 pds. Rem. to be divided into 3 shares, 1 to wife, 1 to daughter Elizabeth, 1 to child unnamed.
Execs: Wife Susanna, Samuel Pennebacker. Wit: William Pennebacker, John DeHaven, Thomas Puhl.

SHERER, VALENTINE. Providence.
Nov 4, 1789. Dec 4, 1789. 1.207
Estate to be sold and divided among Gertrout Schrack, Margaret Miller, Elisabeth Bolton, Catharine Schrack, Mary, John, and Susanna Sherer. Barbara Stein and Magdalena Sherer equally; daughter Susanna to have 50 pds. more than her share. To son John, wearing apparel. To daughter Catharine, 2 pds., 9 s. and to daughter Barbara, 16 pds., 4 s. To daughter Mary, 8 pds., 5 s. and to daughter Magdalena, 18 pds., 4 s. To daughter Susanna, 18 pds., 19 s.
Execs: Son John Sherer and Magdalena Sherer. Wit: Frederick Seltzer, Frederick Isck.

ABRAHAM, ISAAC. Upper Merion.
Feb 15, 1783. Dec 30, 1789. 1.208
To son James, 10 pds. To daughter Miriam Eastburn, wife of John Eastburn, 50 acres, furniture. She to pay to her sister Margaret, 110 pds. Rem. of realty in Upper Merion to daughter Miriam. To daughter Margaret, wife of Benjamin Eastburn, 200 pds. To daughter Dinah Cornog, 210 pds. To son Isaac, rem. of land in Radnor and rem. of estate.
Exec: Son Isaac Abraham. Wit: John Pugh, Jonathan Roberts.

WAGNER, JOHN D. Marlborough.
July 6, 1789. Jan 28, 1790. 1.210
To wife Anna Mary, furniture and maintenance during widowhood. Rem. of personalty and household goods to be sold. Wife to have 1/3 of estate. To son John, value of colt. Rem. to children: John, Catharine, Mary and Hannah equally.
Execs: Andrew Reed, Christian Shade and wife Anna Mary. Wit: Hannes Zepp, Philip Zepp.

CUNNARD, DENNIS. Norriton.
Sept 26, 1786. Feb 15, 1790. 1.211
To wife Lydia, use of whole estate during life. At her death to be sold. To grandchildren: David, Jonathan, Streeper and Rebeckah, children of son Henry, 5 pds. each. To daughter Catharine Abbit, and Rachel Shoemaker, rem. equally. To daughter Catharine, 65 pds.
Execs: Sons in law Wm. Abbit, Isaac Shoemaker. Wit: Amos Ellis, Henry Cunnard, Nathan Potts.

COULSTON, BARNABAS. Plymouth.
June 26, 1778. Feb 18, 1790. 1.212
To wife Elizabeth, personalty and use of realty during life. At her death

to be sold and divided as follows: to son John, 30 pds. Rem. equally to son Edward, daughter Hannah Maulsby and 3 sons in law: James Stroud, David Rittenhouse and David Davis. To son Edward, wearing apparel.
Exec: son John Coulston.
Trustees, son in law James Stroud, stepson James Brooke. Wit: William Stroud, Nathan Potts.

PAUL, ANDREW. Limerick.
June 3, 1789. March 12, 1790. 1.213
To son David's children: John, David and William; daughter Susannah, Hannah, Elizabeth, Samuel, Daniel and Henry whole estate equally.
Exec: Grandson John Paul. Wit: Paul Custer, Frederick Runtz.

GAMBLE, SAMUEL. North Wales.
Jan 15, 1785. March 15, 1790. 1.214
Exr. to sell farm, 30 acres and personalty. To wife Katharine, 1/2 money from sale. Rem. to 5 children: Joseph, Mary, Elizabeth, Hannah and Susannah equally.
Exec: Evan Jones. Wit: Isaac Kolb, Jacob Wismer.

CLAYTON, ELISABETH. Moreland.
June 26, 1789. March 15, 1790. 1.215
To brother John, 5 pds. To sister Hannah Clayton, 20 s. To Elizabeth Childs, daughter of sister Jane Childs, 5 pds. To mother Margaret, interest on 30 pds.; principal at her death to sisters Jane Childs, Dorothy Hallowell and Rachel Jones equally. Rem. to 3 sisters aforesaid.
Exec: Uncle Jonathan Clayton. Wit: Daniel Longstreth, John Engle, John Clayton.

SAUTER, JABOB. Hatfield.
April 7, 1777. March 20, 1790. 1.215
To wife use and profit of estate during life, and certain movables. William and Maria Merkle and brother in law Philip Geisinger to share equally in rem. Share of estate of wife of Jacob Stoffer to be received by Philip Geisinger and the share of the family of Jacob Stoffer to be left to Philip Geisinger to adjust. The share of sisters Barbara and Anna to be received by cousin Deilman Kolb. cousin Martin Weyerman to be caretaker of wife and to be paid for same out of estate.
Execs: John Weyerman, Martin Weyerman. Wit: Abraham Ruth, Jacob Gross.

GEBHARD, MICHAEL. New Hanover.
Dec 22, 1789. March 24, 1790. 1.217
To wife Catharine, household goods, maintenance during widowhood. To son Michael, 20 s. To daughter Mary Magdalena, wife of Frederick Renninger, 1 s. To son in law John Stahl, farm, 45 acres. To grandchild Christina, daughter of John Stahl, bed, bedstead and chest. Rem. of

personalty of daughter Barbara.
Exec: Paul Linsenbigler. Wit: Dewalt Jerger, Christian Bryman.

SUPPLEE, ISAAC. Upper Merion.
Dec 17, 1789. April 24, 1790. 1.218
To wife Elizabeth, income of farm until youngest child is 21. Also 10 acres. Rem. of farm to son John. Son John to have his mother's share after her death. He to pay 70 pds. to children: Ann, Magdalena, Martha and Elizabeth.
Execs: Wife Elizabeth, Jonas Rambo. Wit: Robert Shannon, Andrew Supplee, Andrew Norny.

HAWS, HARTMAN. Limerick.
Sept 9, 1788. May 3, 1790. 1.220
To wife Mary, certain household goods and 6 pds. yearly. To son Daniel, 100 pds. To son Benjamin, 100 pds. To daughter Catharine, 100 pds. To son John, farm. He to pay above legacies. Rem. of personal estate to be sold. To son in law Christopher Smith, 10 acres. He to pay for it.
Execs: Wife Mary, Benedict Garber. Wit: Frederick Sower, John Sower.

PETERS, WILLIAM. Abington.
Feb 19, 1790. May 7, 1790. 1.221
To daughter Margaret Peters, maintenance. To daughter Edith, legacy left by her brother Jonathan 15 pds. also 1 chair, pewter &c. To wife Jane, household goods, stock, 6 pds. yearly and maintenance during widowhood. To daughter Rebeccah, 1 chair, pewter, &c. Exrs. to sell rem. when youngest child is 18. To wife Jane, 60 pds. from sale, rem. of money to daughters Edith and Rebeccah equally.
Execs: Wife Jane, Peter Johnson, Thomas Livezey. Wit: Isaac Waterman, Caleb Hallowell.

SHOEMAKER, RICHARD. Horsham.
May 9, 1786. May 10, 1790. 1.223
To daughters Agnes Mullin and Mary Roberts, all personalty. To son Ezekiel, farm of 136 acres in Horsham. He to pay to daughters 150 pds. each. To granddaughter Sarah Roberts, 35 pds. to be paid by son Ezekiel. To 3 grandchildren: Richard Shoemaker, William Mullin, Richard Roberts, each 10 pds. to be paid by son Ezekiel.
Execs: Son Ezekiel, son in law Cadwallader Roberts. Wit: Joseph Kenderdine, Samuel Shoemaker.

THOMSON, JOHN. Gwynedd.
May 9, 1790. June 12, 1790. 1.224
To wife Margaret, bed, bedding and furniture. To daughter Ganor, part of beds, bedding and pewter. Farm, 123 acres to be sold and money applied as follows: to son Jonah, 20 pds. To son John, 25 pds. To daughter Rachel Wood, 40 pds. To daughter Tacie Haycock, 35 pds. Rem. invested

for support of wife Margaret, at her death equally divided among 5 children: Jonah, John, Ganor, Rachel and Tacie.
Execs: Sons Jonah and John. Wit: Isaac Kolb, Geo. Shoemaker, Walter Hallowell.

FRANCIS, JOSEPH. Abington.
March 17, 1790. July 8, 1790. 1.225
To brother Griffith, all real estate. To mother Sarah, 18 pds. To brother William, 1 pds., 15 s. to brother Griffith, rem. of personalty.
Exec: Brother Griffith. Wit: Joseph Kirk, John Fry, Philip Seams.

CARL, ISAIAH. Providence.
Dec 9, 1789. July 21, 1790. 1.226
To wife Catharine, furniture, maintenance, son Henry to care for her. To son John, 5 s. To son Jacob, 8 d. To daughter Elizabeth, 50 pds., 10 s., 6 d. To daughter Catharine, 200 pds. To son Henry, farm, 110 acres. He to pay aforesaid legacies to daughters. Subject to maintenance of wife. To son Henry, stock and utensils, except bequest to wife.
Execs: Son Henry and Benjamin Dismant. Wit: Henry Dismant, Sophia Davis, Esther Dismant.

HERB, ANTHONY. Frederick.
Oct 6, 1787. July 30, 1790. 1.228
To wife Eva, bed, household goods and furniture. Rem. of personalty to be sold. Land to remain during her widowhood; at her death or marriage to be sold for best advantage of children. If income of rem. of personal and real estate be not sufficient for wife's maintenance, to use principal. At wife's death or marriage rem. of personalty to be sold and divided with proceeds of realty among 8 children.
Exec: Adam Hollobush. Wit: George Michael, John Barkey Sr.

SCHEIFFLE, MATTHIAS. Marlborough.
June 18, 1790. Aug 9, 1790. 1.229
To wife 2 beds, household goods &c. and 54 acres and yearly interest of 100 pds. during widowhood. Rem. to be sold, also aforesaid 54 acres after wife's death or marriage. To son Jacob, 5 pds. To daughter Mally Johnson, 5 pds. To grandson Jacob Johnson, 50 pds. His mother Mally to receive interest until he is of age. To daughter Christina, featherbed, bedstead and side saddle. Rem. to 4 children: George, Matthias, John and christina.
Execs: Philip Gable, Christian Sheid. Wit: Sebstian Gotz, Henry Roshong, John Barkey Sr.

HOOT, CONRAD. Gwynedd.
June 16, 1790. Aug 28, 1790. 1.230
To wife Catharine, and son Henry and daughter Mary equal shares after real and personal estate shall be sold.

Execs: Wife Catharine, Jacob Heister. Wit: Jacob Schwenk, George Gassinger, Anthony Heght.

PHILLIPS, SAMUEL. Upper Merion.
June 2, 1787. Sept 29, 1790. 1.231
To grandson Phineas, son of Joshua, farm, 100 acres. He to provide maintenance for sister Jemima during life. To daughter Rachel, 60 pds. To daughter Leah, 20 pds. To each of her children their share of 52 pds. as they come of age. To daughter Catharine, 30 pds. and to each of her children their portional share of 42 pds. there being 7 children. To daughter Keziah, 142 pds. To son Jonathan, 199 acres. Rem. of estate equally divided among children.
Exec: Son Jonathan Phillips. Wit: James Davis, Jonathan Tucker.

McFARLAND, ELIZABETH. Norriton.
May 18, 1790. Sept 29, 1790. 1.232
Widow of Arthur McFarland. To son John, 2 cows, clock, &c. To son James, bed, bedding and 6 pds. To daughter Elizabeth, wife of Andrew Porter, 1/3 part of table linen. To daughter Margaret, wife of Stephen Porter, 1/3 part of table linen. To daughter Mary, 2 cows, utensils and rem. 1/3 part of table linen. Rem. equally divided between sons John and James, daughters Margaret and Mary, granddaughter Charlotte, daughter of Andrew Porter, granddaughter Elizabeth daughter of Robert Parker.
Execs: Son John and daughter Mary McFarland. Wit: Robert Curry, Jacob Auld.

BOYER, WILLIAM. Frederick.
May 14, 1790. Sept 29, 1790. 1.233
Farm and personalty to be sold other than what if excepted for use of wife Abelona. To wife Abelona, 2 rooms in house during widowhood and work the farm where she lives until sale, she to have maintenance; also income of 100 pds. To son Henry, mare and equal share with other children. To son William, saddle and equal share.
Execs: John Hildebitle, son John Boyer. Wit: Philip Beyer, Peter Bauman, Henry Sasseman.

FRIED, PETER. Lower Salford.
Nov 11, 1788. Sept 29, 1790. 1.235
Books and wearing apparel equally divided among children. Real and personal estate to be sold and money divided into 11 share. Ten shares to children, 1 share to dec. son Abraham's 2 children. Married children to be charged with household goods, children not married when they come of age or marry to have as much as other married children. To Lower Salford Mennonite Meeting, 25 pds. To Skippack Meeting, 25 pds. for use of poor.
Execs: Sons in law Daniel Longenecker, John Bean. Wit: Gabriel Shuler, Joseph Alderffer, John Barkey Sr.

BITTING, MARY. Pottstown.
Dec 21, 1790. Jan 7, 1791. 1.236
To granddaughter Mary Levergood, daughter of Jacob Levergood, wearing apparel and household goods, also 5 pds.; in case of her death to her youngest sister. To 2 grandsons, Jacob and John Levergood, sons of Jacob, 7 pds., 10 s. each. To grandson unnamed, son of John Bitting, $20. Rem. to son John Bitting and daughter Elizabeth Levergood equally, daughters half to remain in hands of exr. and she to receive income. To have principal at her husbands' death; should she die before her husband her share to be divided among her children: Mary, Jacob and John.
Exec: Christopher Shaner. Wit: Henry Warley, Frederick Diller.

HARRY, DAVID. Gwynedd.
Nov 11, 1788. Jan 19, 1791. 1.238
To 2 sisters and brother, Sarah Roberts, Lydia Evans and John Harry, 25 pds. each. To 2 other sisters Jane and Ann, 15 pds. each riding mare. Rem. to brother Benjamin.
Exec: Brother Benjamin Harry. Wit: Owen Thomas, Evan Thomas.

STUART, LAWRENCE. Upper Merion.
Nov 19, 1790. Feb 7, 1791. 1.239
To wife Jane, cow, bed, end of dwelling, maintenance as directed and household furniture. To son John, farm. 107 acres. He to pay legacy to sister Jane. If she applies for it within 2 years, 30 pds. To Jane Nealy widow of John Nealy, 20 pds. out of 100 pds. bond due from William Nealy. Son William to pay said Jane 10 pds. also to wife Jane, 40 pds. out of aforesaid bond.
Execs: Stepson William Nealy and John Wilson. Wit: John Lowry, Jonathan Roberts.

McNEAL, ANTHONY. Moreland.
Feb 5, 1791. March 4, 1791. 1.240
To wife Elizabeth, son Hiram and daughters Margaret and Mary all the beds and bedding equally. To daughters Margaret and Mary, each 50 pds. To son Samuel, 5 pds. Rem. to son Hiram. He to support his mother and allow his sisters to have their home in the house as heretofore until marriage.
Execs: Son Hiram and wife Elizabeth. Wit: Robert Barnes, Stephen Barnes.

TYSON, PETER. Abington.
Aug 16, 1788. March 28, 1791. 1.240
To 2 sons Rynear and Thomas privilege to dig and haul limestone out of quarry on farm for 12 years. To son Peter farm, 180 acres. To 3 sons: Rynear, Thomas and Peter, wearing apparel equally. To each grandchild, 20 s. One-fifth of rem. to heirs of daughter Eleanor, 1/5 to son Rynear, 1/5 to daughter Margaret, 1/5 to son Thomas, 1/5 to son Peter. To 4

children, aforesaid Rynear, Thomas, Margaret and Peter and son in law
Benjamin Hallowell, 16 acres in Moreland with mill.
Execs: Sons Rynear, Thomas and Peter Tyson. Wit: Joseph Lukens,
Abraham Lukens.

HARKER, JAMES. Moreland.
Aug 27, 1790. March 29, 1791. 1.241
To son John, 30 acres on farm in Moreland, he paying half the debt. To
son Jesse, rem. of farm, he paying other half. To son John, 4 pds. To
stepdaughter Sarah Grant, 40 s. To stepdaughter Ann Case, teatable and
40 s. To stepdaughter Letitia Neal, dining table, curtains and 4 pds. To
son Jesse rem. of personalty, he paying the above legacies.
Execs: Anthony Yerkes Jr., Robert Grant, Isaac Cadwallader. Wit:
Michael Ziegler, Henry Sweitzer.

GROVER, JOHN. Upper Merion.
Feb 25, 1788. March 29, 1791. 1.244
To wife Mary all personalty. At her death rem. to be sold. To daughter
Christiana, 50 pds. Rem. divided into 5 equal shares; 1 share to daughter
Ann Hunter, 1 to children of son Christian, 1 to children of dec. son John,
1 to son Joseph and 1 to John Jones.
Execs: James Cochran, John Jones. Wit: Nathan Colflesh, John Johnston.

GROVER, JOHN. Upper Merion, County of Montgomery. Yeoman.
Feb 25, 1788. March 29, 1791. 1.244
To my wife Mary, all personal estate, and all household furniture, cattle,
swine, and implements of husbandry, during her natural life; then to be
divided among my children. To my daughter Christina, 50 pds. specie
(testator makes this conditional on her not marrying John Smith, but
afterwards reconsiders this); after her death, to be divided among my
grandchildren. Rem. of my estate to be devided into 5 shares, one share
to be paid to each of the following: my daughter Ann Hunter. The
children of my late son Christian. The children of my late son John. My
son Joseph. My daughter Christina.
Note: This will is plainly signed, in German script, which has been
carefully recorded, JOHANN JACOB GRAUER. There is no bequest
whatever to a person named John Jones. (Transcribed by Charles R.
Barker.)
Execs: My neighbors Thomas Cochran and John Jones. Wit: Mathias
Colflesh, Jno. Johnston. (Montgomery County Will Book 1 p. 244).

LISMANT, HENRY. Providence.
Feb 16, 1791. March 29, 1791. 1.245
To wife Elizabeth, maintenance, money in her hands to be her dower. To
daughter Elizabeth, 40 pds. and furniture, she to dwell with her brother
John. To son in law Thomas Wilbarham, 40 pds. To son Daniel, 20 acres,
also field adjoining Joseph Tyson, he paying to grandson Henry Dismant,

1/2 Johannes in gold. To son John, home farm, except field to Daniel as directed, reserving grave yard for said use, he paying to daughter Elizabeth as directed 40 pds. also rem. of personalty. To son Benjamin, farm on which he lives except 20 pds. to brother Daniel, he to pay bequest to Thomas Wilbarham.
Execs: Sons Benjamin and John Dismant. Wit: Daniel Stall, Aaron Rambo, Benedict Garber.

CONRAD, DENNIS. Horsham.
March 23, 1789. April 11, 1791. 1.246
To son Isaac, wearing apparel. After sister, Sarah White dies money left by testator's father for her support divided, 1/3 to daughter Mary, wife of Jonathan Lukens, 1/3 to 2 granddaughters Ann Lukens, wife of Azor Lukens and Deborah Conrad equally; 1/3 to daughter Alice Blaker's children. To granddaughters Ann and Deborah, each a case of drawers. To daughter in law Susanna, wife of son John, best bed. Rem. of personalty equally divided, 1/3 to son John; 2/3 to be divided into 3 parts; 1/3 part to daughter Mary; 1/3 to 2 granddaughters Ann and Deborah, remaining to Alice's children. Exrs. to sell 10 acres and money divided; 1/3 to daughter Mary; 1/3 to granddaughters Ann and Deborah, 1/3 to children of daughter Alice. Rem. of farm where son Dennis lives to him. To grandson Dennis Conrad, a part of farm. To son John rem. of farm. He paying to grandson Thomas, 10 pds. and grandson John, 5 pds.
Execs: Sons John and Dennis, son in law Jonathan Lukens. Wit: Benjamin Holt, Christian Christine, Jonathan Jarret.

YERKES, ANTHONY. Moreland.
Feb 27, 1790. April 26, 1791. 1.248
To son Obadiah, maintenance. To daughter Elizabeth Fulton of Virginia, sons Anthony and David, 20 s. each. To son Joseph, 20 pds. To daughter Sarah Grant, 100 pds. To son David, 1 cow. To son Jacob, farm which testator pruchased from father Herman Yerkes, 100 acres and land purchased from brother Elias, 89 3/4 acres.
Execs: Sons Joseph and Jacob Yerkes. Wit: James Fulton, Saml. Ayres, Philip Wynkoop.

JENKINS, PHINEAS. Abington.
May 15, 1789. June 2, 1791. 1.251
To wife Mary, part of furniture, room, 14 pds. yearly. To daughter Sarah Brock, 6 pds. yearly during widowhood. To son Israel, 15 pds. To son Stephen, 10 pds. To granddaughters of son Phineas, Abigail, Ann and Rachel, 20 s. each. To son William's daughters Priscilla, Elizabeth, 3 pds. each and his daughter Willey, 5 pds. To son Jesse all realty subject to payments above. Exrs. to sell personalty to pay legacies except yearly payments.
Execs: Wife Mary and daughter Sarah Brock, and son Jesse.] Wit: George Fisher, John Clayton, Thomas Livezey.

CULP, PHILIP. Springfield.
Feb 26, 1791. June 9, 1791. 1.252
To wife Mary realty and personalty during widowhood. If she marry to have 1/3 part of estate. Rem. equally divided among children.
Execs: Wife Mary and brother Leonard Culp. Wit: John Streper, Henry Snyder.

McCLEAN, ARCHIBALD. Horsham.
Jan 4, 1785. June 15, 1791. 1.253
To wife Ann, horse saddle and birdle, cow, bed, bedding, furniture and income of real estate during widowhood. At her dec. or marriage estate to be sold and divided among 4 children: Joseph, Samuel, William and Edith, when of age. If wife marry 20 pds. yearly to be paid to her during life.
Exec: Son William McClean.

YOUNG, MICHAEL. Upper Salford.
April 10, 1791. June 18, 1791. 1.254
To wife Maria Adelhert all personalty and realty during widowhood. If she marry to take under intestate laws. To son Martin, bible. To son Peter, mare. To daughter Catharine, meadow until wife's death. At wife's death land to be sold, except land sold to son Jacob. To John Hass, grandson, daughter Sophia's share. Share of daughter Catharine to her husband ---- Niess, unless she should be married to another wife, then to her child. Daughter Magdalena's share to her children by Wm. Mayberry.
Execs: Henry Deitz, for John Hass and sons Jacob and Martin Young. Wit: Philip Zingla, Henry Deitz.

KNIGHT, JOHN. Abington.
Dec 17, 1789. June 26, 1791. 1.255
To father Isaac Knight Sr. all estate real and personal.
Exec: Father Isaac Knight Sr. Wit: Humphrey Waterman, John Shriver.

PRICE, EDWARD. Providence.
March 31, 1778. Aug 5, 1791. 1.256
To wife Mary, 60 pds. and 6 d. yearly, also bed, cow &c. room and maintenance, 6 pds.; maintenance during widowhood. To daughter Sarah Dyer, 30 pds. and to discharge of 70 pds. her husband owes testator. To daughter Ruth Thompson, 100 pds. and use of house and land rented to Philip Hoffman and 5 acres field before the door. To son Reese, farm and rem. of estate.
Exec: Son Reese Price. Wit: Lewis Scothron, Robert Holland, Edward Price Jr.

JAMES, ISAAC. Montgomery.
Oct 15, 1789. Aug 6, 1791. 1.257
To daughter Sarah, 100 pds. To daughter Rachel, 10 pds. and 10 pds. for

caring for sister's child. To son in law Benjamin Johnson, 50 pds. To children of daughter Elizabeth, 40 pds. each. To 2 grandchildren, John and Rachel Drake, 200 pds. equally. To Baptist Church at Montgomery, 50 pds., also 10 pds. for minister.
Execs: Sons in law John Drake, Benjamin Johnson. Wit: Edward Lloyd, Edmund Penington.

YEARNHART, HENRY. Upper Bublin.
March 30, 1790. Aug 12, 1791. 1.259
To wife Ann, bed, furniture, income of realty, cow &c. during widowhood. If she marry to have bed, furniture. After wife's death or marriage, sons Jacob and Jesse to have farm. To son Jesse, horse and cart and 12 pds. To daughter Ann, cow and 4 sheep. To 2 daughters Elizabeth and Ann rem. of estate equally.
Execs: Sons Jacob and Jesse. Wit: Joseph Butler, John Cleaver.

MENAN, PATRICK. Whitemarsh.
Jan 8, 1789. Aug 20, 1791. 1.259
To son John Christopher Moier, 5 s. To daughter Mary, 20 pds., furniture, bible &c. To daughter Elizabeth, heifer. To daughter Sarah, 20 pds., heifer, furniture &c. To 3 grandchildren: John, Sarah and Margaret Trump, 7 pds. Rem. to 3 daughters: Grace Wagenor, Mary and Sarah Menan and daughter Elizabeth's children: John, Sarah and Margaret Trump.
Execs: Daughters Mary and Sarah. Trustee, Nathan Potts. Wit: Enoch Marpel, Mary Marpel, Mary Bartleson.

BERNHARD, CASPER. Limerick.
Aug 9, 1790. Sept 13, 1791. 1.260
To wife Mary, all estate. After wife's death, daughter Mary to have house, &c. Rem. to daughter Marilis Kretz. Rem. among 4 children: William, Jacob, Marilis and Maria Bernhard.
Execs: Wife Ann Maria, son in law Henry Kretz. Wit: Leonhard Mewman, Jacob Crous.

HOURST, ELIZABETH. Worcester.
July 8, 1791. Sept 17, 1791. 1.262
To daughter Margaret, wife of Henry Byer, bedstead, wearing apparel, spinning wheel, &c. to son Elias, 1 pds., 5 s. To son Philip, 2 pds., 5 s.
Exec: Son in law Henry Byer. Wit: Leonhard Metz, Stephen Porter.

GERHARD, PETER. Upper Hanover.
March 8, 1791. Oct 10, 1791. 1.262
To wife Susannah, bed, bedstead, furniture &c. To son Jacob, 3 pds. Wife to keep farm, 100 acres and woodland, 40 acres until youngest son Matthias is of age. If daughters Magdalena and Anna shall marry all articles for marriage portion, bedstead, pewter, iron ware and utensils. To

sons Jacob and Matthias, 50 pds. To son Matthias, when of age, 4 tracts containing 165 acres, stock. He to pay 700 pds.; 400 pds. of it to wife Susannah. Rem. of estate after wife's death to 4 children: Jacob, Matthias, Magdalena and Anna.
Execs: Baltzer Shultz, John Shleiffer. Wit: Jacob Yeakle, L. Neuman.

SPRINGER, WILLIAM. Towencin.
Oct 27, 1791. Dec 1, 1791. 1.265
To wife Mary, bed, bedstead and furniture. Rem. of personalty to be sold. Realty to be sold. To wife from personalty, 20 pds. Rem. of money divided as follows: 1 share to wife Mary during widowhood. If she marry to be divided among children. To son John, 1 share, also 1 s. To son Jacob, 1 share. To daughter Barbara, 1 share. To son Daniel, 1 share. To son Henry, 1 share. To sons Joseph and William, 1 share each.
Execs: Henry Kassel Jr., Jacob Kulp, Peter Kulp. Wit: Jarret Godshalk, Henry Pennebacker.

EDWARDS, JOHN. Providence.
March 9, 1791. Nov 26, 1791. 1.267
Personalty to be sold, except what wife receives and maintenance. To Presbyterian Meeting House, 5 pds. After wife's death, farm to be sold. Money to pay legacies to children of granddaughter, Sarah Bean, dec. 50 s. each. To grandson Levi Boyer (Bowyer), 60 pds. To Ann Rambo, wife of Peter Rambo, 50 pds. Rem. of money from sales divided into 4 shares, after 30 pds. deducted to son John. To daughter Elizabeth Boyer, 1 share. [*Annotation states Elizabeth Edwards mar. Thomas Bowyer (son of Stephen) of Montgomery Co., Pa., who d. near Danville, Montour Co., Pa., intestate, 1808*] To daughter Margaret Cornog, 1 share. To son John, 2 shares.
Execs: Son John, Andrew Todd, Joseph Crawford. Wit: Arnold Francis, Benjamin Dismant.

PAWLING, ELIZABETH. Skippack and Perkiomen.
Sept 5, 1791. ___, 1791. 1.269
To grandchild, John Pawling Twaddle, 15 pds. To 3 grandchildren: James, Charles and William Twaddle, 10 pds. each. To granddaughter Rachel Twaddle, 10 pds. to daughter Rachel Reiff, 80 pds. To daughter Deborah Twaddle, bedstead, bedding, furniture. To daughter Rebecca Lynch, pewter. Rem. to be divided among 4 children: Hannah Heister, Deborah Twaddle, Rebecca Lynch and Rachel Reiff.
Exec: Son in law William Twaddle. Wit: Joseph Fitzwater, John DeHaven, Thomas Fitzwater.

MOYER, CASPER. Worcester.
Dec 23, 1791. Jan 6, 1792. 1.270
Personalty to be sold To wife Sarah, 1/3 estate. Rem. to 3 children: Jacob, Mary Geyer, wife of Jacob Geyer and Margaretha Barbary Moyer,

equally.
Exec: Son Jacob Moyer. Wit: Frederick Conrad, Harry Bunn.

SCHUNK, FRANCIS. Providence.
May 19, 1789. Jan 25, 1792. 1.271
To wife Elizabeth, bedstead, furniture, stock, maintenance. To son Christian, 5 pds. To daughter Barbara, bible. To daughter Catharine Seiver, 10 pds. Exrs. to sell farm, 174 acres. Money arising to children: Christian, Barbara Sweitzer, wife of Simon Sweitzer, Francis, Peter, Solomy Ashenfelder, wife of John Ashenfelder, Catharine Seiver, wife of Frederick Seiver and John Schunk equally.
Execs: Son Christian, son in law Simon Sweitzer. Wit: Nicholas Cressman, Francis Hobson.

NYCE, ZACHARIAH. Frederick.
Dec 19, 1791. Feb 2, 1792. 1.273.
To wife Margaret, use of dwelling, cow, sheep, stock, furniture and maintenance. Rem. of personalty to be sold. Money arising to son in law Jacob Arndt. Interest to be paid to wife yearly. To son John, farm and 2 tracts, 205 acres, subject to payments of 800 pds. to be paid to 5 daughters: Mary, wife of Nicholas Gilbert, Catharine, wife of Leonard Leity, Susannah, wife of Michael Slanecker dec., Elizabeth, wife of Jacob Arndt and Margaret Nyce, equally, also to pay money due to heirs of Jacob Nyce. To daughter Margaret, 30 pds. when 18. to granddaughter Nancy Snyder, 6 pds. Exrs. to sell 9 acres 134 perches and money to be divided among sister Susannah Freadley's children.
Execs: Wife Margaret, son John, son in law Jacob Arndt. Wit: Philip Hahn, John Richards.

YOCUM, MARTHA. Upper Merion.
July 8, 1791. Feb 14, 1792. 1.276
Estate to be sold. Money to support children: Reuben and Samuel.
Execs: Peter Matson, William Custer. Wit: Lindsay Coats, Joseph Williams.

MAJOR, ALEXANDER. Gwynedd.
July 14, 1788. Dec 7, 1791. 1.277
To wife Jane, 15 pds. &c. To Presbyterian Congregation of Abington, 50 pds. for new meeting house. To Pennsylvania Hospital, 10 pds. Exrs. to sell farm, 160 acres and personalty. Income from money to be given to wife. After wife's death all money to be divided among children and children of son Peacock as follows: to son Peacock, 5 pds. rem. divided into 9 shares to children of son Peacock, 1 share, 1 share each to sons: James, Ebenezer, John, daughters Margaret, Mary, Hannah, Jane and Elizabeth.
Execs: Joseph McClean, Robert Loller. Wit: Mary Loller, Rachel McClean.

FUCHS, ANNA MARY. Douglass.
May 17, 1791. March 26, 1792. 1.279
To son John, 10 s. besides his share of estate. To daughter Margareth, cow, spinning-wheel and share of estate. Wearing apparel divided among 3 daughters: Catharine, wife of Conrad Fegely, Anna Mary and Margareth Fuchs. Other personalty to be sold and divided among 7 children, those named above and John, Anthony, Matthias and Jacob. Deduction of 1 pds., 2 s., 6 d. and interest from Catharine's share and paid to son Jacob. The same sum also deducted from Catharine's share and divided among 6 other children.
Execs: Sons John and Anthony. Wit: Dewart Yerger, Christian Bryman.

WALTON, JEREMIAH. Moreland.
March 1, 1792. April 1, 1792. 1.281
To wife Mary in lieu of dower, cow, room, maintenance. To son Thomas, piece of land, subject to the payments of 100 pds. to his brother Amos and 3 pds. yearly to his mother during life. Son Thomas to have privilege of timber and stone from farm herein after devised to son Joseph and Isaac. To son Jeremiah, piece of land last purchased from John Lloyd, he to pay 3 pds. yearly to his mother. To son Jonathan, 1 acre of woodland. To sons Joseph and Isaac to be divided, as they shall agree and share alike in value, farm which was testator's father's, except small tract given above, to sons Jonathan and Thomas; Joseph and Isaac to pay following legacies: to their brothers Amos, 50 pds. and 6 pds. yearly to their mother. To their brothers Jonathan and Jesse, 160 pds. each. To son Amos, 160 pds. To 2 sons Jonathan and Jesse, 160 pds. each. To daughter Elizabeth Paxton, 30 pds. besides what she has had. To 4 sons: Thomas, Joseph, Jonathan and Isaac 24 pds. each in lieu of trades. Rem. equally divided among 7 sons. Goods left to wife during life to be sold at her death and divided among all children.
Execs: Samuel Gummere, sons Thomas and Joseph. Wit: Thomas Parry, Benjamin Lloyd, Silas Walton.

BURK, JOHN. Whitpain.
July 24, 1791. April 25, 1792. 1.283
To son Edward, wearing apparel. To daughter Mary, trunk and linen. Rem. to 2 children, equally.
Exec: Owen Thomas. Wit: Benjamin Harry, Joseph Lewis.

PAWLING, JOHN. Skippack and Perkiomen.
Oct 12, 1789. May 15, 1792. 1.284
To wife Elizabeth, bed, bedding, furniture and maintenance, also 30 pds. in cash and 60 pds. yearly in lieu of her dower. Negro boys George and Robin to be free at 21 years of age. Farm of 250 acres to daughter Deborah Twaddle during life. At her death to her children. Farm of 250 acres to daughter Rachel Reiff, during life; at her death to her children. Income of house on Second Street, Philadelphia to daughter Rebeckah

Lynch during life, at her death to her heirs equally. If she shall have no children to the heirs of other 3 daughters. To grandchildren: Nathan and Elizabeth Pennibecker, 200 pds. Rem. of estate equally divided among children of daughter Hannah Heister, wife of John Heister.
Execs: Wife Elizabeth, sons in law Jacob Pennibecker, John Heister, William Twaddle. Wit: Israel Jacobs, George Beyer.

MAGARGEL, WILLIAM. Cheltenham.
July 22, 1786. May 5, 1792. 1.289
To son James, farm, 64 acres, 36 perches. Subject to wife Eleanor's estate during life. He to pay to son William, 50 pds. and to daughter Martha, wife of David Rea, 50 pds. after wife's death or marriage. To daughter Martha, brass kettle. To wife Eleanor, use of farm and personalty. If she marry or die to son William, realty. Personalty equally divided among children.
Execs: Wife Eleanor, sons William and James. Wit: Robert Taylor, Eleanor Taylor, Silas Watts.

PENNEBACKER, HENRY, Skippack and Perkiomen.
May 31, 1792. June 1, 1792. 1.291
To daughters Sebilla and Magdalena, 150 pds. To wife Rebecca, 200 pds. To son Jacob, realty. He to pay above legacies. Rem. to children.
Execs: Sons John, Adam and Frederick. Wit: Henry Hunsicker, Henry Pennebacker.

MILLER, FREDERICK. Marlborough.
March 30, 1784. June 4, 1792. 1.291
To wife Anna Margaret, stock, household goods and personalty during widowhood, and realty, 183 acres. To sons John Adam and Frederick, wearing apparel. To son John Adam. 10 pds. If wife marry or die, realty to 2 sons John and Frederick, for 500 pds. each son to keep 100 pds. and remaining 300 pds. to 3 daughters: Eva, Barbara and Christiana, wife of George Reiter Jr. Rem. divided among 5 children.
Execs.: Sons John Adam and Frederick Miller. Wit: Jacob Long, Ludowig Bottger.

SNYDER, GEORGE ADAM. Gwynedd.
April 10, 1792. June 16, 179. 1.294
To wife Christiana, bed, bedding, furniture, 120 pds., also income of realty until youngest son is 21; or if she marry 25 pds. yearly. To son John, 5 s., &c. He to receive as much as other sons. To sons: Adam, Jacob and George all realty when George is 21. To daughters 75 pds. each. Rem. divided equally among children.
Execs: Robert Loller, son in law Christopher Laash. Wit: Lewis Stanert Jr., Casper Wolf Jr.

FISHER, JACOB. Springfield.

June 9, 1787. Sept 6, 1792. 1.297
To son John, farm. He to pay 500 pds.; also horse. To daughter Mary, cow, bed, bedstead. To daughter Susannah, 30 pds. and cow. Exrs. to sell house in Germantown and personalty. Money to be divided among 6 children: Magdalena Wolf, wife of Bottis Wolf; Christian Fisher, Mary Fisher, Catharine Piper, wife of John Piper; John and Susannah Fisher. Execs: Son John and son in law Bottis Wolf. Wit: Michael Conrad, Jacob Funk, John Funk.

BEYER, GEORGE. Frederick.
March 28, 1792. Aug 4, 1792. 1.299
To wife Catharine, bed, bedstead, furniture and maintenance. She to maintain son Henry in case he is not capable and to have income of estate during widowhood. Personalty to be sold. At wife'e death realty to be sold and rem. divided among 7 children: Henry, George, Anthony, William, Jacob, Catharine and Elizabeth. To daughter Catharine, 34 pds., 7 s., 6 d. To daughter Elizabeth, 23 pds., 14 s. To son George, 21 pds., 12 s., 4 d. To son Anthony, 25 pds., 4 s., 6 d.
Execs: Sons Anthony and William Beyer. Wit: John Hildebitle, Joseph Gross, John Barkey, Sr.

KEELER, MARTIN. Limerick.
May 31, 1790. Oct 1, 1792. 1.301
To wife Hannah, income of estate until son Michael is 21, grain, &c. If wife marry before son is of age, then land to be sold and wife to have 1/3 part. Rem. to be divided among children: Michael, John, Henry, Susanna, Anna and Catharine. Sons to have 5 pds. each more than daughters. In case wife remains widow, she to have income of estate also, bed, bedstead and cow. Exrs. to make deed to Charles Fox for 3 acres.
Execs: Wife Hannah, George Michael. Wit: George Meyer, Philip Coll, Jacob Crous.

ART, YOST. Springfield.
July 1, 1792. Sept 15, 1792. 1.302
To Joseph Keesey, son of Philip Keesey, clock, watch, 65 pds., 10 s., 2 d. To sister Mary Elizabeth Art, of Harenhoot, Saxony, Germany, 50 pds. If she or her children do not apply for it, interest to go to ministers of Moravian Brethren at Bethlehem, Pa. To Williams Burial Ground in Whitemarsh, 4 pds. To Philip Keesey, all cash, household goods and furniture. To children of Philip and Elizabeth Keesey, 1/2 money to be divided among them, after house and land is sold. Other half of money to Philip Keesey. He to have income of house and land until his children are 21. To Philip Keesey, 67 pds., 10 s. Rem. of estate to Philip Keesey.
Execs: Philip Keesey, John Peek. Wit: Michael Conrad, Felix Detweiler, John Ulmer.

KNIGHT, ISAAC. Abington.

March 28, 1792. Oct 3, 1792. 1.304
To son Joshua, 25 pds. To son Isaac, 120 pds. To son in law Jonathan Tyson, 25 pds. To son Mahlon, 100 pds. Exrs. to sell realty and pay above legacies, except son Mahlon's of which Jacob Jeanes is to have the care. To son Isaac, watch. Exrs. to sell personalty. Rem. to children: Isaac, Mary, Sarah and Mahlon and daughter Rebeckah's children.
Execs: Son Isaac, son in law Jonathan Tyson. Wit: Moses Sheppard, Thomas Livezey.

ROBESON, JOHN. Lower Merion.
July 14, 1792. Oct 9, 1792. 1.306
To son Thomas, farm, also interest in Shad Fishery on Schuylkill and rem. of realty, except a half part of interest in a piece of Limestone ground to son Jonathan. To son Jonathan, 6 pds., 10 s. To son Thomas, 10 pds. To son John, 20 pds. to be paid by son Thomas. To granddaughter Abigail, daughter of son John, 20 pds., bed &c. To son John, rem. of personalty.
Execs: Sons Thomas and John Robeson. Wit: Joseph Price, Richard Tunis.

PRICE, JOHN. Lower Merion.
May 14, 1792. Oct 9, 1792. 1.308
To 3 daughters: Hannah, Rebecca and Jane, 1 acre each of farm, also 200 pds. each. To daughter Jane, 150 pds. To daughter Mary Gibson, 100 pds. To granddaughter Lydia, 50 pds. when of age. To grandson John Gibson, 20 pds. To wife Mary, 300 pds. and maintenance, furniture. To son Joseph, 50 acres of farm. To brother in law Robert Holland and Jane his wife, 2 acres of farm. To sister Jane, 5 pds. To son Edward, 5 acres of farm, and 5 acres of woodland. To son John, rem. of farm. To negro servants, Sal and Tom, 3 pds. each and to boy Scipio, 20 s. Exrs. to sell rem. of realty and money divided among children.
Execs: Sons Joseph, Edward and John Price. Wit: Richard Tunis, John Thomas.

HEEBNER, JOHN. Frederick.
Sept 9, 1792. Oct 26, 1792. 1.308
To 7 children: John, Philip, George, Michael, Sophia, Mary and Margarta, all estate equally. To son John, 5 pds.; Michael to have yearly interest of his share.
Execs: Sons John and George Heebner. Wit: Philip Boyer, Henry Sausiman.

PAWLING, HENRY. Providence.
Nov 18, 1791. Nov 3, 1792. 1.310
To son John, 37 acres, adjoining tract given him be deed. To son Nathan, 100 acres, adjoining tract given him by deed. He to pay 300 pds. to exrs. To son Henry, rem. of tract in Providence, with mansion house, between 200 and 300 acres. Subject to the following legacies. To son Benjamin 600 pds. To son Jesse, 600 pds. To son William, 100 pds. To Colonel Henry

Pawling of Kentucky, 20 pds. in token of friendship. To daughter Catharine Stalnford, 275 acres in Lucerne Co., subject to payment of 50 pds. to exrs. Exrs. to sell Connecticut claim and rem. of Wyalusing tract, if proper in their judgment. To daughter Rachel Bartholmew, 200 pds. To grandson Henry Pawling, son of John; and Levi, son of Henry; rem. of money from sale of Wyalusing land. Catfish Island, in Schuylkill, to be sold by exrs. To St. James Church, Providence, 10 pds. out of proceeds of sale of island, to be applied to walling in burying ground. To daughter Catharine, all plate. To brother Barney, 40 pds. and wearing apparel. To son John, walking cane, and silver watch. To exrs. 50 pds. equally. Rem. to sons: John, Henry, Benjamin, Nathan, Jesse and William equally.
Codicil, dated Aug 9, 1792 revokes bequest of farm to son John, it having already been deeded to him and gives Mullatto girl Susannah, 1 calico gown and skirt. Wit: James Vax, Ann Wills.
Execs: Sons John and Henry Pawling. Wit: John Edwards, John Wagonseller, James Vax.

RUSH, DAVID. Montgomery.
Nov 19, 1791. Nov 6, 1792. 1.313
To wife Elizabeth, beds, beding furniture, utensils, grain, stock, 20 pds.; to live in house and have maintenance during widowhood. Realty to be sold when exrs. think best, also personalty not bequeathed. To son George, 10 pds. Rem. to wife Elizabeth and children: George, Barbara and Katharine, equally.
Execs: Wife Elizabeth, brother in law George Telp. Guardians of children John Garner, Abraham Telp. Wit: Abraham Hendricks, Joseph Meyers.

HAGY, JACOB. Whitemarsh.
July 13, 1792. Nov 6, 1792. 1.313
To wife Susanna, 100 pds. and 1/3 part of personalty in lieu of her dower. To son William, 5 pds. To sons: John and Daniel, farm. Daniel to take tract next to Schuylkill with dwelling and paper mill, &c. He to pay John, 300 pds. and John to take the upper part with grist-mill, &c. To sons: Daniel and John, equal shares on the 2 Shad Fisheries on Schuylkill, allowing John the privilege of little house to shelter himself and fishermen. To son John, wearing apparel. To son Daniel, iron plane. To son Jacob Rapine, 1 s. To son in law Samuel Freas, farm in Worcester, he paying to son John, 100 pds. To wife's granddaughter Mary Bays, 20 pds. Rem. to sons Daniel and John equally.
Execs: Sons Daniel and John Hagy. Wit: John Sheppard, Francis Sheetz, Nathan Potts.

KEHL, JOHN. Douglass.
Nov 19, 1789. Nov 8, 1792. 1.315
To son Jacob, 10 pds. Farm, 113 acres to be sold. Money from sale and personalty divided into 3 equal shares. One to son Jacob's children. 1 share to son in law Abraham Bob. 1 share to son Moses.

Execs: Son Moses and son in law Abraham Bob. Wit: John Weiss, Christian Weyman, George Dengler.

KNIPE, JOHN. Gwynedd.
May 24, 1789. Nov 14, 1792. 1.316
To son Daniel, copper Still, hogshead, &c. Books, except wife's to be divided among children, except John and Henry. To son John, 3 pds., 2 s. Realty and personalty to be appraised, each child to have share. Interest of son Henry's share to go to his mother. To son David, farm where testator lived. To son Joseph, 50 acres of farm. To wife Barbara, interest of 50 pds.; maintenance to be paid by son David during widowhood. To daughter Mary's children John and Elizabeth, their mother's share when 21.
Execs: Sons Christian and David Knipe. Wit: Isaac Kolb, Stephen Bloom.

MILLER, ANDREW. Providence.
Sept 13, 1792. Nov 17, 1792. 1.318
To son Jacob, 20 s. To daughter Mary, wife of Dr. Frederick Martin, 20 s. To wife Mary, rem. of estate during life. After her death to be divided as follows: to son Joseph, house and lot where testator lived and 20 acres of farm. Rem. to be sold. Money to be divided into 8 shares, 1 to son Jacob, 1 to son John, 1 to son Philip, 1 to children of son Andrew, 1 to nephew Archibald, 1 each to sons: George, David and Benjamin.
Execs: Wife Mary and Samuel Pennebacker. Wit: Valentine Enrick, Peter Miller, Jacob Schwenk.

KLINE, JOHN. Upper Salford.
Dec 20, 1787. Nov 20, 1792. 1.319
To wife Margareth, personalty, and interest of 200 pds. to be paid by son Jacob. To son Jacob, 300 pds. To children of first wife: Jacob, John, Mary, wife of William Swenk and Salome, wife of Adam Hitlebidle, 1 s. each. To daughter Catharine, wife of Alexander Jamison, 46 pds. 4 s. 6 d. After wife's death estate to be divided into 3 shares: 1 share to daughter Catharine. 1 share to daughter Elizabeth, wife of Henry Croll. 1 share to daughter Susannah, wife of Jacob Gross.
Execs: Wife Margareth, son in law Alexander Jamison. Wit: Christian Bryman, Benjamin Weiser, Henry Muhlenberg.

HENDRICKS, BENJAMIN. Towamencin.
Oct 27, 1792. Dec 15, 1792. 1.320
To wife Catharine, interest of 100 pds. during life, room, maintenance, cow until son Abraham is married. If son Abraham marry he to have house and farm, 88 acres. He to pay 275 pds. He to pay to daughter Susanna, wife of George Becker; to daughter Alice; to daughter Catharine, wife of Henry Fried, to daughter Elizabeth, wife of Peter Weil; and to daughter Barbara, 29 pds., 6 s., 4 d. each. Personalty to be sold, money to be divided among children. To son Abraham, horse, wagon,

harrows, &c. To wife Catharine, bed, bedstead, linen, pewter, 5 pds., &c. To daughter Alice, 15 pds. To daughter Barbara, 15 pds.
Execs: Son Abraham, Gerret Godshalk, Jacob Kolb. Wit: Peter Godshalk, Joseph Hendricks.

ROBERTS, AMOS. Gwynedd.
Aug 22, 1785. Dec 21, 1792. 1.322
To wife Sarah, room, furniture, maintenance, &c. To son Rees, 12 pds. yearly during his mother's life, after that 18 pds. To sons Robert and Charles, 400 pds. To 5 daughters: Mary, Jane, Ann, Sydney and Sarah, 5 pds. equally. To son George, farm, 180 acres, unmarried sisters to live with him; otherwise he to pay them 200 pds. Rem. divided among 7 children.
Execs: Wife Sarah, son George Roberts. Wit: George Maris, John Evans.

HENDRICKS, MATTHIAS. Towamencin.
May 20, 1786. Jan 14, 1793. 1.323
To son Paul, 15 pds. To daughter Margareth, 10 pds. and bible. To wife's children by first husband, Sarah and Catharina, 1 s. each. Rem. to testator's 2 children: Paul and Margareth.
Exec: Garret Godshalk. Wit: Jacob Kolb, Benjamin Hendricks, Ida Hendricks.

SUPPLEE, ISAAC. Upper Merion.
Dec 12, 1792. Jan 14, 1793. 1.324
To Peter Matson's children, 25 pds. equally. To sister Mary, 50 pds. to Benjamin Ramsey's children, 25 pds. equally. To Jacob Supplee's children, 20 pds. equally. To Leonard Lates's children, 20 pds. equally. To nephew Isaac Matson, son of Peter Matson, watch and wearing apparel. Rem. of estate to sister Mary Supplee.
Execs: Peter Matson, Benjamin Ramsey. Wit: Benjamin Ramsey, Benjamin Wager.

FOUST, PETER. Frederick.
Dec 13, 1792. Jan 28, 1793. 1.324
To wife Abelona, farm during widowhood. Personalty to be sold. Interest of money arising to wife. After wife's death realty and personalty that wife received to be sold and divided among 4 children. Daughter Elizabeth's share to be put on interest and at her death given to her children. To son John, 3 pds.
Exec: Son John Foust. Wit: Philip Boyer, Jacob Smith.

CONRAD, JOHN. Norriton.
April 11, 1791. March 9, 1793. 1.326
To wife Ann, personalty and income of realty during life. After wife's death, realty to be sold and money divided as follows: to son Henry, 10 pds. To daughter Sarah, 10 pds. and rem. of money divided among 5

children: Robert, Catharine, Benjamin, Sarah and Henry, equally.
Execs: Sons Benjamin and Henry Conrad. Wit: Thomas Pugh, Jonathan Pugh.

PETERMAN, JACOB. New Hanover.
Jan 19, 1792. Feb 11, 1793. 1.326
Realty and personalty to be sold by exrs., except what wife Mary receives, namely a maintenance, of money arising from sale, wife to have interest of 250 pds. To daughter Maria, 50 pds. To daughter Elizabeth Wise, interest of 50 pds. Rem. divided among 3 sons: Jacob, John and Michael.
Execs: Wife Mary and son Jacob Peterman. Wit: George Snell, Jacob Crous.

SCOTT, GEORGE. Moreland.
Jan 3, 1793. March 18, 1793. 1.327
Personalty to be sold. To son in law Harman Yerkes, income of farm for 1 year. After 1 year, realty to be sold, containing 77 acres and money divided as follows: to daughter Susannah, 24 pds. Rem. to 5 daughters: Mary, wife of John Sharer; Agness, wife of Thomas Muckelhoes; Esther, wife of Thomas Lidyard; Margaret, wife of Harman Yerkes; and Susannah Scott, equally. Money already received by each daughter to be deducted from her share.
Execs: Son in law Harman Yerkes, Samuel Erwin. Wit: John Moore, Derrick Lukens.

DUNBAR, ANDREW. Horsham.
Nov 19, 1785. March 25, 1793. 1.328
To wife Martha, farm, 80 acres, during life. To daughter Martha, wife of Alexander Ramsey, 10 acres and personalty. To daughter Martha, 80 pds. after wife's death. After wife's death, rem. of realty to be sold and 1/2 to daughter Mary Lawrence, and 50 pds. yearly. To daughter Sarah, other half of money from sale. To grandson Andrew Ramsey, 20 pds. To granddaughters: Mary, Martha and Margaret Ramsey, 5 pds. each. To grandsons Alexander and John Ramsey, 5 pds. each.
Execs: Samuel M. Nair, Isaac Parry. Wit: John Mann, Sr., John Mann, Jr.

JOHNSON, MARGARET. Gwynedd.
March 31, 1793. April 11, 1793. 1.330
To daughter Elizabeth, cow, clock. To daughters Barbara and Elizabeth, 100 pds. to be paid by son Henry. To son Henry, 1/2 crown. To son John, 1/2 crown. To daughter Susannah, 10 pds. Rem. divided among 3 daughters: Barbara, Elizabeth and Susannah.
Execs: Son Henry, son in law Walter Howell. Trustees, George Gossinger, Henry Nevil. Wit: Henry Nevil, Enoch Beem.

WRIGHT, JACOB. Horsham.
April 9, 1793. April 26, 1793. 1.331

To wife Jane, personalty and income of realty during widowhood. If she marry, 1/3 part of personalty and 10 pds. from realty yearly. After wife's death or marriage, all estate to sons: John, Joseph, Samuel and Jacob equally, except son Joseph to have 40 pds. more than his brothers. They to pay to daughters Mary and Jane, 100 pds.
Execs: Sons Joseph and Samuel Wright. Wit: John Simpson, Robert Loller.

DUNBAR, SARAH. Horsham.
March 24, 1793. April 29, 1793. 1.332
To mother, what was left to testatrix by father, except the price of a pair of silver shoe buckles, to niece Sarah Ramsey. To sister Mary Lawrence, 2 acres from 1/2 of father's estate. Rem. of land left by father to sister Martha Ramsey. To niece Mary Ramsey, bed, bedstead, linen and cloak. To niece Sarah Ramsey, table linen and rem. of wearing apparel. Rem. of estate to sister Martha's children.
Execs: Isaac Parry, Samuel Mann. Wit: John Shelmire, James Barnes.

KING, PETER. Hatfield.
April 14, 1788. May 11, 1793. 1.333
To son Peter, 5 pds. Exrs. to sell realty and personalty and money to be divided among 8 children: Peter, Martin, Katharine, Barbara, Ann, Elizabeth, Margaret and Mary.
Execs: Brother in law John Funck, daughter Katharine. Wit: David Roat, Abraham Roat, Martin Weyermem.

BREY, GEORGE. Marlborough.
March 23, 1791. May 13, 1793. 1.334
To son Conrad, 5 pds. To son Christopher, 50 pds. To 3 daughters 50 pds. Son John to give to son Jacob a maintenance. Rem. of estate to 9 children: Conrad, George, Windle, Jacob, John, and Christopher, Eva Martha, wife of Melchior Stahl, Elizabeth, wife of Jacob Nicholas and Catharine, wife of Jacob Detweiler.
Execs: Sons Conrad and John Brey. Wit: George Lang, Jacob Lang.

STIMPLE, BENJAMIN. Moreland.
Nov 5, 1792. June 3, 1793. 1.335
To daughter in law Elizabeth Grimes, bedstead, pewter, &c. To son Thomas, walnut chest, &c. To son John, best suit. To daughter Ann, looking glass, &c. Rem. of estate to be sold, money arising to be put to interest until youngest son is 21, then to be equally divided among children.
Execs: Samuel Gummere, John Spencer; they also to be guardians of children. Wit: Jesse Hallowell, Edward Edwards, Joseph Hallowell.

SMITH, HENRY. Frederick.
Oct 14, 1791. June 3, 1793. 1.336

To son George, 20 pds. Estate to be sold and divided as follows: 1/3 to son George; 1/3 to Godfreed Langbine and Margaret his wife; 1/3 to children of daughter Elizabeth, wife of Michael Ninetunhelser, equally. Twenty pds. to be deducted from Godfreed Langbine's share.
Exec: George Mohr. Wit: Richard P. Leedy, Henry Grob.

RITTENHOUSE, MATTHIAS. Wrocester.
June 1, 1793. June 12, 1793. 1.338
To wife Catharine, room, furniture, maintenance, &c. to 2 sons Matthias and Joseph, 2 fars, 1 containing 6 1/2 acres, other 15 acres, equally subject to maintenance of wife and to sisters when married, furniture, &c. To sons Matthias and Joseph, 1 horse each. To granddaughter Susannah Zeigler, 5 pds. Rem. to daughters: Nanny, wife of John Fry; Muney, wife of Jacob Metz; Catharine, wife of Abraham Hubner; Magdalena, Barbara and Sarah.
Execs: Son Matthias, Christopher Zimmerman. Wit: Jacob Rittenhouse, William Rittenhouse, Fred Conrad.

MIERS, JACOB. Cheltenham.
July 7, 1793. July 20, 1793. 1.340
To sons: Jacob and John, realty equally divided. Subject to following legacies. To daughter ann, 140 pds. To daughter Barbara, 140 pds. To daughter Elizabeth, 140 pds. Rem. of personalty to be divided among 6 children.
Execs: Sons Jacob and Frederick. Wit: Benjamin Rowland, David Altemus.

SHOEMAKER, JACOB. Lower Salford.
April 17, 1777. July 24, 1793. 1.340
To wife Susannah, 20 pds. and household goods; interest of 300 pds. during widowhood. If she marry to have interest of 100 pds. After her death to be divided among children. Farm, 140 acres to be sold and personalty also. Wife to have 300 pds. out of it, rem. to children.
Execs: Son Michael and son George. Wit: Daniel Hagy, John Hockman.

REES, EVAN. Providence.
March 3, 1789. July 27, 1793. 1.341
To wife Hannah, bed, furniture. Exrs. to sell farm and personalty when son Evan is 21. Wife to have 15 pds. yearly. If she lives in house, 12 pds. yearly. Rem. of money divided among children. Exrs. to sell land in Berks Co. 11 acres, and other land in Northumberland Co., 217 acres and divided among children. Sons Benjamin and Evan to be sent to school. Rem. to 2 sons Samuel and Daniel, equally.
Execs: Wife Hannah, sons Daniel and Samuel. Wit: Israel Jacobs, Jesse Jacobs, John Jacobs.

POTTS, SAMUEL. Pottstown.
March 5, 1793. July 29, 1793. 1.343

To wife Joanna, wearing apparel, household goods, negro girls, Betty and Peggy, also farm where son Joseph lives, 20 acres, 1/4 part of Warwick Furnace and testator's share of stock and household goods valued to John Rutter and David Potts, Jr. subject to following contracts: to son Thomas, right of ore to supply 1/5 part of Joanna Furnace for which he pays 300 pds.. Also to wife during life money arising from contract to supply ore for 1/4 par of Thomas Bull's contract said Furnace, also to wife income of ore from Rebecca Furnace, all in lieu of her dower. To sons Thomas and Joseph half part of mines in Colebrook Dale, Berks Co., they paying 300 pds. to sister. To daughter Sarah Hobart, 1/8 part of Rebecca Furnace, she paying 400 pds. Rem. to be sold and divided among children, deducting advances. At death of wife bequests to her to be valued, son David to have first choice at valuation, in default of him to each child beginning with others. House and land at Pottstown to be sold at wife's death and divided among children.
Codicil, provides if mine next Jones Mine shall yield copper ore of value, it to go to children: John, Thomas, Joseph and Sarah and privilege of it for copper. Also adds son John to exrs.
Execs: Sons: Thomas, Joseph and David Potts, son in law Robert Loller. Wit: John C. Stocker, David Rutter.

BROOKE, RACHEL. Limerick.
May 29, 1793. July 29, 1793. 1.346
To mother, wearing apparel. To 2 youngest sistrs: Ann and Ruth, testatrix's share of estate left by father, except 5 pds. to sister Hannah Davis's daughter Margaret.
Execs: James Evans, Job Pugh. Wit: Matthias Brooke, James Evans.

SIBERT, SIMON FELIX. Philadelphia.
March 20, 1793. Aug 6, 1793. 1.346
To sister Madam Therese Sophia Sibert, widow of Count of Villefort, all estate.
Exec: Alexander Anderson. Wit: John H. Montulle, Frederick Boulange.

LEVERING, JACOB. Whitpain.
Jan 28, 1793. Aug 1, 1793. 1.349
To poor of Gwynedd Preparative Meeting of Friends, 5 pds. To cousin Catharine Bower, 20 s. To cousin Daniel Levering, farm, 100 acres. To cousin Henry Levering, bible. Rem. of personalty to cousin Daniel Levering.
Exec: Cousin Daniel Levering. Wit: William Evans, Jacob Cope, Samuel Evans.

LANDES, JACOB, SR. Franconia.
May 29, 1787. May 13, 1793. 1.350
To son Isaac, farm, 65 acres and saw-mill. It is valued at 435 pds. He to take his share out and pay rem. 15 pds. yearly. Rem. of estate to be

divided into 9 shares, 1 share each to children: Jacob, Henry Yellis, John, Isaac, daughter Barbara, Elizabeth, Catharine and 1 share to children of dec. daughter Susanna.
Exec: Son Henry Landes. Wit: Rudolph Herley, John Barkey, Jacob Barkey.

WHITMAN, JOHN. Douglass.
May 23, 1793. Aug 12, 1793. 1.351
Estate to be sold. To wife Elizabeth, 1/3 part of estate. To son unnamed, 5 s. To children of first wife: Jacob, John and Maria, rem. of estate.
Execs: Gabriel Kline, Samuel Boyer. Wit: Benjamin Markley, Matthias Warthman, Frederick Beiteman.

WEIREMAN, JOHN. Skippack and Perkiomen.
April 11, 1793. Sept 6, 1793. 1.352
To wife Mary, household goods, cow, 300 pds., maintenance during widowhood. To son John, farm, 150 acres. Rem. to be sold and divided among 6 daughters.
Execs: Son John and son in law Jacob Wissemer. Wit: Christian Haltman, John Barkey, Sr.

FRY, JOSEPH. Towamencin.
Aug 3, 1793. Sept 6, 1793. 1.353
To wife Susanna, bedding, linen, maintenance. When youngest son is of age, realty to be sold. Money divided into 4 equal parts. 1 part to wife. 1 part to son Jacob. 1 part to daughter Margaret. 1 part to son unnamed.
Execs: Wife Susanna, Abraham Godwals. Wit: Isaac Reiner, Jacob Fry, Henry Sweitzer.

SCHEIVE, GEORGE. Hatfield.
Aug 4, 1793. Sept 14, 1793. 1.354
To wife Catharine, 50 pds. and cow, or 7 pds. in lieu of cow according to marriage contract in lieu of her dower. Estate to be divided among children: Margaret, Catharine, Susannah, John, Elizabeth and Martin.
Execs: Son George, son in law George Seiple. Wit: Henry Grob, Robert Loller.

YERKES, JOSIAH. Moreland.
Dec 2, 1791. Oct 1, 1793. 1.355
To son Joshua, 30 s. To son Josiah, 30 pds. To daughter Rebecca Wood, 10 pds. To granddaughter Sarah Boon, cow. To daughter Margaret, 20 s. To daughter Mary, house where testator lived and 2 acres, horse, cow, choice of stock. To son Nathaniel, rem. of realty, 100 acres, and rem. of personalty.
Exec: Son Nathaniel Yerkes. Wit: Silas Watts, George Shelmire.

DAVIS, ROBERT. Gwynedd.

Sept 12, 1793. Oct 5, 1793. 1.356
To Israel, son of brother Hugh, 5 s. To children of brothers John and David: Isaac, Elizabeth, David, Tacey rem. of estate equally.
Execs: Leah Brades and her son Isaac Davis. Wit: Arthur Brades, Thomas Wood, Jacob Hofner.

SCHEETZ, HENRY. Whitemarsh.
Sept 12, 1793. Oct 15, 1793. 1.358
To wife Catharine, house during widowhood, cow, income of 500 pds. during life. Three farms and 2 ten acre lots to be valued and equally divided among children as follows: to son Henry, farm where testator lived. He paying what is over his share to other children. To son Justus, farm in Springfield, he paying what is over his share. Also paying the interest of 30 pds. to his mother. To sons in law John and Ulley Slatter, farm and 2 ten acre lots in Springfield. Personalty to be sold and divided among children. To son Henry, felts, rags. He giving up his part of rags in son Justus's mill. Sons Henry and Justus to pay 6 children: Elizabeth, Catharine, Mary, Ann, Sarah and George, 1/8 part each of dividend in successive years. To son Justus, 500 pds. after wife's death.
Execs: Sons Henry and Justus. Wit: Beonhard Mallharus, Peter Loeser, Jacob Knorr.

MILLER, FREDERICK SR. Marlborough.
Dec 19, 1791. Oct 31, 1793. 1.358
To son Adam, 20 pds. Wit: Jacob Long, Ludowick Goettge.

CADWALLADER, ABRAHAM. Abington.
Sept 2, 1793. Nov 5, 1793. 1.359
To daughters Ruth and Agnes, 60 pds. Rem. of personalty to wife during life, and income of realty until 2 youngest sons Joel and Martin are 21. When son Joel is 21, he to receive farm and pay to his sisters Ruth, Agnes and Martha, 40 pds. each. If son Joel die, farm to be sold and money divided among children, except to wife income of 1/3 part during life. After her death 1/2 of her dower to her children, other half to Preparative Meeting of Friends at Abington.
Execs: Brother in law Abraham Davis, and wife Martha.

RAZOR, JACOB. Providence.
May 28, 1793. Nov 12, 1793. 1.360
To wife Margaret, maintenance, household goods, &c. To 3 children: Abraham, Isaac and Hannah, income of realty. After wife's death realty to be sold and money divided as follows: to son Abraham, 20 pds. and his share. Rem. to be divided among 3 children. Exrs. to make deed to Eleanor Griffith for 4 acres, also to give to Jacob Schwenck a deed. After wife's death household goods to be sold and divided among 3 children.
Execs: Brothers Melker Razor, Michael Razor. Wit: Jacob Weber, Jacob Dismant.

WEINE, JACOB. Limerick.
Dec 20, 1792. Nov 12, 1793. 1.361
To wife Mary, pewter dishes, maintenance, &c. To son Jacob, all estate, and stock.
Exec: Son Jacob. Wit: Jacob Cultz, Joseph Urmy.

McCLINTICK, THOMAS, New Hanover.
Oct 9, 1793. Nov 18, 1793. 1.362
To 3 brothers: Robert, Francis and James, rem. of legacy left to testator by uncle Thomas May. Wit: Christopher Garret, Elizabeth Brooke, John Brooke.

McCAFEE, WILLIAM. Lower Merion.
April --, 1791. Nov 19, 1793. 1.363
To son Thomas, 5 s. To grandson William, son of Thomas, 5 s. To son Robert, 5 s. To son Isaac, 5 s. To son John, 5 s. He to pay to daughter Elizabeth, 10 pds. after wife's death. To son John, watch. To daughter Mary, 5 s. To daughter Jane, 5 s. To wife Jane, rem. of estate. At her death realty to be sold and money divided among Robert, Isaac and Jane.
Execs: Son Robert, son in law John Righter. Wit: Hugh Knox, Bartle Righter, Jacob Libley.

KEYSER, JACOB. Worcester.
Nov 9, 1793. Nov 20, 1793. 1.363
To wife Catharine, bed, &c. To son Samuel, watch, fowling piece. Rem. of personalty to be sold. To wife Catharine and son Samuel all bonds, notes and money arising from sale, equally.
Execs: Wife Catharine, and brother John. Wit: Christian Stouver, Christopher Zimmerman, Henry Hunsicker.

FARRINGER, MARTIN. Whitemarsh.
Dec 26, 1791. Nov 15, 1793. 1.364
To wife Margareth, all estate during widowhood. To son John, 5 pds. To 5 children: John, George, Henry, Martin and dau. Mary Miller all estate, after wife's death, except the children of John Stam shall have an equal share with above named children.
Execs: Sons John and George. Wit: Charles Deshler, Williamsaac Mather.

LEWIS, ISAAC. New Hanover.
Oct 15, 1793. Nov 25, 1793. 1.365
To daughter Elizabeth Coils, 5 s. To son Isaac, 7 pds., 10 s. To son Issachar, 7 pds., 10 s. To daughter Molley, 5 s. To daughter Anna, 15 pds. To daughter Eliner, 3 pds., 10 s. To daughter Elsie, 15 pds. To son Jacob, 18 pds. To wife the interest of 30 pds. At her death principal to be divided among 8 children. Rem. to be equally divided into 9 equal shares after sale of realty 8 shares to children, 1 share to wife Elsie.
Execs: Sons Isaac and Issachar. Wit: Jacob Hoover, Jacob Crous.

KEMPER, JOHN. Perkiomen and Skippack.
Oct 4, 1790. Nov 25, 1793. 1.366
To wife Gertrude, 50 pds., furniture, bed, maintenance, during widowhood. To son Abraham, farm, 85 acres, to be valued to him at 400 pds. He to have 100 pds.; 50 pds. for widow; rem. divided into 5 equal shares. Son Abraham to have 1 share, and 4 daughters each to have 1 share: Susannah, wife of Henry Shat; Mary, wife of William Tyson, Hannah, wife of Henry Kuter and Gertrude Kemper.
Execs: Son Abraham and son in law William Tyson. Wit: Jacob Markley, Henry Markley and Henry Sweitzer.

ARWIN, WILLIAM. North Wales.
Feb 2, 1789. Nov 30, 1793. 1.368
To wife Rebeckah, income of farm, 100 acres during life and use of personalty. To daughter Ellin, 1 pds. To grandchildren, children of son Cadwallader, 20 s. equally. To 3 children: John, Sarah and Elizabeth, farm, 100 acres and personalty after wife's death.
Execs: Son John and daughters Sarah and Elizabeth. Wit: Cadwallader Roberts, Evan Jones.

LIVEZEY, BENJAMIN. Cheltenham.
Sept 1, 1793. Dec 5, 1793. 1.369
To wife and 2 daughters Mary and Hannah, all personalty. To wife all realty, after her death to be divided as follows: to daughters Mary and Hannah, farm in Radnor, Del. Co. they to pay to son John and Esther Pennington, 50 pds. each. To granddaughter Elizabeth Yarnall, 25 pds.
Execs: Daughters Mary and Hannah. Wit: Jonathan Livezey, Benjamin Livezey.

VERNER, GEORGE. Dublin.
Dec 26, 1791. Dec 17, 1793. 1.370
To wife Elizabeth, personalty, except wearing apparel and bible. To grandson George Backman, bible. to sons of daughter Magdalena Backman, wearing apparel equally. To wife Elizabeth, farm where testator lived.
Exec: Wife Elizabeth. Wit: John Mann, Catharine Timanus.

HALLOWELL, JONATHAN. Moreland.
Jan 4, 1793. Dec 23, 1793. 1.370
To wife Elizabeth, income of realty during widowhood for educating 4 children: Martha, William, Samuel and Elizabeth; also 50 pds. for her use. Personalty to be sold. After wife's death or marriage, realty to be sold and divided among 4 children aforesaid.
Execs: Wife Elizabeth and Benjamin Lloyd. Trustee, Nicholas Waln. Wit: Samuel Gourley, Hiram McNiel.

BUTLER, JOSEPH. Upper Merion.

Nov 15, 1790. Dec 25, 1793. 1.372
To wife Sarah, all estate, except following legacies. To son Thomas, horse, mare, cow, wagon, &c. To daughter Sarah, case of drawers, side saddle, 10 pds. &c. To son Jonathan, choice of horse, saddle, 25 pds.
Execs: Wife Sarah, son Thomas and brother in law Joseph Roberts. Wit: John Potts, Christopher Loezer, Jesse Cleaver.

SHOEMAKER, ISAAC. Upper Dublin.
July 30, 1791. Dec 30, 1793. 1.372
To wife Hannah, bed, maintenance, during life. To sons David and Thomas, rem. of estate during widowhood of wife. After her death or marriage to be sold. to son Thomas, 1/3 of money arising from realty. He to pay to son David, 15 pds. Exrs. to have 5 pds. each. To children of Elizabeth Walton, dec. 1/9 part of rem. Rem. of estate to children: Peter, Daniel, Martha, James, David, Mary, Hannah and Rebecca.
Execs: Sons David and Thomas. Wit: John Cleaver, Jonathan Thomas.

PETERMAN, JACOB. Providence.
Oct 4, 1793. Feb 11, 1794. 1.374
To wife Susannah, case of drawers, iron pot, income of realty and part of movables. Rem. of personalty to be sold. Exrs. to sell farm and from money arising to buy small farm for widow and children to live on. If wife marry to take under intestate laws. After wife's death rem. to be divided among 8 children: Elizabeth, Hannah, Mary, Catharine, John, Sarah, Susannah and George as follows: to son John, 35 pds. To son George, 30 pds. Rem. equally divided among 8 children.
Execs: George Hepler, brother John Peterman. Wit: Frederick Isett, John Scharer, Benjamin Dismant.

KATZ, HENRY. Whitemarsh.
May 6, 1783. Feb 15, 1794. 1.375
To wife children, 1/3 of estate, house, garden during widowhood. If she die or marry to son Henry. To wife, household goods, 50 pds. After her death household goods to be divided among children. If she marry to have 1/3 part. To daughter in law Elizabeth, widow of son Conrad, 18 d. To son Henry, paper mill with 17 acres. It to be appraised, he to have 50 pds. Rem. to be divided into 5 parts. Rem. 1 part to each of children: daughter Catharine, daughter Maria and daughter Magdalena, son Henry and grandsons Henry and George, sons of dec. son Conrad. Henry to receive twice as much as George.
Execs: Wife Catharine, son Henry and son in William Hagy. Wit: Daniel Hagy, Jacob Stely.

SHOEMAKER, DAVID. Upper Merion.
Feb 16, 1794. May 10, 1794. 1.376
To brother Peter, saddle. To brother James, boots. To brother Daniel, plow and irons. Money left to testator by sister Margaret, to brothers and

sisters: Peter, James, Daniel, Martha Simpson, Mary Lukens and Hannah Walton, equally. Rem. to brother Thomas.
Exec: Brother Thomas. Wit: John Cleaver, John Steriger.

OBERHOLTZER, HENRY. Hatfield.
July 28, 1791. March 14, 1794. 1.377
To wife Barbara, bed, cow, horse, household goods, &c. use of house and maintenance during widowhood. Son Isaac to receive from wife 5 pds. yearly for privileges. Sons Isaac and Joseph to pay 500 pds., 150 pds. to remain in their hands, wife to receive interest of rem. After her death to be divided among 6 children. To son Joseph, lower part of land, 95 acres 148 perches. To son Isaac, upper part of land, 98 acres 122 perches. To sons: Jacob, John and Joseph and Isaac, 65 pds. each more than daughters. To daughter Catharine, "outset". To Mennonite Meeting at Hatfield, 10 pds. Personalty to be sold. Rem. of money to be divided into 6 shares, to 2 daughters 30 pds. each and rem. to children equally.
Execs: sons John and Joseph. Wit: Jacob Swartz, Abraham Johnson, John Barkey, Sr.

KOONCE, HENRY. Springfield.
Oct 19, 1793. March 14, 1794. 1.380
To wife Anna, all estate for life. At her death to dec. brother Jacob's daughter Barbara Koonce, 3 pds. Rem. to dec. brother Jacob's grandchildren: Jacob and John Miller equally. They to pay to niece Barbara the 3 pds. aforesaid.
Execs: Felix Detweiler, and wife Anna. Wit: Philip Detweiler, Casper Schlatter, Jr.

GEORGES, WILLIAM. Lower Salford.
Nov 15, 1793. March 29, 1794. 1.381
To wife Jacobina, maintenance on estate until son William is of age; then personalty to be sold. Farm, 150 acres to be appraised. Son Abraham to have choice of farm, is [sic] he refuse, then son William. If wife die or marry before son William is of age, then farm to be rented until he is 21 wife to have maintenance during widowhood. Rem. to be divided into 5 equal shares, 1/5 part to wife during widowhood, the other 4 shares to sons: Abraham, William, John and Jacob.
Execs: Brother Abraham Georges, brother in law John Hiltenbeitel. Wit: Ditman Zeigler, Christian Barkey, John Barkey Sr.

JONES, JOHN. Montgomery.
June 26, 1791. March 7, 1794. 1.382
To grandson David Jones, 50 pds. To grandson Jonathan Jones, 100 pds. To son Jonathan, clock. To grandsons: Benjamin and John Jones, children of John Jones, dec. 20 s. each. To stepson Joseph Williams, "Works of William Penn". To son Jonathan, release of a debt of 300 pds. for help given him during the late war between America and Great Britain, he

having already had deeded to him farm in Whitemarsh with mortgage of 600 pds. and release him from the 800 pds. balance of purchase money. Rem. of personalty to daughters: Abigail Shoemaker, wife of Joseph Shoemaker; Sarah, wife of Joseph Ambler, equally. They to pay to granddaughter Sarah Meredith, daughter of Sarah Ambler, 50 pds.
Execs: Sons in law Joseph Shoemaker and Joseph Ambler. Guardian of grandsons David and Jonathan Jones during monority, Samuel Livezey. Wit: Peter Thomson, Jr., Edward Randolph.

DULL, FREDERICK. Plymouth.
Nov 6, 1794. Aug 17, 1795. 1.385
To wife Elizabeth, income of estate, legacies being first deducted. No timber to be wasted, nor principal of personalty to be lessened. To son John, 40 pds. To son Frederick, 40 pds., horse and harness. To daughter Margaret, "outset". To daughter Barbara, "outset". At wife's death, farm, 120 acres to be sold and with rem. of personalty divided in 8 shares as follows: 1 share each to children: Catharine, Margaret, Mary, John, Barbara, Susanna and Frederick. Income of rem. share to daughter Elizabeth.
Execs: Wife Elizabeth and son John. Wit: John Shoup, John Mann.

SPECHT, PETER. New Hanvoer.
March 25, 1795. Aug 24, 1795. 1.385
Mother Barbara to remain on farm and have maintenance during life. Wife Margaret to remain on farm until April 1, 1803, and have income and profits from same, she to maintain mother and educate children, to pay taxes, &c. Farm then to be appraised and divided into 2 equal parts, 150 pds. to remain on each tract and interest paid to wife Margaret in lieu of dower. Rem. of valuation money to be divided into 8 equal parts, 1 part each to children: Adam, Jacob, Magdalena, Peter, Margaret, Elizabeth, Conrad and John. At wife's death, 300 pds. of which she had interest to be divided among children. One of the two tracts of land to son Conrad, he to have choice, the other tract to son John. To Reformed Congregation of New Hanover, 5 pds. Sons to be put to trade of their own choosing at 18, daughters to remain at home.
Execs: Wife Margaret, Jacob Bickle. Wit: Henry Gilbert, Thomas Richards.

MORRIS, JAMES. Whitpain.
Jan 2, 1794. Sept 1, 1795. 1.388
To wife Elizabeth, and children, Joseph and Hannah, each 1/3 part of estate. If children should die under age, their shares to wife, 1/2 to be at her disposal, and the other half to sister Phebe Morris and niece Elizabeth Mifflin.
Execs: Son Joseph Morris, Anthony Morris. Wit: Jacob Roberts.

FISHER, JOSEPH. Douglass.

Sept 31[sic], 1794. Jan 17, 1795. 1.389
To wife Barbara, all estate. Share of land on which mother resides shall be div ided among living brothers and sisters. "Though they shall give something thereof to my wife in remembrance of me as they please".
Exec: Wife Elizabeth. Wit: Bernhard Gilbert, Jacob Huber.

ROBERTS, LEWIS. Abington.
Nov 4, 1782. April 1, 1794. 1.390
To wife Mary, maintenance, from sons John and Lewis. If she marry again, privilege in mansion house and garden and firewood to cease. To son John, grist-mill and 97 acres. To son Lewis, mansion house and 100 acres. Also 1/2 part of wood standing on land bequeathed to son John. To son John, other half of wood. Personalty and farm, 19 acres, adjoining Pennepack Creek to be sold and divided among daughters: Hannah, Ann, Mary, Rachel and Jane. If each share shall be less than 100 pds. to be made up to that amount by sons John and Lewis. If unborn child shall be daughter 100 pds. to be paid by sosn John and Lewis; if a son 300 pds. to be paid by said 2 sons when 21. Sons to learn trade when 16.
Execs: Wife Mary, brother William, cousin George Williams. Wit: Joseph Walker, Jacob Nippes, Silas Watts.

FITZWATER, JOHN. Upper Dublin.
March 14, 1791. April 8, 1794. 1.392
To son John, 40 acres. He to pay to daughter Mary Spencer, 35 pds. To daughter Sarah Lukens, bond and mortgage, given to Matthew Tyson. Matthew Tyson and wife to live in house on said land and have firewood during life. Rem. of estate equally to daughters Mary Spencer and Sarah Lukens, except bonds given by sons Matthew and John.
Execs: Sons Matthew and John. Wit: Isaac Knight, John Cleaver.

JONES, DANIEL. Horsham.
May 6, 1786. April 19, 1794. 1.394.
To wife Phebe, all estate during life, except following: to sons Thomas and David, 20 pds. each when of age. To daughter Elizabeth, 15 pds. when of age. At wife's death, farm to be sold, money equally divided among living children; wife to dispose of personalty in her possession by will. If children should die in minority, then realty equally divided between brother Thomas's children and Isaac Marples's children, Daniel and Jones Marple.
Execs: Wife Phebe, brother in law Nathan Marple. Wit: William Thomas, Martha Marple, Josiah Jones.

GILBERT, JOHN. Moreland.
Oct 19, 1794. April 22, 1794. 1.395
To wife Mary, maintenance and income of 350 pds. in lieu of dower. To daughter Sarah Scout, 50 pds. To daughter Phebe Quickley, 50 pds. To 4 granddaughters: Mary, Martha, Naomi and Rebecca, children of Rebecca Appleton, 50 pds. divided equally. To daughter Mary Dance, 50 pds. To

daughter Marcey White, 50 pds. To daughter Jane Gilbert, 50 pds. To daughter Martha Croasdel, 50 pds. All to be paid after wife's death by 2 sons Jesse and Jonathan. To daughter Jane, 2 acres 20 perches. Rem. to sons Jonathan and Jesse. Wit: John Irwin, Arthur Watts, William Van Horne.

BRAND, JACOB. Limerick.
March 25, 1794. May 19, 1794. 1.396
To wife Hannah, bed, bedstead and maintenance. To son Frederick, farm, 70 acres. Subject to maintenance of wife. Farm at valuation of 600 pds. He to keep 200 pds.; 200 pds. to 4 daughters: Magdalena, wife of Daniel Cryeler, Elizabeth, Hannah and Sophia, equally. Remaining 200 pds. to remain on farm and wife to receive interest during widowhood. To son Jacob, farm, 63 acres and desk. Farm at valuation of 200 pds. He to retain 100 pds. and other 100 pds. to son John. To son Frederick, horse and wagon. To daughter Elizabeth, 10 pds. in addition to 5 pds. she had. To daughters Hannah and Sophia, 125 pds. equally. Estate to remain together and farmed as usual for 6 months. Rem. of personalty to be sold and divided into 8 equal shares, 1/8 part each to wife and 7 children. Execs: Wife Hannah, son Frederick. Wit: Henry Newman, Thomas Richards.

MAJOR, JANE. Gwynedd.
Jan 31, 1794. June 25, 1794. 1.398
To daughter Mary Birney, bolster and 2 pillows. To daughters Hannah, Margaret, and Jane and Elizabeth, wearing apparel. To son Ebenezer, bedstead, table, &c. To daughter Margaret, large chair. To daughters Hannah, Jane and Elizabeth, bed clothes. To son John, pewter quart, pewter plate. To son James, bible and rem. of household goods.
N.B. This was an uncupative will, afterwards comitted to writing by Robert Loller.
Exec: Son in law Alexander McDowell. Wit: Robert Loller, John Irwin.

RITTENHOUSE, HENRY. Norriton.
Dec 11, 1788. Aug 2, 1794. 1.399
To wife Sophia, 15 pds. yearly, furniture and maintenance during widowhood. If she marry furniture to be at her disposal. To son Christopher, 100 pds. Farm to be appraised and son Christopher to have the choice of it at valuation. He to pay off legacies. To grandson John Rittenhouse, 5 pds. Valuation of farm to be equally divided among children. Rem. of estate equally divided among children.
Execs: Son Christopher, Ezekiel Roades. Wit: Robert Curry, Abraham Beyer, Nathan Potts.

KASTNER, ELIZABETH. Whitemarsh.
Sept 7, 1778. Aug 5, 1794. 1.401
Widow of George Kastner. Farm of 15 acres, and 2 stoves to daughter

Agnes Dewees, during widowhood. At her death to be sold and equally divided among 12 grandchildren: John, George and William Streeper, Mary Holman, Hannah Piper, Sarah and Lydia Streeper, William, John and Abraham Dewees, Elizabeth and Christian Dewees. To daughter in law Magdalena Streeper, feather bed, bolster, bible and pewter. Rem. of household goods, wearing apparel and 20 pds. in money to daughter Agnes Dewees. Rem. to daughter Agnes Dewees's children: William, John, Abraham, Elizabeth and Christian Dewees.
Execs: George Streeper, William Dewees. Wit: Levi Trump, Pat. Monan.

HUFTY, MARY. Moreland.
Oct 20, 1793. Aug 21, 1794. 1.402
To son Joseph, use of farm, until son John, is of age, then farm to be equally divided among 4 children: Sarah Neswanger, Jane White, Joseph and John Hufty as tenants in To daughter Sarah, looking glass, candle stand, &c. To daughter Jane, case of drawers, teatable, &c. To son Joseph, feather bed, 10 plate stove, irons, silver buckles and rem. of kitchen furniture. To son John, desk, feather bed, silver watch. To granddaughter Mary Neswanger, feather bed, furnishings, white gown and dimity petticoat. To daughter Sarah, black velvet cloak and rem. of wearing apparel. To daughter Jan, negro man Toley and negro woman Selah. They to have their freedom whenever they pay to exr. the sum of 40 pds. Said money to be applied towards paying testator's debts. Rem. of money to 4 children: Sarah, Jane, Joseph and John equally. To daughter Jane, warming pan. Rem. of estate to son Joseph and daughter Jane, equally.
Exec: Son Joseph. Wit: Isaac Roberts, John Wright, John Watts.

KRAUSS, HENRY. Frederick.
Aug 3, 1785. Aug 30, 1794. 1.403
To wife Anna Mary, bed, bedding and maintenance and 90 pds. To son Michael, farm, 200 acres, he paying 600 pds.; 200 pds. he to keep, the other 400 pds. To sons John Valentine and Henry. To 4 daughters: Margaret, Molley, Eva and Regina, 175 pds. each. To daughter Barbara, wife of John Moore, income of 175 pds. to maintain said daughter. In case of husband's death, principal to be paid to her. If he outlive her, money to go to her children. To son John, 25 pds. Rem. equally divided among 9 children.
Execs: Sons Valentine and Michael. Wit: George Michael, Daniel Krauss, John Barkey.

LEIDY, JACOB. Franconia.
Dec 19, 1791. Aug 30, 1794. 1.405
To wife Barbara, 10 pds., horse, cow, maintenance and interest of 300 pds. To son John, 5 pds. To children of daughter Catharine, as follows: Henry, 10 pds. Jacob, 40 pds. Her 5 daughters 10 pds. each. Rem. of estate to 7 children equally.

Execs: son Jacob, son in law John Fluck. Wit: Charles Shellenberger, Jacob Conware, Henry Shellenberger.

HALLOWELL, WILLIAM. Cheltenham.
Oct 7, 1793. Sept 15, 1794. 1.407
To son Thomas, 6 pds. yearly during life. To son Mattfhew, 6 pds. yearly during life. To son William, 150 pds. To son Rynear's children as follows: Thomas, 30 pds. Mary, wife of John Clayton, 50 pds. Agnes, wife of Joseph Marshall, 5 pds. William, 100 pds. he to receive only income of his. To son John's children: Isaac, 5 pds. Anna and John 100 pds. each. To son Josiah, 150 pds. To son Caleb, clock. To son Chalkey, 10 pds. To son Joseph, farm, 74 acres in Northampton, Bucks Co., during life. At his death to his sons: Joseph, William and John, equally. To son Daniel, home farm, with utensils. He to pay legacies to sons Thomas and Matthew, also to pay 450 pds. to exrs. Rem. to sons: William, Josiah, Daniel, Caleb and Joseph equally.
Execs: sons William and Caleb. Wit: John Thomson and Thomas Livezey.

WALKER, ANNA. Pottstown.
Aug 1, 1794. Sept 24, 1794. 1.409
To son Lewis, 5 s. To son Thomas, 5 s. To daughter Anna Leonard, wearing apparel. To granddaughters Elizabeth Leonard and Anna Walker Leonard, bed-room suit. Rem. to friend David Rutter, to be applied to the support of son David Walker. At his death to be equally divided between son Thomas and daughter Anna Leonard's children.
Exec: David Rutter. Wit: William Thomson, Amos Jones.

DIEMER, MICHAEL. Limerick.
Oct 6, 1793. Oct 2, 1794. 1.411
To wife Catharine, income of 1/4 part of estate. At her death equally divided among 3 children: George, Daniel and Eve. To son George, farm, 100 acres. He to pay 25 pds. more than 1/4 of estate to exrs. To son Daniel, farm, 30 acres in Limerick. To daughter Eve, to be paid by son George, what will amount to 25 pds. less than 1/4 part. Personalty to be sold, money divided among children.
Execs: Isaiah Davis, James Stall. Wit: Adna Evans, Mordecai Evans.

MOYER, ABRAHAM. Providence.
June 28, 1794. Oct 3, 1794. 1.413
To wife Elizabeth, income of estate and maintenance. Personalty to be sold and divided among 4 daughters: Mary, wife of Joseph Shelly; Margaret, wife of George Marsteller; Hannah, wife of George High; Susannah, wife of John Taylor. To grandchildren, 1 Spanish Milled Dollar each in token of remembrance. Rem. divided as follows: 1/4 part to daughter Mary, except 5 pds. of which to son John. 1/4 part to daughter Margaret, and 10 pds. additional. 1/4 part of daughter Hannah. 1/4 part to daughter Susannah.

Execs: Son John, Christopher Zimmerman. Wit: James Adams, Peter Turner, Jacob Auld.

WEITNER, ABRAHAM. Providence.
July 30, 1794. Oct 8, 1794. 1.414
To wife Margaret, 1/3 of personalty and maintenance. To daughter Rachel, bed, bedding. Rem. of personalty to be sold, also farm. To wife Margaret, enough to make up 100 pds. To each of 6 children: George, David, Elizabeth, wife of John Wagonsail, Rachel, Abigail and Deborah, 50 pds. To daughters Abigail and Deborah, each a bed, &c.
Execs: Wife Margaret, and son in law John Wagonsail. Wit: Rachel Hamer, Elizabeth Frame, Israel Jacobs.

FOUT, HENRY. Limerick.
March 4, 1791. Oct 22, 1794. 1.416
To wife Catharine, in lieu of dower, furniture and maintenance. To son Martin, 5 acres, 122 perches in Limerick in addition to 12 acres previously given. To son Henry, farm, 20 acres. At wife's death home farm to be sold. Money equally divided among 4 daughters: Barbara, Susannah, Catharine and Mary.
Exec: Son Martin. Wit: Daniel Baker, William Baker, Benjamin Dismant.

BOEHM, MARY. Marlborough.
Sept 29, 1794. Oct 23, 1794. 1.417
Land and saw-mill to 4 children: John, Mary and William Mock and Betsey Boehm, equally. To Betsey Boehm, rem. of personalty and 50 pds. in money.
Execs: George Schultz, Abraham Schultz.

GOSINGER, GEORGE. Gwynedd.
July 29, 1794. Oct 25. 1974. 1.418
To Barbara Sellers, wife of Leonard Sellers, 10 pds. To Elizabeth, wife of John Hallman, 10 pds. To son in law Henry Hallman, farm, 11 5 acres. He to pay 1000 pds. Income of 1/3 rem. to daughter Susannah; income of 1/3 rem. to daughter Magdalena; income of other 1/3 to daughter Catharine, principal to their children at daughters death. Wearing apparel divided among 3 daughters aforesaid.
Execs: Son in law Henry Hallman, John Hallman. Wit: Jacob Zeigler, Cadwallader Evans.

HOXWORTH, JOHN. Montgomery.
Sept 4, 1794. Oct 25, 1794. 1.421
To brothers Edward and Peter, 50 pds. equally. Exrs. to sell household goods, &c. To brothers Edward and Peter and sisters: Mary, Ann, Elizabeth and Sarah, rem. of estate equally.
Execs: Mother, Elizabeth Hoxworth and brother Edward. Wit: Evan Jones, Theophilus Williams.

GRIM, CONRAD. Upper Salford.
April 10 1792. Oct 30, 1794. 1.422
To wife Maria Barbara, all estate during widowhood, the bringing up of children. If wife marry or die, estate to be appraised and sold by exrs. To sons Daniel and George, 25 pds. each. Rem. of estate equally divided among 3 sons: Philip, Daniel and George.
Execs: Wife Maria and son Philip. Wit: Mc. Croll, Philip Gabrel.

URFFER, GEORGE. Upper Hanover.
April 19, 1794. Oct 31, 1794. 1.424
As testator's mother in law Susannah Kroussin, gave to testator's daughters children, 75 pds. to be paid by testator to said children when of age, exrs. to pay same. To wife Barbara, bed, bedstead and maintenance. Wife to be keep farm, 175 acres for 10 years, when son Baltzer is 21. Tract of land in Milford, 98 acres, to be sold. To son David, weavers loom, and 2 tracts, 191 acres, for consideration of 550 pds. He to keep 150 pds. and pay wife interest of 100 pds. during life, also to pay to son Baltzer, 100 pds. Remaining 200 pds. to 5 daughters, also after wife's death daughters to receive principal of wife's 100 pds. Wife Barbara, to have privilege in house, during life, son David to provide for her. To son Michael, 2 tracts, 35 acres, at consideration of 200 pds. He to keep 150 pds. Remaining 50 pds. he to pay to son Baltzer. To son Baltzer, 150 pds. Personalty to be sold after 10 years. Rem. to 5 daughters: Susannah, Mary, Catharine, Gertrude and Barbara, equally.
Execs: Wife Barbara, brother in law Baltzer Krauss. Wit: Jacob Yeakle.

KRAUSS, HENRY. Frederick.
July 12, 1794. Nov 4, 1794. 1.427
To wife Molley, beds, bedsteads, utensils, 20 pds. and maintenance. Mulatto girl, Dolly to be free when she is of age and have freedom suit. All estate to be sold. Wife to have income of 300 pds. during widowhood, if she marry income of 100 pds. To George Swenck, 15 pds. To Henry Swenck, 10 pds. To Mary Swenck, 10 pds. Rem. to be divided into 4 shares. To children of sister Molly, 1 share. To sister Eva, wife of Jacob Swenck, 1 share. To sister Regina, wife of John Swenck, 1 share. To sister Margaret, wife of Peter Frederick, 1 share.
Execs: Brothers in law John Swenck, George Swenck. Wit: George Yohn Sr., John Barkey, Daniel Krauss.

ENGART, CATHARINE. Upper Dublin.
Jan 9, 1793. Nov 10, 1794. 1.429
To 2 daughters Elizabeth Becher and Mary A. Mack, and granddaughter Mary Cup, wearing apparel equally. Personalty to be sold and money divided into 10 shares. To 8 children, 1 share each. To children of son John, dec. 1 share equally. To children of daughter Margaret Cup, dec. 1 share equally.
Exec: John Jarret, Sr. Wit: John Mann, Peter Steriger.

WILLS, MICHAEL. Plymouth.
July 23, 1793. Nov 19, 1794. 1.430
To wife Jane, all estate during life, then to be at her disposal. To children: Jeremiah, Mary, Rebecca, Michael and John, each a large bible.
Exec: Wife Jane. Wit: Sarah Mather, Pat Menan.

BARRY, RACHEL. Upper Merion.
Oct 11, 1794. Nov 28, 1794. 1.443
To son Samuel, writing desk. To daughter Tacy, wearing apparel, silver shoe buckles and 5 silver teaspoons. To granddaughter Jane, 18 s. when 18. Rem. of estate divided among children, daughter Anstis excepted (she having received what was intended to be paid to her). To sons James and Samuel and to daughters Mary and Lydia, in 1 year after testator's dec. and to sons Richard and Isaac, when 18.
Exec: Son Samuel. Wit: Jonathan Phillips, Jonathan Roberts.

HOUP,[HOUPT] MARGARET. Upper Dublin.
Nov 25, 1794. Dec 4, 1794. 1.432
To son Henry, silver watch. To daughter Catharine, bedstead, chairs, table, &c. To 4 daughters: Lissey, Betsey, Barbara and Catharine, rem. of household goods. Rem. to be divided among 8 children: Henry, Lissey, Jacob, Betsey, Barbara, Samuel, Catharine and Anthony.
Exec: George Dresher. Wit: John Collon, Christopher Loeser.

KASTNER, GEORGE. Upper Dublin.
Dec 15, 1787. Dec 4, 1794. 1.432
Personalty to be divided among brothers and sisters: Samuel, Andrew, Sarah, Elizabeth and Mary, also income of realty during life. To cousin Ann Collins, 1/2 interest in farm, 267 acres; she to take possession immediately after death of survivors of said brothers and sisters.
Exec: Cousin Ann Collins. Wit: Samuel Reall, Sarah Reall.

HARRY, THOMAS. Montgomery.
Dec 12, 1793. Feb 21, 1795. 1.434
To brother John Harry's son Benjamin, 20 pds. To George Weaver 10 pds. To niece Elizabeth Harry, rem. of estate. No legacies to be paid until 1 year after dec. of father and mother of testator.
Execs: William Mullin, Cadwallader Roberts. Wit: Thomas Wilson, Ezekiel Roberts.

PARRY, DAVID. Moreland.
Aug 20, 1794. Dec 11, 1794. 1.435
To wife Martha, all such estate as was her father's and 1/2 of income of rem. during widowhood in lieu of her dower. To son David, rem. of estate, except what shall remian of 140 pds., 1 s., 2 d. after deducting 8 pds., 18 s., 1 d. per annum from present estate which exrs. are to pay to Martha Cumming and Jane Lukens, daughters of brother Stephen Parry, equally.

Execs: Wife Martha, son David, brother Isaac and Samuel Gummere. Wit: Israel Clark, Samuel Lloyd, Lydia Dungan.

CURRY, ROBERT. Norriton.
Aug 23, 1794. Dec 12, 1794. 1.436
To brother Samuel, of Londomdary, Ireland, 5 pds. to nephew Joseph Curry, his son, 5 pds. To wife Mary, rem. of estate during life, to be disposed of at her death as she may think proper, subject to following restrictions: one year after death realty to be sold and payments made from money arising as follows: to Robert Shephard, 50 pds. To Capt. Robert Thomson, 50 pds., also silver sword. To Robert Curry Thomson, 50 pds. To Robert Curry, of Norriton, 30 pds. To Jane Shephard, 25 pds. To Mary, daughter of Archibald Thomson, 25 pds. To purchase a tombstone for testator and his wife and wife's first husband, Robert Thomson, 15 pds.
Codicil gives to Martha Shephard, 5 pds. during life and after wife's death rem. divided among children of Archibald Thomson, Mark Thomson, Martha Shephard, Agnes Darrah, Rebecca Darrah and 1 equal share to the 2 children of Mary Darrah, dec. Also revokes that part of will giving disposal of estate to widow. Wit: to codicil, Christopher Rittenhouse, John Fulton, Jacob Auld.
Execs: Wife Mary, William Armstrong, Martin Thomson. Wit: Archibald Darrah, Christopher Rittenhouse, Jacob Auld.

WOLFINGER, JACOB. Providence.
Nov 27, 1794. Dec 22, 1794. 1.438
To sister Christiana, 5 pds. To brother John, 5 s. To other sister "I not knowing her name properly, but believe it to be Mary Wolfinger", 5 s. To John Reed, 5 pds., axe and hat. To Esther, wife of John Reed, bedstead, &c. To 4 children of John Reed: Susannah, Abraham, Barbara and Mary, 20 pds. equally. To Menonite Meeting House at Skippack, 5 pds. Rem. to be divided each legacy above in proportion.
Execs: Henry Freed, Christopher Zimmerman. Wit: Edward Roberts, Joseph Boyer, Christopher Zimmerman.

GODWALT, ADAM. Towamencin.
May 17, 1792. Jan 5, 1795. 1.439
To wife Fronica, bedstead, furniture, maintenance and 30 pds. To son Henry, farm on Skippack Creek, 102 acres, he paying 300 pds. To son Abraham, other farm, 178 1/2 acres. Sons Henry and Abraham to provide equally for maintenance of wife during widowhood. Son Abraham to pay 600 pds. for his farm. to son Henry, 1 s. and discharge from 150 pds. owing testator. To daughter Catharine, 80 pds. To son Abraham, 10 pds. for use of daughter Catharine. To son in law Abraham Slifer, 1 s. To daughter Elizabeth, 90 pds. and as much as other daughters for marriage outset. To daughter Susannah, wife of David Slifer, 90 pds. To daughter Genio, wife of Joseph Johnson, 80 pds. To daughter Maria, wife of John

Hallman, 80 pds. To daughter Fronica, 80 pds. To daughter Anna, wife of Samuel Hendricks, 80 pds. Rem. equally divided among children.
Execs: Sons Abraham and Henry. Wit: Henry Pannebacker, Yellis Cassel.

DAVIS, SARAH, Upper Dublin.
July 15, 1793. Jan 19, 1795. 1.442
To sister Hannah Trump, income of 150 pds. yearly. To sister Hannah, second best bed and furniture. To nephew Joseph Naylor, 30 pds. To niece Mary Roberts, wife of Job Roberts, 5 pds. To niece Priscilla, wife of John Ambler, 5 pds. To nephew Daniel Jarret, desk. To niece Priscilla Jarret, best bed and furniture. To Mary Ellis, daughter of Robert Ellis, 10 pds. To Ann Jones, daughter of Jacob Jones, 10 pds. To 2 sisters Hannah and Priscilla, wearing apparel, equally. At sister Hannah's death 150 pds. of which she received income to be divided into 2 equal parts. To Mary, Priscilla Ambler, John Naylor, Sarah Brooks, Daniel and Ann Trump, 1 part equally. To children of sister Priscilla Ambler; Daniel, John, Levi and Priscilla, other part equally. Rem. of estate equally to Mary Roberts, Priscilla Ambler, John Naylor, Sarah Brooks, Daniel Trump, Abraham Trump, Daniel Jarret, John Jarret, Levi and Priscilla Jarret.
Execs: Brother in law John Jarret, Job Roberts. Wit: Daniel Longstreth, Samuel Johnson, John Longstreth.

EASTBURN, BENJAMIN. Upper Merion.
Nov 13, 1794. Jan 19, 1795. 1.443
To wife Margaret, 80 pds. money left by her father and 20 pds. yearly during life to be paid by son Samuel, also household furniture and maintenance in lieu of dower. To son Samuel, all estate real and personal, he paying legacies to wife and daughters. To daughter Hannah, 250 pds. To daughter Abigail, 250 pds.
Execs: Wife Margaret, brother John Eastburn. Wit: James Abraham, Peter Supplee.

TYSON, JOHN. Abington.
April 19, 1794. Jan 27, 1795. 1.444
To wife Mary, household furniture and income of estate until son Seth is 16. To son John, silver watch. To son Seth, desk. To 2 sons John and Seth, farm, 121 acres when son Seth is 16. To 2 sons John and Seth, rem. After son Seth becomes of age, wife to have 10 pds. yearly during widowhood. To daughter Mary, 200 pds. to be paid by sons John and Seth.
Codicil, if unborn child is son, to have equal proportion of farm with sons John and Seth, if a daughter to have 100 pds.
Execs: Brother in law Thomas Tyson, brother Isaac. Wit: John Childs, Jesse Fifer.

STANERT, LEWIS. Upper Dublin.
Sept 16, 1794. Feb 1, 1795. 1.446

Exrs. to sell farm. To each son: William, Jacob, John and Lewis, 50 pds. Rem. of estate to 7 children: William, Jacob, John, Lewis, Nancy, Catharine and Hannah equally.
Execs: Robert Loller, sons John and Lewis. Wit: Cornelius Wolf, John Thomson.

FOLTZ, MATTHIAS. Merion.
March 28, 1783. Feb 10, 1795. 1.448
To wife Mary, income of farm, 150 acres, 2 featherbeds, bedsteads, maintenance, &c. To grandson John Bare, 10 pds., wearing apparel, &c. Rem. of personalty after wife has her choice to be sold. After paying legacies, money to be divided among 3 daughters: Barbara Calbflish, Margaret Bare and Mary Ballert, equally. After wife's death, estate to be sold and money divided among 3 daughters.
Execs: Wife Mary, Frederick Crow, Samuel Gloss. Wit: Abraham Walters, George Horn, Andrew Geyer.

BURK, EDWARD. Upper Dublin.
Nov 4, 1794. Feb 21, 1795. 1.449
To daughter Elizabeth Loeser, 100 pds. Rem. of estate to sons Edward and John, equally. Subject to paying daughter Elizabeth, 100 pds. aforesaid.
Execs: Sons Edward and John. Wit: John Trump, Robert Loller.

CUSTER, PAUL. Skippack.
Jan 3, 1795. March 9, 1795. 1.450
To wife Gertraut, bed, bedding, furniture and tenant house, maintenance during life in lieu of her dower and income of 25 pds. yearly from son John during widowhood; at her death to son John. To son Peter, farm, 150 acres and implements. To son Benjamin, 100 pds. to be paid by son Peter. To son Abraham, 100 pds. to be paid by son Peter. To 3 daughters: Elizabeth, Sybilla, and Magdalena, 90 pds. to be paid by son Peter, equally. Also to each daughter 1 cow, bed and belongings. At wife's death articles given her to be equally divided among 3 daughters. Weakly son Harman, to be maintained by son Peter as long as he lives.
Exec: Son Peter. Guardians Harman Umstate, Henry Hunsicker. Wit: Harman Umstate, Benjamin Johnson.

HOFFMAN, JOHN.
Feb 21, 1795. March 9, 1795. 1.452
Nuncupative will. Realty and personalty to be sold. To wife Rebecca, bed, 100 pds. which she received from her father, Abraham Rinard. To son Philip, 30 pds. Rem. divided as follows: to wife, 1/3. to son Philip, 2/3.
Exec: Father in law Abraham Rinard. Wit: William Tyson, Isaac Tyson, Henry Hunsicker.

CLINE, JACOB. Hatfield.

May 30, 1793. May 2, 1795. 1.453
To wife Barbara, 150 pds., personalty and income of farm during life, but if she marry enough furniture for 1 room and 150 pds. in lieu of her dower. To son John, 20 pds. and wearing apparel. To Benjamin Ordey, servant boy, 25 pds., bed and bedding. At wife's death or marriage, farm, 40 acres to be sold, legacies paid, and rem. divided between son John and daughter Catharine. Wit: George Schieve, Evan Jones.

HAUBERGER, NICHOLAS. New Hanover.
March 8, 1795. May 11, 1795. 1.454
To wife Mary Margaret, furniture, income of estate in lieu of dower. To son Peter, silver watch. To son John, silver shoe buckles, and sleeve buttons. To son Daniel, 3 silver spoons. Tombstones on hand to be finished and sold; 1/2 the money for widow, the other half for estate; at wife's death, rem. equally divided among 3 sons: Peter, John and Daniel. Exec: Brother in law John Snell. Wit: Michael Irwin, Thomas Richards.

EGOLF, GEORGE ADAM. New Hanover.
Jan 21, 1796[sic]. May 11, 1795. 1.455
To wife Mary, household goods and maintenance during widowhood. To son Henry, if he accept, and if not to sons: Adam, John, Jacob or Michael, farm, 110 acres, paying 740 pds. If son Henry takes farm he to retain 115 pds. Personalty to be sold. Rem. divided as follows: income of 100 pds. to wife Mary, during life, at her death 6 pds. to each daughter and rem. equally divided among 5 sons. To son Jacob, 125 pds. To son John, 127 pds. To son Adam, 115 pds. To son Michael, 115 pds. To daughters: Catharine, Elizabeth, Anna Margaret, wife of Sigmont Burgert, 50 pds. each. Share of daughter Anna Margaret to be in trust. Rem. to 5 sons.
Execs: Sons Henry and Adam. Wit: Benjamin Markley, Jacob Schneider.

RUTTER, THOMAS. Pottstown.
April 6, 1795. May 25, 1795. 1.458
To wife Martha, 400 pds. yearly, in quarterly payments secured on Warwick Furnace in lieu of dower. At her death principal to revert to estate. Rem. divided among 4 daughters: Mary, Katharine, Ruth and Anna. To wife, 100 pds. at testator's death and 500 pds. within 2 years, also 3/8 of copper ore in iron mines and equal proportion with children of profits from copper mines. To brother John Pyewell, income of 200 pds.; at his death to revert to estate. To cousin and sister in law Anna, wife of Thomas Potts, income of 200 pds.; at her death to revert to estate.
Codicil gives 100 pds. to wife in addition to other legacies.
Execs: Wife Martha, son in law John Clemens Stocker and sons Samuel and David Rutter. Wit: William Potts, Robert Hobart, Robert McClintick.

SHELLENBERGER, JOHN. Hatfield.
March 22, 1794. May 26, 1795. 1.460

To wife Margaret, stock, furniture and 150 pds. To son Charles, 10 pds. Rem. equally divided among sons: Charles, Conrad, Henry, Jacob and Philip, and daughters: Margaret, Elizabeth, Catharine and Eve.
Execs: Son Conrad and son in law George Sheip. Wit: Jacob Rudderton, Jacob Miller.

SNEIDER, JACOB. Cheltenham.
June 7, 1795. June 15, 1795. 1.461
To wife, farm and personalty. After wife's death, farm, to be sold and purchase money divided among children. To grandson Jacob Sneider, 4 pds. Rem. equally divided among wife and 3 children: Conrad, John and Mary.
Execs: Simon Bennett, Benjamin Cottman. Wit: John Shoemaker, Jr., Conrad Sines.

BEANS, THOMAS. Abington.
April 4, 1792. June 17, 1795. 1.462
To wife Elizabeth, 20 pds., room and maintenance. To son Nathan, 1/2 part of farm, he paying to wife 5 pds. yearly and to daughter Jane Miles, 12 pds., 2 s. To son Isaac, other 1/2 of farm, he paying wife 5 pds. and to daughter Jane, 12 pds., 2s. To sons Nathan and Isaac, 2 negro boys, Amram and Israel. To son Thomas, farm, in Southampton, 112 acres, he paying to wife and daughter same sum as son Isaac. To son Thomas, negro boy, Toby. To son Stephen, farm, in Abington, 145 acres, he to give to wife maintenance and to daughter Jane, 12 pds., 10 s. To son Stephen, negro, Sue. To daughter Jane, household goods after wife's death and 50 pds. To grandson Evan Beans, son of Nathan, silver watch. To Phebe Beans, daughter of brother James, 15 pds. Rem. to 4 sons equally: Nathan, Isaac, Thomas and Stephen.
Execs: Sons: Nathan, Isaac, Thomas and Stephen. Wit: Samuel Jones, Richard Whitton.

HENDRICKS, JOHN. Hatfield.
May 7, 1795. July 4, 1795. 1.464
To wife Magdalena, all estate during widowhood. If she marry to have, 1/3 of estate. To daughter Eve, bed, bedstead, 1 cow, &c. To grandchild, Magdalena Georgin, heifer, &c. After wife' death, daughter Eve to have all estate.
Execs: Joseph Overholtzer, John Weirman. Wit: Isaac Overholtzer.

JONES, ISRAEL. Lower Merion.
April 15, 1795. Sept 21, 1795. 1.466
To wife Susannah, all estate during life. After her death to be sold and divided among 6 children: Charles, Griffith, Catharine, Robert, James and Amos.
Exec: Wife Susannah. Wit: Samuel Jones, Mary Bartleson.

HERNER, CHRISTIAN. Upper Dublin.
Feb 15, 1786. Oct 15, 1795. 1.466
To wife Barbara, farm, and use of presonalty also 9 pds. yearly. Sons: John, Christian and Jacob, have already a deed for farm to them. To son Joseph, a lot in Upper Dublin, 24 acres 89 perches, he paying 25 pds. and 300 pds. yearly to wife Barbara. To son Michael, a lot, 24 acres 92 perches, he paying 25 pds. yearly to wife. To son Henry, 20 3/4 acres, he paying 45 pds. To daughter Magdalena, 100 pds. To daughter Barbara, 6 pds. yearly and income of 100 pds.; at her death to daughter Sarah, 100 pds. Exrs. to sell rem. 10 acres. Money arising from sale to be equally divided among sons: John, Christian, Jacob, Joseph, Michael and Henry, equally. After wife's death rem. of personalty to be equally divided among sons. After wife's death farm left to her to be valued, and given to son Henry at valuation.
Execs: Wife Barbara, son Henry. Wit: Casper Soplater (Schlater), Jr., Robert Loller.

SELTZER, NICHOLAS. Gwynedd.
May 18, 1795. Oct 20, 1795. 1.470
To wife Mary, use of farm, bed, bedding and maintenance. After wife's death, farm to be appraised; either to sons, or to be equally divided among them as they shall choose, they to pay valuation. Rem. of personalty to be sold and equally divided among children. To granddaughter Rachel, daughter of Bernard Beaver, 10 pds. when 18. Rem. to be equally divided among children, equally, except son John to have 10 pds. more than other sons, and daughters to have 20 pds. less than sons.
Execs: Son Henry, son in law Casper Slauter. Wit: John Evans, Cadwallader Evans, Jr.

YERKES, SILAS. Moreland.
March 21, 1795. Oct 23, 1795. 1.472
To son Elias, 10 pds. and wearing apparel. To daughter Deborah, wife of Samuel Ayres, 6 pds. To daughter Esther, wife of Charles Ayres, 6 pds. To daughter Elizabeth, wife of Daniel Howell, 6 pds. To son Silas, farm in Moreland, 90 acres, subject to the payment of 60 pds. to daughters[sic] Hannah Yerkes; 1/2 legacies above also. To son Daniel, farm, 76 3/4 acres, subject to payment of other half of legacies above. To son Benjamin, 2 acres, 26 perches. To daughter Hannah, 60 pds., feather-bed, pewter, &c. To son Silas, feather-bed. Rem. of household goods to 4 daughters: Deborah, Esther, Elizabeth and Hannah.
Execs: Sons Silas and Daniel. Wit: George Yerkes, James Dungas, John Watts.

SMITH, JACOB. Frederick.
April 5, 1795. Oct 26, 1795. 1.473
To wife Margareta, farm, during widowhood and household goods. Rem.

of household goods to be sold. If wife marry, realty, 20 acres and personalty to be sold and money equally divided among wife and children. To wife 1/5 part. To son Isaac, 50 pds. to be put on interest for schooling, 1/5 each to 4 children: Isaac, John, Jacob and Abraham.
Exec: Brother in law Jacob Kline. Wit: Johannes Jost, Peter Munner, Henry Sasseman.

CLAYTON, MARGARET. Horsham.
May 4, 1793. Oct 29, 1795. 1.474
To son John, 20 s. Rem. divided into 4 equal parts. To daughter Jane Childs, 1 part. To son John, 1 part. To daughters Dorothy Hallowell and Hannah Jones, 1 part each.
Execs: Son John, son in law George Childs. Wit: Abraham Lukens, Robert Lukens.

WITMAN, MICHAEL. Douglass.
Aug 9, 1795. Nov 4, 1795. 1.475
Estate to be sold when daughter Barbara is 21. To wife, mare, cow, furniture, 1/3 part of personalty and maintenance. She to reside with son Samuel during widowhood. To son Jacob, farm, 90 acres; he to pay 300 pds. and legacy to wife. To son Samuel, farm, 103 acres; he to pay 400 pds. and his share of privileges and legacy to wife Barbara. To daughter Susanna, wife of George Gilbert, 200 pds. To daughter Elizabeth, wife of Barney Gilbert, 200 pds. To daughter Barbara, 200 pds. To son John's children: Jacob, John and Polly, the sum of 300 pds. also a bond of 65 pds. from Samuel McNalley, equally among them.
Codicil gives additional furniture to wife and 50 pds. additional to each daughter: Susannah, Elizabeth and Barbara.
Execs: Wife Barbara, son in law George Gilbert. Wit: Johannes Weiss, Benjamin Markley.

RUSH, HENRY. Marlborough.
Oct 19, 1795. Nov 11, 1795. 1.477
To wife, all estate. Wit: Nicoland Mulbner, Philip Reed.

FLETCHER, SUSANNA. Abington.
Aug 29, 1793. Nov 12, 1795. 1.478
To son Robert, 50 pds. for use of daughter Susanna. To son Thomas, 50 pds. To grandson, Morris Fletcher Sheppard, 25 pds. to sons Robert and Thomas, remaining feather-beds, and 3 chairs, &c. To daughter Elizabeth Ashbridge, clock, feather-bed, wearing apparel. To Robert, Elizabeth and Thomas, rem. of linen, equally. Rem. to be sold and money equally divided among daughter Elizabeth Ashbridge and grandsons: Thomas Morris, Clement Sheppard, children of daughter Hannah, dec. equally; daughter to have 1/2 and 3 grandsons to have other half.
Execs: Daughter Elizabeth Ashbridge and son Thomas. Wit: Thomas Livezey, Moses Shaw.

SHILLIG, PHILIP. Limerick.
May 2, 1795. Nov 24, 1795. 1.479
To wife, bed, bedding and iron pot. Exrs. to sell realty and personalty. Wife to have 1/3 part. Rem. to be equally divided among children, when 21.
Exec: Brother Matthias. Wit: Jacob Fink, Benjamin Dismant.

BOWER, ANDREW. Whitemarsh.
June 24, 1795. Dec 4, 1795. 1.480
To wife, farm, 30 acres during widowhood and goods needed. Rem. of personalty to be sold, and from money arising to 5 grandsons: Andrew, Leonard, John, George and Daniel Kulp each a silver watch and to each daughter: Catharine, Elizabeth and Mary Kulp, a case of drawers. To church at Barren Hill, 20 pds. To each grandchild at the time of marriage, 50 pds. To daughter Elizabeth Kulp, 38 acres. To grandson Jacob, a colt. If wife marry, 30 pds. yearly. After wife's death or marriage, farm and personalty to be divided among grandchildren.
Execs: Wife Elizabeth, son in law Leonard Kulp. Wit: William Shillig, Johannes Fychir.

CASSELBERRY, JACOB. Providence.
Sept 2, 1795. Dec 18, 1795. 1.482
To wife Anna, household goods and maintenance. To son Benjamin, 200 pds. To son Jacob, 200 pds. Dwelling place and tanyard, where son William dwells, to be sold after agreement expires, and equally divided among children. Wife to receive interest of 300 pds. yearly during life; at her death, principal to be divided among children. To sons Benjamin and Jacob, each a watch, when 21. To son Jacob, interest of 200 pds. yearly and 30 pds.
Execs: Wife Anna, and son Richard. Wit: Henry Sweitzer, James Bean, Jesse Bean.

FREEZ, CASPER. Lower Merion.
Nov 22, 1795. Dec 22, 1795. 1.484
To wife Catharine, stove, income of estate and household goods to the amount of 50 pds. during life. To daughter Mary, featherbed, $3, &c. To daughters Eve and Hannah, featherbeds, and 3 pillows. Rem. after wife's death to be divided among children, except deducting from each daughter the value that has been given to 3 married daughters.
Execs: Wife Catharine and brother George Freez. Wit: Algernon Roberts, Peter Ott.

HARTZELL, GEORGE. Franconia.
Dec 9, 1795. Jan 6, 1796. 1.484
To wife Catharine, 2 beds, household goods and maintenance; at her death divided among 4 children: George, Molly, wife of John Gerhard; Catharine, wife of George Heebner and Margaret, wife of Philip Bernett.

To son George, farm, 247 acres and negro man, Cuff for 4 years, he to pay to negro man, 3 pds. yearly and negro woman Betsey, stove, &c. in consideration of 1050 pds.; 300 pds. to remin in his hands, interest to be paid to wife yearly during widowhood. To 3 daughters: Catharine, Molly and Margaret, 75 pds. yearly to be paid by son George. To 2 granddaughters Catharine and Margaret Landis, 50 pds. to be paid by daughter Catharine. Farm and oil-mill in Rockhill, 110 acres, and other tract in Armstrong, Westmoreland Co. to be sold together with rem. of personalty and divided among 4 daughters aforesaid.
Execs: Son George and son in law John Gerhard. Wit: George Hartzell, Henry Michael Shoemaker.

RUMER, HENRY. Upper Dublin.
July 9, 1795. Feb 16, 1796. 1.486
To wife Dorothy, bed, household goods and income of estate during widowhood. If she marry to have 3 pds. yearly. To son: Jacob, Frederick, John and Henry, 15 pds. to be paid after wife's death or marriage. To son Frederick, loom and loom gears, &c. To son Henry, clock. To daughter Dorothy, case of drawers and 15 pds. Exrs. to sell estate after wife's death or marriage and pay above legacies. Rem. to children: Jacob, Catharine, wife of John Kirper; Elizabeth, wife of Jacob Kirper, Frederick, Ann, wife of Christian Greenwolt, each 1/9 part; John, Henry and Dorothy's shares subject to debts they owe testator. Interest of remaining 1/9 part to daughter , wife of Henry Coler.
Execs: Wife Dorothy, son Frederick and son in law Jacob Kirper. Wit: John Heeston, Alexander McDowell.

SCHLATER, HANS CASPER. Upper Dublin.
Dec 9, 1793. Feb 20, 1796. 1.488
To wife Barbara, farm, 52 1/2 acres, interest on lot and household goods during widowhood. To son Casper, 1 acre 9 perches; he paying 10 s. yearly to his mother. To daughter Elizabeth, 10 pds., &c. Rem. of personalty to be sold and money put on interest and paid to wife. If she marry to have bed, furniture and 5 pds. After wife's death or marriage, estate to be appraised and given to son Casper for valuation; if he does not take it to be sold and money divided among children: Casper, Jacob, John and Ulrick and daughters: Catharine, Barbara and Elizabeth.
Execs: Sons Casper and John. Wit: John Mann, Henry Fisher.

WALTON, THOMAS. Moreland.
Jan 6, 1796. March 5, 1796. 1.490
To wife Mary, bed, maintenance to be furnished by son Thomas; also 7 pds. yearly. To son Thomas, house and farm, he to pay to brother Jeremiah, 100 pds. To son Silas, 6 pds. To son Jeremiah, 100 pds. To daughter Sarah, interest of 75 pds. To daughter Elizabeth, 75 pds. To daughters: Mary, Phebe and Anna, 60 pds. each. Rem. to be divided among wife and children.

Execs: Sons Silas, Thomas and Jeremiah. Wit: William Michener, Samuel Gummere, Jonathan Michener.

TYSON, RYNEAR. Abington.
Nov 20, 1793. March 7, 1706. 1.491
To wife Elizabeth, household goods and interest of 200 pds. during widowhood; after her death or marriage, principal to be divided with rem. To daughters Mary and Hannah, 250 pds. each. Rem. to children: Peter, Rynear, Jacob, Benjamin, Thomas, Jesse, Mary and Hannah, equally.
Execs: Sons Peter, Rynear and Jacob. Wit: John Childs, Henry Childs.

WEASNER, GEORGE. Douglass.
Jan 29, 1793. March 12, 1796. 1.492
To wife Gertrude, 100 pds., cow, household goods and maintenance. To son Martin, farm, 103 acres, subject to payment of 400 pds. To daughter Anna Mary, wife of Christian Rudolph, 400 pds. to be paid by son Martin. To sons Henry and George, farm, 63 acres. Rem. after wife's death to be divided among 4 children. To Corporation of the Luthern Church in New Hanover, 10 pds.
Execs: Son Martin, Gabriel Klein. Wit: Jacob Schneider, Benjamin Markley.

ZIMMERMAN, JACOB. Providence.
Dec 15, 1789. March 14, 1796. 1.494
To daughter Hannah, wife of Frederick Stem, 6 pds. To children of daughter Hannah, 6 pds. each. To children of dec. daughter Mary, wife of Andrew Supplee, 6 pds. each. To daughter Catharine, wife of Christian Stouver, 6 pds. To 3 children of dec. daughter Susannah, wife of Frederick Marstellar, 30 pds. equally. To son Matthias, 10 pds. To stepdaughter Sophia, wife of Henry Rittenhouse, 10 pds. To son Christopher, 5 pds. To son John, 80 pds. he to pay to daughter 200 pds. To son Jacob, 5 pds. To wife Susanna, maintenance, by son Jacob.
Execs: Son Jacob, son in law Christian Stouver. Wit: Arnold Zimmerman, Israel Jacobs, Christopher Zimmerman.

SCHLICHER, JOST. Upper Hanover.
Jan 29, 1796. March 17, 1796. 1.496
To 3 sons: Christopher, Henry and George, 26 pds. To son Christopher, farm, 150 acres at valuation of 400 pds. Personalty divided among 8 children.
Execs: son Henry and John Schleiffer. Wit: Philip Lahr, David Schultz.

RAMBO, TOBIAS. Upper Merion.
Jan 29, 1796. March 17, 1796. 1.496
To son Samuel, 40 pds. To son Moses, 165 pds. To daughter Rachel, 60 pds. To daughter Elizabeth, 30 pds. To son Ebenezer, 30 pds. To son William, 30 pds. To granddaughter Sarah, 10 pds. To wife Margaret, 19

pds. yearly, bed, bedding and pewter. Exrs. to sell realty and personalty and income for wife; after her death, to pay legacies.
Execs: Peter Rambo, wife Margaret. Wit: Robert Stuart, Septimus Coats.

SCHULTZ, ANNA. Upper Hanover.
Jan 22, 1795. March 20, 1796. 1.497
To son Balthaser, 20 pds. Rem. divided into 5 equal shares. To son Balthaser, 1 share. To son Christopher, 1 share. To son George, 1 share. To daughter Susannah, wife of Abraham Kreible, 1 share. Remaining share, 30 pds. to son Abraham Dresher, balance to children of Eve Dresher, dec.
Execs: Son Balthaser, and son George. Wit: Abrham Schultz, David Schultz.

BOYER, ABRAHAM. Norriton.
April 6, 1794. March 30, 1796 1.498
To wife Barbara, bed, bedding and income of 300 pds. After wife's death, principal to be divided among children, except daughter Hester Read's share to be put on interest until her husband's death. Estate to be sold, 300 pds. to be put on interest for wife. To son Jacob, 100 pds., 2 horses, wagon, &c. To daughter Susanna, 50 pds. Rem. divided among children: John, Jacob, Abraham, Henry, Andrew, and Barbara.
Execs: Sons John and Jacob. Wit: Robert Curry, Christopher Rittenhouse.

WOLFARTH, NICHOLAS. Marlborough.
April 20, 1788. March 31, 1796. 1.500
To wife Catharine, bed, bedding, clock, household goods and maintenance. Personalty to be sold and to pay following legacies. To son Abraham, 7 pds. To son John, horse, tools for dyeing. To wife Catharine, 1/3 of money. Rem. to 6 children: Abraham, John, Christiana, wife of Henry Daub, Catharine, wife of Peter Daub; Anna Mary, wife of Nicholas Gougler and Margareth, wife of Jeremiah Kirshner, equally. To wife Catharine, farm, 129 acres, during widowhood; if she marry her right to cease; at her death or marriage to 6 children in equal shares.
Execs: Wife Catharine, son in law Henry Daub. Wit: Christian Sheid.

FOGEL, FREDERICK. New Hanover.
July 6, 1795. April 12, 1796. 1.501
To wife Margaret, bed, bedstead, and furniture, 300 pds., she to educate children. Hides now in vats to be tanned and estate turned into money and when son Frederick shall come of age to be equally divided among children. To step daughter Margaret, 12 pds. To son Frederick silver watch, silver shoe buckles, &c.
Execs: Wife Margaret and Sebastian Reifsnyder. Wit: John Richards, Benjamin F. Weinland.

NORMAN, DAVID. Norriton.

March 21, 1796. April 4, 1796. 1.501
To wife Mary, rooms, maintenance, &c. Saw-mill and buildings and 115 acres to be sold and money applied to estate. To son Samuel, 100 pds.; he paying interest to wife. Rem. to be put on interest and wife to have income; at her death equally divided among 3 sons: Jonathan, George and Ezekiel. To son Samuel, rem. of farm; he furnishing maintenance to wife. Son Samuel to pay to each of his sisters: Sarah, Esther, Mary and Elizabeth, 50 pds. Personalty to be sold and money divided among children.
Execs: Wife Mary, son Samuel, William Ellis. Wit: Joseph Roberts, John Meredith, William Potts.

SNOBLE, JOHN. Upper Salford.
April 15, 1795. April 14, 1796. 1.504
Wife to remain on farm and to have maintenance; if she marry will to be void and she to take under intestate laws.
Execs: Wife Catharine, Benjamin Landis. Wit: Mansfield Banton.

STREEPER, LEONARD, Whitemarsh.
June 20, 1795. April 15, 1796. 1.505
To wife Margaret, income of 500 pds., mare, saddle, household goods and income of realty. She to educate minor children until youngest son is of age, then 20 pds. yearly to be paid to her by each of 4 younger sons. To 3 sons: John, Peter and Dennis, 5 s. each. To 2 daughters Sarha[sic] Johnson and Elizabeth Thomas, 75 pds. each; each having had 150 pds. To 4 younger sons: Jacob, Daniel, William and George, farm, 100 acres, also farm, 62 acres purchased of Isaac Norris, also house and farm in Roxborough, 16 3/4 acres; also 3/4 of an acre in Springfield and 1/5 part in Fishery at Port Royal in river Schuylkill, equally, subject to legacy of 20 pds. to wife. To 6 younger daughters: Ann Dull, Rebecca Streeper, Deborah, Mary, Catharine and Susanna Streeper, 100 pds. each. Rem. to 6 younger daughters equally. Home farm to be sold at death of wife and money divided among 6 younger daughters equally.
Codicil empowers exrs. to sell farm of 16 3/4 acres in Roxborough and the income of money arising to wife until youngest daughter Susanna is 18; when said principal is to be divided among 6 younger daughters equally, in addition to other legacies. Codicil dated April 1, 1796.
Execs: Wife Margaret, son Peter, Nathan Levering. Wit: John Huston, Leonard Johnson.

GEORGE, GEORGE. Upper Merion.
Sept 13, 1790. May 7, 1796. 1.508
Baptist Congregation in Tredyfrin, 10 pds.; income for support of ministry. To son William, farm, 60 acres. To son David, farm, 225 acres. To 2 sons aforesaid, 1 negro boy, Nero. To son William, clock. To son David, riding mare. To 3 daughters: Hannah Abraham, Mary Rowland and Jane David, 100 pds. each. Rem. equally divided among 5 children:

William, David, Hannah, Mary, and Jane.
Execs: Sons William and David. Wit: John Lyle, John Elliot, Jacob Wolmer.

McCOLL, WALTER. Whitemarsh.
May 30, 1794. July 10, 1796. 1.509
To wife Mary, house, furniture and 1/3 of crops during life. To son Samuel, farm, 58 acres and utensils. Daughters: Laura, Elizabeth and Catharine, have received their shares.
Execs: John Wilson, Thomas Lancaster. Wit: William Abbett, Thomas W. Pryor.

DAVIS, MARY. Limerick.
Jan 6, 1790. May 10, 1796. 1.511
To son Thomas, clock. Son Thomas, to pay 100 pds. to son Isaiah. Households goods equally divided among sons Thomas and Isaiah.
Execs: Sons Thomas and Isaiah. Wit: Henry Kendall, John Newberry.

GERHARD, ABRAHAM Douglass.
Feb 23, 1795. May 13, 1796. 1.511
To wife Margaret, all realty, 228 acres, during life in lieu of dower. To son Peter and step son David, 30 pds. each. To Elizabeth Zerly, daughter of step son David, 30 pds. Rem. equally divided among children: Peter, Daniel, Catharine, wife of Matthias Hynderleyne, and step children: John, David and Ludowick Zerly.
Execs: Son Peter and step son David Zerly. Wit: George Boyer, Bernhard Yager.

HALLOWELL, ELIZABETH. Moreland.
April 12, 1795. May 28, 1796. 1.513
All estate to children equally on coming of age.
Execs: Brother Samuel Lloyd, Benjamin Lloyd, Samuel Gummere. Wit: Jonathan Knight, Jarret Spencer, John Spencer, Jr.

RYNEAR, JOHN. Whitpain.
Oct 29, 1795. June 4, 1796. 1.514
To wife Barbara, all estate.
Execs: Brother in law Jacob Rex, Samuel DeHaven.

MATSON, ANN. Upper Merion.
Dec 22, 1795. July 25, 1796. 1.515
To son Isaac, 15 s. To daughter Hannah, wife of Philip Dougherty, 15 s. To daughter Mary, wife of Arthur O'Neil, 15 s. To granddaughter Hannah, daughter of Mary, 3 pds. To daughter Ann Marsh's children, 4 pds. each and to her daughter Elizabeth, bed, bedding, &c. To daughter Elizabeth Rambo's children, 3 pds. each. To daughter Esther Rees's children, 4 pds. each, except her son Eli to have 7 pds. To granddaughter

Sarah, daughter of Esther, looking glass. To 4 children of son Peter as follows: to Peter, 7 pds. and clock. To Susanna, 7 pds. to Elizabeth and Hannah, 3 pds. each. To daughters Ann and Esther, wearing apparel, equally. Rem. of estate to be divided among children of daughters Ann Marsha and Esther Rees.
Execs: Son Peter and Natha Potts. Wit: Benjamin Cunrad, Isaac DeHaven.

PHIPPS, JOHN, Whitpain.
Nov 6, 1794. Aug 8, 1796. 1.516
To wife Elizabeth, 30 pds. yearly and maintenance. To son Squire Phipps, 100 pds. To daughter Agnes, 3 pds. yearly; at her death principal to be divided among her children. Rem. to be equally divided. To son Jonathan, 1 part. To son Squire Phipps, 1 part. To daughter Ann Tompkins, 1 part. To daughter Rebecca, 1 part. To children of son Samuel, 1 part. To children of son John, 1 part.
Execs: Sons Jonathan and Squire Phipps. Wit: Rebecca Davis, Nathan Potts, Priscilla Potts.

CLINE, WILLIAM. Montgomery.
Jan 28, 1796. Aug 9, 1796. 1.517
Exrs. to sell farm and personalty. To wife Sarah, all money arising from sale, she to educate children. Guardians of children, Jesse Foulke and Cadwalader Evans.
Execs: Wife Sarah and guardians of children. Wit: Joseph Ambler, Jr., Conrad Cline, Jr., Evan Jones.

HEILICH, GEORGE. Upper Hanover.
June 10, 1796. Aug 22, 1796. 1.517
To wife Barbara, part of personalty, she to have house after agreement expires. Rem. of personalty to be sold. Farm, 160 acres 140 perches to son George at valuation, he to have to wife maintenance. Farm, 145 acres 90 perches to son Peter at valuation. To son George Michael, 25 pds. Rem. to children: George Michael, John George, Henry of North Carolina and George, Adam, Peter, Jacob, Anna and Mary, wife of John Eckel of North Carolina and Eve, Elizabeth, wife of Jacob Klein, Barbara, wife of Ludowig Sheller.
Execs: Wife Barbara, son George, son in law Jacob Klein. Wit: Jacob Muller, Claura George, Adam Blank.

MILLER, CHRISTOPHER. Providence.
July 27, 1796. Aug 25, 1796. 1.520
To wife Mary, cow, 8 pds. and maintenance during widowhood; she to bring up youngest child. Exrs. to sell farm in Pikeland township except 12 acres, also to sell personalty. To son Isaiah, books, farm unsold to be appraised, to deduct 20 acres and rem. to son Isaiah at valuation, he paying 30 pds. yearly. To son Jacob, 20 acres; he paying 20 pds. yearly. To

3 daughters: Catharine, Barbara and Elizabeth, bed and bedding each. Bequest to first wife by her father to be paid to her children. To 3 eldest daughters, 50 pds. each. To son Jacob 150 pds. Rem. of estate equally divided among children.
Execs: Benedict Garber, Charles Garber. Wit: Jacob Garber, B. Dismant.

LIPPINCOTT, JACOB. Abington.
May 3, 1790. Aug 27, 1796. 1.522
To wife Elizabeth, personalty, bond and money on hand. To granddaughter Elizabeth, daughter of Robert Flitcher, and Rachel his wife, 100 pds. when 18. Rem. of estate to children: Robert Flitcher and Priscilla his wife, they paying 10 pds. yearly to Susanna Austin during widowhood. To brother William, 1/2 of income of New Jersey realty. To brother Samuel, other half of income of New Jersey realty, If he does not need it, to his daughter Hannah.
Exec: Wife Elizabeth. Wit: Thomas Livezey, Rynear Tyson, Jr.

ROBERTS, ELIZABETH. Lower Merion.
Sept 6, 1790. Oct 11, 1796. 1.524
To sister Hannah, 10 pds. and cloak. To David Lloyd, bed, bedstead, &c.; after his death, to Elizabeth Robeson, daughter of Jonathan Robeson. Rem. to be sold, money divided among children of nephews of Jonathan Robeson and Jonathan Thomas.
Codicil gives to sister Hannah, 5 pds. and remaining 5 pds. to George Helmbold for use of nephew David Lloyd; and cloak to Eleanor, daughter of nephew Thomas Robeson.
Execs: Nephews Jonathan Thomas and Jonathan Thomas. Wit: Edward Price, Rees Price.

JOHNSON, WALTER. Perkiomen and Skippack.
March 18, 1791. Oct 31, 1796. 1.526
To wife Scyshy, bed, bedstead and household goods. Farm and personalty to be sold, money arisisng to be put on interest for wife during life; at her death to be divided among children. To sons Peter and William, 10 pds. and rem. divided among 7 children: Peter, William, Sarah, wife of Barney Hains,; Mary, wife of John Funck, Magdalena, wife of Gerret Zeigler.
Codicil dated July 28, 1795, gives to sons Peter and William an equal share with other children.
Execs: Son William, son in law Gerret Zeigler. Wit: Michael Zeigler, Abraham Zeigler, Henry Sweitzer.

HENRY, ROBERT. Abington.
Aug 6, 1796. Nov 14, 1796. 1.528
Exrs. to sell farm and personalty and make payments as follows: to Esther Yerkes, wife of Daniel Yerkes, 25 pds. To Jane Worrel, daughter of Demas Worrel, 50 pds. To 5 children of daughter Demas Worrel: Tacy, Elizabeth, Martha, Alice and Isaac, 50 pds. equally. To Trustees of

Presbyterian Church at Abington, rem. of estate.
Execs: John Collon, Samuel Leech. Wit: Baker Barnes, Thomas Livezey.

YERGER, PETER. New Hanover.
May 14, 1796. Nov 30, 1796. 1.529
To wife Barbara, maintenance, to be paid by son who ownes[sic] farm, also interest of 200 pds. and 12 pds. in cash. To son Solomon, 10 pds., beds, &c. To son George, 50 pds. To son Samuel, farm, for 850 pds.; he paying maintenance to wife. To son Samuel, mare, bed, &c. To son David, loom, bed, &c, 100 pds. To oldest daughter 30 pds. on May 27, 1797. To youngest daughter Elizabeth, 50 pds. Rem. of money divided among children. Daughters to be charged with what they received when married. Payments of farm to be divided among children: Elizabeth, George, Solomon, Catharine.
Execs: Tobias Yerger, son George. Wit: Henry Krebs.

JACOBS, ISRAEL, Providence.
Oct 23, 1796. Dec 10, 1796. 1.532
To son John, wearing apparel, desk and bookcase, &c. To daughter Phebe Hobson, case of drawers, teaspoons, &c. To daughter Phebe and son John, table linen, equally. To grandson Thomas Jacobs, "History of Quakers". To granddaughter Hannah Jacobs, 6 silver teaspoons, &c. To son John, farm and 2 tracts, 130 acres, at valuation of 1400 pds. Exr. to sell rem. To son John, 500 pds. To daughter Phebe Hobson, 220 pds. To granddaughter Hannah Jacobs, 122 pds., 10 s. To grandson Thomas Jacobs, 122 pds., 10 s. To daughter in law Lydia Jacobs, 25 pds. To brother Jesse, 10 pds.
Codicil gives to son John, bed, bedstead and to daughter Hannah additional articles.
Exec: son John. Wit: Jonathan Cox, George Pierce, Benjamin Cox, Mary Cleaver.

KREER, HENRY. Moreland.
July 18, 1796. Jan 6, 1797. 1.536
To son David, farm, 36 acres. To grandsons: Andrew, Peter, John, George and Henry, 10 pds. each when of age, with interest. To grandsons Peter and John, wearing apparel and watch. Rem. to son David.
Execs: Son David, Jacob Paul. Wit: Jeremiah Berrel, Harman Yerkes.

SMITH, JOHN. Douglass.
Oct 19, 1787. Jan 25, 1797. 1.536
To wife Elizabeth, room, maintenance, personalty, except what is given to son Conrad, she to have income. To son Conrad, confirmation of farm, 102 acres, already given him; he paying 300 pds. to be divided as follows: to son John, 1/7 part. To son Jacob, 17 part. To daughter Liss, wife of Abraham Stetler, 1/7 part. To daughter Elizabeth, wife of Samuel Keim, 1/7 part. To children of daughter Margaret, wife of Christian Bossler, 1/7

part; 1/2 to her 2 sons by first husband, Christian Berger and other half equally among 5 children by second husband. To daughter Anna Mary, wife of Nicholas Miller, 20 pds. yearly. At wife's death rem. divided as follows: to daughter Margaret, 1 s. Balance divided equally among children and grandchildren. Codicil dated July 3, 1792, gives to daughter Liss' children her share.
Execs: Son Conrad and son in law Nicholas Miller. Wit: Peter Richards, Michael Kepner.

KITSELMAN, JACOB. Upper Merion.
Dec 1, 1796. Jan 30, 1797. 1.539
To wife Margaret, farm, 13 acres during life; at her death to be sold and proceeds divided as follows: to son Jacob, 15 pds. Balance divided equally among 4 children: Jacob, Casper, Margaret Washen and Elizabeth Huzzard. To wife, personalty.
Execs: Sons Jacob and Casper. Wit: William George, James Akins.

SNYDER, LEONARD. Upper Salford.
Feb 26, 1796. Feb 15, 1797. 1.540
To wife Maria Elizabeth, furniture, utensils and income of 100 pds. during widowhood. Rem. equally divided among 6 daughters: Elizabeth, wife of Jacob Shuler; Anna Maria, wife of Jacob Zepp; Christiana, wife of Jacob Hendricks; Margaret, wife of Ulrick Ruckstool; Magdalena, wife of Samuel Shuler; and Barbara, wife of John Stroman. If wife marries, 100 pds. also to be divided among daughters.
Execs: Brother Henry, son in law Jacob Shuler. Wit: Philip Gable, Philip Gable, Jr.

HOGELAND, JOHN. Moreland.
Nov 6, 1796. Feb 25, 1797. 1.541
To wife Cornelia, room, and maintenance in lieu of her dower. To son John, farm, 127 acres and 3 acres bought of Catharine Vansant and 6 pds.; he to pay to his mother, 10 pds. yearly during life and supply her with maintenance; he to pay to his sisters Hannah Vansant Dallen, 90 pds. To daughter Cornelia Deman, 90 pds. To daughter Sarah Loder, 90 pds. To daughter Adrianna, 90 pds. To son Derick, home farm, 145 acres; subject to following payments to his mother, 10 pds. yearly and 450 pds. equally to Hannah Vansant, Cornelia Deman, Sarah Loder, Andriana and Jane. To grandson John Vansant Dallen, 200 pds. to be paid by son Derick. To son Derick, clock; he to give to his brother John, 10 pds. Rem. to be sold, proceeds divided as follows: to daughters 20 pds. each. Rem. equally divided among children.
Execs: Sons John and Derick, son in law Simon Vansant Dallen. Wit: George Newell, Joseph Thornton.

SHANNON, LILY. Norriton.
June 5, 1793. March 14, 1797. 1.543

To son Robert, 10 pds. To daughter Mary Porter, 10 pds. To daughter Rebecca Davis, 10 pds. To sister Agnes Curry, 3 pds. to 3 daughters: Mary, Jane and Rebecca, bedding, wearing apparel, equally. To sons James and William, 50 acres and rem. of personalty.
Codicil gives to daughters Jane and Rebecca, contents of chest.
Execs: Sons James and William. Wit: Ezekiel Rhodes, Peter Lehman, Robert Shannon.

MILLER, JACOB. Gwynedd.
Sept 1, 1796. ____. 1.544
To wife Elizabeth, all personalty. Rem. to Rebecca Young. Wit: Joseph Dance, Thomas Seenky, Gilbert Dance.

SCHLEIFFER, HENRY. Upper Hanover.
June 2, 1796. April 5, 1797. 1.545
To wife Veronica, bed, household goods, except bonds from Abraham Hustard of Upper Milford, she to receive each year enough money from bonds to have maintenance and rem. of money to be divided among children equally: Jacob, John and Abraham, children of daughter Elizabeth, dec. late wife of Ulrick Basler; Mary and Henry Basler, 1 share equally, Mary, wife of Henry Mayer; Veronica, wife of Henry Fried; Anna, wife of Frederick Metzger, each a share.
Execs: Sons Jacob and John. Wit: Jacob Beesctse.

KURR, JACOB. Whitpain.
Sept 4, 1795. April 6, 1797. 1.545
To wife Anna, 150 pds., household goods and maintenance during widowhood, if she marry, maintenance to cease. Rem. to daughters Magdalena, wife of John Rusher and Susannah, wife of John Welker, equally.
Execs: Son in law Jacob Welker, John Wentz. Wit: Job Roberts, Philip Sheneberger.

KASTNER, ANDREW. Upper Dublin.
July 18, 1796. May 4, 1797. 1.547
To Margaret Kastner, daughter of son Thomas, 50 pds. Rem. to Margaret Thomas, she to maintain sisters Sarah and Elizabeth during life.
Execs: Margaret Thomas and her brother David Thomas. Wit: Christian Burns, George Waef.

HARTMAN, GEORGE. Upper Dublin.
July 1, 1794. May 8, 1797. 1.547
To wife Catharine, income of estate during life; at her death divided among daughters Margaret Deets, Mary and Catharine; daughter Catharine to receive 5 pds. more than other daughters. To daughter Catharine, 8 acres; she to pay to daughter Mary, 50 pds. also to pay to daughter Margaret, interest of 50 pds.

Execs: Wife Catharine, George Shelmire. Wit: Lewis Stanert, Robert Loller.

ZIEGLER, ANDREW. Lower Salford.
Sept 10, 1793. May 8, 1797. 1.548
To daughter Elizabeth, wife of Abraham Detweiler, 70 pds. To son Andrew, farm and tract, 130 acres at valuation of 500 pds. he to pay 250 pds. yearly to children. To son Andrew, 25 pds. To sons Dillman and Andrew, rem. of realty, 113 acres at valuation of 330 pds. they to give to son Michael, 10 acres for dwelling place; if he does not marry again; at his death to be sold and divided among children, deducting debts due from him. Rem. of personalty divided into 4 equal parts. To son Dillman, 1 part. To son Andrew, 1 part. To daughter Elizabeth, wife of Abrham Detweiler, 1 part. To children of son Michael, 1 part.
Execs: Sons Dillman and Andrew. Wit: Michael Ziegler, Abraham Ziegler, Henry Sweitzer.

SCHULTZ, GEORGE.
July 30, 1784. May 8, 1797. 1.550
To son Baltzer, 20 pds. Rem. divided into 5 equal shares. To 5 children, 1 share each.
Execs: sons Gregory and Baltzer. Wit: Andrew Krieble, Melchior Krieble.

SCHNEIDER, HENRY. Gwynedd.
March 5, 1795. May 20, 1797. 1.551
To wife Rosina, new house and garden, household goods. To son John, farm, 175 acres in Gwynedd, he to pay 1200 pds.; 300 pds. to his mother or 15 pds. yearly interest for her maintenance. Rem. of 1200 pds. to children as follows: to daughter Rosina, wife of Melchior Reineor, 100 pds. To sons: George, Christopher and Henry, daughter Susannah, Jacob and John, 100 pds. each. Personalty to be sold, each son who has no trade to receive 50 pds. Each son to receive a good horse and 140 pds. of sale money. Rem. to be divided among children equally. At wife's death rem. to be equally divided among children.
Codicil considers 1200 pds. for farm too low, farm to be appraised and each son to have refusal of it in order. Dated March 27, 1797.
Execs: Abraham Krieble and Jeremiah Krieble. Wit: Henry Ricker, James Fitzgerald, Frederick Cunrad.

HOFMAN, ADAM. Worcester.
Dec 6, 1795. May 20, 1797. 1.553
To wife Christiana, bed, bedstead, horse, household goods, 9 pds. yearly during widowhood. To daughters Barbara and Christiana, bed, bedstead and furniture. To 2 sons Adam and Peter, 10 pds. each. To son Adam, rem. of term of lease of farm. Rem. to children: Philip, John, Jacob, Adam, Peter, Baltzer, Paul, Elizabeth, wife of Peter Singer; Maria, wife of Nicholas Slough; Barbara and Christiana, deducting all sums advanced.

Execs: Sons Jacob and Adam. Wit: Anthony Homsher, John Homsher, Frederick Cunrad.

WELLS, PETER. Upper Merion.
Oct 30, 1795. June 3, 1797. 1.555
To child Miriam, furniture. Rem. of estate to wife Lydia.
Exec: Wife Lydia. Wit: Lindsay Coats, Jonathan Roberts.

METZ, LEONARD. Norriton.
Feb 29, 1796. June 30, 1797. 1.555
To wife Mary, income of 1/3 of estate during widowhood. If she marry, 100 pds. in lieu of her dower. to son John, 60 pds., colt, weaving loom, &c. to each unmarried child as much as each married one received. Rem. divided equally among children: Jacob, John, Ann, Esther, Barbara, Mary, Catharine, Abraham, Leonard and Elizabeth.
Execs: son John, Henry Hunsicker. Wit: Joseph Fulton, Nathan Potts.

NEUMAN, HENRY. New Hanover.
July 8, 1797. July 24, 1797. 2.1
Estate to be sold and money divided into 3 parts to 3 children: Henry, dec.; his share to be divided into 2 parts and to his 2 sons, 1 part each. To daughter Martha Elizabeth, 1 share. To daughter Catharine Defrain, 1 share. Daughters to receive 10 pds. each.
Exec: Grandson Edward Conrad. Wit: Jacob Shoener, Jacob Crous.

PAWLING, JOSEPH. Perkiomen and Skippack.
June 20, 1797. July 29, 1797. 2.2
To wife Elizabeth, room and maintenance. To daughter Rachel, wife of Lewis Truckemiller, 50 acres. To son Benjamin 800 pds. and purchase money of farm. To wife, farm, where testator lived; at wife's death to be appraised son Benjamin to have first choice. To daughter Elizabeth, 500 pds. to daughter Hannah, wife of John DeHaven, 500 pds. Rem. to 2 grandsons Joseph, son of Benjamin and John son of Joseph.
Execs: Sons Benjamin and Joseph. Wit: Samuel Pennebecker, Jacob Markley, Henry Sweitzer.

WALTER, ABRAHAM. Lower Merion.
July 6, 1789. Aug 14, 1797. 2.4
To Isaac Warner, all estate; if his wife outlive him to her during widowhood; at her death to children of cousin Walter Walter, dec. and children of cousin Sophia Amos, dec.
Execs: Isaac Warner, Abraham Lewis. Wit: Paul Jones, Lloyd Jones.

CASSEL, HENRY. Towamencin.
May 17, 1797. Aug 14, 1797. 2.5
To wife Margaret, household goods, 50 pds., maintenance and 15 pds. yearly. To son Yellis, plow, wagon, weaver's loom, farm, 131 acres; he to

pay legacy to wife; farm at valuation of 700 pds.; he to keep 100 pds. and to pay following: to wife 75 pds. yearly. Rem. of personalty to 3 children: Yellis, Eve, wife of John Springer and Susanna, wife of George Trumbore. After wife's death, son Yellis to have clock, stove and rem. divided among 3 children.
Exec: Son Yellis. Wit: Jacob Kolb, Jacob Kolb, Jr.

ROBERTS, WILLIAM. Upper Dublin.
Oct 7, 1786. Sept 2, 1797. 2.6
To wife Sarah, 25 pds. cash and 10 pds., 10 s. yearly. Exrs. to sell farm, 15 acres and personalty, money arising exrs. to put on interest, 175 pds. for use of wife; at wife's death, principal to children: Evan, Catharine, Jane, Elizabeth, and William equally, son William's share to be put on interst.
Execs: George Shelmire, John Shelmire. Trustees, Jesse Foulke, Jonathan Thomas. Wit: Robert Loller, Mary Loller.

NAYLOR, JOSEPH. Moreland.
March 31, 1794. Sept 2, 1797. 2.7
Exrs. to sell estate and money divided as follows: to brother John, 5 s. Rem. to wife.
Execs: Wife and father in law Jacob Tompkin. Wit: Isaac Longstreth, Elanora Lukens, Elizabeth Naylor.

FEDLEY, MICHAEL. New Hanover.
Feb 24, 1796. Sept 20, 1797. 2.8
To son Adam, 1 s. he already having had his share. To daughter Elizabeth Acker, 15 pds. To son in law Nicholas Puche, 1 s. To son Jonathan, 15 pds. To son David, 30 pds. To daughter Catharine Schweitser, 35 pds. To daughter Christiana Ryman, 35 pds. To son Michael, 50 pds. To 3 children of daughter Hannah: Sarah, John and Catharine Henrick, 50 pds. To wife Catharine, 1/3 of personalty and maintenance. If sons Jonathan or Michael takes farm to be valued at 550 pds. If not to be divided among 8 children: Elizabeth, Jonathan, daughter Catharine Schweitser, Michael, Christiana Ryman, Magdalena Puche, her share to her 4 children, John, Catharine, Maria and Elizabeth Puche daughter Hannah Henrick, her share to her 3 children: Sarah, John and Catharine.
Execs: son Jonathan, son in law Peter Henrick. Wit: John Beegner, Jacob Crous.

BOUCH, JOHN. Upper Salford.
Oct 13, 1796. Sept 28, 1797. 2.10
To wife Charenah, pewter and realty. At wife's death or marriage, to be sold and divided among children.
Exec: Peter Schwisefort. Wit: Henry Hollobush.

DANCE, JOSEPH. Gwynedd.

Aug 6, 1797. Oct 2, 1797 2.11
To wife Mary, maintenance and income of estate. To 4 children: Gilbert, John, Ann Bewley and Joseph, rem. of personalty. At wife's death divided among children.
Execs: Sons Gilbert and John. Wit: Edmund Penington, John Maince, Jesse Penington.

ZELL, JOHN. Lower Merion.
June 25, 1795. Oct 5, 1797. 2.11
To son David, 400 pds. to be paid by son Jacob. To Amy, daughter of son David, 50 pds., 2 cows, linen, bond and 18 pds. yearly. To Preparative Meeting of Friends at Merion, 3 pds. To son Jacob, farm and all realty, subject to payment of legacies. To sons David and Jacob, wearing apparel.
Exec: Son Jacob. Wit: Thomas George.

GRENWALT, JOHN. Whitpain.
Sept 12, 1797. Oct 10, 1797. 2.12
To daughter Margaret Waggoner, 10 pds. To Margaret, daughter of John Markley, 5 pds. Realty to be sold and money divided among children: Henry, Christian, Elizabeth Clair, Margaret Waggoner and Susanna. Daughter Susanna's share to be put on interest, at her death divided among her children.
Execs: Sons Henry and Christian. Wit: Job Roberts.

GRABER, ULRICH. Upper Hanover.
July 15, 1797. Oct 21, 1797. 2.13
To wife Margaret, 100 pds., household goods and maintenance; at her death to daughter Christiana; rem. to be divided among 4 children. Son Andrew has deed for farm, he to provide maintenance for wife. To daughter Christiana, room. To daughter Eve, 2 cows. To daughters Christiana and Ann Maria, wife of George Long, 100 pds. equally. To daughter Eve, 50 pds. To son Michael, 50 pds.
Execs: Son Andrew and uncle Ludowig Graber. Wit: Ludowig Graber.

OVERLANDER, HENRY. Springfield.
Nov 16, 1796. Oct 28, 1797. 2.15
To wife Fronica, personalty and realty during widowhood; if she marry to have interest of 200 pds. and part of household goods. Realty to be appraised. Farm to son in law Benjamin Campbell and daughter Ann, his wife, at valuation. They to pay to son in law George Jacobs and daughter Christiana, his wife, 1/2 valuation. Rem. to 2 daughters and their husbands.
Execs: Wife Fronica, sons in law Benjamin Campbell and George Jacobs. Wit: Jacob Knorr, George Knorr, Henry Mayor.

SCHULTZE, DAVID. Upper Hanover.
Oct 13, 1794. Oct 30, 1797. 2.16

To wife Elisabeth, bed, bedstead, 1/3 of household goods and maintenance. Daughters not married to receive as much as married daughters did. To daughter Mary, 15 pds. To daughter Rosina, 10 pds. Personalty to be sold and divided among children. Farm, 78 acres, for use of wife and children; one child to keep it at valuation and pay legacy to wife, 50 pds. At wife's death her share to be divided among children. Rem. to 4 daughters: Magdalena, wife of Samuel Loback; Ann, wife of Abraham Clemmer; Mary and Rosina, equally.
Execs: Wife Elisabeth, son in law Samuel Loback. Wit: John Schleiffer, John Schell.

COLLOM, JOHN. Abington.
Sept 29, 1797. Nov 11, 1797. 2.18
To wife Alice, household goods, income of realty, 102 acres. To 3 sons: Jesse, Benjamin and Clement, wearing apparel, equally. Exrs. to sell personalty, money except 1/8 part, to wife and children: Jesse, Benjamin, Clement, Rachel, Hannah and cousin Jonathan Leech, equally. To children of daughter Elizabeth, dec. 1/8 part, equally. At wife's death, farm to be sold, money divided as follows: to son Benjamin and cousin Jonathan Leech, 50 pds. each. Rem. to children, (except 1/7 part): Jesse, Benjamin, clement, Rachel Barnes, Hannah Dean and cousin Jonathan Leech, equally. Remaining 1/7 part to children of daughter Elizabeth, dec.
Execs: Wife Alice, son Jesse, Thomas Fletcher. Wit: Thomas Livezey, Jesse Roberts.

PHIPPS, PETER. Abington.
Jan 26, 1797. Nov 11, 1797. 2.19
To daughter Ann Jones, 100 pds. To daughter Elisabeth Righter, 100 pds. To daughter Mary, 50 pds. To sons Thomas and Joseph, farm, 200 acres, equally, subject to payment of money to daughters. To Mary Townsend, 3 pds., 2 s., 10 d. yearly to be paid by sons Thomas and Joseph. Personalty to 3 daughters: Ann Jones, Mary Child and Elisabeth Righter.
Execs: Sons Thomas and Joseph. Wit: George Williams, Thomas Livezey.

WATERMAN, ISAAC. Abington.
July 27, 1795. Nov 11, 1797. 2.20
To wife Hannah, realty and personalty. To daughter Abigail, wife of Benjamin Hallowell, Jr. 50 pds. To daughter Mary, wife of Watson Playter, 50 pds. To son Joseph, half of farm, subject to wife's estate during life and subject to payment of 230 pds. To son Isaac, rem. of farm, subject to wife's estate during life also to payment of 100 pds. To son Isaiah, 115 pds. to be paid by son Joseph, after wife's death. To son Charles, 115 pds. to be paid by sons, after wife's death. At wife's death, rem. of personalty to be sold and divided among sons, Charles and Isaiah.
Execs: Wife Hannah, son Joseph, cousin Thomas Livezey. Wit: George Williams, John Righter.

ROBERTS, SAMUEL, Providence.
April 8, 1793. Sept 16, 1797. 2.22
To son Samuel, farm, 130 acres. To son Edward, 10 pds. to be paid by son Samuel. To daughter Mary, widow of James Sands, dec., 20 pds. To daughter Elisabeth, wife of John Baker, 20 pds. To daughter Hannah, wife of Michael Horning, 20 pds. To daughter Catharine, wife of William Nelson, 20 pds. To daughter Rebecca, wife of James Curry, 20 pds. To son Arnold, farm, 50 acres, where he now dwells. To granddaughter Catharine, daughter of son John, dec. 10 pds. To granddaughter Hannah, of son John, 10 pds. above legacies paid by son Arnold. Personalty divided among 5 daughters: Mary, Elisabeth, Hannah, Catharine and Rebecca. Exec: Son Samuel. Wit: Derick Casselberry, Norris Jones, Philip Shambough.

SCHWENCK, MATTHIAS. Douglass.
Feb 5, 1796. Nov 20, 1797. 2.23
Personalty to be sold. To wife Catharine, 1/3 part of estate To daughter Maria Magdalena, remaining 2/3 of estate. If she dies under age to brother Andrew.
Execs: And guardian of daughter Maria Magdalena, brother Andrew. Wit: Frederick Beitman, Thomas Richards, John F. Windard.

CLEAVER, ISAAC. Upper Dublin.
Nov 14, 1797. Nov 29, 1797. 2.23
Exrs. to sell farm, 30 acres and pay debts. Rem. to be divided among children. To wife Ann, use of farm and personalty, at her death, realty to be sold. To son Peter, 25 pds. To son Joseph, 50 pds. Rem. divided among 6 children: Peter, Hannah, Joseph, Lydia, Isaac and Mary.
Execs: Sons Peter, Joseph and Isaac. Wit: John Cleaver, Jonathan Thomas.

FITZWATER, THOMAS. Whitpain.
March 10, 1790. Dec 9, 1797. 2.24
To wife Sarah, use of 230 pds.; room and maintenance. Personalty to be sold and realty; money divided among 7 children: George, John, William, Thomas, David, Rachel and Mary. To 5 sons, 230 pds. equally, after wife's death.
Execs: sons George, John and William. Wit: William Robinson, Andrew Knox, Isaac McGlathery.

JONES, BENJAMIN. Whitemarsh.
Oct 7, 1797. Dec 9, 1797. 2.26
To daughter Mary, wife's wearing apparel, &c. Exrs. to sell realty and personalty and money arising applied to purchase of house for wife during life. Rem. to be put on interest and applied towards maintenance for children: Ann, Naomi, Jacob and Samuel. After wife's death, estate equally divided among 4 children, boys to have 2 shares and daughters 1

share each.
Execs: Wife Sarah, Samuel Spencer. Wit: Jesse Trump, Thomas Prayor.

GRUB, JACOB. New Hanover.
Dec 6, 1792. Dec 11, 1797. 2.26
To wife Barbara, 25 pds.,household goods and use of farm during widowhood, 6 pds. yearly. To son Abraham, farm, 130 acres; he to receive deed. To daughter Ruth, 21 pds. and case of drawers. To daughters Hannah and Ruth, wearing apparel, bedding, pewter, &c.
Exec: Son Isaiah. Wit: Jonah Miller, John Cray, John Matthews.

WOLF, JOHN. Whitemarsh.
Aug 16, 1790. Dec 16, 1797. 2.29
Realty and personalty to be sold and money divided as follows: to person who purchaes farm, 1/3 part, wife Mary to receive interest. To wife Mary, household goods. To son John, 5 pds. to son George, 5 pds. To daughters: Christiana, Mary, Barbara and Catharine, 3 pds. each. To granddaughter wife of John Stealy, 40 s. To son Frederick, 10 pds. At wife's death, principal of 1/3 of estate which purchased kept to be equally divided among sons: John, Frederick, George and Benjamin. To son Benjamin, cow.
Exec: Son Benjamin. Wit: Thomas White, Andrew Norney.

THOMAS, DAVID. Providence.
Oct 2, 1797. Dec 23, 1797. 2.30
To son Abel, 125 acres. To son David, rem. of farm. To daughter Anna, use of room and maintenance, while unmarried. To 2 daughters Sarah Longstreth and Anna, 150 pds. to be paid by son Abel. Wife to divide personalty among children. Son David to have right of quarry on son Abel's land.
Execs: wife Mary and son David. Wit: Isaac Jacobs, Mary Ellis, John Jacobs.

TORRENCE, SAMUEL. Horsham.
Dec 16, 1797. Dec 30, 1797. 2.32
To Congregation of Neshaminy, 40 pds. To wife Mary, rem. of estate.
Exec: Samuel Mann. Wit: John Mann, James Wray.

JONES, JOSEPH. Cheltenham.
Feb 25, 1797. Jan 6, 1798. 2.33
To son Jonathan, farm, 50 acres and farm purchased of Henry Gilbert, in Bristol, 19 3/4 acres; he paying to daughter Elizabeth's 6 children: Ann, Mary, Joseph, Isaac, Jacob and Elizabeth Saylor, 60 pds. equally. To Mary Jones, wife of son David, 3 pds. 6 s. 8 d. yearly. To son John, rem. of farm, 85 acres. To daughter Mary, 60 pds. To son Thomas, 110 acres, he pay 60 pds.; 1/2 paid to daughter Mary, other half put on interest for daughter Elizabeth's children, also paying 3 pds. 6 s. 8 d. to daughter in

law Mary Jones, yearly. To 2 sons John and Thomas, bond, equally. Farm, 30 acres, 1/3 part to daughter Mary, 1/3 part to Enoch Roberts, son of daughter Mary, and Joseph Taylor, son of daughter Elizabeth, equally. Remaining 1/3 part to daughter Elizabeth, bed, bedding, &c. Rem. to 3 sons: Jonathan, John and Thomas equally.
Execs: Sons John and Thomas. Wit: Benjamin Rowland, Jacob Albertson.

YEGAR, ELIZABETH, Pottstown.
March 1, 1792. Jan 15, 1798. 2.35
To grandson John Pitting, 1 Spanish dollar. To granddaughter Elizabeth Libegud, 1 Spanish dollar. To son Christian, rem. of personalty and realty.
Exec: Son Christian. Wit: Henry Warley, Sr., Jacob Bechtell.

CROUS, MICHAEL, Frederick.
Dec 4, 1794. Jan 15, 1798. 2.36
To son Michael, bed and maintenance. To grandchildren, 200 pds. equally, to be paid by son Daniel. To son Daniel, farm, 168 acres and personalty. To children of son George, dec. 20 pds. equally. To children of daughter Molly, dec. 20 pds. To children of daughter Elizabeth, dec., 20 pds. To children of daughter Salome, dec., 20 pds. To children of daughter Catharine, dec., 20 pds. To grandson Philip Kern, 10 pds. Son Daniel to pay remaining 100 pds. to grandchildren equally. To son Michae, home farm.
Execs: Michael Crous, Abraham Swenk. Wit: Andrew Berger, Henry Sasseman.

BATE, THOMAS. Montgomery.
July 5, 1790. Jan 20, 1798. 2.39
To son Thomas, farm, 95 acres, he to pay 50 pds. To wife Sarah, use and income of farm, 120 acres during life and furniture. Rem. of personalty to be sold and farm, 120 acres. To son Jesse, 80 pds. and wearing apparel. To 2 daughters Rebecca and Ruth, 20 pds. To 2 daughters Margaret and Hannah, 200 pds. Rem. to 6 children: Jesse, Thomas, Rebecca, Ruth, Margaret and Hannah.
Execs: Son Thomas, Andrew Morgan. Wit: Thomas Morgan, Theophilus Williams, Evan Jones.

WITZ, JACOB. Douglass.
Jan 4, 1798. Jan 30, 1798. 2.41
To wife Mary, all estate.
Exec: Christopher Schaner. Wit: Jacob Drinkhouse, Charles Witz.

WILBERHAM, THOMAS. Limerick.
Dec 17, 1797. Feb 3, 1798. 2.42
To wife Margaret, furniture, use and income of farm during life; at her death to be sold, money divided among children, equally.
Execs: Wife Margaret, Benjamin Dismant. Wit: William Baker.

HOOT, PHILIP. Gwynedd.
Jan 13, 1798. Feb 12, 1798. 2.43
To wife Eve Elizabeth, part of household goods and maintenance, interest of 350 pds. To son Peter, farm, 180 acres, subject to payment to wife, at valuation of 1800 pds. Rem. to John Erhard's children: John, Jacob, Peter, Catharine, wife of John Snyder; Elizabeth, wife of Abraham Weber and 3 children of son Christopher: John, Sarah and Elizabeth. At wife's death, her share to be divided among children.
Execs: Son Peter, sons in law John Snyder, Abraham Weber. Wit: Frederick Conrad, Conrad Gearhart.

WHITE, JAMES. Whitemarsh.
June 15, 1795. Feb 23, 1798. 2.46
Estate to be sold and money divided as follows: to son Thomas, 10 pds. To grandchildren of daughter Nancy, wife of James Edminston, 10 pds. equally. To son Josiah, 10 pds. To daughter Jane, 10 pds. To son James, 15 pds. To daughter Rachel, wife of Thomas Cox, 10 pds. To son David, 10 pds. To grandson Isaiah, son of James, 5 pds. Rem. divided among children.
Execs: Sons James and David. Wit: Jonathan Stout, George Aman.

BURKIRK, ANDREW. Moreland.
Jan 17, 1798. March 28, 1798. 2.47
To daughter Lena, 40 pds. as outset. To 2 daughters Rebecca and Lena, 70 pds. each. To son Cornelius, 2 farms, 40 acres and 9 acres of woodland. Rem. of farm to son Mahlon, he paying legacies to daughters. To grandson Andrew Kurkirk[sic], silver headed cane. To sons Mahlon and Cornelius, wearing apparel equally. To son Cornelius, mare, cow, wagon, bedding, &c. Rem. to be sold and divided among children.
Exec: Son Mahlon. Wit: Isaac Beans, Thomas Beans.

SHITTLER, LUDOWIG. Frederick.
Dec 21, 1797. April 7, 1798. 2.49
To son Ludowig, bible, wearing apparel and farm. woodland; he to pay for farm, 1500 pds.; he to keep his hsare of estate and to pay to daughters in yearly payments 75 pds. each in successive years. To 2 youngest daughters 50 pds. rem. equally divided among 4 children.
Execs: Son in law Jacob Bickel, son Ludowig. Wit: John Zieber, Jacob Grubb, John Barkey, Sr.

GILBERT, BERNARD. Douglass.
Oct 14, 1793. April 16, 1798. 2.50
To wife Mary Elizabeth, bed, bedstead and household goods. To son George, 5 s. To son Bernard, farm and 2 tracts, 76 acres; he paying 600 pds. To wife, interest of 100 pds. yearly and maintenance; at her death, principal divided among children. To son George, 30 pds. To daughter Catharine, wife of Daniel Bob, 30 pds. To son Adam, 30 pds. to daughter

Magdalena, wife of George Stichter, 30 pds. To son Jacob, 30 pds. To son John, 30 pds. To daughter Elizabeth, 30 pds. To son George, 25 pds., 11 s., 1 3/9 d. to each child the above amount until all is paid. rem. of personalty to be sold and interest of 100 pds. paid to wife yearly. To daughters Elizabeth and Mary, marriage portion, each. Rem. of money from personalty to be divided among children: George, Catharine, Adam, Magdalena, Jacob, John, Bernard, Elizabeth and Mary. Farm, 285 1/2 acres in Bethel which testator and son Jacob ownes[sic] to be sold, money divided among children.
Execs: sons George and Adam. Wit: Michael Albrecht, Christian Bryman, Michael Freidmirch.

RUSSEL, JAMES. Lower Merion.
March 4, 1795. April 30, 1798. 2.54
To wife all estate during life. At wife's death to daughter Mary, at daughter Mary's death if she has no heirs to cousin High Henry. Wit: Marsena Alloway, Peter Bechtell.

GODSHALK, JACOB. Skippack and Perkiomen.
Oct 22, 1787. May 7, 1798. 2.55
To wife Helena, all estate. To son Godshalk, all estate after wife's death. Execs: Son Godshalk, Henry Pennebecker, Jr. Wit: Abraham Yerger, Gerred Godshalk.

DENNEHOWER, CATHARINE. Gwynedd.
Nov 12, 1792. May 15, 1798. 2.56
To 3 daughters: Catharine, Elizabeth and Sarah, 3 shares. To 6 children: John, Abraham, Henry, Catharine, Elizabeth and Sarah, rem.
Exec: Son Abraham. Wit: B. Bahtinger, Jacob Fried.

NORTH, ANN. Providence.
Dec 18, 1797. May 15, 1798. 2.56
To daughter Sophia, wearing apparel, bedding, &c. To granddaughter Hannah Humphrey, pewter. To grandson Samuel Davis, 6 pds. To son Joshua, bible. To son John, bible or 15 pds. To son William, bible or 15 pds. To 4 daughters: Sophia, Sarah, Elizabeth and Ann, bonds and notes.
Execs: Son Caleb, Benjamin Dismant. Wit: Benjamin Dismant, Thomas North.

YETTER, JOHN, Whitemarsh.
March 2, 1798. May 26, 1798. 2.58
To wife Ann and daughter Mary, grain and maintenance. To son John, 5 pds. To son Samuel, 20 s. To daughter Amy Lushe, 20 s. To son Ludwick, horse, wagon, farming utensils; he paying to son John, 5 pds. To daughter Mary, household goods, she paying son Samuel and daughters Amy and Catharine their legacies. To son Ludwick, 1/2 of farm. To daughter Mary, 1/2 of farm.

Exec: Son Ludwick. Wit: George Pierce, Sephimers Wood, Nathan Cook.

GRUB, CONRAD. Frederick.
Feb 13, 1786. May 29, 1798. 2.59
To wife Anna, personalty, bonds, notes and maintenance during widowhood. To nephew Jacob Grub, realty, 100 acres; he to give to wife maintenance also 350 pds. he to keep 150 pds. remaining 200 pds. pay to following: to his brother Daniel, 25 pds. To his brother John, 35 pds. To his brother Henry, 35 pds. To his sister Elizabeth, wife of David Wampolt, 25 pds. To brother Abraham, 70 pds. To children of brother George: David and Catharine, 20 pds. equally. To brother Jacob, bond for 25 pds. and note for 6 pds.
Execs: Wife Anna, nephew John Grub. Wit: Jacob Schnider, Michael Croll.

SIDEL, NICHOLAS. Worcester.
April 14, 1798. June 12, 1798. 2.62
Exrs. to sell personalty and realty, 200 acres. Daughter Dorothy to receive interest of her share; at her death whole to be divided among 3 children. To daughter Dorothy, 140 pds., bed, &c. To son Nicholas's son Nicholas, bed. Rem. to 4 children: Nicholas, Elizabeth, wife of Conrad Boyer, Michael and Immanuel. Wit: James Smith, Henry Spare, Frederick Conrad.

REED, PHILIP. Marlborough.
May 9, 1794. July 11, 1798. 2.64
To son Baltsar, farm, 105 acres, at valuation of 300 pds. already conveyed to him, testator having received 51 pds. 1/3 of rem. 83 pds. To son Baltsar. To son Philip, 1/3 part. To daughter Catharine, wife of Yost Shatz's children, 1/3 part. To son Philip, 17 pds. To children of daughter Catharine, 17 pds. To son Baltsar, 5 s. To son in law Yost Shatz, 20 d. To wife Christiana, bed, bedstead, household goods and maintenance during widowhood. Rem. of personalty to be sold and interest given to wife. At wife's death household goods to be divided into 3 parts. To children of son Baltsar, 1/3 part. To son Philip, 1/3 part. To children of daughter Catharine, 1/3 part.
Execs: Philip Gable, son Philip. Wit: W. Wohlsath, Johannes Molherd.

SLOAN, JACOB. Lower Merion.
Oct 3, 1797. July 23, 1798. 2.67
To wife, personalty and farm, 37 acres, she paying 6 pds. yearly. To daughter Barbara, wife of Joseph Campbell, farm at wife's death. Subject to payments of 60 pds. To step daughter Margaret Pettinger, 15 pds. To step daughter Susanna Garret, 15 pds. to step son Amos Pettinger, 15 pds. To step daughter Hannah Fossett, 15 pds.
Execs: Son in law Joseph Campbell, step son Amos Pettinger. Wit: Anthony Levering, Peter Ott, Thomas George.

DAVIS, WILLIAM. Whitpain.
Aug 25, 1798. Oct 4, 1798. 2.68
Estate to be sold and money divided among 5 children: Nancy, John, Sarah, Hannah and Tamer, except son John to have 30 pds. more than his share.
Execs: Son John and daughter Hannah Taylor. Wit: Miles Strickland, Israel Robinson.

BARNES, ROBERT. Moreland.
Aug 23, 1798. Oct 22, 1798. 2.69
Estate to be sold, except 1 acre To son in law Peter Lukens; money divided as follows: to son Samuel, 100 pds.; he paying 20 pds. to granddaughter Elizabeth Barnes, daughter of son Robert. To son Baker, 100 pds. To son Stephen, 100 pds. To son Timothy, 100 pds. To daughter Abigail, 100 pds. To daughter Mary, wife of Peter Lukens, use of 85 pds.; at her death divided among her children. Rem. to be put on interest for wife Abigail; at her death principal divided into 8 shares: 1 share each to sons: Samuel, Robert, Baker and Stephen and Timothy, daughter Abigail, granddaughter Elizabeth Barnes and remaining part income to daughter Mary. To wife, household goods, &c. and estate in New Jersey. Rem. of personalty to be sold; money divided among 5 sons, and daughter Abigail and use of remaining share to daughter Mary.
Execs: Sons Robert and Baker. Wit: Jarret Spencer, Nathan B. Boileau.

KING, THOMAS. Moreland.
April 1, 1794. Nov 1, 1798. 2.70
To wife Ann, household goods and 10 pds. To son Samuel, farm 21 3/4 acres and 2 1/2 acres; subject to payment of 5 pds. yearly to wife, also paying 20 pds. To daughter Ann Vanhorne, and 6 pds. to grandson George King. to son Jonathan, farm 23 1/4 acres; subject to payment of 5 pds. to wife and 10 pds. to daughter Ann. To daughter Mary, 40 pds. and 40 pds. to daughter Martha King. To 3 daughters rem. of personalty. At wife's death, her share divided among children: Samuel, Mary, Martha and Jonathan.
Execs: Sons Samuel and Jonathan. Wit: David Marple, Jonathan Robinson, John Watts.

MARSHALL, GEORGE. Upper Merion.
Sept 5, 1798. Nov 6, 1798. 2.71
To wife Elizabeth, farm and household goods. To children of niece Mary, wife of Lewis Rush of Phila., farm bought of William Levering in Roxborough, equally. To George Atkins, grandson of wife, 500 pds. paid out of personalty. To wife's son Jacob Taylor and her grandchildren; children of Henry Barnwell; after wife's death, farm bought of William Broades with rem. of realty and personalty equally divided among them.
Exec: Benjamin Brook. Wit: Matthias Colflesh, Isaac DeHaven, Benjamin Brook.

ZIEGLER, HESTER.
Oct 28, 1798. Nov 13, 1798. 2.72
To son Michael, copper kettle, &c. To daughter Catharine, wife of Michael Frack, cloak and clothing. To granddaughter Elizabeth, daughter of son Jacob, bed, case of drawers, &c. Rem. of household goods to be sold and money divided into 4 equal parts. To son Michael, 1 part. To son Garret, 1 part. To daughter Catharine, 1 part. To granddaughter Elizabeth Ziegler, 1 part.
Execs: Brother in law Michael Ziegler, Henry Sweitzer. Wit: Jacob Clemmans, Abraham Yerger.

MORRIS, MORRIS. Gwynedd.
Nov 18, 1793. Nov 13, 1798. 2.73
To wife Catharine, bed, bedstead and rem. of estate after legacies are paid. To David Evans' wife, 5 s. To brother James and son Jonathan, 5 s. each. To sister Margaret Edwards, 5 s. To John Kidney, 1 s. To Margaret Stoneburner, 1 s.
Execs: Wife Catharine, Cadwallader Evans, Jr. Wit: Evan Jones, Henry Jones.

BOUTCHER, JOSEPH. Moreland.
Oct 7, 1798. Nov 13, 1798. 2.74
To son Nathaniel, 15 s. To son John, walnut desk. To wife Rachel, bed, bedding, &c., use of estate until youngest child is 10 years or during widowhood. At death or marriage of wife or when youngest child is 10 years; estate to be sold; dower of 150 pds. to be left in hands of purchaser and interest paid to wife during life. At wife's death said 150 pds. divided among 11 children. Rem. of estate to be divided into 16 parts, equally. To son John, 2 parts. To son Benjanin, 2 parts. To son Joseph, 2 parts. To son Elisha, 2 parts. To son Enos, 2 parts. To each daughter: Martha, Sarah, Priscilla, Ann, Elizabeth and Rachel, 10 part.
Execs: Son John and Joshua Comaly. Wit: Jonathan Comaly, Rynear Lukens.

DEAVES, ISAAC. Whitemarsh.
Sept 17, 1798, Nov 26, 1798. 2.76
To daughter Ann, copper kettle, &c., she paying $8. To daughter Martha Lukens, chest and looking glass, she paying $8. To 8 children: Jacob, Thomas, Joseph, Isaac, Samuel, Jonathan, Jesse, and Isreal, said $16, equally. Rem. to 10 children; 8 children aforesaid and daughters: Martha and Ann.
Exec: Son Isaac. Wit: George Pierce, Nathan Cook.

WOELPER, HANNAH. Limerick.
Sept 26, 1798. Jan 1, 1799. 2.77
To grandson Peter Stager, Jr., son of Adam Stager, dec., 3 pds. To 4 children: Peter, Hannah and Philip Stager and Margaret Hooven, and 1

grandchild Peter Stager, Jr., bond 7 pds. 3 d. now in hands of Elizabeth Bondmot in trust. To daughter Margaret, wife of Matthew Hooven, 2 cows and part of wearing apparel. To Barbara, wife of son Peter, petticoat. To Rebecca, daughter of Matthew Hooven, cloak. Bed, bedding, &c. to be divided among 3 sons and 1 daughter. Rem. of wearing apparel to be sold and money divided among 3 sons and 1 daughter aforesaid.
Exec: Jacob Stager. Wit: John Boulton, Nathan Boulton, Isaiah Davis.

COATS, LINDSAY. Upper Merion.
March 30, 1798. Jan 16, 1799. 2.78
To unmarried daughters by first wife, personalty equally. To wife Rachel, farm. To eldest son, farm in Northumberland.
Codicil gives farm given to wife during life; at her death to son Matthias, To son Matthias, horse. To son Lindsay, mare. Mill and mill-house to be sold.
Exec: Wife Rachel. Wit: Slater Clay, John Hughes.

ROBERTS, JOSEPH. Montgomery.
March 2, 1798. Feb 2, 1799. 2.80
To wife Mercy, all estate. To daughter Sarah Conrad, 5 pds. after wife's death. To 7 sons and 1 daughter, all rem. equally divided among them after wife's death; Isaac, Jonathan, Hugh, George, Charles, Septemus, Joseph and Mercy.
Execs: Sons Isaac and Jonathan, John Roberts. Guardians, wife, brother in law Jonathan Pickering, brother Cadwallader Roberts. Wit: David Cleaver, Peter Roberts, Jonathan Cleaver.

DRAKE, GEORGE. Montgomery.
July 11, 1798. Feb 13, 1799. 2.81
To Sarah Williams, Mary Thomas, Jonathan, Elizabeth Hays, Benjamin, Andrew and William, 10 pds. each. To granddaughter Hannah Drake, daughter of son Jonathan, 3 pds. To grandsons Andrew and Thomas Drake, sons of Andrew, 5 pds. each, they to receive interest until 21. Rem. to son John.
Exec: Son John. Wit: Siles Hugh, David Bruner.

ROUTEBUSH, MICHAEL. Upper Hanover.
April 21, 1798. Feb 25, 1799. 2.82
To wife Annamaria, 50 pds. and 18 pds. yearly, bed, &c. To son Michael, farm, 207 acres, 90 perches, at valuation of 1000 pds. paid as follows: 300 pds. he to keep as purchase money; 300 pds. to remain until after wife's death, he to pay interest, remaining 400 pds. divided into 8 payments of 50 pds. each. To son Henry, 100 pds. To daughter Catharine, wife of Daniel Swenk, 100 pds. To son John, 100 pds. To son Michael, 100 pds. At wife's death, 300 pds. to be divided among 4 children. Personalty to be sold, 50 pds. given to wife, rem. divided into 4 parts among 4 children.
Execs: Sons John and Michael. Wit: Daniel Yost, Andrew Yost, John

Detwiler.

LYSINGER, ANDREW. Plymouth.
Dec 29, 1798. March 2, 1799. 2.85
Farm, 55 acres to wife Mary, during life. To son Joseph, 11 acres of farm after wife's death. To son Andrew, 41 acres of farm after wife's death, he to pay to daughter Mary, 105 pds. To son John, 3 acres 8 perches of farm after wife's death. To son Andrew, colt. Personalty to be sold, 5 pds. of it to Beggars Town Church in Germantown. Rem. to wife Mary.
Execs: Wife Mary and son John. Wit: John Hallman, Andrew Normy.

WILSON, JOHN. Franconia.
Feb 7, 1799. March 2, 1799. 2.86
To wife Ann, bed, household goods and 2 rooms and maintenance. Rem. of personalty to be sold. To son John, farm, 125 acres; he paying 1300 pds. To wife Ann, 200 pds. and 12 pds. yearly. To son John, 100 pds. Rem. to sons: William, John and Joseph and daughters: Mary, Jane, Margaret and Ann and grandchildren of son Henry, dec.; Jane, Ann and Tacy, equally.
Execs: Sons John and Joseph. Trustees, Frederick Michael Shoemaker, Matthias Johnson. Wit: Matthias Johnson, John Jones, Jr.

HOLLAS, ABRAHAM. Norriton.
Nov 1, 1796. March 14, 1799. 2.87
To nephew Abraham Hollas, son of Edward Hollas of Ireland, all estate
Execs: Christopher Stuart, Ezekiel Rhodes. Wit: John Baker, Wm. Kidd.

PRITNER, ANTHONY. Radnor.
Jan 31, 1799. March 18, 1799. 2.88
Realty to be sold. To son Anthony Philip Pritner, interest on 200 pds.; at his death 100 pds. to Anthony Blankly and 100 pds. to Hannah Pritner, daughter of John Pritner. Rem. to brothers and sisters: John and Isaac Pritner and Martha Blankly, wife of Richard Blankly, equally.
Execs: Benjamin Brook, John Morgan. Wit: Samuel Powell, J. Elliot.

McKNIGHT, ROBERT. Lowre Merion.
Sept 14, 1795. April 11, 1799. 2.89
To wife, personalty and 1/3 of use and income of realty. Realty in Lower Merion not to be sold until youngest child is 25, then all realty to be divided among children and wife if living to have a share.
Codicil appoints Gavin Hamilton and children exrs. Dated Oct 17, 1795.
Execs: Children.

KEELY, HENRY. Skippack and Perkiomen.
March 22, 1793. April 13, 1799. 2.91
Farm and personalty to be sold and money divided among 11 children. To son Valentine, 50 pds. To each child, 1 share: Valentine, Henry, Conrad,

John, Jacob, Daniel, William, Mary, Elizabeth, Catharine, and Magdalena; son Daniel to receive 30 pds. also.
Execs: Son Valentine and son in law Henry Harley. Wit: John Hoffman, Samuel Pennebacker, William Pennebacker.

LINN, JOHN. Lower Merion.
March 29, 1799. April 21, 1799. 2.91
To daughter Elizabeth Stubert, 5 pds. To grandson John Linn, son of John Jr., 5 pds. To son Jacob, 5 s. Rem. divided among John Linn, Jr., Elizabeth Stubert, Catharine Mattis.
Exec: Grandson John Linn. Wit: Cornelius Holget, Peter Widener.

MARTIN, JOHN, Upper Dublin.
April 9, 1798. April 27, 1799. 2.92
To wife Elizabeth, 200 pds. and 9 pds. yearly during widowhood and household goods, maintenance. Rem. of personalty to be sold and money divided among son Matthias and daughter Elizabeth Trexler. At wife's death, woodland, 20 acres to be sold and divided among 2 aforesaid children.
Execs: Robert Loller, Baltzer Ernst. Wit: Daniel Shoemaker, Peter Steriger.

BISBING, BERNARD. Springfield.
April 4, 1799. April 30, 1799. 2.94
To wife Margareth, household goods, cow, &c. to daughter Elizabeth, bed, bedstead, farm, 115 acres. To son George, cow, &c. At wife's death, farm to be sold and money divided among children: Bernard, Andrew, John, Eve, Margareth, Catharine, Elizabeth, Barbara, Jacob and George, equally. To daughter Eve, wife of Harman Lauer, 10 acres. Realty, 84 acres, to be sold and money divided among children and personalty to be sold, what children have received to be deducted.
Execs: Son John, son in law Robert M. Curtey. Wit: Andrew Fie, George Billger.

SOUR, FREDERICK. Limerick.
Oct 20, 1796. May 2, 1799. 2.95
To wife Margaret, 18 pds. yearly, bed, furniture and maintenance during widowhood. To son John, farm, 118 acres at valuation of 900 pds. To 2 daughters Catharine, wife of Peter Moyer and Elizabeth, wife of Joseph Fry, 100 pds. equally. To wife, interest of 300 pds., at her death principal divided among children. To wife, 100 pds.
Execs: Wife and son John, Simon Sweitzer. Wit: Abraham Bechtell, Henry Sweitzer.

WALTON, JACOB. Moreland.
Sept 3, 1798. May 2, 1799. 2.97
To wife Mary, household goods and maintenance. Sons Isaiah and Charles

to provide maintenance for wife and 12 pds. yearly. To son Isaiah, farm where he lives and part of farm, 61 3/4 acres 22 perches. To son Charles, house and rem. of farm, 68 3/4 acres, 8 perches. To son Jacob, 250 pds. to be paid by sons Isaiah and Charles. To 4 daughters: Ann Penengton, Priscilla Gourley, Elizabeth and Mary, 70 pds. each. Personalty to be sold and money divided among 4 daughters and son Jacob. To son Charles, wearing apparel, &c. To sons Isaiah and Charles, farming utensils and rem. of estate.
Execs: Wife Mary, sons Isaiah and Charles. Wit: Samuel Gummere, Edward Farmer, Rachel Carver.

ELLIS, WILLIAM. Towamencin.
April 23, 1794. May 13, 1794. 2.101
To nephew Amos Ellis, of brother Isaac, 20 pds. To nephew William, of son Isaac, his daughter Mary, case of drawers, &c. To Lydia, daughter of nephew William, bed, &c. To nephew William, farm, 50 acres and rem. of estate.
Exec: Nephew William. Wit: Isaac Shoemaker, Matthew Knox, Isaac McGlathery.

BUCHAMER, JOHN. Hatfield.
April 23, 1794. May 13, 1794. 2.101
To wife Catharine, income of farm during widowhood, furniture and pewter. Son Peter to sell farm, 139 acres, and personalty at wife's death. To 8 children: Jacob, John, Peter, Henry, Catharine, Elizabeth, and Mary, rem. of money equally.
Execs: wife Catharine and son Peter. Wit: Thomas Davis, Jacob Johnson.

MILLER, ELIZABETH. New Hanover.
May 17, 17996. May 14, 1799. 2.102
To daughter Magdalena, 30 pds. and linen. Rem. divided as follows: to daughter Catharine, 1 share. To daughter Gerdraude Wamback, 1 share. To daughter Elizabeth Smith, 1 share. To children of daughter Mary Smith, dec., 1 share. To daughter Magdalena, 1 share. To Hannah Gor, 1 share.
Execs: Sons in law Bartholemew Wamback and John Smith. Wit: Conrad Shunk, Amos Jones.

JONES, ISAAC. Montgomery.
April 11, 1794. May 15, 1799. 2.103
To wife Elizabeth, 2 featherbeds, furniture and farm. To daughter Ruth, 300 pds. and featherbed and bible. To grandchildren of son Daniel and daughter Jane, 20 s. each. To son Isaac, land unsold and rem. of personalty.
Execs: Son Isaac and George Maris. Wit: Nathan Cleaver, John Evans.

ROSENBERGER, HELLENA. Franconia.

July 19, 1793. May 15, 1799. 2.105
To son Yellis, 1 s. To son Henry, 1 s. To daughter Gertrude, wife of Jacob Lantes, 1 s. To daughter Elizabeth, wife of John Alterffer, 1 s. To granddaughter Hellena, wife of Michael Wierman, 50 pds. To granddaughter Anna, daughter of Michael Wierman, 5 pds. when 18. To Benjamin Lantes, clock. To son in law Jacob Lantes, wearing apparel and household goods. Rem. to Benjamin Lantes.
Exec: Benjamin Lantes. Wit: Peter Boorse, Maria Boorse, Jacob Kolb.

JONES, MARTHA. Eastown, Chester Co.
March 29, 1797. June 20, 1799. 2.106
To son Samuel, daughter, granddaughter Sarah, wife of Enoch Jones, granddaughter Martha, daughter of Martha, wife of Lewellin Davis, and Sarha, wife of Roger Davis, principal of 3 certificates, $528.32, equally. To Abner Davis, 50 pds. To 3 daughters: Martha, Elizabeth and Sarah, wearing apparel, equally. To son Thomas, 5 s. To grandson Samuel Jones, and son Griffith, rem.
Exec: Samuel Jones. Wit: David Coler, Christopher Coler.

DAGEN, LUDWICK. Whitemarsh.
June 20, 1799. June 22, 1799. 2.107
Farm, 96 acres, to be kept, until youngest son is 21; after that farm to be sold and money divided among 5 children: Christiana, Eve, Ludwick, Daniel, and John; daughter Eve to have 20 pds. less than a share. Rem. divided among 5 children.
Execs: son Ludwick and sons in law John Hiltner, Michael Hiltner. Wit: William Hiltner, Nathan Potts.

GALLMAN, JOHN. Upper Hanover.
Feb 15, 1783. June 24, 1799. 2.108
To wife Catharine, farm, 81 acres, household goods, furniture, &c. to John Miller, John Daniel Miller (of brother in law Daniel Miller, Sr.) to Mary Catharine Miller and John Miller, children of brother in law Jacob Miller, 5 pds. each. At wife's death, farm and personalty to be sold; 1/2 money to children of brother in law Daniel Miller, Sr. and other 1/2 to children of brother in law Jacob Miller.
Execs: Wife Catharine, brother in law Jacob Miller. Wit: George Heighlick, John Heist, Ulrick Greeber.

WOOD, ISAAC. Upper Dublin.
Feb 8, 1797. June 29, 1799. 2.112
To wife Margaret, household goods, income of farm and income of son Josiah's farm. To son Josiah, 40 acres, he paying 600 pds. after wife's death, rem. of personalty to be sold and money with 600 pds. divided among 4 children: Josiah, Isaac, John and Sarah, as follows: to son Josiah and daughter Sarah, 90 pds. each. Sons Isaac and John, have already received their shares. Rem. equally divided among 4 children.

Execs: Son Josiah and son in law Jonathan Scout. Wit: Robert Loller, John Burk.

LEWIS, ROBERT. Cheltenham.
Sept 15, 1798. June 27, 1799. 2.113
To wife Jane, household goods, and maintenance. To 2 sons David and Amos, farm, equally, they to provide maintenance for wife and to pay 120 pds. To sons Robert and Joseph, 25 pds. each. To 7 daughters: Sarah, Tamer, Mary, and grandsons John, George and Robert Montier, 5 pds. each; to daughters Rachel, Jane, Elizabeth, and Susanna, 10 pds. each; both legacies to be paid by 2 sons.
Execs: Son Robert and son in law Joseph Montier. Wit: Matthew Tyson, Thomas Livezey.

IREDELL, ROBERT. Horsham.
May 20, 1799. July 27, 1799. 2.114
To wife Hannah, maintenance and 24 pds. yearly, personalty and 112 pds. To son John, farm, 100 acres and 7 1/2 acres, woodland; he to provide maintenance for wife. To son Jonathan, rem. of realty, 107 acres; he to pay 1237 pds., 11 s. Son John to pay 1397 pds., 10 s. for farm. To son Robert, 300 pds. To sons John, Jonathan and Seth, 200 pds. each. To son Abraham, 100 pds. To daughter Hannah Comly, 100 pds. To grandson Joseph of son (?) Charles, dec., 50 pds. when 21. Rem. to 6 children: Abraham, Robert, John, Jonathan, Seth, Hannah equally. At wife's death, 400 pds. for her maintenance to be divided among 6 children.
Execs: Sons Robert, John and Jonathan. Wit: Senica Lukens, Joseph Lukens, Abraham Shoemaker.

McGLATHERY, HENRY. Norriton.
Feb 8, 1798. July 29, 1799. 2.117
To granddaughter Maria, 30 pds. To wife Sarah, realty during life. To daughters: Elizabeth, Margaret, Rachel, and Jean, enough added to what they have received to make 100 pds. each. To son Henry, 50 pds. To 2 sons Henry and Mordicai, rem.
Execs: sons Henry and Mordicai. Wit: Jacob Evans, David Supplee, Enoch Supplee.

HERSH, LUDWIG. Marlborough.
July 18, 1799. Aug 14, 1799. 2.118
To wife Catharine, realty and part of household goods. Rem. of personalty to be sold, money divided among 9 children, 3 sons and 6 daughters equally. At wife's death, realty to be sold and rem. divided among 9 children.
Execs: Sons in law Nicholas Hearing, Michael Snyder. Wit: Philip Reed, Philip Reed Sadler.

KIRK, RYNEAR. Upper Dublin.

Aug 27, 1796. Aug 10, 1799. 2.119
To wife Elizabeth, 100 pds., income of farm in Mt. Holly and 10 pds. yearly. Personalty to be divided into 5 equal parts as follows: to grandsons Jonathan and Jesse Roberts of daughter Martha, dec., 1 part equally and 25 pds. each. To 4 daughters: Sarah Tyson, Susanna Roberts, Mary Tyson and Hannah Iredell, 1 part each and 100 pds. each; except to daughter Hannah, 50 pds. To son John, farm, 14 3/4 acres, subject to payment of 10 pds. yearly to wife and to grandsons Jonathan and Jesse Roberts, 25 pds. each, and to daughters: Sarah, Susanna and Mary, 100 pds. each, also to daughter Hannah, 50 pds.
Execs: Brother Jacob Kirk, and son John. Wit: Jacob Kirk, Jr., and John Kirk.

LANE, EDWARD. Providence.
March 1, 1798. Aug 31, 1799. 2.120
To daughter Mary Kendell, 170 pds. To daughter Abigail Couch, 100 pds. To daughter Jane Davis, 120 pds. To daughter Ann Church, 120 pds. and bed, &c. To daughter Eleanor Evans, 250 pds. and 10 acres. To daughter Hannah Bean, 250 pds. To grandson Edward Lane Bean, 50 pds. when 21. To grandson Edward Couch, clock and gun. To granddaughter Ann Lane, featherbed and 1/2 doz. silver teaspoons. To grandson Edward Evans, writing desk. To granddaughter Ann Evans, case of drawers. Rem. of personalty to be divided among 6 daughters: Mary, Abigail, Jane, Ann, Eleanor, and Hannah, equally. To son William, farm; he to pay legacies.
Execs: Son William and son in law William Couch. Wit: James Bean, Edward Evans, Joseph Henry.

CLEAVER, ISAAC. Cheltenham.
Oct 6, 1797. Sept 6, 1799. 2.122
To wife Rebecca, 150 pds. and income of estate. To daughter Hannah, clock; at her death to her son Isaac Tyson. At wife's death, rem. of estate to be sold and money divided as follows: to grandson John Tyson of daughter Agnes, dec., 5 pds. To Rebecca Craft of daughter Agnes, 200 pds. rem. divided into 3 parts. To daughter Hannah, interest of 1/3 part. Remaining 2/3 parts divided among grandchildren: Peter, Rynear, Benjamin, Jesse, Mary and Hannah Tyson, children of daughter Mary, children of daughter Hannah, Rebecca Craft, aforesaid, Isaac Tyson and Rebecca Lukens and children of grandson John Tyson.
Execs: Son in law Thomas Leeck, John Child and Anthony Williams. Wit: Benjamin Mather, Edward Edwards.

CASHO, GABRIEL. Providence.
April 24, 1799. Oct 8, 1799. 2.123
To wife Maria Magdalena, personalty; if she marry realty to be sold and money divided among wife and 7 children: Jacob, Mary, Rebecca, Elizabeth, Sally, Catharine, and John, equally.
Execs: Wife Maria and Henry Boyer. Wit: Francis Swaine, James Wells.

COMBE, THOMAS. Phila.
May 14, 1780. Oct 18, 1799. 2.124
To wife, 1/3 part of household goods. Remaining 2/3 to be divided among 3 daughters: Sarah, Mary, and Hannah. To son Rev. Thomas Combe, library and 3 English Guineas. To grandson John R. Combe, watch and wearing apparel. To grandson Barnet B. Combe, 5 English Guineas. Realty to be sold, money divided as follows: to wife, 1/3 part. Remaining 2/3 parts divided among 3 daughters aforesaid.
Execs: Wife Sarah, daughters: Sarah, Mary and Hannah and brother in law Thomas Rutter. Wit: William Smith, Peter Robinson, Elizabeth Eldny.

GUCKER, PETER. Upper Hanover.
May 16, 1798. Oct 26, 1799. 2.125
To wife Susannah, part of realty and use of personalty. To grandchildren (of daughter Elizabeth, late wife of Henry Sechler) 300 pds. equally divided. To daughter Magdalena, wife of John Detweiler, 300 pds. To daughter Susanna, wife of Henry Sechler, interest of 300 pds.; at her death to her children. To daughter Barbara, wife of Abraham Sell, 300 pds. Rem. of estate after wife's death, equally divided among children: George, Elizabeth, Susannah, and Barbara. Daughter Elizabeth's share to be divided among her children.
Execs: Wife Susanna, son George Cucker. Wit: John Gilbert, John Richards.

CONNER, MARY. Douglass.
Sept 17, 1799. Oct 28, 1799. 2.127
To friend Michael Mauser, realty and personalty, except what is given to son. To son Nedy, 5 s.
Exec: Michael Mauser. Wit: Peter Hauley, Barthw. Wamback.

KOLB, DIELMAN. Worcester.
June 28, 1794. Oct 28, 1799. 2.128
Farm, 208 acres to be sold and personalty. To daughter Magdalena, bedstead, &c. Rem. of estate with money from sale to be divided among children: Martin, Henry, Isaac, Matthias, Daniel, Magdalena, Whilhemina, and Esther, equally; what they have received to be deducted.
Execs: Sons Henry and Matthias. Wit: John Bean, Jr., John Keyser, Frederick Conrad.

WILLIAMS, WILLIAM. Gwynedd.
Sept 23, 1782. Nov 4, 1799. 2.129
To daughter Ann, featherbed, case of drawers, 100 pds., &c. To sons William and John, 100 pds. equally. Farm, 143 acres and rem. of personalty to be sold and money divided among 9 children: Thomas, Enoch, Isaac, William, John, Ann, Elizabeth, Sarah, and Ellin, equally.
Execs: John Evans, son John. Wit: Samuel Castner, Nicholas Riel, Evan Jones.

SPEAR, PHILIP. Worcester.
June 13, 1795. Nov 11, 1799. 2.131
To son Leonard, farm in Providence, containing 59 acres. To daughter Catharine, 115 pds. To daughter Christina, 135 pds. To daughter Mary, 125 pds. To daughter Barbara, 125 pds. To son Benjamin, 200 pds. To son Jacob, 200 pds. To son Daniel, farm where testator lived, &c. To son Henry, farm where testator's father lived. Personalty to be sold; sons Henry and Daniel to pay legacies to their brothers and sisters.
Execs: Son Leonard and son Daniel. Wit: Samuel Gordon, Jacon Garber, Benedict Garber.

MEREDITH, SUSANNA. Upper Merion.
April 20, 1799. Nov 11, 1799. 2.132
To sister Margaret Ray, 1/12 part of estate. To sister Mary McMannamay, 1/12 part. To brother John Meredith, 1/12 part. To David McCallister, son of sister Tamer, 1/12 part. To Polly Care, Susanna Meredith, Jane Meredith and Elizabeth Meredith, daughters of brother John, 1/12 part. To John Meredith, son of brother John, 1/12 part. To nephew Evan Griffith, son of sister Jane, 1/12 part. To Joseph Meredith, and to James Meredith, sons of brother Jesse, 1/12 part each.
Execs: Jonathan Roberts and Samuel Henderson. Wit: Philip Rees, Abraham Jones, Henry Sininger.

LONGBIEN, GODFREY. Limerick.
Feb 13, 1799. Nov 25, 1799. 2.134
To wife Margaret, realty and personalty; at her death to be sold and money divided among heirs: Henry George, heirs John, Godfrey, Elizabeth, Mary Barbara, Catharine, heirs of Margaret and Christian (heirs of John shall receive 1 equal 1/10 part) (heirs of Margaret to receive 1/10 part).
Execs: Son George and son in law George Mohr. Wit: Godrey Salor, John Coal.

ACHABACH, CASPER. Frederick.
Aug 4, 1784. Nov 28, 1799. 2.135
To wife Molly, use of estate during widowhood; if she marry to receive interest of 200 pds. and household goods; rem. equally divided among 3 daughters: Molly, Belinda and Elizabeth; what they have received to be deducted.
Execs: Wife and son in law Henry Sasseman. Wit: Jacob Bergey, John Barkey.

MARKS, PHILIP. Douglass.
April 14, 1796. Dec 9, 1799. 2.136
To wife Eve Catharine, realty and personalty. To daughter Catharine Meyer, 10 pds. To son George Adam, 15 pds. Rem. equally divided among children: George, Catharine and George Adam Marks.

Execs: Wife Eve Catharine and son George. Wit: Frederick Bare, George Stouch.

SCHWARTZ, JACOB. Douglass.
March 9, 1795. Dec 10, 1799. 2.137
To wife Esther, personalty and realty, 50 ac res.
Exec: Wife Esther. Wit: John Landis, Jacob Bowman.

KASTNER, ELIZABETH. Upper Dublin.
Oct 17, 1799. Dec 18, 1799. 2.138
To Susanna Hanway, all estate.
Execs: Jacob and Daniel Hanway. Wit: Edward Fling, Elizabeth Fling, George Thomas.

LEDERACH, HENRY. Lower Salford.
Sept 24, 1799. Jan 1, 1800. 2.139
To Mennonite Meeting, 10 pds. To son John, farm, 132 acres at valuation of 900 pds.; his share to him, 200 pds. he to pay to other children, rem. to be divided among 6 children: Molly, Magdalena, Elizabeth, Henry, Catharine and Anna. Personalty to be divided among children, after unmarried ones have received their marriage share.
Execs: Son John and son in law Abraham Shot. Wit: Godshalk Godshalk, Jacob Ziegler.

AUSTIN, THOMAS. Moreland.
March 13, 1798. Feb 11, 1800. 2.141
To wife Mary, horse and 100 pds. To 2 sons Robert and Jonathan, wearing apparel. To Thomas, son of Benjamin Austin, gold watch. To wife Mary and sons Robert and Jonathan, farm, personalty and farming utensils, &c. for 6 years or wife's death, after that time to be sold and money divided to following: to son Robert, 4/15 part. To children of son Benjamin, 4/15 part. To son Jonathan, 4/15 part. To children of daughter Martha Wollard, 1/15 part and 6 pds. 2 years after wife's death and 6 pds. yearly. To children of daughter Jane Vancourt, 1/15 part and 6 pds. after wife's death and 6 pds. yearly. To grandson Robert Austin Parish, 1/15 part.
Execs: Wife Mary and 2 sons Robert and Jonathan. Wit: Joshua Comly, Samuel Simpson.

GULDY, GALLUS. Norriton.
June 4, 1798. Feb 11, 1800. 2.143
To son David, household goods and farming utensils. To son David's son Gallus, German bible. To son David, sheep. Rem. of estate to sons Casper and David.
Execs: Son David and Nicholas Slough. Wit: Frederick Conrad, Jacob Major.

UNTERGOFFLER, MARY EFA. Frederick.
Sept 27, 1799. Feb 17, 1800. 2.144
To 3 daughters: Efamary, Elizabeth and Annmercy, wearing apparel. Personalty to be sold, money divided among children. Son Jacob to have 5 pds. more than his share.
Execs: Sons Jacob and David. Wit: Jacob Umstead, Henry Sasseman.

WAMPOLE, FREDERICK. Towamencin.
Feb 7, 1798. Feb 17, 1800. 2.145
To wife Catharine, 50 pds., household goods, &c. use of small house, clock, case and bible. At her death, clock, case and bible to son Isaac. To wife, 25 pds. yearly. To son Isaac, farm, 150 acres; he paying to exrs. 600 pds. To son Isaac, 50 pds. To daughters: Catharine, Maria, Eve, Magdalena and son Jacob, 250 pds. each. To exrs. 250 pds. in trust for daughter Elizabeth, she to receive interest; at her death principal to be divided among her children. Rem. equally divided among children: Abraham, Mary, Catharine, Maria, Eve, Magdalena, Elizabeth, Jacob, and Isaac.
Execs: Wife Catharine, sons Jacob and Isaac. Wit: Michael Shoemaker, John Aulthouse.

TAYLOR, MORRIS. Whitpain.
Feb 6, 1800. March 1, 1800. 2.147
To wife Agness, featherbed, &c. Estate to be sold amd money divided as follows: interest of 1/3 part to wife during widowhood; if she marry, 50 pds. To grandson Samuel of daughter Lydia, 10 pds. To sons: Joseph, Morris, David and Jonathan, 40 pds. each. To daughters: Rebecca, Mary and Elizabeth, 40 pds. each. Rem. equally divided among children: Lydia, Joseph, Morris, David, Jonathan, Rebecca, Mary and Elizabeth.
Execs: Sons Joseph and Morris. Wit: Job Roberts, Adam Wertsner.

GILBERT, JANE. Moreland.
Feb 15, 1800. March 6, 1800. 2.149
To sister Martha Croasdill and her 5 children: Anna, Molly, Martha, Jane and Mary, land left by testatrix's father John Gilbert, land to be sold and money divided among them. To niece Jane Croasdill, bedstead, &c. To niece Mary Croasdill, 1 gown. To niece Anna Croasdill, 1 gown. Rem. of wearing apparel to Martha Croasdill and her 5 children. To William Johnson, 5 pds.
Execs: Henry Cuff, Martha Croasdill. Wit: Andrew Scott, William Powers.

SHOEMAKER, JACOB. Upper Dublin.
Dec 27, 1799. March 19, 1800. 2.150
Farm, 24 acres to be sold. To wife Sarah, all estate.
Execs: Wife Sarah and father in law John Conrad. Wit: Benjamin Conrad, John Thomas.

FISHER, JOHN. Whitemarsh.

March 20, 1800. March 27, 1800. 2.149
To wife Catharine, 18 pds. yearly, bedstead, &c. Rem. of estate to be sold, money divided among 9 children: Andrew, George, John, Elizabeth Hart, Catharine, Lewis, William, Ann and Jacob.
Execs: Son Andrew, son in law Andrew Hart. Wit: Leonard Culp, John Hagey, George Pierce.

ENGLES, BENJAMIN. Upper Merion.
March 3, 1800. March 29, 1800. 2.150
To son Thomas, $1. To daughter Agnes, $1. To daughter Hannah, $1. To daughter Catharine, $1. To children: Jacob, Joseph, Benjamin, Moses, Rachel and Jonathan $1 each. Rem. to wife Susannah.
Execs: Wife Susannah and James Akins. Wit: Jacob Auld, Jonathan Cleaver.

BEAN, JOHN. Worcester.
March 10, 1800. April 9, 1800. 2.151
To daughter Mary, beds, &c. To son John, farm 79, acres subject to payment of 640 pds. Money on hand to be divided among 3 children: Mary, John and Henry, wearing apparel and books divided among them.
Exec: Son John. Wit: Peter Johnson, John Bean, John Keyser.

ROBERTS, JOSEPH. Lower Merion.
Nov 29, 1799. April 9, 1800. 2.152
To Joseph Wells, Mary Cotten, Rebecca Ward and Henry Wells, 20 s. each. Rem. of estate to be put on interest and interest paid to brother John, at his death to niece Tacy Jones, wife of Benjamin Jones.
Execs: John Young, Isaac Warner. Wit: Brother John, niece Tacy Jones.

MARKLEY, PHILIP. Norriton.
June 8, 1790. April 14, 1800. 2.155
To wife Mary, maintenance and part of household goods, interest of 400 pds. and 24 pds. yearly, if she marry to have interest of 400 pds. To son Jacob, farm, 79 acres. To son Daniel, farm, 100 acres, grist-mill, at valuation of 275 pds. To son John, farm, 47 acres, subject to payment of 220 pds. To daughter Elizabeth, wife of John Sieber, 400 pds. To daughter Hannah, wife of Matthias Koplin, 400 pds.; what they have received to be deducted. To 3 sons, wearing apparel. To son Jacob, 100 pds. Rem. equally divided among 5 children.
Execs: Wife Mary, and son Jacob. Wit: Isreal Jacobs, Jesse Jacobs, Phebe Jacobs.

AUSTIN, ROBERT. Moreland.
Feb 15, 1800. April 26, 1800. 2.156
To mother Mary Austin, 10 pds. To brother Jonathan, coat and 50 pds. Rem. to sisters Martha Wollard and Jane Vancourt, equally.
Exec: Joshua Comley. Wit: Jacob Paul, Daniel Paul.

MYERS, SUSANN, Cheltenham.
Oct __, 1799. May 12, 1800. 2.157
To mother in law Barbar Surber, 30 pds. To grandson Ajar Conrad, 30 pds. To granddaughter Susanna Conrad, household goods. To son Joseph Hall, 5 s. Rem. to be put on interest and paid to daughter Deborah Hart, wife of John Hart; at her death principal divided among grandchildren. To grandson Matthew Conrad, 1/5 part. To grandson Ajar Conrad, 1/5 part. To granddaughter Susanna Conrad, 1/5 part. To granddaughter Deborah Conrad, 1/5 part. To granddaughter 1/5 part.
Execs: Daughter Deborah Hart, George DeBenneville. Wit: Jonathan Jones, Joseph Jones.

SHANNON, THOMAS. Norriton.
Feb 1, 1800. June 2, 1800. 2.158
To brother Thos. Shannon and Luke W. Morris, 200 pds. in trust for sister Rachel St. Clair; at her death principal divided among her children. To brother Thomas, farm and also 25 acres and personalty.
Execs: Brother Thomas and Luke W. Morris. Wit: Solomon Stewart, Enoch Supplee, Atkinson Farra.

SHANNON, JAMES. Jr. Norriton.
May 17, 1800. July 21, 1800. 2.160
To mother, part of furniture and interest of 800 pds.; at her death to be divided with rem. of estate. To father in law Isaac Knight, 50 pds. To Daniel St. Clair's child, Arthur, gun. Exrs. to put 200 pds. on interest and pay same to Aunt Emelia Shannon. Exrs. to keep household goods in trust for sister Rachel. Rem. of estate, sister to receive 1/2 net proceeds. Other half of proceeds to children of sister Rachel.
Execs: Isaac Knight, Enoch Wheeler. Wit: Benjamin Dewees, Enoch Supplee, Solomon Stewart.

SANDS, RICHARD. Plymouth.
June 26, 1799. July 24, 1800. 2.162
To daughter Esther, featherbed. To son Richard, 5 s. To son Joseph, 5 s. To each child, 5 s. when 21. Rem. of estate to wife.
Exec: wife. Wit: Nathan Cook, Thomas Lawrence.

HENDRICKS, WILLIAM. Abington.
Nov 22, 1796. Aug 2, 1800. 2.163
To wife Catharine, furniture, household goods and maintenance. Rem. of personalty to be sold and realty, money to be put on interest and paid to wife for maintenance. At wife's death, money to be divided among 9 children: Elizabeth, Sarah, Mary, Leonard, Rachel, Hannah, Samuel, John, and Catharine. Daughter Hannah Casey to receive interest of her share; at her death to her children.
Execs: Sons Samuel and John, son in law Andrew Ott. Wit: John Watts, William Wright.

HARRY, JOHN. Whitemarsh.
June 26, 1800. Aug 18, 1800. 2.164
To wife Latitia, household goods. Rem. of personalty to be sold and also realty. To wife, 30 pds. yearly. To son David, 30 pds. To sons David and Rees, 700 pds. each. To 2 daughters Mary Fairlamb and Sarah Lukens, interest of 500 pds.; at their death to be paid to their children. Rem. of estate 1/2 to sons David and Rees and other half put on interest for 2 daughters Mary and Sarah. At wife's death, principal 600 pds. divided among 4 children.
Execs: Sons David and Rees. Wit: Samuel Livezey, William Shepherd.

LUKENS, ABRAHAM. Moreland.
April 26, 1800. Aug 23, 1800. 2.166
To wife Rachel, household goods and 30 pds. yearly. To son Nathan, desk, &c. after his mother's death. To 2 sons Nathan and Robert, wearing apparel. To son Seneca, tools for clock making and Brass. To 3 sons: Seneca, Nathan and Robert, right of realty. To son Nathan, 200 pds. To son Robert and his wife Elizabeth, income of land where they now live. To daughter Gayner Ratcliff, 50 pds. To daughter Lydia Dubre, 100 pds. Rem. of estate divided into 5 equal parts. To son Nathan's children, Lydia, Nathan and Agnes, 1/5 part. To son Seneca, 1/5 part. To son Robert, 1/5 part. To daughter Gayner, 1/5 part. To daughter Lydia Dubre, 1/5 part.
Execs: Sons Nathan and Seneca. Wit: Matthew Grier, Joseph Longstreth, Naylor Child.

STEER, MARY. Whitemarsh.
Nov 15, 1799. Aug 26, 1800. 2.167
To son Frederick, 50 pds. To son George, desk, silver table spoons, &c. To daughter Catharine, wife of Dr. Otto, 25 pds. and wearing apparel. To son Daniel, 50 pds. and household goods. To granddaughter Mary of George Hitner, 1/2 doz. spoons. To granddaughter Mary Otto, 1/2 doz. spoons. To granddaughter Mary of Daniel Hitner, 1/2 doz. spoons. Rem. of estate divided among 3 children: George, Catharine and Daniel, equally.
Execs: Son Daniel Hitner, Henry Scheetz. Wit: George Freise, Andrew Norny.

MAYER, HENRY. Upper Salford.
June 3, 1800. Aug 29, 1800. 2.169
To wife Barbara, 250 pds. and household goods. To son Jacob Mayer, 30 acres at valuation of 100 pds. To son Christian, 30 acres, he paying 8 pds. per acre. Rem. of realty to son Samuel at valuation of 264 pds.; he to maintain wife. To daughter Mary, 50 pds. Rem. of personalty to be sold and divided into 10 parts, to children: Henry, Mary, John, Jacob, Christian, Isaac, Anna, Elizabeth, Barbara and Samuel, 1 part each.
Execs: sons Henry and Christian. Wit: Jacob Landis, Abraham Nice, John Barkey, Sr.

CHAIN, JOHN. Norriton.
March 15, 1800. Sept 12, 1800. 2.171
To granddaughter Ann McCalmont, part of household goods and 50 pds. To granddaughter Mary McCalmont, 6 pds. To grandson Matthew McCalmont, 6 pds. To granddaughter Margaret McCalmont, 6 pds. To Margaret Duff, house, &c. where John Boggs now lives in until she is married. To son Matthew, rem. of estate.
Execs: Son Matthew Chain. Wit: Ezekiel Rhods, John Metz.

SHUTT, JOHN. Worcester.
July 31, 1800. Sept 24, 1800. 2.172
To mother Barbara Shutt, interest of rem.; at her death 50 pds. to nephew John Evans. Rem. to sister Margaret's children, equally.
Execs: Jacob Custer, William Johnson. Wit: Jacob Zimmerman, Joseph Vanfossen.

DOWLIN, PAUL. Horsham.
April 26, 1799. Sept 29, 1800. 2.173
To wife Margaret, maintain and 20 pds. yearly. To son Paul, 10 acres and 88 acres of farm, subject to payment of bond of 50 pds., &c. To son David, 98 acres, he to maintenance wife and subject to her legacy. To grandson Paul Dowlin, son of David, rem. of farm, subject to his father until he is 25 years. To grandsons John and Josiah Dowlin, of son Paul, 25 pds. each. Rem. equally divided among sons David and Paul. Son David to pay to son Paul, 7 pds. 10 s.
Execs: Sons David and Paul. Wit: Isreal Mullin, David Robb.

MOORE, JOHN. Abington.
June 26, 1799. Oct 27, 1800. 2.175
To wife Mary, all estate
Exec: Wife Mary. Wit: Thomas Livezey, John Goodwin, William Francis.

MILLER, BARBARA. Frederick.
Aug 6, 1793. Oct 30, 1800. 2.176
To son Samuel, and daughter Fronica, wife of Abraham Shwenck, all estate equally.
Exec: Son Samuel. Wit: Isaac Barkey, John Barkey, Sr.

EVANS, DAVID. Limerick.
June 28, 1797. Nov 10, 1800. 2.177
To son Owen, farm, 425 acres and personalty. To daughter Sarah, wife of James Garrett, farm, 156 acres 4 perches at valuation of 500 pds. and Jacob amounting to 174 pds. 12 s. and 300 pds. to be paid by son Owen. To daughter Mary, wife of Amos Evans, household goods amounting to 187 pds. 10 s. and 800 pds. to be paid by son Owen. To Charlotte Brooke, daughter of son John, mare, &c. Servant James Dennis to have freedom.
Exec: Son Owen. Wit: Charlotte Brooke, Samuel Evans.

MOORE, JOHN. Moreland.
April 13, 1798. Nov 11, 1800. 2.179
To wife Margaret, 1/3 part of estate. To daughter Elizabeth Fairbee, 20 pds. to nephew Samuel Ayres and Hiram McNealle, rem. of estate in trust for daughter Elizabeth Fairbee, she to receive income; at her death to her children. If she leave no children to be sold and money divided among sisters and brothers in Scotland, Great Britain; Walter, Mary, David and Margaret.
Execs: Nephew Samuel Ayres, Hiram McNeille. Wit: Thomas Snowden, Thomas Livezey.

MATTIS, PETER. Plymouth.
Aug 8, 1800. Nov 18, 1800. 2.180
To son Jacob, $4. To granddaughter Mary of son Jacob, 5 pds. To daughter Mary, wife of Isaac White, use of farm, 2 acres and 70 pds. to be divided among her children. To daughter Elizabeth, wife of William Williams, 110 pds. To son Peter, 160 pds. To grandson Michael Reiff, 30 pds. To grandson David Reiff, 15 pds. Rem. to daughters Mary and Elizabeth and son Peter.
Execs: Sons Jacob and Peter. Wit: Mary Painter, Benjamin Wager.

ROBERTS, OWEN. Lower Merion.
Nov 29, 1799. Nov 27, 1800 2.182
To niece Rebecca Ward, 50 pds. To Henry Wells, interest of 50 pds., at his death divided among his children. To Mary Cotton and Joseph Wells, 20 s. each. To brother John, interest of personalty.
Execs: Brother John and niece Tacy Jones. Wit: John Young, Isaac Warner.

WALKER, MARY. Moreland.
Aug 14, 1797. Dec 13, 1800. 2.183
To daughter Mary, all estate.
Exec: Daughter Mary. Wit: Wm. Tennent, Rynear Lukens.

KORNDERFER, NICHOLAS. Douglass.
Sept 10, 1800. Dec 22, 1800. 2.183
To wife Mary Margaret, interest of money that is now on interest. Estate to be appraised, money put on interest and paid to wife; at her death estate to be sold and equally divided among 3 children: Philip, daughters Elizabeth Miller and Veronica Welker. Son to give to grandson 2 pds. 2 s.
Execs: Wife Mary and Michael Hoover. Wit: George Leonard.

TIMANUS, ROSANNA. Upper Dublin.
Jan 27, 1800. Dec 23, 1800. 2.185
To son Conrad, 20 pds. To daughter Catharine, house and lot at Sassafras and 11th St. Phila. Rem. to daughter Catharine.

Exec: Daughter Catharine. Wit: John Mann, Samuel Mann.

FLETCHER, PRISCILLA. Abington.
Aug 11, 1799. Dec 24, 1800. 2.186
To children: Thomas, Susanna, Hannah, Tacy, Jane and Priscilla, 50 pds. each intrust until they are 21. Daughter Elizabeth had a large share from testatrix's father, Jacob Lippincot, and she to receive nothing. Realty to be sold and money divided among husband Robert Fletcher and children, including Elizabeth, wife of Isaac Hallowell. To daughters wearing apparel.
Execs: George Williams, John Thompson. Wit: Thomas Shoemaker, Thomas Fletcher.

POTTS, CHARLES. Douglass.
Oct 21, 1800. Dec 13, 1800. 2.187
To wife, household goods, wearing apparel, &c. Estated received from father to be sold and money to wife Margaret and son Hartley.
Execs: Brother in law Joseph Potts. Wit: William Geer, George Leonard.

POTTS, STEPHEN. Upper Merion.
Feb 9, 1800. Jan 23, 1801. 2.187
To wife Jane, all estate, at her death to be divided among children: Ann, Esther, Nathan, Alice, Martha and Isaiah.
Execs: Wife Jane and son in law Jonathan Pugh. Wit: John Moore, Nathan Potts.

KENDERDINE, JOSEPH. Horsham.
July 28, 1799. Feb 10, 1801. 2.188
To wife Rachel, income of realty and use of personalty until son Richard is 21; at that time she to have room and maintenance during widowhood; if she marry to have 25 pds. To son Richard, part of farm, 117 acres subject to maintenance of wife. Rem. of realty, 83 acres to be sold, personalty and money divided among daughters: Tacy, Hannah, Mary and Sarah, equally.
Execs: Nephew Joseph Kenderdine, Robert Loller. Wit: Benjamin Kenderdine, Enoch Kenderdine.

KRIEBLE, ABRAHAM. Towamencin.
March 12, 1792. March 16, 1801. 2.190
To wife Susanna, household goods, 500 pds.; if she marry to have 250 pds.; she to receive maintenance from sons Christian and Andrew and to live with them. At wife's death books to be divided among 2 sons. To son Christian, 100 pds. To 2 sons Christian and Andrew, realty, it to be appraised and one son to give to other son 1/2 of valuation and land in Buffalo to be sold and money divided among them. Personalty to 2 sons.
Execs: Melchior Shultze, son Andrew. Wit: Melchior Krieble, Abraham Dresher.

BOORS, JOHN. Towmaencin.
Nov 25, 1793. March 17, 1801. 2.192
To Baptist Meeting in Skippack and Perkiomen, 20 pds. To John Boors, Harman's son, part of wearing apparel and bible. Rem. to be sold and to brothers and sisters as follows: to brother Harman, 1/7 part. To children of Garrett Godshalk, husband of sister Edy, dec.; 1/7 part equally. To John Umstead, 1/7 part. To Arnold Boors, 1/7 part. To Peter Boors, 1/7 part. To brother Henry, 1/7 part. To children of Leonard Hendricks, husband of sister Catharine, 1/7 part equally. To grandson Jacob Hendricks, gun.
Execs: Brother Henry Boors, and grandson John Boors. Wit: Jacob Kolb, Abraham Kolb.

KLINE, PETER. New Hanover.
Aug 31, 1795. April 3, 1801. 2.194
To wife Margaret, all estate.
Exec: Andrew Shiner. Wit: William Reifsnyder, John Richards.

POTTS, ZEBULUM. Plymouth.
Feb 27, 1801. April 4, 1801. 2.195
To wife Martha, all estate. After wife's death, rem. to be divided among children. If 2 sons, William Robert and Daniel help wife on farm until 21 to have 50 pds. more than their share.
Execs: Wife Martha, and son Joseph. Wit: John Hallowell, Nathan Potts.

CUMMING, DAVID. Willow Grove.
April 4, 1801. April 28, 1801. 2.196
To wife Rachel, household goods, farming utensils and income of estate during widowhood; she to provide maintenance for children until they are 18. At wife's death, rem. to be divided among children. Exrs. to sell land in Annwell, N. J., land in Northumberland, land purchased of James West, mills, land in Warwick, land purchased of John Briggs, land at Willow Grove, 10 or 30 acres adjoining land of George Rex, land in Moreland. Exrs. to pay to brother William 6 pds. yearly; at his death to his wife and children, 100 pds. Land to be sold if wife marries. If wife marries to have interest of 1000 pds. Rem. to children: George, Samuel, Solomon, William, Ashey, Rebecca, Rachel, David Blair, Gulichma, Deborah and Thomas. To sister in law Mary Miller, bureau. To Susannah Brownbolt, 3 pds. yearly. Rem. to 11 children, equally. Guardians, brother in law Richard Hopkins, Thomas Worton, John Shoemaker, Nathan Harper.
Execs: Wife Rachel, son George, John Shoemaker. Wit: Mordecia Thomas, William Purdy, Jr.

ADAMS, JAMES. Norriton.
April 13, 1801. May 4, 1801. 2.199
To wife Rachel, interest of estate and household goods; she to keep

children; if she does not keep children to have 1/3 estate. Children to receive their shares at 21 years of age.
Execs: John Edwards, John Major. Wit: Matthew Chain, A. Webb.

WOLFINGER, JACOB. New Hanover.
Feb 23, 1801. May 5, 1801. 2.200
To wife Eve Maria, personalty and maintenance. Realty to be sold, subject to maintenance of wife; money to be divided as follows: to daughter Rebecca Blyban, 50 pds. To daughter Maria Roshon, 25 pds. To grandson Jacob Roshon, 25 pds. To daughter Catharine Zoller, 50 pds. To daughter Ann Ox, 50 pds. Rem. to be divided among 4 daughters: Rebecca, Maria, children of daughter Catharine and daughter Ann. Personalty to be sold after wife's death and money divided among 3 daughters and children of daughter Catharine.
Execs: Henry Hahn, Philip Yost. Wit: Peter Yost, Jacob Crous.

DOTTERER, CONRAD. Frederick.
March 20, 1777. May 12, 1801. 2.202
To wife Magdalena, interest of 300 pds. and maintenance during widowhood; if she marry to have interest of 150 pds., rem. to be divided among children. To son Jacob, 5 pds. Rem. divided among children and grandchildren: Jacob Conrad, John, Abraham, Catharine, Christian, Susanna, Elizabeth and Magdalena and children of son Christian, John and Catharine.
Execs: George Swenck, Samuel Bartolat. Wit: Benjamin Snider, Daniel Boyer, Ludwig Gudller.

DETWILER, FELIX. Springfield.
Dec __, 1793. May 14, 1801. 2.203
To wife Elizabeth, all estate during widowhood; if she marry to have 1/3 part of estate. Estate to be sold, except 4 acres for daughters; rem. equally divided among children.
Exec: Son John. Wit: Henry Fisher, Casper Schlater.

SHAW, SAMUEL. Abington.
Jan 16, 1801. May 28, 1801. 2.205
To brother Joseph, wearing apparel, also Charles. To brother Charles, watch. To sister Martha, teatable, &c. To sister Mary, chest. To friend Jacob Shelmire, chest, deck and cash on hand.
Exec: Jacob Shelmire. Wit: George Shelmire, John Shelmire.

CLIME, SARAH. Montgomery.
Dec 27, 1800. June 1, 1801. 2.206
To son William Morgan, colt. To 3 daughters: Elizabeth, Sarah and Ann Clime, wearing apparel, equally; Mary Hubbs to receive them in trust. To 3 sons: Samuel, John and Jesse Clime, 1 pr. silver buckles, &c. Mary Hubbs to receive them in trust until children are 18. Rem. of estate to be

sold and equally divided among children: William Morgan, Elizabeth, Sarah, John, Ann, and Jesse Clime.
Execs: Son William Morgan, Joseph Hubbs. Wit: Thomas Wilson, Samuel DeHaven.

DEWEES, HENRY. Springfield.
May 15, 1800. June 19, 1801. 2.207
To wife Rachel, room, household goods and maintenance, 30 pds. yearly. To son William, farm, where he lives in Whitemarsh, 7 acres, also 3 pds. To son Henry, 1/4 part of Shad Fishery, 500 pds. &c. To son Jacob, 100 pds. To son John, 100 pds. To son Charles, 250 pds. To son Jonathan, 185 pds. To daughter Sarah Sheetz, 150 pds. To grandsons John and Joseph Steer, 10 pds. each. To daughter Mary Knorr, wife of Christian Knorr, 7 pds. 10 s. yearly; at her death principal to her children. Farm in Springfield, 100 acres to be sold and money to pay legacies, rem. to 8 children, daughter Mary to receive interest of her share.
Execs: Sons Henry and Charles. Wit: John Huston, Jacob Paul.

JONES, ELIJAH. Charlestown.
Feb 4, 1801. June 24, 1801. 2.209
To brother Jacob, 100 pds. To children of brother Benjamin and sister Ann Billew; Mary Dickinson, Ann Jones, Naomi, Jacob, Samuel and Jeremiah Billew. Rem. of realty and money divided among Jacob Jones, Mary Dickinson, Ann Jones, Naomi, Jacob Jones, Jr., Samuel Jones and Jeremiah Billew.
Execs: Brother Jacob Jones, sister Jeremia Billew. Wit: John H. Coats, John Johnson.

ENGARD, JACOB. Upper Dublin.
March 10, 1797. June 27, 1801. 2.210
To daughter Mary, side saddle, 12 pds. To wife Dorothy, rem. of estate during widowhood; if she marry, estate to be sold and wife to receive 1/3 of interest and money divided among 6 children: Jacob, Catharine, Susanna, Mary, Margaret, and Elizabeth, they to receive interest until they are 18.
Execs: Wife Dorothy, son Jacob. Wit: Joseph Lloyd, Jacob Everhart.

CONRAD, JOHN. Moreland.
April 20, 1801. Aug 10, 1801. 2.212
To wife Elizabeth, household goods and 40 pds. for maintenance for herself and son Jonathan. Farm, 48 acres to be sold and rem. of personalty and money divided. To wife Elizabeth, 325 pds. and rem. to be put on interest and wife to receive part for support of son Jonathan; when son is 10 years, wife to receive interest of 1/5 part; if she marry to receive 20 pds. Jonathan Jarret, guardian.
Execs: Father John, David Jarret. Wit: Robert Loller, Joseph Cadwallader.

KITTLER, JOHN. Whitemarsh.
Dec 24, 1799. Aug 25, 1801. 2.
Farm, 116 acres to be sold and money divided as follows: to brother David, 10 pds. To daughter Elizabeth Sharp, widow of Jacob Sharp, 10 pds. To daughter in law Mary Stroud, 5 pds. To grandson John Kittler, son of Andrew Kittler, dec., 35 pds. To daughter in law Mary Kittler, widow of son David, dec., $1. To granddaughter Mary Kittler, 4 pds. 12 s. 6 d. To grandson Samuel Lassly, 30 pds., it to be taken out of his mother's share. To grandson William, 25 pds. Rem. divided as follows: to son Andrew, 2/9 parts. to son John, 1/9 part. To daughter Mary Witz, widow of Jacob Witz, dec., 1/9 part. To daughter Catharine Lassly, 1/9 part. To daughter Sarah, 1/9 part. To daughter Eve Cantwell, wife of James Cantwell, 1/9 part. To daughter Hannah McClay, wife of William McClay, 1/9 part. To daughter Susanna Sharp, wife of John Sharp, 1/9 part.
Codicil datd Jan 23, 1800, only appoints son John as executor.
Execs: Sons Adam and John. Wit: John Huston, Simon Frees.

MESTER, GEORGE. Towamencin.
May 15, 1797. Aug 26, 1801. 2.217
To sister Susanna, farm, personalty to be sold. At sister's death, farm, 34 1/2 acres to be sold, money divided among children of sister Mary, wife of Christopher Reinwalt and children of brother Christopher Mester, equally. Execs: George Anders, Jr., Andrew Krieble, Abra. Krieble's son. Wit: Jacob Kolb, Mordecai Davis, Jacob Kolb, Jr.

MOORE, CHARLES. Montgomery.
Aug 18, 1801. Sept 19, 1801. 2.218
Farm, 100 acres and house in Phila. to be sold and money divided as follows: to nephews Richard and Henry, children of brother Mordecai, dec., 200 pds. each. To children of Margaret Jones, de.c, 300 pds. equally. To 4 nieces: Mary Heston, Rachel Morris, Deborah Jackson and Hannah Moore, 200 pds. each. To Stephen West Moore, and Samuel Preston Moore of brother Richard, 200 pds. each. To niece Hannah Roberts, daughter of brother Richard, 200 pds. To wife Milcah Martha, house in Phila. and rem. of estate. To Gwynedd Meeting, 10 pds. for poor. To Elizabeth Hicks, Charity Williams and William Walton, 60 pds. equally. Execs: Wife Milcah Martha, Cadwallader Evans. Wit: George Weaver, Thomas Wilson, William Walton.

HANNAH, JOHN. Norriton.
Sept 17, 1801. Oct 13, 1801. 2.219
To brother James, 10 pds. and wearing apparel. To Norriton Presbyterian Congregation, 10 pds. To sister Jane Hannah, rem. of estate.
Execs: Sister Jane, Solomon Stewart. Wit: Jacob Gouldy, Isaac McGlathery.

SUPPLEE, MAGDALENA. Worcester.
July 4, 1798. Oct 14, 1801. 2.220
To grandchildren: Magdalena Taylor, Magdalena DeHaven, Magdalena Zimmerman, Magdalena Kastner, Magdalena Tyson, Magdalena Cain, Magdalena Supplee, 5 pds. each. To 2 granddaughters Sarah and Phebe Supplee, daughters of son Abraham, 5 pds. each. To granddaughter Hannah Clare, 40 pds. To grandson Samuel Supplee, desk, he to pay to his brother Nathan, 20 s. To daughters wearing apparel. Rem. to be divided among children: Andrew, Abraham, John, Deborah, Rebecca, Hannah, Rachel and Mary and son in law Jacob Zimmerman, also son Jacob, if he returns.
Execs: Brother Peter DeHaven, Nathan Potts. Wit: Henry Cunrad, Abraham Klaire.

JONES, EVAN. Montgomery.
May 6, 1797. oct 15, 1801. 2.221
To wife Hannah, 600 pds. and household goods. To daughter Hannah, 600 pds. To sons John and Henry, farm, 300 acres; they to provide maintenance for wife. To son Evan, farm, 40 acres and 400 pds. To son John, 40 pds., desk and bible. To son Henry, desk and bible. Rem. divided among children and wife.
Execs: Wife Hannah, sons John and Henry. Wit: Thomas Shoemaker, George Maris, Thomas Shoemaker, Jr.

EVANS, MILES. Norriton.
July 20, 1801. Oct 24, 1801. 2.223
To wife Hannah, horse, household goods, watch and bible. After wife's death, watch and bible to Miles Evans of son Amos. Rem. to children of brother and sister, equally.
Exec: Nephew Job Evans. Wit: Nathan Potts, George M. Potts.

ROBERTS, JOHN. Whitpain.
May 10, 1789. Oct 28, 1801. 2.224
To son Job, farm, 200 acres; he paying to wife Ellin, maintenance and part of household goods. To daughter Sarah, 40 pds. and featherbed. To daughter Ellin, 40 pds. To son Job, 90 acres; he to pay 450 pds. to daughters after wife's death. To 6 daughters: Elizabeth, Ruth, Sarah, Ann, Jane, and Ellin, 1/7 part each to grandchildren: Job, Sarah and William Hallowell, of daughter Mary, 1/7 part equally, also to receive 5 pds. left by father John. To cousin Nehamiah Roberts, wearing apparel. Codicil dated Sept 5, 1797 gives to daughter Sarah a table, revokes part giving 40 pds. &c to daughters and gives them with what they have received equal parts. Daughter Elizabeth's share to her children: Caleb, Tacy, Nathan, Elizabeth, Jonathan and Jane Evans.
Execs: Son in law Nathan Cleaver, sons John and Job. Wit: Cadwallader Evans, John Rowland, John Evans.

CHRISTMAN, GEORGE. Douglass.
Feb 20, 1801. Oct 31, 1801. 2.227
To wife Mary, maintenance, household goods, 50 pds. yearly; at her death to be divided among children, also 6 pds. interest of 150 pds. during widowhood. Farm. to be sold, owner of farm to provide maintenance for wife. Son John, George, Philip, Elizabeth, wife of John Snyder; Solome, wife of Conrad Voegely, Catharine, wife of Peter Boyer, what they have received to be deducted from their equal shares. To son David, 30 pds. To daughter Gertraude, 50 pds. To son Daniel, 50 pds. To son Joseph, 50 pds.
Execs: Son Philip, and son in law Peter Boyer. Wit: George Boyer, Bernard Yeager.

JOHNSON, PETER. Perkiomen and Skippack.
May 14, 1792. Nov 6, 1801. 2.231
To wife Catharine, household goods, 100 pds. Son Benjamin has received farm, 150 3/4 acres; he to provide maintenance for wife. To son Benjamin 100 pds. intrust for daughter Margaret, wife of Henry Yealous. To son in law Henry Yealous, 1 s. To son Christopher, 300 pds. To daughter Gertraude, wife of William Rittenhouse, 100 pds. bond.
Exec: Son Benjamin. Wit: Henry Pennebecker, Henry Hunsicker.

HARRY, JANE. Gwynedd.
Dec 13, 1792. Nov 26, 1801. 2.233
To sister Ann Harry, all estate.
Exec: Sister Ann. Wit: Joseph Lewis, James Lowry.

KAWLER, MARTIN, Marlborough.
April 28, 1798. Dec 7, 1801. 2.234
To stepson in law Christopher Broy, all estate; subject to maintenance of wife, Margaret and testator; he not to sell or own same until after wife's death.
Exec: Andrew Reed Sr. Wit: Philip Reed, Andrew Bosert, Ludwig Auke.

ZIEGLER, PHILIP. SR. Upper Salford.
Nov 7, 1800. Dec 15, 1801. 2.235
To wife Elizabeth, use of farm, 50 acress and personalty, bonds and notes during life. At her death, exrs. to sell farm and personalty; money divided. To sons: Henry, Andrew, John, George, Mark and Philip, 50 pds. each. Rem. divided among sons and daughters Catharine and Elizabeth.
Execs: sons George and Philip. Wit: Dewalt Ness, John Berndt.

BICKLE, LUDWIG. Douglass.
Feb 21, 1792. Dec 29, 1801. 2.336
To wife Barbara, maintenance, interest of 300 pds. and part of household goods during life. At her death, principal 300 pds. and household goods to be divided among children. To son Henry, farm, also 106 acres and 2

acres; subject to maintenance of wife and 340 pds. for use of children. To son in law Samuel Mechlin, 200 pds. Personalty to be divided among children, after deducting what they have received. To son Henry, rem. of land which was purchased of Matthias Hollaback, he paying 5 pds. per acre. To Trustees of Lutheran Congregation in New Hanover, 5 pds. Codicil dated Feb 27, 1792. Son Henry may sell land upon paying for it. Codicil dated Sept 13, 1797. Money charged on the land devised to son Henry to be considered as payment of the legacy bequeathed to him so far as his portion may go.
Execs: Sons Jacob and John. Wit: Bernard Gilbert, John Schnell, John Richards.

GILBERT, DAVID. New Hanover.
Nov 4, 1801. Dec 29, 1801. 2.230
To wife Mary, 20 pds. &c. To brother Anthony, colt. To father Henry Gilbert, realty.
Exec: Brother Henry Gilbert. Wit: Ludwig Linsepegler, John Richards.

BITTING, JOST. New Hanover.
Nov 8, 1793. Jan 26, 1802. 2.240
To son Ludwig, farm, 30 acres. To son Philip, 21 acres, 125 perches at 4 pds. an acre and realty of land 6 acres. To son John, 10 acres, at 4 pds. an acre; at his death to be sold and money divided among his children. Rem. to be sold and money divided among children. To Henry, Joseph, John, Peter and Philip and daughter Sophia each 10 pds. Rem. to be divided among 11 children. To son in law George Bechtell, what is left of daughter Catharine's dec. share. Daughter Rebecca to have full portion, unless she marries again; if she marry to have interest only.
Execs: Sons Henry and Joseph. Wit: Francis Leidig, Samuel Bartolet, Jacob Shoemaker.

RIMBEY, PETER. Providence.
Dec 4, 1801. Jan 30, 1802. 2.242
To wife Margaret, all estate for her maintenance and daughter Elizabeth. At wife's death, realty and personalty to be sold, interest of money for daughter Elizabeth; at her death to be divided among children.
Execs: Son in law Jacob Essig, wife Margaret. Wit: Jacob Buckwalter, Benedict Garber.

DAVIS, REBECCA. Gwynedd.
April 6, 1801. Feb 10, 1802. 2.243
To Rebecca Phillips, daughter of Jonathan Phillips, case of drawers, &c. To James Phillips, son of Jonathan, silver shoe buckles. To Abraham Phillips, lamb. To Alice Phillips, cloak. Rem. to Jonathan Phillips.
Execs: Cousin Jonathan Phillips. Wit: Job Roberts, William McCoy.

KEPPLE, HENRY. Upper Salford.

Nov 11, 1801. Feb 12, 1802. 2.244
Realty and personalty to be sold and money divided among 6 children: Peter, Catharine, Elizabeth, Martin, Margaret and Christina. To 3 children: Henry, Catharine and Elizabeth of daughter Margaret, wife of Jacob Long, 10 pds. each.
Execs: Son Martin, son in law Jacob Doub. Wit: Philip Gable, Jacob Fillman

ROBESON, THOMAS Lower Merion.
Dec 16, 1801. Feb 13, 1802. 2.245
To wife Ann, personalty.
Execs: Algernon Roberts, Joseph Price. Wit: Benjamin Holland, James Winter.

RICHARD, JOHN. Whitemarsh.
Oct 5, 1797. March 15, 1802. 2.246
To wife Mary, household goods, &c. Land to 3 sons, to be appraised, son Jacob to have 100 pds. deducted, each son to pay his mother 1/3 part of interest of value. To son Jacob, home farm in Gwynedd, subject to maintenance of wife and interest. To son Leonard, farm where he lives in Roxborough, 11 3/4 acres, subject to maintenance and interest to wife. To son John, farm in Whitemarsh, subject to maintenance and interest. To daughter Catharine Richard, featherbed, side saddle, &c. To church at Barren Hill, 10 pds. To son in law Henry Katz, husband of daughter Margaret, 1/6 of valuation of realty and personalty, after deducting 100 pds. and 130 pds. for 3 sons, subject to interest to wife. To daughter Catharine, 1/6 part of valuation. To wife 1/3 part of interest from 1/6 of valuation of estate; 2/3 to daughter Mary Lentz, wife of William Lentz, after wife's death to receive whole of interest. Exrs. to sell land in Cressham, and 9 acres purchased on Peter Heysler. Rem. to be sold.
Execs: Son in law Henry Katz, sons John and Leonard. Wit: John Huston, Andrew Kates.

RAMBO, GUNNER. Limerick.
Jan 23, 1802. March 30, 1802. 2.251
To son Abraham, farm, 20 acres and 75 pds.; son Eli to pay him 25 pds. To son Eli, farm, 56 acres 14 perches, except 2 acres 105 perches to son John, subject to payment of 100 pds. to son Moses and to sons Abraham and Aaron, 25 pds. each. To son Eli, farm, 5 acres 102 perches. To son Aaron, 1 pd. 10 s. To son John, farm, 88 acres, also 2 acres, 105 perches and personalty, except notes, &c. Rem. of notes, bonds, books, after paying debts to 5 sons: Moses, Aaron, John, Abraham and Eli.
Execs: Sons Aaron and John. Wit: John Boulton, Levi Boulton.

BELTZ, JACOB. Limerick.
Dec 20, 1800. April 13, 1802. 2.252
To son John, plough, bedstead, &c. To son Philip, bed. To son George,

bed, &c. To daughter Christina, bed, bedstead, &c. To 4 sons: Jacob, John, Philip, and George, wearing apparel. Rem. of estate to be sold and money divided among children. Sons to receive 2 shares; daughters to have 1 share: Jacob, John, Philip, George, Elizabeth Baker, Maria Fisher, Hannah Michael and Christina.
Codicil dated Dec 20, 1801. Son John to keep 3 sheep, 2 for daughter Christina and 1 for son George. To daughter Christina, linen. Wit: John Harst, Jacob Crous.
Execs: Sons John and Philip. Wit: Jacob Crous.

YERGER, DEWALT. Douglass.
Jan 20, 1802. April 20, 1802. 2.255
To wife Maria Margaret, all estate, except bequests. To Elizabeth Sance, daughter of Daniel Sance, dec.; 100 pds. after wife's death. To Corporation of the Lutheran Congregation of New Hanover, $30, after wife's death.
Execs: Wife and Conrad Fegoly. Wit: David Zarley, Benjamin Markley.

DISMANT, JOHN. Providence.
Dec 28, 1801. May 11, 1802. 2.56
To brother Daniel Dismant, realty; he to give land he owns, formerly owned by William Dismant to his brother Benjamin; except meadows. If Daniel will not give up land; then to brother Benjamin, 1/2 of realty. To Daniel, personalty, except household goods which are to be divided among mother and sister Elizabeth, son Daniel to provide maintenance for mother. To sister Margaret Wilberham, 60 pds. to be paid by sons Daniel and Benjamin. To sister Elizabeth Dismant, 120 pds.
Execs: Brothers Daniel and Benjamin. Wit: Michael Moyer, Daniel Stall.

SHEID, GEORGE. Marlborough.
April 30, 1802. May 21, 1802. 2.257
Estate to be sold and money divided among 8 children. To daughter Elizabeth, bed, &c. Rem. equally divided among children: Daniel, Elizabeth, John, Jacob, George, Mally, Joseph and Henry.
Execs: Brother in law Jacob Boyer. Wit: Henry Snider, John Nice.

KERTEL, ANNA MARIA. Germantown.
April 25, 1794. May 27, 1802. 2.258
To daughter Margaret, wife of George Walter, wearing apparel. Books divided among 3 children: Margaret, wife of George Walter; Jacob and Paul Grosscup. Rem. of estate equally divided in 4 shares to Margaret Walter, Jacob and Paul Grosscup, and to children of son Christopher Grosscup. 1 share, after deductions.
Execs: Son Paul, son in law George Walter. Wit: Henry Smoyer, T. Huber.

BARE, JOHN. Douglass.

Jan 19, 1802. June 2, 1802. 2.259
To wife Elizabeth, all estate; she to raise children; if she marry, 1/3 of estate. Rem. 2/3 of estate to children.
Exec: Wife Elizabeth. Wit: Harman Reifsnider, William Burner.

OTTINGER, CHRISHOPHER. Cheltenham.
Aug 13, 1799. May 7, 1802. 2.260
To daughter Dorothy, 1250 pds., clock, at her death to grandson Christopher Ottinger. To son William Ottinger, 500 pds., watch, books and wearing apparel. To daughter Rachel Keyser, 500 pds. To daughter Sarah Hubbs, 500 pds. To granddaughter Dorothy McCalla, 500 pds. to grandson Aaron Keyser, 500 pds. To grandson Christopher Keyser, 500 pds. To grandson Nathan Keyser, 500 pds. To grandson William Keyser, 500 pds. To granddaughter Mary Keyser, 500 pds. To granddaughter Sarah Keyser, 500 pds. To granddaughter Rachel Ottinger, 500 pds. To granddaughter Mary Ottinger, 500 pds. To servant Henry Forst, 15 pds. To Sarah Nash, wife of Joseph Nash, 100 pds. To John Nash, William and Daniel Nash, of Joseph Nash, 25 pds. each. To Catharine Schreiver, daughter of George Schreiver, 50 pds. To Margaret Rex, daughter of cousin Margaret Rex, $20. To Deacons of Presbyterian Church in Germantown, 150 pds. To Andrew Redheifer, interest of 100 pds.; at his death principal to be paid to children of grandson Christopher Keyser. Rem. of realty to gandsons: Christopher, Charles, Isaiah, John and Alexander Ottinger, sons of William Ottinger. Rem. of personalty to 14 grandchildren.
Execs: Son William and Robert Loller. Wit: John Minnigh, Samuel Funck.

SMITH, ROBERT. Plymouth.
May 23, 1800. June 8, 1802. 2.263
To wife Mary, household goods, 60 pds. yearly. Land in Westmoreland County, to be rented, after then to be sold; interest from money to son Robert; at his death principal to his children. To son Robert, 7 pds. 10 s. yearly, for 10 years, after that 15 pds. yearly. Tract in Westmoreland to be rented and sold; interest from money to daughter Rachel. To grandson Robert Smith Steel, interest of tract of land. To daughter Rebecca, 100 pds. Personalty to be sold and money together with 200 pds. from rent of Phila. house to be divided among 4 children: Esther, wife of Ephraim Steel; John, Rebecca and Rachel.
Execs: Mary Smith, daughter Rebecca smith, son in law Ephraim Steel, Andrew Porter. Wit: Stephen Porter, John McFarland, Elizabeth Porter.

HORNING, LUDWICK. Skippack and Perkiomen.
Jan 30, 1797. June 10, 1802. 2.266
To wife Catharine, household goods, maintenance and 300 pds. To son Peter, 1 s. Son John has received farm at valuation of 800 pds., rem. he to keep. To daughter Margaret Creater, 100 pds. To daughter Barbara Hall, 100 pds. To daughter Elizabeth Heffilfinger, 100 pds. Rem. to be

divided among 7 children: Michael, John, Eli, Jacob, Margaret, Barbara and Elizabeth.
Execs: Sons John and Jacob. Wit: Henry Hunsicker, Isaac Hunsicker, Fred. Conrad.

LUTZ, ADAM. Whitpain.
Jan 13, 1802. June 21, 1802. 2.268
To wife Anna Maria, 100 pds., household goods, use of farm. Personalty to be sold and interest to wife. At wife's death, farm to be sold and equally divided among 4 sons: Peter, George, Jacob and Adam. To Katharine and Philip, 5 s. my two eldest children. To 3 grandchildren: Elizabeth, David and Adam Billew of daughter Elizabeth, 50 pds.; they to receive interest until 21. Rem. to be divided among 5 children: Peter, George, Jacob, and Adam Lutz, Mary, wife of John Riddle.
Execs: Son Jacob, John Wentz. Wit: Streeper Connard, William Wells.

GODSHALK, CATHARINE AND JANE. Towamencin.
Aug 18, 1795. June 26, 1802. 2.271
Estate to last living. Then to brothers and sisters in 13 shares. To Jacob Godshalk's heirs, 1 share. To William Godshalk's heirs, 1 share. To Syken, her heirs, 1 share. To Margaret, wife of Henry Kassel, 1 share. To Garret Godshalk, 1 share. To Magdalena, 1 share. To Mary, 1 share. To Matthias Hendricks, 1 share. To John Godshalk, 1 share. To Anna, wife of Melchior Yoder, 1 share. To Eve, wife of Jacob Swartz, 1 share. To Peter, 1 share.
Execs: Brother Peter Godshalk, Jr., Matthias Stouffer. Wit: Godshalk Godshalk, John Swartz, Garret Godshalk.

ULRICH, JACOB. Whitemarsh.
May 15, 1802. July 17, 1802. 2.272
To niece Ann Rivercom, 1 1/4 acres, stove, household goods. To son Jacob 157 pds., 8 s. 6 d. and 42 pds. 10 s. 6 d. To negro girl Jenny, 2 suits of clothes, $4 yearly and 1 acre. To nephew Jacob Ulrich, 100 pds. when 23. To children of aunt Mary Gilberts, 10 pds. equally. To Corporation of the Union School, 20 pds. To Congregation of Puffs Church, 15 pds. To mother, 7 pds. yearly, out of bond. To sell 1/2 of farm in Delaware and personalty. Rem. of estate to sister Mary Acoff.
Execs: Henry Scheetz, Ezekiel Hill.

FEGLEY, GEORGE. Douglass.
June 18, 1802. July 24, 1802. 2.275
To sister Sarah Fegley, 100 pds. To cousin Conrad Fegley, rem.
Exec: Cousin Conrad Fegley. Wit: Conrad Shunk, David Zerley.

WALTON, JEREMIAH. Abington.
Sept 4, 1801. Sept 10, 1802. 2.276
To wife Margaret, household goods, and income of rem. of estate. To 2

sons Isaac and James, wearing apparel. To son Isaac, Cleaning Mill, stove, &c. To son James, stove. Rem. of personalty to be sold. After wife's death, 1/2 of estate to 2 sons James and Isaac. To 3 daughters: Ann Mitchener, Rachel Ackley and Sarah Hallowell, 1/2 of estate.
Execs: 2 sons Isaac and James. Wit: Benjamin Parry, Samuel Walton, Thomas Parry.

REIBER, CATHARINE. Upper Hanover.
March 28, 1894. Sept 27, 1802. 2.277
To Christopher Scholtz, stove, &c. To Baltzer Meishter, "Erasmus Sermons", &c. To 7 children of Christopher Sholtz, 2 Spanish Dollars, each. Rem. of personalty to be sold. To Christopher Scholtz, 1/3 of estate. Remaining 2/3 of estate to brother Jacob Reiber of York County.
Exec: Christopher Scholtz. Wit: Maria Scholtz, Rosina Scholtz.

DAVID, MARGARET. Gwynedd.
Sept 22, 1802. Oct 13, 1802. 2.279
Land in Gwynedd, for use of school for poor children, near Friends Meeting House. To Thomas Lewis, rem.
Exec: Cadwallader Evans. Wit: Joseph Meredith, Joseph Lewis.

THOMAS, JERUSHA. Moreland.
March 7, 1802. Nov 9, 1802. 2.279
To brother William Robinson, farm, 4 acres; subject to 15 pds. to sister Martha Whitton. To niece Martha Austin, income of rem. of realty, 4 acres. To niece Martha Austin, bible, saddle, &c. To Robert Robinson, son of Jonathan Robinson, 14 pds. with interest. To Ann Robinson, of son Jonathan Robinson, 5 pds. with interest. To niece Rachel Trump, 6 pewter plates. To niece Mary Whitton, pewter dish. To niece Amy Whitton, pewter dish, &c. To sister Martha Whitton, bed, bedding, &c. Rem. of estate to Jonathan Robinson, William Robinson, Martha Austin, equally.
Execs: Brother William Robinson, John Dean. Wit: William Roberts, William Ayres, John Watts.

SHEPARD, JAMES. Plymouth.
May 18, 1802. Nov 10, 1802. 2.281
Realty and personalty to be sold; money divided. To wife Martha, 500 pds. To son Robert, 8 s. 3 d. To daughter Mary Edwards, widow of Samuel Edwards, dec., 6 pds. yearly; at her death, principal 100 pds.; 30 pds. to her children, rem. to son Thomas and Jane Fulton, wife of John Fulton, son Thomas, daughter Martha Davis, wife of James Davis and son William, equally. To daughter Martha Davis, interest of 1/5 part of rem. To son Thomas, Jane Fulton, James and William, rem.
Codicil May 19, 1802. Daughter Martha Davis to receive principal.
Execs: Wife Martha, John Huston. Wit: Joseph Corson, John Blee.

REESE, MARGARET. Upper Merion.
Aug 2, 1802. Nov 23, 1802. 2.285
Farm, 3 acres and personalty to be sold and money divided among: Griffith Reese, George Reese, Hannah Reese, Ann Reese, Alexander Reese and 102 pds. 10 s. equally. Griffith Reese to keep George Rees' share in trust.
Exec: Nephew George Reese. Wit: James Akins, Philip Reese, George Reese.

PARRY, Isaac. Horsham.
July 2, 1802. Nov 25, 1802. 2.286
To wife Grace, 100 pds. and 40 pds. yearly, during widowhood; if she marry 20 pds. yearly. To son Samuel, 50 pds. Farm to be valued, son to take it for valuation; subject to 400 pds. yearly for wife; if sons do not take farm; to be sold and money to be divided among children. Guardians, Samuel Gummere, nephew Isaac Parry.
Execs: Wife Grace, sons Isaac and Samuel Parry. Wit: John Gummere, Lydia Gummere.

ROBERTS, BARBARA. Abington.
Oct 21, 1801. Dec 11, 1802. 2.288
To son John, 20 pds. To granddaughter Barbara Roberts, daughter of son John, 20 pds. &c. to granddaughter Sarah Walton, 15 pds. To son Jesse, 20 pds. To grandsons Jonathan Roberts and Samuel Roberts, of son Jesse, 10 pds. each. To grandson Amos Harner (Harmer), 10 pds. To grandson Chalkey Harner, 5 pds. To grandsons John and Charles Parry, 10 pds. each. To daughter Elizabeth Parry, horse, &c. To 2 daughters Mary and Elizabeth, rem. of household goods and wearing apparel. Rem. to 5 children: John, Isaac, Jesse, Mary Thomas anad Elizabeth Parry, equally.
Execs: Son Jesse, daughter Elizabeth. Wit: George Williams, John Williams.

BARTLESON, JAMES. Whitpain.
Nov 9, 1802. Jan 4, 1803. 2.289
To son Samuel, clock. To wife Catharine, income of farm, 16 1/2 acres, until son Samuel is 21. If wife marries to have 1/3 of estate. To son Samuel, farm, subject to payment of 2/5 of value to sister Maria; wife to receive 1/3 of value.
Execs: Wife Catharine, Job Roberts. Wit: David DeHaven, Job Roberts.

JONES, JOSHUA. Montgomery.
Jan 14, 1800. Jan 11, 1803. 2.290
Personalty to be sold. To Baptist Church in Montgomery, $100. To Joseph Hubbs, $100. To niece Dorothy Van Horn, $30. To nephew Enoch Jones, and Nathaniel Jones, $40 each. To children of brother Daniel, dec., and children of brother Thomas, dec., rem. equally.
Execs: Joseph Hubbs, nephew Joshua Jones. Wit: Joseph Lunn, Robert

Loller.

REIFSNIDER, WILLIAM. Douglass.
Dec 20, 1802. Jan 12, 1803. 2.292
To wife Elizabeth, farm, 108 acres and 8 acres of woodland and household goods. Rem. of estate to be sold and money divided as follows: to wife 1/2 of estate; she to receive interest; at her death to children. Other half of estate to children after deductions.
Execs: Brother Peter Reifsnider, brother in law Andrew Shiver. Wit: Ulrich Stall, George Bechtell, Peter Richards.

URMY, HENRY. Norriton.
Dec 10, 1802. Jan 22, 1803. 2.293
To wife Magdalena, 120 pds. also 300 pds., &c. during widowhood; if she marry to be divided among 4 children: John, David, Barbara and Isaac. Rem. of estate to 4 children.
Execs: Wife Magdalena, Henry Teany. Wit: John Edwards, John McSeland.

ZIMMERMAN, ARNOLD. Worcester.
April 8, 1802. Feb 1, 1803. 2.295
To wife Mary, household goods, interest of 250 pds. To son Jacob, 5 s. To son William, 300 pds. To daughter Rachel, wife of John Marsteller, 100 pds. To daughter Mary, 130 pds. &c. To daughter Sarah Baar, 10 pds. To son Christopher, farm in Worcester, 120 acres at valuation of 700 pds. To son Christopher, 300 pds. from 700 pds. Rem. of valuation equally divided among 11 children. To 2 daughters 100 pds.
Execs: Sons Jacob, William, and Christopher. Wit: Matthias Rittenhouse, John Roosen, Henry Hunsicker.

STAUFFER, JOHN ULRICH. Worcester.
Sept 20, 1800. Feb 15, 1803. 2.296
To wife Catharine, farm and personalty. To daughter Jenny, wife of Henry Roosen, farm, 20 pds. after wife's death at valuation of 240 pds. Daughters Jenny and Dorothy, wife of Matthias Moyer, to have dividends equal to sons Christian and Garret. Rem. equally divided among 4 children: Christian, Garret, Jenny, and Dorothy.
Execs: Son Garret, son in law Henry Roosen.

FEAGLEY, PHILIPBINA. Douglass.
Jan 7, 1803. Feb 15, 1803. 2.297
To daughter Mary, 15 pds. To daughter Rosana, petticoat. Rem. of wearing apparel to 2 daughters Mary and Rosana. Rem. of estate equally divided among children, except son George, he to have 15 pds. less than other children: Nicholas, John, Mary, Barnt, Rosana, Conrad and George.
Execs: Sons Nichols and John. Wit: Henry Davidson, George Leonard.

NARACKER, JACOB. Springfield.
Nov 21, 1798. Feb 15, 1803. 2.299
To wife Anna, bed, household goods. Realty to be sold; money put on interest for wife; at wife's death, interest to daughter Margaret Surber, now Margaret Cressman; at her death principal to 7 grandchildren children of step daughter Ann Mary, Jacob, Elizabeth, John, Joseph and Margaret Surber.
Execs: Jacob Surber, John Detwiler. Wit: John Huston, William Huston.

HICKS, WILLIAM. Springfield.
Dec 2, 1797. March 19, 1803. 2.300
To wife Barbara, cow, household goods and house and land in Chestnut Hill, maintenance, 20 pds. yearly and 50 pds. To son William, wearing apparel, 5 s. To daughter Mary, 100 pds. Personalty to be sold, money divided. To daughter Mary Hicks, 1/3 part. To grandchildren: Catharine, Sarah, Mary, William, Barbara Hicks, Christopher Rex, Ann, Margaret and William Rex, 2/3 part equally. To daughter Mary, farm at valuation of 1200 pds. to grandchildren. To William Hicks, 144 pds. and to 8 aforesaid grandchildren, 132 pds. each with interest.
Execs: Daughter Mary and brother Nicholas Hicks. Wit: Matthew Tyson, Jonathan Tyson, Thomas Livezey.

FRANCIS, ARNOLD. Providence.
April 15, 1802. April 2, 1803. 2.302
Realty and personalty to be sold; money to wife Elizabeth; at her death to children.
Codicil to daughter Catharine, 10 pds. more than other children.
Execs: Sons Thomas and John. Wit: John Edwards, James Whiteside.

TENNIS, SAMUEL. Towamencin.
Nov 27, 1802. April 5, 1803. 2.303
To daughter Magdalena, 70 pds. To daughter Levina, 150 pds. To daughter Hannah, 250 pds., household goods, &c. To grandson Humphrey Hughes, 1 acre. To grandson Samuel William Hughes and Israel Jones, 10 pds. To son William, farm, 105 acres. Rem. of estate to grandchildren of son Israel: Samuel, Rachel, Mary, Israel and William and great grandson Samuel Tennis, equally. To son Israel's widow, 6 pds. yearly. To grandchildren: Abraham Levina, Francis and Samuel Lukens, 25 pds. each. To grandson Israel Tennis, 10 pds. To above grandchildren, 90 acres in tract No. 3. Rem. of estate to son William.
Exec: Son William. Wit: Henry Smith, Sr., Henry Smith, Jr.

SELL, HENRY. New Hanover.
April 20, 1802. April 15, 1803. 2.306
To wife Anna Mary, household goods, 12 pds. yearly and maintenance. To son John, farm, in Upper Hanover, 105 acres for 1050 pds. and maintenance of wife. Personalty and woodland in Douglass, 10 acres 30

perches to be sold. Valuation money and sale money to be divided among 9 children: Elizabeth, wife of Michael Mull, Catharine, Barbara, Magdalena, Philip, Margaret, wife of John Barred, Henry, John, Anna Mary, wife of Michael Routebush, equally. To son John, 100 pds.
Execs: Son John, son in law Michael Routebush. Wit: Henry Borneman, Jacob Welker, Daniel Yost.

LUKENS, WILLIAM. Horsham.
Sept 9, 1798. April 28, 1803. 2.309
To wife Elizabeth, maintenance, 250 pds. yearly during widowhood; if she marry to 4 daughters: Sarah, Martha, Mary and Rachel. Sons Benjamin and Joseph to provide maintenance for wife. To 3 daughters: Sarah, Martha, and Rachel, 30 pds. each. To daughter Mary, 130 pds. yearly until she marries. Children: William, Elizabeth, Jonathan, David, Thomas and Daniel, have had their shares. Rem. to sons Benjamin and Joseph.
Execs: Wife Elizabeth, sons Jonathan and David. Wit: Samuel Gummere, Jonathan Iredell.

THOMAS, OWEN. Whitpain.
July 24, 1801. April 20, 1803. 2.310
To wife Grace, 600 pds., bond 50 pds. and 6 pds. yearly during widowhood and maintenance. To sister Jane, room, &c. To brother Evan, 40 pds. To brother Robert, 50 pds. To brother Evan's children: Margaret and Susanna, 40 pds. each, to David, Joseph, Evan and Rachel, 30 pds. each. To nephew John Hallman, of Phila., 50 pds. To nephew John Thomas, 100 pds. and interest. To Grace Rogers, 20 pds. To Job, desk and 40 pds. To nephew Samuel Thomas, farm, 100 pds.
Codicil give to wife, household goods; Job to have legacy if he lives in house.
Execs: Wife and Samuel Thomas. Wit: Benjamin Harry, Joseph Lewis.

SHAFFER, JACOB, SR. Marlborough.
Feb 7, 1803. May 11, 1803. 2.312
To wife Elizabeth, farm and personalty during widowhood; if she marry estate to be sold and money divided. To son Jacob, 10 pds. To daughter Catharine, 10 pds. and bible. To son George, 5 pds. To 6 children rem. of estate: Henry, Andrew, William, Jacob, Susanna and Catharine.
Execs: Son William, son in law George Geiger. Wit: Henry Snider, Philip Gable, Jr.

CASSEL, JOHN. Worcester.
Jan 27, 1802. May 24, 1803. 2.313
To wife Catharine, bonds, personalty and maintenance. Son Jacob to pay wife 15 pds. yearly. To son Jacob, farm, 116 acres at valuation of 450 pds.; he to keep 200 pds. Rem. of valuation to 4 sons and children of dec., daughter Mary, wife of Peter Johnson. To son Yellis, 200 pds. To son Henry, 200 pds. To daughter Mary dec., heirs, 200 pds. Son Yellis, Henry,

Peter Johnson, and John to pay wife 20 s. yearly. Rem. to be equally divided into 5 shares to Yellis, Henry, John, Jacob and children of daughter Mary.
Execs: 2 sons Yellis and Henry. Wit: John Bean, Bolser Heebner.

MAY, SARAH. Pottstown.
June 28, 1798. June 29, 1803. 2.315
House and lot in Phila. on Almond Street to Thomas, Samuel and Nathaniel Holland, children of brother Nathaniel Holland, 1/2 and other half to Mary, Sarah and Joanna Holland. To Thomas, Samuel and Nathaniel, Mary, Sarah and Joanna Holland, 800 pds. equally. To nephew John and Joseph Potts, 100 pds. in trust for niece Sarah Hobart. To Samuel Conby and Joseph Tatnal, 50 pds. for Friends Meeting at Wilmington. To exrs. 25 pds. for Friends Meeting at Exeter. To exrs. 25 pds. for Friends Meeting at Pottstown. To Hugh Judge, 50 pds. To Rebecca Patrick, 100 pds. To Sarah Hockley, 50 pds. and to Doctor Francis Potts, 100 pds. To Thomas and Sarah, children of James May, 50 pds. each to to Herrcretta Potts, daughter of the late Thomas Potts, 25 pds. To Martha Capman, 50 pds. Exrs. to pay 10 pds. for schools. To sister Joanna Potts, rem. of estate.
Execs: Sister Joanna, if she dies before testatrix, her children: John, Thomas, Joseph, and David, son in law Robert E. Hobart. Wit: John Schaffer, Jacob Dunknouse, Peter Bastress.

POTTS, Isaac. Cheltenham.
May 22, 1803. July 2, 1803. 2.318
Realty to be sold and divided among children: Edward, Samuel, Joanna, Martha, Ruth, Rebecca and Deborah. Son Edward to be charged with bond. To wife, estate at time of marriage in North Wales, and 60 pds. yearly. To daughters plates, equally. To son Samuel, watch. To William Savery, gold headed cane.
Execs: Brother in law Jacob Paul, son in law John Paul, sons Edward and Samuel. Wit: Benjamin Rowland, Thomas Shoemaker.

VANDERSLICE, ANTHONY. Providence.
May 6, 1803. July 4, 1803. 2.319
To 2 grandsons Jacob Custer, son of Peter Custer and daughter Rebecca and Anthony Vanderslice, son of John Vanderslice dec., farm in Limerick, 300 pds. equally. To wife Elizabeth Vanderslice, income of farm in Providence and Skippack 348 acres, use of house &c. during widowhood. To daughter Rebecca, farm 348 acres, subject to maintenance of wife.
Execs: Peter Custer, son in law John Umstead, Jr. Wit: William Smith, Adolph Pennepacker.

REIMER, PETER. Perkiomen and Skippack.
June 30, 1803. July 14, 1803. 2.321
To Samuel Hatfield, farming utensils. To brothers Haines and Ludiwg, all

estate. To Elizabeth, wife of Solmon Grimling Sr., Catharine or widow Corper, Barbara, wife of Tobias Heppler, nephew Philip Reimer, son Ludwig, personalty equally. To Samuel Hatfield, 2 acres.
Exec: Henry Hunsicker. Wit: Henry Been, Henry Sweitzer.

ISET, FREDERICK. Providence.
July 4, 1801. July 23, 1803. 2.322
To wife Rebecca, bed, maintenance and interst of 300 pds. To 2 sons Jacob and Frederick, wearing apparel, farm 100 acres in Providence, at valuation of 800 pds. To daughter Barbara 1 share, grandson John Shunk to have 10 pds. of his mother's share, and granddaughter Rebecca Shunk, 5 pds. of her mother's share. To son Jacob, 1 share. To son Frederick, 1 share. To daughter Elizabeth, 1 share. To daughter Hannah, 1 share. To grandson John White, 40 pds.
Execs: Son Jacob, John Roudebush. Wit: John Essig, Jacob Garber, Benedict Garber.

HINES, SAMUEL. Hatfield.
June 1, 1803. Aug __, 1803. 2.323
To wife Elizabeth, household goods, &c. Estate to be sold and money divided. To wife Elizabeth, 50 pds. Daughter Mary, wife of William McCasin (Annotation states "McCown" in original will, error for McEwen) and daughter Elizabeth, widow of Philip Wentz, dec., have received their shares. To daughters: Margaret Hines, Ann, Hannah and Eleanor Hines, 50 pds. each. To son Matthew, 50 pds. To son Samuel, 50 pds., mare, colt. Rem. of estate to wife and 6 daughters, 2 sons.
Execs: Wife and John Todd. Wit: Isaiah Thomas, John Taylor.

BINDER, MOSES. New Hanover.
May 20, 1796. Aug 19, 1803. 2.325
To wife, household goods, maintenance, &c. To 2 eldest sons of daughter Catharine, realty at 1400 pds. after wife's death. Personalty to be sold, if more than 700 pds. plus to children of daughter Catharine Wentz, 2 eldest sons to receive nothing. To wife Anna, 1/3 interest to children: Jacob, Hannah, Anthony, Frederica, Catharine, John and Anna Mary.
Execs: Son John, Jacob Gilbert. Wit: Bernhart Gilbert, Jr., Bernhard Gilbert, Sr.

YOUNG, ANDREW. Marlborough.
Nov 20, 1799. Aug 20, 1803. 2.326
To son Michael, farm in Upper Hanover, 130 acres and household goods, subject to payment of 600 pds.; he to keep 300 pds. To son Abraham, farm in Marlborough, 200 acres; he to provide maintenance for family and at valuation of 1000 pds. To son Henry, land in Phila. at valuation of 100 pds. To wife Susanna, household goods, maintenance, interest of 200 pds. To 6 daughters: Gertraude, wife of Henry Bosert, Elizabeth, wife of Peter Dinnigh, Barbara, wife of John Achey, Margaret and Anna, Maria and

Susanna, 200 pds. each and rem. to 9 children.
Execs: Sons Michael and Andrew. Wit: Ludwig Arche, John Boligh, Daniel Yost.

NEIMAN, GEORGE. Douglass.
May 4, 1801. Aug 27, 1803. 2.330
To wife Barbara, interest of 1/3 part of estate. To granddaughter Polly Bunn, of daughter Mary Bunn, chest, &c. which came from Germany. To sons Philip and John, wearing apparel, equally. To son Peter, $25. Rem. to Philip, John and daughter Mary.
Execs: Sons Philip and John. Wit: John Fritz, Samuel Baird.

COULSTON, EDWARD. Norriton.
June 9, 1803. Aug 30, 1803. 2.331
To wife, income of farm in Plymouth and household goods during widowhood. After wife's death or marriage, estate to be sold and divided among children: John, Barnabas, William, Thomas, James, Elizabeth and Mary.
Execs: 2 sons William and Thomas. Wit: Simon Armstrong, John Armstrong.

JOHNSON, BENJAMIN.
Aug 1, 1803. Sept 2, 1803. 2.332
Realty in New Jersey, to be sold. To 2 brothers John and William, $200 each. To sister Ann Woolsey, $50. Rem. of estate divided among 2 brothers John and William and 2 sister Catharine Watkins and Elizabeth Scout.
Execs: Brother John and Ephraim Woolsey. Wit: Joseph Carr, Robert Dunlap, Isaac Tomkins.

MARIS, GEORGE. Gwynedd.
July 17, 1803. Sept 10, 1803. 2.333
To wife Jane, household goods, maintenance, 30 pds., 48 pds. yearly, and interest of 800 pds. To son William, 4 tracts, first purchased of Jesse Evans, except 10 acres; second purchased of Rowland Evans; third purchased of Margaret and Hannah Jones, fourth, 9 3/4 acres. To son George, 3 tracts, rem. of land purchased of John Troxel, second purchased of Thomas Evans and 18 acres, subject to payment of 20 pds. yearly to wife. To brothers: Levi Foulke, Jesse Foulke, nephew William Foulke, John Evans, Jr. and Cadwalader Evans, 6 tracts, 146 1/2 acres in trust. To daughter Ann and Jane, income of tracts, 60 acres, 70 perches; at their deaths to children and grandchildren, equally. To daughter Rebecca, income of 71 acres, subject to waterways and 3 pds. yearly to daughter Ann and Jane each and 6 pds. to wife. At her death to William, George, Ann, Hannah and Jane, grandson Jesse Maris, and children of daughter Susannah. To daughter Susannah, 5 tracts, 2 lots, 3 acres, 1 lot, 9 acres, 1 lot 2 1/2 acres, 1 lot 2 acres at her death to her children, also interest

of 100 pds. or 10 acres. To Levi and Jesse Foulke, William Foulke, John Cadwalader Evans, 600 pds. in trust for daughters Ann and Jane; they to pay the interest of 200 pds. to wife and interest of 400 pds. to daughters Ann and Jane. To daughter Susannah, interest of 200 pds. and to wife interest of 100 pds. at her death, principal to her children. To daughter Hannah, 550 pds. To grandson Jesse Maris, 200 pds. and 300 pds. To son William, horse, and to son George, horse, farming utensils. To daughters Ann and Jane, household goods. To daughter Judith Maris, 12 pds. Rem. to children: William, George, Ann and Jane. Trustees, Levi and Jesse Foulke, nephew William Foulke, John and Cadwalader Evans.
Execs: Sons William and George, Cadwalader Evans, Jr. Wit: John Evans, George Roberts, Joseph Meredith.

HENDRICKS, JOHN. Limerick.
July 4, 1803. Sept 2, 1803. 2.342
To wife Margaret, house, household goods, maintenance, ii of 125 pds. To son Peter, house, three tracks of land; 2 in Limerick, 123 acrs, the other one in Hanover, 10 acres, he to provide maintenance for iwfe and also 150 pds. to son Jacob, farm in Limerick, 48 acre. To daughter Mary Magdelena, wife of Jonathan Feadley, 200 pds. after deductions are made. Personalty to be sold and money to be divided among wife oand 3 children, at her death her share to be divided among 3 children.
Execs: Sons Peter, Isaac Davis. Wit: Abraham Shwink, Benjamin Markley.

BROOKE, JONATHAN. Lower Merion.
Jan 4, 1801. Oct 3, 1803. 2.344
To son James, wagon, part of farm. To daughter Hannah Cumley, part of farm, at her death 1/4 part each to sons James, Samuel and 1/4 to children of daughter Hannah, the other 1/4 to son Nathan. To granddaughter Clarissa Brooke, daughter of son Nathan 25 pds. To granddaughter Mary Brooke, 25 pds. To granddaughter Hannah Cumley 25 pds. To grandsons Charles and William Brooke, rem. of money from farm equally. Wearing apparel to son Samuel, rem. of household goods to be sold, and money divided among 3 children.
Execs: Son James, nephew Benjamin Brooke. Wit: John Jones, Job Pugh.

HALLMAN, HENRY. Perkiomen and Skippack.
Jan 31, 1800. Oct 10, 1803. 2.346
To son Henry and son Anthony and daughter Catharine, wife of Jacob Creasamer, daughter Christiana, wife of Jacob Snyder, daughter Mary, wife of Matthias Ritter, 5 pds. each. To son Abraham, 100 pds. To son Daniel, 95 pds. Rem. of estate to be divided among 6 sons and 4 daughters: Jacob, Benjamin, John, Isaac, Daniel, Sarah, wife of Christian Mattis, Margaret, wife of Jacob Iset, Elizabeth, wife of Jacob Frontfield, Susanna, wife of John Groves.
Execs: Sons Jacob and John. Wit: Henry Hunsicker, John Tyson.

LUKENS, JESSE. Horsham.
Sept 27, 1803. Nov 7, 1803. 2.347
Estate to wife Elizabeth.
Execs: Wife Elizabeth, brother in law Isaac Kirk. Wit: George Child, Isaiah Lukens.

MAGILL, WILLIAM [JR.] Moreland.
Oct 17, 1803. Nov 15, 1803. 2.348
To wife Mary, 25 pds.; 5 pds. yearly, household goods. To wife and daughters: Sarah, Elizabeth, Hannah and Mary, furniture, wearing apparel to sons William and James. To son William, desk and share in Union Library of Hatborough. To son James, one acre in Hatborough. To son William, also one acre, subject to maintenance of wife. Rem. personalty to be sold and lot of 8 acres in Bucks Co., 47 acres, in Moreland, money to be divided among 6 children.
Eexec: Wife Mary, Robert Loller. Wit: Robert Dunlap, Joseph Carr.

BOILEAU, ISAAC. Moreland.
Jan 10, 1801. Nov 15, 1803. 2.350
To wife Racheal, maintenance 30 pds. yearly, household goods. To son Nathaneal B., farm, 107 acres, subject to maintenance of wife. At wife's death, clock to daughter Ann Follwello. To daughter Ann Follwello, 30 pds. yearly, 1/2 to be paid by daughter Sarah Wilson, other half by daughter Racheal Barns, to daughter to pay $20 yearly. To daughter Sarah Wilson, farm where she now lives, containing 64 acres, 14 perches, subject to payment of 250 pds. to children of daughter Ann. To daughter Racheal Barns, where she lives and track of 2 3/4 acres 8 perches, subject to payment of 15 pds. yearly. To daughter Ann Follwello, 250 pds. To children of daughter Ann, $20 to her mother yearly, at daughter Racheal's death, her husband to have use of farm of 64 acres 14 perches, if she outlives her husband, to her children. To negro Jack, house, and 4 acres of land; at his death, to grandson Samuel Barns. To son Nathaneal B. personal estate, subject to a payment of 30 pds. to the Presbyterian Church, Abington.
Exec: Nathaneal B. Boileau. Wit: James Oglevie, Robert Loller.

FISHER, GEORGE. Abington.
April 11, 1803. Nov 17, 1803. 2.354
Personalty to be sold, and lot in Abington and money divided as follows: 1/3 to wife Christina, wife to receive interest of the other 2/3. To Charlotte, daughter of Racheal Phipps of Abington, 2/3 part.
Execs: Wife Christina, Jos. Webster. Wit: Thomas Livezey, John Clayton.

SHADE, HENRY. Whitpain.
Aug 17, 1803. Nov 24, 1803. 2.356
To wife Margaret, 15 pds., household goods, interest of 300 pds., estate to be sold and money divided among 5 children: Jacob, Henry, John,

George, Susanna, wife of Peter Bush. At wife's death 300 pds. to be divided among 5 children.
Execs: John Wentz, Frederick Conrad. Wit: Garret Bean, Jacob Bean.

HARMAN, JOHN. Hatfield.
Nov 17, 1803. Nov 30, 1803. 2.355
To cousin Martin Funk, watch. To sister Elizabeth's son John Freitz, gun, etc. To sister Mary's son Henry Clime, 105 pds. when 21. To Sarah Coil, 10 pds. when 18.
Exec: Uncle John Funk. Wit: Edmund Pennington, John Funk.

ROBERTS, JOHN. Lower Merion.
Aug 12, 1803. Dec 2, 1803. 2.359
To Pennsylvania Hospital, 50 pds., 50 pds. for Building School near Friends Meeting House, in Lower Merion; 10 pds. to Quaker Burying Grounds. To nephew John Roberts, 18 pds. when 21. To niece Lydia, daughter of brother Algernon Roberts, 500 pds. To nephew Isaac Roberts, desk, watch, wearing apparel and 180 pds. To niece Gainor, household goods and 240 pds. To niece Anna Roberts, 10 pds. To niece Elizabeth Roberts, 10 pds. To nephew Algernon Roberts, 10 pds. and chest. To nephew [blank] 10 pds. etc. To nephew John Robert, son of brother Benjamin, 50 pds. To William Palmer, son of sister Tacy, 100 pds. To brother Washington, millwright tools and 100 pds. To niece Mary Oxford, 50 pds. To William Palmer, 50 pds. To nephew Asher, 50 pds. To nephew George Palmer, nephew of Chas. Palmer, 25 pds. To niece Tacy Palmer, daughter of Joseph Palmer, 25 pds. To John Roberts, son of brother Edward, 150 pds. when 21. Rem. to nephew George Roberts.
Exec: Brother Algernon Roberts. Wit: Joseph Price, Titus Yerkes.

WINTERS, JAMES. Lower Merion.
Sept 18, 1793. Dec 10, 1803. 2.361
To nephew Benjamin Holland, farm 80 acres, at his death, to his son James Holland, subject to maintenance of wife during widowhood. To nephew John Fisher, 20 shillings, paid by nephew Benjamin.
Execs: Nephew Benjamin Holland, Llewelyn Young. Wit: Archibald Menzus, James Brown, James Thompson.

RAMBO, AARON. Providence.
Nov 25, 1803. Dec 23, 1803. 2.362
Farms to be rented to son William, farm bought of John Guardner subject to the payment of 125 pds. To son John, farm where testator lives, subject to the payment of 175 pds. Personalty to be sold. To daughter Elizabeth 300 pds. when 21. Rem. to be divided among 3 children.
Execs: Brother Levi, Henry Pennebecker. Wit: Jacob Wismer, Jacob Carl.

HORNING, JOHN. Providence.
Oct 13, 1803. Dec 24, 1803. 2.364

To wife Elizabeth household goods, income of farm and lands during widowhood. If she marry to have interest of 300 pds.. To son Jacob, farm, at valuation. If he refuses to , next son. If sons refuse farm to be sold. Money to be divided as follows: 50 pds. to sons each, remaining part to be divided among all children. Farm 17 acres to be sold; woodland 4 acres. Personalty to be sold and money divided, 100 pds. to each son. To son Jacob Horning, horse, saddle, etc. To son Ludwick, horse, saddle. Rem. of sons 27 pds. each. Rem. divided among children.
Execs: Sons Jacob and Ludwick. Trustees Henry Hunsicker, Jacob Hallman, Garret Stoffer. Wit: Henry Hunsicker, Henry Fry. John Tyson.

LLEWELYN, MARTHA. Lower Merion.
June 3, 1791. Jan 17, 1804. 2.366
To grandson Joel Carpenter, son of daughter Elizabeth wife of John Young, money from farm, in Lower Merion and 100 pds. If he dies before he is 21; 100 pds. to be divided among children of John Young; Mary Griffith, Martha and John. To daughter Elizabeth 50 pds. to daughter Aridena wife of Llewelyn Young, 10 pds. To son Morris, 40 pds. To grandson Joel Carpenter, feather bed, etc. To daughter Elizabeth, table. To son Morris, rug, etc. To granddaughter Martha Young, of Llewelyn Young, drawers. Rem. of among Ariadna, Morris and Elizabeth.
Execs: Lindsay Coats, Jonathan Carmalt, Jr. Wit: William Hagy, Henry White, Philip Fritz.

HOLT, BENJAMIN. Horsham.
Oct 3, 1797. Feb 10, 1804. 2.367
To wife Margaret, household goods, etc. To son Charles, 2 horses, plow, etc., he to provide maintenance for wife, he to receive income of farm. Personalty to be sold and divided among daughters: Martha Barnes, Grace Fell, Joanna Christine, and Hannah Ryon's children and son Thomas Holt's children, equally. Abner Holt to receive half of his mothers share. To daughter Sarah Watkins $1.00 to be paid by son Charles. To sons Jesse and Charles farm 100 acres, at wife's death or marriage subject to the payment of 50 pds. each and to be divided among daughters and grandchildren.
Execs: Jesse and Charles. Wit: Benjamin Cadwalder, Nathan Holt, Nicholas Martin.

MANGOLD, GEORGE ADAM. Marlborough.
April 23, 1799. Feb 13, 1804. 2.369
Estate to be sold (except to daughter Catharine, bed, etc.) To daughter in law Catharine widow of son George Adam, 7 pds. Rem. to be divided among 4 grandchildren: Catharine, Christopher, George Adam, Joseph of son George Adam.
Execs: Jacob Karver, Nicholas Miller. Wit: Adam Yost, Peter Renninger, Frederick Zolig.

FISHER, GEORGE. Abington.
April 11, 1803. Feb 14, 1804. 2.370
To brothers John, Joseph and Malachi, wearing apparel, equally. Personalty to be sold except household goods, and lot, and money to be divided as follows: to wife Christina 1/3 remaining 2/3 put on interest for wife at her death, principle to Charlotte daughter of Rachel Phipps.
Execs: Wife Christine, Joseph Webster. Wit: Thomas Livezey, John Clayton.

CHRISTMAN, JACOB. Limerick.
Feb 16, 1804. March 13, 1804. 2.371
To wife Elizabeth use of farm, household, furniture, during widowhood. If she marries 1/3 estate. Personalty to be sold and money divided into 9 shares, among children after wife's death or marriage, farm to be appraised 1/3 part to son Henry, 1/3 part to son Jacob, 1/3 part to son Daniel at appraisement and money divided among 9 children: Henry, Jacob, Daniel, George, John son in law John Nice, daughter Catharine, daughter Susanna, wife of Abraham Turner, daughter Susanna share to be put on interest. At her death to her children sum of 40 pds. To daughter Magdelena late wife of Nicholas Iches 4 children, 10 pds.
Execs: Sons Henry Christman, and Daniel Christman. Wit: Henry Hahn, George Brant, Isaiah Davis.

NEVIL, AGNESS. Gwynedd.
Dec 28, 1803. March 10, 1804. 2.374
To son Jacob 20 s. To daughter Shelah wife of Frederick Coughar, 20 s. To grandchildren of son Peter, 20 s. equally. To grandchildren of son Adam, 20 s. equally. To grandchildren of daughter Elizabeth, 20 s. equally. To son Henry, rem. of estate.
Exec: Henry Hallman. Wit: Jacob Heisler, Jr., Abijah Miller.

YOUNG, NICHOLAS. Upper Hanover.
July 20, 1801. March 14, 1804. 2.375
Personalty to son Henry. Exrs. to provide maintenance for son Henry, at his dath rem. of estate to his children.
Execs: Son in law George Hilegass, and grandson Michael Young. Wit: Henry Smith, Peter Bowman.

SHAUL, JOHN. Upper Dublin.
Feb 5, 1804. March 21, 1804. 2.377
To wife Elizabeth, household goods, $80, use of farm, $80 yearly during widowhood. To sister Anna Bruner, $66.67. To Thomas Clemmens wearing apparel. To granddaughter Elizabeth Clemmens, $133.60 when 18. To German Reformed Church in Whitpain $26.67. At wife's death or marriage farm to be sold. Personalties to be divided into 4 parts: to sister Anna Bruner one part. To brother Adam Shaul's son John Shaul one part. To brother Jacob Shaul's grandchildren, children of Michael Tatt,

one part. To brother Conrad John Shaul, one part.
Execs: Christopher Loeser, Samuel Mann. Wit: Isaac Mann, Joel K. Mann.

ZIEGLER, CHRISTOPHER, SR. Providence.
Nov 7, 1796. April 24, 1804. 2.379
To son Micheal, horse. Rem. divided into 10 parts: to son Micheal one part. To children of son John one part. To children of son Andrew one part. To son Christopher one part. To children of daughter Catharine wife of Benjamin Mayer one part. To daughter Hannah wife of Martin Landis one part. To daughter Elizabeth wife of Samuel Bower one part. To daughter Barbara wife of David Buckwalter one part. To daughter Susanna wife of Jacob Weiss one part. To daughter Deborah wife of David Longenecker one part.
Execs: Sons in law Samuel Bower, David Buckwalter. Wit: Jacob Longacre, Jacob Garber.

ANDERS, GEORGE, SR. Towmaencin.
Oct 27, 1803. April 24, 1804. 2.381
To wife Anna Barber, maintenance, household goods, use of farm. To son George, farm, 150 acres, at valuation of 1500 pds. subject to maintenance of wife. Wife to receive interest of 1500 pds. to daughter Susanna Yeakle, 20 pds. Rem. of money to be divided into 5 parts: to son George one part. To daughter Susanna and Anna Seidle 92 pds. each. To 4 sons: Abraham, Andrew, George and John, rem. of money from farm equally. At wife's death her share to 6 children.
Execs: Sons Abraham and Andrew. Wit: Melchior Schultz, Andrew Krieble.

HAIR, BENJAMIN. Horsham.
Jan 19, 1804. April 24, 1804. 2.383
To son Matthew, personalty, farm, subject to the payment of legacies. To daughter Jane Taylor 100 pds. To daughter Elizabeth Hair 100 pds., bed, etc. To daughter Sarah Simpson 100 pds. To grandson Amos Tolbert 80 ps. when 21. To granddaughter Anna Roberts wife of Ezekiel Roberts 50 pds. To son John 2 s. 6 d. To daughter Mary Doyle wife of Stephen Doyle 2 s. 6 d. To daughter Anna McDougal 2 s. 6 d. To daughter Elizabeth, case of drawers.
Execs: Son Matthew, son in law John Simpson. Wit: Paul Dowlin, William Neellin.

LIEBENUGH, ADAM. New Hanover.
Feb 16, 1804. April 27, 1804. 2.385
To wife Christina, personalty. To son Jacob, woodland, 6 acres 52 1/2 perch at valuation of 50 pds. to sons Matthias, John, Peter, 50 pds. each. Rem. of estate at wife's death equally divided among children. To son Jacob one part. To son John one part. To son Peter one part. To daughter Elizabeth wife of Charles Neiman one part. To grandchildren of daughter

Catharine wife of William Kepner, one part equally.
Execs: Sons Matthias, and Peter. Wit: Charles Guiger, Peter Richards.

KEEPAR, BERND. Skippack and Perkiomen.
Feb 13, 1804. May 4, 1804. 2.386
Estate to be sold, if son John and Samuel do not take farm money to be divided into 4 parts: to son John one part. To son Samuel one part. To daughter Elizabeth wife of Daniel Schrach one part. To daughter Margaret one part. To daughter Elizabeth 30 pds. To daughter Catharine wife of Samuel Hatfield, 15 pds. To grandson Bernd, 50 pds. when 21.
Execs: Sons Samuel, son in law Philip Reimer. Wit: John Rawn, Abraham Grater, Henry Sweitzer.

PRISE, DANIEL. Lower Salford.
June 8, 1802. May 7, 1804. 2.388
Estate to be divided among children: John, George, William, Daniel and Hannah, wife of John Clemmens, Elizabeth widow of Jacob Weidner.
Execs: Sons John and Daniel. Wit: Michael Shoemaker, Jacob Shoemaker.

BERKHEIMER, LEONARD. Upper Salford.
____, 1802. May 14, 1804. 2.389
To second wife Catharine farm, 20 acres, household goods, during widowhood. If she marries estate to be sold. To children of son William 25 pds. each. To children of son Andrew 15 pds. each. Rem. of estate equally divided among other five children: George, Philip, Henry, Solomy wife of Valentine Mungesser, Magdeline, wife of Samuel Goodnight, equally.
Execs: Eldest son George and Philip Gable. Wit: John Hilbelitel, William Shletora.

KOLB, JOHN GEORGE. New Hanover.
Jan 6, 1804. May 23, 1804. 2.391
To wife Magdelena, household goods, 5 pds. To son Samuel, farm, 110 acres, 97 perches and 30 acres of woodland in Douglass. He to provide maintenance for wife, subject to the payment of 1400 pds. He to keep 100 pds. to pay to wife's interest of 100 pds. To son George, rem. 26 acres, 56 perches at valuation of 300 pds. He to keep 100 pds. Personalty to be sold, money divided among children as follows: to daughter Magdelena, 100 pds. To son Peter, 100 pds. To daughter Maria, 100 pds. At wife's death her share to be divided among children: Magdelena, Peter, Samuel, Maria, George, Elizabeth, Henry, Moses, Catharine and Jacob.
Execs: Sons Samuel and George. Wit: John Billing, Anthony Keel, and Daniel Yost.

BRANT, ADAM. New Hanover.
____, 1801. June 13, 1804. 2.395
To wife Abigail, household goods, use of farm during widowhood. Personalty to be sold. To grandsons Samuel Keepner and Henry clock,

tools, equally. At wife's death, farm to be sold and personalty and money divided among 3 children: Samuel, Henry and Elizabeth Keepner, except 50 pds.; interest of 50 pds. to be paid to daughter Mary Gome.
Exec: Jacob Shantz. Wit: Philip Yost, George Leonard.

SHOEMAKER, WILLIAM. Cheltenham.
Oct 4, 1799. June 18, 1804. 2.396
To wife Hannah, 100 pds. To wife Hannah, household goods. Estate to be sold and money divided as follows: Rem. to 11 children: Abraham, Daniel, Jesse, Sarah, Lydia, William, Susanna, Joseph, Elizabeth, Malachi and Mary, equally. Daughter Sarah to have maintenance from children if necessary.
Execs: Wife Hannah, sons Abraham and Daniel. Wit: Esther Nusgrove, Joseph P. Nusgrove and Susanna Shoemaker.

CLEAVER, JOHN. Upper Dublin.
Aug 30, 1799. July 24, 1803. 2.398
To wife Hannah, household goods, 9 pds. yearly during widowhood. To son John, mare, and 30 pds. To sons Jesse and John wearing apparel, equally. Rem. equally divided among 3 children: Rebecca Woollin, Jesse and John.
Execs: Sons Jesse and son in law Joseph Woollin. Wit: Daniel Shoemaker, Thomas Shoemaker.

YOUNG, ROWLAND.
Feb 12, 1803. July 24, 1804. 2.399
Real estate to sons John and Andrew. Son Andrew to pay 7 pds. per acre yearly, to his mother, also 50 pds. yearly until all is paid. Son John to pay 25, pds. yearly and 7 pds. 10 s. per acre. To wife 50 pds. also to receive interest of 200 pds. yearly and son Andrew to provide maintenance. Personalty to 8 children: Catharine, Magdelena, Henry, Christina, Rosanna, Margaret, John and Andrew equally.
Execs: Sons John and Andrew. Wit: George Vogle, John Bender.

AMBLER, JOHN. Montgomery.
March 1, 1797. July 25, 1804. 2.402
To son John 104 acres, 81 perches, subject to the payment of 250 pds. To son Jesse 35 acres and track in Bucks Co., 38 acres, 46 perches and 40 pds. etc. To daughter Gainor, 100 pds. and feather bed, etc. To daughter Tacy, 100 pds. and feather bed, etc. To daughter Susanna 100 pds. and feather bed, etc. Rem. of estate to 7 children: Joseph, Edward, Jesse, Gainor, Tacy and Susanna.
Execs: Sons Joseph and Edward. Wit: John Evans, William Collom, Alexander Forman.

EVANS, JACOB. Norriton.
May 30, 1804. July 27, 1804. 2.403
To wife Hannah, household goods. To son Enoch 90 pds. and colt, interest

of 88 pds.; wife to receive interest of 44 pds. at her death son to receive interest. To son Jonathan, 25 pds. interest of 175 pds. He to receive interest of 87 pds. 10 s. until wife's death. To son Jonathan's wife, stove. To son George, 70 pds. etc. To daughter Eleanor 200 pds. wife to receive interest of 100 pds. To son Jonathan 200 pds. wife to receive interest of 100 pds. To daughter Elizabeth 200 pds. wife to receive interest of 100 pds. To niece Tacy Styer, 15 pds. Rem. of estate divided among 3 sons: George, Enoch and Aaron. Land of son Samuel now deceased, to son Enoch.
Execs: Wife Hannah, sons Enoch and Aaron. Wit: Enoch Supplee, Nathan Potts.

SHUPERD, CHRISTOPHER. Whitemarsh.
March 23, 1793. Aug 4, 1804. 2.407
To sons: John, Christopher, Philip and Christian, 7 pds., 10 s. To daughters: Margaret, Christina, feather beds, etc. To son Christian, bible. Rem. of books divided among 4 sons. Use of realty to son Christian and daughters Margaret and Christina for one year. Estate to be sold and money divided among children: John, Christopher, Philip, Christian, Eve, Mary, Elizabeth, Margaret and Christina.
Execs: Sons John and Christian. Wit: Daniel Hagy, Paul Bishop, Jacob Jones.

KARVER, JACOB. Upper Hanover.
June 3, 1797. Aug 21, 1804. 2.409
To wife Elizabeth, all estate during widowhood. To son Nicholas Miller, husband of daughter Catharine, farm. At wife's death or marriage at valuation of 550 pds. To son Jacob, farm bought of George Heist in Lower Milford at valuation of 300 pds. To son John Adam 10 pds. Rem. divided among 3 children.
Execs: Son John Adam, son in law Nicholas Miller. Wit: Adam Schneider, George Ewalt.

RICHARDS, CHARLES. Worcester.
March 5, 1803. Aug 25, 1804. 2.410
To brother George wearing apparel. To wife Mary, household goods. Interest of rem. of estate during widowhood. Estate to be sold and wife to receive interest. At wife's death or marriage estate to brother George Richards.
Execs: Brother George Richards, Joseph Henry. Wit: John Roosen, Christopher Zimmerman.

HOFMAN, CHRISTOPHER. Lower Salford.
March 28, 1795. March 6, 1804. 2.412
To Abraham Kriebel, son of Christopher Kriebel, cupboard. To Alms Box of Schwenchfelder, estate 10 pds. To 3 children of Abraham Kriebel: Isaac, Christian and Mary 5 pds. each. Personalty to be divided into 3

equal shares: to 5 children of sister Anna 1/3, to sister Rosina's 3 children 1/3, to Christopher Kriebel, son of Abraham Kriebel, 1/3.
Codicil dated March 17, 1798 to Susanna daughter of Abraham Kriebel, 5 pds.
Execs: Balthaser Schultz, Jacob Yeakle. Wit: Melchior Kriebel, Melchior Schultz.

BOWER, DANIEL. Douglass.
June 24, 1804. Oct 5, 1804. 2.414
Personalty to be sold. Estate to wife, at her death to 2 children, Henry and John.
Execs: Wife and brother in law Jacob Gable. Wit: Henry Swinehart, John Richards.

WENTZ, FREDERICK. Worcester.
Feb 3, 1798. Oct 31, 1804. 2.415
To wife Appellonia, household goods, interest of 500 pds. Income of farm, and farm containing 200 acres. Personalty to be sold, and money divided as follows: to 7 children: Peter, Philip, Catharine, wife of John Knipe, Magdelena, wife of John Erhard Hoot, Nancy, wife of John Ginkiner, Barbara, wife of Philip Stong, Susanna, wife of John Bieber, equally. Daughter Magdelena to receive interest only. Daughter Nancy to receive interest of 100 pds. as part of her share.
Execs: Frederick Conrad, Joseph Tyson.
Codicil dated Oct 7, 1800. Heirs of daughter Susanna and Magdelena, receive their shares.
Execs: Frederick Conrad, John Wentz, son of brother Abraham.
Wit: Nicholas Martin, Joseph Tyson, Frederick Conrad.

AUSTIN, JONATHAN. Moreland.
March 10, 1802. Oct 24, 1804. 2.419
Estate to be sold. To wife Martha 1/3 part of estate. Rem. of estate to be put on interest and paid to wife yearly in trust for daughter Mary until she is 21. To daughter Mary 2/3 part of estate when 18.
Exec: Joshua Comly. Wit: Edward B. Potts, John Roberts.

MASON, PETER. Springfield.
June 16, 1802. Nov 2, 1804. 2.420
To friend John Stott, 300 pds. To wife Mary all estate.
Exec: Wife Mary. Wit: Nicholas Kline, George Billger.

LEECH, THOMAS. Upper Dublin.
Sept 4, 1804. Nov 5, 1804. 2.421
To wife's son Isaac Tyson and friend Silas Yerkes, wearing apparel equally. To brother Joseph 3 incomes of lots in Philadelphia, amounting to $32 annually. At his death, to nephew and nieces, children of brother Isaac and Samuel, and sister Mary, namely: Isaac Leech, Racheal Mather,

Rebecca Austin, Martha Shoemaker, Richard T. Leech, Rebecca Leech, Samuel Leech, Esther McClean, equally. To brother Joseph interest of 50 pds. To wife's grandson Leech Tyson, silver watch. To nephew Isaac Leech, bible. To niece Rebecca, spoons, etc. To wife Hannah, household goods. Farm in Upper Dublin. At wife's death to wife's son Isaac Tyson, farm 99 acres, 102 perches subject to the payment of 1000 pds. To sister Rebecca Erwin, 50 pds. rem. of 1000 pds. to said nieces and nephew equally. Personalty to be sold, wife to receive interest. To wife's daughter Rebecca Lukens, 20 pds. at wife's death. To wife's grandson Leech Tyson, 25 pds. To wife's granddaughter Rebecca Tyson, 25 pds. To wife's grandson, John Tyson, 20 pds. To wife's grandson, Seth Tyson, 20 pds. To wife's granddaughter Hannah Tyson, 20 pds. Rem. to wife's son Isaac Tyson.
Exec: Thomas Livezey. Wit: Matthew Tyson, Ryner Tyson.

YOST, PHILIP. New Hanover.
Jan 3, 1797. Nov 12, 1804. 2.423
To wife Veronica, household goods. Son John to provide maintenance for wife. To son John, 100 pds. To son Harmon, 100 pds. To son Philip, 70 pds. To 3 sons, wearing apparel, equally. Rem. of estate among 8 children: John, Harmon, children of daughter Catharine Reifsnyder, namely: Philip, Mary, Andrew, Veronica, Elizabeth, Catharine, one share. Elizabeth Missamer, Philip, daughter Solomy Barlinger, Magdelena Messamer, Racheal Ortlip one share each. At wife's death personalty to be sold and divided among 8 children.
Codicil dated Jan 9, 1802. Daughters shares to descend to children.
Execs: Sons John and Philip. Wit: Isreal Ortlip, Jacob Crous.

LOESER, JOHN. Whitpain.
May 2, 1803. Nov 12, 1804. 2.427
To wife Margaret, household goods, use of estate during widowhood. If she marries to receive 8 pds. Estate to be sold and money divided among 8 children: Elizabeth, Christian, Mary, Sarah, Margaret, John, Racheal and Catharine.
Execs: Wife and son Christian, brother Christopher. Wit: Christopher Loeser, Morgan Morgan.

AYRES, SAMUEL. Moreland.
April 2, 1804. Dec 3, 1804. 2.428
To wife Deborah, household goods. To son William, farm, 7 3/4 acres and lot 3 acres at valuation of 7 pds., 10 s. to wife yearly. After son Hiram is 21. Son William to receive bonds and wheelwright tools. Personalty to be sold. Wife to receive interest, and income of farm. To wife 15 pds. yearly, 1/2 to be paid by son William other half by son Hiram. To son Hiram when 21 farm and rem. of plantation bought of Thomas Austin and 2 acres bought of George Brooks. To daughter Esther, cow. At wife's marriage or death, income of farm bought of Benjamin Yerkes. To

daughter Elizabeth 50 pds. When son Hiram is 22 to daughter Elizabeth 300 pds. To brother Charles, wearing apparel. Rem. of estate to 4 children: William, Esther, Elizabeth and Hiram, equally.
Execs: Son William and Hiram McNeal. Wit: William Dean, Jesse Harker, John Watts.

MORRIS, WILLIAM. Gwynedd.
Sept 2, 1804. Dec 7, 1804. 2.431
To brother George, wearing apparel, saddle, etc. To nephew George Wilson, watch. To sisters Anna and Jane, riding mare. Rem. of personal estate to mother. To mother real estate in Gwynedd, subject to debts. At mother's death to nephew Jesse Morris, subject to the payment of 1200 pds. To cousin Margaret, 100 pds. Rem. of estate to children of sisters Anna and Susanna. Trustees, uncle Levi Foulke, Jesse Foulke.
Execs: Cousin William Foulke, Cadwalder Evans. Wit: Edward Jenkins, Rob. I. Evans, Jr.

DERDINGER, CATHARINE. Providence.
Nov 5, 1804. Dec 15, 1804. 2.433
To brother Lawrence Bausman, personal estate. To Jacob Cummins, 25 pds. To Reform Church at Trappe, 6 pds. Real estate to be sold. Money to brother Lawrence.
Exec: Francis Swaine. Wit: Frederick A. Muhlenberg, Geo. Kepler, Philip Schreder.

BOYER, PETER. Frederick.
Nov 5, 1804. Dec 15, 1804. 2.434
To wife Catharine, household goods, interest of 300 pds. Estate to be sold and mondey divided among children: Catharine, Elizabeth, Charles, Sarah and Peter equally.
Execs: Brothers George and Jacob. Wit: Jacob Hawk, Jacob Boyer.

KULP, DILMAN. Skippack and Perkiomen.
Aug 14, 1802. Dec 20, 1804. 2.434
To wife Hannah, personal estate. At wife's death, personalty to be sold. To children of daughter Sarah deceased, 5 pds. each. To son Jacob, wearing apparel, and carpenter tools, and $10, 1/2 money in house, and other 1/2 to daughter Susanna. To grandson Dilman Kulp, 5 pds. Rem. of divided among divided among 3 children: Jacob, Susanna and Margaret; Margaret to receive 300 pds. less than other children.
Execs: Henry Kulp, Henry Hunsicker. Wit: William Dismant, Benjamin Dismant.

CUSTER, JACOB. Worcester.
March 29, 1803. Dec 24, 1804. 2.436
To son Jacob, land in Worcester. He to pay to sons Peter, Samuel and Joseph 400 pds. equally and he pay to wife Elizabeth interest of 400 pds.

and maintenance. To wife Elizabeth, household goods. Son Jacob to pay to 4 sisters, 100 pds. equally. Rem. of estate to be sold and money divided among 7 children: Peter, Samuel, Joseph, Catharine, Mary, Rebecca and Anna equally.
Execs: Sons Peter and Joseph. Wit: Joseph Tyson, Cornelius Tyson.

NANNA, WILLIAM. Whitpain.
July 8, 1798. Jan 16, 1805. 2.437
To wife Sarah, household goods. Rem. of personalty to be sold, wife to receive interest. To nephew William Nanna, carpenter tools. Real estate to be sold and money put on interest, for wife Sarah. At wife's death, estate to be sold and money divided among nephew William, Sarah Stringer, and Tacy Nanna, equally.
Execs: Christopher Loeser, Job Roberts. Wit: Miles Abbett Isaac Cleaver.

RESH, ELIZABETH. New Hanover.
Aug 4, 1804. Feb 5, 1805. 2.438
To daughter Catharine, household goods. Rem. of estate to be sold and money divided in to 2 equal shares. To daughter Catharine, one part. To son in law Andrew Swartz, one part, in trust for grandsons of daughter Barbara, deceased.
Exec: Brother Abraham Delp. Wit: George Shwink, Thomas Bolig, Daniel Yost.

BARTOLET, SAMUEL. Frederick.
Dec 20, 1804. Feb 11, 1805. 2.440
To wife Elizabeth, all estate until daughters Esther and Elizabeth are 18. If she remains a widow. When daughters are 18, personalty to be appraised, wife to live with mother in law Susanna Fry, and to receive interest of 300 pds. yearly during widowhood. If she marries to receive interest of 200 pds. To sons John and Daniel, farm in Frederick, 184 acres, 40 perches subject to maintenance of wife, at valuation. To each child 500 pds. when 21. Son Samuel to receive 75 pds. more than other sons. To son Daniel 75 pds. more than other sons. To daughter Susanna 50 pds. To daughter Esther and Elizabeth, 50 pds. At wife's death personalty to be sold and money divided among children: Abraham, Jacob, Samuel, John, Daniel, Susanna, Esther and Elizabeth. 5 acres of woodland to be sold.
Execs: Wife Elizabeth, sons Abraham and Samuel. Wit: Francis Leidig, Benjamin Markley.

PAUL, JOSEPH. Whitemarsh.
Sept 27, 1803. March 16, 1805. 2.443
To children of brother Jacob Paul, household goods equally. To sister Margaret, widow of John Neatsmith, principle and interest in farm. To brother Jacob, incomes of land. To nephew Joseph Paul, of brother Jacob, land in Germantown, 45 acres subject to the payment of 300 pds. to

brother Jonathan, and 300 pds. to sister Anna, and Thomas. To Joseph Paul, 40 acres in Roxborough. To Joseph Paul, son of Jacob 12 1/2 acres in Whitemarsh. To brother Jacob and his son Samuel, land in Whitemarsh, subject to the payment of 300 pds. to nephew John Paul, and 300 pds. to nephew Joseph Paul. To brother Jacob, and his Samuel, land in Upper Merion. Rem. of realty to be sold and money with rem. of estate to be divided into 4 parts. To children of brother John, deceased, one part. To children of brother Jonathan, one part. To children of brother Jacob, one part. To children of brother Isaac Potts, deceased, one part.
Execs: Brother Jacob Paul, and his son Joseph Paul. Wit: John Evans, Cadwalder Evans, Jr.

EVANS, ELIZABETH. Gwynedd.
May 13, 1804. March 16, 1805. 2.445
To Margaret Hubbs, chest. To nieces Mary Hubb and Margaret Hubb, wearing apparel equally. To Jesse Foulke, William Foulke and James Jones, Jr., part of land in Gwynedd, 1/2 a. in trust for Preparative Meeting of Friends, in Gwynedd. To brother John, rem. of land in Gwynedd, and personalty.
Exec: Brother John. Wit: William Morris, Cadwalder Evans, Jr., Edward Jenkins.

THOMAS, DAVID.
____. March 25, 1805. 2.446
To sons Aubrey, Thomas and William Thomas, all estate. To daughter Martha, 35 pds. To daughter Lydia, 50 pds. and cow. To daughter Eleanor, 50 pds. and cow. To daughter Hannah Yocum, 5 pds. To grandson William Yocum, 5 pds.
Execs: John Jones, son Aubrey. Wit: Samuel Evans, Rosannah Rhoads.

MALSBERGER, JACOB. New Hanover.
Jan 13, 1805. April 2, 1805. 2.447
To wife Catharine, household goods, farm, until son Joseph is 21. Rem. of personalty divided as follows: son Joseph to receive interest of 150 pds. when 21. To daughter Elizabeth, 150 pds. Rem. divided as follows: to wife Catharine, 1/3 part. To children of daughter Catharine, 1/7 part. To son Jacob, 1/7 part. To daughters Susanna, Peggy, Mary, Elizabeth and son Joseph 1/7 part each. To son Joseph, farm, when 21 subject to valuation. Wife to receive interest of 1/3 of valuation. To children of sister Catharine, 1/6 part of remaining 2/3. Rem. divided into 5 equal parts. To Jacob, Mary, Susanna, Edward, Peggy and Elizabeth, one share each. At wife's death her share divided among 6 children.
Execs: Wife Catharine, and son Joseph. Wit: Andrew Shaner, George Lenoard.

WALTON, MARY. Upper Dublin.

June 10, 1799. April 11, 1805. 2.449
To son Silas, bible and 5 s. To grandson John Walton, 5 s. To son Jeremiah, 5 pds. Rem. of estate to be divided into 4 parts. To daughter Elizabeth, one part. To 3 other daughters: Mary Bond, Phoebe Shoemaker, Amy Clark, one share each.
Execs: Son Silas, and son in law Daniel Shoemaker. Wit: Thomas Hallowell, Samuel Gummere.

HOUGH, EDITH. Montgomery.
Aug 22, 1804. April 16, 1805. 2.450
To son Silas, land left of brother Silas Hart. He to pay 25 pds. to son Thomas, and 25 pds. to granddaughter Edith of son John. To granddaughter Susanna Crispen, feather bed, and wearing apparel to granddaughter, Mary Dickinson, trunk, etc. Rem. of estate divided among grandchildren: Mary Dickinson, Edith Hough, charlotte Hough, Myra Gilbert, Sarah Hough, Nancy Hough, equally.
Codicil dated Feb 2, 1805. Mary Dickinson's share to her daughter Caroline. [*Annotation states Mary lately dec. ? Eli Dickinson father of Caroline.*]
Execs: Son Silas, and nephew Joseph Hart. Wit: Charles Humphrey, Henry Weaver.

JOHNSON, BENJAMIN. Worcester.
June 18, 1800. April 19, 1805. 2.452
To wife Susanna, household goods, and interest of 100 pds. during widowhood. To sons: William and Joseph, farm, and 100 pds. each. To daughter Catharine, part of household goods. Rem. divided among children: Isaac, Peter, John, Racheal, Elizabeth and Catharine. Son Isaac to receive 50 pds. less than other children.
Execs: Henry Hunsicker, Benjamin Johnson. Wit: John Hunsicker, John Tyson.

McCREA, JOSEPH. Norriton.
May 19, 1800. April 27, 1805. 2.453
To wife Mary, farm, 77 3/4 acres and household goods. To son John farm, 121 acres and 10 acres subject to the payment of 100 pds. To daughter Margaret, and at her decease 50 pds. To grandsons Joseph White, and John White. To son John, Bible. To daughter Jane, 200 pds. To daughter Hannah, 10 pds. To daughter Margaret, farm of 15 acres and interest of 100 pds. To daughters Margaret and Rebecca, clock. At wife's death, farm to daughter Rebecca, subject to the payment of 5 pds. to Rebecca Smith. Rem. of estate to two daughters Margaret and Rebecca.
Execs: Wife Mary, son John, and daughter Rebecca. Wit: Benjamin Rittenhouse, David McNeeley, Frederick Conrad.

HAAF, CHARLES. Skippack and Perkiomen.
July 13, 1802. April 29, 1805. 2.455

To son Jonah, farm, 100 acres and 30 acres bought of Elizabeth Patton, subject to 210 pds. and interest, to widow of David Rinerd, of Limerick, and 100 pds. To granddaughter Catharine Wireman, when 21. To grandson Charles Wireman, land 32 acres when 21 and rem. of track adjoining said son Jonah's land. To granddaughter Sarah Wireman, 400 pds. when 21. To granddaughter Catharine Wireman, 400 pds. when 21. To 2 granddaughter Sarah, and Catharine, pewter, etc., equally. To Charles Wireman, rem. Personalty to be sold.
Execs: Son Jonah, son in law, Jacob Wireman. Wit: John Hollabush, Samuel Evans.

WILLS, JANE. Plymouth. Jan 29, 1804. May 2, 1805. 2.458
To son Michael, farm, 175 acres in Plymouth, and all reality subject to the payment of the following. To grandson Michael Mather, and to granddaughter Jane McCalla, the son and daughter of my late daughter Elizabeth, 50 pds. each. and to grandchildren of son John, Sarah, Jane and John, 50 pds. each, and 50 pds. with interest, to Lawrence Egbert; 50 pds. with interest to Benjamin Rambo; 87reatl pds., 10 s. with interest to John Markley, and to daughter in law Mary Wills, widow of son Jeremiah, 100 pds. to grandson Michael Wills of son Jeremiah 50 pds. Rem. of estate to son Michael. [*William Gabb is married to granddaughter Rebecca, daughter of son Jeremiah, daughter Mary Whiteman has received deed for 25 acres in Plymouth, wife of ___; daughter Rebecca Mather, wife of Michael who has received a like quantity.*]
Execs: Son Michael and kinsman Thomas Wilson, Sr. Wit: Jesse Wager, Charles Ramsey.

SPEES, ANTHONY. Douglass.
Nov 21, 1804. May 22, 1805. 2.460
To wife Margaret, household goods, and maintenance. To son Daniel, farm, and 2 tracks in Douglass, containing 103 acres subject to the payment of 600 pds. and to wife Margaret maintenance, and 6 pds. yearly. To daughter Catharine, wife of Moses Kehl, 25 pds. To daughter Mary Margaret, wife of George Deugler, 25 pds. To children of daughter Christiana, deceased, wife of George Gucker, 25 pds. and rem, 200 pds. to son Daniel. Rem. divided among children and grandchildren.
Execs: Sons in law Moses Kehl, and George Dengler. Wit: Henry Geyer, John Bickel, Peter Richards.

GARRETT, CHRISTOPHER. New Hanover.
Nov 14, 1801. May 23, 1805. 2.463
To wife, household goods. To daughter Elizabeth Davis, 10 pds. To son James 20 pds. Rem. of estate to be sold and money divided among 5 children: James, Elizabeth, Ruth, Thomas and Hannah, except 400 pds. wife to receive interest. At wife's death 400 pds. divided among children.
Execs: Wife and son Thomas and James Wit: Sarah McClintick, Robert McClintick, John Brooke.

SANDS, ELIZABETH. Plymouth.
Feb 12, 1805. May 30, 1805. 2.464
To daughters Esther and Elizabeth, household goods, and wearing apparel. To son Aaron, stove. When daughter Elizabeth is 21, farm to be sold and money divided among children: Esther, Richard, Joseph, William, Isaac, Jacob, Ezra, Aaron and Elizabeth. Rem. to sons.
Exec: Son Joseph. Wit: Hilary Norny, Andrew Norny.

COLLEY, ABIGAIL. Plymouth.
Jan 18, 1805. June 1, 1805. P66
To son Jonathan, 5 pds. To grandson Alexander and Jonathan 25 pds. To granddaughter Alice Colley, bed, etc. To granddaughter Rebecca Pennington, 11 pds., 5 s. To granddaughter Abigail Wager, 5 pds. To granddaughter Abigail Pennington, 5 pds. To Preparative Meeting of Friends 5 pds. To daughter Mary Wager, 1/2 of wearing apparel. To granddaughters Mary Wager, use and interest of rem. of estate
Execs: son in law Benjamin Wager, Nathan Potts. Wit: William Armstrong, John Armstrong.

WAMPOLE, CATHARINE. Towanemcin.
Feb 7, 1804. Feb 25, 1805. 2.467
To grandson Frederick Wampole of son Jacob, 20 pds. etc. To granddaughter Catharine, wife of John Adam Cressman, 10 pds. etc. To granddaughter Catharine, of son Abraham 10 pds. etc. To granddaughter Catharine, of Jacob Kline, 10 pds. etc. To granddaughter Catharine, of Daniel Kop, 10 pds. etc. To granddaughter Catharine of son Jacob 6 pds. etc. Wearing apparel to 4 daughters: Catharine Hartzel, Maria Eve Kop, Magdalena Kline and Elizabeth Benner. Rem. to 5 children.
Execs: Son in law Ludwig Benner. Wit: Michael Shoemaker, Abraham Andrews.

THOMAS, EVAN. Whitpain.
Jan 18, 1805. March 14, 1805. 2.469
To daughter Rachel, household goods. To son David, farm, 100 acres subject to legacies. To daughter Margaret $150. To daughter Susanna, $80. To John, Samuel Joseph, Rachel and Evan, $115 each.
Exec: Son David. Wit: Robert Thomas, John Shearer, Joseph Lewis.

FETZER, FREDERICK. Gwynedd.
May 20, 1800. July 22, 1805. 2.470
To son John, 50 pds. To daughter Elizabeth Moreham's children: Rachel, Elizabeth, Joseph and John, 10 pds. each. Rem. of estate to 4 children: Andrew, John, Isaac, and daughter Eve Bisbing.
Execs: Sons Andrew and John. Wit: Job Roberts, George Land.

SIDDONS, ANTHONY. Whitpain.
June 18, 1805. Aug 13, 1805. 2.471

To granddaughter Jane Tyson, bed, etc. To granddaughter Maria Biddle, spoons, etc. To grandson, Isaac Biddle, wearing apparel. Rem. of estate to be sold and divided among 2 granddaughters Jane Tyson and Maria Biddle.
Execs: Evan Evans, Job Roberts. Wit: David DeHaven, Joseph Richards.

MARTIN, RACHEL. Douglass.
March 30, 1795. Aug 13, 1805. 2.472
To niece Rachel Lewis, table, etc. To niece Mary Culp, pewter. To niece Rachel Culp, 5 pds. To niece Rachel Ives, beding, etc. To niece Mary Ives, saddle, etc. Farm in Charleston, Chestor County, to be sold and money divided among 3 sisters: Elizabeth Lewis, Susanna Culp and Rebecca Ives.
Exec: William Ives. Wit: Jesse Ives, Samuel Baird.

EDWARDS, ROBERT. Horsham.
Jan 26, 1801. Aug 13, 1805. 2.473
To son John, 18 pds. To son Edward, 33 pds. To son David, 8 pds. Estate to be sold and money divided among children as follows: to sons: John, Edward, David, 1/5 part each. Rem. divided among 2 daughters Elizabeth and Ann.
Execs: Sons Edward and David. Wit: Hugh Foulke, Cadwalder Foulke, Jr.

JENKINS, JOHN. Gwynedd.
May 24, 1805. Aug 29, 1805. 2.474
To wife interest of 400 pds. and household goods. To daughter Sarah, 200 pds. To daughter Elizabeth, 300 pds. To son Owen, 100 acres subject to the payment of 20 pds. yearly to School at Hatfield. To step daughter Margaret Clayton, 30 pds. To son Jesse, 50 acres. To son John 100 acres subject to maintenance of wife and 400 pds. At wife's death, her legacy to daughter Elizabeth, Margaret Clayton and daughter Sarah. To son Edward, 65 acres. Rem. divided among children.
Execs: Sons Jesse and John. Wit: William Hoffman, Abijah Miller, Joseph Lewis.

EVANS, MARY. Gwynedd.
May 25, 1802. Aug 30, 1805. 2.476
To children: William and David Hillis and [Ann Pugh?] Pug, and Mary Baldwin, children to sister Ann Hillis, 20 pds. each. To Abigail Walton and Mary Reymy, children of sister Margaret, 10 pds. To Hannah Spencer, 10 pds. To niece Phebe Wood, 10 pds. To Sarah Geary, 10 pds. To Samuel Evans, 10 pds. To Joseph Evans, stove and 5 pds. To Thomas Evans, 8 pds. To Thomas Foulke, son of Joshua, 5 pds. To Abraham Uptecrave, 10 pds. To John Harboe of Limerick, 1/2 income of farm. To children of sister Anna and Margaret, rem. of estate.
Execs: Levi Foulke, Joseph Shoemaker. Wit: Joseph Lewis, Ann Rhoads.

SHICK, LUDWIG. Douglass.

Nov 23, 1800. Sept 16, 1805. 2.478
To mother, household goods and maintenance. To sons Henry and Frederick, reality at valuation of 500 pds. To mother, interest of 100 pds., remaining 400 pds. to 4 children: Barbara, wife of Christian Barbow, Rosina, wife of Ludwig Benner, Elizabeth, wife of John Gilbert, and son John.
Execs: Sons John and Henry. Wit: Samuel Moyer, John Wien.

KLINE, GABRIEL, Lower Salford.
Jan 20, 1805. Sept 16, 1805. 2.480
To wife Elizabeth, household goods and interest of 800 pds. To sons: Isaac, John, Jacob and Gabriel, 10 pds. Rem. of estate among children and grandson.
Execs: Sons Isaac and John. Wit: Joseph Tyson, Samuel Harley.

HUGHES, OWEN. Towamencin.
Aug 28, 1805. Sept 21, 1805. 2.481
To wife Elizabeth, 24 pds. and household goods. To daughters Elizabeth and Ann privileges and house. To son John, 220 pds. To son Isaac, 220 pds. To son Owen, 200 pds. To daughter Catharine, 120 pds., at wife's death. To daughters: Sarah, Elizabeth and Ann, 100 pds. and 20 pds. each at wife's death. To granddaughter Sarah, of Levi Hughes, 20 pds. To son Edward, farm, 148 acres subject to privileges of wife. Rem of estate to son Edward.
Execs: Sons John and Edward. Wit: Benjamin Van Fossen, Henry Snyder.

REITER, GEORGE MICHEAL. Upper Hanover.
April 20, 1805. Sept 21, 1805. 2.482
To 2 sons Micheal and John, 50 pds. each. To daughter Margaret, 50 pds. Farm to be divided into 3 parts and valued, and sons and sons in law to have right of acceptance, if they accept same to be sold. Rem. of estate divided into 11 parts. To children of son George, one part. To daughter Catherine, widow of John Conrad Reller, one part. To children of deceased daughter Elizabeth, wife of John Wetzel, one part. To Eve, wife of Frederick Sano, but now of Peter Heebner, one part. To daughter Martha, one part. To children of deceased daughter Mary Elizabeth, wife of Peter Kline, one part. To Barbara, wife of George Adam Blank, one part. To son Micheal, one part. To son John, one part. To daughter Mary, wife of Frederick Wilhalm Geisenheimer, one part. To son Peter, one part. To grandson George Reiter, 20 pds. to be paid by son George. To daughter Eve, 100 pds. Rem. to 2 sons and one daughter. To wife Catharine, household goods and 100 pds.
Execs: Sons Micheal and John. Wit: Philip Reed, Adam Bosert, Conrad Hillegass.

TYSON, RYNEAR. Abington.
Sept 2, 1805. Sept 23, 1805. 2.486

To nephew Rynear Tyson of brother Peter, 100 pds. To sisters Mary Hallowell and Hannah Thomas, 45 pds. each, yearly. At their death 750 pds. to their children. To brothers Peter and Benjamin, personal estate, and reality, subject to legacies.
Execs: Brothers Peter and Benjamin. Wit: Thomas Livezey, Joseph Lukens.

LEIBENGUTH, JOHN. Douglass.
July 14, 1805. Oct 12, 1805. 2.487
Rem. of farm and household goods, to wife Elizabeth. At wife's death farm to be sold and money divided among 5 children: Ann, Rachel, Solomon, Samuel and Thomas.
Execs: Wife Elizabeth and George Keyser. Wit: Henry Yohn, John Miller, Peter Richards.

MARPLE, ENOCH. Norriton.
Sept 21, 1805. Oct 15, 1805. 2.489
To wife Mary, rem. of estate.
Exec: Wife Mary. Wit: Richard Corsen, Andrew Norny.

WARNER, ISAAC. Lower Merion.
July 6, 1805. Oct 29, 1805. 2.489
To wife Hannah, all estate. To Robert Smith, one feather bed, $80 etc. To cousin William Warner, 67¢. To cousin Isaac Roberts, at wife's death, wife's share.
Execs: Cousin Isaac Roberts, and Abel Thomas. Wit: Henry Colflesh, Benjamin Holland.

BEEN, HENRY. Worcester.
Oct 18, 1803. Nov 12, 1805. 2.491
To son John, 100 pds. To grandchildren: John, Henry and Peter Been, 10 pds. each and personalty. To grandchildren: Margaret, Elizabeth, and Susanna, 5 pds. each. Extra money divided among John and Jacob.
Exec: Son John. Wit: Peter Johnson, John Been.

McCOLOUGH, JAMES. Moreland.
Aug 31, 1805. Nov 12, 1805. 2.492
To nephews, William and John McColough, of Ireland, 20 pds. each. To Nathan Kinman's wife Jane, 20 pds. To nephew James McColough, 5 s. To Elizabeth Shaw, lot and buildings. To Isaac Daniel, 3 pds. Rem. to nephew William McColough, of Philadelphia.
Execs: William McColough. Wit: Jacob Thaw, John Wright.

BLARE, JONATHAN. Worcester.
Oct 5, 1805. Nov 21, 1805. 2.493
To wife rem. of estate.
Execs: Wife and Mordecai Jones. Wit: Daniel Shoemaker, Bandal Osborn.

LEVERING, MARGARET. Springfield.
___, 1802. Dec 11, 1805. 2.494
To niece Mary Sturges, household goods. To sister in law Elizabeth Levering, close press. To John Rasor, stove. To Barnabas Colston, cow, and rem. of household goods.
Execs: Barnabas Colston, Peter Streeper. Wit: Peter Streeper, Barnabas Colston.

ADAMS, MARGARET. Horsham.
April 23, 1796. Dec 16, 1805. 2.495
To sister Sarah, wearing apparel. To Elizabeth, of son in law James Dunn, 5 pds. To grandson James Dunn, 10 pds. to William Dunn, 5 pds. Rem. of estate to daughter Margaret Dunn.
Exec: James Dunn. Wit: John Fisher, Jr., Hiram McNeill.

HANIS, JOHN. Montgomery.
Feb 27, 1799. Dec 23, 1805. 2.496
To son Isaac, 15 pds. To granddaughter Elizabeth Hanis, of son John, 15 pds. To grandson Samuel Hanis, 15 pds. To grandson Benjamin Hanis, 15 pds. To grandson John Hanis, 15 pds. To grandson Jacob Hanis, 15 pds. Children of son Isaac, to have equal share. Rem. of estate divided among grandchildren and children.
Execs: John Hanis and James Wilson. Wit: Thomas Wilson, John Hanis, and Jacob Medera.

STERIGER, PETER. Upper Dublin.
Jan 4, 1804. Jan 17, 1806. 2.498
To wife Elizabeth, interest of rem. of estate At her death or marriage, divided among children: Margaret, John, Mary, David, Elizabeth, Peter, Martha, Sarah, and William equally.
Execs: Edward Burk, and wife Elizabeth. Wit: Joshua Wood, Jonathan Scout.

WILLIAMS, ANTHONY, Cheltenham.
April 23, 1805. Jan 20, 1806. 2.499
To wife Rachel, 60 pds. yearly, maintenance of 1015 pds., household goods. To son Joseph, farm, where he lives, in Whitemarsh and Springfield, except 10 acres to sons John and Anthony, and subject to the payment of 20 pds. yearly to wife. To son Joseph, 1/2 farm of 230 acres and 140 perches in Bald Eagle. To son John, farm in Cheltenham, except lot to son Anthony subject to the payment of 20 pds. yearly to wife. To son John 1275 pds. etc. To sons John and Anthony, lot 5 acres, 10 perches. To son Anthony lot and buildings in Cheltenham subject to mortgage and other half of farm, and subject to 20 pds. to wife yearly. To son Anthony 1745 pds. Rem. of personalty to sons John and Anthony.
Execs: Wife Rachel, sons Joseph, John and Anthony. Wit: Benjamin Mather, Edward Edwards.

SHOEMAKER, GEORGE. Cheltenham.
Dec 27, 1805. Jan 25, 1806. 2.502
To nephew Charles Roberts, $500. To brother Isaac Shoemaker, $500. To wife Sarah, farm, 96 acres, 10 perches subject to personalty and subject to the payment of above legacies.
Execs: Wife Sarah, brother in law Joseph Bird. Wit: Thomas Shoemaker, Silas Yerkes.

ROBERTS, JOHN. Merion.
April 2, 1765. Jan 20, 1806. 2.504
To son John, farm, of 55 acres. To wife Susanna, room and maintenance. To son Isreal 20 pds. To daughter Phebe, 10 pds. To children: Robert, Elizabeth, Jane, Mary and Hannah 5 s. each. To wife Susanna, rem. of estate
Execs: Wife Susanna, and son John. Wit: John Roberts, John Price and John Kite.

MILES, SAMUEL. Cheltenham.
____, 1805. Jan 29, 1806. 2.505
To exrs. $2000 for executing will. To daughter Hannah, wife of Joseph B. McKean, farm in Cheltenham (except part divised to daughter Mary Miles) containing 108 acres. To daughter Mary Miles, part of farm, 41 acres, 146 perches and land purchased of Richard Lake, 22 acres, 122 perches and land purchased of John Jones, containing 25 acres, 8 perches subject to mortgage of 500 pds. To daughter Mary, one share in Philadelphia Library. To Joseph B. McKean, John Miles and Joseph Miles, lands in Spring Township (except land where son Samuel lives). To be sold and money to be put on interest for Abigail Potts, wife of Thomas Potts, and her children. To Joseph B. McKean, K Miles and Joseph Miles, land purchased of John Hopson, 300 3/4 acres and other lands to be sold and interest to daughter Abigail Potts and children. To Joseph B. McKean, John Miles and Joseph Miles, farm, where son William lives, 150 acres and 150 acres received from brother Richard in trust for son William and his wife and children. To sons: John, Joseph, and Charles, 7 tracts adjoining Furnace Lands. To son Samuel house, where he now live, in Milesborough. To exrs. $1000 for executing son Samuel's will. To son Joseph lot in Milesborough, No. 1. watch, and $1000 etc. To Joseph B McKean, John Miles and Joseph Miles, $4444.44 in trust for daughter Rebecca, widow of son James and her children. To sister Hannah, $133.33 yearly. To daughter in law Rebecca Miles, and her children, $3066.67. To exrs. rem. of land to be sold and money divided among legatees. To daughter Abigail household furniture. Rem. of estate to sons: Samuel, William, Vister Miles, John Miles, Joseph and Charles Miles, daughter Hannah McKean, Abigail Potts and heirs of son James.
Codicil dated Dec 28, 1805. Exrs. to pay daughter Abigail's share to her or her children. Son Samuel's share to go to the rem. of estate. To Lowry Miles widow of son Samuel $133.33, quarterly.

Execs: Son in law Joseph B. McKean, son Joseph Miles. Wit: Benjamin Rowland, John Moore, and Benjamin Rowland, Jr.

BURKEY, SUSANNA. Franconia.
Nov 30, 1805. Feb 20, 1806. 2.515
To daughter Elizabeth Burkey, 50 pds. To son Abraham 250 pds. he to receive interest. To daughters: Mary, Magdalena, and Sarah, household goods, and wearing apparel, and rem. of estate.
Exec: Son John. Wit: Henry Furman, Michael Shoemaker.

TYSON, JOSEPH. Providence.
July 6, 1805. Feb 10, 1806. 2.516
To wife Mary personal estate and household goods, use of farm, until son Isaac is 21. Then real estate to be appraised, sons to have choice if not taken to be sold, and money divided among 6 sons: Jacob, Jona, Peter, Joseph, Joshua, and Isaac. After wife's and daughters legacies are deducted. To wife interest of 500 pds. to each daughter 150 pds.
Execs: Son Joseph and Henry Pennybecker. Wit: Benjamin Bean, John Thomas.

KASTNER, SAMUEL. Gwynedd.
Feb 21, 1806. Feb 28, 1806. 2.518
To Gwynedd Preparative Meeting, 10 pds. Rem. of personal estate divided among Elizabeth Miller and Rebecca Cooly. To Elizabeth Miller, 1/2 of farm, 81 acres. At her death to Rebecca Cooly. To John Cooly and Rebecca his wife, other half of farm. Exrs. to make deed for 116 acres in Upper Dublin.
Execs: Daniel Lukens, Amos Lewis. Wit: Job Roberts, Ellis Cleaver.

LUKENS, JOHN. Towamencin.
Sep 10, 1805. March 11, 1806. 2.520
To son John, farm, 110 acres. To son Isaac, farm, in Gwynedd 90 acres. Each son to pay 300 pds. to estate. To son Levi, 200 pds. and bond of 400 pds. To daughter Martha 200 pds. To grandson John Pawling, 5 s. Sons John and Isaac to pay 50 pds. yearly to son Levi of Virginia, and 50 pds. to daughter Martha. Rem. of personalty to be sold and money divided among sons: John, Isaac and Levi and daughter Martha. To son John, horse, etc.
Execs: Son John and Abraham Dresher. Wit: Henry Smith, Sr., Henry Sweitzer.

HUNSPERGER, CHRISTIAN. Franconia.
Jan 9, 1806. March 11, 1806. 2.521
To wife Catharine, household goods. To son Frederick, farm, in Franconia, 103 acres at valuation of 1000 pds. to be paid to wife, and maintenance. To son Abraham, 30 pds. To son Christian 12 acres or valuation of the same. To children: Abraham, Christian, Jacob, Frederick, Anna and

Catharine, rem. of estate equally.
Execs: Son Frederick and Abraham Clemmer. Wit: Micheal Shoemaker, Jacob Leidig, George Snyder.

CONRAD, ELIZABETH. Lower Merion.
Aug 2, 1804. March 26, 1806. 2.523
To 4 children: Rachel Sibley, John Conrad, Andrew Wilfong, and Elizabeth Bare, farm, 7 acres equally. Rem. of estate divided among 4 children.
Execs: Son John, son in law Jacob Sibley, John Wilfong, and John Bare. Wit: Owen Jones, Jonathan Jones.

ARMSTRONG, WILLIAM. Norriton.
Feb 11, 1805. March 31, 1806. 2.524
To 3 sons and daughter of brother Simon: William, John, James and Mary, 100 pds. each. Rem. of estate to be sold and money divided among: Ephraim, William, and Joseph Armstrong, and sisters: Mary, Sarah, Elizabeth, Margaret, Hannah, Rebecca and heirs of Ephraim, of Norriton, equally.
Exec: Brother Joseph Armstrong. Trustees, Frederick Conrad. Wit: William Shannon, Daniel Bare, Elizabeth Shannon.

EASTBURN, MARY. Abington.
Nov 14, 1803. April 5, 1806. 2.526
To daughter Rebecca interest of 300 pds. at her death her heirs to receive 100 pds. other 200 pds. to 2 sons Amos and David. To daughter Rebecca, household goods. To daughter Mary Phillips, 50 pds. and household goods. To daughters Rebecca and Mary, wearing apparel, etc. To son Amos, 100 pds. To son David, 100 pds. To grandson Joseph Eastburn, of son Samuel, 20 pds. To 5 sons: Joseph, Benjamin, Samuel, John and James, 5 pds. each. To granddaughter Mary Eastburn, of son James 5 pds. Rem. of divided among divided among son James, and daughter Mary Phillips.
Execs: Son John and daughter Rebecca. Wit: John Wilson, Oliver Wilson, John Wilson, Jr.

KRICKPAUMB, ELIZABETH. Lower Merion.
Jan 5, 1804. April 14, 1806. 2.527
To son Philip, 5 s. To daughters Elizabeth and Nancy, 5 s. each. Rem. of personal estate divided among children: Mary Conrad, and Barbara.
Execs: Son Conrad, son in law Seth Schnider.

CAMPBELL, THOMAS. Lower Merion.
April 3, 1806. April 23, 1806. 2.528
To sister Jane Stewart, wife of Francis Stewart, 10 pds. To sister in law Barbara Campbell of brother Joseph, 50 pds. Real estate to be sold and money divided among 5 children of deceased brother Joseph, Margaret, James, Elizabeth, Jacob and Joseph equally.
Execs: Algernon Roberts and Lloyd Jones. Wit: Andrew Anderson, Paul

Jones, Silas Jones.

FAMOUS, JOHN. Upper Merion.
April 21, 1806. May 5, 1806. 2.529
To wife Catharine, farm, during widowhood. At her death or marriage, to be sold and money divided as follows: to son William 5 pds. Rem. equally divided among children: John, Andrew, Jacob, George, Mary and Maria. To wife, personal estate.
Execs: Sons John and Andrew. Wit: David George, Samuel George, and Jonathan Roberts.

SMITH, ANDREW. New Hanover.
Sept 19, 1795. May 13, 1806. 2.531
To wife Catharine, household goods, and interest of 200 pds. and maintenance. To son , 250 pds. To daughter Anna Mary wife of John Smeck, 200 pds. To daughter Catharine, wife of Frederick Nevil, 130 pds. To daughter Magdalena, wife of John Dengler, 210 pds. To daughter Elizabeth, wife of John Spengler, 250 pds. To 2 grandson, John Newman and Jacob Newman, 150 pds. equally. To son Henry, farm, 173 acres, 136 perches subject to maintenance of wife. Rem. divided among sons: John, Andrew, and Henry. Farm purchased of Jacob Kop to be sold.
Execs: Sons John and Henry, and son in law John Dengler. Wit: George Bucher, John Richards.

SHELMIRE, JACOB. Moreland.
Sept 28, 1805. May 13, 1806. 2.533
To wife Martha, interest of 100 pds. for 3 years, after that to receive interest of 1/4 of estate also. To 3 sons: John, Samuel and Lewis, 1/4 part of estate each. At wife's death her share to be divided among children.
Execs: Son Samuel and brother John. Wit: George Shelmire, John Retherford.

SHEPERD, WILLIAM. Plymouth.
July 11, 1805. May 20, 1806. 2.535
To son William, farm, he to pay following legacies. To wife, 60 pds. yearly, and interest of 500 pds. at her death. Interest of 500 pds., divided among 5 children, equally. To son John, and daughters 400 pds. each. Daughter Catharine to receive interest only. rem. of estate to be divided among children. Wearing apparel to 3 sons. Rem. of personalty to be sold and divided among 5 children.
Execs: Sons John and William, and son in law David Lukens. Wit: John Van Dike, Samuel Livezey, Jacob Van Dike.

KENDIG, JOHN. Franconia.
Dec 26, 1800. May 29, 1806. 2.537
To wife Susanna, 50 pds. and household goods, and use of farm. To son Abraham, farm, 160 acres subject to maintenance of wife and 650 pds. To

daughter Magdalena, interest of 300 pds. to son John, bible. To son Joseph, mare. Rem. of divided among divided into 5 shares: to Abraham, John, Joseph, Fronica, her children to receive her share, and to children of daughter Susanna, wife of Jacob Echtle, and one share each.
Execs: Sons Abraham and Joseph. Wit: Micheal Shoemaker, Jacob Godshall.

ROBERTS, JOHN. Lower Merion.
Dec 10, 1800. June 2, 1806. 2.539
To nephew Joseph Wells, 20 s. To nieces Rebecca Ward and Mary Coton, and nephew Henry Wells, 20 pds. each. To niece Tacy Jones, wife of Benjamin Jones, rem. of estate.
Execs: Tacy Jones, William Davis. Wit: John Young, Isaac Warner.

SHINER, ANDREW. Douglass.
March 24, 1806. June 6, 1806. 2.540
To wife Juliana, household goods, and maintenance, and use of farm, At her death to be sold and money divided as follows: to son Henry 50 pds. Rem. divided among children.
Execs: Wife, son in law John Reifsnyder. Wit: Harman Reifsnyder, Peter Richards.

KEER, GEORGE. Cheltenham.
Dec 18, 1804. July 16, 1806. 2.541
To wife Rachel, income of estate, during widowhood. After wife's death or marriage estate to be divided into 9 parts. To daughter Elizabeth Keller, 1/9 part. At her death to her children. To daughter Sarah Plunket, one part. To daughter Mary Kinckle, one part. To John Shoemaker, and Thomas Webb, one share in trust for daughter Hannah Keer. To daughter Ann Blyler, one share. To daughter Rachel Keer, one share. To son George, one share. To daughter Margaret, one share. To grandchildren of George Haas and Ann Haas, of daughter Jemima, one share equally.
Execs: Son George and John Shoemaker. Wit: Jacob Mayer, Jacob Fetty, Jr.

SNYDER, JACOB, SR. Worcester.
May 24, 1794. Aug 6, 1806. 2.544
To wife Christina, interest of 200 pds. during widowhood and household goods. Rem. of estate to 3 daughters: Elizabeth, Catharine and Margaret, equally. At wife's death her share divided among 3 daughters.
Execs: Son John and Frederick Conrad. Wit: Henry Ricker, John Sebolt, Frederick Conrad.

MILLER, MARTIN. Lower Meron.
Oct 23, 1801. Aug 8, 1806. 2.546
To daughters Maria and Margaret, farm 5 acres. Rem. of estate to wife Susanna, at her death to 4 children: John, Mary, Margaret and Henrietta.

To daughter Henrietta, lot and privelege of other farm.
Execs: Wife Susanna and daughter Margaret, and Philip Sheaff. Wit: Nicholas Pechin, Benjamin H. Smith.

JONES, JOHN. Montgomery.
May 1, 1802. Aug 19, 1806. 2.548
To Gwynedd Preparative Meeting, 100 pds. To nephew Caleb Foulke, Sr., 50 pds. To niece Priscilla Foulke, 50 pds. To niece Lydia Spencer, 60 pds. etc. To nephew John Jones, Sr., 40 pds. To nephew Isaiah Jones, 20 pds. To cousin John Lewis, 20 pds. To nephew Evan Jones, 40 pds. To Elizabeth Walton, 3 pds. To sister in law Hannah Jones, silver spoons, etc. To niece Hannah Jones, bed, etc. To Hannah Jones and Priscilla Foulke, wearing apparel. To niece Hannah Jones and nephews John Jones, Henry Jones and Evan Jones, rem. of estate.
Exec: Nephew John Jones, Jr. Wit: James Shoemaker, Thomas Shoemaker, Jr.

MARIS, JOHN. Gwynedd.
____. Sept 10, 1806. 2.549
Farm to be sold and from money, Mother to receive 1000 pds. To sister Anna, 150 pds. To sister Jane, 100 pds. To sister Hannah, 50 pds. To sister Susanna, 200 pds. To sister Rebecca, 100 pds. Farming utensils to mother and sisters Anna and Jane.

DISMANT, BENJAMIN.
June 7, 1804. Sept 29, 1806. 2.550
To son Henry, $1.00. To son William, farm, of 50 acres at his death to grandson John Dismant. To son William, rem. of farm and personalty. To sons John and Benjamin, wearing apparel. To granddaughter Maria, bed, etc. To grandson Benjamin, case of drawers.
Exec: Son William. Wit: Benjamin Dismant, Christian Dismant.

CONRAD, JOHN. Horsham.
Sept 22, 1806. Oct 7, 1806. 2.551
To wife Susanna, maintenance, household goods, $80 yearly. To son Dennis, farm, subject to maintenance of wife, and $80 yearly. Personalty to be sold and money divided as follows: to grandson Jonathan, 100 pds. To son Jonathan, 150 pds. To son Dennis, 150 pds. Rem. divided into 4 parts. To son Jonathan, one part. To son Dennis, one part. To daughter Anna, 1/4 part. To daughter Hannah, interest of 1/4 part.
Execs: Sons Jonathan and Dennis. Wit: William Park Sr., Hiram McNeill.

SCHNEIDER, PETER. Plymouth.
April 26, 1806. Oct 10, 1806. 2.554
To son Henry, 300 pds. To son Samuel, 5 pds. To daughter Sophia, 300 pds. To daughter Christiana, interest of 300 pds. To German Lutheran Church in Whitpain, 10 pds. Personalty to be sold. To son Seth, house

and 1/2 of farm. To son John, farm, where he now lives and other 1/2 of farm; at son John death, his share divided between sons Henry and Seth. To son Henry, lot. To son Seth, lot, and use of limekiln. To son John, rem. of limestone. Rem. of estate divided among children.
Execs: Sons Henry and Seth. Wit: Benjamin Rambo, Nathan Potts, Benedict Potts.

SHEPERD, JOHN. Whitemarsh.
March 5, 1800. Oct 18, 1806. 2.557
To wife Eleanor, household goods, and maintenance, and 1/2 of income of estate. To son James, ground in Philadelphia, subject to 1/2 income of wife. To daughter Mary Conrad, lot in Philadelphia, subject to 1/2 of income to wife. To son James, and daughter Mary, farm in Whitemarsh, subject to 1/2 of income to wife. Rem. of estate to son James and daughter Mary.
Execs: Son James and wife Eleanor, and daughter Mary Conrad. Wit: Henry Katz, Sr., Jacob Dewees, John Hendricks.

ULYCH, MARGARET. Upper Dublin.
March 30, 1805. Nov 4, 1806. 2.559
To son Adam, 200 pds. To Christina Acuft, and Elizabeth Acuft, of daughter Mary, bed, and wearing apparel. To 5 children, Jacob, William, Joseph, Christina and Elizabeth Acuft, of daughter Mary, linen, etc.
Execs: Son in law Jacob Acuft, and George Haag. Wit: Casper Schlater, Joseph Acuft.

BROOK, MATTHEW. Providence.
Nov 3, 1806. Nov 14, 1806. 2.560
To son George, 300 pds. To daughter Sarah, 1000 pds. Farm to be sold. Rem. of divided among estate, sons William and George equally.
Execs: 4 sons: William, Thomas, George and Matthew. Wit: John Brook, Matthew Brook.

MATTES, JOHN JACOB. Plymouth.
Sept 14, 1803. Nov 19, 1806. 2.561
To wife Catharine, household goods and maintenance. To son Christopher, tools. Rem. of personalty to be sold and farm 85 acres and money to wife, for maintenance of children. To son Christopher, 100 pds. To son Philip, 50 pds. To son John, 25 pds. To son David, 25 pds. Wife to receive interest of 600 pds. At wife's death her share divided among 7 children: Catharine, Christopher, Philip, Maria, Hannah, John and David. Rem. of estate divided among 7 children.
Execs: Wife Catharine, and sons Christopher and Philip. Wit: George Berkimer, Frederick Dull.

GEORGE, ELIZABETH. Lower Merion.
March 25, 1800. Dec 1, 1806. 2.563

To Ann Ledom, wife of Isaac Ledom, gown, etc. To Eleanor Supplee, wife of Jonathan Supplee, gown, etc. To sister in law Susanna Jones, 30 pds. etc. To sister Hannah Williams, 30 pds. To brother Jacob Jones, 100 pds. etc. To sister in law Mary Jones, rem. of wearing apparel, etc. To niece Rebecca George, table, spoons, and 30 pds. To niece Sarah George, table spoons. To niece Hannah Foulke, widow, 10 pds. To nephew Algernon Roberts, 40 pds. To nephew John Roberts, 5 pds. To nephew Algernon, watch. To nephew Benjamin H. Smith, 30 pds. To Mary Davis, 30 pds. To Elizabeth, daughter of niece Rebecca George, buttons, to her sister Ann, table, to her sister Hannah, table, to her sister Jane, looking glass. To niece Mary Oxford, 10 pds. etc. To Anna Roberts, 10 pds. etc. To Martha Sancey, 10 pds. To Meeting House in Lower Merion, 15 pds. Rem. of estate to fund for building school.
Execs: Brother Jacob Jones, and nephew Algernon Roberts. Wit: Jacob Morris, Anthony Levering.

MOSER, GEORGE. Gwynedd.
July 2, 1805. Nov 21, 1806. 2.566
To wife Margaret, maintenance and 100 pds. and interest of 400 pds. To George Lever of Philip Lever, $40. To Benajah Bradford, of Samuel Bradford, $40. To Margaret Young, of John Young, $40. Personalty to be sold and farm 65 acres. To brother Christian Moser, wearing apparel, and 100 pds. Rem. of estate to 2 brothers Peter and Christian, and sister Barbara Neuman.
Codicil dated Aug 22, 1805. To wife Margaret, stove, and 50 pds. etc.
Execs: Brothers Peter and Christian. Wit: Melchior Schultz, John Anders.

RICHARDSON, JOEL. Abington.
Nov 1, 1806. Dec 31, 1806. 2.568
Farm to be sold 48 acres, 129 perches. To sister Sarah, 20 pds. To brother William, 100 pds. to sister Eleanor, 70 pds. Rem. of estate to brother Jonathan Richardson.
Exec: Jonathan Richardson. Wit: Joseph Waterman, Isaiah Waterman.

DETWILER, JOHN. Perkiomen and Skippack.
Nov 11, 1801. Nov 18, 1806. 2.559
To Minnonite Society in Skippack, 10 pds. Realty to be sold. Personalty to be sold among children, except wearing apparel. To sons: Abraham, Jacob and John, wearing apparel. To grandchildren, one Spanish dollar, each. To 3 sons aforesaid, 50 pds. each. Rem. of estate divided among children: Abraham, Jacob, John, Susanna, wife of Henry Kolp, Barbara, wife of Isaac Cassel, Mary, wife of John Landes, Elizabeth, wife of Nicholas Holderman, Hester, wife of Henry Hunsicker, Sarah, wife of John Moyer, Catharine, wife of Jacob Longacre, Hannah, wife of Jacob Benner, Magdalena, wife of Abraham Gotwals, and Salomy, wife of John Corner, equally. Daughter Susanna, to receive interest. To son in law Henry Hunsicker, German bible.

Execs: Son in law Henry Hunsicker, son Jacob. Wit: Isaac Hunsicker, John Tyson.

SUPPLEE, ANDREW. Norriton.
March 5, 1803. Dec 20, 1806. 2.571
To wife Susanna, household goods, 80 pds., 19 pds. yearly and maintenance. To son David, part of farm, with buildings and 50 pds. subject to 6 pds. yearly to wife. To son Enoch, rem. of land, subject to 10 pds. yearly to wife, and maintenance. To daughter Margaret Jones, 400 pds. subject to 3 pds. yearly to wife. To son Enoch, rem. of personalty.
Execs: Wife Susanna, and sons David and Enoch. Wit: Isaiah Bryden, Jacob Moyer.

NICE, JOHN. Upper Salford.
July 17, 1806. Dec 24, 1806. 2.573
To wife Maria Elizabeth, interest of 131 pds. and maintenance during widowhood. Rem. of Jacob to be sold for use of children and grandchildren. Estate to be divided among 4 children. To children of daughter Barbara, deceased, wife of John Heinneman, one part. To children of son George, deceased: Frederick, John and Franocia, one part. To daughter Elizabeth, one part. To son John, one part.
Execs: Philip Gable, and George Hartzel. Wit: Martin Keepler, John Shoemaker.

FISHER, CHRISTIAN. Abington.
Dec 18, 1806. Jan 9, 1807. 2.575
To niece Rebecca Mershon, daughter of sister Rebecca, 100 pds. To heirs of nephew William Coates, deceased, 50 pds. To niece Rachel Thomason, daughter of sister Susanna, 20 pds. Wearing apparel to sisters Rachel and Mary Logan, wife of Joseph Logan, equally. Rem. of estate to niece Rebecca Mershon.
Execs: George Williams, John L. Williams. Wit: John Clayton, William Grant.

MARIS, JANE. Gwynedd.
Oct 6, 1806. Jan 17, 1807. 2.576
To daughter Ann, 300 pds. To daughter Jane, 300 pds. To daughter Rebecca, 50 pds. To grandson Jesse Maris, 25 pds. To children of daughter Hannah, 75 pds. equally. To children of daughter Susanna, 50 pds. equally. Rem. of estate to daughters Ann and Jane, equally.
Codicil dated Nov 17, 1806. Daughter Jane being deceased, her share divided as follows: to daughter Ann, 75 pds. To children of daughter Hannah, 100 pds. To children of daughter Susanna, 75 pds. To daughter Rebecca, 50 pds. To grandson Jesse Maris, 25 pds. To sister Priscilla Foulke, 70 pds. To sister Lydia Spencer, 30 pds. To brother Levi Foulke, 50 pds. Rem. of estate to daughter Ann.
Execs: Brothers Levi Foulke, and Jesse Foulke. Wit: Cadwalder Foulke,

Edward Jenkins.

WISLER, JACOB. Upper Hanover.
May 12, 1806. Jan 20, 1807.
To wife Esther, household goods, and 10 pds. Rem. divided among children equally, except heirs of daughter Elizabeth, wife of Samuel Kean, to have nothing.
Codicil dated Aug 28, 1806. Son in law Henry Boyer to be charged with bond, 45 pds.
Exec: Son John. Wit: Andrew Greber, Jacob Fry.

DEAVS, JOHN. Whitemarsh.
Jan 8, 1807. Jan 30, 1807. 2.579
To wife Elizabeth, real estate and 1/2 of personalty. Rem. of personalty to be sold. At wife's death, farm to be sold. To sister Anna Deavs, at wife's death 40 pds. To brother Thomas, wearing apparel. Rem. of estate at wife's death, equally divided among brothers and sisters: Thomas, Ann, Joseph, Isaac, Martha Lukens, Samuel, son of Jonathan Deavs, Jesse and Isreal.
Exec: Brother Isaac. Wit: Ezra Comfort, David Shoemaker, George Peirce.

RAMBO, ABRAHAM. Upper Merion.
Nov 6, 1806. Feb 2, 1807. 2.581
To wife Ann, estate, until daughter Harriet is 15, then to be sold, except household goods to wife. Rem. divided as follows: to wife Ann, 1/3 part. To son Charles, 1/3 part. To son aaron, rem. To 3 daughters: Eleanor, Magdalena, and Harriet, other 1/3 of estate.
Execs: Wife and Jacob Shainline. Wit: George B. Holstein, John Famous.

LEVERING, PETER. Plymouth.
Nov 17, 1806. Feb 16, 1807. 2.583
To wife Hannah, rem. of estate
Execs: Wife Hannah, and John Hartman. Wit: John Hallowell, Joseph Thomas.

SHEPERD, MARTHA. Providence.
April 24, 1804. Feb 21, 1807. 2.583
To son Thomas, 5 pds. To son Robert, 5 pds. To daughter Mary, 5 pds. To daughter Jane, 200 pds. To son William, 67 pds. to grandson Joseph Davis, French Crown. Rem. of estate divided among 2 sons, James and William, and daughter Mary.
Execs: John McFarland, Nathan Potts. Wit: Matthias Boyer, Leonard Van Fossen.

BOSSERT, ADAM. Marlborough.
Jan 26, 1807. Feb 26, 1807. 2.585

To wife Margaret, household goods, maintenance use of house and 12 pds. during widowhood. son Henry to keep 100 pds. of purchased money of farm for his share. To son Adam, land 205 acres at valuation of 1300 pds. and 300 pds. to be put on interest for wife, during widowhood. Rem. of estate to 7 children: Henry, Adam, Elizabeth, John, Catharine, Robert and Philip.
Execs: Brother in law Henry Smith, George Mumbower. Wit: Charles Walter, Philip Reed.

GREBER, ANDREW. Upper Hanover.
March 24, 1804. March 7, 1807. 2.588
To six grandchildren of daughter Anna Margaret, deceased, wife of John Nicholas Meeth, 50 pds. equally. To son Ludowig, enough to make his share 122 pds. To son Andrew, enough till he receives 122 pds. and all children receiving same amount. Rem. of estate divided into 8 equal parts. To son Ludowig and Andrew, and daughter Mary Lizabeth, wife of Dieter Royer, and son Henry one share each. To children of daughter Anna Margaret, one share. One share to Eve now wife of Lorenz Kern. To Christina, wife of Peter Stachler, one share. To son John, one share.
Execs: Sons Ludowig and Henry. Wit: Andrew Greber, Peter Heilig.

PENNEBACKER, ANN. Providence.
June 12, 1797. March 14, 1807. 2.590
To son Derich, 5 s. To daughter Catharine, 20 pds. etc. To daughter Elizabeth, close press. To 4 daughters: Margaret, Catharine, Elizabeth and Hannah, linens, etc. Rem. of estate divided among 6 children: sons Jacob and Samuel and 4 daughters.
Exec: Son Jacob. Wit: Jacob Garber, John Garber.

FRY, ELIZABETH. Abington.
March 5, 1807. March 16, 1807. 2.591
To nephew Henry Meser, stove. To niece Elizabeth Shop, gown. To niece Catharine Meser, wife of Conrad Meser, and Magdalena Krier, wife of Peter Krier, shawl, and rem. of wearing apparel. Realty to be sold. To nephew Henry Meser, rem. of estate.
Exec: Nephew Henry. Wit: Benjamin Foster, Elizabeth Faribee.

KERR, ANNAOTILE. Whitpain.
Sept 26, 1799. April 7, 1807. 2.592
To sister Mary Hoover, gown, and 50 pds. etc. To 2 granddaughter. Nancy Hockamiller, and Mary Hockamiller, 50 pds. each, linen etc. Rem. of estate to son Jacob Hockamiller.
Exec: Son Jacob. Wit: John Wentz, Philip Sheneberger.

MOORE, THOMAS. Whitemarsh.
Jan 21, 1807. April 10, 1807. 2.594
To wife Barbara, income from 1/3 of estate. Personalty to be sold and

farm, money put on interest for children for 10 years. Marble Quarry to be sold. rem. of estate after 10 years, to be sold and money divided among children.
Execs: John Bennett, brother in law Henry Lynigar. Wit: George Peirce, Joseph Leedom, Harman Yerkes.

STEWART, SOLOMON. Norriton.
Jan 18, 1807. April 10, 1807. 2.596
To wife Hannah, household goods, and interest of 700 pds. and maintenance. To 3 brothers: Joseph, Robert and John, 100 pds. each, at wife's death. To cousin John Stewart, interest in saw-mill, and land etc. To brother Thomas, rem. of reality, and household goods. Farm to be sold.
Codicil: wife to have servant girl.
Execs: Wife Hannah, Stephen Porter, and John Stewart. Wit: Enoch Supplee, William Atchinson, Neal Conway.

ROSHON, PHILIP. Limerick.
Dec 12, 1807. April 11, 1807. 2.597
Estate to be sold, rem. divided into 5 parts. To sons: Peter, Jacob, Henry, Maria, wife of John Dar, Elizabeth, wife of Henry Agalmose, one share each. To sons Peter and Jacob, 30 pds. To son Henry, 10 pds. more than his share.
Execs: Sons Peter and Jacob. Wit: John Markley, John Nagle.

GYER, HENRY. New Hanover.
Jan 30, 1807. April 18, 1807. 2.599
To son Conrad, watch, etc. To daughter Elizabeth, household goods. To daughter Mary, household goods. To wife, 1/3 of estate, during widowhood. Rem. of estate divided among children.
Codicil dated Jan 10, 1807. All estate to be sold.
Execs: Michael Kratz, and Jacob Brendlinger. Wit: George Erb, Benjamin Messemer.

SAYLOR, VALENTINE. Providence.
Nov 13, 1805. April 30, 1807. 2.602
Estate to be sold. To wife Catharine, $106, maintenance and household goods. To son Peter, 300 pds. To son John, 300 pds. To son Valentine, 300 pds. To son Joseph, 300 pds. To daughter Mary Sowers, 200 pds. To daughter Catharine Sowers, 200 pds. To daughter Barbara Shafor, 200 pds. To daughter Hannah Highley, 200 pds. To daughter Elizabeth Botersuay, 200 pds. To daughter Sarah Spear, 200 pds. To granddaughter Mary Berkimer, 100 pds. Rem. of estate divided among children.
Execs: Son Peter, John Botersuay. Wit: John Edwards, Matthew Dell.

TAYLOR, CATHARINE. Merion.
Sept 18, 1796. March 25, 1807. 2.604
To daughter Elizabeth Righter, wearing apparel, beds, etc. To daughter

Hannah Mitchel, pewter. To son Lewellyn Joe Taylor, silver coins. To son John, bible. Rem. to be sold.
Execs: Son John and daughter Elizabeth. Wit: Isaac and Philip, Jonathan Garnalt, Jr., Hannah Carnalt.

HESTON, REBECCA. Gwynedd..
Feb 24, 1807. May 18, 1807. 2.605
To Preparative Meeting of Friends, in Gwynedd, 12 pds. To children of sister Susanna Heston, 5 pds. each. Rem. of estate to nephew Jesse Morris, and children of sister Hannah Wilson, and Susanna Heston.
Execs: Levi Foulke, Jesse Foulke. Wit: Cadwalder Roberts, Jr., Nathan Evans.

EARNEST, BALTZER. Cheltenham.
Dec 19, 1806. May 30, 1807. 2.607
To daughter Susanna Rush, 55 pds. To daughters Elizabeth Beek and Mgdalena Kisseller, 55 pds. each. To grandson Baltzer Earnest of son Baltzer, 25 pds. To son Baltzer Earnest 400 pds. To daughter Magdalena Kisseller, clock, etc. To daughter Catharine Hahn, interest of 50 pds. at her death, principal to grandson Henry Earnest. To son Henry, 350 pds. To 3 daughters: Susanna Rush and Elizabeth Beck, and Magdalena Kisseller, rem. of estate.
Execs: Sons Henry and Baltzer. Wit: Thomas Livezey, George Fitzwater.

WEBB, PAUL. Philadelphia.
June 26, 1802. Jan 29, 1807. 2.609
To Rector, Church Wardens and Vestry men of United Episcopal Churches of Christ, George and St. Peters Church in Province, 700 pds. Execs: Samuel Wheeler and Thomas Cumpston. To exrs. 50 pds. Wit: Joseph Donaldson, Leonard Snowden, Joseph Eastburn.

JACOBS, SAMUEL. Providence.
Aug 13, 1806. June 6, 1807. 2.610
To son Jeremiah, 40 acres subject to 300 pds. To son John, 40 acres subject to 300 pds. To son John, $65. etc. To son Jesse, 324 pds., 7 s., 6 d. To daughter Catharine, 300 pds. To wife Elizabeth, 300 pds. and household goods. To wife and son Richard, income of use of rme. of farm. Rem. of estate to son Richard, subject to maintenance of wife.
Execs: Wife Elizabeth and son Richard. Wit: Isaac Tyson, Isreal Einghurst.

SATZELER, FREDERICK. Providence.
April 19, 1801. July 7, 1807. 2.613
To wife Elizabeth, household goods, and maintenance, 8 pds. If she marries to have 40 pds. To son John, loom. To daughter Hannah, household goods, and 40 pds. To son Philip, 60 pds. Rem. of estate divided among children: Frederick, John, Margaret, Hannah, and Elizabeth.

Execs: Sons Philip and John. Wit: John Prizer, Henry Shelly, Benedict Garber.

SHUNK, FRANCIS. Trappe.
May 19, 1807. July 7, 1807. 2.614
To Rebecca Vanderslice, farm, and personalty.
Exec: Rebecca Vanderslice. Wit: Jacob Fry.

COLLUM, ALICE. Abington.
June 17, 1806. July 18, 1807. 2.615
To nephew Jonathan Leech, bed, etc. To granddaughter Elizabeth Robinson, bed, etc. To granddaughter Jane Blake, bed, etc. To granddaughter Alice Worrel, bed, etc. To daughter Rachel Banes and daughter in law Martha Collom and granddaughter Elizabeth Robinson, and Jane Blake, linen, equally. Rem. of estate to be sold and money divided as follows: to daughter Rachel Barnes, 1/3. To daughter in law Martha Collom, 1/3. To granddaughters: Elizabeth, Jane and Alice, 1/3.
Execs: Son in law Barker Barnes, and Thomas Webster. Wit: William M. Tetement, Susanna Tetement, and Mary Webster.

CLINE, MICHAEL. Lower Merion.
____. Aug 19, 1807. 2.617
To children of son Henry, 30 pds. equally. To children of son Matthias, 30 pds. equally. To daughter Barbara Cline, 3 acres, and household goods. To son John, rem. of realty and personalty.
Execs: Sons John and Peter and Barbara. Wit: Bartle Bartlesom.

MAY, FREDERICK. Upper Salford.
June 20, 1807. Aug 27, 1807. 2.618
To wife Lutina, household goods, and maintenance and 5 pds. yearly. To step daughter Eva Margaret, 5 pds. To son Christian, farm, 100 acres and rem. of personalty.
Exec: Son Christian. Wit: Philip Zirgler, John Egg, and John Barkey.

TORBET, SAMUEL. Plymouth.
Aug 6, 1791. Aug 27, 1807. 2.620
To father and mother, Thomas and Elizabeth, income of estate, at their death to brothers and sisters.
Execs: Brothers Thomas and James, and Joseph Crawford. Wit: Andrew Marowine, Godfrey Bachus.

CONRAD, PETER. Whitpain.
April 10, 1794. Oct 6, 1807. 2.622
To wife Hannah, 18 pds. and household goods. Estate to be sold and money divided among 2 daughters Tacey Styer, and Catharine Conrad. Codicil dated Dec 14, 1796. To wife Hannah, 30 pds. instead of 18 pds.
Execs: Son in law John Styer, and Catharine Conrad. Wit: Henry

Schneider and Nathan Potts.

FOSTER, GEORGE. Abington.
Jan 29, 1807. Oct 7, 1807. 2.623.
To wife Rebecca, maintenance and 24 pds. and household goods. To daughters: Ann, Martha Jodon, and Christian Shade, Rebecca Johnson, Amelia and Esther Fitzwater, 50 pds. each. To sons George and Benjamin, 84 acres, 82 perches, subject to legacies of daughters. To sons George and Benjamin, wearing apparel, and personalty.
Execs: Sons George and Benjamin. Wit: Amos Hallowell, Thomas Livezey.

SPERRY, JOHN. Gwynedd.
Aug 28, 1807. Oct 8, 1807. 2.625
To wife Elizabeth, 9 pds. yearly. To son Jacob, farm, etc., subject to 900 pds. Rem. of estate to be sold and divided into 5 equal parts. To children of George, John, Jacob, Margaret and Peter. Sons George and John to be charged with what they have received.
Execs: Son Jacob and Hugh Foulke. Wit: Cadwalder Foulke, Jr., Christian Smith.

DEAN, WILLIAM. Moreland.
July 18, 1806. Oct 16, 1807. 2.627
Estate to be sold and divided as follows: to wife Mary one part; 1/2 of rem. to son John. Rem. divided among children: Joseph, Benjamin, William, Samuel, and Sarah.
Execs: Joseph and Hiram NcNeill. Wit: Amos Addis, William Jennings.

CARL, JACOB. Upper Providence.
July 20, 1807. Oct 24, 1807. 2.628
To wife Christian, household goods, and use of farm. At wife's death, farm, to be sold and money divided among children: John, Barbara, Isaiah, Peter, Katie, and Elizabeth, Hannah and Abraham.
Execs: Wife Christina, sons Isaiah and Peter. Wit: John Hiltebriltel, Jacob Garber, Benedict Garber.

WIAND, ELIAS.
March 14, 1806. Oct 21, 1807. 2.630.
To wife Scharlota, use of farm. To son David, farm, 1500 pds. At wife's death, he to pay to daughters. To children of Lumbacks, 35 pds. Abraham Heil, 70 pds. Frederick Boyer, 70 pds. To Sibilla, 70 pds. To children of Henry Carl, 70 pds. To Catharine, 80 pds. etc. Son Andrew to provide maintenance for daughter Sibilla.
Execs: Wife Scharlota, and son Andrew. Wit: Samuel Evans, Owen Evans.

WHITE, JABEZ. Horsham.
Feb 16, 1807. Oct 24, 1807. 2.632
To wife 10 pds. yearly. To 3 daughters: Mary Hannah, and Lydia, 300 pds.

To Jane Thomas, wife of John Thomas, $100. To daughter Edith Carr, $30. Rem. of estate to 3 sons: John, Ayres, and Joseph, equally. To brother Joseph, wearing apparel.
Execs: Son John and son in law Samuel Tomkins, and Richard Shoemaker. Wit: Enoch Kenderdine, Thomas Kenderdine.

PENNEBECKER, REBECCA. Perkiomen and Skippack.
Oct 18, 1807. Nov 7, 1807. 2.633
To daughter Sibilla, wife of of Isreal Newberry, 1/2 of wearing apparel and 6 pds. To daughter Magdalena, 5 pds. To son Benjamin, 5 pds. To son Henry, 5 pds. To son Jacob rem. of estate.
Exec: Son Jacob. Wit: Henry Hunsicker, John Johnson.

KNOX, ANDREW. Whitpain.
June 6, 1806. Nov 5, 1807. 2.634
To wife Isabella, household goods, and maintenance, interest of 500 pds. At wife's death, personalty divided between daughters Martha and Mary. To son Robert, realty, except 45 acres subject to the payment of interest of 500 pds., to wife, and maintenance of wife and brothers John and James. At wife's death, son Robert to pay sons John and James, 18 pds. each, yearly. To daughter Mary, wife of David McNeily, 45 acres subject to 200 pds. interest of 100 pds. to sons James and John, and except of other 100 pds. to daughter Martha. To daughter Martha, household goods, etc. To son James, horse. To son John, horse. To son Andrew, $100. Rem. of estate to 6 children: David, Abner, Andrew, John, James, and Martha. Trustees, Frederick Conrad, Jacob Yost, Abraham Yost.
Execs: Wife Isabella, son Robert, and son in law David McNeily. Wit: Jacob Yost, Andrew Yost, Frederick Conrad.

EVANS, JOHN. Gwynedd.
Sept 14, 1807. Nov 6, 1807. 2.638
To son John, farm, 192 acres, feather bed, etc. To son Cadwalder, farm, and 2 tracts, 281 acres, household goods, subject to 500 pds. to grandsons Robert and John. To Levi Foulke, Jesse Foulke, and John Jones, Jr., 25 pds. in trust for Friends Meeting House. To Elizabeth Evans, 10 pds. To Jane Long, 10 pds. To son Cadwalder, 2/3 part, 50 acres, at valuation and pay to grandsons John and Robert. To grandsons, John and Robert, 500 pds. to be paid by son Cadwalder, and 1/2 valuation of 50 acres, 20 perches, other half of valuation to son Cadwalder, and 1/2 of rem. of estate To son John, 200 pds. To grandson Robert, 1/2 part of the remaining 1/2 part. To grandsons, Rowland and Evan, 200 pds. To grandson John, rem.
Execs: Son Cadwalder, and grandson Robert. Wit: John Wilson, Jr., Edward Jenkins.

CARR, WILLIAM. Horsham.
Sept 29, 1807. Dec 19, 1807. 2.640

Real estate to be sold, 147 acres, rem. of money to wife, Mary, until all the land is sold. To daughter Elizabeth, 50 pds. and household goods. Rem. of household goods, to wife Mary, and rem. of real estate for 8 years. To daughter Elizabeth, 100 pds. After 8 years, real estate to be sold, wife to receive 1/3 of interest. To sons 150 pds. each, and interest of 100 pds. Rem. to daughter Elizabeth, sons: Michael, Joseph, and Daniel, equally.
Execs: Wife and brother Joseph. Wit: Samuel Mann, John Carr.

HOUSER, ALBERT. Whitemarch.
Nov 9, 1799. Dec 24, 1807. 2.641
To wife Christina, farm, 20 acres, household goods and 5 pds. To son Allbright, horse, and farm, at valuation. If sons refuse to be sold and personalty; money divided among 4 children. To son Allbright, and daughter Mary, 10 pds.
Execs: Sons, Allbright, and Matthias. Wit: Casper Schlater, John Caler.

MATTSON, PETER. Upper Merion.
Oct 4, 1807. Dec 24, 1807. 2.642
To wife Catharine, use of real estate, until son Samuel is 16, then to 3 sons, they to provide maintenance, and household goods. To son Peter, 10 acres and other land. To son William, 15 acres. To sons Isaac and John, real estate subject to 10 pds. to grandson Peter of son Isaac, and 27 pds., 10 acres to exrs. To 3 sons: Robert, Job, and Samuel, rem. of realty, equally. To son Jonathan, $4.00. To 4 daughters: Susanna, Hannah, Elizabeth and Ann, 25 pds. each. To daughter Ann, case of drawers. To 4 daughters rem. of personalty.
Codicil dated Nov 6, 1807. To 3 sons, land along run, and land purchased of Matthias Colflesh, 2 acres, 131 perches and other realty.
Execs: Son Peter and Jonathan Rambo, and Nathan Potts. Wit: Joseph Rattiff, Benedict D. Potts.

SPEITLE, JOSEPH. Douglass.
Oct 14, 1800. Jan 2, 1808. 2.645
To wife Barbara, 200 pds. and household goods. To children, one share, each of estate.
Exec: Son in law Christian Romcich. Wit: Henry Richards, Matthias Richards.

EDGE, MARY. Horsham.
Feb 23, 1807. Jan 19, 1808. 2.646
To Jacob E. Jarrett, 300 pds. etc. To Charles Jarrett, 300 pds. when 21. To Mary Jarrett, bed, etc. To Sarah Jarrett, looking glass, $30, etc. To Susanna Jarrett, bed, etc. Rem. of estate divided among sister Rachel's children: Jacob, Mary, Charles, Sarah, Susanna. To 3 sisters, wearing apparel.
Execs: William Jarrett, Jacob Tomkin, Jr. Wit: William Jarrett, and Jacob

E. Jarrett.

SHOEMAKER, JOHN. Cheltenham.
Aug 30, 1805. Jan 23, 1808. 2.647
To wife Martha, household goods, and farm, interest of 150 pds. yearly. To nephew John Shoemaker, son of brother Joseph, watch. To Trustees of Friends Boarding School, in Westown, 50 pds., interest paid to wife. To son John, farm and other land, subject to the payment of yearly rent. To daughter Elizabeth, wife of Peter Robeson, 500 pds. and 60 pds. yearly, 1000 pds. to her children. To daughter Elizabeth, land in Cheltenham, at her death to her children, or to sons Charles and John. To son in law Peter Robeson, bond, 500 pds. To son Charles, clock, and farm. Rem. of personalty to 3 children: Charles, John, and Elizabeth.
Execs: Sons Charles and John. Wit: Thomas Livezey, John Fitzwater.

YERKES, JOSEPH. Moreland.
Nov 22, 1807. Jan 21, 1808. 3.1
To son Anthony, household, and real estate, subject to maintenance of Sarah Ashton. At his death to Susanna Yerkes, wife of son Anthony. To grandson Joseph Tomkins, house and lot in Philadelphia. 1/2 of money to son Anthony, from house, other half to grandson. Guardian of grandson, Joseph Ely. To granddaughter Elizabeth Lukens, $4000, when 21. John Shoemaker, Jr. Guardian of granddaughter. Rem. of estate to Susanna Yerkes.
Execs: Hugh Ely, John Shoemaker, and son Anthony. Wit: Jesse Harper, Sarah Wells.

GRESMER, CATHARINE. Upper Hanover.
Nov 10, 1790. Feb 9, 1808. 3.4
To Catharine, wife of John Gresmer, household goods. To Frederick Gresmer, clock. To children of Michael Hillegas, 50 pds. equally. To John Hillegas, 5 pds. To Eve, wife of of George Horlacker, 5 pds. To George Hillegas, 5 pds. To sister Catharine Gresmer, interest of rem. of estate
Exec: George Horlacker. Wit: Owen Garver, Peter Halaffer.

REIFF, GEORGE. Lower Salford.
Jan 21, 1808. Feb 13, 1808. 3.6
To wife Elizabeth, household, and 100 pds. and 60 pds. and interest of 1200 pds. At her death principle 1200 pds. divided among 6 children. Rem. of estate equally divided among 6 children: Abraham, George, Jacob, Daniel, Joseph, and Elizabeth, wife of of Christian Detwiler. Trustees Michael Zeigler and Henry Hunsicker.
Execs: Sons George Reiff and Jacob Reiff. Wit: Michael Zeigler and Henry Hunsicker.

OTTINGER, JOHN. Springfield.
June 1, 1802. Feb 29, 1808. 3.7

To son John, farm, 155 acres and household goods, wearing apparel, and personalty. To wife Margaret, privilige of house, son John to provide maintenance. Income of farm where Henry Stout lives and 3 pds. yearly. To daughter Sarah, farm, purchased of John Slingofflin, 53 acres subject to 1/2 of land to wife. To daughters: Elizabeth, Dorothy, Catharine, Ann and Sarah, 200 pds. each. To wife Margaret, 100 pds. To Ann and Rebecca, 15 pds. Rem. divided into 7 equal shares. Rem. divided among wife, son and 5 daughters.
Execs: Son John and son in law John Burk. Wit: A. Heyser, and William Heyser.

HANNAH, JANE. Norriton.
March 3, 1808. March 11, 1808. 3.11
To Hannah White, daughter of Abner and Jane White of Providence, 20 pds. To Robert White, 60 pds. To servants of Mary McCrea, 50 pds. equally. To Rebecca Smith, 5 pds. To Norriton Presbyterian Church, 10 pds. To Mary McNeely, wife of Daniel McNeely, bed, etc. Rem. of estate divided among niece Ann Hannah, and nephew John Hannah.
Execs: Hannah Stewart, and Robert and William White. Wit: John McCrea, Jane White.

GEYER, WILLIAM. Upper Hanover.
Aug 22, 1805. March 12, 1808. 3.12
To wife Anna Mary, household goods, and rem. of estate. To son Henry 20 pds. etc. To son Conrad 20 pds. etc., and daughter Catharine 10 pds. Rem. divided among 5 children: John, Michael, Henry, Conrad, and Catharine.
Exec: Son Conrad. Wit: Henry Borneman, John Detwiler.

POTTS, JOHN. Upper Dublin.
Dec 14, 1801. March 16, 1808. 3.14
To wife Hannah, income of estate, during widowhood. If she marries, 20 pds. yearly. To sons Thomas and Jesse, 50 acres. To son Jonathan, rem. of farm. To daughter Elizabeth, 24 pds. to be paid by 3 sons and maintenance. Rem. of estate to 3 sons and daughter equally.
Codicil dated Nov 22, 1807. Appoint son John as exr. instead of Jesse, who is deceased.
Execs: Sons Thomas and Jesse. Wit: Nathan Potts, Priscilla Potts.

BROWN, JOSEPH A.
Sept 15, 1807. April 2, 1808. 3.17
To wife Sarah, income of estate until daughter Mary is 21, Then 2/3 divided among 3 daughters.
Execs: Wife Sarah, Stephen Paterson. Wit: A. Brown, Elizabeth Brown.

SWENK, NICHOLAS. Lower Salford.
March 7, 1806. April 7, 1808. 3.18

To wife Anna Barber, 20 pds. and household goods, and 2 3/4 acres and 4 acres, 98 perches, interest of 400 pds. To son George, farm, 150 acres at valuation of 800 pds. To son George, 100 pds. of valuation. To son Jacob, 100 pds. To daughter Elizabeth, wife of Abraham Markley, Mary, wife of Michael Wagner, Barbara, wife of John Ot, 100 pds. equally. To granddaughter Elizabeth, wife of John Zeigler, 100 pds. Interest of 200 pds. to sons: George, Jacob, and to children of daughter Elizabeth and granddaughter Elizabeth Zeigler, equally. To granddaughter Mary, of son George, cow, etc. Son George to provide maintenance for wife. To daughter Mary Magdalena, wife of Andrew Gample, interest of 200 pds. To son Martin, 5 pds. To sons George and Jacob, books. Rem. of estate to sons Jacob and George, 1/4 part each, and granddaughter Elizabeth, wife of Abraham Markley, Mary wife of Michael Wagner, Barbara, wife of John Ot, 1/4 part to granddaughter Elizabeth 1/4 part. Trustees; Jacob Rife, Sr.
Execs: Sons George and Jacob. Wit: Michael Shoemaker, Samuel Harley, Isaac Kline.

ROBERTS, HUGH. Lower Merion.
Aug 17, 1801. April 8, 1808. 3.22
Personalty to be sold and farm, 130 acres. To Pennsylvania Hospital, 100 pds. To Philadelphia Dispensary, for Poor, 50 pds. To Pennsylvania Society, for Abolition of Slavery, 20 pds. To Preparative Meeting of Friends, in Lower Merion, 20 pds. To School House, 15 pds. To Algernon Roberts, and David Roberts, 15 pds. for School House. To John Roberts, and his sister Rebecca Roberts, 80 pds. each. To cousin Hannah Roberts, 80 pds. To Jonathan Robeson, and Thomas Robeson, 40 pds. each. To Rebecca wife of William Ward, 30 pds. To Mary, wife of John Cotton, 30 pds. To John Rawlins, 80 pds. To Ruth, wife of John Rawlins, 80 pds., feather bed, pewter, etc. To Nathan Rawlins, watch. To Anna Rawlins, bible. To Henry Wells, 40 pds. and 1/2 of wearing apparel. To Jacob Wells, 1/2 of wearing apparel. To Hugh Ward, son of William and Rebecca, 5 pds. To children of Jonathan Robeson: Conrad, Joseph, Ann, Elizabeth, and Mary, 5 pds. each. To 6 children of John Roberts, namely: Jeshu Roberts, Hannah Price, Sarah Thomas, Jane Tunis, Thaman Roberts, and Ann Trimble, 5 pds. each. To Algernon Robers, 30 pds. and to John Roberts, Millwright. To Sidney Jones, daughter of Phineas Roberts, 10 pds. and Mary, wife of Titus Yerkes, 10 pds. To Ellen Thomas, wife of Abel Thomas, 10 pds. To Anna Rawlins, wife of Nathan Rawlins, 5 pds. Rem. of estate to John Roberts, Rebecca Roberts, Jonathan Robeson, Rebecca Ward.
Codicil dated Jan 10, 1808. To Ruth Rawlins, wife of John Rawlins, 80 pds. made void. To Jonathan Jones, and William Hagey, 400 pds. They to pay Ruth Rawlins, interest yearly.
Execs: Algernon Roberts, and Jonathan Robeson. Wit: John Righter, Isaac Warner, Thomas George.

GEHRY, JACOB.
Oct 24, 1797. April 13, 1808. 3.27
To wife Gertrude, household goods, maintenance 150 pds. Son Jacob to provide maintenance for wife. To sons: Jacob, John, Peter and Michael, wearing apparel, equally. To daughters: Catharine, Elizabeth, and Rebecca, at wife's death, wearing apparel equally. Personalty to be divided among children, and grandchildren as follows: Jacob, John and Peter 250 pds. each. To son Michael, 250 pds. To daughters 125 pds. each. To children of daughter Ann Maria, late wife of John Hillegass 125 pds. equally. To daughter Catharine, wife of John Wagner, 1/2 of her share of estate, other half to her children of first husband, Michael Hillegas deceased. To children of John Adam, deceased, his share equally.
Execs: Sons Jacob and John. Wit: Casper Yeakel, Baltzer Schultz.

HALLOWELL, BENJAMIN. Abington.
Sept 14, 1799. April 13, 1808. 3.32
To 3 sons: Peter, Benjamin, and Isaac, wearing apparel. To son Peter, 12 pds. and interest of 100 pds. yearly, and farm 21 acres. At his death to his children. To son Benjamin, farm, where he lives, 1/2 of plantation in North westerly part except 6 acres subject to 200 pds. To son Isaac, farm, and other 1/2 of plantation, subject to 300 pds., clock, etc. To daughter Tacy, wife of Ryner Lukens, 250 pds. To daughter Martha, wife of John Michener, 250 pds. To grandchildren 20 s. each. To 2 daughters Tacy and Martha, 1/2 of rem. of estate, other half as follows: to daughter Mary's children 50 pds. rem. to daughter Sarah's children, and daughter Mary's child equally.
Execs: Sons Benjamin and Isaac. Wit: Thomas Livezey, John Tyson.

TRUMP, MICHAEL. Upper Dublin.
Jan 7, 1800. May 2, 1808. 3.34
To son Abraham, 75 pds. To son Jesse, 12 pds. To daughter Grace, 175 pds. To daughters Elizabeth and Lydia, 150 pds. each. To daughter Hannah, 130 pds. To grandsons: Michael Trump, son Jesse Trump, and Jesse Moore, 10 pds. each. To son John 400 pds. at his death 200 pds. to granddaughters Sarah and Anna, of son John. To Ann, 150 pds. To Sarah, 50 pds. To sons Abraham and Jesse, rem. of estate.
Execs: John Jarrett, Thomas W. Pryer. Wit: Thomas Shoemaker, Levi Jarrett.

MOYER, CHRISTIAN. Upper Salford.
April 1, 1808. May 7, 1808. 3.
To wife Nanny, 300 pds. and household goods. To son Henry, 1/2 of realty, at valuation of 12 pds., 10 s. per acre. To son Abraham, other half of realty, at valuation of 13 pds., 10 s. per acre. Personalty to be sold and money divided among 6 children: Henry, Abraham, Molly, Susanna, Magdalena, and Christian. Daughter Magdalena to receive interest.
Execs: Sons Henry and Abraham and brother Samuel Moyer. Wit: George

Hartzell, Jacob Landes.

FOX, MARGARET. Lower Merion.
July 14, 1807. May 18, 1808. 3.42
To daughter Margaret Lynch, and her husband Christopher, interest and dower of estate by husband George Fox.
Exec: Christopher Lynch. Wit: Jacob Lintz, Llwellyn Young, Margaret Lintz.

FRITZ, JOHN. Douglass.
Feb 8, 1804. May 31, 1808. 3.43
To wife Mary, interest of 300 pds., household goods, and maintenance. To son Martin, farm, 104 acres and 10 acres in Douglass, at valuation of 1200 pds. To son Martin, 150 pds. and 300 pds. To son Jacob, 300 pds. To daughter Catharine Linderman, 260 pds. To daughter Mary, 260 pds. To daughter Magdalena, 260 pds. To daughter Elizabeth, 260 pds. Rem. of estate to be sold and divided among sons Peter, Martin, and Jacob and daughters: Catharine, Mary and Elizabeth.
Execs: Brother Martin, son Peter. Wit: John Wambach, Jacob Yocum, Bartholomew Wambach.

BROOKE, MARK. Upper Merion.
March 15, 1808. July 5, 1808. 3.48
To wife Elizabeth, interest of estate, during widowhood. If she marries 1/3 estate. To children Louisa, and Anna, 2/3 of estate when of age.
Execs: Father Benjamin Brooke, and father in law Jesse Bean. Wit: John Jones, Richard Roberts.

LANE, ROBERT. Providence.
Aug 13, 1802. July 6, 1808. 3.50
To 4 daughters: Sarah Fox, Elizabeth Shannon, Rebecca Pawling, and Mary Shannon, estate etc. following legacies. To granddaughter Rebecca McFarland, spoons, and 50 pds. To granddaughter Rebecca Fox, bed, curtain. To granddaughter Rebecca Pawling, spoons and 10 pds. To Rebecca Pawling, and granddaughter Rebecca Fox, shoe buttons. To servant Minney, 10 pds. and interest of 20 pds. To daughter Mary Shannon, feather bed, etc.
Exec: Son in law Thomas Shannon. Wit: Andrew Todd.

STEWART, WILLIAM. Upper Merion.
May 4, 1808. July 25, 1808. 3.52
Estate to be sold. To Presbyterian Church, 1/2 of estate. To sister, Jane, 100 pds. To Elizabeth, wife of Matthew Downes, 50 pds. To Mary, wife of Matthew Downes, 40 pds., bed, etc. To Robert, son of Matthew Downes, 40 pds. To Mary Campbell, 40 pds. Rem. of estate to School House, for Poor Children.
Execs: John Davis, and Matthew Roberts. Wit: Jonathan Roberts, Sr.,

Frances Murphy, Jonathan Roberts, Jr.

CLINE, BARBARA. Hatfield.
March 15, 1806. Aug 8, 1808. 3.55
To grandson Henry Cline, bonds, etc., amounting to 178 pds., feather bed, etc., cash. To granddaughters Mary Allebough and Barbara Rosenberger, wearing apparel, equally. To Mary Allebough, saddle, etc. To grandson Henry Cline, close press.
Exec: Philip Shellenber. Wit: Edmund Pennington, William Johnson.

HELMBOLD, GEORGE. Lower Merion.
May 20, 1808. Aug 11, 1808. 3.57
To wife Elizabeth, all estate during widowhood. Mill House, etc., to be valued at $2100 and oldest son each child to receive a share of valuation. If wife marries 1/3 of estate. To son George, 1/2 share. To son Conrad, one share. To son Henry, one share. To son Joseph, one share. To son Jacob, one share. To son Charles, one share. To daughter Mary, wife of John Gray, of Virginia, one share. To daughter Elizabeth, one share.
Exec: Wife Elizabeth. Wit: Algernon Roberts, Paul Jones, Jr.

THOMAS, GRACE. Whitpain.
Feb 2, 1808. March 10, 1808. 3.60
To nephew Robert Jones, of brother Joshua, 50 pds. To nephew Abraham Jones, 50 pds. To nephew Isreal Jones, 50 pds. To Grace Rogers, daughter of niece Priscilla, 300 pds., household goods, etc. To widow of William Jones, Elizabeth, 30 pds. To Grace Jones, of nephew Robert Jones, feather bed, etc. To Anthony Prichard, of nephew Anthony, 20 pds. To Job Thomas Rowry, 30 pds. To Ann Roberts, wife of Abraham Roberts, 10 pds. To Mary Potts, widow of Jesse Potts, 10 pds. To Hannah Jones, 15 pds. To Hannah Hall, wife of Jervice Hall, 20 pds. Rem. of household goods, to Hannah Meredith, wife of Joseph Meredith, Grace Rogers and Ann Ambler, wife of Joseph Ambler, equally.
Execs: Grace Rogers, and Samuel Thomas. Wit: Christian Moser, David Thomas.

WILSON, JOSEPH. Lower Merion.
July 11, 1808. Aug 23, 1808. 3.62
To wife Sarah, all estate during widowhood. At wife's death estate to be sold and money divided among children equally.
Execs: Wife and brother John Wilson, and friend John Arwin. Wit: William Thomas, John Graham.

SHOEMAKER, THOMAS. Gwynedd.
Jan 27, 1808. Aug 24, 1808. 3.64
To son George, 30 pds. To son Jacob, watch. To son Thomas, farm, 109 acres, subject to 200 pds. farm, 180 acres to be sold. Rem. of estate divided among children: Joseph, George, Abraham, and Mary, equally.

Execs: Sons Joseph and Thomas. Wit: John Jones, Jr., Henry Jones, Evan Jones, Jr.

SHAMBACK, VALENTINE. Providence.
Dec 1, 1796. Sept 5, 1808. 3.66
To daughter Mary, wife of John Hugler, 500 pds. To daughter Dorothy, wife of John Pennebecker, 500 pds. To Anna Benson, 10 pds. yearly. To son Philip, realty, subject to legacies. To son Philip rem. of estate Codicil dated Dec 29, 1804. To daughter Mary and daughter Elizabeth, deceased, 150 pds. Daughter Dorothy's share to her children.
Exec: Son Philip. Wit: Zacharias Rittenhouse, Peter Saylor.

GILLER, JOHN, SR. Limerick.
July 21, 1800. Sept 10, 1808. 3.68
To wife Susanna, farm and household goods. Rem. of personalty to be sold. Estate to be sold at wife's death and money divided among children except sub-daughter Magdalena wife of Sinson Ruth, to receive $60 less than one share. To her son Conrad Niman, $60.
Execs: Sons Conrad and John. Wit: Samuel Pennebecker, Samuel Evans.

THOMSON, MARGARET. Gwynedd.
Nov 26, 1797. Sept 15, 1808. 3.71
To daughters Geanor Thomson, and Rachel, widow, 15 pds. equally. Rem. of estate to 5 children: Jonah, John, Geanor Thomson and Rachel widow of Race Haycock.
Exec: Thomas Shoemaker. Wit: John Harris, Thomas Shoemaker.

SORBER, JOHN. Springfield.
Sept 6, 1805. Oct 7, 1808. 3.72
To son Jacob, loom etc. To daughter Christiana, household goods, and $66.67. To daughter Elizabeth VanWinkle, wife of Peter VanWinkle, $13.33. To daughter Margaret Williams, wife of Benjamin Williams, $13.33. To son Jacob, farm, 4 acres. At valuation. To daughter Christiana, 1/5 part of rem. To daughter Elizabeth, 1/5 part. To daughter Margaret, 1/5 part. To son Jacob, 1/5 part. To 7 grandchildren of son John, deceased, 1/5 part equally.
Execs: Son Jacob and daughter Christiana. Wit: John Huston, Jacob Miller.

BISBING, GEORGE. Whitpain.
Feb 15, 1808. Oct 12, 1808. 3.76
To George Bisbing, of son John deceased, 250 pds. To George of son Michael, deceased, 250 pds. Rem. of personalty to Charles Hugler, for use of daughter Rosannah wife of Adam Workeiser, Elizabeth, wife of Henry Brockholder, Margaret, wife of Moses DeHaven, Susanna, wife of Andrew Fetzer, equally. To Charles Kugler, farm, 202 1/2 acres and farm, 230 acres in trust for 4 daughters equally.

Execs: Jacob Weber, John Schlater. Wit: Jacob Gilbert, John Caler.

HILTNER, WILLIAM. Whitemarsh.
March 13, 1805. Oct 14, 1808. 3.80
To son John, 10 pds. To daughter Hannah, household goods, and 15 pds. To son Jacob at wife's death 15 acres of valuation of 15 pds., 13 s., 4 d. to each child. Rem. of estate to be sold and money divided among 6 children: Mary, John, Michael, Elizabeth, Margaret, and Hannah.
Execs: Wife Agnes, sons John and Jacob. Wit: George Pierce, Philip Fie.

ARMITAGE, ENOCH. Horsham.
Sept 5, 1808. Oct 18, 1808. 3.82
To wife Mary, household goods. Rem. of personalty to be sold. To Enoch Carey, of sister Hannah, 25 pds. To Armitage Kenderdine, of daughter Rachel, 110 pds. Rem. of personalty divided among daughters Elizabeth and Rachel. To daughter Elizabeth, farm, 54 acres, subject to the payment of 15 pds. yearly to wife, during widowhood, and 15 pds. yearly to daughter Mary. Rem. of farm to daughter Rachel, 12 acres of land purchased of Joseph Kirkbride, subject to 15 pds. yearly to wife and 15 pds. to daughter Mary yearly and 1000 pds. to daughter Elizabeth.
Execs: Son in law Samuel Bright, Thomas Kenderdine. Wit: Eli Kenderdine, Hiram McNeal.

ROSENBERGER, JOHN. Hatfield.
Dec 28, 1805. Oct 19, 1808. 3.85
To wife Christina, 175 pds. and household goods, and maintenance. To son Benjamin, 50 pds. To son Martin's children: John, Elizabeth, and Mary, 60 pds. equally. Rem. of personalty to be sold and divided among 6 children: Henry, John, Benjamin, Daniel, Abraham and Catharine.
Execs: Sons John and Abraham. Wit: Michael Shoemaker, Peter Conver.

GRUB, GEORGE. Pottstown.
Nov 17, 1807. Oct 19, 1808. 3.87
Estate to be divided among daughters Elizabeth and Susanna. To Edward Potts, 5 pds.
Execs: Brother Abraham Grub and Abraham Scheloff. Wit: Edward Potts, Abraham Zimmerman.

LOLLER, ROBERT. Moreland.
June 4, 1808. Oct 25, 1808. 3.88
To wife Mary, household goods, wearing apparel, 400 pds. incomes of estate and 100 pds. yearly. To brothers: James, Alexander, and William, and sister Grace Townsand, 100 pds. each. To Robert Stephens, 50 pds. To daughters of Mary Stephens, deceased, 50 pds. equally. To Mary Iredell, 12 pds. yearly. To Mary Iredell, share in Union Library of Hatboro. To Union Library Germany of Hatboro, $20. To Trustees of Presbyterian Church of Abington, 50 pds. To Norristown Academy, 50

pds. To Ann Moody, 10 pds. To Mary Gossly, 10 pds. To Elizabeth
McClean, wife of nephew Joseph McClean, 10 pds. To Elizabeth Powel,
10 pds. To Samuel Hart, of Joseph Hart, deceased, books, etc., and 75
pds. To brother James, watch. To Nathaniel B. Boileau, telescope. Rem.
of estate after wife's death to Nathaniel B. Boileau, in trust for Academy
to be erected in Hatboro. Rem. of estate for Academy.
Exec: Nathaniel B. Boileau. Wit: James Aglevia, Samuel Cossly.

KEHR, FREDERICK. Douglass.
May 16, 1803. Nov 1, 1808. 3.91
Personal and real estate to wife Anna. At her death divided among
children and grandchildren: John, Frederick, Catharine, and deceased
daughters children.
Exec: Son John. Wit: Mary Willauer, Christian Willauer.

LAND, MICHAEL. Montgomery.
Dec 10, 1804. Nov 1, 1808. 3.93
To wife Ann, household goods, and 25 pds. yearly. Rem. of estate to be
sold. Rem. of estate as follows: to son John, 200 pds. To daughter
Christiana, 150 pds. To 2 granddaughters Sallie daughter of Catharine,
and Sarah of daughter Eve Wagoner, 10 pds. each. Rem. of estate to 7
children: Catharine, George, Michael, Eve, wife of George Wagoner,
Jacob, Christiana, and John, equally. At wife's death, principle and rem.
divided among 7 children.
Execs: John Huston, and son Jacob. Wit: William Huston, and Peter
Hinkle.

BRIDSON, HANNAH. Lower Merion.
Oct 22, 1808. Nov 4, 1808. 3.96
To daughter Sarah Larkin, wearing apparel, etc. To son George, bed, etc.
To grandson William Larkin, $30.
Execs: Daughter Sarah. Wit: Frances Scheetz, Benjamin Holland.

KINDERDINE, JANE. Horsham.
Dec 31, 1802. Dec 17, 1808. 3.97
Rem. of estate to son Eli.
Execs: Son Eli, and Enoch Kinderdine. Wit: Robert Loller, Mary Smyners.

BURNEMAN, CHRISTIL. Limerick.
June 13, 1804. Feb 7, 1809. 3.98
Personalty to be sold and divided among children. They to provide
maintenance for wife. Realty to be sold, 1/4 part of purchased money
divided among children, except son Daniel, he to receive 400 pds. at wife's
death. To daughter Mary, bed, etc., and 10 pds. yearly. At wife's death,
rem. divided among children: Henry, John, Barbara, and Mary. Guardians
of son Daniel, Isaac Markley and John Barlow.
Execs: Sons Henry and John. Wit: Matthew Brooke, John Slighter.

SCHMIT, THOMAS. New Hanover.
To Evangelist Lutheran Church, 20 pds. To Evangelist Calvinist Church, 3 pds. To sister's son Barnd Getz, 20 pds. To brothers son John, 20 pds. To brother Conrad, 50 pds. To widow of Anna Maria Miller, farm, 20 acres and 50 acres and household goods.
Exec: Jacob Mecklin. Wit: Harman Ache, Jacob Mecklin, John Amen.

JOHNSON, ESTHER. Gwynedd.
Feb 16, 1809. March 3, 1809. 3.103
To daughter Ellen Evans, 2 lots 18 acres and 8 acres. To daughter Ann Yexley, 2 lots 80 acres and 3 acres. To daughter Mary Scarlet, 4 lots, 12 acres woodland, 4 acres, 21 acres and 8 acres. To son Samuel, 2 lots, 18 acres and 12 acres, 42 perches. Personal estate to be sold and money divided among 4 children: Ann, Ellen, Samuel and Mary.
Codicil: Daughter Ann's estate divided among 3 children, 100 pds. divided among daughter Mary, and son Samuel and granddaughter Esther Evans.
Execs: Son Samuel and Cadwalder Evans, and Alice Cleaver. Wit: Jacob Roberts, Samuel Cleaver.

NANNA, ABRAHAM. Upper Merion.
May 20, 1805. March 7, 1809. 3.108
To son Reese, farm, household goods, wearing apparel. To granddaughter Susanna Nanna, of son Reese, land purchased of William Peters, and Richard Rockley, 15 acres etc. To daughter Hannah, wife of John Wentz, farm in the tenure of Thomas Lukens, at her death among her children. To daughter Elizabeth, wife of David Conard, farm in Merion, in the tenure of John Tenany, containing 60 acres. To daughters Hannah and Elizabeth, 32 acres of land. Rem. of realty to grandchildren of son Reese and daughter Hannah and Elizabeth. To grandson Abraham Wentz, watch. Rem. of estate divided among 3 children: Hannah, Reese and Elizabeth.
Execs: Evan Lewis, John Wentz, John Hughes, and Job Pugh. Wit: John Jones, Charles Jones.

BLARE, MARY. Worcester.
Feb 14, 1809. March 27, 1809. 3.112
To Mary Baker, 30 pds. and 5 pds. yearly. Farm. 1 acre, 20 perches to be sold. To Mordecai Jones, 10 pds. To Jonathan Jones, clock, etc. To wife, tea table. To Elizabeth Jones, 10 pds. etc. To Martha Jones, 5 pds. To Mary daughter of Daniel Shoemaker, bed, etc. To Catharine, of Daniel Shoemaker, beds, etc. To Elizabeth Shoemaker, cupboard, etc. To Rosanna Miller, stove and 5 pds. To Jonathan Jones, 3 chairs. To Daniel Shoemaker, rem. of personal estate. To Mary Osborn, arm-chair. To Daniel Shoemaker, bond. Rem. of estate to nephews and nieces: Jacob, David, Henry, and Casper Goldy, Christian, Mary and Catharine, and Jacob, and Daniel Baker, equally.
Exec: Mordecai Jones. Wit: Adam Homshire, Joseph Lewis.

MORRIS, MARGARET. Whitpain.
April 18, 1806. March 27, 1809. 3.114
Estate to be sold and money divided among children: Christina, Susanna, Catharine, Mary, Elizabeth, and John equally.
Execs: Son in law Benjamin Corson, and Amos Ellis. Wit: Henry Conard, Andrew Norney.

TYSON, GRACE. Upper Dublin.
March 3, 1809. April 8, 1809. 3.117
To sister Mary, interest of 50 pds. To sister, Elizabeth Edwards, 25 pds. To Thomas Tyson, 50 pds. To sister Priscilla Butler, rem. of estate.
Execs: Brother Thomas Tyson and Levi Jarrett. Wit: James Barnes, John Marple.

FREAS, GEORGE. Whitemarsh.
Sept 14, 1808. April 10, 1809. 3.118
To wife Sarah, 200 pds. To son Samuel, 200 pds. and bond 250 pds. To son Simon, 300 pds., lots, and buildings where I now dwell, amounting to 1000 pds. subject to the payment of 300 pds. To son Jacob, 5 pds. and bond 300 pds. Son George to pay to daughter Mary, rem. of 300 pds. After daughter Mary's death, her share to be divided among her children. To daughter Elizabeth Snyder, wife of Samuel Snyder, 15 pds. yearly. Son Simon to pay to daughter Elizabeth, 250 pds. To Henry Snyder, bond, 50 pds. At daughter Elizabeth's death, her share to be divided among her children. To George Katz, 10 pds. To daughter Catharine, wife of Philip Fye, 250 pds. and 50 pds. bond. To granddaughter Charlotte Wyland, 18 pds. yearly, When daughter Catharine is 18, son George to pay 399 pds. annaully. To Catharine Stout, late wife of son Philip Freas, 20 pds. Rem. of estate divided among 7 children, equally.
Execs: Son George, and son in law Philip Fye. Wit: William Steeley, Daniel Snyder.

AKEHUFF, DAVID. Whitemarsh.
Jan 1, 1802. April 22, 1809. 3.123
Exrs. to pay debts, and funeral expenses. To wife Mary, household goods, and wearing apparel, farm, where I now live. To son Jacob Akehuff, wearing apparel. Rem. of money divided among 6 children: Jacob Akehuff, Susanna Ruben, Rachel Shelmire, Margaretta Loazer, Mary Williams, Sarah Hearsh, widow of William Rex. To granddaughter Mary Rex, $20 when twenty. To grandson Jesse Rex, $20 when twenty. Rem. of estate to be divided among 6 children, equally.
Execs: son Jacob Akehuff, and son in law George Shelmire. Wit: Christopher Ottinger, Casper Schlater.

GILBERT, JONATHAN. Cheltenham.
July 7, 1808. April 24, 1809. 3.126
To wife Dedemiah, household goods, and 30 pds. and 48 pds. yearly in 1/2

yearly payments. Exrs. to sell land where I now live in Cheltenham, purchased of Isaac Potts, containing 200 acres, 100 perches. Rem. of estate be sold, except that which wife received. To 6 children: John, Jesse, Charles, Israel, Jonathan and William, 800 pds. yearly. At wife's death, rem. of estate divided among children.
Execs: Sons Jesse, John, and Charles. Wit: Thomas Livezey, Samuel Funk.

THAW, MARY. Abington.
April 2, 1809. May 1, 1809. 3.128
To brother Charles Thaw, bible. To sister Martha Shelmire, silver spoons, and silver tongs and wearing apparel. Personal estate to be sold and money divided into 3 equal parts. To brother Charles Thaw, one part. To sister Elizabeth, one part. To sister Martha Shelmire, one part.
Exec: Sister Martha Shelmire. Wit: Anthony Benezet, Jeremiah Berrell, William Hece, and Henry Berrell.

PAUL, JACOB. Abington.
Jan 13, 1809. May 22, 1809. 3.131
Estate to be sold and money divided among children. To wife Esther, household goods, and 100 pds. to be paid to her annually, and interest of money from children and grandchildren of son Daniel, and daughter Mary Ann, until son Jonathan is 15. To daughter Susanna, $50. To daughter Jane, $50. To son Jonathan, $100. Daughter Mary Tredal deceased, her share of $200 to her children. Daughter Ann Thornton deceased, her share of $160 to her children. Rem. of estate to be divided into 9 equal parts. To children of son Daniel, one part. To children of daughter Mary, one part. To children of daughter Ann, one part. To son Thomas, one part. To son Sutton, one part. To daughter Elizabeth, one part. To daughter Jane, one part. To daughter Susanna, one part. To son Jonathan, one part.
Execs: Thomas Fletcher, and Joshua Comly. Wit: Jacob Thomas, Moses Lukens.

DUBRE, REBECCA. Moreland.
Nov 17, 1807. June 12, 1809. 3.135
To daughters Margaret and Rebecca, wearing apparel, equally. To granddaughters, $1.00 each. To daughter Rebecca Knight, household goods. To 3 granddaughters: Hannah, Sarah, and Martha Dubre, 5 pds. each. If either die, their portion to be given to daughter Rebecca Knight. To daughter Margaret Thomas, 1/4 part of rem. and 5/6 to be equally devided between son Jacob Dubre and daughter Rebecca Knight.
Execs: Son Jacob and Charles Holt. Wit: Charles Holt, Lydia Zimmers, and Samuel Zimmers.

EGG, JOHN. Upper Salford.
Jan 30, 1809. June 20, 1809. 3.137

To wife Dorothy, household goods, and 150 pds. Rem. of estate equally divided among 9 children: Conard, Darius, John, Anna, widow of Martin Miller, Catharine widow of Simon Adams, Margaret, wife of Joseph Storm, Magdalena, wife of Nicholas Buch, Sabella, wife of Mark Zeigler and Fanny. To daughter Catharine, 150 pds. Exrs. shall be appointed guardians of daughter Theresa, and shall give interest of 150 pds. To son John, 25 acres land with interest. Wearing apparel divided equally among 3 sons. Estate to be sold.
Execs: Darius Egg, son in law Nicholas Buck. Wit: John Roller, Jacob Bear, Cadwalder Foulke.

RUSH, PETER, Cheltenham.
June 10, 1809. July 8, 1809. 3.141
To daughter in law and 4 daughters: Hannah Rush, Elizabeth, Hannah, Louisa and Mary, household goods. To daughter Elizabeth, feather bed, etc. Estate to be sold and money divided among children and grandchildren, namely: Hannah Rush, Elizabeth Rush, Sarah Kirk, Martha Bartolet, Hannah, Louisa and Mary equally. Granddaughter Sarah Kirk shall have $130 less than others. To Martha Bartolet, $100.
Execs: Daughter in law Hannah Rush, and John Thomsen. Wit: Thomas Shoemaker, Joseph Bener.

BARLEY, RUDOLPH. Lower Salford.
May 14, 1796. Aug 1, 1809. 3.144
To wife Mary, farm, and household goods and 150 pds. Estate to be sold and money divided among equally children. To son, Jacob, farm, where I now dwell, 120 acres subject to the payment of 30 pds. yearly. To son Abraham, rem. of farm, subject to the payment of 25 pds. yearly. Farm in Lower Salford, divided equally among sons: Henry and Samuel, subject to the payment of 25 pds. yearly. To son in law Frederick Dill, bible.
Execs: Sons Rudolph and Jacob. Wit: George School, Henry Landis, Isaac Landis.

ROBERTS, JONATHAN. Upper Merion.
May 16, 1809. Aug 22, 1809. 3.149
To daughter Mary Roberts, farm, and household goods. If she remains unmarried, Exrs. to pay 20 pds. in 1/2 yearly payments. To son Matthew Roberts, 1/2 of farm, purchased of John Meredith. To son Jonathan Roberts, rem. of farm. To son John Roberts, 1,500 pds. To 4 grandchildren: Roberts Moore, Mordecai Moore, Anna Maria Moore, and Hannah Bartholomew Roberts, 25 pds. each, when 18 and to grandsons when they are 21. To children, books, divided equally. Rem. of personal estate to my sons Matthew and Jonathan Roberts, equally.
Execs: Sons Matthew of and Jonathan. Wit: Jonathan Phillips, Jonathan Cleaver, Phineas Phillips.

CLEAVER, William. Upper Merion.

Nov 29, 1802. Aug 22, 1809. 3.152
To wife Mary, farm, during widowhood, and personal estate. To son Jonathan, real estate. To sister Elizabeth, 400 pds.
Execs: Wife Mary, and son Jonathan. Wit: Jonathan Phillips, Richard Moore, Joseph Walker.

SHEARER, VALENTINE. Whitpain.
July 30, 1799. Sept 14, 1809. 3.154
Exrs. to pay debts and funeral expenses. To daughter Maria, wife of Henry Geysingheimer, farms, in Whitpain, Norriton, and Worcester, containing 159 acres. To children of daughter Margaretta, 100 pds. to be paid yearly when 21. To granddaughter Rachel Berkhymer, 25 pds. If she remains with wife until 18. To son Valentine, of brother Ludwick, 5 pds. If children die, under age aforesaid, their share to be yearly divided among sister and brothers, subject to the payment of 30 pds. only unto wife Maria. To wife Maria, farm, and household goods, and rem. of estate.
Execs: Wife Maria, and son in law Henry Geysingheimer. Wit: Frederick Conrad, Jacob Clemens, Rachel Berkhammer.

MILLER, FREDERICK. Whitemarsh.
Sept 5, 1809. Oct 4, 1809. 3.159
To wife Eve Miller, all estate. To nephew Godfrey Hamlet, son of sister Elizabeth, rem. of estate.
Exec: Isaac Williams. Wit: George Peirce, William Goulston.

CLEAVER, NATHAN. Montgomery.
April 29, 1804. Oct 16, 1809. 3.160
To wife, 400 pds. and household goods, and farm, and 12 pds. paid to her yearly. To son Jonathan Cleaver, 30 pds. To son Salathiel, 30 pds. To grandson Amos Griffith, 30 pds. when 21. To 3 sons: Jonathan, Nathan, and Salathiel Cleaver, farms, in Montgomery, and Horsham, containing 160 acres purchased of John Evans, and sisters. Rem. of estate divided among 3 sons equally.
Execs: 3 sons: Jonathan, Nathan, and Salathiel Cleaver. Wit: Hugh Foulke, Isaac Jones.

ALLBRIGHT, MICHAEL. Douglass.
May 18, 1807. Oct 24, 1809. 3.163
Estate to be sold. To wife Elizabeth, land in douglass, and household goods. Rem. of personal estate divided among 6 children: Conrad, Catharine, Tobias, Michael, Maria, Elizabeth.
Execs: Sons Tobias, and Michael. Wit: Abraham Eshbach, Barney Gilbert.

DETWILER, HENRY. Perkiomen and Skippack.
Jan 22, 1809. Oct 31, 1809. 3.165
To Henry Bean, bonds, and 150 pds. Estate to be sold and money divided among 4 sons: John, Jacob, Henry and Isaac.

Execs: Sons Henry and Isaac. Wit: John Tyson, Henry Updegrove.

MORRIS, SARAH. Whitemarsh.
July 26, 1809. Nov 13, 1809. 3.167
To daughter Susanna, 25 pds. To granddaughter Anna, wife of Charles Hallow, 25 pds. To Mary Trimble, wife of William Trimble, 25 pds. To Rebecca Johnson, $40. To Mary Phipps, $20. To sisters, wearing apparel, and linens. To sister Hannah Kirkbride, household goods. To 3 nieces, rem. of household goods. To David Wilson, riding chair, etc. To niece Sarah, feather bed, etc. To niece, Sarah, silver spoons. Rem. of estate divided into 10 equal parts, among: Samuel, John, Stephen, Oliver, David, and Isaac. Remaining 9/10 parts divided equally among 6 brothers and 3 sisters: Elizabeth, Rachel and Rebecca.
Exec: Brother John Wilson. Wit: Thomas Lancaster, Jacob Thorp.

RIGHTER, BARTLE. Lower Merion.
Oct --, 1807. Nov 14, 1809. 3.170
To wife Charlotte, all estate. To daughters: Hannah, Mary, Rebecca, Catharine, and Elizabeth, 25 pds. when 21. After wife's death, daughter Elizabeth to receive feather bed, etc. To grandson Bartholomy Katch, 5 pds. when 21. Rem. of estate divided among 3 sons: William, Rudolph, and Joseph.
Execs: Son Rudolph, and George Jarrett. Wit: Algernon Roberts, and John Roberts.

CRAVIN, HELENA. Moreland.
March 15, 1809. Nov 14, 1809. 3.172
After funeral expenses are paid, rem. of residue divided among 4 sons: William, James, Isaac, and Thomas Cravin. To daughters: Ann, Catharine, Rose, Lena, and Christiana, household goods, equally.
Execs: Son in Law Mahlon V. Booskirk. Wit: John Shelmire, John Rhoads.

KATES, ANDREW. Whitemarsh.
Oct 28, 1809. Dec 4, 1809. 3.173
To wife Catharine, cow, household goods, during widowhood. She bringing up children and maintaining testators mother, Margaret Kates, if she marries again 1/3 part of estate. Rem. to be equally divided among children: Elizabeth, Sarah, Jacob and Philip.
Codicil dated Nov 2, 1809. To 2 sons, and wife privilege of taking real estate at appraisement.
Execs: Catharine Kates, and Leonard Lear. Wit: Jacob Kolp, Nathan Potts.

BEWLEY, NATHAN.
Nov 24, 1807. Dec 14, 1809. 3.176
To wife Hannah, beds, etc., and household goods. Rem. to be sold at public sale, and out of proceeds $160 to wife, to maintain son John to the

age of 7 years. Income of rem. to be hers during life. At her death to 4 children: Mary, Isaac, Hannah, John.
Exec: George Fitzwater. Wit: Ebenezer McDowell, Josiah Wood.

WATERMAN, PHINEAS. Cheltenham.
March 7, 1809. Feb 6, 1810. 1809. 3.178
To wife Rebecca, farm, in Cheltenham, until son John is 14. When 2 sons Isaac, and John are 14, farm, to be sold, proceeds as follows: to wife, 1/3 after her decease, to 2 sons, Isaac and John, remaining 2/3 divided equally among 5 children: Joseph, James, Charles, Isaac, and John.
Execs: Rebecca Waterman, Thomas Shoemaker. Wit: Zenas Large, Richard M. Shoemaker.

TYSON, William. Skippack.
May 18, 1805. Feb 19, 1810. 3.180
To son Matthias, Joseph and daughters Ann, widow of Jacob Casselbury, daughter Magdelane, deceased, wife of Richard Umsted, daughter Mary deceased, wife of Jacob Shoemaker, daughter Elizabeth, wife of Henry Peters, daughter Barbara, deceased, wife of Michael Zeigler, to son John, daughter Catharine, wife of Abraham Huntsperger, sons William and Isaac, 1/11 part of estate each. Personal estate to be sold.
Execs: Sons John and Isaac Tyson. Wit: Jacob Casselbury, Thomas Bean.

EGOLF, MARIA ELIZABETH. New Hanover.
May 26, 1798. Feb 21, 1810. 3.183
To daughters Catharine, Elizabeth Egolf, all estate. They paying to each daughter 5 s. each as follows: Simon Boyer's wife, Jacob Egolf, Michael Egolf, Adam, and Henry, and John, 5 s. each.
Exec: Daughter Catharine. Wit: Adam Warthan, Anthony Bitting.

SCHULTZ, DAVID. Upper Hanover.
Dec 21, 1809. Feb 26, 1810. 3.184
To daughter Juliana, 30 pds. and household goods. To son Gabriel, stock, household goods. Rem. to 2 daughters Christine, and Juliana, equally. Real estate to Gabriel, he paying to sisters 150 pds.
Execs: Isaac Schultz, Jeremiah Schultz. Wit: George Schultz, William Schultz.

KEYSER, ANDREW. Perkiomen and Skippack.
March 30, 1809. Feb 28, 1810. 3.186
To wife Sarah, household goods, and income of 400 pds. Exrs. to sell land. Rem. equally divided among children: John, Jacob, Samuel, Rachel, wife of Barned, Elizabeth, wife of John Markley, Molly, wife of Isaac Markley, Sarah, wife of John Bruckenmiller, Susanna, wife of Peter Warner.
Execs: Son Jacob, son in law Peter Warner, Henry Hunsicker. Wit: Jacob Hallman, Isaac Dettra.

HAWK, DAVID. Lower Providence.
Nov 19, 1808. March 12, 1810. 3.188
To son Jacob, 2 pds. To son John, 2 pds. To son in law Samuel Gordon, 390 pds., 10 s. To son Joseph's 5 children, 40 pds. when of age. To son Isaac, 350 pds. To son Abraham, farm, 147 acres he to pay above legacies. To son George, 2 pds.
Execs: Sons George and Isaac. Wit: Matthew Dill, Henry Wismer, Andrew Jack.

SANDMAN, LAWRENCE. Moreland.
Feb 5, 1810. March 14, 1810. 3.189
To wife Mary, household goods, use of house, 29 acres of land, income of 300 pds. during widowhood. To son Lawrence, and Michael, 350 pds. To son Christian, 350 pds. To each son, John and George, 100 pds. To son Jacob, 200 pds. To daughters Mary and Elizabeth, 100 pds. each. Rem. equally divided among 4 sons: Jacob, Charles, William, and Henry.
Execs: Son Christian, and Hiram McNeill. Wit: John Nodds, James Carrell.

LINSENBIGLER, PAUL. New Hanover.
April 12, 1809. April 4, 1810. 3.193
To wife Anna Maria, household goods, and 1/3 personal estate and income of 200 pds. during widowhood. If she marries interest of 500 pds. and 1/3 personal estate. To 2 sons, Abraham and Paul, farm, 41 acres at 10 pds. per acre. To 2 other sons Samuel and John, farm, of 100 acres subject to the payment of 400 pds. Rem. equally divided among children income only of her share to daughter Maria Margaret, during her life. To Jacob Stouffer, part of estate.
Execs: Brother John Sloanecker and Anthony Fuchs. Wit: Barney Fegley, Jonathan Richards.

McBEATH, William. Norristown.
Feb 11, 1810. April 9, 1810. 3.198
To son James, 20 pds. To step-daughter Mary Martin, 12 pds. To Nathan Potts, 3 pds. Rem. daughter Jane Shearer, of County Tyrone, Ireland.
Execs: Levi Pawling, Isaiah Wells, Samuel Patterson. Wit: George M. Potts, Benjamin Rambo.

RENNINGER, WENDELL. New Hanover.
Dec 15, 1804. April 12, 1810. 3.200
To son Conard, 2 farms, 106 acres and 32 acres, 70 pds. respectively, he to pay to wife Margeretha, income of 150 pds. yearly, also maintenance. To sons: Jacob, Wendell and John, Conard, and George, 12 pds. each. Over and above equal shares and rem. to be divided equally among sons and daughters. Son Peter's wife Elizabeth to have 1/3 part of what he would get balance to his child George. After wife's death, estate to be divided equally among children.

Execs: Sons Jacob Renninger, and Conard Renninger. Wit: Jacob Makcline, and John Gilbert.

SMITH, JOHN. New Hanover.
Jan 30, 1807. April 14, 1810. 3.203
To son Peter, $1.00 To son John, $1.00 To daughter Margaret, wife of Jacob Romfeld, $1.00 To granddaughter Elizabeth Romfeld, 50 pds. To daughter Maria, wife of Andrew Ohl, $1.00 Rem. divided among children: Jacob, George, Elizabeth, wife of John Stahl, Catharine, wife of Jacob Yerber, Susanna, wife of John Schneider, Barbara, wife of Henry Shellenberger, grandsons John and William Lin, children of daughter Maria, 1/2 equal share each with testators children.
Codicil dated Feb 26, 1810. To daughter Maria, 100 pds. she being then a widow, to be deducted from the share of 2 grandsons, John and William Lin.
Execs: Son George Smith, son in law John Schneider. Wit: Peter Bastres, Peter Richards, Samuel Pennebecker and Joseph Rendell [Kendell?].

FITZGERALD, JOHN. Worcester.
Nov 23, 1809. April 18, 1810. 3.206
To wife Rosanna, household goods, etc. To sons, John and James, farm. They to keep their mother during life. Pay for mortgage 120 pds. and to pay to son Peter and daughter Elizabeth, son Matthias, daughter Barbara, daughter Sophia, $20.00 each.
Execs: Sons Peter and John. Wit: Cornelius Tyson, William Bachtekeruh.

LEHMAN, GEORGE. Norriton.
Feb 20, 1810. April 21, 1810.
To daughter Magdalena Boaz, cow, household goods. To son John, cow, and wearing apparel. To granddaughter Elizabeth, feather bed, $6.00. Rem. to be sold, and equally divided among children: Peter, John, Elizabeth, Magdalena, and Abraham's children, equally.
Execs: Son John, and son in law Matthias Boaz. Wit: Enoch Supplee, George Evans.

LOLLER, MARY. Moreland.
April 16, 1810. April 23, 1810. 3.209
To Samuel Hart, 50 pds. To his daughter Mary Hart, 10 pds. To nieces Mary Iredell, and Edith Powell, rem. of estate equally.
Exec: N. B. Boileau. Wit: James Oglevia, Mary Swisher.

JONES, JACOB. Lower Merion.
Sept 30, 1803. April 26, 1810. 3.211
To wife Mary, 100 pds. and household goods etc. To Lydia daughter of nephew Algernon Roberts, to have desk after wife's death. To nephew Owen, and Jonathan Jones, sons of brother Owen, deceased, and to each of Owen's daughters 5 pds. each. To relative Benjamin Hays Smith,

grandson of testators sister Mary Hays, deceased, 300 pds. To Mary Davis, granddaughter of sister Mary, 100 pds. To nephew Edward Roberts, son of Rebecca Roberts, 10 pds. To Mary Axford, 10 pds. granddaughter of sister Rebecca. To niece Rebecca George, daughter of sister Hannah Williams, 100 pds. To Samuel and Robert Bond and Hannah Hacker, children of niece Eleanor Bond, deceased, 100 pds. divided equally. To relative Elizabeth, wife of Henry Calflesh, 10 pds. to her daughter Esther, and daughter Mary (Calflesh), 10 pds. To Gainor Roberts, daughter of Algernon, 10 pds. To Martha Sankey, 10 pds. to nephew Humphrey Owen, of New of Jersey, 10 pds. and to his widowed daughter 10 pds. and his son Joshua Owen, 10 pds. To wife Mary, rem. during widowhood. To Exrs. 50 pds. in trust. To Lower Merion Preparative Meeting of Friends, for alterations, 50 pds. To Trustees appointed by Lower Merion Preparative Meeting of Friends, 50 pds. income to repair Meeting House, and Grave Yard. At wife's death house and lot in Lower Merion to Jonathan Jones, Algernon Roberts, Henry Bowman, Jonathan Roberts, and David Roberts, in trust for erecting a School House, also 800 pds. in money, also 500 pds. income to be applied to hireing a teacher and in support of a free school. To nephew Algernon Roberts, rem. of farm, after death of wife, in trust for his 2 sons John and Isaac Roberts. Also Lime Quarry, in Plymouth. To Merion Preparative Meeting, 10 pds. in trust towards a dwelling house for care taker of meeting house. Rem. to wife Mary.

Codicil dated Oct 10, 1807. Rem. of estate after wife's death to Trustees of School.

Execs: Wife, Mary, nephew Algernon and Benjamin Hays Smith. Wit: Lloyd Jones, Anthony Levering.

COCHRAN, MARY. Lower Merion.
May 10, 1802. April 28, 1810. 3.219
To niece Jane Linsey, bed, etc. To nephew William Cochran and 2 nieces Jane Linsey and Mary Roberts, rem. of estate.
Codicil dated April 15, 1810. Share of William Cochran, now deceased, to Nancy Maris, niece of brother Thomas Cochran's wife to take share and share alike in the estate.
Execs: Brother Thomas Cochran. Wit: William Horn, Joseph Price.

LYNN, JOSEPH. Cheltenham.
Oct 6, 1802. April 28, 1810. 3.221
To wife Sarah, household goods, income of rem. of estate. During her life, after her death, 5 s. To daughter Sarah Wilson, 5 s. To son Franklin Lynn. Rem. of estate to other children: Joseph, Jeremiah, John, William, Esther and Mary equally.
Execs: Wife Sarah, and sons Joseph and John Lynn. Wit: Benjamin Rowland, Jacob Myers.

TOWMILLER, CHRISTOPHER. Lower Merion.

Dec 19, 1809. May 14, 1810. 3.223
To wife Mary, all estate. At her death or marriage, equally divided among children, except son John is to receive 1 acre less than others, son Christopher to have nine months school each year.
Exec: Wife Mary. Wit: John Smith, James Bryson.

MATHER, JOSEPH. Montgomery.
Sept 2, 1809. May 15, 1810. 3.225
To grandson Joseph Evans, 5 pds. To grandson William Ambler, 5 pds. To 2 grandsons, Edward and Andrew Ambler, 8 pds. divided equally. To son in law and daughter Edward and Ann Ambler, rem. of estate.
Execs: Son in law Edward Ambler. Wit: William Ambler, Joseph Ambler.

HARRY, BENJAMIN. Gwynedd.
April 23, 1810. May 28, 1810. 3.226
To niece Mary Evans, 150 pds. To niece Ruth Evans, 350 pds. To niece Rebecca Evans, 150 pds. To niece Ann Evans, 150 pds. To Curtis son of niece Ruth, 200 pds. To sister Ann, use of personalty, and real estate except what is given to sister Lydia, 31 acres after her death to her children. To niece Mary Lukens, $20. To relative Lydia Gibson, 150 pds. To nephew of George Roberts, to niece Jane Castner, to children of niece Ann Wilson, to niece Sidnah Roberts, 1/5 part all sale of real estate after the death of sister Ann, the other 1/5 part to George Roberts, to use for the support of nephew Robert Roberts. One other of the 3 equal parts divided into 4 equal parts, one to nephew David Harry, one to nephew Rees Harry, one to niece Mary Fairlamb, one to nephew David Harry for the maintenance and support of niece Sarah Lukens. Rem. of 3rd. part divided into 6 equal parts. One to niece Mary Evans, one to nephew Owen Evans, one to niece Ruth Evans, one to niece Rebecca Evans, one to niece Ann Evans, one to children of nephew Reese Evans.
Execs: George Roberts, Owen Roberts, David Harry. Wit: Samuel Thomas, Cadwalder Evans.

RAWLINS, JOHN. Lower Merion.
March 22, 1810. June 21, 1810. 3.230
To wife Ruth Rawlins, personal estate, house and lot bought of Isaac Thomas, during life. At her death 3 lots, 25 acres to be sold. To granddaughter Mary Rawlins, daughter of Margaret Rawlins, 5 pds.
Execs: Sons John and Nathan Rawlins. Wit: Mersena Allaway, Mordecai Davis, and John Davis.

BRADFIELD, Abner. Cheltenham.
June 17, 1810. July 21, 1810. 3.232
To wife Phebe, household goods, etc., $10 and maintenance, house and lot during widowhood, also $80. by 1/2 yearly payments by children. To children: William, Samuel, Isaac, Mahlon, John, and Rachel, as tenant in common all farms, all real estate subject to the payment of wife Execs:

Sons William and Samuel. Wit: Thomas Livezey, John Fitzwater.

KEYSER, DERICK. Springfield.
Aug 12, 1804. July 6, 1810. 3.235
To wife Rachel, $533.33 also income of $21.33, and household goods. To son Aaron, $266.67. To daughter in law Catharine Keyser, wife of Christopher Keyser, $13.33. To sons Nathan and William, $266.67. To daughter Mary, $186.67. To daughter Sarah, $186.67. rem. divided among 5 children, equally: Aaron, William, Sarah, Christopher, Mary, also wife's share, after her decease or marriage to children, equally.
Execs: Son Aaron, wife Rachel, and John K. Duy. Wit: Jacob Dutweiler, John Ottinger.

SCHNEIDER, CHRISTIAN. Hatfield.
May 17, 1810. Aug 10, 1810. 3.238
To wife Mary, 600 pds. yearly at the interest of 5%. Rem. of estate divided equally among 5 brothers and 2 sisters. To brothers and sisters of 1st wife, 50 pds. each. Real estate to be sold, after wife's death, money divided among brothers and sisters.
Codicil dated, July 14, 1810. To wife Mary, farm, during widowhood. To the congregation of Schwneksfelters, 100 pds.
Execs: George and Henry Schneider. Wit: Jacob Oberholtzer, Frederick Ratzel.

HARMON, PETER. Hatfield.
July 30, 1810. Aug 11, 1810. 3.241
To aunt Elizabeth Funk, 5 pds. To sister Mary Kline, 5 pds. To brother David Harmon, one suit of wearing apparel. Rem. of property divided equally among brothers and sisters: Abraham Harmon, Catharine Heston, Elizabeth Fritz, and Mary Kline.
Exec: Brother Abraham Harmon. Wit: John Funk, Isaac Morris.

SEIWELL, ANTHONY. Pottstown.
April 23, 1810. Aug 22, 1810. 3.243
Exrs. to sell all personal property, except that which wife has received. To wife Mary, all money arising from sale of estate.
Execs: Wife, and father in law Conrad Mock. Wit: James Harris, Henry Hahn.

PLIEM, CHRISTIAN. New Hanover.
Oct 6, 1798. Aug 24, 1810. 3.244
To son Christian, all estate. To 4 daughters: Mary, Elizabeth, Esther, and Eve, 260 pds. each. To grandson Christian Freatz, 30 pds. To son Christian Pliem, rem. of estate. To daughter Mary, 50 pds.
Exec: Son Christian. Wit: Nicholas Miller, Conrad Mock, George Leonard.

STRUKER, CHRISTIAN. Franconia.

May 29, 1810. Sept 1, 1810. 3.247
To sister, Elizabeth, household goods, and interest of money at 5%. To brother Jacob, wearing apparel.
Execs: Isaac Meyer, Ralph Meyer. Wit: Michael Shoemaker, Daniel Haga.

WILSON, THOMAS. Norriton.
July 3, 1810. Sept 3, 1810. 3.249
To wife Isabella, household goods, and interest of bank stock. To son James, 365 pds. To daughter Mary Sands, wife of William Sands, 150 pds. To daughter Ann Jordon, wife of Thomas Jordon, 150 pds. To daughter Isabella Harrison, wife of Jada Harrison, 150 pds. To daughter Ann Wilson, 5 pds. To daughter Margaret Harwood, wife of John Harwood, $1.00. To grandson Matthew Wilson, 50 pds. To grandson John Wilson, 50 pds. To granddaughter wife of Anthony Burk, 50 pds. To granddaughter Margaret Harwood, $1.00. To granddaughter Sarah Ann Haley, $1.00. To granddaughter Ann Haley, $4.00. To Thomas Taylor, lot in Trenton. To granddaughter Eleanor Taylor, wife of Thomas Taylor, full share of estate. Rem. of estate to be divided equally among sons and daughters: James, Mary, Ann, and Isabella.
Execs: John McCrea, and son in law John Harwood. Wit: William Thomas, Philip Beck, John McCrea.

HEPPLER, GEORGE. Upper Providence.
July 23, 1810. Sept 10, 1810. 3.252
To son George, 80 pds. and wearing apparel. To daughter Catharine, 30 pds. and household goods. To daughter Hannah, spinning wheel, and 50 pds. Rem. of estate divided equally among children. To daughter Mary, one share. To daughter Susanna, one share. To daughter Margaret, one share, and Exrs. shall pay to daughter Margaret 250 pds. To son George, one share. To daughter Catharine, one share.
Exec: David Dewees, Esq. Wit: Joseph Vanderslice, Jacob Schwenk, Benedict Garber.

BOORSE, HENRY. Towamencin.
July 12, 1808. Sept 24, 1810. 3.254
To Elders of Skippack and Towamencin Minnonite Meeting, 50 pds. To Jonas Boorse, chest, etc. Exrs. to sell tract of woodland in Franconia. Rem. of estate divided equally among children.
Execs: Daniel Boorse, John Boorse. Wit: Paul Hendricks, Henry Hunsicker.

ARWIN, JOHN. Gwynedd.
May 11, 1810. Oct 3, 1810. 3.256
To wife Hannah, household goods, 30 pds. yearly. If she marries, to have 10 pds. yearly. To Cadwalder Arwin, 50 pds. and 250 pds. equally divided among step-children: Jacob, Jonathan, Joseph and John McCrory, and Hannah Nile. Estate to be sold. To Cadwalder Roberts, Jr., Hugh Foulke,

Ellen Roberts, and Jacob Albertson, rem. of estate, equally.
Exec: Israel Robinson. Wit: Nicholas Brile, George Hortler.

MOORE, MARGARET. Moreland.
Oct __, 1807. Oct 10, 1810. 3.258
To daughter Elizabeth, wearing apparel. To niece Maria McNeill, beds, etc. To niece Minnie, chest of drawers. Rem. of personal estate to be sold. To 2 nephews, William Ayres, and Hiram McNeil, 1/3 of said husband's share. All real estate to daughter Elizabeth when 21.
Execs: William Ayres, Hiram McNeill. Wit: Peter Saureman, Daniel Yerkes.

ADAMSON, JOHN. Horsham.
June 17, 1806. Nov 15, 1810. 3.260
To daughter Ellon, 3 pds. yearly. To son Robert, farm, and household goods and wearing apparel, and 100 pds. To daughter Sidney, 100 pds. part, of farm, and household goods. To son Amos, horse, etc. Rem. of household goods divided equally among 2 sons, Robert and Amos.
Execs: Sons Robert and Amos. Wit: William Mullen, Hugh Foulke, Jonathan Cleaver.

HOFF, MICHAEL. Pottsgrove.
Aug 6, 1810. Dec 3, 1810. 3.263
To wife Eleanor, all estate.
Execs: Wife, Eleanor, and son in law Samuel Ludwig. Wit: John Taylor, John Boyer.

SHOEMAKER, DAVID. Whitemarsh.
March 24, 1807. Dec 7, 1810. 3.265
To wife Jane, household goods, and 30 pds. Exrs. to sell all real estate. To 4 daughters: Ellen, Margaret, Ann, and Mary, legacies equally.
Execs: Son in law Ezra Comfort, Jonathan Cleaver, and brother in law Job Roberts. Wit: Samuel Maulsby, Septimus Wood.

TENNENT, WILLIAM M.
Jan 9, 1810. Dec 8, 1810. 3.268
To wife Susanna, and a negro girl, named Hannah Marvil, estate. And household goods, and $5000. After her death to equally William Tennent Rodgers, and $1000 to nephew Ravard Rarney Rodgers. To niece Ann Stewart, bed, etc., and $1000. To William Tennent Rodgers, son of nephew William Rodgers, $1000. To William Tennent Austin, son of Susanna Austin of Connecticut, $1000. To niece Maria Eleanor Stewart, watch, and land of 2 acres and rem. of estate.
Execs: Wife Susanna, and niece Maria Eleanor Stewart, and John Morrison, Esq. Wit: Harmon Yerker, Silas Yerkes.

BENDER, LUDWIG. Douglass.

July 4, 1805. Dec 22, 1810. 3.270
To wife Anna Margaret, farm, and household goods. Estate to be sold, subject to the privileges of wife and 200 pds. shall be equally divided among 8 children: Catharine, Fronica, Margaret, Elizabeth, Ludwig, John, Christina, and Anna Maria, daughter Fronica to have share annually. To son Ludwig, 60 pds. To son John, 60 pds.
Execs: Son Ludwig Bender, and son in law George Huber. Wit: Benjamin Markley, Andrew Young.

RAMBO, JONATHAN. Upper Merion.
Nov 24, 1810. Dec 26, 1810. 3.273
To wife Rachel, all estate and household goods. Exrs. to sell lot, containing 4 acres adjoining lands of John Hughes. To 2 daughters Catharine and Margaret, and son Jonathan money from lands, divided equally among them, when daughters are 18 and son 21. To 2 daughters case of drawers etc. Rem. equally divided among children.
Execs: Wife Rachel, and brother Peter Rambo, and Matthias Holstein. Wit: Benjamin Ramsey, Nathan Potts.

PAUL, ELIZABETH. Abington.
Nov 13, 1810. Dec 27, 1810. 3.276
To sister in law Jane Paul, widow of James Paul, $100. To sister in law Lillie Paul, widow of Sutton Paul, table cloth, etc., and $50. To sister in law Jane Paul, bed, etc., and 1/2 wearing apparel, and $250. To sister Susanna Paul, other half of wearing apparel. Rem. of estate divided among sisters Susanna, Jane and brother Jonathan equally.
Exec: Thomas Fletcher. Wit: Joseph Iredell, C. F. Hallowell.

CANE, ROBERT. Plymouth.
Aug 31, 1810. Jan 7, 1811. 3.278
To wife Barbara, all estate, after wife's death, real estate to be sold and money divided among children: Mary, Elizabeth, John, and James, and grandson Charles Wayne.
Exec: Son John. Wit: William Armstrong, Nathan Potts.

WAMBOLD, DANIEL. Upper Salford.
March 19, 1810. Jan 9, 1811. 3.279
Wife to stay on premises till son Henry is 21. To son David, 35 acres of woodland subject to the payment of $25. To sons Henry and David, farm, where I now live, subject to the payment of 25 pds. yearly. Rem. of estate divided into 11 equal parts. To John, 1/11 part. To George, 1/11 part. To Daniel, 1/11 part. To Elizabeth, 1/11 part. To Catharine, 1/11 part. To David, 1/11 part. To Barbara, 1/11 part. To Mary, 1/11 part. To Margaret, 1/11 part. To Jacob, 1/11 part. To Henry, 1/11 part.
Execs: Son George and son in law Abraham Kolb. Wit: John Benner, Jacob Daub.

RINGFIELD, WENDLE. Whitpain.
March 31, 1809. Jan 12, 1811. 3.282
To wife Margaret, household goods, wood lot in Whitpain to be sold, interest of money from sale of real estate. Interest of money from estate divided equally among daughter Maria's children: John, William, Catharine, and George when 21. To 3 grandchildren, interest of money from estate: Samuel Bartleson, Maria Bartleson, and Nancy Yelter, equally when 21 (children of deceased daughter Catharine). Daughter Mary widow of Jacob Walter and her children : John Walter, William, Catharine, and George Walter.
Execs: Wife Margaret, Charles Kugler, of Philadelphia. Wit: Abraham Wentz, and John Wentz.

HAUSER, MICHAEL. Philadelphia.
May 19, 1806. Feb 19, 1811. 3.287
To nephew John Echel, windsor chair maker, of Philadelphia, apprentice. To John Hunsicker, chairmaker and Ritchell son of daughter Rachel, $266.67 and silver watch. To daughter Elizabeth, wife of Henry Hoffman, $20. To Henry Jacoby, interest of rem. of estate during life of daughter Richell, his wife. To grandchildren, rem. of estate equally. Children of Henry and Richell.
Exec: Robert Smith, Esq. Wit: James Sellers, Charles Bowman.

ZOLLER, CHRISTIAN. New Hanover.
April 9, 1809. Feb 18, 1811. 3.289
To wife Margaret, household goods, and interest of 400 pds. annually to be paid by son Jacob. All estate to be sold and money divided equally among children: Francis, Margaret, Catharine, Sophia, Maria, Elizabeth, and Mary, except 25 pds. which son George is to have.
Codicil dated Sept 12, 1810. To sons Francis and Jacob, legacies and money from sale, divided equally among sons Francis' children.
Execs: Son Jacob Zoller, and son in law Henry Knoup. Wit: Benjamin Markley, Henry Kribs.

LUKENS, ELIZABETH. Horsham.
Sept 28, 1809. Feb 19, 1811. 3.292
Exrs. to keep 100 pds. and interest thereof to be paid annually to daughter Rachel Walton, during her life, at her death equally divided among her children. To 4 granddaughters: Elizabeth Griffith, Elizabeth Lukens, daughter of Joseph Lukens, and Catharine and Tacy Lukens, daughters of Abraham Lukens, 20 pds. each. Rem. of estate to 2 daughters Sarah Hallowell and Martha Lukens, equally.
Execs: Sons Jonathan and David Lukens. Wit: Amos Lewis, Jesse Lukens.

FOULKE, CALEB. Gwynedd.
Sept 12, 1809. Feb 20, 1811. 3.293
To sons Caleb and Charles, all estate, in trust for their mother during her

widowhood.
Execs: sons Caleb and Charles. Wit: Jesse Foulke, Cadwalder Evans.

RUTH, HANNAH. Pottsgrove.
Jan 26, 1810. March 12, 1811. 3.294
All property to children: John, Charles, Nathaniel, Philip, Mary, and Elizabeth, equally divided among them, except two beds, and wearing apparel, which daughters Mary and Elizabeth receive. All personal estate to be sold at public sale, except things mentioned above.
Exec: Jacob Rhoads. Wit: John Taylor, Henry Warley.

LUKENS, PETER. Towamencin.
Feb 22, 1811. March 16, 1811. 3.296
To son Jesse, farm, in Gwynedd, clock, etc. To 3 sons: Jesse, Jonathan, and Peter, wearing apparel, equally. To 3 daughters: Susanna, Martha, and Edith, household goods, equally. To son Jonathan, 400 pds. 1/2 to be paid in one year. To son Peter, 400 pds. 1/2 to be paid in one year. To son Jesse, and daughters Susanna Iredell and Martha Shoemaker, and Edith Scott, farm, and lands in Towamencin.
Execs: son Jesse Lukens, and son in law Robert Iredell. Wit: Cadwalder Evans, Andrew Kreibel.

DOTTERER, MICHAEL. Frederick.
July 16, 1808. March 18, 1811. 3.298
To wife Catharine, household goods, and 25 pds. Estate to be sold at public sale and money shall be divided among children and grandchildren. To 3 children of son Peter Dotterer, 300 pds. equally. To daughter Philibina, wife of Henry Mower, interest of 150 pds. to be paid annually. To 6 children: Philip, Michael, John, Conrad, Maria, and Catharine, principle of 150 pds. to be divided among them equally.
Execs: Sons Michael and Conrad, and Jacob Houck. Wit: Benjamin Markley, Anthony Bitting.

RAMBO, BENJAMIN. Norristown.
Feb 28, 1811. April 15, 1811. 3.301
To wife Martha, all estate and farm, in Upper Merion, until son Charles is 21, and household. If she marries, she shall receive the sum of 10 pds. yearly. to daughters Jane and Elizabeth, 100 pds. Exrs. to make repairs to farm after repairs are made, Exrs. to put rem. of money in interest for use of son Charles. To son Charles, farm, he attains the age of 21 and rem. of estate subject to the privilege of mother.
Exec: Nathan Rambo. Wit: W. H. Holstein, Nathan Potts.

SHOEMAKER, BENJAMIN. Cheltenham.
Dec 29, 1810. April 15, 1811. 3.304
To daughter Jane Hallowell, 15 pds. yearly, and after her death, to her children, 100 pds. to be equally divided among them. To Thomas

Shoemaker, 15 pds. yearly for use of daughter Jane Hallowell. To children of daughter Rebecca, 100 pds. equally. To children of daughter Mary, 100 pds. equally. To granddaughter Amy Hallowell, 100 pds. To granddaughter Rachel, daughter of Eli Shoemaker, 100 pds. when 18, If she dies her share to be equally divided among Nathan Shoemaker, Comly Shoemaker, and the heirs of Benjamin and Robert Shoemaker, deceased. Rem. of estate divided into 4 equal parts. To son Nathan, 1/4 part. To son Comly, 1/4 part. To children of son Robert Shoemaker, 1/4 part. To children of son Benjamin, remaining 1/4 part.
Execs: Sons Nathan and Comly. Wit: Isaac Leech, Joshua Paxon.

DRAKE, JOHN. Montgomery.
March 29, 1811. May 29, 1811. 3.306
To wife Rachel, farm, in Montgomery and personal estate. To brother Thomas Drake, part of real estate. To niece Hannah Drake, rem. of plantation. To niece Rachel Roberts, 40 pds. To nephew Andrew Drake, 5 pds. To nephews: John, James, Drake, 5 pds. and rem. of money to wife. Exrs. to sell stock at public sale.
Execs: Niece Hannah Drake, and George Warren. Wit: Levi Drake, Enos Lewis, Evan Jones.

MATSON, PETER. Upper Merion.
April 8, 1811. May 23, 1811. 3.309
To wife Ann, all estate, until son Elijah is 21, and use of house. To son Elijah, land, subject to the payment of daughter Abigail's share of 100 pds. in 2 years, and estate shall be equally divided among sister Susanna Mathers.
Execs: David Brooke, and James Anders. Wit: Lawrence Ramsey, Jacob Ramsey, and Nathan Potts.

MACK, ELIZABETH. Philadelphia.
July 20, 1808. June 1, 1811. 3.311
To children of son William Mack, 162 pds., 10 s. equally. To granddaughter Rebecca Zeigler, 45 pds. and to each of other 5 children, namely: William, Elizabeth, Mary, Catharine, and Jacob, 33 pds., 6 s., 8 d. To Jacob Culp, Margaret Culp and Elizabeth Culp, 33 pds., 6 s., 8 d. To other granddaughter Lydia Lentz, 45 pds. To daughter Hannah Weaver, wife of Adam Weaver, 200 pds. To daughter Margaret Fox, 5 pds. Rem. of estate to grandson William Weaver.
Exec: William Weaver. Wit: Henry Hallman, Daniel Kopp.

KENDELL, JOSEPH. Limerick.
May 21, 1811. June 7, 1811. 3.314
Estate to be sold and land in Frederick to be sold containing, 100 acres. Wife to estate at valuation of 100 pds. To wife, 900 pds. If she remains a widow, 400 pds. during her life. From son Samuel's share to be deducted $600. From son John's share to be deducted 100 pds. From daughter

Elizabeth's share to be deducted 100 pds. To 8 children: Samuel, Mary, John, Elizabeth, Joseph, Philip, Christopher, and Henry, rem. of estate, equally.
Execs: Son in law Henry W. Conrad, and Samuel Grop, Esq. Wit: William Smith, Abraham Hallman, and Henry Kihl.

LEYDICH, FRANTZ. Frederick.
April 18, 1811. June 10, 1811. 3.317
Estate to be sold. To wife Christina, house, and household goods, and 500 pds. To son Jacob, 1400 pds. To 3 sons: Philip, John and Henry, 300 pds. To daughter Catharine, 100 pds. To daughter Elizabeth, 113 pds., 15 s. Rem. of estate after wife and daughters sums are deducted divided equally among 6 children: Philip, John, Henry, Catharine, Elizabeth, and Magdalena.
Execs: Sons Philip and Jacob. Wit: Jacob Zoller, Benjamin Markley.

CONRAD, DAVID. Norriton.
Dec 6, 1807. Aug 9, 1811. 3.320
To wife Elizabeth, household goods. To son Reese, 200 pds. when 21. To daughters Lydia and Nancy, rem. of money from estate, equally, when 18.
Execs: Isaac McGlathery, Jonathan Conrad. Wit: Francis Hovan, John Custer.

HAMER, MARTHA. Providence.
July 5, 1797. Aug 12, 1811. 3.321
To granddaughter Martha Brook, household goods, and 20 pds. when 25. To granddaughter Martha Shunk, 10 pds. when 25. To grandson Martha Schrack, 10 pds. when 18. To granddaughter Martha Hamer, 10 pds. when 18. To son James Hamer, 5 pds. To daughter Sarah, spinning wheel, etc. To granddaughter Elizabeth Brook, wearing apparel. Rem. of estate to be equally divided among 3 daughters: Elizabeth, Mary, and Sarah.
Exec: Son James. Wit: Jesse Jacobs, Benjamin Cox, John Jacobs.

LEECH, HANNAH. Upper Dublin.
Jan 22, 1805. Aug 13, 1811. 3.324
To grandchildren: John Tyson, Seth Tyson, and Hannah Tyson, 10 pds. To daughter Rebecca Lukens, wearing apparel, feather bed, etc. To son Isaac Tyson, rem. of estate.
Exec: Son Isaac Lukens. Wit: Thomas Livezey, Silas Yerkes.

WYNKOOF, THOMAS. Moreland.
July 25, 1811. Sept 2, 1811. 3.325
To sisters Hannah and Mary and brother Cuffee, $5.00. To mother Belinda, rem. of estate.
Execs: Cornelius Wynkoof, and Isaac Warner. Wit: Jacob Yerkes, and Anthony Yerkes.

WELTZ, MICHAEL. Springfield.
Aug 14, 1805. Sept 30, 1811. 3.327
To daughter Susanna, bed, etc., and 50 pds. To son George, looms, etc.
Execs: Son George, and Jacob Lentz. Wit: Christopher Yeakle, Jacob Peterman.

BOORSE, HARMAN. Towanencin.
Dec 5, 1801. Oct 1, 1811. 3.331
To wife Susanna, household goods, and 15 pds. yearly. To son Peter, 17 pds., 10 s. yearly. To son Peter, farm, where I now dwell, containing 82 acres subject to the payment of 440 pds. of said son Peter. To son Peter, 300 pds. after wife's deceased, shall be equally divided among 6 daughters and remaining 150 pds. to son Peter, shall pay it in 3 yearly payments, the 1st shall be paid in 2 years, after wife's decease. To son Peter, implements. To daughter Elizabeth, household goods. Rem. equally divided among children: John, Peter, Margaret, Anna, wife of Abraham Hendricks, Catharine, wife of Samuel Metz, Sibilla, wife of Jesse Lewis, and Elizabeth.
Execs: Sons John and Peter. Wit: Henry Hunsicker, Joseph Hendricks.

WARD, JOSEPH. Upper Providence.
Sept 15, 1811. Oct 23, 1811. 3.333.
To wife Mary, all estate, real and personal.
Exec: Wife Mary Ward. Wit: Thomas Pears, Benjamin Rees.

ROBERTS, JOSEPH. Norriton.
Oct 9, 1806. Nov 13, 1811. 3.335
To son Isaac, farm, 100 acres and household goods, etc. To son John, grist mill, saw-mill and farm, 72 acres. He to pay to granddaughter Mary Roberts, daughter of son Joseph 200 pds. To daughter Hannah Ellis, rem. of real estate, 27 acres. She paying to Rachel Roberts, widow of son Joseph, 50 pds.
Execs: Sons Isaac and John and son in law Amos Ellis. Wit: Nathan Potts, Seth Chapman.

WENTZ, JOHN P. Upper Salford.
Oct 1, 1811. Nov 22, 1811. 3.338
To wife Mary Magdalena, personalty, as she may chose, rem. to be sold, as well as real estate. Wife to have income during life, and principle if necessary. Rem. to 5 children: John, Jacob, Mary Magdalena, Elizabeth, and Catharine.
Execs: Wife Mary Magdalena, and Jacob Herring. Wit: Andrew Reed, Christian May.

PHIPPS, DANIEL. Whitpain.
Aug 10, 1811. Nov 22, 1811. 3.341
To wife Catharine, income of estate until son George shall be 18 years of

age, then to be sold, household goods, and 1/3 estate and $30 additional each year. In case of her death or marriage payment of $30 annually to cease. To 3 sons: Jonathan, Abraham, and George, 50 pds. each. Rem. of estate to 10 children: Priscilla, Margaret, Rachel, Jonathan, Elizabeth, Abraham, Catharine, Ann, Maria, and George, after death of wife her share to be divided equally among children.
Execs: Wife Catharine, and son Jonathan. Wit: Job Roberts, Jacob Gerhart.

KEARN, MARY. Gwynedd.
June 27, 1810. Dec 4, 1811. 3.343
To 3 grandchildren, heirs of Philip Kearn, deceased: Christian, John, and Margaret, $10 each. Rem. of estate to be divided equally among 3 children: Adam, Margaret, widow of Henry Hober, and Catharine, wife of George Shive.
Execs: Son Adam, and son in law George Shive. Wit: David Bruner, John Wentz.

WITCOMB, ANN. Upper Dublin.
Aug 1, 1811. Dec 11 1811. 3.345
To daughter Margaret Rapp, wearing apparel, cow, household goods, etc. To daughter Ann Engle, $5.00. To granddaughter Catharine Engle, $40.00. Rem. of estate to sons Joseph and John Witcomb, and Margaret Rapp.
Execs: Sons Joseph and John. Wit: Thomas Livezey, and Henry Scheetz.

YERKERS, STEPHEN. Moreland.
July 28, 1811. Dec 23, 1811. 3.347
To wife Rebecca, income of estate, during life. To son Samuel, 50 acres of farm. Rem. to be sold and of the money, 600 pds. to son Joseph. Rem. divided into 3 equal parts. One to daughter Rebecca. One to daughter Rachel. One to 3 children of deceased daughter Elizabeth, wife of Eli Morgan, namely Mary, Emma, and Thomas.
Execs: Son Samuel, and George Shelmire. Wit: William Redding, Jesse Willard.

WUNDERLICH, GEORGE. Franconia.
April 6, 1808. Jan 3, 1812. 3.349
To wife Eva Margaret, money and bonds, and household goods which she brought me and interest of 50 pds. during widowhood. To grandson Jacob, son of George Wunderlich, all rem.
Exec: Son George. Wit: Michael Shoemaker, John Gerhart.

ROBERTS, REBECCA. Lower Merion.
Dec 10, 1800. Feb 3, 1812. 3.351
To nephew Joseph Wells, 5 s. To niece Rebecca Ward, 15 pds. To niece Mary Cotton, 10 pds. To nephew Henry Wells, 15 pds. and to his

daughter Elizabeth, 10 pds. and bedding, etc. To Rebecca Jones, daughter of Benjamin and Tacy, case of drawers, and pewter. To Tacy Jones, rem. of estate.
Execs: Tacy Jones, and William Davis. Wit: Aaron Keech, Mordecai Davis, John Young, and Isaac Warner.

IREDELL, HANNAH. Horsham.
March 6, 1811. Feb 17, 1812. 3.353
To daughter Hannah Comly, silver spoons, etc. To granddaughter Rebecca Kirk, brass hand irons. To son Seth, 50 pds. To children of deceased children: Rebecca, Charles and Gainor, to each set, 500 pds. divided equally among them. To son John, franklin stove, etc. To son Jonathan, 10 pds. To daughter in law Hester Iredell, interest from estate of son Abraham. Rem. of estate to son Robert and daughter Hannah Comly, equally.
Execs: Sons John and Jonathan. Wit: Joseph Lukens, John Jarrett.

NICHOLS, FRANCIS. Pottsgrove.
April 21, 1810. Feb 19, 1812. 3.355.
To daughter Anna Maria Nichols, house and lot and 12 acres and 1500 pds. and tract of land containing 1054 acres and 67 perches. To daughter Harriet Nichols, house and lot, containing 3 and 4 acres and 1500 pds. To daughters Anna Maria and Harriet, woodland in Chester County. To daughter Martha Nichols, 1500 pds. to be put on interest and paid to her yearly. To William Francis Nichols, farm, 1058 1/2 acres. To Arthur St. Nichols, farm, 1058 1/2 acres. To Francis and Michael Nichols, tract of land containing 1003 3/4 acres. To William Francis Nichols, Arthur St. Nichols, Francis Nichols, and Michael Nichols, 300 pds. each. To housekeeper Elizabeth Sockritter, 100 pds. To present housekeeper, Elizabeth Parker. To Martha Nichols, bed, etc. To William Francis Nichols, gown, etc. To Francis Nichols, gown, etc. To Michael Nichols, one case of pistols. To Arthur, silver sword. To daughters Anna Maria, and Harriet, books, etc., equally.
Execs: Charles Biddle, Esq., Bird Wilson, Esq. Wit: Jacob Drinkhouse, Robert McClintuck.

BRITTAIN, JOHN. Abington.
Aug 16, 1809. March 6, 1812. 3.359
To wife Martha, household, and interest of estate. To son Peter, bible. To daughter Elizabeth, looking glass. After wife's death, Exrs. to sell estate. To son Jacob, 200 pds. when 21. Rem. of estate divided among children: Peter, Thomas, Elizabeth, Sarah, Rachel, and Hannah, equally.
Execs: Son Thomas, and Abednego J. Whitten. Wit: John Trump, William Robinson, and Abednego J. Whitten.

CRAFT, ANN. Cheltenham.
Dec 21, 1810. March 6, 1812. 3.362

To daughter in law Alice Craft, wearing apparel. To granddaughter in law Mary Craft, wife of Jonathan Craft, rem. of wearing apparel. To granddaughter Agnes Craft, sheets, etc. To granddaughter Elizabeth Craft, sheets, etc. To granddaughter Ann Tyson, feather bed, etc. To granddaughter Hannah Tyson, looking glass. To granddaughter Hannah Tyson, case of drawers, and household goods, and wearing apparel. Money to be divided into 5 equal parts. To son John Craft, 1/5 part. To son Jacob Craft, 1/5 part. To daughter Hannah Tyson, 1/5 part. To grandson Silas Yerkes, 1/5 part. To granddaughters Agnes and Elizabeth Craft, remaining 1/5 part.
Exec: Son John Craft. Wit: Isaac L. Mather, Bartholomew Mather, Jr.

DYER, ELIZABETH. Moreland.
Jan 26, 1807. March 18, 1812. 3.364
To son John Dyer, $2.00 yearly. To son James Dyer, $2.00 yearly. To daughter Elizabeth Dyer, $50. To daughter Deborah Dyer, household goods. To grandchildren, moned divided as follows: to grandson Moses, bible and $100. To granddaughter Deborah, $100. To grandson Edward, $3.00. To son Joseph $10.00 yearly and rem. of estate.
Exec: Joseph Dyer. Wit: John Hogeland, and Deborah Hogeland.

CHUTT, BARBARA.
March 3, 1812. April 7, 1812. 3.366
Rem. of estate after furneral expenses and debts are paid divided equally among all the children, equally.
Exec: Son in law Valentine Hunsicker. Wit: Henry Sweitzer, Abraham Zeigler.

SHERMAN, MARGARET. Montgomery.
Feb 26, 1811. April 9, 1812. 3.368
To niece Rebecca, watch, bible, and wearing apparel, etc. To Exrs. 5 pds. each, for their services. To Trustees of Presbyterian Church of Abington, rem. of estate, and 150 pds.
Codicil dated Jan 1, 1807. The portion to the Trustees of the Presbyterian Church of Abington, shall be applied to their successors.
Codicil dated Feb 6, 1811. To niece Rebecca, 6 pds. annually.
Execs: John Mann, N. B. Boileau, John Morrison. Wit: Samuel Leech, Richard Leech, and Samuel Leech, Sr.

JEANS, JACOB. Moreland.
Dec 1, 1799. May 1, 1812. 3.372
Household goods, divided equally among children: Isaiah, William, Amos, Elizabeth, Jane, Leah, Rachel, and Anna. Rem. of estate divided between sons: Isaiah and Williams Jeans subject to the payment of legacies. Rem. of sums from legacies to daughters: Elizabeth, Jane, Leah, Rachel, and Anna and son Amos. To daughters Leah, Rachel and Anna, 50 pds. each. To daughters 100 pds. to be paid by sons after wife's death. To son Amos,

312 pds. to be paid by sons Isaiah and William, after sons Amos is 21 and after he attains the age of 23 he shall receive 212 pds. To wife Leah, $200 yearly, during widowhood and privileges of farm.
Execs: Sons Isaiah and William. Wit: R. Whitehead, Bob Whitehead, William Harting, and Benjamin Brown.

REES, JOHN. Upper Merion.
April 1, 1811. May 6, 1812. 3.375
To son Philip, farm, 13 acres and farming utensils and household goods. To William Carver, lot, and 13 acres. To daughter Abigail, 13 acres, 50 pds. To grandchildren, 150 pds. when 21. To Elders of Radnor Meeting, $20. To May Cake, $20. when 18. Rem. of estate collected by Exrs. and to be put in interest and amount equally divided among grandchildren.
Execs: Sons Philip and son in law Thomas Loury. Wit: William Custer, David Brooke.

KERN, LORENTZ.
March 3, 1812. May 6, 1812. 3.378
To wife Eve, all estate and household goods, until son John is 18. If she marries before son John is 18 estate to be sold. to daughter Mary, bed, etc. To daughter Eve, bed, etc. To daughter Leity, bed, etc. Rem. of money from estate divided among children, equally: Henry, Margaret, widow of Henry Steler, Elizabeth wife of John Jacoby, Magdalena, wife of John Bittenbender, Mary, Eve, Leity, and John.
Execs: Wife Eve, and son in law John Jacoby. Wit: Henry Greber, Jacob Schneider.

BENSON, ANNA. Lower Providence.
Feb 23, 1812. May 6, 1812. 3.381
To daughter Nancy, wife of John Bunner, wearing apparel. Exrs. to divide household goods equally among granddaughters: Elizabeth, and Eleanor Roberts, and daughter of John Roberts, and money equally divided into 3 equal shares, among daughter Nancy, wife of John Bunner, Elizabeth Bunner, daughter of John Bunner, and Eleanor Roberts, daughter of John Roberts.
Execs: Peter Saylor and Amos Pennebecker. Wit: Isaac Hawk, Abraham Shutt.

MOCK, GEORGE. Upper Hanover.
May 24, 1811. May 18, 1812. 3.382
To wife Esther, 100 pds. yearly and household goods, and dwelling during widowhood. To son John, all lands in Douglass, containing 150 acres subject to the payment of 300 pds. To son George Mock, all lands in Upper Hanover, containing 150 acres subject to the payment of 1600 pds. Rem. of estate shall be equally divided among 6 daughters: Catharine, wife of Henry Hoffman, Margaret, wife of Conrad Geizer, Elizabeth, wife of Philip Christman, Esther, wife of Jacob Fisher, Margaret, wife of Adam

Eberhard, and Veronica.
Execs: Sons John and George. Wit: Adam Hittle, George Bechtel.

PENNEBACKER, JOHN. Upper Providence.
Aug 1, 1808. May 22, 1812. 3.387
To granddaughter Mary, walnut chest, and farm in Upper Providence, containing 70 acres. To wife Catharine, rem. of estate, after debts are paid. To grandson John, rem. of land, subject to the payment of $40 yearly to wife Catharine. To son Adolf, all estate.
Execs: son Adolf, and Samuel Grop. Wit: John Winter, and Henry Martin.

CAPEL, HENRY. Perkiomen and Skippack.
Oct 28, 1796. May 27, 1812. 3.389
To brother Zeller, of son Henry, farm, in Perkiomen and Skippack. To brother Herbert, 25 pds. To daughter Elizabeth, 5 pds. yearly. Rem. of estate shall be distributed among the poor.
Execs: Herbert Capel and Henry Capel. Wit: Henry Capel, son John and Henry Hunsicker.

FRICK, PETER. Hatfield.
July 15, 1808. June 9, 1812. 3.392
To children, nephews, and uncles and Catharine, wife of John all land. Son John to have 1425 pds. To Catharine, wife of John 40 pds. and guardian. To children of son John, money as follows: to son Peter, 90 pds. To son John, 88 pds. to son Henry, 82 pds. To son Samuel, 76 pds. To daughter Ann, 70 pds. To children of nephew Michael, 70 pds. equally. To children of son Michael, money as follows: to daughter Peggy, 70 pds. To son Jacob, 70 pds.
Exec: Martin Funk. Wit: John Funk, Abraham Hunsberger.

WELKER, GEORGE. Upper Hanover.
Aug 9, 1811. June 5, 1812. 3.394
To wife Margaret, household goods, and 600 pds. yearly and interest of 36 pds. and 12 pds. paid out of personal estate. Estate to be sold and rem. of money divided among youngest son, when 21. To sons George and John Welker, rem. of estate equally. To sons George and John Welker, 2 tracts of lands in Upper Hanover, containing 80 acres subject to the payment of 300 pds. and 600 pds. to stand for widow.
Execs: ____. Wit: George Hillegass, Jacob Welker.

RACOB, CHRISTIAN. Towamencin.
Jan 27, 1808. June 27, 1812. 3.399
To Christian Racob, son of brother Nicholas, 100 pds. After 3 years rem. divided equally among brother Frederick's children. To brother Joseph Racobs, of Alleghany County, 100 pds. To daughter Mary, 100 pds. To daughter Elizabeth, 100 pds. To Daniel Racob, 100 pds. To John Racob, 100 pds. If either die their share to be equally divided among brothers

and sisters. To daughter Susanna, 50 pds. To Catharine Racob, 25 pds. To John Racob, 25 pds. To Frederick Racob, Jr., 25 pds. To Jacob Fry, tract of land in Catawissa, containing 126 acres. To Trustees of School House, 50 pds. To Jacob Fry, all shoemaker tools. To Wolf Wisler, wearing apparel. Rem. of estate equally divided among children of brother Frederick.
Execs: Joseph Tyson of Worcester and Joseph Fry, of Towamencin.
Execs: William Gotshalk, Jacob Stouffer.

PRICHARD, JOSEPH. Whitpain.
May 17, 1812. July 29, 1812. 3.401
To wife Mary, income of land after sale of real estate, 150 pds. to be put in interest by step sons: John Harvey and Samuel Harvey for use of step son Thomas Harvey while his wife is living. Rem. of estate equally divided among : James Harvey, John Harvey, William Harvey, Samuel Harvey, Thomas Harvey, my step sons and Mary Slingluff my step daughter and her daughter Hannah Slingluff.
Execs: Wife Mary, and step sons John, Samuel and Thomas Harvey. Wit: Job Roberts, and Samuel Ashmead.

MISSEMER, CASSIMER. Pottsgrove.
Jan 2, 1810. Oct 10, 1812. 3.404
To son George, 75 acres of land and 750 pds. 300 pds. divided equally among children. To daughter Margaret, close press, etc. To son Jacob, 1/2 of 50 acres. To son Frederick, plow land, containing 5 acres. rem. of land divided among children, except George, Henry and Margaret. To daughter Margaret, bed, and wearing apparel. Rem. of estate divided equally among 3 daughters: Elizabeth, Hannah, and Catharine.
Execs: Son Jacob and Francis Bickney. Wit: Joseph Bitting, Samuel Evans.

WEBSTER, MARGARET. Upper Moreland.
July 8, 1811. Aug 11, 1812. 3.408
To Cornelia Vansant, wife of Henry Vansant, wearing apparel. To Rebecca Vansant, blue quilt. To niece Phebe, feather bed, etc. To Amelia Allimus, black silk gown, etc. To Eleanor Jones, gown, etc. To Margaret Todd, clock, etc. To Elizabeth Duffield, 1/2 of wearing apparel. To Hannah Jones, scissors, and chain. To Hannah Yerkes, sheets, etc. To Margaret Yerkes, quilt, etc. To brother Oliver beds, etc., and interest from all money and rem. of estate. To Margaret Yerkes, case of drawers, and rem. of wearing apparel. To Benjamin Yerkes, 15 pds. to James Yerkes, 20 pds. To brother Henry Vansant, 1/4 part of rem. of personal estate Rem. of estate to Joshua Jones.
Exec: Joshua Jones. Wit: Joshua Krewson, Clarissa Krewson.

BEAN, JOSHUA. Providence.
May 11, 1812. Aug 21, 1812. 3.410

To Joshua Bean, $500 when 21. To nephew James Bean, rem. of estate.
Exec: Nephew James Bean. Wit: Daniel Morgan, William Casselbury.

POTTS, JAMES. Upper Dublin.
July 30, 1812. Aug 27, 1812. 3.411
To wife Elizabeth, all estate, and $20 annually. To son David, $200 when 21 and interest thereof to his mother during widowhood. To 3 children: Jane, Davie and Thomas, money from estate, equally.
Execs: Wife Elizabeth, and George Fitzwater. Wit: Elizabeth Updegrove, Josiah Wood.

YOST, DANIEL. Whitpain.
Dec 21, 1811. Sept 3, 1812. 3.413
To sons Jacob and Abraham, plantation and 4 tracts of land, containing 114 acres subject to the payment of 14 s., 1 d. To sons Isaac and Abraham, tools. To sons Jacob and Abraham and daughters Mary and Sarah, 250 pds. To daughters Mary and Sarah, bed, etc. To sons Jacob and Abraham, 220 pds. Rem. of estate divided equally among children: Jacob, Peter, Abraham, Mary and Sarah. To son Peter, 376 pds., 17 s.
Execs: Sons Peter, and Abraham. Wit: Randal Osborn, Abraham Phillips, Fred Conrad.

GORDON, GEORGE. Montgomery.
Oct 15, 1810. Sept 10, 1812. 3.416
To wife Elizabeth, household goods. Exrs. to put 500 pds. on interest for wife during widowhood. To son John, plantation in Montgomery, woodland containing 5 acres. To son Jonathan, $30 yearly. To son Jonathan, rem. of lands containing 86 1/4 acres. To son John, $30. yearly. To daughter Sarah, wife of John Newberry, 250 pds. To grandson George Newberry, 50 pds. To daughter Elizabeth, 300 pds. To son John, farm, and household goods. Rem. of estate divided equally among children.
Execs: Sons John and Jonathan. Wit: Nathan Roberts, Cadwalder Foulke, and Margaret Foulke.

WIREMAN, JOHN. Hatfield.
Oct 22, 1811. Oct 10, 1812. 3.421
To brother Abraham, silver watch. To sister Sophia, umbrella. Rem. of property to cousin Abraham Ruth.
Exec: Isaac Morris. Wit: John Funk, Isaac Morris.

HOMER, WILLIAM. Upper Dublin.
Jan 20, 1806. Oct 15, 1812. 3.423
To wife Mary, household goods, privilege of using house. $60 annually during her life. To granddaughter Elizabeth, rem. of household goods. To son William, house, and farm, containing 140 acres during life. To his daughter Elizabeth, at the age of 25 to have 40 pds. After son William's decease his share to be divided among children. To daughter Mary

[*annotation adds Ryon?*], 200 pds. To daughter Elizabeth [*annotation adds Dubre*], 200 pds. To daughter Jona, 175 pds. with bond 25 pds. Rem. of estate divided among my grandchildren: Homer Dubre, David Davis and William Hallowell each 40 pds. and share with the rest.
Execs: Son in law Joseph Hallowell and son William Homer. Wit: Jesse Hallowell.

GERGES, ABRAHAM. Perkiomen.
March 30, 1812. Oct 24, 1812. 3.426
To wife Elizabeth, tract of lands containing 10 acres. Personalty to be sold. Exrs. to sell plantation and 2 tracts of land and money from them shall be divided as follows: to heirs of brother Conrad, 1/5 part. To heirs of sister Mary, wife of John Hildabiale, 1/5 part. To heirs of brother William, 1/5 part. To heirs of brother Henry, 1/5 part. To heirs of sister Saloma, wife of Abraham Berga, 1/5 part. To wife during widowhood, 1/2 of estate, which was valued at $2666.67. Rem. of money to be put on interest and divided in the following manner: to heirs of sister Catharine, wife of Philip Fisher, 1/7 part. To heirs of brother Henry Zeigler, 1/7 part. To heirs of brother Andrew, 1/7 part. To heirs of brother George, 1/7 part. To heirs of brother John, 1/7 part. To heirs of brother Mark, 1/7 part. To heirs of brother Philip, 1/7 part.
Execs: Abraham Kile, David Allabach. Wit: Jacob Sorver Tyson.

LUKENS, JOHN. Lower Providence.
Oct 12, 1812. Nov 3, 1812. 3.430
To daughter Mary, saddle, feather bed, etc. To daughter Catharine, saddle, $28 and feather bed. Exrs. to sell both real and personal estate at public sale. Rem. of estate divided among children: Abraham, Francis Gurney, Samuel, Lavina, wife of Jesse Brocke, Maria, wife of Peter Pricerer, and Catharine, Catharine and Mary to receive their shares when 21.
Execs: Francis Gurney Lukens, and son in law Jesse Brooke. Wit: Joseph Henry, and William Casselbury.

MOORE, JOHN. Upper Merion.
Feb 14, 1803. Nov 16, 1812. 3.433
To son John 5 pds. and to his children 5 pds. each when 21. To grandchildren: Morris Stephens, and David Stephens, 30 pds. when 21. To son Jonathan, 110 pds. To 3 children of Jonathan Moore, 10 pds. when 18. To Thomas Moore, 10 pds. when 21. To son in law Abijah Stephens, 5 s. To John Evans, 5 pds. To granddaughter Jane Moore, silver chains, etc. To John Moore, cow. To son Richard, clock, and rem. of estate except 55 pds. To John Moore and his 5 children.
Execs: Son Richard, and Jonathan Cleaver. Wit: Hannah Jones, and Israel Jones.

PAUL, JAMES. Moreland.

July 24, 1812. Nov 24, 1812. 3.435
To son David, 400 pds. when 21. Rem. of estate to wife, Martha Paul. If she marries to children.
Exec: Martha Paul. Wit: Robert Milne, Thomas Stemple, Herman Daniels.

DeHAVEN, JOHN. Whitpain.
May 15, 1799. Dc 18, 1812. 3.437
To son David, farm, containing 44 acres and land in Skippack, containing 12 acres. To wife Elizabeth, use of house, and 15 pds. yearly and featherbed, household goods. To daughter Lydia Wents, 20 s. To 4 grandchildren: Jonathan, Samuel, Levi, and Jacob Wentz, 150 pds. as follows: to Jonathan 60 pds. To grandsons Levi and Samuel, and Jacob 30 pds. each. Rem. of estate to son David DeHaven.
Execs: Wife Elizabeth and son David. Wit: Morgan Morgan, and Samuel Slingloof.

MATSON, CATHARINE. Upper Merion.
Nov 25, 1812. Dec 2, 1812. 3.439
To daughter Hannah bed, etc. To daughter Ann, bed, etc. To son Samuel, money from sale of cow to be put on interest until son Samuel is 21 years of age. If he dies his share divided equally among 3 daughters: Hannah, Elizabeth and Ann. Exrs. to rent farm where I now live after my death and money from the rents to be divided among 3 daughters: Hannah, Elizabeth, and Ann, equally. To son: William, Jonathan, Isaac, Robert, John, and Job, 5 s. each.
Exec: David Lukens. Wit: William Matson, Jonathan Matson.

REINEWALT, MELCHIOR. Towamencin.
Nov 2, 1810. Dec 18, 1812. 3.441
To wife Rosanna, household goods, and 100 pds. yearly. To son Jonas, tools, etc. Rem. to children equally. Exrs. to make appraisement of property and son Jonas and daughter Lydia shall keep as much as they choose until son Jonas is 21 years of age. And rem. shall be divided equally into 3 shares, among wife and 2 sons. To son Jonas lot in Towamencin containing 46 1/2 acres.
Execs: Andrew Kriebel, and brother in law Jacob Snyder. Wit: Henry Snyder, Frederick Conrad.

KNEEDLER, JACOB. Horsham.
June 3, 1809. Jan 11, 1813. 3.445.
To wife, household goods, $40 yearly during widowhood. To son Jacob, Bible. To son Joseph, sermon book. To son Samuel, silver watch. To sons: Jacob, John, Joseph, and daughter Elizabeth, 40 pds. to sons: George, Daniel, Adam, William and Samuel, remaining 50 pds. To John Kneedler, 50 pds. to son John Deim, 10 pds. to Elizabeth Lentz, daughter of Nicholas Lentz, 5 pds. towards her education. To Philip Curemen, $20. To John Ambler, farm in Gwynedd, where he now dwells, subject to the

payment of 40 s. per year. Exrs. to pay the said person or persons of the Congregation of the Church of Upper Dublin 10 pds. Rem. of estate to be sold except 1 acre and money divided among 9 children: Elizabeth, Jacob, John, George, Joseph, Daniel, Adam, William and Samuel Kneedler equally. 100 pds. shall be given to daughter Elizabeth at the time a division shall take place.
Execs: Sons Jacob and Joseph and John Singer. Wit: Job Roberts, and Charles Mather.

FETTER, RACHEL. Moreland.
Feb 4, 1806. Jan 23, 1813. 3.450
To son Michael, feather bed, etc. and 50 pds. To son William Fetter, desk. To daughter Cathrine Benner 1/2 dozen silver tea spoons. To daughter Ann, feather bed, etc. To granddaughter Mary Benner, daughter of George, 1/2 dozen chairs and shawl. To granddaughter Rachel, small tea table. To granddaughter Ann 4 silver tea spoons. Rem. of estate divided among 3 daughters: Rachel, Catharine and Anna, equally. To son George, 9 pds. yearly for rent due which has not been settled.
Execs: Son George and son in law John Heritage. Wit: Joshua Comly, Christian Snyder, John Worthington.

INGHART, MARY. Upper Dublin.
Jan 11, 1811. Feb 2, 1813. 3.452
To son Adam, and his heirs, 27 pds. To grandson John, son of Adam. 10 pds. To sister Margaret, 10 pds. and their money put on interest for their benefit. Rem. of estate to daughters Catharine and Anna, to be divided equally. House and lot in Upper Dublin to be sold.
Execs: Casper Schlater, and George Peirce. Wit: Samuel Livezey, Jacob Albertson, George Peirce.

MOYER, JACOB. Lower Salford.
July 11, 1809. Feb 3, 1813. 3.454
To sons Jacob and Joseph, all estate and land containing 166 acres subject to the payment of 15 pds. per acre yearly. After other years payment the sum of 200 pds. to be equally divided among 7 children: Susanna, Christian, Jacob, Maria, Abraham, Sarah, and Joseph. To wife, 50 pds. and children to give money when ever necessary 50 pds.
Execs: Sons Christian and Jacob. Wit: Jacob Kolb, Joseph Alderfer.

MOSTELLER, MICHAEL. Germantown.
___, 1776. Feb 16, 1813. 3.457
To John Hesser, money for the support of my father Peter Mosteller, if he dies before money is exponded to sister Sully and other sisters.
Execs: John Hesser, and Jonathan Custard. Wit: John Burk, Daniel Burk.

POLIZ, VALENTINE. Upper Providence.
Jan 29, 1813. Feb 20, 1813. 3.458

To wife Elizabeth, farm, and household goods, and 50 pds. Rem. of estate to be sold and money divided equally among children, excepting daughter Catharine. To son Henry, 30 pds. more than rest of children. To son David, 5 acres for erecting a house, subject to the payment of 50 pds. Execs: Son Jacob and wife Elizabeth. Wit: John Shantz, George Schwenk.

RHOADS, EZEKIEL. Norriton.
Feb 16, 1809. March 2, 1813. 3.463
To wife, 100 pds. to be paid to her with 30 days and household goods. To son Ezekiel, tract of land containing 100 acres subject to the payment of 900 pds. to 7 daughters and also 15 pds. yearly to wife. To son Abraham, land purchased of Elizabeth Norris, subject to the payment of 150 pds. to sisters. To son Joseph, land in Norriton containing 25 acres, 5 perches. The several sums of money amounting to 1750 pds. are to be divided as follows: to daughters: Eleanor, Elizabeth, Margaret, Lydia Barbara, Hannah, and Anna, 250 pds. each. To daughter Eleanor, clock. To daughter Barbara, and Anna, 20 pds. each. Rem. of estate to sons Ezekiel and Joseph equally. They paying to daughters Barbara and Anna, 30 pds. Execs: Sons Abraham, and Ezekiel, and Joseph. Wit: Joseph Tyson, William Zimmerman.

JOHNSON, MARY.
Dec 16, 1812. March 16, 1813. 3.465
To granddaughter Mary Carver, $21.33, and bed, etc. To daughter Hannah Supplee, second gown, and skirt. To son Abner Hughes, $16. etc. To daughter Elizabeth Carver, $16. To grandson Jesse Carver, $8. Exrs. to pay all debts and funeral expenses. Rem. of estate divided among 3 children: Hannah Supplee, Abner Hughes, and Elizabeth Carver, and granddaughter Mary Carver, equally.
Execs: son Abner Hughes and William Carver. Wit: John Roberts, and Samuel Henderson.

STOUFFER, GARNET. Perkiomen.
March 24, 1812. March 13, 1813. 3.467
To wife Margaret, household goods, and 125 pds. to be paid to her by son John. To daughter Catharine, wife of Jacob Speer, lot and 275 pds. Rem. of estate divided among 3 children, equally. Daughter Catharine's share to be kept in the hands of the Exrs.
Execs: Sons Dillman and John. Trustee, Henry Hunsicker. Wit: Garnet Hunsicker, and Henry Hunsicker.

ENZEST, PHILIP. Upper Dublin.
Aug 23, 1811. March 31, 1813. 3.469
Estate to be sold. To Mary Houser daughter of Elizabeth Willhelms, $40, when 21. Rem. of estate divided as follows: to son Philip, 1/9 equal part. To son in law Joseph Ramsey and Barbara his wife, 1/9 equal part. To Jacob Houpt and Catharine, his wife, 1/9 equal part. To son Nicholas, 1/9

part. To daughter Mary Long, interest of 1/2 of those equal parts, and after her death her share divided among children. To daughter Dorothy, interest of those equal parts, and after her death divided among her children, equally. To William one equal part. To daughter Elizabeth one equal part and her daughter Mary equally. To son Peter, one equal part. To grandson William Frat, 1/2 equal part.
Exec: Henry Scheetz. Wit: Abraham Lukens and Catharine Hocker.

SMITH, HENRY. Lower Merion.
Nov 15, 1811. April 6, 1813. 3.471
To granddaughter Mary Clawson, $266.67 when 21. If she shall die her share to be divided equally among children. To daughter Christina, household goods. Estate to be sold and money divided equally among children: Joseph, Henry, William, John, Christina, and Mary.
Execs: Sons Joseph and Henry. Wit: Jacob Kolb, David Kulp.

SAHLER, PERTER. Limerick.
Sept 12, 1807. May 17, 1813. 3.473
To wife Sarah, house old and interest of 400 pds. To children: John, Elizabeth, Catharine, and Susanna, all estate. To son John, wearing apparel, and 1/5 part of estate. To daughters: Elizabeth, Catharine and Sarah, 1/5 part equally. To daughter Susanna, 1/5 part.
Execs: Son John Sahler, and son in law Henry Walt. Wit: George Nyce, Benjamin Markley.

SPENCER, JAMES. Upper Dublin.
Oct 17, 1812. May 18, 1813. 3.476.
To wife Elizabeth, all property, and 50 pds. and 3 cords firewood, and 25 pds. yearly. To son Abner, stove pipe etc. To son William, tract of land in Upper Dublin, 36 3/4 acres and 1/4 rem. of personalty. To grandson Josiah Spencer, tract of land 25 acres, 143 perches during life. To be held in trust. To children of son James' 1/4 part of estate. To son James, 1/2 of wearing apparel. To daughter in law Mary, share of son Josiah's estate. To grandson Morgan Spencer, tract of land in Upper Dublin, containing 33 acres, 50 perches. Rem. of estate divided among son James' children, equally when 21. Grandson Morgan to pay to daughter in law Mariam Spencer, 9 pds. annually. To daughter Elizabeth Shoemaker, 2 tracts of land in Upper Dublin, and 1/4 part of estate. And rem. of personal estate. To son Abner, farm, where I now dwell, subject to the payment of 15 pds. yearly, and 1/4 part of estate.
Codicil dated March 6, 1813. To Exrs. tract of land in Upper Dublin. To grandsons 2 acres of land and money divided equally among children of son James, equally.
Execs: Sons William and Abner. Wit: Thomas Livezey, Rynear Fitzwater.

ROOP, JACOB. Montgomery.
April 3, 1813. May 24, 1813. 3.486

To Isaac Markley, all estate.
Execs: Jacob Capel, and Isaac Markley. Wit: John Thomas, Henry Hartman.

NACE, JACOB. Springfield.
Sept 1, 1812. May 25, 1813. 3.488
To wife Mary, all estate. To stepchildren all land in Whitemarsh, 1 2/4 acres. Rem. of estate divided equally among children.
Execs: Son Jacob Nace and step son Jacob Dager. Wit: John Husten, and Jacob Husten.

COX, JONATHAN. Upper Providence.
May 5, 1813. June 3, 1813. 3.490
To sister Sarah, deed of 10 acres of land. To sister Mary Cox, 500 pds. and household goods. To Susanna Abel, 400 pds. To brothers William and Jonathan, $10, each. To brother Joseph Cox, all estate.
Execs: Brother Joseph Cox, and sister Sarah Wilson. Wit: John Hunsberry, John Jacobs.

SELEER, MARY. Gwynedd.
July 1, 1811. June 14, 1813. 3.492
To son John, 10 pds. To son Henry, 20 pds. To son Jacob, 10 pds. To son Abraham, 10 pds. To grandson Elis, 5 pds. Rem. of money divided among children, equally.
Exec: Son John. Wit: John Roberts, Jesse Ambler.

NAUGLE, JACOB. New Hanover.
May 11, 1812. June 17, 1813. 3.494
To wife Grace, all estate. To Aaron Lenderman, land in Hanover.
Execs: Wife Grace, and John Buckwalter. Wit: Peter Yost, Samuel Evans.

WAMBOLD, JACOB. Franconia.
Dec 11, 1812. June 26, 1813. 3.495
To wife Barbara, household goods, and 300 pds. yearly. To son Jacob, farm, 60 acres subject of the payment of 1200 pds. and 1644 pds. paid in yearly payments and pay to wife 120 pds. To son George, 1/4 equal part of estate and 100 pds. To daughter Barbara, wife of Henry Benner, 1/4 equal part of estate. To daughter Catharine, wife of Jacob Benner, 1/4 equal part of estate. Exrs. to make public sale of rem. of estate.
Execs: Son George, and son in law Henry Benner. Wit: Michael Shoemaker, John Gerhart.

BAKER, GEORGE. Norriton.
Feb 26, 1813. June 26, 1813. 3.499
To daughter Sarah, household goods, and 300 pds. to be paid to her by son Frederick. To son Frederick, farm, during term of single life. To daughter Nancy, wife of John Shade, 100 pds. to be paid to her by son

Frederick. To son Frederick, tract of land in Norriton, containing 172 acres subject to the payment of 440 pds. to sisters Sarah and Nancy. Rem. of money after debts and funeral expenses are paid equally divided among son John and daughters Sarah and Nancy.
Execs: Son Frederick, and Frederick Conrad. Wit: Jacob Derrick, Nathan Custer.

KEPHART, ADAM. Limerick.
Aug 14, 1810. July 3, 1813. 3.500
Estate to be sold and money from sale to be put on interest for wife, and she to receive 200 pds. annually, 12 pds. to be paid within one year after my decease. To daughter Eve, wife of John Kephart, $200. Rem. of estate to 6 children: daughter Eve, Andrew, John, Adam and Christian, and daughter Elizabeth, equally.
Execs: John Newman, and Michael Dotterer. Wit: Jacob Reifsnyder, Benjamin Markley.

KEER, RACHEL. Cheltenham.
May 16, 1809. July 6, 1813. 3.504
To son George Keer, $267. Debts anf funeral expenses to be paid. To son George, family bible. To granddaughter Rachel, bed, etc. Rem. of estate equally divided among children.
Exec: John Shoemaker. Wit: Charles Shoemaker, Eli Berril.

BROOKE, JOHN. Limerick.
June 20, 1813. July 16, 1813. 3.506
To wife Mary, house and lot, where I now dwell in Limerick, containing 38 acres and household goods, and $48 yearly. To daughters Mary and Ann, bed, etc. Rem. of household goods, divided equally among children: Mary, Ann, John, and William. To son Jesse, tract of land. To son Robert, tract of land. To daughter Elizabeth and Thomas, and Jesse, tract of land equally valued at $1200. Rem. of estate divided as follows: to grandchildren: Elizabeth, Thomas, and Jesse, 1/9 part. To daughter Rachel, wife of Owen Evans, 1/9 part. To son Robert, 1/9 part. To Nathan, Harriet, and Elizabeth, and Charlotte, 1/9 part each. To daughter Charlotte, wife of James Evans, 1/9 part. To daughter Mary, 1/9 part. To daughter Ann, 1/9 part. To son John, 1/9 part. To son William, 1/9 part. If any of these shall die their share divided among children.
Execs: Wife Mary, and son Robert, and son in law Owen Evans, and James Evans. Wit: James Harris, James Brooke.

HUGHES, ATKINSON. Horsham.
Aug 3, 1813. Aug 30, 1813. 3.509
To son Thomas, 10 acres. To son Atkinson, 3 acres. To son Thomas, and Atkinson, rem. of estate. To wife Jane, farm, and household goods. To daughter Ruth, 6 pds. yearly. To daughter Susanna 100 pds. and 100 pds. to be equally divided among children. To daughter Martha, 100 pds. To

daughter Elizabeth, 100 pds. To daughter Jane, 100 pds. Rem. of estate to Exrs.
Execs: Sons Thomas and Atkinson. Wit: Hugh Foulke, Joseph Kenderdine, and Robert Sutton.

STARE, ROSANNA. Worcester.
Aug 29, 1813. Sept 4, 1813. 3.512
To daughter Deborah, wearing apparel, and household goods. Rem. of estate Exrs. to sell and money divided among children.
Exec: Henry William Conrad. Wit: Michael Brunner, Frederick Conrad.

PALMER, THOMAS. Horsham.
Dec 11, 1812. Sept 11, 1813.
To wife, Tacy, farm, and household goods, and $107 yearly during widowhood. To son George, 55 acres subject to the payment of $53.50 and $60 yearly. Rem. of estate to son John and William. To son John and William, each a horse. To daughters Lydia and Susanna, $1200 each.
Execs: Sons George and Charles. Wit: Nathan Lukens, and Hiram McNeill.

LUKENS, JOHN. Towamencin.
June 19, 1811. Sept 18, 1813. 3.517
To wife, horse and feather bed, and interest of 1500 pds. To 2 grandchildren, John and Edith, 100 pds. when 22. To son George, farm, where I now dwell, containing 100 acres subject to the payment of 1500 pds. Rem. of estate to 3 sons: David, George, and Joel equally.
Execs: Sons David, George, and Joel. Wit: Cadwalader Evans, Jr., Charles Jenkins.

OSBORNE, JANE. Whitpain.
May 3, 1803. Oct 2, 1813. 3.519
To brother Robert, 45 pds. If he dies his share to be divided equally among children. To brother Evan two bonds of 15 pds. and 30 pds. against him. To nephew John Hallman, 40 pds. To John, son of brother Evan, 20 pds. To Margaret, child of brother Evan, case of drawers, and feather bed, etc. To David, child of brother Evan, cow, and 20 pds. Rachel Evans. To Joseph and Evan, children of brother Evan, 10 pds. each. If Evan die his share to be divided equally among John, David and Joseph. To Sarah Thomas, 10 pds. To Job Thomas, 40 pds. to Samuel Thomas, 100 pds. Rem. of estate divided equally amoang 3 nieces: Margaret, Susanna, and Rachel Thomas.
Codicil dated May 3, 1803. To children of John Hallman deceased, 50 pds. each, when 21 and 18 years.
Exec: Samuel Thomas. Wit: Joseph Lewis, Benjamin Markley.

SORBER, JACOB. Hatfield.
Feb 5, 1812. Oct 11, 1813. 3.522

To wife Catharine, household goods, and 100 pds. To son Jacob, and John, 150 pds. each. To daughter Elizabeth, 100 pds. Rem. of estate to son Philip and David and 2 granddaughters Elizabeth and Catharine, equally. To granddaughter Catharine, 50 pds.
Execs: Sons Philip and David. Wit: Edward Hoxworth, John Hoxworth, and Frederick Conrad.

LEVERING, ELIZABETH. Plymouth.
Aug 30, 1812. Oct 12, 1813. 3.524
To 3 daughters wearing apparel, equally. To daughter Alice Cox, 2 acres of land. To grandson Joseph, son of Peter, interest of $100 annually. Rem. of estate to be sold and money equally divided among children: Mary, Magdalena, Peter, Alice, shares of Alice and Magdalena to be left in the hands of the Exrs. until 21.
Execs: Son William Levering and William Shepherd. Wit: Levi Evans, Cadwalder Foulke.

SAYLOR, HENRY. Limerick.
May 8, 1809. Nov 9, 1813. 3.527
To wife Susanna, farm, and household goods. To son Henry lands in Limerick, and Providence, he paying to sister Susanna 100 pds. Exrs. to sell property and money to be put on interest until son Henry is 21. To step daughter Hannah, 10 pds.
Execs: Samuel Evans, and Samuel Grop. Wit: Michael Razer, and John Rambo.

SKEEN, SAMUEL. Pottsgrove.
Aug 3, 1813. Nov 11, 1813. 3.529
To wife Jamima, household goods, and farm, and 125 pds. yearly. Estate after 2 months of my decease to be sold and money divided among children: Peter, Mary, Samuel, William, Elmer, equally.
Execs: Sons Peter and Samuel. Wit: John Schneider, Jacob Tuchs.

REIFSCHNEIDER, SEBASTIAN. New Hanover.
March 20, 1810. Nov 5, 1813. 3.531
To wife Catharine, household goods, and 500 pds. yearly, during widowhood. To son John, 300 pds. To son Jacob, 300 pds. To son Abraham, 300 pds. to son David, 300 pds. To daughter Catharine, 100 pds. To daughter Elizabeth, wife of Abraham Dotterer, 108 pds. To daughter Magdalena, wife of Nicholas Swoyer, 145 pds., 10 s. and daughter Catharine to have interest of 200 pds. and after her decease divided among children, equally: Isaac, Sarah, Dotterer. To children of daughter Magdalena, 145 pds., 10 s. To daughters: Hannah, Susanna, and Lidia, 300 pds. when 18.
Execs: Wife Catharine, and sons John and Jacob. Wit: Tobias Yerger, and John Reigner.

HAUCK, JACOB. Frederick.
July 15, 1813. Nov 15, 1813. 3.534
To wife Margaret, interest of plantation and farm, containing 135 acres and household goods, and interest of 300 pds. yearly during widowhood. To son John, $30. To wife, all estate, after her death to be sold and interest of 1400 pds. divided equally among 11 children: Jacob, John, Henry, George, Daniel, Charles, Molly, Elizabeth, Margaret, Sarah, and Catharine, equally.
Execs: Sons Jacob and Henry. Wit: Benjamin Markley, Ludwig Schultz.

JONES, MARY. Pottstown.
July 28, 1813. Nov 17, 1813. 3.538
To daughter Sarah Jones, 200 pds. and silver spoons, etc. To daughter Ann Mintzer, silver coffee pot, etc. To 3 children: Joseph, William and Ann, house in which testator lived, etc. Rem. equally divided among all children: Catharine, wife of Frederick Smith, George Leaf, Joseph, William and Ann Mintzer and Sarah Jones. Estate to be sold reserving 1/2 acre. To Hannah Reifsnyder, $50.
Execs: Sons George, and son in law Jacob Smith. Wit: Jacob Drinkhouse, William Thomas.

WAGNER, PETER. Montgomery.
Dec 14, 1812. Nov 26, 1813. 3.540
To wife Mary, personal estate. She and son John to have real estate during their lives. Rem. after selling real estate. To daughter Elizabeth, 1/5. To children of deceased son Balter, 1/5. To children of son Peter, 1/5. To son Frederick, 1/5. To son George, 1/5. Son John to be maintained out of estate if principle be used. To daughter Dorothy, and Catharine, nothing at their request.
Execs: Wife Mary, and Isaac Wambold. Wit: Abraham Johnson, Lewis Grater.

STONG, PHILIP. Worcester.
Dec 12, 1802. Dec 3, 1813. 3.543
To wife Barbara, income of 300 pds. rem. and maintenance, household goods, etc. To son Philip Stong, tract of 26 acres also 5 acres woodland. To son Frederick, home farm, 132 acres subject to the payment of legacies. To sons: Jacob, Philip, Henry, Conrad, and Frederick, 100 pds. each, amount already received to be deducted. To 5 daughters, 150 pds. each. Rem. of estate divided among 11 children.
Codicil dated May 31, 1807. Share of daughter Susanna Johnson in the hands of executors in trust, after her death to her children.
Execs: Sons Philip Conrad and Frederick. Wit: Frederick Conrad, John Hamsher, and Abraham Weber.

FRITMER, JOHN. Lower Merion.
Dec 6, 1813. Dec 18, 1813. 3.550

To wife all estate.
Execs:___. Wit: William Thomas, John Kinzie.

BOYER, PHILIP. New Hanover.
Nov 24, 1810. Dec 31, 1813. 4.1
Wife Margaret shall live on farm, 3 years after my decease. Exrs. to sell land. Estate to be sold and money divided among 12 children: Susanna, Catharine, George, Henry, Mary, Elizabeth, Philip, John, William, Sally, Jonah, and Margaret, when 21. To wife Margaret, household goods, and 400 pds. annually.
Execs: Wife Margaret, George Boyer, and George Beyderman. Wit: Jacob Dengler, Conrad Geist.

NORRIS, CHARLES. Norriton.
July 28, 1813. Jan 5, 1814. 4.3
To daughter Mary, tract of land containing 170 acres. To daughter Deborah, tract of land containing 229 acres. To daughter Hephzibah, tract of land where I now dwell containing 30 acres. To mother in law Hephzibah Gardner, privilege of living in house where I occupy and $50 yearly during widowhood. To sister in law Keziah Gardner, $240 yearly and after her death $240 among daughters Deborah, and Hephzibah, equally. Rem. of estate to daughters Doborah, and Hepzibah, equally.
Exec: Albanus Logan. Wit: David Schrack, John Buttetswa, and Matthew Dill.

STETLER, CHRISTIAN. Frederick.
Feb 12, 1812. Jan 15, 1814. 4.5
To wife Catharine, farm, and household goods, and 500 pds. during widowhood. If she marries interest of 250 pds. and 10 pds. within 2 months after my decease. To son Adam, farm, where I now dwell containing 129 acres and interest of 1500 pds. yearly. To son Christian, bed, etc., and interest of 600 pds. yearly. Estate to be sold and money to be equally divided among children: Henry, Abraham, Adam, and Salomi.
Execs: Sons, Henry, Abraham, and Adam. Wit: Philip Leydich.

ROSHON, PETER. [Annotation states "*Pierre Ruchon.*"] Frederick.
Feb 11, 1804. Feb 14, 1814. 4.9
Estate to be sold and money divided among 6 children, equally except daughter Christina, 35 pds. to be deducted. To son Henry, 1/6 equal part. To son John, 1/6 equal part. To daughter Elizabeth, wife of Christian Wannamaker, 1/6 equal part. To daughter Catharine, wife of Jacob Scheifly, 1/6 equal part. To daughter Christian, wife of Jacob Estenmiller, 35 pds. To daughter Molly, 35 pds. over and above her equal 1/6 part.
Execs: Henry Roshon, and John Roshon. Wit: Benjamin Markley, Philip Boyer, Jr.

RICHARDS, MARIA. Lower Providence.

April 6, 1814. April 16, 1814. 4.11
To Martha Lally, $20, etc. To niece Sally Richards, $20, and wearing apparel. To Menonist Congregation of Skippack, $6. Rem. of goods to be sold and money to be put in a head stone for my grave.
Execs: Christopher Zimmerman. Wit: William Casselberry, and John Hunsicker.

THOMAS, JOHN. Plymouth.
Aug 3, 1812. April 7, 1814. 4.12
To wife Mary, money arising from estate. To daughter Grace, 200 pds. To daughter Mary, 200 pds. To son Daniel, 260 pds. to daughter Sarah, 250 pds. To son Samuel, 150 pds. To son John, 150 pds. To 6 grandchildren: James, Allen, Thomas, Catharine, Mary, and Sarah Wood, 150 pds. equally. To grandchildren living at my decease, $100 each. Rem. of estate to daughters: Grace, and Mary, and son Daniel Thomas, equally.
Exec: Son Thomas. Wit: George Peirce, Jacob Albertson.

HEDRICK, PETER. Upper Salford.
___, 1812. May 3, 1814. 4.14
To wife Catharine, all estate, during widowhood. If she marries, to have 1/3 equal part, and rem. divided equally among children: Peter, Abraham, Christian, Jacob, Henry, John, Michael and Catharine. To son Michael, $10 and 6 acres, 9 perches.
Execs: John Driesbauch, Christian Hedrick. Wit: William Andich, Jacob Gable.

WYNKOOP, CATHARINE. Moreland.
Oct 15, 1811. May 7, 1814. 4.15
To son Isaac, bond of $536.36, etc. To son Cornelius, sheets, etc. To son Abraham, table cloth, etc. To daughter Rebecca, wearing apparel, bed, etc. To grandson John, clock. To granddaughter Catharine, 1/2 dozen tea spoons. To granddaughter Catharine, basket of tea ware. Rem. of estate divided equally among grandchildren.
Exec: Mahlon Booskirk. Wit: Isaac Warner, Jane Hunter.

UPDEGROVE, ANN. Lower Providence.
Feb 15, 1814. May 16, 1814. 4.17
To Hester Reed, wearing apparel, bed, etc. If there is amy money left after paying expenses, to daughter Ann, wife of Jacob Clemmons.
Exec: William Casselberry. Wit: Jacob Fronfield, and James Bean.

JUNKIN, ANNA BARBARA. Springfield.
Dec 10, 1811. May 16, 1814. 4.18
To grandson Jacob, $125. To granddaughter Susanna Heydrick, wife of Abraham Heydrick, $125 and trunk, and wearing apparel. Rem. of estate to grandson Jacob, and granddaughter Susanna, equally. To grandson Jacob and granddaughter Susanna, all real estate, equally.

Execs: Granson in law Abraham Heydrick, and John Huston. Wit: Abraham Heydrick, John Stanberger, Isaac Carmalt.

EMERICH, VALENTINE. Skippack and Perkiomen.
Jan 25, 1810. May 26, 1814. 4.20
To wife Elizabeth, farm, and household goods, and interest of 150 pds. during widowhood, and wearing apparel. To son John's 5 children, 5 s. each. To son George, one equal share of estate. To daughter Catharine, interest of 50 pds. and after her death to her children, equally. To daughter Dorothy interest of 150 pds. To son Philip, one equal share of estate, and wearing apparel. To daughter Elizabeth, interest of one equal share of estate and after her death to her children, equally. To Michael Climer, 5 s. To Mary Baker, interest of 50 pds. and after her death to her children. To granddaughter Catharine, interest of 25 pds.
Execs: John Rahn, and Jacob Rosenberger. Wit: Andrew Todd, and Samuel Grop.

LANDES, ISAAC. Franconia.
April 4, 1814. June 3, 1814. 4.23
To wife Catharine, household goods. To sons John and Henry, farm, of 77 acres and 1500 pds. equally. Rem. of estate to be sold and money divided among children equally: John, Henry, Elizabeth, Mary, and Anna.
Execs: Sons John and Henry. Wit: Michael Shoemaker, and Abraham Harley, and Jacob Landes.

OBERHOLTZER, JACOB. Franconia.
Dec 30, 1813. June 3, 1814. 4.26
To wife Elizabeth, household goods, and farm. To son John, tract of land containing 10 acres. To grandchild Gehman, 120 acres subject to the payment of 150 pds. yearly.
Execs: Son in law Samuel Gehman. Wit: Michael Shoemaker, John Sechler.

HARPLE, CATHARINE. New Hanover.
May 30, 1806. June 13, 1814. 4.28
To daughter Barbara, large iron kettle. Rem. of estate to 3 children: daughter Barbara, Anna Maria, wife of Daniel Swinehart, and Christina, wife of Michael Bender, and daughter in law Catharine Harple, widow of son Jacob, divided into 4 equal parts, as follows: to daughter Barbara, 1/4 equal part. To daughter Anna Maria, 1/4 equal part. To daughter Christina, 1/4 equal part. to daughter in law Catharine, 1/4 equal part.
Exec: Jacob Brendlinger. Wit: Benjamin Markley, and Peter Esterline.

REX, CHRISTIAN. Springfield.
Oct 31, 1807. Aug 22, 1814. 4.29
To wife Margaret, all money and all estate, $3033.33. To sister Catharine, $16, yearly. to 6 grandchildren: Ann, Margaret, William, Jesse,

Christopher, and Mary, $133.33 each. To Sarah Harsh, $133.33. To son Jesse, $800. To Charles Dunnet, $133.33. 1/4 of estate to son Jesse. Remaining 3/4 to be equally divided among 6 children of son William Rex: Anna, Margaret, Jesse, William, Christopher and Mary.
Execs: Wife Margaret, and Charles Dunnett and son Jesse Rex. Wit: George Dunnett, and Jacob Yeakle.

BUCKAMMER, CATHARINE. Hatfield.
May 6, 1808. Aug 26, 1814. 4.32
To granddaughter Elizabeth, 100 pds. and household goods. Rem. of estate to children: Jacob, John, George, and Henry and Catharine, and Elizabeth, equally. Wearing apparel to be equally divided among daughters Catharine and Elizabeth.
Codicil dated Jan 14, 1809. To daughter Catharine, equal share of estate.
Execs: Frederick Conrad, and Jacob Heister, Jr. Wit: William Hendricks, and Jacob Wishler, Jacob Heisler, and James White.

BENDER, JACOB. Providence.
July 14, 1814. Sept 6, 1814. 4.34
To wife Elizabeth, house and 6 acres. To Jacob and Catharine, and Mary, 6 acres each. Rem. of estate to be sold.
Execs: Wife Elizabeth, and William Sowers. Wit: George Schwenk.

RUTH, JOHN. Pottsgrove.
Feb 21, 1814. Oct 3, 1814. 4.36
To wife Alana, rem. of estate during life.
Exec: Jacob Schantz. Wit: George Leider, and Jacob Drinkhouse.

JONES, MARTHA. Montgomery.
March 7, 1812. Oct 13, 1814. 4.37
Exrs. to pay to sister Ann Jones, interest of estate. To sister Susanna, $50. To daughter Rebecca, wife of John Jones, $50. To niece Susanna, daughter of sister Hannah, 150 pds. To brother Jonathan Jones, and sister Ann Jones, 300 pds. each. To brother Jonathan Jones, rem. of estate.
Execs: Ann Jones, and brother Jonathan Jones. Wit: Joseph Price, and Titus Yerkes.

WILLIAMS, JESSE. Whitemarsh.
Dec 1, 1812. Oct 3, 1814. 4.39
To wife, 1/2 of personal estate, and other half to be sold equally among 3 daughters.
Execs: Brother Richard, William, and Jacob Albertson. Wit: Joshua Paxon, and Joseph Foulke.

JEANS, JESSE. Whitemarsh.
July 27, 1814. Oct 29, 1814. 4.40

To wife Mary, household goods. To 3 daughters: Elizabeth, Esther, and Margaret, $667. To 4 daughter: Sarah, Mary, Hannah, and Rebecca, $800. To son William, lot of 7 1/2 acres. Rem. of estate to sons William and Isaac.
Exec: Son Isaac. Wit: Leonard Steyer, George Potts, and Nathan Potts.

COCHRAN, JAMES. Lower Merion.
Sept 17, 1807. Oct 31, 1814. 4.41
To wife Margaret, all estate. To sister in law Catharine Davis, $20. To sister in law Elizabeth Davis, 50 pds. To sister in law Jane Morris, 50 pds. To nephew Robert Cochran, 100 pds. To niece Lydia Morris, 30 pds. To niece Anna Morris, 100 pds. To son in law John Lindsay, Works of Travel, in 8 volumns, and rem. to 2 children, Jane Lindsay, and Mary Roberts, equally.
Execs: Jane Lindsay, and Mary Roberts. Wit: John Horn, Henry Colflesh.

GILBERT, HENRY. New Hanover.
April 25, 1810. Nov 4, 1814. 4.44
To wife Barbara, household goods, and maintenance, and income of 200 pds. during life. To son Anthony, farm, 103 acres subject to the payment of 1500 pds. To each son 50 pds. Rem. of estate divided among children, equally, share already received to be deducted.
Execs: Son Henry and son in law Michael Swinehart. Wit: Jacob Bickel, and John Richards.

SMITH, CHRISTOPHER. Moreland.
Dec 16, 1812. Nov 12, 1814. 4.48
To wife Hannah, entire estate.
Execs: Wife Hannah Smith, and Benjamin Lloyd. Wit: Jeremiah Walton, Joseph Prior, and Jonathan Michener.

GILKESON, ANDREW. Upper Dublin.
June 12, 1813. Nov 25, 1814. 4.49
To wife Edith, $200 annually, and household goods, etc., as she may choose. To son James, farm, 57 acres he paying to daughter Edith, $200, $400 to daughter Esther, to wife, Edith, annually, $56, and at her death to pay $200 to Edith Wyce, wife of Jacob Wyce, and $200 to daughter Esther. To son Elias, house and 5 acres, land subject to $10 annually to wife, Edith, also $100 in cash to Elias. To son Andrew, house and lot, subject to $10 annually to wife, Edith, note, $381.33 to be cancelled. To son Samuel, dwelling, of 11 acres of land in which testator lived subject to the payment of $400 to daughter Edith. To daughter Edith, $800. To daughter Jane Fitzwater, $400. To daughter Harriet, $700 and $56 yearly to wife Edith. to son Joseph, farm, 7 acres subject to the payment of $8.00 annually to wife, Edith. Estate to be discharged of debt of $565.
Exrs. to sell rme. of real estate, out of which income of $1000 to wife Edith, during her life. Rem. equally divided among sons: James, Elias,

Andrew, Samuel, Joseph, and daughters: Edith, Esther and Harriet.
Codicil dated Dec 16, 1813. to daughter Esther, $300. To daughter Harriet, $300.
Execs: Sons James, Andrew, and Samuel Gilkeson. Wit: Job Roberts, Charles Mather.

LUKENS, JOSEPH. Whitemarsh.
May 18, 1811. Dec 5, 1814. 4.53
Debts and funeral expenses to be paid. To wife Mary, beds, household goods, interest of 500 pds., during widowhood, all furniture, she chooses, to take and income of 500 pds. In case of her marriage, to son Lukens and daughter Tacy Weber, equally. To wife, also dwelling and maintenance. To brother Job Lukens, 20 pds. To son, wearing apparel, and farm, 198 acres. To son in law Jacob Weber, and wife Tacy Weber, farm, on which they reside, in Whitpain, 115 acres. To daughter Tacy Weber, 800 pds. Rem. of estate to son Lukens, and daughter Tacy Weber, equally divided.
Execs: Son and son in law Jacob Weber. Wit: Thomas Livezey, and Philip Smith.

PETERMAN, JACOB. Plymouth.
Jan 6, 1813. Dec 9, 1814. 4.56
To wife Ann, use and income fo estate, during widowhood. If she marries only legal dower. To son Joseph, and Priscilla, his wife, house where I live 2 acres, 64 perches. To son Joseph, 150 pds. To 6 grandchildren, of deceased daughter Ann, wife of John Davis, 100 pds. each. Rem. of estate to son James Peterman, and daughter Hannah Whiteman, son to have 100 pds. more than daughter Hannah.
Execs: Ann and son in law John Whiteman, Alexander Ramsey. Wit: Priscilla Potts and Nathan Potts.

MARPLE, ABEL. Moreland.,
Sept 3, 1814. Dec 10, 1814. 4.59
To wife Eleanor, use of household goods, and use of 1/3 of farm. To daughter Eliza, wife of Isaac Banes, Jr., farm. To son David, other farm, in Hatboro, 50 acres. To son David, rem. of estate.
Execs: Wife Eleanor, Thomas B. Montanye. Wit: Samuel Shoemaker, John Potts.

MILLER, BARBARA. Upper Providence.
Oct 31, 1814. Dec 17, 1814. 4.60
To daughter Mary, all estate.
Exec: Benjamin Cox. Wit: Matthew Dill, John Umstad.

ENGARD, WILLIAM. Upper Dublin.
March 18, 1807. Dec 17, 1814. 4.61
To wife Elizabeth, income of estate, during life, at her death to son William, 3 acres of land. To daughter Catharine, income of other 5 acres

from the decease of wife. Rem. equally divided among son William, and daughter Catharine.
Exec: Edward Burk. Wit: Josiah Wood, Jonathan Scout.

TYSON, JONATHAN. Abington.
Sept 6, 1814. Dec 27, 1814. 4.62
To 2 sons Elijah, and Jonathan, wearing apparel, equally. To wife Hannah, personal estate, she brought, bond of $1000 and household goods, and $700 and $200 yearly to be paid to her by children. To son Elijah, farm, in Abington, 52 acres, 20 perches. To daughters Elizabeth Shaw, and Rebecca Scholfield, 49 acres, 61 perches in Abington, subject to payments to wife. To son Jonathan, land farm, 98 acres, 110 perches subject to payment to wife. Rem. to 4 children: Elijah, Jonathan, Elizabeth, and Rebecca equally.
Execs: Son Jonathan, son in law Samuel Scholfield. Wit: Thomas Livezey, John Combs, and Benjamin Tyson.

LAW, JOSEPH. Norriton.
Nov 22, 1814. Dec 29, 1814. 4.67
To daughter Rebecca, wife of Peter DeHaven, income of 400 pds. To son James, 500 pds. To Norriton Presbyterian Church, 50 pds. To John Christy McChrea, 50 pds. To Hannah Stewart, 10 pds. To John Stewart, 10 pds. To Robert Darrah, 10 pds. To John McChrea, 10 pds. To Eleanor Dunlap, 10 pds. To Catharine McChrea, 10 pds. To Ann Darrah, 10 pds. Rem. of estate for the purpose of taking children of persons unable to care for the same, in Norriton Township.
Execs: John McChrea, John Stewart, and Hannah Stewart. Wit: Joseph Barr, John Hartle, and William L. Shannon.

RYMEWALT, CHRISTOPHER. Towamencin.
March 1, 1813. Jan 2, 1815. 4.70
To wife Maria, household goods, maintenance, and income as per Articles of Agreement. To son Christopher, farm, subject to the payment of 600 pds. to wife. Rem. equally divided among children: David, Christopher, Abraham, Susanna, wife of Christian Schneider, Rosanna, Maria, wife of Godfrey Bossum, Rachel, Catharine, Elizabeth, wife of John Erb, Magdalena, and Nancy. Rem. after decease of wife, to children, equally.
Execs: sons Christopher, and Abraham, and Mordecai Davis, and John Kulp. Wit: Mordecai Davis, Frederick Conrad, and John Davies.

UMSTAD, MARY. Worcester.
Aug 11, 1808. Jan 6, 1815. 4.73
To Mary Driechler, 150 pds. To John Nise, son of Anna Umstad, 15 pds. Rem. to 3 children, equally.
Exec: Henry Custer. Wit: Levi Custer, and Henry Hunsicker.

KNOX, MATTHEW. Whitpain.

Dec 5, 1814. Jan 18, 1815. 4.74
To wife Isabella, income of estate, during life. To son William, 200 acres of land, in Mercer County, Pa. To 2 sons Daniel and George, other tract of land 200 acres in Crawford County, Pa. to son John, $1.00 to have full share. Rem. to children, equally.
Exec: Ebenezer Rambo. Wit: John Meredith, Isaac McGlathery, and Charles McGlathery.

HALLMAN, GEORGE. Whitpain.
Nov 10, 1814. Jan 27, 1815. 4.76
To wife Sarah, estate, till youngest child becomes of age. To daughter Mary Hallman, household goods. To son Samuel Hallman, cow. To son Anthony Hallman, bible. Rem. of estate equally among wife and children: Mary, Samuel, Anthony, William, and Weikle.
Execs: Father in law Samuel Weikle, and brother Henry Hallman. Wit: John Slingluff, and A. Keyser.

STOUT, JOHN. Cheltenham.
Jan 15, 1815. Jan 28, 1815. 4.77
Estate to be sold and divided equally among 8 children: John, Elizabeth, William, Peter, Henry, Frederick, George, and Jacob Stout, deducting sums already given each.
Execs: Sons John and Peter. Wit: Robert McCurdy, and Thomas Livezey.

TOMKINS, ANNA. Horsham.
Jan 16, 1815. Jan 30, 1815. 4.79
To 2 sons Jacob E. and Benjamin D. all estate, subject to payments of debts.
Execs: Sons Jacob and Benjamin. Wit: Joshua Paul, and Hiram McNeill.

DYER, JOSEPH. Moreland.
Jan 9, 1813. Feb 7, 1815. 4.81
To wife Mary Ann, household goods, etc., use and profits on North East side of Bribery Road, except 44 acres and maintenance and $40 yearly. To son Samuel, farm, 33 1/2 acres, also 11 1/2 acres. To son Joseph, 20 1/2 acres of land, and 6 acres, 50 perches of land subject to the payment of 125 pds. to be paid to Exrs. To son James, farm, of 153 acres. To son Philip, rem. of land subject as aforesaid. To son Samuel, interest in lands in Rhode Island, and Massachuetts. To daughter Elizabeth Dupue, 200 pds. etc. To daughter Mary, household goods, and 250 pds. etc. To daughter Phebe, bed, and household goods, and 250 pds. To daughter Susanna, bed, and household goods, and 250 pds. To sons James, and Philip, books equally. Rem. of estate to 4 daughters: Sarah, Mary, Phebe and Susanna.
Execs: Christian Schneider, Edward Dyer. Wit: Thomas Margerum, John Comly.

BROWN, WILLIAM. Upper Dublin.
Dec 16, 1814. Feb 13, 1815. 4.89
To 6 older children: Margaret, Elizabeth, Thomas, Jane, and Mary and Esther, $1.00 each. To 3 younger children: Sarah, Lydia, and William, to be deducted. Rem. of estate to wife Mary.
Exec: Wife, Mary Brown. Wit: John Shay, John Collom.

MARIS, ANN. Gwynedd.
Sept 20, 1813. Feb 13, 1815. 4.90
To nephew Jesse, 12 pds. To nieces Maria and Jane Herton, 100 pds. equally. Rem. of estate to sister Hannah Wilson.
Exec: Brother in law John Wilson. Wit: Nathan Roberts, Charles, F. Jenkins.

KOLB, JOSEPH. New Hanover.
Sept 2, 1812. Feb 13, 1815. 4.91
To wife Mary, house and 5 lots, and household goods, and maintenance, during life. To son George Michael Kolb, farm, he to pay 460 pds. of which wife is to receive annual income, after her death to be divided among 6 sons: George Michael, George, Peter, Joseph, John and Christian. To son John, farm, 120 acres at 11 pds. per year, in several payments. Rem. of estate to be sold and divided as follows: to son Michael Fry, son of daughter Susanna, 50 pds. To Hannah Mourer, daughter of daughter Magdalena Lock, 50 pds. To Mary Mourer, daughter of daughter Mary, deceased, 50 pds. To sister Susanna Smith, 20 pds. Daughter Sarah to have outset the same as other daughters. To son George Michael, 1/13 part of rem. To son George, 25 pds. more than 1/13. To son Peter, 100 pds. less than 1/13. To son Joseph, 1/13 part. To son John, 25 pds. less than 1/13. To son Christian, 1/13 part. To daughter Elizabeth, income of 1/13 part. To daughter Catharine, interest of 50 pds. less than 1/13 part. To daughter Margaret, 1/13 part. To daughter Magdalena, 50 pds. less than other 1/13 To daughter Barbara, 50 pds. less than other 1/13. To daughter Sarah, 1/13 part.
Execs: 2 sons George Michael, and John. Wit: Benjamin Markley, Michael Hilbert.

NEISE, JOHN, New Hanover.
March 29, 1813. Feb 17, 1815. 4.97
Estate to be sold, interest to son Abraham, about 110 acres at $20 per acre in several payments. To 4 daughters: Elizabeth, wife of John Kepner, Margaret, wife of Peter Koons, Eve, wife of Emanuel Soliday, Dinah, wife of Jacob Fryer, 150 pds. each. Daughter Catharine deceased, and daughter Mary Richards wife of John Richards, have full share. Rem. divided among 5 sons: John, Jacob, Henry, Michael, and Abraham, sums given after to be taken into account.
Execs: Sons Henry and Abraham, and Benjamin Markley. Wit: Henry Krebs, and Peter Esterline.

TYSON, MATTHEW. Abington.
July 5, 1800. Feb 15, 1815. 4.99
To wife Sarah, 20 pds. yearly, during widowhood, use of room household goods, and maintenance. To son Jonathan Tyson, farm, 150 acres 1/2 interest in meadow in Springfield, subject to the payments to wife. To son Rynear Tyson, 208 acres in Springfield, subject to the paymemts to wife. Rem. to 3 daughters: Catharine, Elizabeth, and Sarah, equally.
Codicil dated May 27, 1809. Ratifies and makes additional request to wife.
Execs: Sons Jonathan and Rynear. Wit: Robert Loller, Matthias Lear.

FISHER, HENRY. Upper Dublin.
Aug 18, 1813. Feb 18, 1815. 4.105
To wife Sarah, during widowhood, all estate, if she marries, one bed, and 520 pds. for her portion. Children to have refusal of farm, on term of appraisement. In case of a refusal to each son, 50 pds. To daughter Sabina, 37 pds., 10 s. Rem. equally divided among children. Deceased daughter Catharine Trexler, share to be divided among her children.
Execs: Wife Sarah, and Casper Schlater. Wit: Christina Hernar, Jacob Acuff.

YERGER, TOBIAS. New Hanover.
Feb 23, 1813. March 6, 1815. 4.106
To son Samuel, farm, 218 acres for 1600 pds. of which wife Catharine shall have income of 300 pds. To daughter Elizabeth, wife of John Smith, 433 pds., 6 s., 8 d. To daughter Magdalena, wife of David Harpel, 433 pds., 6 s., 8 d. To daughter Margaret, wife of John Reifsnyder, 433 pds., 6 s., 8 d. At wife's death her 300 pds. to be equally divided among 4 children: Elizabeth, Magdalena, Margaret, and Samuel. To wife Catharine, household goods, and maintenance. Rem. of estate equally divided among children: Elizabeth, Magdalena, Margaret, and Samuel.
Execs: Sons Samuel and son in law John Reifsnyder. Wit: Peter Miller, H. Schneider, Jr.

COX, THOMAS. Whitemarsh.
July 14, 1814. March 8, 1815. 4.109
To daughter Mary, 100 pds. To daughter Sarah, 100 pds. children of son James as follows: to daughter Anna, 10 pds. To son John, 10 pds. To son Thomas Jefferson Cox, 10 pds. To daughter Rachel, 10 pds. To son James, 10 pds. All to be placed on interest during minority. Rem. of estate equally divided between 2 daughters Mary and Sarah.
Exec: Jacob Gilbert. Wit: John Slingluff, Frederick Reif.

REIF, JOHN. Horsham.
Aug 25, 1811. March 14, 1815. 4.110
To son John and Joseph, Jacob, and Samuel, $1.00 each. To daughter Mary, 100 pds. Rem. equally divided among daughter Mary and daughter Jane.

Exec: Son Jacob. Wit: John Wilgus, Hiram McNiell.

BOORS, SUSANNA. Towamencin.
June 4, 1805. March 16, 1815. 4.111
To son Jonas, 25 pds. Rem. of estate equally divided among 2 sons Daniel and Jonas.
Execs: Sons Daniel and Jonas Boors. Wit: Jacob Kulp and David C. Kulp.

NAGLE, GRACE. Pottsgrove.
Feb 10, 1815. March 28, 1815. 4.112
To niece Mary Bechtel, wife of John Buckwalter, all estate.
Exec: John Buckwalter. Wit: Samuel Evans, and Samuel Tyson.

STAFF, FREDERICK. Norriton.
Sept 6, 1802. April 6, 1815. 4.113
To Jacob Singer, all estate.
Exec: Jacob Singer. Wit: John Thomas, Joseph Thomas.

KNIGHT, ISAAC. Abington.
March 7, 1815. April 11, 1815. 4.113
To wife Sarah, 70 pds. yearly, during widowhood, household goods, and maintenance, $100 in cash, also dower, due from Daniel St. Clair, also 75 pds. to purchase a horse, 5 rooms in house, etc. with furniture. If she marries to forfeit everything except 80 pds. yearly. To Flora Conroe, colored, 6 pds. yearly during life. To Trustees of Friends Meeting in Abington, 12 pds. yearly to keep graves in repair, should son in law James Worth survive granddaughter Mary Elizabeth Worth, 60 pds. yearly during life. To Exrs. 200 acres, land in Abington in trust for profits for same for granddaughter Mary Elizabeth Worth. Rem. to Mary Elizabeth Worth. If Mary Elizabeth Worth die, without issue, rem. of estate as follows: to Joshua and Jonathan, sons of brother Joshua, 2/9 equal parts. To sister Mary's children, Jonathan and Elizabeth, 2/9 part. To sister Rebecca's daughter Elizabeth, 1/9 part. To 3 of sister Sarah's children: Elizabeth, Elijah, and Rebecca, 2/9 part, equally. To brother Mahlon, rem. 2/9 part.
Execs: Son in law James Worth, and nephew Jonathan Cleaver. Wit: Joseph Lukens, Thomas Livezey.

MILLER, JACOB. Springfield.
Dec 1, 1803. May 29, 1815. 4.117
To wife Nancy, household goods, and proceeds of all estate, during widowhood. But if she marries to have $20 and furniture. To son Jacob Miller, farm, where he lives. To son John Miller, 15 acres of land. Rem. equally divided among 2 sons, except $20.
Execs: Sons Jacob and John. Wit: John Mann, and Christopher Loeser.

McDOWELL, ALEXANDER. Upper Dublin.

Dec 1, 1813. May 29, 1815. 4.118
To wife Margaret, household goods, and profits of estate. To daughter Nancy, part of plantation, if she and daughter die, estate to be sold. To son Major, 20 pds. and 100 pds. to be put in interest to be paid yearly to wife. Rem. of estate divided equally among 9 children.
Execs: John Mann, and son Major. Wit: Thomas Butler, and Peter Engart.

RAMBO, SARAH. Upper Merion.
March 4, 1811. Feb 13, 1815. 4.119
To sons John and Jeremiah, 5 pds. each. To granddaughter Sarah Stewart, household goods. To daughter Hannah, use and profits from estate. To son John, 10 acres of land. To grandsons James, and Robert, rem. of estate.
Execs: Matthias Holstein, and Jacob Shenline. Wit: Michael Rambo, and Nathan Potts.

SISLER, JOHN. Montgomery.
March 3, 1815. May 15, 1815. 4.120
To wife Catharine, farm, and household goods, and 24 pds. yearly. Real estate to be sold and rem. divided among sons and daughters: Isaac, Jesse, Mary, Elizabeth, and Rachel, equally. To wife Catharine, $40 and watch. To daughter Mary, $60.
Execs: Sons Isaac and John. Wit: Andrew Layman, and Jonathan Heist.

RENNINGER, JACOB. Douglass.
Jan 6, 1815. June 12, 1815. 4.122
To wife Elizabeth, farm, and household goods, and 300 pds. yearly. To son John, farm, containing 85 acres subject to the payment of 750 pds. To daughter Elizabeth, 40 pds. yearly. To son Henry, 40 pds. yearly. To daughter Maria, 40 pds. yearly. To son John, 40 pds. yearly. To daughter Susanna, 40 pds. yearly. To son Jacob, 40 pds. yearly. To Jacob Bowman, son of deceased daughter Magdalena, 40 pds. yearly. To son John, smith tools. Estate to be appraised and sold after 5 weeks after my decease.
Execs: Son John and son in law John Bender. Wit: Abraham Sechler, and Abraham Oberholtzer.

ACHE, HARMON. Marlborough.
March 26, 1812. June 15, 1815. 4.123
To wife Maria, household goods, and 30 pds. yearly to be paid by son John. Personal estate to be sold and money divided among children: Jacob, Ludwig, Valentine Ache.
Execs: Sons Jacob and John. Wit: Jacob Lester, Anthony Bitting.

PRUTZMAN, ADAM. Limerick.
Jan 26, 1804. June 19, 1815. 4.125
To wife Catharine, household goods, and interest of real estate. To son David, 50 pds. To daughter Hannah, 25 pds. To son Adam, 100 pds. and

rem. divided into 5 equal parts. To daughter Mary, 1/5 part. To son Jacob, 1/5 part. To children of son Adam, 1/5 part. To son Frederick, 1/5 part. To son David and his children, 1/5 part. If daughter Hannah die, her sum of 100 pds. to be divided into 5 equal parts. To children and grandchildren, interest of 1/6 part. To children, wearing apparel, equally. Codicil dated, April 12, 1812. Dr. William Smith to be Exrs. instead of son Frederick.
Execs: Sons Jacob and Frederick, son in law John Kepler. Wit: Matthew Brooke, and William Brooke.

PAWLING, JOHN. Lower Providence.
Nov 10, 1813. June 24, 1815. 4.127
To daughters: Elizabeth, and Rachel, and Fanny, farm, for use of 10 years and household goods. Proceeds from sale to all children: Margaret, Eleanor, John, Elizabeth, Rachel, and Fanny, equally. To son John, tract of land in Bedford County, containing 100 acres. Rem. of estate to all children.
Execs: Son John, and Nathan Pennebecker. Wit: Henry and William Pawling.

HENDRICKS, ANNA MARIA. Towamencin.
Aug 2, 1811. Aug 14, 1815. 4.129
To son Thomas, farm, where I now dwell, containing 36 acres. Exrs. at request of daughter to sell premises for her maintenance. To grandchildren, rem. of residue, equally. Rem. of estate to William and Ann Sampey.
Exec: Mordecai Davis. Wit: David Kulp, Christian Stauffer.

FOULKE, LEVI. ggg.
___. Aug 14, 1815. 4.130
To wife, farm, and $300 worth of household goods, and $32 yearly to be paid by Exrs. To son William, tract of lands containing 14 and 25 acres. To 4 grandchildren: John, Levi, Anna, and William, $100 each when 21. To son William, rem. of estate.
Exec: Son William. Wit: George Potts.

ROBERTS, ISAAC. Abington.
Nov 24, 1814. Sept 2, 1815. 4.133
To son Isaac Roberts, 23 acres of land and horse, and 25 pds. To son William Roberts, rem. of plantation, where on I now dwell, containing 50 acres. To daughter Sarah, legacies, and 150 pds. To daughter Ruth, 150 pds. To daughter Mary, 150 pds. To daughter Tacy, 150 pds. To daughter Hannah, 150 pds. Trustees, son in law Isaac Walton, and Samuel Scholfield. Tp grandson Charles, 25 pds. and interest of 1700 pds. that son William is to pay. Rem. of estate, Exrs. to make sale and to be sold.
Execs: Sons William and Isaac, and Thomas Shoemaker. Wit: Samuel Scholfield, and Richard Roberts.

FITZWATER, RYNEAR. Upper Dublin.
Aug 25, 1815. Sept, 4, 1815. 4.135
To Mother, Hannah, $80 yearly. Trustee, George Fitzwater, and John Fitzwater, to hold in trust a piece of land in Upper Dublin, for Burying Ground of the Fitzwater family, and 100 pds. towards repairs, and 1/2 to be put on interest for payment on household goods. To brother John Fitzwater, $500. To sister Jane Tyson, $500. To children of brother Thomas deceased, namely: Sarah, Hannah, and Catharine, $500, equally divided. To brother Jacob Fitzwater, personal estate, subject to the payment of just debts and funeral expenses.
Exec: Brother Jacob Fitzwater. Wit: Thomas Livezey, and George Fitzwater.

RAPINE, ANNA. Springfield.
Aug 30, 1815. Sept 20, 1815. 4.137
To daughter Elizabeth, household goods, and rem. of estate to be sold, and money to be put on interest for son Reuben, until he becomes of age.
Exec: William Shane. Wit: John Taylor, and Samuel Cressman.

LINDEBERGER, JOHN. Springfield.
March 14, 1815. Sept 25, 1815. 4.138
To wife Mary, household goods, and interest of $300 in cash during widowhood. Exrs. to give principle sum to children, equally.
Execs: Wife Mary, and Joseph Miller. Wit: Christian Keyser, and A. Keyser.

CLENNAH, WILLIAM. Lower Providence.
Sept 16, 1815. Oct 3, 1815. 4.140
Estate to be sold and money remaining to be kept by Exrs. and divided in the following manner. To daughter Mary, $1.00 and $30 at my decease. To daughter Susanna, $1.00. To wife Elizabeth, at my decease, shall have rem. of money kept in the hands of the Exrs. and put on interest and paid annually to wife Elizabeth. Until son Thomas is 21, then Thomas Perfirm to have $160, and wife Elizabeth to have income of the rem. during widowhood, after wife's death son William to have what wife received.
Execs: Joseph Crawford, and William Horn. Wit: John Francis, and Robert Shannon.

HAWKINS, JESSE.
Sept 1, 1814. Oct 9, 1815. 4.141
To 4 sons: Isaac, Amos, James, and William, to have all lands and paying to 6 daughters as follows: to daughter Rebecca Roberts wife of William, 210 pds. To daughter Hannah Jenkins, 210 pds. To daughter Rachel Blake, 210 pds. To daughter Keziah Hawkins, 245 pds. and 45 pds. is given as interest of household goods. To daughter Elizabeth Hawkins, 245 pds. To daughter Mary, 245 pds. to be paid to her by Exrs. when 21.

Exrs. to pay to grandson Jesse Roberts, $20. To grandchildren Jesse Hawkins, and Jesse Jenkins, $20, equally divided, and put on interest until 21, when the amount is to be paid to them by Exrs.
Execs: Sons Isaac, Amos, James, and William. Wit: John Wright, and Isaac Jenkins.

BECHHART, CONRAD. Frederick.
April 20, 1814. Oct 11, 1815. 4.143
To wife Catharine, land in Frederick, containing 22 acres, 100 perches and household goods, and interest of 300 pds. To son Benjamin land, containing 22 acres, 100 perches, and interest of 450 pds. Son Henry to farm plantation where I now dwell, containing 130 acres and 50 perches and rem. of residue divided among children: Christian, Adam, Benjamin, Mary, wife of Peter Swinford, Catharine, wife of Daniel Hollaburk, Susanna, wife of John Dengler, equally.
Execs: Son Benjamin and son in law Peter Swinford. Wit: John Groff and Christian Souder.

DeHAVEN, DAVID. Whitpain.
Sept 4, 1815. Oct 18, 1815. 4.147
To wife Magdalena, household goods, and $32 yearly, to be paid by Exrs. on the first day of April, of every year. Rem. of estate after expenses are paid to be divided in the following manner. To son John, 2/5 equal part. To son Isaac, 1/5 equal part. To daughter Rachel, 1/5 part. To son David, 1/5 part. Job Roberts to be guardian.
Execs: Son John, and brother in law Isaac Zimmerman. Wit: Jesse Barnes, Cadwalder Foulke.

ARMSTRONG, SIMON. Plymouth.
Sept 13, 1815. Oct 24, 1815. 4.150
To son Joseph, 50 pds. To son James, 800 pds. To daughter Mary, 800 pds. and at daughters death, her share to be equally divided among 3 children: William, John, and Anna. To son Joseph's children, 150 pds. each: James, John, Joseph, Jane, and Mary. To son William, rem. of estate. All estate both real and personal to be left in the hands of Exrs.
Exec: Son William Armstrong. Wit: James Pugh, Joseph Armstrong.

GRIM, GEORGE. Upper Providence.
Sept 14, 1815. Oct 31, 1815. 4.152
To wife Elizabeth, all estate, and household goods, and maintenance, after wife's death property to be divided among children: Elizabeth, Adam, and Mary, when 21.
Codicil dated Sept 3, 1815. To wife Elizabeth, farm.
Execs: Wife Elizabeth, and brother in law Peter Lehman. Wit: John Favinger, and Isaac Hallman.

RAMBO, MARTHA. Upper Merion.

Aug 18, 1815. Nov 4, 1815. 4.154
To son Charles, 5 pds. To daughters Jane and Elizabeth, profits and rem. of residue. Personal estate to be sold.
Exec: Brother John Supplee. Wit: Nathan Potts, and Ebenezer Rambo.

JONES, HENRY. Montgomery.
Oct 16, 1815. Nov 7, 1815. 4.158
Exrs. to sell land containing 28 acres in Wissahickon. To wife Jane, household goods and 300 pds. and 200 pds. yearly to be paid unto her on the 10th day of April, yearly during widowhood. To son Lewis, gold watch, and walnut desk. To son Clement, silver watch, $500, and family bible. Wife to dispose of wearing apparel. Farm 172 acres to be sold. Rem. equally divided among 3 sons: Lewis, Clement, and John.
Execs: Evan John, and Cadwalder Foulke. Wit: Richard Roberts, Thomas Shoemaker, and Morgan Morgan.

MOYER, GEORGE. Limerick.
Aug 16, 1815. Nov 9, 1815. 4.160
To wife Catharine, use of house, and household goods, and maintenance etc. To son George, farm, 100 acres subject to the payment of $1200. To son Benjamin, 22 acres of land subject to the payment of 6 pds. per acre. To daughter Catharine, wife of George Swink, 500 pds. Rem. to wife. Rem. to 3 children: Catharine, George, and Benjamin, equally.
Execs: Sons George and Benjamin. Wit: John Herstine, Peter Fry, and George Moyer.

McCOOL, SAMUEL. Whitemarsh.
July 3, 1815. Nov 13, 1815. 4.164
To wife Barbara, income of $400 during widowhood, if she marries said money to go to grandchildren. To Sabella Cerreher, wife's niece, before and after, $200. To daughter Mary, $100. Rem. equally divided among sons: Jonathan, Walter, and Samuel, and daughters: Mary, Alevia, Elizabeth, and Rachel. to Matthias Waxeller, $25. To his wife, Letitia, $20.
Execs: Justus Scheetz, and Job Roberts. Wit: William Dewees, William Hoffman.

JONES, SILAS. Loer Merion.
Dec 11, 1812. Nov 14, 1815. 4.166
To daughter Hannah Supplee, 10 pds. to daughter Hester Craft, 100 pds. To daughter Sarah Price, 10 pds. To daughter Mary Marquedant, 100 pds. To 5 grandson, children of daughter Ann Leedom, deceasd: Jesse, John, Silas, George, and Isaac, 100 pds. equally. To 3 grandchildren of daughter: Hannah, Jane, Hester, and Sarah, 90 pds. equally. Rem. to sons: Charles, Silas, and Cadwalder.
Execs: Sons Charles, Silas, and Cadwalder. Wit: Joseph Price, and John Elliott.

HOXWORTH, PETER. Hatfield.
April 6, 1812. Nov 20, 1815. 4.168
To each of 6 older children: Israel, William, Eleanor, Mary, Sarah, and Margaret, 50 pds. To the 2 younger daughters Rachel and Anna, 10 pds. each. To wife Ann, farm, household goods, and maintenance, and interest of money bequeathed to daughters until they become of age. If she remain my widow also the rem. of personal estate, should she marry to 2 younger sons Peter and Jesse.
Execs: Son Israel, and wife Ann. Wit: Jesse Roberts, and David Ruth.

LYLE, JOHN. Upper Merion.
Nov 8, 1815. Nov 27, 1815. 4.171
To daughter Elizabeth Wood's children, 400 pds. equally to be paid by son Francis Lyle. To daughter Mary Kirkpatrick, 200 pds. to be paid out of land conveyed to son Francis. To son Walter Lyle's children, 200 pds. to be paid by son Benjamin, out of land which was given him. To daughter Martha's children, 200 pds. to be paid by son Benjamin. To son Charles, 100 pds. to be paid by son Benjamin. To Abi, $40 yearly during life, to be paid by son John, out of land conveyed to him. To daughter Abi, place called Glasley on Lancaster Pike, and household goods. To daughter Elizabeth, chest. To daughter Mary Kirkpatrick, bed, etc. To son Francis, clock. To son John, clothes. To daughter Elizabeth, dinning table.
Codicil. Inter Alia after rem. to be divided equally among 6 children: Francis, John, Benjamin, Mary, Margaret, and Abi.
Execs: Son Francis, and son in law Robert Wood. Wit: Jonathan Cleaver, Matthew Roberts, and Nathan Potts.

ROBERTS, JESSE. Abington.
Oct 16, 1815. Dec 2, 1815. 4.175
To wife Mary, household goods, etc., and $40 and 42 pds. yearly during widowhood. And principle 700 pds. to all children: Jonathan, Jesse, Samuel, Mordecai, James, and William, equally at her death. To grandson George, of Jonathan, lot at Edge Hill. Rem. to 6 children: Jonathan, Samuel, Jesse, Mordecai, James, and William. Sums loaned to sons to be deducted from their shares.
Execs: Wife, Mary and sons Mordecai and James. Wit: Thomas Webster, and William Roberts.

BINDER, JACOB. New Hanover.
April 24, 1815. Jan 15, 1816. 4.178
To wife Susanna, household goods, and maintenance, income of 800 pds. to be paid by son Jacob. Rem, equally divided among 6 children: Michael, Jacob, John, Henry, Elizabeth, wife of Anthony Fush, Susanna, wife of George Erb. Son George to receive no more than has already been given to him.
Exec: Jacob Brendlinger. Wit: John Shlonecker, George Fry.

ROBERTS, ALGERNOR. Lower Merion.
March 23, 1815. Jan 19, 1816. 4.180
To wife, farm, till April 1st, and $3000 in trust for the use of daughter Anna. To son Isaac Warner Roberts, farm, on payment of $10,000 toward legacies. To son George W. Roberts, farm as described, should he die before becoming of age, $500 to sons: John, Algernon S. and Edward, each. Rem. divided among his mother and brothers: Algernon S. and Edward, and sister Tacy, Elizabeth, and Lydia. To daughter Lydia, $4067.67. To daughter Gainor, $5360. To Elizabeth, Algernon and Edward, and Tacy, $6000 each. To son John Roberts, $500. To son Isaac live stock, implements, etc.
Execs: Sons John and Isaac. Wit: Paul Jones, John Levering.

SHINLINE, MAGDALENA. Norriton.
June 28, 1807. Jan 22, 1816. 4.187
To 2 daughters Catharine Shinline, and Magdalena Norris, household goods, etc. To 4 daughters: Dolly, Susanna, Catharine, and Magdalena, wearing apparel and rem. To grandson Andrew Preast, 30 pds. Rem. equally divided among sons Jacob and 4 daughters.
Execs: Brother Nicholas Bower, and son in law Jacob Singer. Wit: Benjamin Conrad, John Thomas.

STAUFFER, ULRICH. Norriton.
Oct 30, 1815. Jan 30, 1816. 4.189
To wife Hannah, house, and maintenance, etc., income of 2000 pds. To daughter Rachel and son in law Isaac Oberholtzer, farm, in Norriton. Rem. of estate to children: John, Christian, Rudolph, Henry, Abraham, Catharine, wife of John Wisler, share of deceased daughter Mary, wife of John Fried, to her children, Elizabeth, wife of David Fittels, Hannah, wife of Benjamin Frieder, Sarah, wife of Jacob Grove, Rachel, wife of Isaac Oberholtzer.
Execs: Sons Christian and Rudolph. Wit: Joseph Tyson, Cornelius Tyson.

THOMAS, MORDECAI. Moreland.
Sept 5, 1813. Feb 13, 1816. 4.193
To wife Elizabeth, household goods, income of estate during life. To daughter Rachel, $500 and furniture. To daughter Ann, $500. To son Samuel, $600. To children of son John, deceased, bond of 200 pds. and $450 at death of wife. To grandson David Parry, $50 at death of wife. Rem. equally divided among children: Jonathan, Elizabeth, Jacob, Hannah, Tacy, and Martha. To grandson Reuben Thomas, china faced watch.
Execs: Sons Jonathan, Jacob, and Samuel, and son in law Joseph Iredell, Michael Trump, and Isaac Michener. Wit: Isaac Tomkins, James Hawkins.

ROBERTS, CADWALDER.
Nov __, 1814. Feb 21, 1816. 4.195

To son Richard, farm, 150 acres he to have 250 pds. To son Ezekiel, each to sons Ezekiel and Cadwalder, and daughters Agnes, and Mary, 500 pds. for the use of son Edward, and 500 pds. for use of son Joseph. To daughter Agnes, case of drawers, etc. Rem. of money arising from sale of farm, 250 pds. each to sons Ezekiel Cadwalder, and daughters Agnes, and Mary. Rem. to son Richard. Wearing apparel to be divided among 7 children. Trustees, nephew George Roberts, and Jacob Albertson. Exec: Son Richard. Wit: Job Roberts, and William Mullin.

WEBER, BENJAMIN, SR. Worcester.
Feb 14, 1816. Feb 22, 1816. 4.198
To daughter Rebecca, household goods, and 100 pds. To son Jacob, farm, 31 acres. Estate to be sold and money given to 7 daughters equally: Catharine, wife of Frederick Searfoss, Elizabeth, wife of John Shearer, Mary, wife of George Shade, Susanna, wife of Joseph Hahn, Hannah, wife of Adam Flech, Anna, wife of Jonathan Gouldy, and Rebecca and Mary. Execs: Son Jacob and Frederick Searfoss, and John Shearer. Wit: Jacob Snyder, John Wentz.

REINER, HENRY. Lower Providence.
Sept 24, 1810. Feb 26, 1816. 4.206
To wife Susanna, household goods, and 1/6 part of rem. To each of 4 children: Elizabeth, wife of Jacob Garber, Hannah, wife of William Garber, Susanna, and Mary, wife of Jacob Rittenhouse, 1/6 of estate. To son John, 300 pds. Remaining 1/6 part to heirs of son John.
Execs: Sons in law Jacob Garber and Jacob Rittenhouse. Wit: Abraham Reiner, and Philip Reiner.

FRANCE, NANCY. Upper Dublin.
Jan 24, 1816. Feb 28, 1816. 4.202
To brother Paul France, 25 pds. to his wife, Mary, black silk gown. To brother Paul's daughter Lydia, and Mary, best bed. To brother Paul's son Simon, the sum of 1 pds., 17 s., 6 d. To brother Nicholas, 10 pds. To brother Tobias, 10 pds. to son John, 10 pds. To sister Elizabeth Hoxworth, 9 pds. To brother Jacob, new suit. Rem. as follows: one share each to brothers: Paul, Nicholas, Tobias, and sisters Elizabeth.
Exec: Brother Nicholas France. Wit: John Roth, Joseph Everhart.

SMITH, WILLIAM. Upper Providence.
Feb 23, 1816. Feb 29, 1816. 4.204
To Jacob Bower, and Henry Lyle, and Elizabeth Lyle, $50 each. To James Stinson, $400. To 4 brothers in law: David Evans, Benjamin Evans, Matthew Evans, and Joseph Armstrong, 450 each. To Mary Evans, $40. To brother James Smith, gold watch. And to his wife Catharine, $50. To friend Joseph Henry, in trust for Mary McCoy, daughter of sister Mary Williams, $400. Rem. 1/3 each to brother Price Smith's children of sister Mary Williams, and children of brother Smith, deceased.

Execs: Joseph Henry, and John Jacobs. Wit: Isaac Huddlesome, and Elizabeth Boggs.

REIFF, JACOB. Lower Salford.
Oct 16, 1802. May 1, 1816. 4.207
To wife Catharine, 1000 pds. and household goods, and maintenance, during widowhood. To son Jacob, 100 pds. in cash and 500 pds. borrowed of son John, several years ago. To son John, mill, and farm, 114 acres in Lower Salford, subject to the payment of 1800 pds. To son Benjamin, farm, 226 acres subject to the payment of 1600 pds. To daughter Catharine, 200 pds. To daughter Elizabeth Weber, 200 pds. To daughter Anna Detwiler, 200 pds. Rem. to 7 children: Jacob, John, George, Benjamin, and daughters: Anna, Elizabeth, and Catharine, equally.
Execs: Sons Jacob and Benjamin Reiff. Wit: Jacob Bergey, Bernard Frien.

SCHNELL, GEORGE. Limerick.
April 8, 1814. March 4, 1816. 4.215
To wife Anna Dorday, household goods, 1st money from real estate to son Jacob and George, daughters Christina, and Mary. 2nd money to son Samuel, and daughters: Elizabeth, Hannah and Salome. To daughters Hannah, and Salome, household goods, such as daughters Christina and Mary has received, after wife's death rem. to be sold and divided equally among 8 children.
Execs: Sons Samuel and George. Wit: Jesse McCollester, John Scheide, and George Erb.

BLIM, CHRISTIAN. Pottsgrove.
June 4, 181?. March 20, 1816. 4.217
To sons John and Jacob, farm, in Pottsgrove, 400 acres of land, at 12 pds., 10 s. per acre. Rem. divided equally among: Christian, Jacob, Philip, John, Jacob, Maria, wife of David Latshaw, and son in law Samuel Myer, husband of daughter Susanna, deceased.
Execs: Sons John and Jacob. Wit: George Bechtel, and Nicholas Miller, and Peter Richards.

WALKER, MARY. Philadelphia.
Jan 24, 1815. April 10, 1816. 4.219
To sister Susanna Dungan privilege of house in Moreland, containing 21 acres subject to the payment of $100. To niece Peggy Lewis all estate. To niece Charlotte, 10 acres of land. Rem. of plantation to nephew Amos Dungan subject to the payment of 1/3 part.
Exec: sister Susanna Dungan. Wit: Joshua Comly, Jonathan Potts.

FUNK, JACOB. Cheltenham.
Sept 15, 1802. April 16, 1816. 4.221
To wife Anna, household goods, and maintenance, and interest of 600 pds. at rate of 5% yearly. to son John, farm, 64 acres, 24 perches. To

daughters: Barbara, Mary, Anna, and Elizabeth, 1/6 equally, part of net proceeds.
Execs: Sons John and Samuel. Wit: Michael Seppert, John Minnich, and Jacob Knox.

ZENTMAN, GEORGE. Montgomery.
April 15, 1816. April 27, 1816. 4.225
To wife, all estate.
Exec: John Harris. Wit: Joseph Quinn.

SORBER, JACOB. Springfield.
April 12, 1816. May 9, 1816. 4.226
To nephew Jacob Sorber, $266.67. To sons John and Joseph, $213.33. To John Sorber, gold watch. To sister Elizabeth, 10 acres of land. To sister Margaret, 4 acres of land. Rem. of land divided equally among 4 nieces.
Exec: John Huston. Wit: George Mock, John Miller.

MARTIN, RICHARD. Cheltenham.
Feb 24, 1815. May 13, 1816. 4.228
To wife Rebecca, household goods, and 40 pds. To daughter Rachel, 15 pds. To Martha Shoemaker, 100 pds. To son Richard Shoemaker, 75 pds. To daughters Martha Shoemaker and Rebecca Shoemaker, 25 pds. each. To nephew Richard, 25 pds. To Mary Stokes, wife of Joshua 25 pds. To Clement Sheppard, 25 pds. To Joseph Thomas, son of Nathan Thomas, 25 pds. and wearing apparel. To David Ramson, rem. of estate.
Execs: Thomas Shoemaker, and Justus Berrell, Jonathan Thomas. Wit: Isaac Paxson, Peter Lukens.

MILLER, SUSANNA. Lower Merion.
Oct 17, 1812. May 14, 1816. 4.229
To son John, land, in Haverford. To granddaughter Margaret Sheaf, wearing apparel, bed, etc. To son John, rem. of estate.
Execs: Son John and Jonathan Jones. Wit: Owen Jones, and Cornelius Smith.

McMAIR, SAMUEL. Horsham.
April 15, 1816. May 16, 1816. 4.231
To wife Mary, household goods, and $100. To son John, farm, where on I now dwell, in South Hampton. To son Samuel, farm, where on I now dwell, subject to the payment of $100 yearly to wife. To son James, 122 acres of land subject to the payment of $100 yearly to wife. To daughter Ann, wife of Silas Carver, $1334. To daughter Mary Long, wife of Hugh Long, $1334. To daughter Rebecca, bed, etc. Personal estate to son John, and Samuel McMair. To daughters Ann and Mary, 61 acres equally.
Execs: Sons John, Samuel, and James. Wit: Samuel Mann, and Azor Oberholtzer.

MOYER, MICHAEL. Upper Providence.
Aug 12, 1814. May 17, 1816. 4.234
To son Peter, all estate, interest of 300 pds. Rem. of estate divided among daughters: Polly, Elizabeth, Margaret, and Deborah.
Execs: Paul Ferye, and George Quinn. Wit: Henry Pennebecker, Jacob Clemmens.

DETWILER, JOHN. Upper Hanover.
April 27, 1816. June 10, 1816. 4.236
To wife Molly, household goods, and interest of 600 pds. yearly. To Samuel Freed, 200 pds. To Jacob Sechler, 50 pds. To wife of Henry Smith, 200 pds. To brother Jacob Detwiler, 200 pds. To Benjamin Sells, 300 pds. To sister Barbara Moyer, interest of 300 pds. Rem. of money to wife.
Exec: Michael Roudenbush. Wit: Henry Smith, George Hillegass.

JONES, JACOB. Whitemarsh.
Oct 2, 1809. June 11, 1816. 4.239
To wife Sarah, profits and maintenance of land in Whitemarsh. To Friends School in Plymouth, 200 pds. for the purpose of schooling poor children or children of such parents who may not be in circumstances to give them a suitable education. To Baptist Meeting of Roxbury, 50 pds. To Baptist Meeting of Lower Merion, 50 pds. To John Jones, wearing apparel. To Sarah Jones, a girl brought up with John Coats, 100 pds. when 21 years. In case of her death the aforesaid sum to Samuel Jones, son of brother Benjamin Jones, and his heirs. To Alice Major, daughter of brother Benjamin Jones, 50 pds. To each of Samuel Lloyd's children, of his first wife, 46 pds., 13 s. 4 d. To Daniel Baloo, son of sister Ann Baloo, 100 pds. To sister Rachel, 40 pds. To Jeremiah Baloo, 300 pds. To John Jones, son of brother John Jones, 100 pds. To Jacob Jones, 300 pds. Codicil dated, Oct 7, 1809. In case of death of nephew Jacob Jones, of brother Samuel Jones, his share will be equally divided. To sister Ann, 100 pds. of their shares. Rem. equally divided among legatees, mentioned in will.
Exec: Samuel Maulsby. Wit: George Peirce, and Isaac B. Peirce.

SPRINGER, JACOB. Towamencin.
May 7, 1816. June 12 1816. 4.242
To wife Susanna, farm, where I now dwell, until son Morris is 21, and household goods. Rem. divided equally among children.
Execs: Jacob Wampole, and Abraham Stover. Wit: Benjamin Hendricks, Abraham Hendricks.

MORGAN, ANDREW. Hatfield.
Nov 17, 1815. June 4, 1816. 4.246
To son Daniel, $2000 and wearing apparel. To daughter Rebecca, household goods. To granddaughter Matilda Evans, $800 when 21. To

granddaughter Elizabeth Beans, $800 when 21. If either of them die, their shre to be equally divided among children Daniel and Rebecca. To granddaughter Theodore, prayer book. To grandson Andrew, bible. To Daniel and Rebecca, farm, 107 acres. Rem. of estate to children, Daniel and Rebecca Morgan.
Exec: Son Daniel. Wit: Thomas Morgan, Owen Jenkins.

SLIFER, JOHN. Upper Hanover.
Nov 8, 1813. June 17, 1816. 4.248
To wife Esther, household and 10 pds. Exrs. to keep 300 pds. and give to wife yearly. Rem. of estate divided in equal shares. To son John, 1/3 part. To son Daniel, 1/3 part. Remaining 1/3 part to heirs of daughter Elizabeth.
Execs: Sons John and Daniel. Wit: Wendel Weand, Abraham Bechtel.

YERKES, CONRAD. Lower Salford.
April 13, 1813. June 18, 1816. 4.250
To 4 daughters: Margaret, wife of Philip Faus, Elizabeth, wife of George Snyder, Catharine, wife of John Scheder, and Mary, wife of John Reese, rem. of estate, equally. To wife Margaret, all estate
Execs: George Hartzell, and Benjamin Reiff. Wit: Jacob Croll, George Betz.

LEVERING, BENJAMIN. Plymouth.
Sept 20, 1815. July 5, 1816. 4.252
Estate to be sold. To wife Sarah, 851 pds. To Baptist Meeting of Roxbury, $50 to be applied towards keeping grave yard in repair. To brother Joseph Levering, wearing apparel, and $150. To Samuel Spencer, silver watch. To Rebecca Guilinger, $40. To mother in law Mary Spencer, $100. Rem. of estate to wife Sarah.
Execs: Alexander Crawford, and Thomas Shepard. Wit: George Peirce, and Jacob Hall.

PRICE, REESE. Lower Merion.
Feb 3, 1810. July 18, 1816. 4.254
To wife Hannah, $200 yearly and household goods, and farm. To son: Edward, Enoch, and Charles, and daughters: Mary and Sarah, 1000 pds. each. To son Thomas, tract of land in Lower Merion, containing 100 acres. To son Isaac, tract of land. To 7 children: Edward, Enoch, Charles, Mary, Sarah, and Isaac, and Thomas, 1000 pds. each.
Execs: Sons Isaac and Thomas. Wit: Jonathan Jones, Samuel Pugh.

JOHNSON, JACOB. Marlborough.
Nov 26, 1813. July 26, 1816. 4.258
To wife Philipbena, farm, in Marlborough, containing 53 acres and household goods, and interest of money.
Exec: Philip Reed. Wit: Jacob Hartinstain, Jacob Freas, and John Feries.

OTTINGER, JOHN. Springfield.
March 16, 1810. July 29, 1816. 4.261
To wife Hester, farm, and household goods, during widowhood, and if she marries, Exrs. to sell personal estate and divided money among wife and 4 children.
Execs: Wife Hester, and Jacob Holgate, and Aaron Keyser. Wit: Henry Hallman, and William Keyser.

RICHARDS, PETER. Upper Salford.
March 5, 1816. July 27, 1816. 4.262
To wife, and children, household goods, and 6 pds. in cash, during widowhood, and interest of 250 pds.
Execs: Sons Peter, and Philip. Wit: John Keller, and John Auchy.

COLTMAN, ROBERT. Cheltenham.
July 14, 1812. July 27, 1816. 4.266
To son William, $100. To son John, all estate. Thomas Copner, Ephraim, Fenton, and John Stell, guardians of son John, until he arrives at the age of 21 years. Rem. of estate to sons John and William. To children of Thomas Copner, $800 equally. To Ephraim Fenton, $800. To Thomas Forest, $800. To John Stell, $800.
Execs: Thomas Copner, Ephraim Fenton, and Thomas Forest and John Stell. Wit: Samuel Thomas, Joel Mann.

DAUB, HENRY. Whitemarsh.
Aug 1, 1813. Aug 3, 1816. 4.268
To wife Christina, farm, and household goods, and $20 and $80 yearly to be paid by Exrs. in quarterly payments, of $20 each. After wife's death, farm, 1/2 acre of land shall be valued and amount of such valuations shall be divided into 5 equal parts. To daughter Catharine, wife of Christopher Hocker, 1/5 part, and after her death her share to be divided equally. To daughter Molly, 1/5 part. To daughter Christina, 1/5 part.
Codicil To daughter Molly, 1/5 part of all estate Rem. to wife Christina.
Execs: Son Henry, and Andrew Geyser. Wit: Jacob Geyer, and Jacob Frick.

HOFFMAN, DANIEL. Gwynedd.
Jan 1, 1812. Aug 13, 1816. 4.273
To daughter Sarah, wife of Frederick Worner, tract of land. Rem. of estate to sons Daniel and Jesse, equally. To wife, use of plantation.
Exec: Thomas White. Wit: Samuel Martin, John Jenkins, and Edward Jenkins.

BROWN, CAEPER. Upper Providence.
May 21, 1813. Aug 24, 1816. 4.275
Estate to be sold and proceeds to be given to children: John, Elizabeth, Samuel, Jacob, and Isaac, to son David's children, when 21.

Exec: Son John. Wit: John Grop, and Samuel Grop.

BELINDA, JANE. Moreland.
Sept 22, 1808. Sept 5, 1816. 4.277
To daughters Hannah, and Mary, wearing apparel, equally. To daughter Mary, 1/3 of estate. To children of daughter Hannah, 1/3 part.
Exec: Isaac Warner. Wit: Semen Barnes, and Thomas Warner.

LUKENS, ELIJAH. Upper Dublin.
June 21, 1816. Sept 14, 1816. 4.278
To wife Rebecca, farm, and household goods, and $4000. To nephew Joseph Lukens, tract of land containing 130 acres. To sister Agnes Fletcher, $5333.33, annually, and interest of money to daughter Sarah, $5333.33 to be divided equally among children. To brother William Lukens, $5333.33. Rem. of estate to be sold and money equally divided among: Sarah, and Charles Lukens, and William, Tacy and brother Rynear.
Execs: Thomas Fletcher, and Thomas Livezey. Wit: Nathan Comly, and Jonathan Bright.

HAGLER, GEORGE. Upper Salford.
Jan 12, 1814. Sept 23, 1816. 4.281
To wife Christina, 100 pds. and household goods. To son Jacob, 50 acres of land in Lower Salford, subject to the payment of 10 pds. per acre. To sons Abraham, and David, rem. of farm, containing 200 acres. To sons: George and Peter and daughter Hannah, wife of Christian Rohr, woodland in Lower Salford, subject to the payment of 150 pds. To daughter Elizabeth, 150 pds. To daughter Barbara, interest of 700 pds. annually. Rem. of estate equally divided among 4 children: David, Abraham, Catharine, Elizabeth.
Execs: Sons Peter and Abraham. Wit: Edmund Flinn, William Fitzgerald, and Michael Shoemaker.

LOESER, CHRISTOPHER. Upper Dublin.
Sept 9, 1816. Sept 30, 1816. 4.__
To the Vestery of Whittemarsh Episcopal Church, $300. To wife Elizabeth, income and profits of estate, and after wife's death Exrs. to sell all estate. To cousin Jacob Cook, $50. To children of Thomas Yoany, $100, equally and rem. of estate equally divided among children of Christian Loeser.
Execs: Christian Loeser, nephew William Burk. Wit: Joseph Fitzwater, and Casper Schlater.

DRAKE, RACHEL, Montgomery.
March 24, 1814. Oct 11, 1816. 4.286
To niece Rachel Roberts, wearing apparel, and $100. To daughter Rachel Drake of brother Levi, rem. of wearing apparel. Rem. of estate to niece

Hannah Drake.
Execs: Niece Hannah Drake, and George Weaver. Wit: John Weaver, and Evan Jones.

COLER, JOHN. Whitemarsh.
Oct 8, 1816. Oct 28, 1816. 4.287
To wife Barbara, house, and household goods, and after expenses are paid and after wife's decease, money divided equally among children.
Execs: Casper Haughter, and Casper Coler. Wit: John Kinney, Ulrich Schlater.

ACUFF, JACOB. Upper Dublin.
Sept 19, 1816. Oct 28, 1816. 4.288
To wife Mary, $500 and household goods, money to be paid by Exrs. during widowhood and 75 pds. annually.
Codicil dated, Sept 19, 1816. 50 pds. to be charged to son William on account of his trade.
Exec: Son David. Wit: Joseph Detwiler, and Jacob Ulrich.

MARTIN, JOHN. Gwynedd.
May 4, 1815. Oct 29, 1816. 4.289
To wife Hannah, interest of 1/3 of estate. Estate to be sold and money divided among children: Anna, Elizabeth, Mary, Jacob, Lydia, John, Charles, and Hetty.
Execs: George Martin, and Abraham Schneyder. Wit: John Martin, Joseph Knipe, Benjamin Kulp.

CUSTER, EVE. Worcester.
Feb 23, 1801. Oct 30, 1816. 4.293
To daughter Catharine, silver watch. To 6 children: Henry, Levi, Cornelius, Catharine, Anna, and Mary, rem. of estate.
Execs: Sons Henry and Levi. Wit: Joseph Tyson, and Jacob Zimmerman.

UMSTEAD, RICHARD. Lower Providence.
Sept 17, 1816. Nov 7, 1816. 4.294
To sister Hannah, 12 pds. yearly, after my decease, 200 pds. To granddaughters Mary, and Sarah, $100. To grandson Richard Morgan, $100 and to have 6 months schooling. To daughter Anna Morgan, household goods. Rem. of estate to be sold and proceeds to go to the payments of expenses and legacies. To daughter Anna Morgan, 2000 pds. To daughter Alice, 120 pds. yearly, and 2000 pds. to be put on interest for daughter until 21.
Execs: Jacob Umstead, and Michael Corbitt. Wit: Joseph Skenn, and John Evans.

EVANS, AMOS. Upper Dublin.
July 19, 1816. Nov 14, 1816. 4.297

To wife Mary, personal estate. To 4 children: Edward, Owen, John, Mary, lands in the state of Ohio. Exrs. to pay to wife's son James McKinney, $60. Rem. of estate divided equally among step daughter Rachel Holt, and 4 children.
Execs: Sons John and Edward. Wit: Amos Lewis, Jesse Lukens.

MILLER, LEONARD. Upper Hanover.
Feb 7, 1816. Nov 25, 1816. 4.298
To wife Margaret, household goods, and interest of 450 pds. After wife's death 450 pds. to be equally divided among 10 children: Henry, Frederick, Charles, William, Samuel, Josiah, Catharine, Sarah, Elizabeth, Lydia. To son Henry, $40 yearly. Rem. of estate to be sold. to son Frederick, weaving loom. To daughter Sarah, bed, $25 etc.
Execs: Son ina law George Boyer, and Jacob Fry. Wit: Philip Reed, Michael Rieter.

HARTZELL, ULRICH. Upper Salford.
March, 5, 1810. Nov 27, 1816. 4.301
To son and daughter farm, where I now dwell, and personal estate, and son to pay to daughter 500 pds. To daughter 500 pds. to be paid by son Jacob.
Exec: Son Jacob Hartzell. Wit: George Emert, and Abraham Allebach.

RHOADS, JOHN. Moreland.
Nov 14, 1816. Nov 30, 1816. 4.302
To wife Sophia, $450 and household goods. To daughter Elizabeth, $30. To daughter Mary, $30. To daughter Rachel, $100. To daughter Sophia, $200, bed, etc. To daughter Susanna, $100, bed, etc. To son John's children, $5. each. To son William $500 and wearing apparel, and rem. of estate to be sold and money divided among sons and daughters children equally.
Exec: Son William. Wit: Silas Roney, and Mahlon V. Booskirk.

FRY, WILLIAM. Montgomery.
April 1, 1816. Dec 23, 1816. 4.304
To 4 grandchildren, of daughter Catharine, Theophilus, John, Elizabeth, and Eleanor Williams 4 pds. each to be paid to them of son John Fry. To son John, 1/3 of farm.
Execs: Sons Enoch, and John Fry. Wit: John Gordon, Nathan Hanas, and Thomas Morgan.

WIEANT, YOST. Upper Hanover.
Oct 28, 1815. Nov 28, 1816. 4.306
To wife Barbara, all estate and interest of 300 pds. To son Daniel, tract of land containing 120 acres subject to the payment of 600 pds. yearly, and farming implements. To son Wendel, 7 s. , 6 d. Rem. of estate to be sold and money after expenses are to be equally divided among 9 children:

Susanna, Catharine, John, Henry, Elizabeth, Daniel, Samuel, Maria, and Michael.
Execs: Sons Henry and Daniel. Wit: Daniel Shleiffer, and Abraham Bechtel.

SHOEMAKER, EZEKIEL. Horsham.
Jan 30, 1796. Dec 3, 1816. 4.309
To wife Hannah, household goods, 125 pds. yearly. To son Joseph, 10 pds. yearly. To grandson Ezekiel son of Joseph Shoemaker, 20 pds. To daughter Ann, 10 pds. To daughter Jane, of daughter Ann, 20 pds. To granddaughter Sarah, 20 pds. To son Richard, farm, containing 136 acres and rem. of personal estate.
Execs: Sons Joseph and Richard. Wit: Sons Joseph and Richard.

MULLIN, WILLIAM. Horsham.
July 11, 1816. Dec 31, 1816. 4.311
To son William, farm, in Horsham, containing 100 acres. To daughters Mary and sarah, all residue of land. Son William to pay to daughters Mary and Sarah, $400 yearly.
Execs: Son William and son in law Jesse Reuben, and Jesse Shay. Wit: Richard Shoemaker, Richard Roberts.

DeHAVEN, MARY. Skippack.
Dec 10, 1816. Dec 31, 1816. 4.313
To daughter Mary, wife of William Keller, wearing apparel. To children, rem. of wearing apparel, equally. Rem. of estate to be sold.
Exec: Peter Saler. Wit: Barbara Umsted, and Mary Rittenhouse, and Rebecca DeHaven.

KIRKPATRICK, MARY. Upper Merion.
Nov 18, 1816. Jan 9, 1817. 4.314
Exrs. to place a head and foot stone at the grave of daughter Elizabeth, her name and age engraved on it. To sister Abi McLemon, wearing apparel, $6 yearly. To niece Elizabeth Bones, her son Melson Bones, bed, etc., and $25. To nephew Francis McLemon, $10. To niece Mary, $15. To nephew Walter Lyle, son of Francis, $50. To niece Martha Lyle, daughter of Francis, $25. To nephew B. Rush Lyle, $25. To sister Mary, widow of Walter Lyle, $10., residue of estate.
Exec: Brother Francis Lyle. Wit: Matthew Roberts, and John Elliott.

BOYD, WILLIAM. Norristown.
Jan 6, 1817. Jan 10 1817. 4.316
To son James, and daughter Mary, and grandson William, $230 to be put on interest and divided equally among them. To daughter Mary, $40. To daughter Betsey, watch.
Execs: Son in law Peter Keyser and son Alex. Wit: Joseph Leedom, and Hugh Dickson.

253

HANGEN, JACOB. Franconia.
March 22, 1815. Jan 11, 1817. 4.318
To sons George and John, wearing apparel, equally. Estate to be sold and money divided among children: George, John, Jacob, Catharine, wife of Jacob Cope, Elizabeth, wife of Philip Sholl, Barbara, wife of William Wirl. Execs: Sons George and John. Wit: Michael Shoemaker, Jr., and Michael Shoemaker, Sr.

AUSTIN, SUSANNA. Upper Dublin.
May 16, 1813. Jan 13, 1817. 4.319
To sister Mary Kirk, and Mary Hallowell, wearing apparel, equally. To nephew Isaac Tyson, 100 pds. To Rebecca Edwards, wife of Edward Edwards, 50 pds. To daughters Elizabeth, wife of Anthony Williams, and Agness Craft 50 pds. equally. To Sarah Tyson, 20 pds. To Thomas Tyson, 10 pds. To Susanna Worth, 100 pds. To Elizabeth Krier, 20 pds. To niece Priscilla Michener, 10 pds. To John Kirk, 10 pds. To Joseph Kirk, 10 pds. To Isaac Kirk, 10 pds. To Mary Marple, 10 pds. To Elizabeth Worth, household goods. To niece Rachel Bewley, wife of John Bewley, interest of 50 pds. to be paid annually by Exrs. To niece Susanna Hallowell, interest of 50 pds. to be paid annually by Exrs. To sister Mary Kirk, and nieces Sarah and Susanna, rem. of estate equally.
Execs: Nephew Isaac Tyson, and brother John Tyson. Wit: Thomas Livezey, John Fitzwater.

BARLOW, JOHN.
Dec 30, 1816. Jan 13, 1817. 4.321
To sister Rebecca Corbin, 100 pds.
Execs: ____. Wit: Matthew Brooke, and John Schlichter, and Abner Barlow.

STERN, JOHN. Worcester.
Aug 27, 1812. Jan 17, 1817. 4.322
Estate to daughter Salomi, and maintenance.
Execs: Christopher Zimmerman, Richard Casselbury. Wit: Frederick K. Conrad, Frederick W. Conrad.

CHECK, MAGDALENA. Towamencin.
June 15, 1813. Feb 17, 1817. 4.323
To William Hendricks, estate.
Exec: William Hendricks. Wit: Thomas White, and James White.

WEAVER, ABRAHAM. Whitemarsh.
Feb 21, 1808. March 15, 1817. 4.324
To wife Elizabeth, household goods, and $500. Rem. of estate to children: William, and Hiltner, equally.
Exec: William Weaver. Wit: Thomas Morris, and John Dager.

WHITE, THOMAS. Plymouth.
March 18, 1817. March 31, 1817. 4.325
To wife Mary, 1/2 of real estate for her use and benefit. To 7 children rem. of estate, equally divided among them, except 2 sons, Solomon and John of which they are to have $100 and rest of other children to have 10 pds. each.
Execs: Sons Solomon and John. Wit: David Trexley, Barnard Coulston.

ROSENBERGER, DANIEL. Franconia.
Feb 11, 1817. March 31, 1817. 4.326
To wife Dorothea, household goods. To son Henry, Martyr Book. To son Samuel, watch. Exrs. to make sale thereof as soon as convenient and money from sale to wife, and sons Samuel and Henry.
Execs: Wife Dorothea and Daniel Rosenberger. Wit: Henry Rosenberger, and Michael Shoemaker.

SHOEMAKER, ELIZABETH (*annotation states "nee Deaves"*). Whitemarsh.
Nov 24, 1816. April 10 1817. 4.328
To son George Shoemaker, $300. To brother Thomas, $500, if he dies his estate to be divided among children: Thomas, Mary, Isaac, George, Margaret, Elizabeth, and Barbara. To 7 daughters of Michael and Margaret Newbold, $70 each. To husband Jonathan Shoemaker, all estate.
Execs: Husband Jonathan Shoemaker, and Samuel Maulsby. Wit: Peter Robeson, Isaac Roberts.

HAGY, JOSEPH. Lower Merion.
April 14, 1817. April 26, 1817. 4.329
Estate to be sold, except household goods, which is given to wife Ann. To wife Ann, all money arising from the sale of estate, and maintenance.
Exec: Brother William Hagy. Wit: John Duy, and Daniel Nippes.

BARNWELL, MARY. Lower Merion.
Feb 19, 1817. April 26. 1817. 4.331
To daughter Letitia, all money that can be levied out of property, except $50. To Ann Roudenbaugh, rem.
Exec: Peter Picheon. Wit: Michael Burns, and Nathan Dotterer.

SHOEMAKER, JOHN. Cheltenham.
Sept 23, 1814. May 6, 1817. 4.332
To wife Jane, all estate, $1000, and household goods, and farm, and utensils, and $400 per year. To brother Charles Shoemaker, farm, subject to the payment of $400 yearly. To Elizabeth Robeson, farm. To brother Charles all lands, subject to the payment of $2600 towards payment of legacies. To Jonathan Shoemaker, interest of $300. To cousins: John, Ann, Abigail, $400 each. To Richard Mather, $200. To children of Jonathan

Shoemaker: Isaac, David, Charles, and George, $400 each. To children of Betsey Boone, $400 each. To David Shoemaker, $400. To Mary Evans, $400. To Nathan, Ann, and Martha, children of Thomas Shoemaker, $400. each. To children of sister Carolina Plurner, $400 each. To cousin Ann Maul, $400. To Dr. John Moore, and Catharine, his wife, $1000. To Richard Mott, of New York, $500. To Benjamin White, books, $200. To John Shoemaker, $100. To Hannah Tolan, $50. To Elizabeth Donald, $30. To Treasurer of Committee of Boarding School at Westtown, of my title, and interest in the mill built on School Farm, which cost me $500. To Treasury of Asylum, $500. To William Berrel, silver watch. To Joseph Boster, $100. To Thomas Cockburn, $100.
Execs: Wife Jane, and brother Charles Shoemaker, and William Shoemaker. Wit: Daniel Fletcher, and Eli Berrell.

RUDY, FREDERICK. Upper Salford.
March 23, 1814. May 15, 1817. 4.336
To wife Charlotte, household goods, and 30 pds. yearly. To son Philip Rudy, farm, containing 60 acres and farm, containing 7 acres in Rock Hill, County, subject to the payment of yearly interest unto wife Charlotte. To 8 children: Jacob, Philip, Frederick, Catharine, wife of Andrew Boyer, Polly, wife of Henry Boyer, and Maria, wife of John Boyer, Christiana, wife of Abraham Rober, Charlotte, wife of Isaac Cressman, 100 pds. each in yearly payments, which is to be paid by son Philip, till the sum of 600 pds. is fully paid off. To son Frederick, farm, containing 40 acres subject to the payment of 500 pds.
Execs: Son Jacob, and Jacob Smith. Wit: Abraham Scholl, Frederick Wannamaker, George Hartzell.

WAMBACK, BARTHOLOMEW. Pottsgrove.
May 20, 1803. May 19, 1817. 4.340
To son John, lands, in Douglass, and 1400 pds. To wife, interest of 600 pds. yearly. To son John, bible, and clock, etc. To grandson Bartholomew, watch. [*Annotation states the names of wife and 6 daughters given in will.*]
Execs: Wife, and son John. Wit: Aloses Yocum, and Stinson Ruth.

EVANS, DAVID. Lower Merion.
March 25, 1814. May 20, 1817. 4.344
To wife Mary, and to son Nathan, use of estate, during widowhood, and to son Nathan, 2/3 part of estate. To son David, $100. To daughter Sarah, $50. To sons Monroe, and Thomas, $100 equally.
Exec: Son Nathan Evans. Wit: Jacob Bealer, and Thomas Bealer.

WILLAUER, CHRISTIAN. Upper Hanover.
March 7, 1817. June 5, 1817. 4.345
To wife Mary, 5 s. To sister Elizabeth, $100. to sons Samuel, and Jonathan, books, etc., equally. Rem. of estate to sons Samuel and

Jonathan.
Exec: Solomon Fris. Wit: Conrad Brey, and Andrew Garber.

MILLER, ADAM. Marlborough.
Dec 26, 1815. June 12, 1817. 4.348
All estate to be sold and money divided among 8 children.
Execs: Sons Frederick and Adam. Wit: Philip Reed, and George Bohr.

GARBER, BENEDICT. Upper Providence.
June 12, 1813. June 14, 1817. 4.350
To granddaughter Deborah, 40 pds. To granddaughter Anna, 40 pds. To granddaughter Lydia, 40 pds. To granddaughter Elizabeth, $20. To granddaughter Mary, $10. To granddaughter Hannah, $10. To granddaughter Sarah, $20. To grandson Benedict, $40, when 21. To granddaughter Catharine, 100 pds. Rem. of estate divided among 3 sons: Jacob, Charles and Benjamin Garber, equally. To son Jacob, one share. To son Charles, one share. To son Benjamin, one share.
Execs: Sons Jacob and Charles. Wit: John Roudenbush, and Paul Fry.

SEIWELL, CATHARINE. Pottstown.
Jan 9, 1811. June 18, 1817. 4.352
Estate to be divided into 7 equal parts. To children of John Seiwell, 1/7 part. To children of daughter Elizabeth, 1/7 part. To son John Seiwell, 1/7 part. To son Henry, 1/7 part. To daughter Maria, 1/7 part. To daughter Catharine, 1/7 part. To children of Anthony Seiwell, 1/7 part.
Exec: Son Valentine. Wit: John Yost, and Daniel Kroltz.

KEYSER, NATHAN. Springfield.
Jan 24, 1817. July 10, 1817. 4.353
To wife Mary, all estate. To son Derrick, rem. of estate, when 21.
Execs: Brother Aaron Keyser, and William Keyser. Wit: John Kepner, and Peter Van Winkle.

PHIPPS, JAMES. Abington.
Feb 28, 1817. July 31, 1817. 4.354
To wife Sarah, household goods, interest of money and maintenance. To daughter Abigail, farm, containing 100 acres.
Exec: Wife Sarah. Wit: Thomas Fletcher, and Isaac Walton.

HEEBNER, CHRISTOPHER. Norriton.
Jan 2, 1802. Aug 2, 1817. 4.356
To wife Susanna, household goods, and 400 pds. and remaining shares to be equally divided among 4 children. To daughter Sarah, farm, and 500 pds. To son John, farm, containing 100 acres subject to the payment of 30 pds. to wife. To son Abraham, farm, in Moreland, containing 120 acres subject to the payment of 1500 pds.
Codicil dated July 12, 1814. 3 sons each, Abraham, John, and Christopher,

may retain 100 pds. To daughter Sarah, 600 pds.
Exec: Son Abraham. Wit: John Cassel, and Jacob Cassel.

MARTIN, MARTHA. Cheltenham.
Sept 12, 1810. Aug 19, 1817. 4.360
To daughter Rachel, $200. To daughter Rebecca, $300. To daughter Martha, $300. To granddaughter Martha, $100. To granddaughter Rebecca, $100. To daughter Martha, wearing apparel.
Execs: Sons Isaac, and grandson Richard. Wit: Thomas Shoemaker, and Samuel Robinson.

VANDERSLICE, THOMAS. Upper Providence.
July 24, 1817. Aug 22, 1817. 5.1
Tract of land where I dwell to be sold, containing 240 acres. To son Jacob, tract of land, containing 40 or 50 acres. To son Joseph, $500. To son Edward, 50 pds. to be paid annually by Exrs. and to be put on interest. To son Jacob, 5 pds. To grandson Jacob, silver watch. To granddaughter Ann, bureau, in my bed room. To mother, 30 pds. annually. To wife Mary, 5 pds. to son Thomas, black boy, named Bob. To daughter Mary, negro girl. Rem. of estate to be sold and money divided among sons: John, Thomas, Mark, Augustus, and daughter Mary, equally.
Execs: Brother in law George Peirce, and Mary Robeson, and Levi Pawling. Wit: Samuel Gartley, and Jesse Jarrett.

DRAKE, THOMAS. Montgomery.
July 24, 1817. Aug 25, 1817. 5.3
To sister Sarah, $100. To sister Mary, $100. To brother Jonathan, $100. To sister Elizabeth, $100. To brother Jonathan, $100. To brother Andrew, $1000. To brother William, $100. To sister Hannah, $100. To niece Hannah, tract of land.
Exec: George Martin. Wit: Silas Hough, and Henry Harris.

SPRINGER, JOHN. Towamencin.
April 25, 1805. Aug 27, 1817. 5.4
To son Jacob, farm, subject to the payment of 1000 pds. After his decease 390 pds. to be divided equally among brother John Springer, and sisters Elizabeth and Margaret, and rem. divided into 4 equal parts. To son Jacob 1/4 part, and he is to pay to brothers and sisters, rem. 600 pds. paying 75 pds. each year. To daughter Gertrude, 10 pds.
Codicil dated June 10, 1815. In case of death of son Jacob, all money to son John.
Execs: Son John and Jacob. Wit: Frederick Conrad, and John Hendricks, and Charles Hendricks.

HALLMAN, WILLIAM. Whitemarsh.
May 18, 1817. Sept 1, 1817. 5.6
To wife Mary, farm, and household goods. To daughter Sarah, 6 pds.

yearly. To 3 daughters: Mary, Sarah, and Elizabeth, are not to have any portion of their share until 18 years of age.
Execs: Daughter Mary, and Henry Hallman, and George Streper. Wit: George Streper, and Weiss.

ROBERTS, EDWARD. Whitpain.
May 12, 1817. Sept 7, 1817. 5.8
To son Amos, rem. of estate.
ExeIsaac: Amos Roberts, and Enos Roberts. Wit: Samuel Wentz, and Thomas Humphrey.

WARNER, CHRISTIAN. Montgomery.
Aug 16, 1809. Oct 10, 1817. 5.9
To wife Catharine, household goods, and interest of monies. To sons Dewalt and John, 200 pds. each. To son Peter, 300 pds. To daughters Hannah and Catharine, 200 pds. each.
Codicil dated Nov 10, 1817. To son John Warner, $100.
Execs: Sons Dewalt and Peter. Wit: Frederick Conrad, and Henry Conrad.

SWARTZ, JOHN. Franconia.
Nov 12, 1817. Oct 10, 1817. 5.12
To wife Anna, household goods, and interest of 600 pds. at 5%. To son Joseph, 80 acres of land in Franconia. To son Philip, rem. of farm, subject to the payment of $60 per acre. To son Abraham, 8 acres of woodland. Rem. of estate to all children: Henry, John, Jacob, Abraham, Joseph, Samuel, Philip, and Elizabeth, and Mary, equally.
Execs: Sons Abraham, and Henry. Wit: Jacob Zehman, and Henry Bergey, and Michael Shoemaker.

CURWIN, JOHN. Montgomery
June 26, 1817. Oct 15, 1817. 5.14
Estate to father John Curwin.
Execs: Richard Mason, and Eleanor Evans. Wit: Richard Mason, and Eleanor Evans.

NASH, WILLIAM. Moreland.
July 11, 1817. Nov 17, 1817. 5.15
To son William, 1/3 of estate. All estate to sister Mary Jones, wife of Owen Jones. To son Joseph, $100. To daughter Susanna, $60. Charles Spencer and Jacob Walton to be guardians of 2 children William and Susanna.
Execs: Jarrett Spencer, Hiram McNeill. Wit: Isaiah Walton, and John Johnson.

DAVIS, JOHN. Whitpain.
April 26, 1814. Dec 2, 1817. 5.17

To daughter Rachel, household goods. Estate to be sold and money to be given to children in 3 equal payments.
Execs: George Martin and son Thomas. Wit: Henry Schneider and Andrew Fetzer.

HARRY, ANN. Gwynedd.
Jan 29, 1814. Dec 2, 1817. 5.18
To Dr. Curtis Evans, son of niece Ruth Evans, all real estate, containing 50 acres subject to the payment of 40 pds. To niece Ruth Evans, sherry table stand. To niece Mary Evans, looking glass. Rem. of household goods to be divided equally among nieces: Mary, Ruth, and Rebecca. Rem. of estate divided equally among nephew Owen Evans and his sisters Mary and Rebecca, each. 40 pds. to Samuel Walter grandson to niece Rebecca, at 21.
Exec: Dr. Curtis Evans. Wit: Job Roberts, William Walter.

SWARTZ, ANDREW. Lower Salford.
May 31, 1817. Dec 8, 1817. 5.19
To wife Catharine, household goods, and 300 pds. After wife's death, equally divided among children. To son Abraham, tract of land containing 45 acres subject to the payment of 1000 pds.
Execs: Sons Isaac and Andrew, Jacob, and Abraham. Wit: Benjamin Reiff.

WILLIAMS, JOSEPH. Upper Merion.
Dec 21, 1814. Dec 9, 1817. 5.23
To grandsons: Joseph Jarret, Joseph Thomas, and Joseph Conrad, 100 pds. each. To daughter Elizabeth, 50 pds. To Ann Moyer, $50. To Meeting of Friends at Plymouth, 100 pds. To daughter Sarah, 1/3 part of estate, and other 1/2 to her children, equally. To daughter Ann interest of 1/3 of estate. To 5 children, 1/3 part of estate, equally. To daughter Mary, 1/3 part of estate
Execs: Son in law John Iredel, and Joseph Lukens. Wit: George Potts, and Samuel Thomas, and Nathan Potts.

BARNES, ELIZABETH. Upper Merion.
Nov 25, 1817. Dec 13, 1817. 5.25
Exrs. to see that a head and foot stone be placed on my grave.
Exec: Francis Lyle. Wit: Francis Lyle, Benjamin Lyle, and John Elliott.

PILGER, LUDWIG. Franconia.
Oct 19, 1795. Dec 26, 1817. 5.26
To wife Magdalena, 100 pds. and household goods. Rem. of estate to be divided among sons: George, Henry and Ludwig, and daughters: Magdalena and Charlotte, equally.
Exrs.: Wife Magdalena, and son George. Wit: Michael Sholl, and George Gerhart.

WILSON, THOMAS. Montgomery
Nov 14, 1817. Dec 27, 1817. 5.27
To daughter Hannah, $20 an farm, containing 12 acres. To daughter Elizabeth, 12 acres of land and bed, etc. To daughter Margaret, 100 pds. and bed, etc. Son James to pay to son William, $10 annually. To son William and son Thomas, wearing apparel, equally.
Codicil dated Nov 14, 1817. Son Thomas shall keep a cow for daughter Hannah. To daughters Elizabeth and Margaret, certain part of estate.
Execs: Jacob Cassel, and son Thomas. Wit: Evan Jones, and John Weaver.

YERGER, ANDREW. New Hanover.
Nov 20, 1817. Jan 5, 1818. 5.31
To wife Philipina, household goods, and interest of 800 pds. annually. Estate to be sold and money divided among children: John, Daniel, David, Abraham, Joseph, Matthias, Margaret, Catharine, and Conrad. To son Daniel, farm, containing 86 acres subject to the payment of 20 pds. per acre. To son David, farm, containing 90 acres. To son Abraham, farm, containing 250 acres subject to the payment of 30 pds. per acre.
Execs: Michael Abrecht, and son John. Wit: Philip Boyer, and Samuel Yerger.

FAIRES, WILLIAM. Willow Grove.
Sept 24, 1817. Jan 8, 1818. 5.34
Household goods to be sold. To son John, all estate.
Execs: Son John, and Hiram McNeill. Wit: George Rex, Abraham Justice.

SHOEMAKER, ISAAC. Norriton.
Nov 17, 1811. Jan 21, 1818. 5.36
To wife Rachel, all estate. To son Dennis, $466.66. To son Isaac, $266.66. To son David, $266.66. To granddaughter Lydia, $133.33. To daughter Margaret, interest of 1/7 part of estate.
Execs: Sons Dennis and Isaac Shoemaker, son in law John Roberts. Wit: William Ellis, and Jonathan Thomas.

HIGHMAN, BARBARA.
May 22, 1812. Feb 4, 1818. 5.38
To daughter Mary, wearing apparel. To granddaughters household goods, equally. To son Peter, 10 pds. to be put of interest. Rem. of estate equally divided among children.
Exec: Son John. Wit: William Long, and John Bunn.

GRATER, JOHN. Perkiomen and Skippack.
March 5, 1805. March 27, 1818. 5.39
To wife Margaret, household goods, and interest of 400 pds. To son Lewis, farm, containing 120 acres subject to the payment of 1200 pds. To daughter Elizabeth, 50 pds. To son John, 20 pds. To son Lewis, 20 pds. Rem. of estate equally divided among children: Mary, wife of George

Hubler, John, Abraham, Lewis, Catharine, wife of Dillman Seigler, and Elizabeth, wife of Henry Hallman, equally. Execs: Sons Abraham and Lewis. Wit: John Tyson, and Jacob Horning, Isaiah Lewis.

WENTZ, JOHN. Whitpain.
May 1, 1817. March 28, 1818. 5.41
To wife Hannah, farm, household goods, and 200 pds. in cash and $180 annually. Rem. of estate to be sold. To son George, $100. To son Samuel, $150. Rem. of money from sale of estate divided among children: Abraham, George, Samuel, Daniel, Rebecca, Hannah, Albert, and Susannah, equally. Wife to be guardian of minor children.
Execs: Sons Abraham, George, Samuel, and Daniel. Wit: Jacob Hurst, and Henry Hurst.

SHOEMAKER, SAMUEL. Moreland.
Sept 7, 1816. April 2, 1818. 5.44
To Samuel Shoemaker, farm, containing 8 square perches of land. To wife Agnes, rem. of estate, household goods. To sister in law Martha, dwelling house. To niece Agnes Comly, farm, containing 25 acres subject to the payment of $500. To Asa Comly, farm, containing 55 acres subject to the payment of $500. To nephew Nathan Shoemaker, 1000 pds. To niece Agnes, 200 pds. To Asa Comly, 300 pds. To Isaac Williams, 50 pds. To George Williams, 50 pds. To Joshua Phipps, 50 pds. To Rachel Phipps, 25 pds. To Joseph Phipps, 50 pds. To Elizabeth Parry, 50 pds. To John Thomson, 100 pds. To sister Mary's grandchildren, the children of Frederick Altemus, 100 pds. equally. To brother Jacob Shoemaker's children, 80 pds. equally. To Ezekiel Shoemaker, 80 pds. To Mary Thomas, wife of Enoch Thomas, 50 pds. To Comly Shoemaker, 100 pds. To Jonas Hallowell, 50 pds. To Thomas Shoemaker, 300 pds. To Nathan Shoemaker, 100 pds. To Thomas Shoemaker's 2 daughters Ann and Martha, 10 pds. each. To Joseph Shoemaker, 20 pds. To Thomas Shoemaker Cowper, 20 pds. To Charles Shoemaker, 10 pds. To John Shoemaker, 10 pds. To Jane Shoemaker, widow of Benjamin Shoemaker, deceased, and 4 children, 100 pds. equally. To Martha Shoemaker, widow of Robert Shoemaker, deceased, and her 2 daughters, 30 pds. equally. To her son Richard Shoemaker, 50 pds. To Nathan Shoemaker's 4 daughters: Lydia, Rachel, Rebecca, and Sarah, 100 pds. equally. To sister in law Martha Shoemaker, 100 pds. To sister in law Grace Conrad, 20 pds. To her children, 100 pds. equally. To sister in law Jane Lukens, children as follows: to Martha Lukens, 50 pds. To Abraham Lukens, 20 pds. To Lydia Livezey, 15 pds. To Agnes Lukens, 15 pds. to George Shoemaker, 30 pds. To Amy Hallowell, 10 pds. To Rebecca Ross's 3 children, 100 pds. each. To Nathan Comly, 15 pds. To John Radcliff, 50 pds. To Robert Radcliff, 50 pds. To Joseph Radcliff, 50 pds. To Robert Radcliff, 50 pds. To Joseph Radcliff, and his 6 children, 5 pds. each. To Mdary Harner, wife of Amos Harner, 50 pds. To Elizabeth Cadwalder, widow of Joseph Cadwalder, 30

pds. To Benjamin Cadwalder, 10 pds. To David Kinsey, 10 pds. To William Fallous, 10 pds. To Grave Yard, 10 pds. for use and repairs. Rem. of estate to Nathan Shoemaker, and Thomas Shoemaker, equally.
Execs: Wife Agness, and Thomas Shoemaker, and Comly Shoemaker.
Wits: Samuel Shoemaker.

LEVERING, DANIEL. Whitpain.
July 29, 1817. April 6, 1818. 5.47
To wife Susanna, all estate, after wife's death to daughter.
Exec: John Heist. Wit: Henry Freedley, and Matthias Fetter.

SHIPE, HENRY. Hatfield.
March 31, 1818. April 8, 1818. 5.48
To wife Mary, household goods. Estate to be sold and money divided among 2 daughters Mary and Elizabeth.
Execs: Son Abraham, and Frederick Ratzell. Wit: Jacob Ruth, and John Kerrdig.

SAMES, SOPHIA. Whitpain.
Feb 27, 1818. April 11, 1818. 5.49
To 3 children, and Sophia Wentz, rem. of estate.
Execs: Son Jesse, and Thomas Humphrey. Wit: John Hurst, and Jacob Hurst.

POTTS, JOANNA. Pottstown.
Dec 26, 1808. April 11, 1818. 5.50
To daughter Sarah Hobart, wearing apparel. To Tacy Coats, 50 pds. To Peggy Cook, and negro Thomas Jackson, 10 pds. each. To son in law Robert Hobart, 1/5 part of daughter Sarah's amount. To sons Thomas and David, and John, 1/5 part of estate.
Codicil dated July 15, 1810. To Elizabeth, $2000. To son John, bond, and note of land.
Execs: Sons: John, Thomas, and David, and Joseph, and son in law Robert Hobart. Wit: Adam Drinkhouse, and Jacob Drinkhouse, and George Leaf.

OTTINGER, MARGARET. Springfield.
Dec 15, 1808. April 14, 1818. 5.55
To granddaughter Margaret, household goods, and farming utensils, and 10 pds. To daughter Anna, bed, etc. To daughter Rebecca, $50. To daughters Anna and Rebecca, wearing apparel, equally.
Exec: Aaron Keyser. Wit: William Keyser, John Ottinger.

KIRK, JOSEPH. Horsham.
Nov 25, 1816. April 18, 1818. 5.56
To nephew Thomas, $20. To nephew John, $10. To niece Sarah, $10. To nephew Joseph, $40. To Joseph Wood, $40. To Joseph Kirk, $40. To Joseph Walter, $15. To Thomas Harany, use of watch, at his death to son

Joseph. To niece Anna, dictionary, and gold Guinea. To niece Mary, bible. To sons and to 4 sisters, wearing apparel, equally. Exrs. to sell lot of land in Moreland, containing 2 acres. Rem. of estate divided equally among 4 sisters: Ann, Mary, Susanna, and Sarah.
Execs: Joseph Wood, and Isaac Longstreth. Wit: Benjamin and Charles Longstreth.

BURD, ELIZABETH. Pottsgrove.
April 17, 1817. April 22, 1818. 5.58
To sister Jane, $600. To brother James, $600. To sister Margaret, $400. Rem. of estate to brother Joseph Burd.
Execs: Brother in law Jacob Hubley, and Joseph Burd. Wit: Edward Hubley and Sarah Hubley.

FENNELS, ELIZABETH. Philadelphia.
____. May 10, 1818. 5.59
To Mary Fennell, wearing apparel.
Exec: Thomas Elliott. Wit: William Lentz, and Robert Fennells.

REINWALD, BALTHASER. Towamencin.
April 25, 1804. May 18, 1818. 5.59
To daughter Sarah, clock, etc. Rem. of estate to daughters Sarah and Regina. To son in law Andrew Ander, farm, containing 59 acres subject to the payment of 600 pds. To son Henry Snyder, 100 pds.
Execs: Son in law Henry Snyder, and Andrew Ander. Wit: Melchior Schultz, and George Anders.

BECHTEL, GEORGE. Pottsgrove.
June 9, 1809. May 18, 1818. 5.61
To wife Hannah, to have use of house, and household goods, and interest of 400 pds. To sons: Samuel, George, John, Peter, Jacob, David, and William, 200 pds. each. To son George, 500 pds. Rem. of estate divided equally among children.
Codicil dated June 9, 1809. $300 to remain in place. To each of sons: Samuel, John, George, Peter, Jacob, David, and William, 200 pds. each.
Execs: Brother in law John Yocum, and George Bechtel. Wit: Peter Richards, and Jacob Drinkhouse.

SMITH, HANNAH. Horsham.
July 4, 1817. May 19, 1818. 5.65
To sister in laws Mary and Elizabeth, wearing apparel. To brother Samuel, and his children, money arising from sale of farm, equally. To Hannah Spencer, daughter of James Spencer, bed, etc. Rem. of estate to brother Samuel, and 1/4 part to son Isaiah, and 2/4 part, rem. to brother Isaac Walton.
Exec: Benjamin Lloyd. Wit: George and Charles Spencer.

JONES, MORDECAI. Whitpain.
May 6, 1816. May 30, 1818. 5.66
To wife, 40 acres, of land. To Benjamin Wentz, 36 acres of land subject to the payment of 12 pds. yearly. To son Jesse, tract of woodland, containing 2 acres, 40 perches. To Mordecai Wentz, and Sophia, his wife, 9 3/4 acres. To Maria Coplin, 3 3/4 acres. To Elizabeth Jones, $100. To Maria Coplin, $200. To Jonathan Jones, 50 pds. To brothers children, $200 equally. To wife, 4 acres of woodland.
Execs: Jonathan Jones, and son Jesse. Wit: Jonathan Jones, and Abraham Wentz.

MOYER, JACOB. Upper Hanover.
May 8, 1818. June 16, 1818. 5.67
To wife Elizabeth, all estate.
Execs: Wife Elizabeth, and son Samuel. Wit: Jacob Atom.

SEASHOLTZ, DAVID. New Hanover.
Jan 21, 1800. June 20, 1818. 5.68
Estate to be sold.
Exec: Son Jacob. Wit: Daniel Hoffman.

LONGACKER, ISAAC. Norriton.
June 20, 1818. July 4, 1818. 5.70
Estate to be sold and money put in interest for wife, Catharine.
Execs: Wife Catharine, and George Henry. Wit: Nathan Potts, Mary Corson.

KULP, JACOB. Towamencin.
Jan 30, 1813. July 18, 1818. 5.71
To wife Mary, household goods, during widowhood, income of $64 yearly. Rem, equally divided among 8 children: Elizabeth, Abraham, Catharine, Mary, Jacob, David, Susanna, and Nancy.
Execs: Sons Jacob and David. Wit: Jacob Godshall, Abraham Stover.

STROMAN, HENRY. Marlsborough.
July 20, 1818. Aug 17, 1818. 5.73
To wife Elizabeth, during widowhood, all estate. Rem, equally divided among children: John, Henry, Jacob, Joseph, Anna, wife of John Borkman, Elizabeth, wife of Henry Weaver, Maria, wife of Peter Shuck, Christina, wife of Jonas Tyson. Share of son John, to be divided into 3 equal parts. To his children: Henry, Charles, Polly, wife of Henry Shuler. Share of daughter Elizabeth to be inherited by her daughter Elizabeth Shaeffer, after her mothers decease.
Execs: John Auchy, Philip Reed. Wit: William Fuller, John Bentz.

BITTING, ANTHONY. New Hanover.
Nov 8, 1811. Aug 17, 1818. 5.74

To wife Magdalena, use of dwelling house, and household goods, and maintenance. Rem, divided among 3 children: Archibald, Maria, wife of Barney Dotorow, deceased, and Sarah, wife of George Sensendeffer.
Execs: Wife Magdalena Sensenderfer. Wit: Christian Fryer, and George Yerger.

NEISS, ABRAHAM. Upper Salford.
Aug 8, 1813. Aug 18, 1818. 5.76
To wife Magdalena, household goods, income of 300 pds. To son Philip, farm, 111 acres and income of 2500 pds. and maintenance. Rem, divided among children.
Execs: Sons John and Abraham. Wit: John Auchy, Jacob Landers, and Michael Shoemaker.

KRAUSS, SARAH. Upper Hanover.
June 19, 1817. Aug 18, 1818. 5.78
To daughter Polly, 15 pds. and table. Rem. to 7 children, equally.
Execs: David Schultz, and Isaac Schultz. Wit: Jeremiah Krauss, Christopher Schultz.

HICKS, BARBARA. Springfield.
March 25, 1809. Aug 28, 1818. 5.79
To daughter Mary, household goods. To grandson William Hicks, clock. To granddaughter Sarah Hicks, bureau, etc. To daughter Mary, and granddaughters Barbara Hicks, and Margaret Huston, wearing apparel. To granddaughter Barbara, beds, etc. To granddaughter Margaret Huston, cover lid. Rem. of estate to grandchildren: William, Sarah, Barbara Hicks, Christopher and William Reese, Ann Bradfield, Margaret Huston, Ann Bradfield share to rem. in the hands of nephew Christopher Loeser. Farm to be sold, proceeds to daughter Mary Ottinger, 1/4 at her death to be divided among grandchildren: William, Sarah, and Barbara Hicks, remaining 3/4 part to grandchildren.
Execs: Christopher Loeser, Thomas Livezey. Wit: Rynear Tyson, John Cleaver.

WILLIAMS, SAMUEL. Gwynedd.
July 11, 1818. Sept 12, 1818. 5.82
To Peter Saylor, and his wife Ann, mother of testator, all estate.
Exec: Step father Peter Saylor. Wit: Job Roberts, and Jesse Spencer.

BOURQUIN, HENRY. Worcester.
May 29, 1818. Sept 17, 1818. 5.83
To friend Charles Bisson, all estate.
Exec: Charles Bisson. Wit: Amos Weber, Frederick Conrad.

EVANS, THOMAS, Gwynedd.
July 5, 1813. Sept 18, 1818. 5.84

To daughter Tacy, 100 pds. farm, 128 acres, to be divided among children. Rem. divided among 6 children.
Execs: Caliph Evnas, Nathan Evans, Cadwalder Roberts. Wit: Job Roberts, George Sheive.

BARTMAN, ADAM. New Hanover.
Dec 15, 1812. Sept 25, 1818. 5.86
Estate equally divided among children: Margaret, widow of John Hinderlighter, sons: Adam, Jacob, and daughter Christina, wife of Henry Rumfield, and daughter Catharine Bartman, equally. To son Michael's children, 7 s., 6 d., each, and daughter Maria and son John one equal share, each.
Exec: Son Adam. Wit: Henry Linsenbigler, Matthew Richards.

GREGER, GEORGE. Whitpain.
Feb 9, 1812. Oct 17, 1818. 5.87
To wife Catharine, bed, household goods, and maintenance. To son Abraham, farm, 116 acres subject to the payment of 1600 pds. Farm in Plymouth 50 acres to son George, he to pay 800 pds. To Trustees of Boehm's Church, 5 pds. Rem. of estate divided equally among children: Abraham, George, Margaret, Catharine, Elizabeth, children of Barbara Hoot, namely: Catharine, Elizabeth, Rebecca, Philip George, one share to children of daughter Mary Roff, namely: Margaret, Mary, William, Elizabeth.
Execs: Sons Abraham, George, and son in law David Styer. Wit: Job Roberts, Charles Mather.

SHANNON, THOMAS. Norriton.
Dec 26, 1810. Oct 27, 1818. 5.89
To son John, farm, in Norriton, subject to the payment of 300 pds. to daughter Rebecca, wife of John McFarland. To granddaughter Elizabeth Henry, 125 pds. To son Samuel, farm, in Norriton, 75 acres riding horse, etc. to son William, 20 acres in Norriton. To daughter Rebecca, in addition to gifts, 300 pds. To granddaughter Elizabeth, 125 pds. Rem. equally divided among 4 children: John, Samuel, William. and Rebecca McFarland.
Execs: Sons John, Samuel, and William. Wit: Frederick Conrad, and Henry W. Conrad.

ARMSTRONG, WILLIAM. Plymouth.
Oct 14, 1818. Oct 28, 1818. 5.92
To brother Joseph, $100. To sister Mary Percy, lot in Plymouth, 19 acres. To children of Joseph and John Armstrong, $166.67 To nephew William Armstrong, son of brother James, house and lot in Norristown. To nephew Augustus, son of brother James, desk. To sister Mary Percy, interest of mortgate of $400, at her death principle to niece Jane Bartlesome. To nephew William Bartlesome, legacy at the decease of his mother Mary. To brothers Joseph and James wearing apparel. Rem,

divided as follows: interest of 1/3 to brother Joseph. At his death to his children. interest of 1/3 to brother James, at his death to his children, interest of 1/3 to sister Mary, at her death equally to her children.
Execs: Cousin Joseph Armstrong, and George N. Potts. Wit: Thomas Pugh, John Roberts.

SHANNON, JOHN. Lower Providence.
Feb 7, 1818. Oct 29, 1818. 5.94
All estate to be sold, proceeds divided among 8 children: Martha, Amelia, Robert, John, Benjamin, Amos, Mary, and Jane, equally. Shares of Martha and Amelia to be diminished, 180 and 200 pds. respectively, on account of money advance them.
Execs: Son Amos, and son in law Samuel Horning. Wit: Benjamin Evans, Nathan Potts.

EATON, JOSEPH.
July 5, 1817. Oct 29, 1818. 5.95
All estate, to wife Rebecca.
Exec: Wife Rebecca. Wit: Thomas Strafford.

PLACE, FREDERICK. Limerick.
June 29, 1815. Oct 9, 1818. 5.96
All estate to wife Ann, after her death equally divided among children: John, Henry, Peter, Benjamin, and Margaret, Mary Cressman and Ann. To son of Jacob Place, no bequest he being provided for.
Execs: Sons John and Henry. Wit: Matthew Brooke, and John S. Missimer.

McMAIR, MARY. Horsham.
Jan 3, 1817. Nov 16, 1818. 5.97
To son John, bed, etc. To daughter Ann Cravin, choice of beds, etc. To son James, bed, etc. To son Samuel, beds, and household goods. To daughter Rebecca, gowns, and china ware. Rem. of wearing apparel to 2 daughters Ann Cravin and Mary Long, equally. Rem. of estate to sons: John, Samuel, and James.
Execs: 3 sons: John, Samuel, and James. Wit: Samuel Mann, and Isaac Mann.

REIMER, LUDWICK. Frederick.
Sept 6, 1818. Nov 18, 1818. 5.99
To wife Susanna, house and maintenance. To son John, house and 15 acres of land. To grandson Jacob Pennebecker, 50 pds. Rem. to 3 children: Philip, Elizabeth, and Magdalena, equally.
Exec: Son John. Wit: Jacob Reifsnyder, Daniel Krauss.

BARNES, JAMES. Upper Dublin.
Oct 7, 1818. Dec 9, 1818. 5.100

To wife real estate during life, after her death, to Joseph Heaton, $1000.
To Samuel Meyers, $200. To daughter Lydia, $800. To James Barnes,
$30. To Sarah Spencer, daughter of James Spencer, $30. To James, B.
Griffith, son of James Griffith, $30. To Joshua Frazer, $300. Farm, 100
acres valued at $10,000 to Joseph Heaton, he to pay legacies.
Execs: Sarah Barnes, Joseph Heaton, George Fitzwater. Wit: Thomas
Livezey, and Jacob Fitzwater.

WEEST, CASPER. Lower Merion.
Aug 13, 1813. Dec 19, 1818. 5.101
To wife Mary, $200 yearly. To 2 grandchildren Francis and Mary Weest,
after death of wife, $30, each, for use, during minority, and $500 each
when 21. Rem. to daughter Elizabeth.
Exec: Daughter Elizabeth. Wit: Samuel Stearne, Thomas Anderson.

RHOADS, ROSANNA. Norriton.
June 15, 1797. Dec 31, 1818. 5.102
To Rosanna Jones, daughter of Abraham Jones, 10 pds. silver spoons etc.
To nephew Issacher Rhoads, 10 pds. To nephew Abraham Rhoads, 5 s.
Rem. to nephew Zebedee Rhoads.
Exec: Zebedee Rhoads. Wit: Nathan Potts, Priscilla Potts.

SINGER, PETER. Norriton
March 19, 1817. Jan 2, 1818. 5.104
To wife, income of estate, during widowhood. To daughter Margaret, cow,
and household goods. To son Jacob, $35. Rem. to wife, during widowhood.
At her death, 4/5 there of to children: John, Margaret, Elizabeth, wife of
Jacob Weber, and son Jacob, equally income of 1/5 to daughter Christina,
wife of Jacob Labold, at her death to her children, equally, if she survive
her husband, to have principle sum.
Execs: Son John Singer, and son in law Jacob Weaver. Wit: John Thomas,
Joseph Thomas.

JONES, JOSEPH. Lower Merion.
Nov 24, 1818. Jan 19, 1819. 5.105
To wife Eleanor, all estate.
Exec: Wife Eleanor. Wit: William H. Elliott.

ROSHON, PETER. Pottsgrove.
Dec 13, 1818. Jan 27, 1819. 5.106
Farm, 70 acres, to son Samuel, subject to the payment of 600 pds. and
interest of 400 pds. to be paid to wife, yearly, during widowhood. At wife's
death to be paid to daughter Elizabeth. To her son John, 100 pds. and at
her death 400 pds. divided equally among son Jacob and son Samuel, and
grandson Peter. Remaining 1/4 to sons Jacob and Samuel, and daughter
Elizabeth, and grandson Peter.
Execs: Christian Mattis, and son Samuel. Wit: T. B. Harris, and Daniel

Chrisman.

McCLEAN, WILLIAM. Horsham.
June 20, 1817. Jan 30, 1819. 5.108
To daughter Rachel, room and certain privileges as described, household goods, wearing apparel, and maintenance, and $80 annually, while in life. Rem. of estate to son Moses.
Exec: Son Moses. Wit: Atkinson Hughs, and Hiram McNeill.

GERHART, NICHOLAS. Franconia.
Jan 15, 1819. Feb 1, 1819. 5.111
To brother Matthias, all presonal estate, either in money or wearing apparel, etc.
Exec: Jacob Moyer. Wit: Peter Moyer, and Nicholas Shoemaker.

ARMSTRONG, JAMES. Norristown.
Jan 8, 1819. Feb 8, 1819. 5.112
To Elizabeth Patterson, $100. Rem. of estate to Ann Armstrong.
Execs: Wife Ann, and Hugh Dickson. Wit: William Mitchell, and Hugh Dickson.

DUNLAP, WILLIAM. Abington.
Dec 8, 1818. Feb 16, 1819. 5.114
Estate to be sold and money from sale of estate to mother and 2 sister Elizabeth and Ann.
Execs: John Morrison, and Nathaniel B. Boileau. Wit: Samuel Leech, and Samuel Happerset.

McLERNON, ABY. Upper Merion.
May 11, 1818. Feb 16, 1819. 5.115
To daughter Mary, household goods, and wearing apparel, and 1/2 of estate. To son Charles, other 1/2 of estate.
Exec: Francis Lyle. Wit: Robert Moore, Mordecai Moore.

SHULER, SAMUEL. Upper Salford.
Dec 19, 1818. Feb 17, 1819. 5.116
To daughter Sarah, bed, and cow. To daughter Hester, $40, to be put on interest for her bed and cow. To sons Jacob and Daniel, $20 each. To wife Magdalena, household goods, and interest of 150 pds. during widowhood. Rem. of estate divided equally among children: John, Samuel, Jacob, Daniel, and daughters Margaret, Maria, Elizabeth, Catharine, Sarah, and Hester.
Execs: Joseph Groff, and John Richards. Wit: Jacob Nice, and Philip Zepp.

WAGNER, FREDERICK. Northern Liberties.
June 27, 1818. Feb 20, 1819. 5.118
To wife Isabella, interest of $2400 annually, and household goods, after

her death, $2400 to be equally divided among children Jacob and Elizabeth.
Exec: Brother in law Samuel Rossetter. Wit: Samuel Simson, and George Pleas.

WILLS, MARY. Norristown.
March 27, 1815. March 9, 1819. 5.119
To brother Michael, 1/2 part of house and lot in Norristown. Rem. of estate to Michael Wills.
Exec: Michael Wills. Wit: Levi Pawling, George Reighter.

SPATZ, JOHN. Pottsgrove.
June 8, 1818. March 15, 1819. 5.121
To wife Elizabeth, farm, during widowhood, and household goods. 20 acres of land after my decease to be equally divided among daughters: Susanna, Sarah, Maria, and Rachel.
Execs: Wife Elizabeth, and John Reifsnyder. Wit: Benjamin Reifsnyder, and Andrew Spatz.

ZIMMERMAN, JACOB. Worcester.
Dec 16, 1805. March 18, 1819. 5.122
To daughter Mary, curtains, and looking glass. To 3 daughters: Mary, Magdalena, and Elizabeth, pewter ware, and 10 pds. each. to son John, 1/3 of personal estate, and remaining 2/3 shall be divided among children: Arnold, Elizabeth, Mary, Magdalena, equally. To John Zimmerman, farm, where I now live, containing 100 acres.
Execs: Sons John and Arnold. Wit: Joseph and Cornelius Tyson.

WALTON, MARY. Moreland.
Nov 19, 1818. March 27, 1819. 5.124
To daughter Elizabeth, wearing apparel, and beds, etc. To sons Amos, Jeremiah, and Isaac, $100 each. To son Isaac's 2 daughters Lydia and Ann, $30 each. Rem. of estate to sons: Joseph Jeremiah, Jonathan, Jesse, and Isaac, and daughter Elizabeth, equally.
Execs: Sons Amos and Isaac. Wit: Isaiah and Jacob Walton.

LUKENS, ABRAHAM. Whitemarsh.
Nov 22, 1818. March 31, 1819. 5.125
To wife Martha, household goods, and $200 yearly. Sons to pay the Exrs. a reasonable among of money for rent of farms. To sons, wearing apparel, equally. To son Joseph, working horse, etc. To sons Charles, and Joseph, $1000 each.
Execs: Son Joseph, and son in law Jacob Fitzwater. Wit: Philip Sellers, and Thomas Lukens.

ADAMSON, ROBERT. Horsham.
March 10, 1819. April 3, 1819. 5.128

To wife Tabitha, house, and household goods. To all children, $50 each. To daughter Ann, case of drawers. To daughter Esther, $40. To daughter Rebecca, feather bed, etc. To son Thomas, 100 pds. To daughter Ann, 100 pds. To daughter Esther, 100 pds. To daughter Rebecca, 100 pds. To sons Charles, Jonathan, and Thomas, farm. Rem. of estate to sons: Jonathan, Charles, and Thomas, each.
Execs: Sons Jonathan, Charles, and Thomas. Wit: William Mullin, and Joseph Foulke.

EWING, WASHINGTON.
April 30, 1819. April 3, 1819. 5.130
To Thomas Miller, all estate, after expenses are paid.
Execs: Jacob Aman, and Jacob Force.

GIVEN, JOHN. Norriton.
May 8, 1818. April 7, 1819. 5.131
To Elizabeth, and Hannah, and Mary Shrack, $150 equally. To Elizabeth Reese, daughter of Benjamin Reese, $60. To Kitty Slaugh, bible, and rem. of estate.
Execs: William Hamill, and Jesse Bean. Wit: Stephen Porter, and Christopher Rittenhouse.

BERGY, CHRISTIAN. Lower Salford.
April 3, 1813. April 9, 1819. 5.132
To son Christian, farm, and 1800 pds. To daughter Margaret, 50 pds. To daughter Barbara, 100 pds. To daughter Sarah, 6 pds. Exrs. to put 200 pds. on interest for daughter Margaret. Rem. of estate divided into 11 parts as follows: Catharine, wife of Christian Holderman, Philip, Jacob, Margaret, Barbara, Sarah wife of Joseph Butterweek, Ann, wife of Abraham Holderman, John, Elizabeth, wife of Jacob Tyson, and Christian.
Execs: Sons Abraham and John. Wit: Benjamin Gilderger, and Dillman Zeigler.

LICK, WILLIAM. New Hanover.
Aug 8, 1818. April 13, 1819. 5.133
To wife Catharine, all estate.
Execs: ____. Wit: Frederick Gilbert, and Samuel Roff.

GODSHALK, GODSHALL. Lower Salford.
Feb 20, 1809. April 15, 1819. 5.134
To wife Sarah, all estate, and interest of 300 pds. yearly. To son Jacob, farm, containing 37 acres. Rem. of estate divided equally among children. To son Jacob, one share. To daughter Elizabeth, one share. To daughter Hebena, one share.
Execs: Son Jacob and son in law David Allebach. Wit: Garrett Hunsicker.

YERKES, JACOB. Moreland.

Feb 9, 1819. April 23, 1819. 5.136
To wife Sarah, tract of land, containing 10 acres and household goods. To 2 daughters $333.33, equally.
Execs: Son in law John Hogeland, and Joseph Yerkes. Wit: George Fetter, and Thomas Montany.

THOMAS, NATHAN. Abington.
March 20, 1819. April 26, 1819. 5.138
To wife Sarah, 1/3 of net proceeds. Estate to be sold. Rem. of estate divided among children.
Execs: 3 sons: George, Jacob, and Jesse. Wit: John Leech, and Matthew Conrad.

MEREDITH, JOHN. Plymouth.
Jan 9, 1813. May 11, 1819. 5.139
To son David, tract of land in Plymouth, containing 127 acres, 148 perches, subject to the payment of $1000 legacy. To son John, tract of land in Plymouth, containing 157 acres, 23 perches, subject to the payment of $3000 legacy. To son Joseph, tract of land, in Plymouth, containing 72 acres, 12 perches. To son Aaron, tract of land in Plymouth, containing 68 acres, 56 perches ss $3000 legacy.
Execs: Sons: David, John, Aaron, and William Ellis. Wit: William Abatt, John Thomas, Allan Corson.

ANDERS, ABRAHAM. Worcester.
June 10, 1815. May 12, 1819. 5.143
To Benjamin, farm, containing 125 acres subject to the payment of 1300 pds. To son Abraham, farm, containing 100 acres subject to the payment of 1500 pds. To daughter Rosina, 4 acres of woodland, subject to the payment of 1200 pds. All books, to be divided equally among children. Rem. of estate divided among children, equally.
Execs: Sons Benjamin and Abraham, and son in law Christopher Dresher. Wit: Balser Heebner, and Melechior Schultz.

SHAIN, JOHN. Abington.
May 20, 1819. May 31, 1819. 5.145
Estate to be sold.
Exec: Charles Dewees. Wit: Jesse Wright, and Joseph Webster.

HOFFACRE, MICHAEL. Whitpain.
April 26, 1819. June 5, 1819. 5.147
Share to 4 children, as follows: to John, 1/4 part. To daughter Susanna, 1/4 part. To daughter Elizabeth, 1/4 part. To daughter Mary, 1/4 part.
Execs: Son John, and son in law Philip Hoffacre. Wit: Christopher Wentz, and Job Roberts.

LLOYD, BENJAMIN. Moreland.

April 16, 1819. June 9, 1819. 5.147
To wife Elizabeth, household goods, and $1500. To son Benjamin, 2 1/2 share. To son Jesse, 2 equal shares. To son John, 2 equal shares. To daughters Rachel, and Elizabeth, one share each
Execs: Sons Benjamin and Jesse, and son in law John Melone, and Mark Balderson. Wit: Isaac Walton, and Isaac Perry.

HALLOWELL, DOROTHY. Upper Dublin.
April 26, 1819. June 14, 1819. 5.149
To son Joseph, interest of $250. To daughter Margaret, rem. of estate.
Execs: John Bright, and Joseph Kenderdine. Wit: Thomas Lukens, and Samuel Dresher.

MASTERSON, HENRY. Whitemarsh.
Nov 6, 1818. June 15, 1819. 5.150
To wife Elizabeth, household goods. To daughter Sarah, equal part of estate. Estate to be equally divided among children. To daughter Sarah, cherry bureau. To brother John, silver watch.
Execs: Christopher Tennent, and Peter Keiger. Wit: Hugh Dickson, and John Masterson.

SCOTT, ALEXANDER. Worcester.
June 26, 1818. June 22, 1819. 5.151
To wife Jane, household goods, and maintenance. To son Israel, farming utensils, and $300.
Execs: Wife Jane, Richard Roberts, George Roberts, and son Israel. Wit: Job Roberts, and Amos Griffith.

MARKLEY, BENJAMIN. New Hanover.
Feb 10, 1819. June 20, 1819. 5.153
Estate to be sold and money from sale divided into 5 equal parts. To wife Hannah, 1/5 part. To son Jonah, 1/5 part. To daughter Mary, 1/5 part. To daughter Sarah, 1/5 part. To daughter Elizabeth, 1/5 part. To Hannah Sholl, 25 pds. To daughters Elizabeth and Rebecca, 25 pds. each. To niece Anna, 50 pds. To grandson Joshua Markley, books, etc.
Execs: Jacob Miller, Frederick Conrad, brother John Markley, and son in law Philip Boyer. Wit: Henry Daub, and Jacob Klemmer, and Abraham Dotero.

OVERDORFF, JACOB. Upper Hanover.
May 26, 1819. July 24, 1819. 5.154
To wife Regina, household goods. To sons John and George, 1200 pds. each.
Execs: Brother in law Henry Roth, and Abraham Gehman. Wit: George Zeigler, and Peter Stout.

PEIRCE, GEORGE. Plymouth.

Jan 18, 1814. July 29, 1819. 5.156
To wife Rebecca, use and proceeds arising from estate, and $10.67 to Exrs. for their services. To wife, household goods. To daughter Mary, $1000 to be put on interest. To grandson George Peirce, $1000.
Execs: William Hallowell, and Samuel Maulsby. Wit: David Lukens, and Michael Wills.

KURTZ, VALENTINE. Limerick.
Aug 16, 1818. Aug 6, 1819. 5.157
To wife Sarah, household goods, and farm. To daughter Susanna, 200 pds. To daughter Mary, 200 pds. To daughter Eleanor, 200 pds. Remaining 200 pds. To daughter Elizabeth's sons, and 200 pds. to daughters of daughter Elizabeth. To son Valentine, farming utensils.
Execs: Valentine Kurtz, and Michael Duttereo. Wit: Matthew Brooke and George Beltz.

ELMS, GEORGE. Lower Providence.
March 29, 1819. Aug 7, 1819. 5.159
To wife Mary, household goods, and estate to be sold.
Exec: Peter Saylor. Wit: Christian Sower, and Arnold Saylor.

JOHNSON, HENRY. Montgomery.
April 1, 1819. Aug 12, 1819. 5.160
To wife Mary, household goods, and farm, containing 100 acres. To son Jesse, $100. Rem. of money arising from sale of estate divided into 9 equal parts. To son Edward, 1/9 part. To daughter Margaret, 1/9 part. To son John, 1/9 part. To daughter Elizabeth, 1/9 part. To daughter Hannah, 1/9 part. To children of daughter Susanna, 1/9 part. To daughter Martha, 1/9 part. To son David, 1/9 part. To son Jesse, 1/9 part.
Execs: Son Jesse, and John. Wit: Jacob Cassell, and Jacob Bruner.

JARRETT, JOHN. Upper Dublin.
March 8, 1806. Aug 18, 1819. 5.162
To wife Rachel, household goods, and bond of 200 pds. farm, during widowhood. To Daniel Jarrett's 3 children: Joseph, Martha, and Chalkey, 100 pds. each. To son John Jarrett, 996 pds., 16 s., 3 d. To Ann Jones, 100 pds. To son Levi, rem. of estate, and farm, 120 acres.
Codicil dated Oct 10, 1813. To wife Rachel, tract of woodland, and wearing apparel. Guardians of daughter Priscilla, brother David Jarrett, and Isaac Perry.
Exec: Son Levi. Wit: William Jarrett, and Jesse Trump, and Thomas Livezey.

YOST, JOHN. Pottsgrove.
July 8, 1819. Aug 30, 1819. 5.164
Real estate to be sold. Wife Mary to have use and privilege of farm, and household goods. To daughter Rachel, $82 and part of household goods.

To daughter Sarah, $180 and part of household goods. To sons John and Jacob, $180 each, proceeds $75 to each of them over and above their shares.
Execs: wife Mary, and sons John and Jacob. Wit: Philip Yost, and Jacob Drinkhouse.

ACKLEY, THOMAS. Moreland.
May 24, 1817. Aug 31, 1819. 5.165
To John Ackley, all estate. To daughter in law Rachel Stemple, $20. To Lydia and Lousia, $10 each. Rem. of estate divided into 9 equal parts.
Exec: John Ackley. Wit: Peter Rhoads, and Gilbert Gace.

GRIFFITH, HOWELL.
Dec 8, 1817. Sept 13, 1819. 5.166
To wife Alice, all estate and after death, all she possess among children.
Execs: ____. Wit: George Wack.

WENSLEY, DANIEL. Plymouth.
June 13, 1819. Sept 25, 1819. 5.167
To wife Mary, all estate.
Exec: Wife Mary. Wit: Allen Corson.

BURNSIDE, WILLIAM. Montgomery.
March 13, 1817. Oct 8, 1819. 5.168.
To son Francis Burnside, 1/2 part of estate, and farming utensils. To grandson William Burnside, $500. To granddaughter Amelia, $500. Rem. of estate to sons Thomas and Francis, equally. All bonds to be given to son William, for $1000.
Execs: sons Thomas and Francis. Wit: Thomas Dyer, and John Evans.

JONES, JOHN. Montgomery.
May 17, 1814. Oct 21, 1819. 5.169.
To Evan Jones, and Richard Shoemaker, tract of land.
Execs: Evan Jones, and Richard Shoemaker. Wit: Morgan Morgan, William Amblers, and Cadwalder Foulke.

UMSTAD, JOHN. Upper Providence.
Sept 18, 1819. Oct 27, 1819. 5.171
To son Jonas, all lands, he pay to son John, $4000.
Execs: Son Jonas, and grandson John and Thomas Francis. Wit: Abraham Brower, and Andrew Ambler.

STREPERS, MARGARET. Whitemarsh.
Nov 1, 1817. Nov 1, 1819. 5.162
To son George, $66.67. To daughter Susanna, bed, etc. To 6 daughters: Ann, wife of John Dull, Rebecca, widow of James Harvey, Deborah, widow of William Yerkes, Mary, wife of Jonathan Jones, Catharine, wife of

James Monahon, and Susanna, wearing apparel, equally divided.
Execs: Son George, and son in law Jonathan Jones. Wit: George Martin, and Jacob Dewees.

MANN, JOHN. Upper Dublin
June 12, 1816. Nov 15, 1819. 5.174
To wife, household goods, and farm, containing 28 acres. Exrs. to pay to wife, $133, after my decease. To son John, $1667. To daughter Mary, $1067. To daughter Martha, $1067. To son William, $1067. To daughter Elizabeth, $1466. To son James, $800. To son Joseph, $800. To daughter Sarah, $1466, and household goods.
Execs: Sons John and Joel K. Wit: Samuel and Isaac Mann.

WILLIAMS, GEORGE. Abington.
March 17, 1819. Nov 19, 1819. 5.176
To son John, $8500. To son George, farm, in Abington, subject to the payment of $3000 to daughter Hannah. To daughter Hannah, $600. To son Thomas, $8500, to purchase a farm for him. To daughter Elizabeth Harper, $2400. To daughter Sarah Brown, $2200.
Execs: Sons John L. and George and Thomas. Wit: Thomas Shoemaker, and Samuel Rowland.

CONRAD, SAMUEL. Horsham.
May 17, 1819. Nov 27, 1819. 5.177
To wife Grace, use of house and lot, $40 annually, during widowhood. To daughter Hannah, household goods. To son Samuel, $250. Rem. of real estate equally divided among 4 daughters: Sarah, Hannah, Ruth, and Priscilla. Rem. of personal estate to children, 4 daughters and 2 sons: Samuel, and Cornelius, equally.
Execs: Sons Samuel and Cornelius. Wit: Richard Shoemaker, and Joseph Kenderdine.

DETWILER, MARTIN. Gwynedd.
Oct 10, 1811. Dec 3, 1819. 5.178
To wife Maria, household goods, and 50 pds. and 150 pds. out of real estate, and maintenance. If real estate to be sold wife, to receive 550 pds. in goods and money. To German Meeting House and grave yard in New Brittain, 25 pds. Rem. to 6 sons and 5 daughters: Christian, Jacob, Samuel, Abraham, Joseph, Benjamin, Hannah, wife of Henry Rosenberry, Susanna, wife of Isaac Rosenberry, Mary, wife of John Price, Sarah, Barbara, wife of George Cassel.
Execs: Sons Jacob and Abraham. Wit: Thomas Kneedler and Jacob Cassel.

MURREY, STEPHEN. Horsham.
Oct 30, 1815. Dec 14, 1819. 5.179
To wife, personalty, use of real estate during widowhood. If not sufficient house and lot be be sold, and she to receive income. Rem. at her death to

be divided among children.
Execs: Wife Jermina, during widowhood, son Thomas, and Isaac Longstreth. Wit: Isaac Shoemaker, Dennis Conrad.

TENNENT, SUSANNA. New York.
March 6, 1819. Dec 17, 1819. 5.180
To brother Dr. John R. Rodgers, income derived from father John Rodgers. To niece Joanna Rodgers, daughter of John Rodgers, $500. To nephew William Dorgers, $500. To Mary E. Stewart, $500. To Ann T. Stewart, $500, also bed, household goods. To William Morison, $100 to purchase piece of plate suitable to inscribe for himself. To Princeton Theological Seminary, $400. Rem. to brother John Rodgers.
Exec: Brother John Rodgers. Wit: Stephen Beaton, William Mandeville, Philip S. Brinkerhoff.

SHAY, JOHN. Horsham.
April 13, 1818. Dec 10, 1819. 5.182
To wife Mary, use of dwelling, household goods, and maintenance. To son John, mill, and 4 acres of land, he to pay mortgage 400 pds. and $40 yearly to wife Mary, during widowhood. To son John, 400 pds. to pay said mortgage. To son Jesse, homestead, 5 acres subject to the payment of $40 annually to his mother, during widowhood. To son Jesse, also 16 acres of land in Horsham. To son Jonathan, farm on which he lives subject to the payment of $40 annually to his mother, during widowhood. To son Jonathan, also $2160, to satify a mortgage on his farm. To 2 sons Thomas and William, farm, subject to the payment of annually $80. To their mother, during widowhood. To daughter Mary, household goods, and $2000. To son Thomas, clock and desk. Rem. equally divided among 5 sons.
Execs: Sons Jesse, Jonathan, and Thomas. Wit: Joseph Perry, Hiram McNeill.

MOORE, ELIZABETH. Horsham.
Dec 19, 1819. Dec 22, 1819. 5.185
To daughter Hannah, obligations against Joseph Lukens, and George Dunnet, wearing apparel, and personal property.
Execs: Son Jesse, and son in law Joseph Bealer. Wit: Ann and Isaac Tomkins.

WOOD, SOPHIA. Whitpain.
____. Dec 28, 1819. 5.186
To son Ezekiel Wood, house, and 3 acres of land. To grandchildren: Elizabeth, Jacob, and Catharine Matthias, children of daughter Mary, 15 pds. to be paid to son Ezekiel. To Christiana Thomas, wife of Howell Thomas, 3 pds. To granddaughter Catharine Matthias, 25 pds. to be paid by son Ezekiel. To Elizabeth Snyder, wife of Henry Snyder, 3 pds. Personal estate divided equally among son Ezekiel and granddaughter

Catharine. Rem. 1/2 to son Ezekiel the other 1/2 to 3 grandchildren, aforesaid.
Exec: Son Ezekiel. Wit: Henry Schneider, and John Conrad.

WILLARD, JESSE. Moreland.
Aug 15, 1818. Jan 4, 1820. 5.187
To wife Margaret, $300, household goods, and maintenance. To 2 sons Isaac, and Thomas, $1.00 each. To 2 sons David, and Duffield, $40 each. To daughter Esther, household goods. Income to wife and 4 sons. Minor children to be deducted, boys to become apprentices, they to have principle aforesaid to become to. If wife marries again, 1/3 interest, during life. Guardians, Benjamin Yerkes, Sr., William Ayres.
Codicil dated, April 6, 1819. To wife, $200, additional.
Execs: Wife Margaret, and William Ayres. Wit: William Redding, Anthony Yerkes.

CUNNINGHAM, GEORGE. Uper Merion.
Nov 19, 1819. Dec 27, 1819. 5.190
To wife Elizabeth, all estate, real and personal.
Exec: Wife Elizabeth. Wit: Samuel Henderson.

MITCHELL, WILLIAM. Norristown.
Dec 22, 1819. Jan 10, 1820. 5.191
To brother Joshua, wearing apparel. To sister Rebecca Strowman, feather bed, and household goods. To niece Mary Litsinger, bed, etc. To William Boyd Perkins, furniture. Rem. as follows: to brother Thomas, 1/5 part. To brother Jacob, 1/3 part of rem. To sister Rebecca, 1/3 part of rem. To brother Joshua, 1/3 part.
Execs: Brother Jacob and nephew Thomas D. Mitchell. Wit: William Powell, Charles Jones.

COMFORT, EZRA. Whitemarsh.
April 14, 1812. Jan 26, 1820. 5.192
To wife, use of house, and farm, household goods, and maintenance, 10 pds. yearly during widowhood. If she marry, privileges and uses. To daughter Elizabeth, 100 pds. To daughter Mercy Paxson, 100 pds. To daughter Grace Gillinghamn, 100 pds. To son John, 100 pds. To daughter Alice, 100 pds. To wife Alice, 20 pds. yearly, to be paid by son Ezra. To son Ezra, rem.
Execs: Wife Alice, and son Ezra. Wit: Job Roberts, Jonathan Cleaver.

SNYDER, VALENTINE. Frederick.
Sept 18, 1814. Feb 7, 1820. 5.194
To wife Anna Maria, house and household goods, and maintenance. William Ammerman to be provided for at the expense of estate. Farm, 150 acres land to son Jacob Snyder.
Exec: Son Jacob. Wit: George Nice, and Henry Krebs.

BEANS, ISAAC. Moreland.
Sept 7, 1814. Feb 14, 1820. 5.195
To son Thomas, tavern, and farm, subject to the payment of 500 pds. each to granddaughter Mary Bean Michener, daughter of deceased Mary, at her death to children of daughter Margaret. To son John, farm, in Moreland. To daughter Margaret, farm, subject to the payment of 5 pds. step mother Elizabeth Bean. Daughter Margaret to pay to step mother sums directed in fathers will. To son Isaac, farm, in Moreland. To grandson Isaac, desk, and gold guinea. To daughter Margaret, silver ware, and beds, etc.
Execs: Sons Thomas, John, and Isaac. Wit: Seneca Lukens, Hiram McNeill.

FUNCK, JOHN. Hatfield.
April 27, 1815. Feb 21, 1820. 5.197
To son John, $50. To son Henry, $50. To the poor, 5 pds. To Free School of Hatfield, 5 pds. Rem. equally divided among 8 children: Martin, Samuel, John, Henry, heirs of daughter Margaret, Samuel, Mary, and John Delp, Mary Elizabeth, and Catharine.
Execs: Sons Martin and John. Wit: Abraham Blumsberger, John Frick.

HUBLER, JOHN. Perkiomen.
Dec 29, 1819. Feb 29, 1820. 5.198
Estate to 3 children: Henry, Isaac, and Elizabeth.
Execs: Samuel Gehman, and Andrew Zeigler. Wit: William Rile, John Halteman.

STREEPER, PETER. Whitemarsh.
Oct 26, 1819. Feb 10, 1820. 5.199
To wife, during widowhood, dwelling, maintenance, income of 500 pds. during life. To 2 daughters Elizabeth and Sarah, what they have had. To grandson Streeper Carr, son of daughter Mary, deceased, $500, when of age. To son in law Robert Carr, $4.00 Real estate to be divided into 3 equal parts, and give to Daniel, Barnabas, and Peter, at valuation, paying unto other sons Leonard, John, and Samuel, and 4 daughters: Catharine, Rebecca, Elizabeth, and Sarah, equally, share at valuation. At wife's death her dower to be equally divided among children. Guardian, George Martin.
Execs: Wife Christiana, and sons Leonard, and Daniel. Wit: George Bisbing, and Joseph Kirkner.

LUKENS, JONATHAN. Horsham.
Aug 29, 1818. March 7, 1820. 5.201
To wife Mary, dwelling, and maintenance, and household goods, and $160 annually, during life, at her death, household goods, equally divided among 2 daughters Elizabeth and Alice. To daughter Elizabeth, $2000. To daughter Alice, $2000. Rem. equally divided among 2 daughters Elizabeth

and Alice. Rem. of personalty to children. Rem. of estate to son William, subject to privilege of wife Mary.
Execs: Son William, and son in law John Jarrett. Wit: Mary and Hiram McNeill.

JAMES, HOWELL. Plymouth.
July 23 1819. March 23, 1820. 5.203
To 3 daughters $7.08. Homestead 3 acres to son Seth. Wife Christina, 1/3 of the income of said lot during widowhood. To daughter Elizabeth and Mary James, each, $33.33.
Exec: Son Seth. Wit: Ann Coulston, and Samuel Johnson.

WAULT, BARBARA. Upper Salford.
May 2, 1816. March 30, 1820. 5.204
Farm, 57 acres, to be sold and money divided equally among children. Personalty to be divided equally among children: Jacob, Catharine, Elizabeth, Mary, Barbara, Margaret, Christiana, Susanna, and Sophia.
Execs: Son Jacob, and son in law Samuel Cressman. Wit: Michael Shoemaker, and Peter Roudenbush.

MEGARER, JOHN. Abington.
Nov 3, 1818. April 3, 1820. 5.205
To son Joseph, $180. To children of Hannah Mount, $180, equally. To son Allen, $200. To children of daughter Sarah Stephens, $150, equally. To son Isaac, $200. To son Jonathan, $200. To daughter Rebecca, wife of John Casky, $200. To children of son John, $100, equally. To David Stephens, $50. To son Jesse, $13.34. Rem. of the above legacies in the same ratio.
Execs: Son Allen, and Mark Watson. Wit: John Strowman, William Weepert.

FLECK, ADAM. Gwynedd.
April 29, 1815. April 29, 1820. 5.207
To wife Maria Margaret, household goods, and interest of 1500 pds. To son Daniel and Jacob, tracts of lands containing 140 acres, 91 acres. To son Adam, remaining tracts, subject to payment of $32 annually to Leah Brodes. Money arising from the valuation of real estate divided equally among children. To son Thomas' children, 1/8 equal share. To daughter Margaret, 1/8 equal part. To daughter Mary, wife of Frederick Rumor, 1/8 equal share. To daughter Catharine, wife of Jacob Hoover, 1/8 equal share. To daughter Susanna, wife of Jacob Weber, 1/8 equal share. To each of 3 sons in law, 200 pds. Rem. of estate equally divided among children.
Execs: Sons Daniel and Jacob, and John Clemens. Wit: John Marshall, Philip Hoover, and Frederick Conrad.

CLEMENS, GERHART. Lower Salford.

Aug 6, 1813. May 6, 1820. 5.210
To wife, household goods. To 5 children, rem. of estate: Jacob, Elizabeth, wife of George Reiff, Sarah, wife of Jacob Reiff, and Catharine, wife of Jacob Shoemaker, and Henry.
Execs: Sons Jacob and Henry. Wit: Henry Hunsicker, and Abraham Hunsicker.

CONRAD, JOHN. Whitemarsh.
June 24, 1811. May 11, 1820. 5.211
To wife Sarah, household goods, 40 pds. yearly. Exrs. to pay to daughters Priscilla and Esther, 100 pds. each. Rem. of estate divided among children: Priscilla, Esther and Sarah.
Execs: Daughter Sarah, and son in law George Dunnett. Wit: William Jeanes, and Peter Wilson.

MARKLEY, JOHN. New Hanover.
Oct 14, 1819. May 16, 1820. 5.212
To wife Elizabeth, tract of land containing 12 acres and farm, and interest of 1500 pds. annually. To sons Andrew and Benjamin, all lands, in New Hanover, subject to payment of 500 pds. and horse and wagon. Rem. of estate divided equally among children. To daughter Barbara, wife of John Kurtz, one share. To daughter Elizabeth, wife of Jacob Neice, one share. To daughter Susanna, wife of George Neice, one share. To daughter Maria, one share.
Execs: Sons George, Benjamin, and Abraham Markley. Wit: Peter Boyer, Adam Worthman, and Frederick Conrad.

AMAN, GEORGE. Whitemarsh.
April 4, 1818. May 22, 1820. 5.215
To wife Barbara, household goods, and interest of 500 pds. yearly, rem. of estate divided equally. To son Arnold, one share. To daughter Magdalena, one share. To son Joseph, one share. To son George, one share. To granddaughter Mary Hank, one share. To son John, one share.
Execs: Sons Arnold and George. Wit: George Zorn, and Henry Daub.

CLAYTON, JONATHAN.
July 14, 1817. May 29, 1820. 5.216
To wife Mary, $266.67, and farm, and household goods. To son Jonathan, after death of mother, $270. To son John, tract of land in South Hampton, and $2272. To son Joseph, $2272. To son Jonathan, $2272. To daughter Mary Knight, farm, where I now dwell, containing 26 acres, 36 perches, and $2222. To son Abraham, rem. of estate.
Execs: Sons: John, Abraham, and Jonathan. Wit: George Pawling, Joshua Comly, and Franklin Comly.

TYSON, RYNEAR. Abington.
Sept 18, 1818. June 6, 1820. 5.220

To wife Rebecca, farm, during widowhood, and household goods, and 1/3 part of estate. To sons Mahlon, and William, tract of land, containing 90 acres subject to payment of $2000. Rem. of estate to be sold and rem. divided among children, in equal shares.
Execs: Son William and John Tyson. Wit: Jonathan Lukens, and Thomas Livezey.

CHRISMAN, GEORGE. Franconia.
April 27, 1820. June 21, 1820. 5.222
To wife Hannah, household goods, and interest of 200 pds. yearly. To daughter Margaret, 337 pds. To grandchildren: William, Elizabeth, Jacob, Mary, and Hannah, Kulp, 237 pds., 10 s. each. To daughter Magdalena, 75 pds. To daughter Catharine, 337 pds., 10 s. To wife Susanna, 337 pds., 10 s. To daughter Elizabeth, 337 pds., 10 s. To son George, farming utensils, farm, containing 100 acres subject to payment of 200 pds. 262 pds., 10 s. to be paid as follows: to daughter Magdalena, 37 pds., 10 s. To daughter Margaret, 37 pds., 10 s. To daughter Susanna, 37 pds., 10 s. To daughter Catharine, 37 pds., 10 s. To daughter Rebecca, 37 pds., 10 s. To daughter Elizabeth, 37 pds., 10 s. To son John, 37 pds., 10 s. To daughter Maria, 37 pds., 10 s. To son George, 37 pds., 10 s. To son George, 200 pds. To daughter Mary, 75 pds. when 21. Rem. of estate to be sold and money divided equally among children. Son John and daughter Maria, to have German and English schooling.
Execs: Sons George and Michael Snyder. Wit: Peter Gerhart, Abraham Benner, and Henry Cope.

BARR, JACOB. Upper Providence.
Jan 9, 1818. July 28, 1820. 5.226
To wife Susanna, household goods, and rem. of personalty. To Emeline Streit, 5 silver table spoons. To Catharine Epting, $500. To sister Margaret, $10, and bed, to each of her children $10. Rem. of estate to sister Susanna's children equally.
Execs: Wife Susanna, and William Mintzer. Wit: Benjamin Johnson, and Samuel Smith.

HUBER, CHARLES. Upper Hanover.
July 3, 1820. Aug 2, 1820. 5.228
To wife Betsey, household goods. To son John, rem. of estate, after paying expenses.
Exec: Son John. Wit: Henry Wiand, and Daniel Wiand.

REES, PHILIP. Upper Merion.
Oct 1, 1801. Aug 4, 1820. 5.229
To nephew Jeremiah Cross, $100, and wearing apparel. To Exrs. Jonathan Cleaver, tract of land in Upper Merion. To brother Isaac, and sisters Susanna, and Mary, and Rachel, 100 pds. each. To wife, rem. of estate.

Exec: Jonathan Cleaver. Wit: William Carver, and Abner Hughes.

MAYBURY, WILLIAM. Marlborough.
Jan 8, 1819. May 27, 1820. 5.230
To son William, 4000 pds. and wearing apparel, and gold watch. To Catharine Zinch, 750 pds. and choice of household goods, and use of farm. To Charles Quillman, and George Quillman, 750 pds. each. To sister Molly, 300 pds. To brother William tract of land in Marlborough. To daughter Rebecca, 50 pds. and clock, etc. To daughter Elizabeth, 50 pds. To daughter Anna, 75 pds. To son Thomas, 50 pds. To sisters: Sophia, Rebecca, Lydia, Nancy, table cloths, each. Rem. of estate to be divided equally among children.
Codicil dated May 5, 1819. To son William tract of land containing 30 acres, 13 perches.
Exec: Philip Reed. Wit: Henry Roshong, and Adam Hillegass, and Tobias Sellers.

SCHULTZ, ANNA. Upper Hanover.
Aug 7, 1820. Sept 4, 1820. 5.234
To Juliana Alhouse, $20. To son Gabriel Schultz, rem. of estate.
Execs: Son Gabriel, and Henry Alhouse. Wit: Isaac Schultz, and Casper Schultz.

PAUL, ANN. Cheltenham.
April 30, 1820. Sept 4, 1820. 5.234
To sister Mary, $50. To brother Jonathan, equal share of brother John's estate. To Sarah Paul, bureau. To Mary Paul, and Sarah Mitchell, wearing apparel, equally. Rem. of estate to Sarah Paul, Elizabeth, Ann and Jane Paul, children of brother Jonathan Paul, and Joseph Knight, $60 each, and rem. of estate.
Execs: Daniel Fletcher, and Charles Shoemaker. Wit: Jane Shoemaker, and Jacob Omensetter.

SCHULTZ, ROSIANA. Upper Hanover.
April 15, 1820. Sept 4, 1820. 5.236
Estate to be divided into 7 equal parts. To brother George, one part. To children of brother Andrew, one part. To sister Barbara, one part. To brother Matthew, one part. To sister Susanna, one part.
Exec: Christain Yeakle. Wit: George Schultz, and Matthias Schultz.

LLOYD, JOHN. Lower Merion.
Oct 26, 1819. Sept 6, 1820. 5.237
To daughter Elizabeth, $1.00. To son Jesse, $1.00. To Eleanor Jones, legacy left by sister Sarah and $20.
Exec: Eleanor Jones. Wit: Philip Fretz, and Elijah Elwell.

EVANS, OWEN. Whitpain.

March 3, 1816. Sept 9, 1820. 5.239
To Dr. Curtis, one share, and gold buttons. To Mary Davis, feather bed, etc. Rem. of estate to sister Rebecca.
Execs: Rebecca Evans, and Benjamin Morgan. Wit: David Styer, and William Walter.

WOOD, JOHN. Moreland.
July 31, 1820. Sept 14, 1820. 5.238
To wife Mary, farm, and household goods, and $100. To sons Joseph and John, farm, containing 104 acres. Rem. of stock, to sons, each. To daughter Ann, bed, etc., and $650. To daughter Sarah, $500.
Execs: Sons Joseph and John. Wit: Casper Kizar, and Isaac Parry.

ROBINSON, ISAAC.
March 11, 1820. Sept 28, 1820. 5.240
To wife Jane, all estate. To granddaughter Jeanette all lands, and $50.
Execs: Wife Jane, and daughter Sarah. Wit: Thomas Butler, and Jonathan Wood.

KOLB, JACOB. Upper Salford.
July 24, 1813. Sept 28, 1820. 5.241
To wife Anna, household goods, and interest of 500 pds. at 5% interest. To son Jacob, farm, containing 80 acres. Rem. of estate to children, equally.
Execs: Michael Shoemaker, and Benjamin and Abraham Alderfer.

STALFORD, ELIZABETH. Hatfield.
Feb 4, 1819. Oct 7, 1820. 5.243
To sister Sarah, 6 silver tea spoons. To Cephas, rem. of estate.
Exec: Sister Mary. Wit: Jesse, John, and Thomas Davis.

DULL, CHRISTIAN. Gwynedd.
May 26, 1820. Oct 13, 1820. 5.244
To wife Elizabeth, household goods. To son Christian, wearing apparel. Rem. of estate to be sold. To grandson John Dull, $300.
Execs: ____. Wit: Daniel Kneedler, and George Thomas.

WISMER, JOSEPH. Gwynedd.
Oct 13, 1820. Oct 28, 1820. 5.247
To wife Barbara, all estate, and 50 pds. To daughter Esther, $30. To son Joseph, $30. To son Jacob, $30.
Execs: Son Joseph, and son in law Jacob Ruth, and John Aulthouse. Wit: Evan Jones, and Andrew Lehman.

GERHART, NICHOLAS. Whitpain.
Sept 2, 1811. Nov 3, 1820. 5.250
To son Barnabas, 50 pds. To son Jacob, 50 pds. To son Philip, 50 pds. To

grandchildren, each, 15 pds. Rem. of estate to 3 sons: Barnabas, Jacob, and Philip.
Execs: Son Peter, and Philip Shenberger. Wit: Job Roberts, and John Wentz.

LLOYD, JOHN. Horsham.
April 5, 1819. Nov 6, 1820. 5.251
To wife Sarah, $100. Estate to be sold. Rem. of estate divided into 6 equal parts.
To son Joseph, 1/6 part. To son Abraham, 1/6 part. To son Cadwalder, 1/6 part. To daughter Hannah, 1/6 part. To daughter Mary, 1/6 part. To daughters Lydia and Ann, 1/6 part each. To son Joseph, $5.00. To son Abraham, $5.00. To son Cadwalder, $3000. To grandson John, $250. To grandson Cadwalder, $50.
Execs: Son Cadwalder, and son in law Isaac Walton, and Hiram NcNeill. Wit: Frederick Sollada, and Mary McNeill.

McCLINTUCK, ROBERT. Pottstown.
May 8, 1818. Nov 14, 1820. 5.254
To mother, $200. To niece Ann, $200. To Robert McClintuck Harris, $100.
Execs: John Frick, and Samuel Shafer. Wit: Jesse Rees, and William Mintzer.

STEMPLE, WILLIAM. Plymouth.
Nov 4, 1820. Nov 15, 1820. 5.255
To nephew John, 1/2 of plantation. To Mary Davis, $1500.
Execs: Samuel Thomas, and Samuel Maulsby. Wit: Thomas Leedom, and George Potts.

HULLS, ISAIAH. Cheltenham.
Nov 1, 1820. Nov 16, 1820. 5.256
To wife Sarah, all estate, and household goods, and $2000.
Execs: Son in law Alex McCalley, and Aaron Keyser. Wit: James Gentle, Jesse McCalla.

HOLDERMAN, HENRY. Perkiomen.
Oct 25, 1820. Nov 23, 1820. 5.258
To wife Elizabeth, 400 pds. after wife's death divided among children, and grandchildren, equally. Rem. of estate divided among children. To son Christian, one share. To son Abraham, one share. To son John, one share. To son Jacob, one share. To children of daughter Margaret, one share. To daughter Elizabeth, one share. To daughter Hannah, one share. To daughter Catharine, one share.
Execs: Sons Christian and John. Wit: Thomas Zucht, and William Kili.

DOTTERA, CATHARINE. Frederick.
April 23, 1816. Dec 2, 1820. 5.259

Estate to be sold and money divided as follows: to son Conrad, 50 pds. and rem. equally divided among children: John, Conrad, Maria, wife of of Jacob Smith, Catharine, wife of Wendel Wiant.
Exec: Son in law Wendel Wiant. Wit: Benjamin Markley, and Philip Zepp.

KENDERDINE, RICHARD. Horsham.
Nov 8, 1820. Dec 5, 1820. 5.260
Estate to be sold. To wife, 1/3 of income and profits, of estate, and rem. to children: Sarah, Anna, David, Richard, Rachel, Elizabeth Paul, equally. Execs: Richard Shoemaker, and Elizabeth Kenderdine. Wit: Isaac Longstreth, and Joseph Kenderdine.

FARRINGER, JOHN A. Lower Providence.
Aug 20, 1820. Dec 20, 1820. 5.261
To wife Elizabeth, all lands, containing 89 acres. To daughter Christina, 400 pds. to granddaughter Elizabeth, bed, etc. To granddaughter Catharine, 5 pds. After wife's death rem. of estate to be divided equally among children, in 6 parts. To son John, 1/6 part. To daughter Mary, 1/6 part. To daughter Christina, 400 pds. To granddaughter Elizabeth, bed, etc. To granddaughter Catharine, 5 pds. After wife's death rem. of estate to be divided among children, in 6 equal parts. To son John, 1/6 part. To daughter Mary, 1/6 part. To daughter Christina, 1/6 part. To daughter Elizabeth, 1/6 part. To daughter Catharine, 1/6 part. To son Frederick, 1/6 part.
Execs: Son John, and son in law Peter Lehman. Wit: Philip Riner, and H. Geisenhainer.

MALSBERGER, CATHAREINE. Pottstown.
May 28, 1818. Jan 3, 1821. 5.263
To granddaughter Mary, beds, etc. To son Jacob, one equal share. To son Joseph, 1/7 equal share. To daughter Mary, 1/7 equal share. To children of daughter Catharine, 1/7 share. To daughter Susanna, 1/7 share. To Anthony Hooky, 1/7 share.
Execs: Sons Jacob and Joseph, and son in law Anthony Hooky. Wit: Peter Richs, and George Leaf.

FRANTZ, TOBIAS. Whitpain.
Jan 1, 1821. Jan 10, 1821. 1821. 5.265
Estate to be sold. To sons Enos, Jesse, and Aaron, wearing apparel, equally. To daughter Sarah, 1/2 doz. silver tea spoons, and all mothers wearing apparel. Guardians, of son Jesse, David Thomas, and Peter Root. Guardians of son Aaron.
Execs: ____. Wit: Henry Greenwalt, and Matthias Felter.

ALDERFER, JOHN. Lower Salford.
March 5, 1817. Jan 11, 1821. 5.266
To son John, tract of land containing 77 acres. To wife Elizabeth, interest

of 600 pds. yearly.
Execs: Benjamin and Abraham Alderfer. Wit: Isaac and Joseph Alderfer, and Henry Clemens.

MAURER, PETER. Upper Hanover.
Dec 27, 1816. Jan 20, 1821. 5.268
All personal estate to be appraised. To daughters Margaret and Mary, 30 pds. each. To grandson Peter, 15 pds. To daughters Margaret and Mary, 300 pds. each. To grandson Peter, 300 pds. To grandchildren: George, Polly, and Paky, 300 pds. equally.
Execs: Grandson Peter Kolb, and George Hillegass. Wit: George and Jacob Maurer.

KLINE, CATHARINE.
Aug 4, 1820. Jan 22, 1821. 5.269
To 3 daughters: Elizabeth, Catharine, and Mary, all estate. Rem. of estate divided among 5 children [only 4 named?]: Abraham, Elizabeth, Catharine, and Mary, equally.
Execs: ____. Wit: Charles Hendricks, and Samuel March.

THOMAS, ENOCH. Cheltenham.
March 20, 1817. Jan 27, 1821. 5.270
To wife Mary, personalty and real estate. To daughter Elizabeth, 5 pds. To son Enoch, 5 pds. To son Samuel, tract of land in Abington, containing 1 acre, 8 perches. To son William, farm, containing 4 acres. To son Elijah, rem. of farm. To grandson William, tract of land.
Execs: Sons Samuel, William, and Elijah Thomas. Wit: William Powell, and James Harner.

FRY, JOHN. Lower Providence.
Feb 28, 1820. Jan 30, 1821. 5.272
To wife Anna, household goods, and money arising for sale of estate to be equally divided among children. To sons John and Isaac, farm, in Lower Providence. To daughter Barbara, 75 pds. To daughter Catharine, 175 pds. and remaining 100 pds. to be divided among wife, and children.
Execs: Sons John and Jacob. Wit: John Zoller, Peter Warner and Andrew Todd.

TYSON, THOMAS. Abington.
March 17, 1815. Feb 13, 1821. 5.274
To wife Sarah, farm, and household goods, and $400. Exrs. to put on interest 100 pds. for wife. To 6 daughters: Mary, Sarah, Eleanor, Elizabeth, and Hannah, and Susanna, 100 pds. equally. To son Thomas, clock, and tract of land containing 123 acres, 140 perches. To daughters Eleanor, and Elizabeth, tract of land containing 103 acre subject to payment of $40 yearly. To son Thomas, wearing apparel. To 6 daughters aforesaid, 300 pds. each. To daughter Mary, tract of land in West

Moreland, containing 200 acres.
Execs: Son Thomas and daughter Mary. Wit: John Tyson, and John Kirk.

SHELMIRE, CATHARINE. South Hampton.
April 11, 1820. Feb 15, 1821. 5.279
To daughters Ann and Mary, wearing apparel, equally. To sons Abraham and Daniel and Benjamin, $50, each. To grandson George Rutherford, $10. To granddaughter Elizabeth, $10. To daughter Ann, blue chest. To son Abraham, bible, and 6 silver tea spoons. Rem. of estate to son Benjamin.
Execs: Son Benjamin, and Hiram McNeill. Wit: John Kruson, and William Lewis.

JOHNSON, WILLIAM. Moreland.
Dec 2, 1820. Feb 19, 1821. 5.280
To wife Sarah, household goods, and interest of money. To daughter Mary Roney, $1.00. Rem. of estate to other children.
Exec: Son Charles. Wit: Charles Ferry, and Samuel Shoemaker.

FOULKE, PRISCILLA. Gwynedd.
Jan 20, 1821. Feb 22, 1821. 5.281
To sister Lydia Spencer, wearing apparel. To niece Priscilla, $133.33, and silver tea spoons, and feather bed, etc. To children of sister Lydia, $266.67. To nephew Edward Foulke, $200, and feather bed, and bible, etc. To niece Susanna, feather bed, etc. Rem. of residue equally divided among children. To niece Edith, large oval dinning table. To brother Jesse, interest of a certain bond, of 100 pds. To Preparative Meeting of Friends, in Gwynedd 50 pds. to be applied towards building a new building. Rem. of estate to sister Lydia.
Execs: Edward Foulke, and Jesse Spencer. Wit: William and George Foulke.

FOULKE, JESSE. Gwynedd.
Feb 22, 1821. April 2, 1821. 5.282
To nephew Edward Foulke, tract of land subject to payment of 1200 pds. To niece Susanna Foulke, $500. To nephew George Foulke, $500. To Preparative Meeting of Friends, $200. Rem. of farm, containing 150 acres to nephew Jesse and William. To niece Priscilla Spencer, feather bed, etc. To nephews Edward and Jesse, all wearing apparel, equally.
Execs: Nephews Edward and Jesse. Wit: Job Roberts, and Joseph Evans.

FREGELE, GEORGE. Douglass.
March 20, 1821. April 19, 1821. 5.285
To wife Amelia, household goods, 1/3 of personalty and interest of 200 pds. To son Daniel and Jesse, all lands.
Execs: Son Daniel and Jesse. Wit: Matthias Yorgey, and Henry Sassaman.

JONES, JONATHAN. Lower Merion.
March 15, 1821. April 24, 1821. 5.287
To wife Mary, household goods, and farm. To son Owen, farm.
Execs: Wife, and Joseph Warner. Wit: Owen Jones, and Joseph Brookefield.

EGBERT, LAWRENCE. Plymouth.
Nov 11, 1820. April 4, 1821. 5.289
To wife Sarah, household goods, and interest of $4000. To sons Thomas and David, 500 pds. To children: George, Sarah, and Susanna, 500 pds. each. To sons Thomas and David, $400. to daughter Sarah, $100 and rem. divided equally among children.
Execs: Sons: George, Thomas, and David. Wit: Thomas Cowden, and Jacob Ritter.

McNEAL, THOMAS. Moreland.
Feb 21, 1821. May 14, 1821. 5.291
To wife Elizabeth, household goods, and maintenance. To daughter Rebecca, feather bed, etc. Rem. divided equally among daughter Rebecca, and son John.
Execs: Isaac Tomkins, and son John. Wit: Isaac Beans.

HAWS, FREDERICK. Springfield.
May 11, 1819. May 14, 1821. 5.292
To wife, interest and income of estate, and household goods, after wife's death to children: Ann, John, Samuel, Margaret, Hannah, Elizabeth, Rachel, and children of daughter Catharine, equally.
Execs: Daughter Hannah, and John Heister. Wit: Henry Prise, and Frederick Haas.

PORTER, ELIZABETH. Norriton.
Aug 20, 1815. May 21, 1821. 5.294
To daughter Harriet, all estate.
Exec: Daughter Harriet. Wit: Atkinson Farra, Samuel Farra.

IVES, WILLIAM. Pottstown.
Dec 15, 1814. May 22, 1821. 5.295
To son Thomas, 1/4 part. To daughter Rachel, 1/4 part. To son Jesse, 1/4 part, and $180.67. To Mary Parver, $139. To daughter Rachel, household goods.
Execs: Sons Thomas, and James. Wit: Henry and Peter Leibenguth.

BRAND, GEORGE. Pottsgrove.
June 2, 1819. May 25, 1821. 5.296
To son Samuel, farm, containing 137 acres. To daughter Elizabeth, 100 pds. To son Benjamin, 500 pds.
Execs: Sons Benjamin and Samuel. Wit: Henry and Jacob Crous, and

Henry Schneider.

EGBERT, ELIZABETH. Springfield.
April 9, 1821. June 1, 1821. 5.299
To Eleva Rees, silver spectacles. To niece Ann Rees, rem. of personalty.
Exec: Ann Rees. Wit: George Martin, and John Righter.

SINGER, JOHN. Gwynedd.
May 13, 1821. June 7, 1821. 5.300
To William Reiley, 25 pds. To Elizabeth Hartzell, 25 pds. to Samuel Fleshocer, 25 pds. And 25 pds. for taking care of children if Gwynedd, and this sum to be left in the hands of the Trustees of St. Peter's Church. To Boem's Church, 200 pds. To St. Peter's Church, 200 pds. To George Lightcap, tract of land. To Henry and John Spary, 25 pds.
Execs: ____. Wit: George Sheirer, and Joseph Foulke.

KENDERDINE, RACHEL. Horsham.
Jan 13, 1821. June 8, 1821. 5.302
To daughter Tacy, wearing apparel. To daughter Mary, lot of land. To daughter Sarah, feather bed.
Execs: Joseph and Enoch Kenderdine. Wit: John and Jesse Shay.

MORRIS, WILLIAM. New Brittain.
Dec 26, 1816. June 6, 1821. 5.303
To wife Ann, use and profits of estate. To granddaughter Mary, spinning wheel.
Exec: Son Isaac. Wit: Abner Morris, and Jacob Evans.

JONES, CATHARINE. Upper Merion.
July 9, 1819. June 12, 1821. 5.305
To son Peter, $266.67, and to his children, $133.33, equally. To son Jonathan's children, $213.33 equally. To granddaughter Margaret's children, $213.33 equally. To grandson Jesse Roberts, $53.33. To daughter Rebecca Roberts, $533.33. To daughter Catharine, $266.67. To brother Jonah, $100.
Execs: Sons Peter, and son in law Richard Roberts. Wit: George Potts, and William Yocum.

LINENBOCH, JOSEPH. Plymouth.
June 21, 1821. June 12, 1821. 5.307
To daughter Esther, $5.00. Rem. divided into 3 equal parts. To son Jacob, 1/3 part. To son in law John Hallman, remaining 1/3 part. To daughter Hannah, 1/3 part.
Execs: Son Jacob, and John Hartman, and Daniel Davis. Wit: John Brant, and Samuel Davis.

YERKES, FRANKLIN. Moreland.

Oct 18, 1820. June 30, 1821. 5.308
To wife Margaret, all estate, and after her death to her children. To sons: Silas, George, and John, 1/8 part of estate. To daughters: Elizabeth, Susanna, and Hester, and Mary, 1/8 part of estate. To daughters Hester and Mary, $50. each.
Exec: Son Silas. Wit: Jacob Achuff, and Daniel Colladar.

BUTLER, SARAH. Lwer Providence.
March 11, 1808. June 19, 1821. 5.310
To son John, all estate.
Exec: Jonathan Roberts. Wit: Henry and William Pawling.

SPAID, CHRISTIAN. Marlborough.
April 6, 1810. July 4, 1821. 5.321
To wife Barbara, household goods, and interest of 200 pds. after wife's death divided among children, equally.
Execs: Jacob Boyer and son Jacob. Wit: Thomas Snyder, and Philip Gable.

LLOYD, SARAH. Horsham.
March 31, 1821. July 23, 1821. 5.312
Estate to be sold.
Execs: Cadwalder Lloyd, and nephew Davis Lloyd. Wit: Hiram McNeill, and Nathal Itole.

DeHAVEN, SAMUEL. Horsham.
July 13, 1819. July 24, 1821. 5.313
To wife Catharine, household goods, and farm, containing 4 acres. To grandson Isaac, 4 acres. To son Abraham, $3. and tract of land containing 85 acres subject to payment of 130 pds. Rem. of estate to be sold and money divided among 4 daughters.
Execs: Son David, and son in law Jacob Wright. Wit: Jacob Cassel, and Paul Dowlin, Jr.

ROSENBERGER, JOHN. Montgomery.
April 15, 1797. July 27, 1821. 5.318
To wife, household goods. Rem. of estate divided among wife and children, equally. To daughter Hannah, interest arising from sale of land. To grandson John, 1/2 of money, from sale of land.
Execs: ____. Wit: Ludwig Stagner, and Evan Jones.

FILLMAN, JACOB. Limerick.
Nov 7, 1815. March 24, 1821. 5.320
Estate to be sold and money divided into 9 equal parts. To son Jacob, 1/9 part. To daughter Catharine, 1/9 part. To son John, 1/9 part. To son Henry, 1/9 part. To daughter Christina, 1/9 part. To son Frederick, 1/9 part. To son Philip, 1/9 part. To son Abraham, 1/9 part. To daughter Hannah, 1/9 part. To daughter of son Jacob, 10 pds.

Execs: Sons Jacob and Abraham. Wit: Matthew Brooke, and Daniel Krous.

HAHN, PHILIP. New Hanover.
March 20, 1806. aug 13, 1821. 5.321
Estate to be sold. To wife Margaret, part of dwelling house. Rem. of estate to 3 daughters: Catharine, Susanna, and Margaret.
Execs: Sons Philip and John. Wit: John Boyer.

WISLER, MARY. Towamencin.
Nov 25, 1820. Aug 14, 1821. 5.323
To Sarah Row, wife of Abraham Benner, clock, etc. To Mary Benner, $50. To Elizabeth Row, $12. To brother Paul, $2.00. To brother John, $2.00. Rem. of estate to be sold and divided into 6 equal parts. To sister Elizabeth, one part. To sister Rachel, one part. To Amos Evans, one part. To Jesse Lewis, one part. To sister Susanna, one part. To brother Abraham Benner, one part.
Execs: Daniel Boorse, and Jesse Lewis. Wit: John Boorse, and Benjamin Hendricks.

CHRISTIAN, CHRISTIAN. Horsham.
Oct 8, 1819. Aug 21, 1821. 5.324
To son George, gun. To grandsons and great grandsons, wearing apparel. To granddaughter Rachel, $50. Rem. of estate to be sold and money divided into 5 equal parts. To son George, 1/5 part. To daughter Sarah, 1/5 part. To children of son Thomas, 1/5 part. To daughter Elizabeth, 1/5 part. To daughter Ann, 1/5 part.
Execs: Son George, and daughters: Sarah, Elizabeth, and Ann. Wit: Seneca Lukens, and Hiram McNeill.

HILTNER, JONATHAN. Whitemarsh.
July 25, 1821. Aug 31, 1821. 5.325
To wife Christian, use and profits of estate. To son John, $100. To daughter Mary, $100. To sons George and Charles, silver watch each. After wife's death, rem. of estate divided equally among 4 children: John, Mary, George, and Charles.
Execs: Wife Christian, and son John. Wit: George Potts and Philip Fie.

MILHOOF, CATHARINE. Douglass.
May 21, 1808. Sept 7, 1821. 5.327
To Lutheran Congregation in New Hanover, rem. of money from estate after expenses are paid.
Exec: Jacob Bickle. Wit: Isaac Feather, and Jonathan Richards.

RUTH, JACOB. Hatfield.
Nov 1, 1817. Sept 18, 1821. 5.328
To wife Mary, household goods, and interest of 800 pds. Rem. of estate

divided equally among children: Isaac, Jacob, John, Sarah, wife of David Sellers, Catharine, wife of Abraham Cassel, Magdalena, wife of Jacob Keller, Mary, wife of James Yocum, and Elizabeth, wife of Christian Atherholt.
Execs: Son Jacob and son in law James Yocum. Wit: Abraham Shipe, and Jacob Oberholtzer.

ROSENBERGER, DAVID. Hatfield.
March 7, 1821. Sept 19, 1821. 5.329
To wife Barbara, household goods, and farm. To son Henry, tract of land containing 108 acres and 156 perches subject to payment of 1500 pds. To son John, tract of land containing 86 acres, 113 perches subject to payment of 1500 pds. To daughter Froney, farm, containing 78 acres subject to payment of 145 pds. and of which 400 pds. she may keep. To 8 grandchildren: Jacob, David, Mary, Ann, Deborah, Barbara, Frederick, and Henry, 400 pds. to be paid as follows: to son Jacob, 50 pds. yearly. To son David, 50 pds. yearly. To daughter Mary, 50 pds. yearly. To daughter Deborah, 50 pds. yearly. To daughter Barbara, 50 pds. yearly. To son Frederick, 50 pds. yearly. To son Henry, 50 pds. yearly. Rem. of real estate to daughter Susanna.
Execs: Wife Barbara, and sons John and Henry. Wit: Jacob Rosenberger, and Samuel Detwiler.

HEISTLER, JACOB. Gwynedd.
Feb 8, 1821. Oct 21, 1821. 5.334
To Exrs. $50. each. To son John, family bible, and tract of land containing 134 acres subject to payment of 1000 pds. Rem. of estate divided into 4 equal parts. To daughter Elizabeth, 1/4 part. To daughter Catharine, 1/4 part. To daughter Nancy, 1/4 part. To daughter Susanna, 1/4 part.
Execs: Son Daniel and son in law Henry Aulthouse, and Jacob Bisbing. Wit: Emanuel Steitel, Evan Jones.

CLAY, SLATOR. Upper Providence.
May 16, 1821. Oct 15, 1821. 5.336
To son Charles, farm.
Exec: Son Charles. Wit: Joseph Henry.

ANDIG, WILLIAM. Upper Salford.
April 6, 1821. Oct 13, 1821. 5.337
Estate to be sold and money divided among children.
Exec: John Hoering. Wit: Isaac Gerhart, and John Auchy.

HIGHLEY, JOHN. Lower Providence.
Dec 6, 1819. Oct 18, 1821. 5.338
To daughter Mary Patterson, wife of Robert Patterson, lot in Upper Providence, and after her death equally divided among children. To daughter Elizabeth, wife of Joseph Rittenhouse, $266.67. To son Jacob

Highley, bible, and clock, and 3 years after my decease, rem. of estate divided into 5 equal parts. To son Henry, 1/5 part. To daughter Mary, 1/5 part. To daughter Elizabeth, 1/5 part. To son Jacob, 1/5 part. To son John, 1/5 part.
Execs: Son Jacob and Joseph Crawford. Wit: Joseph Teany, and Curtis Evans.

TYSON, MARY. Limerick.
Sept 15, 1818. March 21, 1821. 5.339
To granddaughter Phebe Korl, amount of a bond of son Joseph, dated Jan 18, 1818, for $144.72. To daughter Barbara, farm, where I now dwell, subject to payment of $400, and $25 and part of household goods. To daughters wearing apparel, equally, and household goods. To Mary Ann Rambo, blue chest.
Execs: Son Peter, and son in law William Dismant. Wit: Daniel and Esther Stall, and Thomas Dougherty.

SNYDER, HENRY. Marlborough.
March 27, 1819. Oct 23, 1821. 5.340
To wife Christina, household goods, and interest of 500 pds. and 25 pds. yearly. To daughter Catharine, wife of Philip Gabel, 7 pds. Rem. of estate divided into 7 equal parts. To son George, 1/7 part. To son Jacob, 1/7 part. To children of son Henry, 1/7 part. To daughter Margaret, 1/7 part. To daughter Christiana, 1/7 part. To children of daughter Elizabeth, 1/7 part. To son Henry, 1/7 part.
Execs: Son Jacob and son in law Philip Gabel and Samuel Zeigler. Wit: Philip Reed, and Jacob Sheid.

SMITH, MARGARET. New Hanover.
July 29, 1820. Oct 25, 1821. 5.343
To daughter Sophia, 15 pds. To sn Jacob's daughter Sarah, 5 pds. To granddaughter Diana, rem, of property. Rem. of estate divided into 3 equal parts. To children of deceased daughter Margaret, 1/3 part. To children of daughter Elizabeth, 1/3 part. To grandsons Jacob and Peter, 1/3 part.
Exec: Son in law Henry Fillman. Wit: Jacob Overdorf, and John Zan, and Jenry Sassaman.

LEWIS, AMOS. Upper Dublin.
Oct 9, 1820. Oct 26, 1821. 5.344
To daughter Jane Jones, farm, containing 10 acres. To daughter Ellen Lukens, farm, containing 105 acres, 100 perches. To sister in law Mary Hubbs, $600 to be put on interest and to be paid to her yearly. To daughter Jane, $2000.
Execs: Daughter Jane, and son in law Jesse Lukens. Wit: Daneil Shoemaker, and Ellis Cleaver.

BROADES, ARTHUR. Montgomery.
Feb 7, 1809. Oct 26, 1821. 5.346
To wife Leah, 1/3 of rents, and income of realty. To daughter Mary, tract of land containing 24 acres. To son Peter, tract of land containing 83 acres.
Execs: Son Peter, and John Jones. Wit: Benjamin Free, Joseph Keyser, and R. Whitehead.

HEISTER, JOHN. Pottstown.
April 11, 1820. Oct 29, 1821. 5.347
To son Jonathan's children: John, Thomas, 375 acres. To son John, tract of land containing 153 acres and $1155. To children of daughter Elizabeth, tract of land containing 3 acres. To daughter Catharine, house and lot, containing 400 acres and $3879. To daughter Rachel, house and lot, containing 7 acres and $4777.
Execs: Son John and son Samuel. Wit: Jacob Drinkhouse, and William Mintzer, and Jacob Hubley.

EVE, ADAM.
June 19, 1809. Nov 8, 1821. 5.352
To wife, all estate, both real and personal. To son Abraham, $40. Rem. of estate divided equally among children. Exrs. to pay to John Michener, son of daughter Christina, 25 pds.
Exec: Son Daniel. Wit: George and William Holstein.

LUKENS, MARY.
June 29, 1819. Nov 9, 1821. 5.353
To brother George, bond, $220. To brother Charles, 100 pds. To brother George Roberts, for benefit of brother Robert Roberts, 100 pds. To Sidney Roberts, 100 pds. To niece Sidney, $50, and feather bed, etc. To niece Sarah, $50. To niece Mary, silver table spoons.
Execs: Brother George and William Foulke. Wit: Charles Lukens, and Samuel Livezey.

WARE, DAVID. Upper Providence.
Oct 17, 1821. Nov 9, 1821. 5.354
To wife Rachel, all estate.
Exec: Jeremiah Billew. Wit: Abraham Reiff, and Matthew Dill.

SCHOENER, JOHN. Pottstown.
Dec 31, 1819. Nov 9, 1821. 5.355
To wife Maria, all estate. To children of George Painer, 100 pds. equally. To children of deceased daughter Susanna, 100 pds. equally. To daughter Elizabeth, 150 pds.
Execs: Son John and Jacob Drinkhouse. Wit: Henry and Lewis Warley.

McCLEAN, RACHEL.

Aug 24, 1821. Nov 15, 1821. 5.357
To nephew John McClean, $666.66. To niece Mary McClean, $200. To niece Rebecca McClean, 1/3 part of wearing apparel, and feather bed, etc. To John McClean, 1/3 part of wearing apparel, and feather bed, etc. Rem. of household goods, to nieces: Rebecca, Jane, and Rachel McClean.
Exec: Moses McClean. Wit: Joseph and Robert Kenderdine.

WILSON, JOHN. Whitemarsh.
Feb 17, 1818. Nov 15, 1821. 5.358
To wife Sarah, household goods, and $88 yearly. To 3 daughters: Rebecca, Elizabeth, and Sarah, 20 acres of woodland. To 3 daughters: Rebecca, Elizabeth, and Sarah, $100 each. To son Joseph, $1040. To son John, 54 acres, 20 perches of land. To son Amos, 50 acres of land.
Execs: Sons Amos, David, and daughters Rebecca and Elizabeth. Wit: Samuel Livezey, and Josiah Albertson.

YERKES, REBECCA. Moreland.
Feb 16, 1807. Nov 23, 1821. 5.362
To daughter Susanna, $25. Rem. to be divided among sons and daughters: Isaac, and David, and Mary, Rebecca, and Sarah, equally. Execs: Sons Elias, Isaac, and Arthur. Wit: David Yerkes, and Thomas Michener.

HALLOWELL, THOMAS. Moreland.
April 27, 1820. Nov 24, 1821. 5.363
To wife Martha, house and household goods. To son Thomas, farm, containing 109 acres. To John Jones, looking glass, etc. To son Ezra, silver can. To Isaac Shoemaker, dozen tea spoons. To son Thomas, and son in laws George Shoemaker, and John Thomson and Thomas Shoemaker, and Isaac Shoemaker, farming utensils, equally. Exrs. to pay to grandchildren, $4.00 each.
Execs: Son Thomas, and son in law George Shoemaker. Wit: Grove Mitchell, and Samuel Shoemaker.

BOWER, NICHOLAS. Norriton.
Nov 27, 1821. Dec 10, 1821. 5.365
To daughters Elizabeth, and Margaret, $30. each. To daughter Sarah, feather bed. Rem. of estate divided as follows: 2/3 to Sarah Fulton. 1/3 to Christiana Teany.
Exec: Nicholas Slough. Wit: Joseph Armstrong, and Jacob Albright.

EGOLF, JOHN. New Hanover.
Nov 2, 1 1821. Dec 11, 1821. 5.366
To brother Adam, personalty.
Exec: Brother Adam. Wit: John Reifsnyder, and Jacob Schneider.

CLEAVER, MARY. Upper Merion.
Aug 6, 1810. Dec 12, 1821. 5.367

To daughter Elizabeth, $533.33, and household goods. To daughter in law Rebecca Cleaver, wearing apparel. To granddaughter Mary Rambo, feather bed, etc. To son Jonathan, rem. of estate.
Exec: Son Jonathan. Wit: Jonathan and Phinehas Phillips, and Joshua Tyson.

BOWMAN, ROGER.
May 5, 1807. Dec 17, 1821. 5.368
To son Henry, farm. To daughter Hannah, 150 pds. To granddaughter Ann, 20 pds. To granddaughter Jane, 400 pds. To grandsons: Joshua, and John, 100 pds. each.
Exec: Son Henry. Wit: Gideon and Benedict Malin.

SHOEMAKER, JANE. Plymouth.
Nov 12, 1819. Dec 28, 1821. 5.369
To husband David Shoemaker, 400 pds. and personal estate, to daughters: Ellen, Margaret, Ann, and Mary, equally.
Execs: Cadwalder Foulke, and John Jones. Wit: Job Roberts, and Charles Mather.

KROUSE, JEREMIAH. Upper Hanover.
Aug 4, 1821. Dec 21, 1821. 6.1
To son Nathan, all land, subject to payment of 1600 pds. To 2 daughters beds, etc. To wife Magdalena, house, during widowhood.
Execs: Son Nathan, and George Krouse. Wit: David Schultz, and Jacob Gerhart.

PRICE, HANNAH. Lower Merion.
Feb 12, 1818. Dec 12, 1821. 6.3
To daughter Sarah, wearing apparel, and bible. To son Enoch, 5 shares of stock. To sons Edward and Thomas, 3 share of stock, each. To son Charles, $200. To sons all household goods, equally. Rem. of estate divided among sons: Edward, Isaac, Enoch, Thomas, and Charles, and daughter Sarah.
Execs: Son Isaac, and Joseph Price. Wit: Titus and Mary Yerkes, and Ann Moore.

KARR, ROBERT. Whitemarsh.
Nov 17, 1821. Jan 15, 1822. 6.5
To wife, household goods, and maintenance. All estate to son Streeper.
Exec: Son Streeper. Wit: Allen Corson, and John Conrad.

FREDERICK, HENRY. Upper Salford.
Dec 8, 1821. Jan 21, 1822. 6.7
Estate to be sold. To wife Catharine, household goods, and 1/3 of estate, and other estate divided among children, equally: Charles, George, Jacob, Henry, Catharine, and Joseph.

Execs: John Frederick, and brother in law Joseph Hendricks. Wit: Jacob Meyer.

VANDERSLICE, AUGUSTUS. Upper Providence.
Jan 31, 1822. Feb 5, 1822. 6.8
To brother Joseph, all property. To brother Joseph, $1.00. To brother Marcus, $1.00. Rem. of estate divided into 5 equal shares. To brother John, one share. To brother Edward, one share. Remaining 1/5 share to brother Jacob.
Exec: Brother John. Wit: A. Thomas, and Samuel Spencer.

SAYBOLD, PETER. Pottsgrove.
July 22, 1810. Feb 13, 1822. 6.9
To wife Ann, all estate.
Exec: Wife Ann. Wit: John and Nathan Brooke.

WYNKOOF, GARRETT. Moreland.
Oct 23, 1818. Feb 20, 1822. 6.10
To wife Ann, $200 and farm, and household goods. To granddaughter Margaret, use of farm. To grandsons, part of estate.
Execs: Christian Snyder, and Hogland and Hiram McNeill. Wit: Frederick Sollady, and Jacob Warner.

BECHTEL, JOSEPH. Pottsgrove.
Nov 4, 1821. Feb 23, 1822. 6.12
To wife Catharine, household goods, and farm, and 1/2 of all income, and $50.
Exec: Jacob Blim. Wit: Aaron Keyser, and John Molsberger.

KEHL, BARBARA. Upper Hanover.
Dec 24, 1821. Feb 25, 1822. 6.14
Personal estate to be sold. To grandchildren of son Jacob, 1/8 part of estate. To daughter Barbara, 1/8 part. To daughter Anna, 1/8 part. To daughter Eve, 1/8 part. To granddaughters: Elizabeth, Catharine, Barbara, Anna, and Eve, wearing apparel, equally.
Exec: Son in law George Kolb. Wit: Jacob Hillegass, and Henry Stier.

LIVEZEY, THOMAS ESQ. Upper Dublin.
Jan 16, 1819. Feb 25, 1822. 6.16
To Thomas Fletcher, Thomas Shoemaker, wearing apparel, equally. To Joseph, son of uncle Joseph deceased and John Livezey, son of uncle Benjamin (had 712 acres of land in Luzerne Co.) deceased, $200 each. To John Fitzwater, all law books. To nephew Robert Livezey, son of brother Daniel deceased, books. To sister Susanna, $100 yearly. To niece Catharine, daughter of sister Esther, $300. To step brother David, and step sister Rachel and Elizabeth, $100 each. To nephew and niece Charles and Esther, children of sister Mary deceased, $150 each. Nephew John

deceased son of brother Jonathan deceased, Esther, Susanna, and Ann, children of brother Jonathan deceased. Robert, Jonathan, Sarah, Isaac, Deborah, Thomas, Ezra children of brother Daniel deceased. To nephew Robert Livezey, $150. To George Leonhart, $100. Rem. of estate divided among children, equally: Samuel, Esther, Rebecca, Joseph, Thomas, and Jonathan children of sister Susanna.
Execs: Robert Livezey, and John Fitzwater. Wit: Christopher Dresher, and John Whitecomb.

LEIDICH, CHRISTIAN. Frederick.
Oct 1, 1816. Feb 26, 1822. 6.17
To 3 daughters: Catharine, Elizabeth, and Mary, household goods, equally. Rem. of estate divided among 6 children: Philip, John, Henry, Catharine, Elizabeth, and Mary, each.
Exec: Son in law Philip Zeiber. Wit: Benjamin Markley and Benjamin Johnson.

BOYER, PHILIP. Upper Salford.
Jan 22, 1822. March 11, 1822. 6.19
To wife Sophia, household goods, and 1/2 of all income. To son Michael, all real estate.
Execs: Brother in law Daniel Boyer, and John Croll. Wit: Jacob Croll and Benjamin Reiff.

KLINE, JACOB. Lower Salford.
Nov 15, 1821. March 5, 1822. 6.20
To wife Mary, house and tract of land containing 145 acres. 100 pds. to be put on interest for to be divided among children.
Execs: Wife Mary, and son Abraham. Wit: Henry Kolb, and Isaac Kline, and Joseph Alderfer.

KEISEL, JACOB. Springfield.
Jan 13, 1822. March 6, 1822. 6.21
To wife Hannah, household goods, and maintenance. To grandson, $133.33. To son Christian, $50. To son Enoch, $100. To daughter Susanna, $50. Rem. of estate after expenses are paid divided among children.
Execs: Sons Christian and Enoch. Wit: Daniel Snyder, and Jacob Bisbing.

VANFOSSEN, BENJAMIN. Towamencin.
Feb 14, 1822. March, 20, 1822. 6.23
To wife Frania, household goods, and farm, 20 pds. yearly. To 3 sons, all wearing apparel, equally. To 3 sons, 100 pds. each. Rem. of estate divided equally among 7 children: Matthias, John, Benjamin, Margaret, Anna, Barbara, and Eleanor.
Execs: Matthias, and Jacob Kulp. Wit: Joseph Snyder, and Jonas Reinwalt.

ZEIGLER, MICHAEL. Perkiomen and Skippack.
Jan 24, 1809. April 3, 1822. 6.26
To son Abraham, dwelling place, containing 104 acres subject to the payment of 1500 pds. Rem. of estate divided into 7 equal parts. To son Jacob, 1/7 part. To son Isaac, 1/7 part. To son Abraham, 1/7 part. To son Dillman, 1/7 part. To daughter Catharine, 1/7 part. To daughter Elizabeth, 1/7 part. To daughters of son Michael, 1/7 part. To grandsons William and Andrew, 15 pds. each.
Execs: Sons Jacob and Abraham. Wit: Garrett, and Andrew Zeigler, and Henry Sweitzer.

HUNSBERGER, PETER. Franconia.
Oct 12, 1820. April 22, 1822. 6.28
To wife Dorothea, household goods, and 250 pds. and farm, containing 80 acres. Rem. of estate divided into 6 equal parts. To son Christian, 1/6 part. To son John, 1/6 part. To son Samuel, 1/6 part. To daughter Susanna, wife of Isaac Zeigler, 1/6 part. To daughter Anna, wife of Michael Lander, 1/6 part. To daughter Hannah, wife of John Landes, 1/6 part.
Execs: Sons Christian and John. Wit: Abraham Benner, and Samuel Schelle, and Henry Cope.

SAUDER, CHRISTIAN. Franconia.
Oct 24, 1821. April 22, 1822. 6.29
To son Christian, farm, containing 48 acres subject to the payment of 13 pds. for each acre. Rem. divided among children. To daughters Elizabeth, Barbara, household goods, equally.
Execs: Son Christian, and brother Henry Sauder. Wit: Frederick Huntsberger, Christian Benner, and Henry Cope.

JACOBS, ELIZABETH. Skippack.
June 4, 1821. April 25, 1822. 6.31
To children: Richard, John, Jesse, Jeremiah, Nancy wife of Jacob Horning, Catharine, wife of John McCrea, 50 pds. each. To 2 daughters Nancy and Catharine, wearing apparel, equally. Personal estate to be sold and money divided among children.
Codicil dated, Jan 28, 1822. To daughter Nancy's children, 50 pds. each. To Jesse, Nathan, Jeremiah, Catharine, 10 pds. each.
Exec: Son Richard. Wit: Peter Prizer, and John Allabough.

CONARD, HANNAH. Whitpain.
Aug 8, 1813. May 6, 1822. 6.32
To grandson Peter, rem. of estate, and household goods.
Execs: Son in law Caleb Evans, and Henry Conard. Wit: Henry Carney, and John Conard.

BAKEWELL, WILLIAM. Lower Providence.

April 16, 1812. May 20, 1822. 6.33
To wife Rebecca, interest of 1/3 part of proceeds from sale of estate, and household goods. To son Thomas, all lands. To son William, 400 acres of land. To 3 daughters: Eliza, Sarah, and Ann, rem. of household goods. To son Thomas, books, etc., and gun. Rem. of estate to 6 children.
Execs: Son Thomas, and wife, Rebecca, and daughter Eliza. Wit: Henry Pawling, and Philip Spare, and Anthony Whitby.

SMITH, HENRY. Frederick.
Nov 8, 1818. May 22, 1822. 6.35
To son Peter, tract of land in Frederick, containing 150 acres subject to the payment of 2400 pds. All household goods, to be sold. To son Daniel, $1.00 in addition to what he has received. To 9 children, 1/9 part each of estate.
Execs: Son John and Philip Reed. Wit: Henry Kerr, and Peter Hillegass.

MEYER, BENJAMIN. Douglass.
Jan 1, 1819. June 3, 1822. 6.37
Estate to be sold. To daughter Barbara, 100 pds. and bed, etc.
Execs: Son in law Henry Eshbach, and Henry Beyers. Wit: John Bauer, and Philip Christman.

LEECH, SAMUEL. Cheltenham.
June 12, 1817. June 17, 1822. 6.38
To wife Ann, dwelling and household goods. To Rebecca, wife of Rev. Joseph Patterson, small silver watch, and $96 yearly. To sons Richard, and Samuel, $1600 yearly. To son Richard, desk, and book case. To son Samuel, clock.
Execs: Sons Richard, and Samuel. Wit: Thomas Tyson, and Hiram McNeill.

HARTMAN, MICHAEL. Montgomery.
March 30, 1822. July 15, 1822. 6.41
To wife Elizabeth, lot, containing 6 acres, 111 perches, and tract of woodland containing 4 1/2 acres and interest of $50 annually, and household goods. To nephew Michael Hartman, 3 lots of land subject to the payment of $50. To German Lutheran Church, in Hilltown, 100 pds. to Michael Harner, $40. To niece Catharine, wife of Martin King, $30. Remaining 300 pds. to be divided among legatees. To wife's grandchildren of daughter Margaret, 100 pds. equally. To brothers of son Michael, 25 pds. To children of brother Frederick, interest of residue.
Execs: Michael Steever, Andrew Reed, and Philip Hartzel. Wit: Jacob Cassel, and George Weisel.

SHOEMAKER, AGNES. Moreland.
Dec 13, 1819. Aug 20, 1822. 6.44
To Sarah Shoemaker, 3/4 part of estate. To Benjamin Shoemaker,

remaining 1/4 part. To niece Rachel, 30 pds. To William Follows, 50 pds. To Mary Shoemaker, 10 pds. To nephew Nathan Lukens, interest of his bond. To niece Agness Comly, rem. of estate.
Exec: Samuel Shoemaker. Wit: Thomas Shoemaker, and Comly Shoemaker.

LOVE, STEPHEN. Horsham.
May 31, 1822. July 26, 1822. 6.45
To wife Sarah, household goods, and use and profits of estate. To Gorman, son of Thomas, $1000. To Stephen Love, $500. To children of Francis Beard, $500, equally. To William, Thomas, John Love, of Ohio, $500 equally. To nephew Andrew Love, $500. To James Williamson's daughter Sarah, $300. To Sarah Allen, $300.
Exec: Hiram McNeill. Wit: David Dowlin, and Thomas Vansant.

KOLB, JOHN. Skippack and Perkiomen.
June 6, 1822. Aug 21, 1822. 6.46
To father Martin Kolb, farm, at valuation of 1400 pds. subject to the payment of 425 pds. To wife Elizabeth, and daughter Elizabeth, all estate.
Exec: Father in law George Reiff. Wit: Henry Kolb, and Henry Hunsicker.

JOHNSON, WILLIAM. Upper Providence.
May 26, 1810. Sept 14, 1822. 6.47
To wife Barbara, 1/3 of personalty, and interest of 400 pds. If she marries interest of 200 pds. and after her death divided equally among children.
Execs: Son Jacob and brother in law Garret Zeigler. Wit: Henry Hunsicker, and Jonathan Routebuch.

WEIREMAN, JONATHAN. Hatfield.
Aug 13, 1821. Sept 30, 1822. 6.48
To son Abraham, farm, 153 acres. To son in law John Delp, grist mill, and tract of land containing 76 acres subject to the payment of 1000 pds. To son Abraham, weavers loom, and bible, and wearing apparel. To daughter Nancy, book, called "Wandering Soul". To daughter Barbara, 88 pds., 13 s. 8 d. To son Michael, 53 pds., 14 s. 2 d. To daughter Sophia, 139 pds., 18 s. 7 d. To daughter Mary, 150 pds., 17 s., 3 d.
Exec: Son Abraham. Wit: David Wisler, and David Kulp.

RICHARD, PETER. Upper Salford.
Aug 30, 1822. Sept 30, 1822. 6.50
Estate to be sold. To wife Sarah, rem. of estate.
Execs: Brother John and Jacob Smith. Wit: Frederick Grimley, and George Hartzell.

KENDERDINE, JOSPEH. Horsham.
Aug 29, 1822. Oct 1, 1822. 6.51
To wife Hannah, household goods, and $50 quarterly. To son John, $3.00.

To son Justinian, $3.00. To son Joseph, $3.00. To son Charles, $3.00. To
daughter Hannah, $2.00. To daughter Mary, $2.00. To daughter Sarah,
$2.00. To daughter Elizabeth, $2.00. To daughter Rebecca, $2.00.
Guardian Joseph Kenderdine.
Execs: Sons John and Justinian. Wit: Isaac Longstreth, and John Jarrett.

EVANS, AMOS. Limerick.
Sept 24, 1822. Oct 11, 1822. 6.52
To wife Mary, use and benefit of house and household goods, and farming
utensils, and tract of land containing 131 acres, 84 perches. To daughter
Sarah, $500. To children of Eleanor Frick, tract of land containing each
31 acres, 84 perches. To Edward Galony, 4 share of stock of the Reading
Railroad. To Jacob Lewis, 3 shares. To Benjamin Frisk, 3 share. Rem. of
estate to be sold.
Execs: Mary Evans, and Owen Evans, and Thomas Evans, Jr. Wit:
Samuel Evans, and William Towers.

TRUNER, DAVID. Montgomery.
Jan 14, 1822. Oct 12, 1822. 6.58
To son John, Works of Jacob Denner. To son Jacob, bible. To all children,
rem. of books, equally. To son David, one feather bed, etc. To all sons,
wearing apparel. To daughter Margaret, large chest. To son David, $100.
To grandson Henry, $10. Rem. of estate to children: John, Jacob, David,
Abraham, Margaret, and Joseph, equally.
Exec: Evan Jones. Wit: John Griffin, and Cadwalder Roberts.

HOLLOWBUSH, HENRY. Limerick.
____. Oct 21, 1822. 6.59
Estate to be sold.

LAYMAN, THOMAS. Gwynedd.
Dec 13, 1820. Oct 12, 1822. 6.59
To wife Catharine, use of household goods, and all money. To daughter
Mary, $5.00. To daughter Elizabeth, $5.00. To son Casper, $5.00. To son
Thomas, $5.00. To daughter Sarah, $5.00. Rem. of estate to son Andrew,
and daughter Sarah, equally.
Exec: Son Andrew. Wit: Henry Stern, and William Hibblehouse.

BATE, THOMAS. Montgomery.
Jan 4, 1822. Oct 12, 1822. 6.60
To daughter Margaret, $100. To 3 youngest daughters $270., and chest,
etc. To grandsons Albert and Jackson, wearing apparel, equally.
Execs: Evan Jones, and Thomas Morgan. Wit: Nathan Harrar, and
William Fry.

DOWERS, MARY ANN. Springfield.
Oct 8, 1822. Oct 17, 1822. 6.62

To sister Matilda, trunks, and wearing apparel, watch, etc.
Exec: Abraham Heydrick. Wit: Abraham and Susanna Heydrick.

ROSS, THOMAS. Norristown.
July 4, 1816. Oct 23, 1822. 6.62
To grandson Thomas, cyclopedia. To grandson Thomas, desk, and book case, etc. To niece Sarah, stock. To daughter Elizabeth, house, in Philadelphia.
Codicil, dated July 4, 1816. To niece Sarah, stock of 5 shares in Philadelpia Bank.
Execs: son in law Richard Maris, and Caleb Newbold. Wit: Jesse Curtis Clay, and Joseph Thomas, and Levi Pawling.

WHITEHEAD, HANNAH. Montgomery.
Aug 10, 1822. Oct 23, 1822. 6.64
To aunt Mary, all personal estate.
Execs: ____. Wit: Nicholas Wanomaker, and John Sperry.

DRESSHER, GEORGE. Upper Dublin.
Dec 7, 1804. Oct 25, 1822. 6.64
To wife Mary, 24 pds. and interest of 400 pds. during widowhood and household goods. To son Christopher, 50 pds. To daughter Mary, 200 pds. To son Christopher, and Samuel, all realty.
Execs: Sons Christopher and Samuel. Wit: John Bright, John Nines, and Conard Kline.

HORTENSTINE, JOHN. Lower Providence.
Aug 20, 1822. Oct 29, 1822. 6.66
To wife Mary, all estate. After wife's death, divided among children: Eli, George, Henry, John, Joseph, Rachel, Susanna, Mary, Catharine, and Mary, equally.
Exec: Son John. Wit: Joseph Crawford, and Jonathan Shearer.

HUMPHREY, THOMAS. Montgomery.
April 21, 1820. Nov 25, 1822. 6.75
Personalty to be sold. To daughter Rebecca, $50. To nephew Thomas, case of pistols. To son in law Samuel, silver mounted sword.
Execs: Wife Euphemia, and Samuel Wentz, and daughter Rebecca. Wit: Frederick Conrad, and Frederick Markley.

HOLLOWBUSH, HENRY. Limerick.
Oct 21, 1822. Nov 25, 1822. 6.76
Real estate to be sold. Rem. of estate divided into 5 equal parts. To daughter Mary's children, one share. To son John, one share. To son Peter, one share. To son Henry, one share. To son Jacob, one share. To daughter Susanna, one share.
Execs: Son John, and William Tower. Wit: Samuel Evans, and William

Hollonbush.

ROBERTS, JESSE. Norristown.
June 8, 1822. Nov 25, 1822. 6.77
To 3 daughters: Rachel, Sarah, and Hannah, all estate. To daughter Rachel, tract of land in Norristown. To daughters Sarah, and Hannah, tract of land.
Execs: Daughter Rachel, and George Holstein. Wit: Benjamin Evans, and Thomas Miller.

ZOLLER, MARGARET. New Hanover.
Nov 13, 1815. Nov 27, 1822. 6.78
To sons George and Jacob, and Francis, wearing apparel, equally. Rem. of estate divided among children: Francis, Margaret, wife of Abraham Grub, Catharine, wife of Conrad Mauck, Molly, wife of Philip Bitting, Sophia, wife of Henry Crows, Elizabeth, wife of Jacob Crows, and Maria, wife of Ludwig Stark.
Exec: Son in law Henry Crows. Wit: Ludwig Lensinbegler, and Jonathan Richards.

CRATOR, JACOB. Montgomery.
Dec 23, 1820. Nov 28, 1822. 6.79
To wife Catharine, household goods, and house. Personal estate to be sold and money given to wife, and 350 pds. To son John, and Peter, and Catharine, rem. of estate, equally.
Execs: Martin Funk, and Christian Stegnor. Wit: Isaac Morris, and Peter Benner.

FEGELY, PETER. Douglass.
____. Nov 28, 1822. 6.80
Estate to be sold, and money divided among children: Peter, John, Christian, Polly, wife of Henry Bichel, and Elizabeth, wife of Abraham Stetler, equally.
Execs: Son Peter, and son in law Abraham Stetler. Wit: John Bechtel, and Jacob Allebach.

JONES, PAUL. Lower Merion.
Sept 20, 1820. Nov 29, 1822. 6.81
To son Enoch, tract of land containing 11 acres, 10 perches. To daughter Susanna, $1800. To daughter Ellen, feather bed, and $60 worth of furniture. To daughter Sarah, $1800. To daughter Phebe, $1800. To daughter Jane, $1800. To son Rees, $1800. To Anthony Levering, $666.67. To son Enoch, $1000. To son Lloyd, $1000. To granddaughter Phebe, $50. To granddaughter Phebe Smith, $50. To grandson Paul, $50. To grandson William, $50 and bible. Rem. of estate to sons Enoch and Paul.
Execs: Son Paul, and daughter Ellen. Wit: Charles and Silas Jones, and John Levering.

STEINROOK, CHRISTIAN. Pottstown.
March 18, 1820. Nov 29, 1822. 6.83
To wife, household goods, and interest of 400 pds. Personal estate to be sold, except wearing apparel. To son John, 50 pds. To son Christian, 50 pds. To son Samuel, 50 pds. Wearing apparel equally divided among sons John and Samuel. To Joseph Spidle, $50. To daughter Margaret, $50. Rem. of estate divided into 5 equal parts. To son John, 1/5 part. To son Samuel, 1/5 part. To son Christian, 1/5 part. To daughter Margaret, 1/5 part. To daughter Anna, 1/5 part.
Execs: Sons John and Samuel, and son in law Peter Moser. Wit: George Leaff, and John Reifsnyder.

SCHELEOP, VALENTINE. Frederick.
Jan 13, 1822. Nov 30, 1822. 6.84
To wife Feronica, household goods, and interest of 1000 pds. yearly. To son Daniel, farm, in Frederick, containing 164 acres subject to the payment of 10 pds. per acre and 1000 pds. Remaining 520 pds. to be divided equally into 3 parts. To son Abraham, 1/3 equal part. to daughter Catharine, wife of George Smith, 1/3 equal part. To 3 grandchildren: Samuel, Sarah, and Maria Kurtz, 1/3 part.
Exec: Son Daniel. Wit: Henry Daub, and John Hoffman.

LESHER, RACHEL. Pottstown.
Sept 9, 1820. Dec 2, 1822. 6.86
To nephew James Lesher, and nieces Hester and Rachel, equal part of estate. To niece Hester, silver tea spoons. To niece Rachel, silver tea spoons, and household goods. To niece Susanna, silver tea tongs. To nephew William, bed, quilt. To Catharine Lesher, widow of William Lesher, interest of $200 yearly, during widowhood, and after her death divided equally among children.
Execs: Peter Hertzog, and Joseph Miller. Wit: John Taylor, and Christian Reiner, and Edward Stiles.

RICHARDSON, JOHN. New Hanover.
Sept 18, 1816. Dec 3, 1822. 6.87
Estate to be sold. To daughter in law Salome, $300 yearly. To daughter in law Nancy, $20 yearly.
Execs: Sons Mark and George. Wit: Adam Worthman, and Peter Fritz.

WARING, ELIJAH. Philadelphia.
Feb 22, 1821. Dec 9, 1822. 6.89
To wife Sarah, use and profits of rents and bond, and household goods. To son Elijah, bible, and watch, etc. To brother Edward, $600. To William Allen, and Joseph Allen, $600, each. To nephew Samuel, $100. To Richard Smith, $300. Rem. of estate to son Elijah.
Codicil dated, Feb 22, 1821. To brother Edward, interest of 500 pds.
Execs: Samuel Emlen, Richard Smith, Daniel Elliott, and brother Edward.

Wit: Benjamin Bryant, Thomas Lynd, and Mordecai Lewis.

GEORGE, GEORGE. Horsham.
Aug 12, 1822. Dec 12, 1822. 6.95
To wife Margaret, $24, and household and use of farm, during widowhood. To daughter Catharine, $50. To daughter Mary, $130. To daughter Eliza, $50. To daughter Elizabeth, $50. To granddaughter Elizabeth, $50.
Execs: Son in law Isaac Fetzer, and Samuel Mann. Wit: Joseph and Robert Kenderdine.

UMSTED, HARMAN. Limerick.
Oct 5, 1819. Dec 14, 1822. 6.96
Estate to be sold and rem. divided into 6 equal parts. To son Joseph, 1/6 part. To son Thomas, 1/6 part. To son Arnold, 1/6 part. To son David, 1/6 part. To daughter Mary, 1/6 part. To son Jacob, 1/6 part.
Execs: Sons: Thomas, Joseph, Arnold, and David. Wit: Peter Longaker, and Jacob Rittenhouse.

COLTMAN, JOSEPH. Moreland.
June 30, 1822. Dec 17, 1822. 6.97
To wife Jane, household goods, and use of house. Rem. of estate to be sold and money given to daughter Ann.
Exec: Thomas Shoemaker. Wit: Anthony Yerkes and Hiram Ayres.

BOWER, SAMUEL. Douglass.
Feb 23, 1820. Dec 26, 1822. 6.99
To wife Elizabeth, 350 pds. Rem. of estate divided equally among children, John, Samuel, Andrew, Susanna, Barbara, Deborah, Elizabeth, and Anna.
Execs: Sons John and Andrew. Wit: William Weiss, and Jacob Allabach.

FITZWATER, SARAH. Whitpain.
Oct 1, 1817. Dec 30, 1822. 6.100
To daughter Rachel, $40. To daughter Mary, 30 pds. To grandson Jesse, 10 pds. and interest. To granddaughter Sarah, buff colored bed quilt. Household goods, to be divided among daughters Rachel and Mary. To granddaughter Mary, case of drawers. To granddaughter Sarah, dinning table. Rem. of estate divided among sons: George, John, William, Thomas.
Execs: Son William and daughter Mary. Wit: Israel and John Robinson.

KLINE, JOHN. Hatfield.
Oct 9, 1822. Jan 4, 1823. 6.101
To wife Mary, household goods, and use of farm. To Sarah, wife of Abraham King, $100. Guardian, John Funk.
Execs: Abraham Harman, and Abraham King. Wit: John Frich, and Henry Shellenberger, Cadwalder Foulke.

PORTER, JOHN. Norriton.

Sept 21, 1814. Jan 7, 1823. 6.107
To wife Mary, all estate, and after her death to be equally divided among children: Robert, Margaret, John, Joseph, and Benjamin.
Execs: Wife Mary, and Stephen Porter. Wit: William Hamill, and William Bean.

HEIST, JOHN. Upper Hanover.
Oct 8, 1822. Jan 14, 1823. 6.104.
To wife Anna, household goods, and farming utensils. To daughter Elizabeth, 62 pds., 10 s. To daughter Maria, 62 pds., 10 s. To 9 children: Henry, George, Conrad, John, Peter, Magdalena, Christina, Maria, and Elizabeth, 150 pds. each. To sons: Henry, George, Conrad, and daughter Magdalena, 50 pds. each. To son John, and daughter Christina, and son Peter, and daughters Mary and Elizabeth, 50 pds. each. To Peter Keiber, $30.
Execs: Sons Peter, John and George. Wit: Jacob and Peter Miller.

EVANS, PETER. Montgomery.
July 6, 1818. Jan 6, 1823. 6.106
To son John, books, and 150 pds. To son David, 250 pds. and desk. To son Septimus, household goods. To son Peter, 250 pds. and desk, and book case, and wearing apparel. To daughter Lydia, 200 pds. To daughter Sarah, 400 pds. and feather bed, etc. To grandson Jonathan, 80 pds. Codicil dated, May 25, 1819. To daughter Lydia, 50 pds. and feather bed. To daughters Lydia and Sarah, stock.
Exec: Son John. Wit: Walter Evans, Owen Jenkins, and Evan Jones.

SHUNK, CHRISTIAN. Limerick.
Oct 4, 1820. Jan 18, 1823. 6.108
To son Abraham, 100 pds. To granddaughter Mary, $100.
Execs: Samuel Gross, and William Towers. Wit: William Dismant, and Frederick Schrauder.

SCHULTZ, ABRAHAM. Upper Hanover.
May 12, 1822. Jan 24, 1823. 6.109
To wife Regina, household goods, and 500 pds. To son Joseph, tract of land containing 10 acres, 12 perches.
Execs: Sons Adam and Isaac. Wit: Matthias Gerhart, and Jeremiah Meshter.

EVANS, JAMES.
Nov 28, 1822. Feb 1, 1823. 6.111
To wife Mary, use of house and household goods. To son Mark, tract of land containing 112 acres. To daughter Elizabeth, 150 pds. To Exrs. 9 pds. each. To son Samuel's 4 children, 40 pds. To grandson Jesse, 10 pds. To granddaughter Eliza, 10 pds. To granddaughter Maria, 10 pds. To grandson George, 10 pds. To daughter Ruth Missimer, 150 pds.

Execs: Sons James and Mark, Wit: Jacob Hubley, and James Evans.

SAMMS, ANN. Moreland.
Aug 14, 1806. Feb 5, 1823. 6.113
To 3 daughters: Mary, Ann, and Sarah, wearing apparel. To son in law John Wood, feather bed, etc. To son John, interest of money and rem. of household goods.
Execs: Son Thomas, and son in law John Wood. Wit: Benjamin Lloyd, and Elizabeth Lloyd.

MILLER, MARGARET. Moreland.
May 14, 1818. Feb 11, 1823. 6.114
To Margaret McClean, feather bed, etc., and $1000. To John and Mary McCahron, $200, each. To William, John, and Mary McCahron, $100 each. To Hetty Kerr, $100. To Lydia McClean, rem. of estate.
Execs: Alexander McClean, and Hiram McNeill. Wit: Michael Fetter, and James Hawkins.

JOHNSON, JOHN. Perkiomen and Skippack.
Dec 21, 1821. Feb 14, 1823. 6.115
To wife Barbara, farm, containing 75 acres and household goods. To son John, farm, containing 41 acres. To children: Jacob, Benjamin, John, Magdalena, Catharine, Barbara and Anna, 200 pds. each.
Execs: Son Jacob and William Slotterar. Wit: Henry and Joel Hunsicker.

MECKLER, JACOB. New Hanover.
Oct 22, 1822. Feb 14, 1823. 6.116
To wife Catharine, household goods, and maintenance, during widowhood, and 1/2 of money and rem. to be kept in place for wife.
Execs: John Aldeman, and Michael Dross. Wit: Ferderick Gilbert, and Philip Boyer.

BOOZ, MATTHIAS. Gwynedd.
Jan 17, 1823. Feb 15, 1823. 6.118
To wife Catharine, case of drawers, and household goods, and all realty. To son Samuel, and daughter Phoebe, $50 each. Rem. divided among children: Catharine, Jacob, Margaret, Matthias, Conrad, and John, Mary, Phoebe, and Samuel, equally. To daughter Phoebe, 1/2 dozen red chairs.
Execs: Sons Jacob and Samuel. Wit: George and John Heist.

SHEID, CHRISTIAN. Montgomery.
Feb 6, 1823. Feb 23, 1823. 6.119
To housekeeper Catharine Frasher, $500 and household goods. To Catharine, daughter of Peter Frasher, $200. To son Jacob, $16. To wife Susanna, $1.00.
Execs: Daniel Jacoby, and Jacob Weidemoyer. Wit: Charles Garber, and George Sheid.

GLOESS, DANIEL. Douglass.
Dec 4, 1822. Feb 27, 1823. 6.120
To wife Sarah, household goods. To brother Jacob, wearing apparel. All estate which has not been bequeathed to be sold.
Exec: Daniel Miller. Wit: Henry Zuber, and Frederick Schoenly.

HAHN, JOHN. New Hanover.
Feb 9, 1823. March 7, 1823. 6.123
To wife Catharine, tract of land containing 30 acres. To son Joseph, $200. To son William, rem. of realty.
Execs: Richard Jacobs and William White. Wit: Nicholas Slough, and Jesse Griffith.

ESHBACH, CATHARINE. Hartford.
Oct 2, 1809. March 10, 1823. 6.125
Estate to be divided into 4 equal parts. To son Jacob, 1/4 part. To son Abraham, 1/4 part. To daughter Susanna, 1/4 part. To daughter Elizabeth, 1/4 part.
Execs: Son Jacob and son in law John Bower. Wit: Isaac Barton, and Jacob Allebach.

VAN COURT, CORNELIUS. Moreland.
Jan 21, 1823. March 10, 1823. 6.125
To wife Elizabeth, household goods, and 100 pds. yearly. to daughter Sarah, mahogany dinning table. To son John, desk, etc. To daughter Maria, large chest, looking glass, etc. To Hannah, bed. To son William wearing apparel. Rem. of estate to be sold. To son Jonathan's son Charles, 25 pds. Rem. divided equally among children.
Execs: Son in law Stacy Thomas, and Hiram McNeill. Wit: William Ayres, and William White.

PAWLING, HENRY. Lower Providence.
July 5, 1817. March 21, 1823. 6.127
To son William, tract of land containing 250 acres. To son Henry, 150 pds. Rem. of estate to son Levi and 1/4 part to each of the children.
Execs: Son Levi and son in law James Milnor. Wit: Jonathan Farmer, and Joseph Thomas.

SPARE, HENRY. Worcester.
Feb 24, 1823. April 16, 1823. 6.130
To son William, farm, of 130 acres.
Exec: Son William. Wit: David McCrea, and Hannah Spare, and Frederick Conrad.

SCOTT, SUSANNA. Moreland.
June 15, 1821. June 21, 1823. 6.131
To sister Margaret, wearing apparel. To niece Susanna, table coverlet

cotton and wool. Rem. of estate to be equally divided among 5 nieces: Elizabeth, Susanna, Hester, Margaret, and Mary. Execs: Niece Elizabeth and Hester. Wit: Ann and Maria Stewart.

DeHAVEN, JONATHAN. Upper Merion.
Oct 4, 1822. April 21, 1823. 6.132
To brother John DeHaven, tract of land where I dwell. To brother John and Peter, all personal estate.
Execs: Jonathan John, and Peter DeHaven. Wit: Lawrence Ramsey, and Randolph Supplee.

GODSHALK, MARGARET. Towamencin.
April 10, 1823. April 23, 1823. 6.132
To brother William, all estate.
Execs: Jacob and William Godshalk. Wit: Jacob Metz, and John Tyson.

EVANS, HANNAH. Philadelphia.
Sept 9, 1822. May 14, 1823. 6.133
To son Jonathan, $5.00. To son George, $5.00. To daughter Eleanor, $5.00. To granddaughter Emiline, $5.00 To grandsons Isaac and Edward Davis, $5.00. To granddaughter Rachel, $5.00. Rem. of estate to son Enos.
[*Annotation: The original reads: to my daughter Eleanor Harper. To my granddaughter Emmeline Evans, child of my son Nathan Evans, deceased. To my grandson Isaac R. Davis and Edward M. Davis, children of my daughter Elizabeth deceased. To my granddaughter Rachel Evans. Mr. E. Wood Jan 4, 1922.*]
Exec: Son Enos. Wit: John Piper, George Benner, and John Hackett.

LANDES, JOHN. Franconia.
To wife 100 pds. to be paid by son Jacob. To son Jacob, dwelling house and 82 acres. To children: Jacob, Abraham, Mary, wife of Christian Moyer, 500 pds. equally.
Execs: Son Jacob and son in law Christian Moyer. Wit: Michael Shoemaker, and John Landes and Abraham Detwiler.

HOUGH, SILAS. Montgomery.
May 12, 1823. June 10, 1823. 6.136
To wife Elizabeth, family bible, and gold watch, and interest of rem. of estate. To Philadelphia Baptist Association, $1000. To Baptist Church of Montgomery, $100. To niece Susanna, interest of $200. To nieces Sarah, Ann, and Charlotte, $50 each. To grand nephew William and John Crispen, land containing 17 acres.
Execs: Wife Elizabeth, and brother in law John Hart, and Rev. Joseph Mathias, and Rev. Thomas B. Montanye. Wit: Evan Jones, and John Eder.

RENNINGER, MAGDALENA. Upper Hanover.
Oct 22, 1822. June 6, 1823. 6.138

To daughter Elizabeth, all estate. Wit: Jonas Borger, and David Seesholtz.

ROBERTS, JOHN. Montgomery.
April 1, 1815. June 20, 1823. 6.139
To nephew Mordecai tract of land containing 35 acres. To nephew Charles, farm, containing 200 acres. To nieces Jane and Martha, farm, containing 1 1/4 acre, equally. Tract of land containing 521 acres to be divided into 6 parts. To nephew John, 1/6 part. To nephew Eldad, 1/6 part. To niece Mary, 1/6 part. To niece Ann, 1/6 part. To sons and daughters of brother Mordecai, 1/6 part each. Remaining 1/6 part to be sold. To half sister Elizabeth, $50. To John Mullen, $50. To Ann Thomas, $50. To Benjamin Hancock, $50. to Robert Jones, $50. To James Chapman, $50. To granddaughter Juluan Chapman, $50. To Trustees of North Wales Meeting, $50. To brother Mordecai, wearing apparel. Rem. of estate to nephew Mordecai.
Execs: William Foulke, and Cadwalder Foulke. Wit: George Roberts, and David Ambler.

SORVER, PHILIP. Hatfield.
June 15, 1803. June 21, 1823. 6.141
To wife Margaret, house, and household goods, and $32. To daughters and granddaughters interest that shall arise after decease of wife.
Execs: Son in law Edward Jenkins, and brother John. Wit: Peter Hoxworth, and Thomas Davis.

BROOKE, JAMES. Upper Merion.
Oct 18, 1822. July 18, 1823. 6.143
To wife Ann, all estate.
Execs: William Jones, and Peter Rambo. Wit: Benjamin Brooke, and Samuel Humphreys.

CRAIG, DANIEL. Norriton.
April 2, 1823. July 19, 1823. 6.144
To wife Jane, household goods. To son James, oil mill, and tract of land subject to the payment of $500. To 3 daughters: Jane, Hannah, and Hannah, $1000, each. To daughter Joanna, $500.
Exec: Son Lewis. Wit: Joseph Thomas, and William Zimmerman.

LONG, HUGH. Upper Merion.
July 1, 1823. Aug 7, 1823. 6.146
To wife Elizabeth, household goods, after wife's death estate to be sold and money divided among children: Alexander, Lewis, William, Hugh, Isabella, equally.
Execs: Jonathan Roberts, and wife Elizabeth. Wit: D. Wolmer, Joseph Thomas, and Andrew Crawford.

WISMER, HENRY. Lower Providence.

313

Aug 23, 1823. Sept 6, 1823. 6.148
To wife Mary, house and household goods. Personal estate to be sold.
Execs: Wife Mary, and John Shearer. Wit: Thomas Francis, and Peter Wissler.

YORGY, HENRY. Douglass.
May 4, 1816. Sept 20, 1823. 6.148
To wife Catharine, household goods, and 460 pds. to 6 children: Peter, Mathias, Henry, John, Ann and Mary, each 200 pds. Rem. of estate to aforesaid 6 children.
Exec: George Bucher. Wit: George Renninger, and Peter Fegle.

FULMORE, GEORGE. Abington.
Sept 11, 1823. Oct 7, 1823. 6.150
To son George, 150 pds. Rem. of money after expenses are paid to be divided among 3 children: son George, and daughters Mary and Elizabeth.
Execs: Jacob Fulmore, and son in law Jonathan Bright. Wit: Israel Hallowell and Joshua Ward.

KENDALL, HENRY. Limerick.
March 4, 1822. Oct 7, 1823. 6.151
To wife Mary, $80 yearly, and house, and household goods. To son Joseph, tract of land. To grandson Henry, 200 pds.
Exec: Son Joseph. Wit: Samuel Groff, and William Towers.

CASSEL, ISAAC. Perkiomen and Skippack.
March 18, 1813. Oct 16, 1823. 6.152
To wife Magdalena, household goods, and 50 pds. and dwelling house, and interest of 450 pds.
Codicil dated Jan 15, 1821. To son Abraham, 1500 pds. instead of 800 pds. To each of 3 sons, 50 pds. and 56 pds. to be equally divided among children.
Execs: Sons John and Jacob. Wit: Frederick Conrad, Jr., and Frederick Conrad, Sr.

SHOEMAKER, JANE. Cheltenham.
Aug 12, 1823. Oct 17, 1823. 6.155
Real estate to be sold. To Jane Downing, Susanna Fairbanks, Lydia Baldwin, and Tacy Ashbridge, each, $500. To Thomas Ashbridge, $500, interest thereof to be paid to Jane Maris. To sister Sarah, $300, and to each of her children, $200 and to sister Sarah, gold watch and silver coffee pot. To Abigail Shoemaker, Catharine Moore, and Sarah Lea, $200, each. Rem. of proceeds from sale divided equally among brothers and sisters. To Elizabeth Barrett, $300. To Mary Fletcher, silver coffee pot. To Sarah Govett, and Eleanor Berrel, $200, each. To John Saxon, $100. To Jane Hallowell, $50. To Ann Livezey, $50. To Hannah Bosler, $50. To Elizabeth McDonald, $50. To Leah Carr, $50. To Elizabeth Robeson,

$1000, and silver can. To Susan Sansom, table cloth. To Daniel Fletcher, riding carriage. To John and Isabella Wilson, each a bed stead. Rem. of household goods, and farming utensils to Samuel Charles Shoemaker.
Execs: Peter Robeson, and Charles Shoemaker. Wit: Richard Shoemaker, and Jacob Omengetter.

RIEFF, GEORGE. Perkiomen.
Sept 8, 1823. Oct 20, 1823. 6.158
To wife Ann, house, and household goods, and $60 annually. To sons: Israel, Jacob, and Samuel, 50 pds. each. Proceeds from sale and real estate to wife. To 5 younger children: Israel, Jacob, Samuel, Mary, and Rebecca, interest when they arrive at age.
Execs: Wife Ann, and Jacob Custer. Wit: John Winter, and John Hammil.

KRATZ, ISAAC. Lower Salford.
Dec 16, 1817. Oct 23, 1823. 6.159
To wife Maria, 300 pds. and household goods. To son Isaac, 1600 pds.
Exec: Son in law Henry Clements. Wit: Benjamin, Abraham, and Joseph Alderfer.

WEISNER, MARTIN. Douglass.
Sept 6, 1823. Oct 24, 1823. 6.161
To wife Elizabeth, 6 pds. annually, and household goods. To sons Henry and David, realty. To son John, 100 pds. To son George, 100 pds. To daughter Catharine, 100 pds. To daughter Elizabeth, 100 pds. To son John, 50 pds. To daughter Catharine, 50 pds. To daughter Elizabeth, 50 pds. Rem. of estate divided equally among children.
Execs: Sons Henry and David. Wit: Henry Swinehart, and John Stauffer.

GUY, JONATHAN. Gwynedd.
Jan 8, 1807. Oct 28, 1823. 6.162
To wife Barbara, all estate.
Exec: Wife Barbara. Wit: Rachel Lewis, and Joseph Lewis.

SHOEMAKER, JOSEPH. Gwynedd.
Aug 28, 1823. Oct 30, 1823. 6.163
To wife Martha, $1200, and household and income of $1000 and after her death $1000 to be divided equally among children. To son Abraham, $700. To son Jesse, $1500. To son Charles, $1200, and desk. To daughter Lydia, 600 pds. and silver watch. To 3 sons: Abraham, Jesse, and Charles, wearing apparel, equally. Estate to be sold. Rem. to wife, and children.
Execs: Son Jesse, and son in law Isaac Jeans. Wit: George and Thomas Shoemaker.

MILLER, ELIZABETH. Lower Providence.
Oct 16, 1822. Oct 30, 1823. 6.164
Estate to be sold and money divided among grandchildren. To sons:

Benjamin, John, and Samuel, 50 cents each. To 3 daughters: Elizabeth, wife of Thomas Hugh, Catharine, wife of John Corson, Mary, widow of Jonathan Jones, 50 cents each.
Execs: Jonathan Croll, and William White. Wit: John Force, and Philp Riner.

WELLS, LYDIA. Upper Merion.
March 26, 1810. Oct 30 1823. 6.166
To niece Mary Roberts, wearing apparel. To niece Sarah Moore's son Robert, chest of drawers. To niece's son Mordecai, bed, etc. To nieces, daughter Ann, and Mary, small chest of drawers. To 3 children of niece Sarah Moore, rem. of estate, equally.
Execs: Nephew Matthew Roberts, and Jonathan Roberts. Wit: Jonathan Philip, and Jonathan Cleaver.

DAVIS, ISAIAH. Pottsgrove.
March 7, 1823. Nov 1, 1823. 6.167
Farm to be sold, where I now dwell, containing 47 acres, 28 perches. To wife Sophia, bed, etc. To daughter Mary, bed, etc., and 100 pds. Rem. of estate divided into 6 equal shares. To son Thomas, one share. To daughter Ann, wife of Benjamin Casselberry, one share. To daughter Rebecca, wife of Jacob Casselberry, one share. To 3 grandchildren, one share. To daughter Esther, wife of George McElhney, one share. To daughter Mary, one share.
Execs: Son Thomas, and George Richard. Wit: Frederick Conrad, and Christian Hatfield.

POTTS, MARY. Pottstown.
July 17, 1821. Nov 4, 1823. 6.168
To son in law Joseph Potts, 100 pds. and silver coffee pot. To grandson James Hartley, colored silver tankard. To granddaughter Mary P. Smith, pint silver tankard. To daughter Sarah, silver tea pot. To daughter Harriet, silver bowl. To granddaughter Lousia, silver cream pitcher, and 1/2 dozen silver tea spoons, etc. To grandson David, silver soup ladle. To granddaughter Mary, silver sugar dish. Rem. of estate after expense are paid divided among daughters: Sarah, and Harriet, equally.
Execs: ____. Wit: Jacob Drinkhouse, and Mary Graham.

MOORE, RICHARD. Upper Merion.
Sept 11, 1823. Nov 5, 1823. 6.169
To wife Abigail, use of farm, and $2000, and use of $3000 annually, and household goods until daughter Eliza is 18 years old. To son Edwin, farm, containing 35 acres. To son Samuel, farm. To daughter Eliza, $3000.
Execs: Brother in law Peter Supplee, and Jonathan Cleaver. Wit: Jonathan Roberts, Robert Moore, and Alexander McCraig.

SPECHT, JACOB. New Hanover.

Oct 24, 1823. Nov 13, 1823. 6.171
To wife Catharine, household goods, and income of estate, during widowhood, and 10 acres of land.
Execs: Peter Fritz, and Michael Schweinhart. Wit: Matthias Gilbert, and George Richards.

KROUSE, DANIEL. Frederick.
Dec 3, 1814. Nov 21, 1823. 6.173
To wife Margaret, household goods, and house, and interest of $350 pds. Personal estate to be sold and money divided among children: Sarah, wife of George Adam, John, Daniel, Molly, wife of Frederick Wald, Rebecca, wife of Emrich, equally.
Execs: Sons Daniel and Jacob. Wit: Sarah Boyer, and Benjamin Markley.

NORMAN, MARY. Whitpain.
June 27, 1823. Nov 22, 1823. 6.174
To daughter Sarah, 450. To daughter Esther, $50. To daughter Mary, $100. To son Samuel, bond of $62. To son Jonathan, $50. To son Ezekiel, $50. To grandson Mahlon, bond of $81. To 3 grandchildren: Mary, Margaret, and Jacob, $1.00 equally. To granddaughter Mary, case of drawers. Rme. of wearing apparel, and bedding to daughters Sarah and Mary.
Execs: Daughter Sarah, and son in law Thomas Butler. Wit: William Ellis.

CASSELBERRY, ANN.
Feb 21, 1820. Nov 24, 1823. 6.175
Wearing apparel, to be equally divided among children. To son William, farm, where I now dwell, containing 1/2 acre. All personal property to be divided among children.
Exec: Son William. Wit: Peter Warner.

IREDELL, ROBERT. Montgomery.
Oct 7, 1823. Nov 27, 1823. 6.176
To wife Susanna, 1000 pds. and farm, and household goods. To 3 daughters rem. of household goods, equally.
Codicil dated July 22, 1823. To wife Susanna, $50 immediately after my death. Rem. from farm, to be divided equally among 3 daughters. To Jacob Fitzwater, $400.
Execs: Wife Susanna and son in law Thomas Shoemaker. Wit: Cadwalder and Franklin Foulke.

FREEDLEY, HENRY. Pottstown.
Sept 25, 1823. Nov 27, 1823. 6.180
To wife Catharine, household goods. To daughter Elizabeth, 2 tracts of lands, subject to the payment of $1000. To daughter Harriet, 1/2 equal part of estate.
Execs: Sons Jacob and John, and Samuel. Wit: Peter Bastres, and R. E.

317

Hobart.

WATERMAN, HANNAH. Abington.
Oct 6, 1822. Nov 29, 1823. 6.182
To son Joseph, 50 pds. To son Isaiah, farm, containing 100 acres and $40. To grandchildren: Isaac, Agnes, Mary, and John, 40 pds. equally. To daughter Priscilla, 40 pds. To granddaughter Eleanor, 20 pds. To son Isaiah, profits of plantation. To granddaughter Hannah, table cloth. Rem. of estate to sons Joseph, and Isaiah, equally.
Execs: sons Joseph and Isaiah. Wit: William Grant, and Joel Cadwalder.

WILSON, ENOS. Franconia.
Feb 11, 1823. Dec 5, 1823. 6.183
To sister Eleanor, $80 and watch. Rem. of estate to father.
Exec: Father. Wit: Jonah Miller, and William Wilson.

AMOS, ABEL. Lower Merion.
Nov 2, 1823. Dec 6, 1823. 6.184
To wife Margaret, all estate. To mother Elizabeth, $5.00. To brother Abraham, and his wife, $5.00. To brother Walter, $5.00. To sister Hannah, wife of Andrew Foy, $5.00. To sister Agnes, wife of George Razor, $5.00.
Execs: Wife Margaret, and sons Amos and John. Wit: John Sinket, and Francis Murphy.

ADMINISTRATIONS

McCLINTICK, ALEXANDER. Oct 16, 1786. Sarah McClintick, adm.
McCLEARY, THOMAS. March 18, 1793. Archibald Darrah, adm.
McCLINTOCK, THOMAS. New Hanover. Nov 18, 1793. Robert McClintock, adm.
MAYBURRY, THOMAS. Pottsgrove. May 13, 1797. Rebecca Mayburry, John Warder, Thomas Warder, adms.
MORGAN, WILLIAM. April 30, 1792. Anthony Crothers, adm.
McCAMMAN, WILLIAM. Norriton. Oct 8, 1793. Ezekiel Rhods, adm.
NEWBERRY, ANN. Worcester. April 1, 1795. Jesse Bean, adm.
NYCE, GEORGE. Frederick. Dec 12, 1790. John Nyce, George Nyce, adms.
NEIMAN, HENRY. June 15, 1790. Mary Neiman, adm.
NEIMAN, JACOB. New Hanover. March 23, 1790. Andrew Bittle, Jacob Neiman, adms.
NICHOLASON, JOHN. March 9, 1791. John Neidigh, Christian Bryman, Adms.
OBERTIER, PHILIP. Towamencin. Oct 31, 1794. Elizabeth Obertier, adm.

NANNA, REESE. Plymouth. Feb 9, 1786. Christian Steer, adm.
OBERHOLTZER, SAMUEL. Towamencin. Nov. 14, 1791. Barbara Oberholtzer.
PROTZMAN, CONRAD. Providence. April 7, 1788. Barbara Protzman, George Sherff, adms.
PAUL, DAVID. Limerick. Dec 4, 1789. Samuel Pennepacker.
PAUL, DANIEL. Limerick. Dec 7, 1792. Catharine Paul, Paul Custer, adms.
POTTS, DAVID. March 17, 1798. Joseph Potts, Jr., adm.
PITT, ELIZABETH. Sept 15, 1794. John Pitt, adm.
POTTS, EDWARD B. June 13, 1799. Francis R. Potts, adm.
POLAND, GEORGE. Montgomery. Sept 22, 1786. Elizabeth Poland, adm.
PENNEBECKER, HENRY. Skippack and Perkiomen. June 9, 1792. John Pennebacker, adm.
PRUTZMAN, HANNAH. Limerick. Aug 13, 1792. Jacob Prutzman, adm.
PALMER, JOHN. Horsham. Dec 5, 1785. Thomas Palmer, George Palmer, adms.
PHIPPS, JOHN. Whitpain. Feb 23, 1790. John Phipps, Sr., adm.
PAWLING, JOHN. Skippack. May 17, 1790. Elizabeth Pawling, John Heister, adms.
PAUL, JOSPEH. Horsham. Nov 10, 1794. Esther Paul, adm.
PAWLING, NATHAN. Providence. April 17, 1795. Willimina Pawling.
PETERS, SAMUEL. March 18, 1793. Archibald Darrah, adm.
PHIPPS, SAMUEL. Cheltenham. May 16, 1793. Ann Phipps, adm.
QUEE, SETH. Upper Dublin. Nov 27, 1786. John Jarret, adm.
PENNEPACKER, WYAND. Upper Hanover. April 14, 1795. Henry Pennepacker, adm.
RELLER, CONRAD. Upper Salford. Oct 23, 1795. Catharine Reller, George Reller, adms.
RAMBO, GEORGE. Upper Merion. March 28, 1786. Mary Rambo, Jonas Rambo, adms.
ROW, GEORGE. Jan 23, 1793. Nicholas Cressman, adm.
RIDDLE, GEORGE. Oct 10, 1797. Thomas Riddle, adm.
ROBINSON, JAMES. Plymouth. Dec 27, 1785. John Robinson, Jonathan Colley, adms.
RAMBO, JEREMIAH. Jan 25, 1791. Sarah Rambo, John Rambo, adms.
ROBERTS, JOHN. Upper Merion. Jan 25, 1791. Isaac Davis, Joseph Roberts, adms.
RALLWAGON, J. FREDERICK. Douglass. March 23, 1791. Ludwick Shick.
RAMSEY, JAMES. May 29, 1792. Jacob Swink.
RAMBO, JOHN, SR. Upper Merion. July 18, 1794. Elizabeth Rambo, John Rambo, adms.
ROBINSON, JOHN. Lower Merion. May 20, 1795. Mary Robinson, adm.

RICHARDSON, JONATHAN. Oct 31, 1795. Margaret Richards, Joel Richards, adms.
RUTH, JACOB. Hatfield. Feb 12, 1798. John Evans, adm.
RUSSEL, JAMES. Lower Merion. April 30, 1798. Isaac Watkin, adm.
REINHART, LAWRENCE. Feb 12, 1798. Jacob Schneider, adm.
REX, MARGARET. Gwynedd. Feb 17, 1785. William Rex, adm.
ROBERTS, MARY. March 7, 1786. William Nanna, adm.
REESE, PHILIP. Upper Merion. Oct 24, 1784. Enos Reese, adm.
RICHARDS, PATRICK. March 18, 1793. Archibald Darrah, adm.
ROWEN, PATRICK. March 18, 1793. Archibald Darrah, adm.
RITTENHOUSE, WILLIAM. Worcester. Oct 19, 1792. Margaret Rittenhouse, Jacob Rittenhouse, adms.
REX, WILLIAM. Springfield. June 22, 1795. Jesse Rex, Jacob Acoff, adms.
ROBERTS, WILLIAM. Abington. July 3, 1795. Isaac Roberts, Jesse Roberts, adms.
REILEY, WILLIAM. Norriton. July 30, 1798. Samuel Bard, adm.
SHAINLINE, ANDREW. Upper Merion. Dec 27, 1785. Magdalena Shainline, Nicholas Bower, adms.
STREPER, ABRAHAM. Lower Merion. Oct 9 1792. Mary Streper, Joseph Price, amds.
SHOEMAKER, BENJAMIN. Cheltenham. Oct. 30, 1793. James Shoemaker, Benjamin Shoemaker, Eli Shoemaker, adms.
SPARE, BENJAMIN. Worcester. Jan 20, 1798. Mary Spare, Daniel Spare, Jacob Beyer, adms.
STALL, CHRISTIAN. Providence. March 2, 1786. Daniel Stall, adm.
SOWER, CHRISTOPHER. Oct 11, 1788. C. Zimmerman, adm.
STEER, CHRISTIAN. Whitemarsh. Jan 21, 1791. Mary Steer, George Hitner, adms.
STEWART, CHRISTOPHER. Norriton. June 15, 1799. Elizabeth Stewart, Wm. Henderson, Jr., adms.
SCHULTZ, GEORGE. Upper Hanover. May 10, 1797. Gregory Schultz, Baltzer Schultz, adms.
SHOEMAKER, GEORGE. Cheltenham. Dec. 26, 1798. George Shoemaker, Richard Roberts, adms.
STYER, JACOB. Whitemarsh. May 2, 1791. Elizabeth Styer, Henry Styer, adms.
SWISEFORT, JOHN. Marlborough. Aug 29, 1791. Mary Swisefort, Peter Swisefort, adms.
SMITH, MICHAEL. Mar 9, 1786. Mary Smith, William Smith, adms.
SWANNER, MARGARET. Nov 25, 1793. Matthias Guist, adm.
SCHNIDER, NICHOLAS. Frederick. May 13, 1799. Benjamin Schnider, Nicholas Schnider, adms.
SCHRIEVER, PHILIP. Lower Merion. Oct 17, 1798. Ann Schriever, adm.
SUTCH, WILLIAM. Horsham. Nov 6, 1786. Mary Sutch, Benjamin Sutch, adms.

TYSON, ABRAHAM. Abington. April 11, 1796. Thomas Tyson, adm.
TYSON, ABRAHAM, JR. Abington. Dec 12, 1796. Abraham Tyson, Sr., John Tyson, adms.
THURNINGER, BENJAMIN. Aug 30, 1797. George Pfleager, George Bechtell, adms.
THOMPSON, HANNAH, Norriton. March 23, 1790. Robert Thompson, adm.
TENNIS, ISRAEL. Towamencin. Dec 30, 1790. Jane Tennis, adm.
TOMPKINS, JONATHAN. Whitemarsh. June 12, 1786. Ann Tompkins, adm.
THAW, JOHN. Abington. April 10, 1795. Benjamin Thaw, adm.
TODD, MARTHA. Moreland. Dec 30, 1797. William Todd, adm.
TREXLER, PETER. Lower Merion. Nov 18, 1784. Catharine Trexler, adm.
THOMAS, RICHARD. Lower Merion. May 15, 1798. Ann Thomas, adm.
UPDEGROVE, ABRAHAM. Perkiomen. Jan 5, 1788. Henry Updegrove, adm.
VERNER, ELIZABETH. June 25, 1799. Henry Timanus, adm.
UMSTEAD, HENRY. Perkiomen. Dec 6, 1788. John Umstead, Herman Umstead, adms.
VANDERSLICE, JACOB. Pottsgrove, April 29, 1793. Thomas Vanderslice, William Thomas, adms.
WARNER, ANTHONY. Lower Merion. Sept 29, 1798. Rachel Warner, adm.
WICK, BALTHAZAR. March 28, 1787. Christian Dull, adm.
WISLER, CASPER. Oct 24, 1785. John Wolf Wisler, adm.
WEIGNER, CATHARINE. Perkiomen. Jan 29, 1787. Henry Smith, adm.
WELKER, DIETRICK. Providence. May 16, 1786. William Rittenhouse.
WARD, DENNIS. March 18, 1793. Archibald Darrah, adm.
WEEK, GEORGE. Gwynedd. Oct 30, 1784. Margaret Week, George Schellinger.
WEASNER, GEORGE. May 10, 1796. Morton Weasner, Gabriel Cline, adms.
WOELPER, HANNAH. Limerick. Jan 1, 1799. Matthew Hoover, adm.
WYANT, JACOB. Gwynedd. March 10, 1785. Jacob Wisemer, William Rex, adms.
WEBER, JACOB. Worcester. June 29, 1791. Christian Weber, Abraham Weber, Benjamin Weber, Eve Weber, adms.
WOOD, JOSPEH. Whitemarsh. Oct 25, 1791. Thomas Morgan, adm.
WOLMER, JACOB. June 13, 1793. Daniel Thomson, adm.
WHITMAN, JOHN. Douglass. July 4, 1793. Michael Whitman, adm.
WINTER, PETER. Lower Merion. March 26, 1788. Benjamin Holland, adm.
WENTZ, PETER. Whitpain. Oct 16, 1793. Joseph Tyson, Mordecai Jones, adms.

WAGGONER, PETER. Norriton. July 18, 1797. Catharine Waggoner, John Fleek, adms.
WILSON, THOMAS. Douglass. April 10, 1797. Catharine Wilson, adm.
WALTON, THOMAS. Moreland. Aug 19, 1797. Silas Walton, Samuel Gummere, adms.
WHITE, WILLIAM. Oct 13, 1794. John White, adm.
WRIGHT, WILLIAM. Lower Merion. Oct 13, 1795. Tacey Wright, adm.
WALLACE, WILLIAM. Pottsgrove. June 13, 1798. Elizabeth Wallace, Amos Jones, adms.
YEAKLE, BALTZER. Towamencin. May 18, 1789. Abraham Yeakle, Abraham Andrews, adms.
ZIMMERMAN, CONRAD. Marlborough. Jan 1, 1786. Jacob Zimmerman, Matthias Sheively, adms.
ZIGLER, DILLMAN. Lower Salford. Oct 18, 1794. Jacob Ziegler, adm.
ZIEGLER, ANDREW. Oct 18, 1794. Andrew Ziegler, Jacob Ziegler, Dillman Ziegler, adms.
YERKES, ELIAS. Moreland. March 25, 1799. Elias Yerkes, Isaac Yerkes, adms.
ZERN, FREDERICK. Whitemarsh. Mar 11, 1793. John Zern, Jacob Zern, adms.
ZINSENDENFER, MARTIN. New Hanover. Oct 19, 1784. Conrad Kneeley, Michael Kneely, adms.
MORGAN, THOMAS. Hatfield. Aug 19, 1799. Thos. Morgan, Jr., adm.
BOYLE, JOHN. Upper Merion. Aug 26, 1799. William Henderson, adm.
BARTLESON, LEVI. Upper Merion. Aug 26, 1799. Mary Bartleson, adm.
STELTZ, JOHN. Berks County. Sept 28, 1799. John Snell, adm.
ARCHIBALD, ALEXANDER. Norriton. March 18, 1793. Archibald Darrah, adm.
ALLEBACH, ABRAHAM. Hatfield. Oct 30, 1794. Catharine Allebach, Jacob Longacre, adms.
ALDERFER, JACOB. Lower Salford. Jan 20, 1798. Frederick Alderfer, Isaac Alderfer, adms.
ACKLEY, MORDECAI. Moreland. Nov 12, 1798. Rebecca Ackley, adm.
ADAM (Negro). Oct 28, 1796. Ginn Cain, adm.
AMBROS, RUTH. (No papers.)
ALLINGER, STEPHEN. Lower Merion. March 2, 1792. George Stout, adm.
BELL, ANN. Norriton. Oct 13, 1790. Abraham Morgan, Deborah Page.
BELL, ANDREW. Norriton. March 18, 1793. Archibald Darrah, adm.
BOORS, ARNOLD. Towamencin. Jan 18, 1795. Henry Boors, Jacob Kolb, adms.
BARTLESON, BARTLE. Norriton. May 17, 1794. James Bartleson, Robert Knox, adms.
AUSTIN, THOMAS. Moreland. Nov 13, 1798. Joshua Comley, William West, adms.
BILLEW, DANIEL. Moreland. May 11, 1789. Rebecca Billew, adms.

BURRES, DANIEL. Whitpain. Nov 13, 1798. Job Roberts, adm.
BARRET, CASPER. New Hanover. Aug 17, 1796. (No papers.)
BARTLESON, ENOS. Montgomery. June 20, 1791. Mary Bartleson, Edward Jenkins, adms.
BARTLESON, EZRA. Plymouth. Aug 4, 1796. George M. Potts, adm.
BARD, FRANCIS. Frederick. April 22, 1788. Gottfried Saklor, adm.
BOULLONGE, FREDERICK. Whitpain. Jan 25, 1798. Catharine Boullonge, Israel Robinson, adm.
BOLIN, GEORGE. Montgomery. Sept 22, 1786. Elizabeth Bolin, adm.
BEAKLEY, GEORGE. Pottstown. April 1, 1795. Frederick Matthew, adm.
BEIDEMAN, GEORGE. Douglass. Nov 20, 1797. Catharine Beideman, Adam Beideman, adms.
BEWLEY, GEORGE. Upper Merion. Jan 7, 1799. Isaac Bewley, adm.
BATES, HUMPHREY. Montgomery. Feb 20, 1785. James Hamer, adm.
BOYER, HENRY. Gwynedd. July 30, 1792. Margaret Boyer, adm.
BROWER, ISAAC. Dougalss. Dec 19, 1796. Henry Gabel, Abraham Brower, adm.
BARTLESON, JOHN. Norriton. March 20, 1786. Mary Bartleson, David Waggoner, adms.
BISHOF, JOHN. Marlborough. Oct 27, 1786. Andrew Reed, adm.
BURKHARD, JOHN GEORGE. New Hanover. Feb 28, 1789. David Burkhard, Tobias Yerger, adms.
BARTLESON, JANE. March 25, 1789. Abner Bartleson, Bartle Bartleson, adms.
BEAN, JOSHUA. Providence. Oct 5, 1793. William Lane, adm.
BORELAN, JAMES. Plymouth. April 15, 1794. John Pugh, John Edwards, adms.
BEWLEY, JOHN. Upper Merion. Jan 7, 1799. Isaac Bewley, adm.
BERKEY, MARY. Lower Salford. May 11, 1798. Christian Berkey, adm.
BOURDMAN, MOSES. Providence. May 29, 1792. Jacob Swenk, adm.
BROOKS, MICHAEL. Norriton. March 18, 1793. Archibald Darrah, adm.
BRAND, MICHAEL. New Hanover. Aug 16, 1794. Philip Brand, adm.
BARTLESON, NICHOLAS. April 12, 1790. Abner Bartleson, Bartle Bartleson.
BOORS, PETER. Lower Salford. May 24, 1797. Mary Boors, Matthias Stouver.
BRADY, PATRICK. Plymouth. Oct 10, 1798. Patrick Mulveny, adm.
BRADY, PATRICK. Plymouth. Oct 12, 1799. Hugh Brady, Nathan Chapin, adms.
BROOKE, SAMUEL. Upper Merion. Feb 2, 1792. Elizabeth Brooke, Jesse Brooke, adms.
BROWN, SOLOMAN. Norriton. March 18, 1793. Archibald Darrah, adm.
BROWN, SAMUEL. Norriton. Oct 30, 1798. Williamina Brown, John Brown, adms.

BARNS, THOMAS. Horsham. Nov 11, 1784. Elizabeth Barns, Thomas Barns, adms.
BURRAS, THOMAS. Norriton. March 18, 1793. Archibald Darrah, adm.
CRAIG, ANNE. Norriton. March 17, 1787. Thomas Craig, adm.
CUMMIUS, CHARLES. Norriton. Feb 25, 1789. Herman Yerkes, adm.
COOMBS, DAVID. Abington. Dec 20, 1787. George Webster, adm.
COLSTON, DAVID. Norriton. May 28, 1791. Ezekiel Rhods, adm.
CRISTY, DENNIS. Norriton. March 18, 1793. Archibald Darrah, adm.
CRESSMAN, DANIEL. New Hanover. March 20, 1795. Abraham Bechtel, Isaac Lantz, Nicholas Cressman, adms.
CARROLL, DANEIL. Norristown. (No papers.)
COMFORT, ELIZABETH. Franconia. Oct 8, 1785. Abraham Benner, adm.
CANNON, FORGUS. Norriton. March 18, 1793. Archibald Darrah, adm.
CRAFT, GEORGE. Abington. Feb 19, 1798. John Tyson, Rebecca Craft, John Craft, adms.
CONRAD, HENRY. Worcester. Aug 3, 1788. Magdalena Conrad, Frederick Conrad, adms.
CLEMMER, HENRY, SR. Franconia. June 2, 1791. Abraham Clemmer, Henry Clemmer, adms.
COOK, HENRY. Norriton. March 18, 1793. Archibald Darrah, adm.
CLINE, HENRY. Lower Merion. June 28, 1799. Elizabeth Cline, John Cline, adms.
CADWALADER, ISAAC. Moreland. Nov 19, 1793. Daniel Longstreth, John Longstreth, adms.
COGGINS, JONATHAN. Gwynedd. June 1, 1785. Mary Coggins, adm.
COULSTON, JOHN. Norriton. Feb 1, 1785. Elizabeth Coulston, William Coulston, adms.
CUSTARD, JOHN. Whitpain. Feb 22, 1794. Sarah Custard, Henry Styer, adms.
CUSTER, JOHN. Skippack. Dec 19, 1794. John Umstead, adm.
COLFLESH, JOHN. Upper Merion. Oct 13, 1795. Matthias Coleflesh, Edward Skippen, adms.
CUNRAD, LYDIA. March 30, 1796. David Cunrad, adm.
CULP, LEWIS. Whitemarsh. Sept 4, 1797. Elizabeth Culp, adm.
CROLL, MICHAEL. Upper Salford. Feb 8, 1796. Jacob Croll, Frederick Conrad, adms.
CUSTER, PETER. Worcester. Feb 15, 1799. Margaret Custer, adm.
COULSTON, SAMUEL. Whitpain. Aug 20, 1785. Israel Coulston, adm.
COWDEN, SAMUEL. Upper Merion. Oct 6, 1792. Hester Cowden, adm.
COULSTON, WILLIAM. Norriton. May 17, 1790. Eve Coulston, Ezekiel Rhodes, adms.
CLARK, WILLIAM H. March 18, 1793. Archibald Darrah, adm.
CASTLE, YELLIS. Towamencin. Dec 7, 1793. Hobert Castel, Abraham

Castel, adms.
DIFFENDEFFER, ABRAHAM. Worcester. Feb 10, 1795. George Lilling, adm.
DEEN, ADAM. Whitpain. Oct 17, 1797. Catharine Deen, Mordecai Jones, adm.
DAVIS, DAVID. Lower Merion. June 29, 1790. Llewelwyn Young, adm.
DEVAN, DAVID. June 27, 1792. Levi Bartleson, adm.
DAVIS, ELIJAH. Providence. Feb 17, 1785. Elizabeth Davis, Thomas Davis, adms.
DAVIS, EDWARD. Whitemarsh. May 5, 1788. Jesse Davis, Ezekiel Davis, adms.
DAVIS, ELISHA. Providence. Dec 30, 1789. (No papers.)
DAVIS, EDWARD. Providence. March 23, 1795. Mary Davis, William Davis, adms.
DRESHER, EVE. June 3, 1797. Abraham Dresher, adm.
DALLIKER, FREDERICK. Upper Hanover. Feb 12, 1799. John Dotterer, adm.
DETWEILER, FELIX. Springfield. April 11, 1827. Frederick Detweiler.
DAVIS, GAINOR. Gwynedd. June 20, 1788. Jesse Foulke, adm.
DETWILER, JACOB, JR. Upper Hanover. March 15, 1787. Conrad Bress, George Roth, adms.
DAST, JACOB. June 29, 1790. Jeremiah Yeakle, adm.
DEHAVEN, JOHN. Limerick. March 20, 1797. Jonathan Feadley, adm.
DUNGAN, JOSEPH. Hatfield. Dec 26, 1797. Rachel Dungan, Silas Hough, adms.
DOTTERER, MICHAEL. Frederick. Oct 2, 1786. John Heebner, adm.
DAVIS, MARMADUKE. Moreland. May 21, 1789. James Davis, adm.
DILL, MARGARET. Limerick. Dec 28, 1790. Daniel Rees, adm.
DAVIS, MARY. Plymouth. March 2, 1797. Elizabeth Davis, adm.
DAVIS, REBECCA. Jan 2, 1793. William Hanna, adm.
DILL, ROBERT. Limerick. March 31, 1794. Moses Hobson, adm.
DAVIS, THOMAS. Plymouth. Jan 23, 1789. Lydia Davis, James Wood, adms.
DEWEES, WILLIAM. March 23, 1790. Robert Shannon, adm.
DUBRE, WILLIAM. July 1, 1792. Moses Sheppard, adm.
DAVIS, WILLIAM. Dec 12, 1796. Enoch Miller, adm.
ENGLE, CATHARINE. Douglass. Feb 4, 1785. Peter Richards, adm.
ENGART, CATHARINE. Upper Dublin. Aug 5, 1794. Philip Engart, adm.
EVANS, DAVID. Limerick. Feb 5, 1786. John Snider, adm.
EVANS, EZEKIEL. Norriton. Jan 24, 1785. Samuel Horton, adm.
EVANS, HUGH. Gwynedd. Jan 14, 1792. George Maris, Levi Foulke, adm.
EVANS, JONATHAN. Lower Merion. Jan 27, 1785. Elisha Evans, William Evans, adms.
EARNEST, JOHN. Cheltenham. March 7, 1796. Catharine Earnest, Henry Earnest, adms.

ESSIG, MARGARET. Aug 20, 1785.
ESHBACH, MARGARET. New Hanover. Dec 31, 1789. Valentine Bargert, adm.
ELLIS, MARY. Whitpain. July 22, 1799. Adam Feadley, adm.
EVANS, NEHEMIAH. Lower Merion. June 15, 1797. Susannah Evans, adm.
ELLIS, RACHEL. Whitpain. Aug 7, 1792. Amos Ellis, adm.
EDWARDS, SAMUEL. Upper Merion. Feb 11, 1799. Nathan Edwards, adm.
EDWARDS, THOMAS. Upper Merion. Sept 27, 1786. Elizabeth Edwards, Nathan Edwards, adms.
FULTON, ANDREW. March 18, 1793. Archibald Darrah, adm.
FUNCK, ABRAHAM. Franconia. July 18, 1796. Elizabeth Funck, John Funck, adms.
FRY, CREMONA. Sept 24, 1790. Robert Lewis, adm.
FLEMMING, CHARLES. Lower Merion. April 17, 1793. Robert McDowell, adm.
FISHER, CONRAD. Douglass. Oct 13, 1788. George Bechtel, adm.
FABRICIUS, FREDERICK. Plymouth. Nov 24, 1784. Margaret Fabricius, adm.
HIGH, FREDERICK. Providence. Aug 9, 1788. Elizabeth High, Jacob Casselburry, adms.
FISHER, GEORGE. Upper Hanover. Dec 27, 1791. Joseph Fisher, Wyndle Wyant, adms.
FRANCIS, GRIFFITH. Abington. Feb 5, 1795. William Francis, adm.
FRITZ, GEORGE. New Hanover. Dec 29, 1796. Isaac Shantz, adm.
FOUST, HENRY. Norriton. Oct 26, 1784. Anna Foust, Jacob Vanfossen, adms.
FEGALLY, HENRY. New Hanover. Aug 20, 1792. John Fegally, George Fegally, adms.
FURMAN, JOHN. Franconia. April 2, 1787. Henry Furman, George Nice, adms.
FISHER, JOHN. Upper Hanover. Nov 10, 1787. Catharine Fisher, Philip Gabel, adms.
FRONEFIELD, JOHN. Skippack. Jan 19, 1790. Mary Fronefield, adm.
FISHER, JOHN. March 18, 1793. Archibald Darrah, adm.
FRANKENBERG, JOHN. March 18, 1793. Archibald Darrah, adm.
FREDERICK, JOHN. Douglass. Nov 25, 1793. Elizabeth Frederick, Michael Frederick, adms.
FITZWATER, JOHN. Upper Dublin. Oct 17, 1795. Hannah Fitzwater, John Fitzwater, adms.
FISHER, PETER. Limerick. March 25, 1789. John Weise, adm. Jan 25, 1791. Anthony Bitting, adm.
FRANCIS, RACHAEL. May 15, 1792. Thomas Francis, adm.
FURGUSON, SAMUEL. March 18, 1793. Archibald Darrah, adm.
FABER, THEOBALD. Upper Hanover. April 29, 1789. Barbara Faber, Jacob Bright, adms.

GILBERT, BENJAMIN. Moreland. Feb 25, 1789. Herman Yerkes, adm.
GOTWALTS, FRONICA. Towamencin. Dec 14, 1799. Joseph Johnson, Henry Gotwalts, adms.
GROVER, GEORGE. Lower Merion. Oct 23, 1787. (No papers.)
GODSHALK, GARRET. Towamencin. Nov 18, 1796. Andrew Ziegler, Godshalk Godshalk, adms.
GEYER, HENRY, SR. Douglass. Jan 28, 1785. Henry Geyer, adm.
GROVER, JOHN. Feb 15, 1791. Jacob Grover, adm.
GRIFFITH, JOSEPH. Gwynedd. Feb 4, 1792. Amos Griffith, Jehu Evans, adms.
GOODMAN, JOHN. Lower Merion. June 15, 1797. Elizabeth Goodman, adm.
GALLMAN, JOHN. June 24, 1799. Catharine Gallman, adm.
GRESNER, WILLIAM. Upper Hanover. Dec 29, 1787. Catharine Kriesemer, George Horlacker, adms.
HEEBNER, ANNA. Worcester. Dec 9, 1784. Melchior Shultz, Melchior Krieble, adms.
HALLMAN, ANTHONY. Springfield. Dec 27, 1791. William Hallman, adm.
HARKIN, ALEXANDER. Jan 16, 1795. Robert Patterson, adm.
HERBERGER, ANDREW. Springfield. Nov 17, 1797. Abraham Heydrick, Christian Herberger.
HEISER, BALTZER. Frederick. Feb 17, 1786. Margaret Heiser, Peter Richards, adms.
HUMPHREYS, BENJAMIN. Lower Merion. June 19, 1792. Joseph Price, Edward Price, Richard Tunis, adms.
HAUS, BENJAMIN. Limerick. Jan 4, 1798. Elizabeth Haus, Daniel Haus, Christopher Sheffe, adms.
HALL, CEASER. April 30, 1792. Anthony Crothers.
HUBRAND, CHRISTOPHER. March 18, 1793. Archibald Darrah, adm.
HOBSON, FRANCIS. Limerick. Nov 27, 1792. Moses Hobson, adm.
HILBART, GEORGE ADAM. New Hanover, Jan 24, 1785. Henry Fryer, adm.
HARDY, GEORGE. March 18, 1793. Archibald Darrah, adm.
HALL, HENRY. Providence. March 20, 1786. Barbara Hall, Henry Hunsicker, adms.
HAMILTON, HUGH. Perkiomen. March 25, 1786. Samuel Jacobs, adm.
HOGLAND, JOHN. Jan 24, 1793. George Hocker, adm.
HALLOWELL, JOHN. Abington. Sept 25, 1793. Martha Hallowell, William Hallowell, John Thompson, adms.
HART, JOHN, SR. Whitemarsh. May 30, 1795. John Hart, Andrew Hart, adms.
HERCHER, JOHN. Frederick. Feb 8, 1796. Michael Kuntz.
HIMER, MAGDALENA. Dec 27, 1792. Joseph Spikle, adm.
HAUS, MARY B. Limerick. May 13, 1793. Isaiah Davis, adm.
HENDERSON, MATTHEW. March 21, 1796. William Henderson, adm.

HOUPT, MARY. Worcester. Aug 11, 1797. Benjamin Johnson, adm.
HARG, MATTHEW. Moreland. Nov 13, 1797. John Thomas, adm.
HEDRICK, NICHOLAS. Upper Salford. Oct 26, 1784. Peter Hedrick, Sr., Peter Hedrick, Jr., adms.
HEPP, SEBASTIAN. Upper Salford. Jan 3, 1786. Barny Hart, adm.
HEILEY, SUSANNA. Providence. May 28, 1792. John Heily, adm.
HOLT, THOMAS. Sept 12, 1797. Sarah Holt, adm.
JAG, DAVID. New Hanover. Dec 28, 1787. Matthew Richards, David Burkard, adms.
JONES, DAVID. Cheltenham. Nov. 10, 1792. Mary Jones, adm.
JONES, EVAN. Worcester. March 10, 1794. Mordecia Jones, adm.
JONES, GEORGE. Abington. Sept 21, 1797. Elizabeth Jones, John Stevens, adms.
JONES, HUGH. Lower Merion. Oct 13, 1790. John Jones, adm.
JOHNSON, JOHN. March 18, 1793. Archibald Darrah, adm.
JONES, JOHN. Moreland. April 24, 1797. Samuel Gummere, adm.
JONES, JOHN. Cheltenham. April 22, 1799. Jonathan Jones, Priscilla B. Jones, adms.
JONES, RACHEL. May 24, 1791. Amos Jones, adm.
KEYSER, ANDREW. Cheltenham. Nov 9, 1786. Mary Keyser, Joseph Norman, adms.
KEYSER, CHRISTOPHER. Upper Hanover. March 29, 1796. Jeremiah Krauss, Barbara Schultz, adms.
KOLB, DILLMAN. Perkiomen. Dec 20, 1785. Lydia Kolb, Henry Kolb, adms.
KINNARD, ESTHER. Moreland. Dec 30, 1796. Emanuel Kinnard, adm.
KROESEN, FRANCIS. Moreland. Jan 4, 1796. Mary Kroesen, adm.
KENNEDY, FRANCIS. Moreland. Dec 27, 1808. Robert Kennedy, David Kennedy, adms.
KREIBLE, GEORGE. Lower Salford. Oct 11, 1792. Hester Kreible, Andrew Kreible, adms.
KEPNER, HENRY. New Hanover. Nov 1, 1785. Mary Kepner, adm.
KLINE, HENRY. Lower Merion. June 28, 1799. Elizabeth Kline, John Kline, adms.
KREIBLE, MELCHIOR. Gwynedd. May 17, 1790. Melchior Kreible, Jr., Abraham Anders, adms.
KREPS, MICHAEL. New Hanover. June 6, 1791. Catharine Kreps, Jacob Zeber, Philip Hahn, adms.
KASTNER, MARY. Gwynedd. Sept 9, 1793. Jacob Miller.
KNIGHT, NICHOLAS. Whitemarsh. Nov 13, 1787. Elizabeth Trump, adm.
KRIESEMER, WILLIAM. Upper Hanover. Dec 29, 1787. Catharine Kriesemer, George Horlacker, adms.
LEAR, ADAM. Limerick. Aug 24, 1789. Margaret Lear, adm.
LENTZ, CHRISTOPHER. Springfield. Aug 16, 1794. Barbara Lentz, Jacob Lentz, John Lentz, adms.
LEVI, DAVID. Upper Hanover. March 1, 1785. Margaret Levi, adm.

LAWLER, DOROTHY. Douglass. May 21, 1792. Valentine Hornater, adm.
LEOSER, ELIZABETH. Upper Dublin. Sept 26, 1794. Christopher Leoser.
LONGENACRE, HENRY. Limerick. Oct 5, 1796. Elizabeth Longenacre, David Longenacre, adms.
LEWELLYN, JOHN. Lower Merion. March 28, 1786. Morris Lewellyn, Lewellyn Young, adms.
LONG, JACOB, JR. Marlborough. Jan 4, 1791. Margaret Long, adm.
LUTHER, JOHN. Feb 18, 1792. George Wiess, adm.
LOWDERBACK, JOHN. Providence. June 19, 1792. John Gish, adm.
LLOYD, JAMES. Moreland. Nov 19, 1793. Samuel Lloyd, adm.
LLOYD, JOHN. Gwynedd. May 15, 1799. Benjamin Llloyd, Thomas Shoemaker, adms.
LONG, MARY CATHARINE. Nov 11, 1785. George Long, Jacob Long, adms.
LANTIS, MARTIN. Douglass. Feb 20, 1799. John Lantis, William Weiss, adm.
LOCHMAN, NICHOLAS. Limerick. Aug 13, 1792. Valentine Curtz, adm.
LEOSER, PETER. Upper Dublin. Aug 30, 1794. Christopher Leoser, Christian Leoser, adms.
LLOYD, REBECCA. Plymouth. Dec 9, 1794. John Lloyd, Philip Lloyd, Mary Lloyd, adms.
LEWIS, SEPLITHAH. Gwynedd. Dec 27, 1786. Joseph Lewis, adm.
MILLER, ANN. May 15, 1786. Henry Miller, adm.
McFARLAND, ARTHUR. Norriton. July 25, 1789. Elizabeth McFarland, John McFarland, Stephen Porter, adms.
MOYER, ABRAHAM. Limerick. Nov 28, 1794. Catharine Moyer, adm.
MOWRER, ANDREW. Upper Hanover. Aug 25, 1794. John Mowrer, Jacob Mowrer, adms.
McCLINTOCK, ALEXANDER. Upper Merion. Dec 3, 1795. James Stewart, adm.
McCLAINE, ANN. Horsham. Oct 19, 1796. William McClane, adm.
MINTZER, ENGLEBERT. Douglass. March 24, 1791. Mary Mintzer, adm.
MURFEY, EDWARD. March 18, 1793. Archibald Darrah, adm.
MOYER, GEORGE. Marlborough. Jan 8, 1795. Hannah Moyer, adm.
MILLER, GEORGE. Upper Hanover. Dec 18, 1798. Jacob Miller, Solomon Freis, adms.
MAXFIELD, HENRY. March 18, 1793. Archibald Darrah.
MOYER, JACOB. Upper Salford. Oct 27, 1785. Margaret Moyer, Jacob Cressman, adms.
METZ, JOHN. Towamencin. May 31, 1790. Jacob Metz, Jacob Boyer, adms.
MAYBURRY, JOSEPH. March 23, 1791. Isaac Bechtell, adm.
MEHARD, JOHN. Norriton. Feb 4, 1792. James Adams, adm.

McKENNEY, JAMES. Feb 18, 1792. George Wiess, adm.
MARIS, JESSE. July 19, 1792. George Maris, Owen Foulk, adm.
MARGARGEL, JACOB. Providence. Feb 6, 1793. Jacob Dilworth, Joseph Margargel, adms.
McDARNET, JAMES. March 18, 1793. Archibald Darrah, adm.
MINNET, JAMES. Providence. May 12, 1795. Priscilla Minnet, adm.
MARIS, JONATHAN. Gwynedd. April 17, 1797. George Maris, adm.
McDOWELL, JAMES. Whitpain. Feb 18, 1799. Mary McDowell, Wm. McDowell, Jr., adms.
McKENNEY, MORRIS. Feb 18, 1792. George Wiess, adm.
MARTSLOFF, PHILIP. Towamencin. May 26, 1788. Eve Martsloff, adm.
MILLER, PHILIP. New Hanover. June 25, 1789. John Richards, adm.
MILLER, PETER. Jan 11, 1791. Christian Gross, adm.
KEYSER, CHRISTOPHER. Springfield. Oct 12, 1799. Catharine Keyser, Aaron Keyser, adms.
CONWELL, ROBERT. Cheltenham. Oct 14, 1799. Sophia Conwell, adm.
WAGONSELLER, JOHN. Providence. Oct 14, 1799. John Wagonseller, Peter Wagonseller.
ARMSTRONG, BENJAMIN. Philadelphia. Oct 19, 1799. Joseph Armstrong.
KASTNER, ANDREW. Upper Dublin. Oct 28, 1799. Cadwallader Evans, Amos Lewis, adms.
MOYER, JACOB. Norriton. Oct 13, 1799. Susanna Moyer, Jacob Moyer, adms.
SPENCER, JOHN. Moreland. Oct 31, 1799. Jarret Spencer, Jesse Foulk, adms.
WALT, CASPER. Upper Salford. Nov 27, 1799. Barbara Walt, Jacob Walt, adms.
BRANT, FREDERICK. Limerick. Dec 7, 1799. Jacob Brant, adm.
KEYSER, HENRY. Douglass. Dec 9, 1799. Elizabeth Keyser, George Keyser, adms.
TIMANUS, HENRY. Upper Dublin. Dec 23, 1799. Samuel Mann, adm.
GRUB, SAMUEL. Lower Salford. Jan 15, 1800. Andrew Grub, Joseph Alderfer, adms.
DETWELLER, JOSEPH. Skippack. Jan 15, 1800. George Shoemaker, adm.
LONGSTROTH, THOMAS. Moreland. Jan 23, 1800. Catharine Longstroth, John Longstroth, Thomas Longstroth, adms.
CUSTER, HARMAN. Worcester. Feb 3, 1800. Jacob Custer, Henry Custer, adms.
WEASNER, LEONARD. Douglass. Feb 10, 1800. John Weasner, adm.
BURCKART, DAVID. New Hanover. Feb 10, 1800. Elizabeth Burckart.
COMLEY, JOHN. Upper Merion. Feb 25, 1800. Jacob Colflesh, adm.
EGELMAN, HENRY. Limerick. March 3, 1800. Henry Egelman, adm.
HILLIGAS, PETER. Upper Hanover. March 10, 1800. Frederick Hist,

George Hist, adms.
KUGLAR, PAUL. Lower Merion. March 17, 1800. Sarah Kuglar, John Kuglar, adms.
BEAN, JOHN. Norriton. March 25, 1800. Jesse Bean, adm.
COULSTON, ELIZABETH. Whitpain. March 28, 1800. Isreal Coulston, adm.
MARKLEY, ABRAHAM. Skippack and Perkiomen. April 7, 1800. Benjamin Markley, John Markley, adms.
HOLMAN, DANIEL. April 23, 1800. Jacob Holman, adm.
MARCH, DANIEL, SR. Limerick. April 22, 1800. Daniel March, Jr., adm.
TARRANCE, MARY. Philadelphia. May 15, 1800. Nathan Edwards, adm.
REIFSNYDER, MICHAEL. Douglass. June 15, 1800. John Reifsnyder, adm.
PRIEST, HENRY. Norriton. July 18, 1800. Matthias Priest, George Priest, adms.
HITNER, GEORGE. Plymouth. July 23, 1800. Hannah Hitner, adm.
CUSTER, PAUL. Worcester. July 31, 1800. John Custer, Jonas Custer, adms.
SMITH, JANE, alias ROBERTS, JANE. Aug 13, 1800. John Roberts, adm.
BYDEMAN, ADAM. Aug 13, 1800. Fronica Bydeman, Frederick Bydeman, adm.
MATTHEWS, JOHN. Towamencin. Aug 27, 1800. Mary Matthews, adm.
VAN BURKIRK, JACOB. Gwynedd. Sept 1, 1800. Mary Van Burkirk, Philip Hahn, John Shermer, adms.
TOY, MARY. Providence. Sept 6, 1800. Peter Keen, adm.
EVANS, ELIZABETH. Lower Merion. Sept 13, 1800. David Evans, adm.
HOWELL, WALTER. Gwynedd. Sept 13, 1800. Elizabeth Howell, George Howell, adms.
BURNSIDES, JAMES. Washington, DC. Oct 6, 1800. William Burnsides, John McCrea, adms.
ROBERTS, REES. Gwynedd. Oct 6, 1800. George Roberts, Joseph Lewis, adms.
PAWLING, BENJAMIN. Skippack and Perkiomen. Nov 5, 1800. Rebecca Pawling, Joseph Pawling, adms.
WILLS, JEREMIAH. Norriton. Nov 24, 1800. Mary Wills, Michael Wills, adms.
KING, JOHN. Upper Salford. Dec 1, 1800. Joseph Hendricks, Christian Weber, adms.
WHITCOMB, JOHN. Upper Dublin. Dec 6, 1800. Ann Whitcomb, Joseph Whitcomb, adms.
REX, ELIZABETH. Germantown. Dec 11, 1800. Jacob Rex, adm.
HENDERSON, ALEXANDER. Upper Merion. Jan 3, 1801. Samuel

Henderson, Nathaniel Jones, adms.
THOMSON, JAMES. Douglass. Jan 8, 1801. William Thomson, adm.
BOGART, CORNELIUS. March 7, 1801. Daniel Deal, adm.
CRAFT, BARNET. Abington. March 14, 1801. John Craft, adm.
THOMPSON, ROBERT. March 18, 1801. Archibald Darrah, Benjamin Thompson, Mark Thompson, adms.
UMSTEAD, HENRY. Providence. March 31, 1801. John Umstead, adm.
JONES, JONTHAN. Whitemarsh. April 14, 1801. Susanna Jones, Isaac Jones, Abraham Yerkes, adms.
UPDEGROVE, EDWARD. Towamencin. May 5, 1801. Elizabeth Updegrove, John Potts, adms.
SAVAGE, GEORGE. May 11, 1801. Jeremiah Savage, adm.
EVANS, GEORGE. Whitemarsh. May 12, 1801. John Brooke, adm.
RUTH, ABRAHAM. Hatfield. May 13, 1801. Abraham Ruth, John Funck, adms.
BEAVER, BARNEY. Gwynedd. May 28, 1801. Susanna Beaver, Jacob Pruner, adms.
PRETZMAN, HENRY. Providence. Jan 18, 1801. Benjamin Cox, adm.
ACKLEY, THOMAS. July 18, 1801. Samuel Gummere, Isaac Walton, adms.
WELLS, EDWARD. Whitpain. July 25, 1801. William Wells, Levi Wells, adms.
BRANT, JOHN. Limerick. Aug 11, 1801. Jacob Brant, adm.
WENTZ, PHILIP. Gwynedd. Aug 15, 1801. Elizabeth Wentz.
McDOLE, ALEXANDER. Whitemarsh. Aug 29, 1801. Elizabeth McDole, John McDole, adms.
EGBERT, LAWRENCE. Whitemarsh. Sept 5, 1801. Lawrence Egbert.
ERB, CASPER. New Hanover. Sept 5, 1801. Henry Erb, George Erb, adms.
WALDON, JOHN. Oct 3, 1801. Magdalena Waldon.
CAMPBELL, JOSEPH. Oct 13, 1801. Barbara Campbell.
MOORE, CATO. Nov 10, 1801. Anthony Bitting.
TYSON, RYNEAR. Abington. Nov 10, 1801. Rynear Tyson, adm.
BLACKWOOD, SAMUEL. Moreland. Nov 16, 1801. Jonathan Lloyd.
BRANT, HANNAH. Limerick. Nov 28, 1801. Jacob Brant, Henry Croll, adms.
SNYDER, NICHOLAS. Limerick. Dec 4, 1801. Ann Snyder, adm.
RUE, ANN. Dec 8, 1801. Nicholas Bower, adm.
JARRET, JOSEPH. Horsham. Dec 14, 1801. Rachel Jarret, Jonathan Jarret, David Jarret, adms.
BENGETT, SARAH. New Hanover. Jan 12, 1802. Molly Bengett, adm.
FULTON, JAMES. Moreland. Jan 27, 1802. Daniel Paul, adm.
PRICE, JOHN. Lower Merion. Feb 8, 1802. Jane Price, Joseph Price, adms.
SUCH, MARY. Upper Dublin. Feb 18, 1802. John Collom, adm.
PRICKART, JOHN. Moreland. Feb 20, 1802. George Rex, adm.

DEWEES, HENRY. Springfield. Feb 27, 1802. John Dewees, Jonathan Dewees, adms.
BRADFORD, SAMUEL. Providence. March 4, 1802. Mary Bradford, Jacob Longacre, adms.
SLOANE, JAMES. Whitpain. March 10, 1802. James Sloane, adm.
KRUP, MARY. Lower Salford. March 30, 1802. Jacob Krup, George Swenk, adms.
STEMPLE, LYDIA. Plymouth. April 9, 1802. Jesse Foulk, adm.
TAYLOR, JOSEPH. Whitpain. April 9, 1802. Susanna Taylor, Jacob Engel, adms.
THOMAS, ISAAC. Bucks County. May 20, 1802. John Roberts, adm.
WISE, PETER. Upper Dublin. May 17, 1802. John Wise, adm.
JARRET, DANIEL. Upper Dublin. May 31, 1802. Ann Jarret, Levi Jarret, adms.
MAYBURRY, SILVANAS. Aug 9, 1802. Jacob Bortman, adm.
POTTS, MARTHA. Plymouth. Aug 27, 1802. Joseph Potts, Joseph Thomas, adms.
HOUSER, JACOB. Whitemarsh. Sept 3, 1802. Robert Porter, adm.
EVANS, ADNA. Limerick. Sept 21, 1802. Athamar Evans, Ruth Evans, adms.
WALT, GEORGE. Frederick. Sept 25, 1802. John Swenck, adm.
WALKER, MICHAEL. Sept 25, 1802. Mary Walker, adm.
MARTIN, ELIZABETH. Upper Dublin. Sept 29, 1802. Matthias Withe, adm.
CLEMMER, HENRY. Hatfield. Oct 14, 1802. Mary Clemmer, John Clemmer, adms.
MORRIS, JOSHUA. Abington. Oct 23, 1802. Sarah Morris, Thomas Fletcher, Oliver Wilson, Robert Fletcher, adms.
ZEARFOS, FREDERICK. Oct 25, 1802. Benjamin Zearfos, Frederick Zearfos.
BROOKE, JONATHAN. Limerick. Nov 3, 1802. Susanna Brooke, Benjamin Brooke, adms.
SCHNIDER, HENRY. New Hanover. Nov 9, 1802. John Schnider, Peter Richards, adms.
SHANTZ, ISAAC. New Hanover. Nov 13, 1802. Barbara Shantz, Abraham Shantz, John Shoemaker.
PAWLING, ELIZABETH. Skippack and Perkiomen. Dec 23, 1802. William Shannon, Jonathan Jones, adms.
HOLSTEIN, SAMUEL. Upper Merion. Jan 10, 1803. Matthias Holstein, George Holstein, adms.
MADDON, BERNARD. Upper Merion. Jan 28, 1803. John Cotton, adm.
SWANER, PETER. Limerick. Feb 1, 1803. Anna Swaner, John Herstine, adms.
FITZWATER, MATTHEW. Upper Dublin. Feb 2, 1803. George Fitzwater, Joshua Tyson, adms.
DUPORTAIL, LEWIS L. Feb 3, 1803. Isaac Huddleson, adm.

YERKES, JOHN. Feb 4, 1803. Harman Yerkes, John Yerkes, adms.
SNYDER, CATHARINE. New Hanover. Feb 15, 1803. George Boocher, adm.
BUTLER, SARAH. Upper Dublin. Feb 15, 1803. Thomas Butler, Jonathan Butler, adms.
HOXWORTH, PETER. Hatfield. Feb 16, 1803. Peter Hoxwroth, Israel Hoxworth, adms.
ROBERTS, SAMUEL. Providence. March 2, 1803. Lydia Roberts, Arnold Roberts, Edward Roberts, adms.
PAUL, DANIEL. Moreland. March 15, 1803. Margaret Paul, Jacob Paul, Israel Warner, adms.
JENKINS, JESSE. Gwynedd. March 16, 1803. Levi Jenkins, Hugh Coustly, adms.
JENKINS, JOHN. Gwynedd. March 19, 1803. John Jenkins, Edward Jenkins, John Hughes, Peter Wentz, adms.
SWENCK, GEORGE. Frederick. March 21, 1803. Jacob Swenck, Abraham Markley, adms.
SWENCK, JOHN. Frederick. March 21, 1803. Abraham Swenck, George Swenck, adms.
ADAMS, SIMON. Upper Hanover. April 18, 1803. Catharine Adams, Theodore Egg, adms.
EVANS, JAMES. Providence. April 9, 1803. Ann Evans, Owen Evans, adms.
ROBERTS, CATHARINE. Plymouth. April 13, 1803. Thomas Bradley, adm.
PAINTER, CATHARINE. May 10, 1803. Jacob Painter, adm.
BEEN, HENRY. Skippack and Perkiomen. June 6, 1803. Maria Been, John Been, Henry Esbeship, adms.
EVANS, EVAN. Montgomery. June 25, 1803. Lydia Evans, Cadwallader Evans, adms.
BEAN, ADAM. Worcester. July 7, 1803. John Bean, adm.
REIMER, RACHEL. July 14, 1803. John Heiser, Jacob Heiser, adms.
FRY, JOHN. Abington. Juy 21, 1803. Elizabeth Fry, John Stephens, adms.
HARPLE, LUDWICK. Providence. July 26, 1803. John Harple, Ludwick Harple, adms.
SHRIVER, GEORGE. Abington. Aug 25, 1803. John Shriver, Benjamin Shriver, adms.
CRAWFORD, WILLIAM. Upper Merion. Aug 29, 1803. Anna Crawford, Matthew Crawford, adms.
WILSON, ANN. Franconia. Sept 14, 1803. Joseph Wilson, adm.
ROOSEN, HENRY. Worcester. Sept. 24, 1803. Jane Roosen, John Roosen, adms.
SHEPER, DANIEL. Whitemarsh. Oct 3, 1803. Elizabeth Sheper, Charles Nice, adms.
POTTS, SARAH. Cheltenham. Oct 5, 1803. Levi Foulke, adm.
WAGNER, SUSANNAH. Montgomery. Oct 20, 1803. Henry Wagner,

adm.
HOLT, SARAH. Horsham. Oct 25, 1803. Enoch Jenderdine, adm.
McCLEAN, WILLIAM. Norriton. Nov 2, 1803. Isaac Powell, adm.
McCLEAN, SAMUEL. Norriton. Nov 2, 1803. Isaac Powell, adm.
EVANS, PETER. Lower Merion. Nov 16, 1803. Mary Evans, Levi Evans, adms.
GRIMLEY, JOHN. Limerick. Dec 16, 1803. Frederick Grimley, adm.
HALLOWELL, JOB. Plymouth. Dec 8, 1803. Hannah Hallowell, William Hallowell, adms.
WOOLMAN, JOHN. Horsham. Dec 14, 1803. Lewis Woolman, John Woolman, adms.
WILDBAHN, CHARLES FREDERICK. Gwynedd. Feb 3, 1804. Samuel Sybrana, adm.
HEEBNER, JOHN CHRISTOPHER. Worcester. Feb 14, 1804. Abraham Heebner, adm.
SHOEMAKER, MARTHA. Cheltenham. Feb 14, 1804. Jacob Paul, adm.
SIMPSON, WILLIAM. Moreland. Feb 14, 1804. Amos Simpson, Thomas Fletcher, adms.
LANDIS, YELLIS. Franconia. Feb 21, 1804. Jacob Landis, Isaac Landis, adms.
LLOYD, ELIZABETH alias VELVET, ELIZABETH. March 2, 1804. Andrew Todd, adm.
WHITE, JANE. Whitpain. March 19, 1804. Elizabeth White, Justus Scheetz, adms.
SNYDER, BENJAMIN. Frederick. March 20, 1804. Elizabeth Snyder, Samuel Boyer, adms.
SNYDER, JOHN. Cheltenham. April 26, 1804. Phebe Snyder, Thomas Livezey, adms.
HUGHES, LEVI. Skippack and Perkiomen. April 26, 1804. Rebecca Hughes, Joseph Tyson, adms.
KEPLER, REBECCA. Skippack and Perkiomen. April 26, 1804. John Kepler, Philip Reimer, adms.
SIBLEY, RUDOLPH. Lower Merion. May 18, 1804. John Price, William Hagay, adms.
McKNIGHT, DAVID. Worcester. June 16, 1804. Samuel Bell, adms.
LLOYD, SARAH. Abington. July 9, 1804. Joseph Thomas, adm.
BERKEY, JOHN. Upper Salford. July 26, 1804. Jacob Berkey, Abraham Berkey, adms.
LLOYD, SARAH. Abington. Aug 14, 1804. Benjamin Lloyd, adm.
SIMPSON, JOHN. Horsham. Aug 21, 1804. John Simpson, Benjamin Hough, adms.
HARMAN, PHILIP. Upper Merion. Sept 17, 1804. Jacob Harman, Conrad Ruple, adms.
YERKES, ANTHONY. Moreland. Oct 19, 1804. Mary Yerkes, Robert Yerkes, Joseph Yerkes, adms.
ROBERTS, ELI. Whitpain. Oct 27, 1804. George Roberts, adm.
DuPORTAIE (see DuPortail), LEWIS LIBEQUE. Oct 19, 1804. John

Craig, adm.
LOCK, PETER. Upper Hanover. Nov 7, 1804. Eve Lock, John Lock, adms.
RYMAN, DANIEL. Providence. Dec 11, 1804. Henry Ryman, adm.
RYMER, LEWIS. Providence. Dec 11, 1804. David Rymer, adm.
McCACHAN, SARAH. Upper Merion. Dec 15, 1804. Isaac Abrahams, adm.
HINES, MATTHEW. Horsham. Dec 31, 1804. William Hines, adm.
RUTH, SAMUEL. New Hanover. Jan 3, 1805. John Ruth, adm.
GOODMAN, CONRAD. Lower Merion. Jan 8, 1805. Elizabeth Goodman, adm.
WITMAN, SAMUEL. Douglass. Feb 4, 1805. Barney Gilbert, George Horner, Jr., adm.
FRY, SUSANNAH. Frederick. Feb 25, 1805. George Grow, Adam Grow, adms.
ROBINSON, JOHN. Upper Dublin. March 2, 1805. Samuel Bobinson, George Lukens, adms.
DICKHOWKE, HENRY. Providence. March 20, 1805. Jacob Wismer, adm.
ENYARD, CHARLES. Abington. March 25, 1805. Abraham Enyard, adm.
McGLATHERY, JOHN. Whitpain. March 25, 1805. Isaac McGlathery.
RICE, LEWIS. Norristown. March 25, 1805. Michael Mather, adm.
ARMSTRONG, EPHRAIM. Norriton. April 10, 1805. Joseph Armstrong, Ephraim Armstrong, William Armstrong.
HOUP, SAMUEL. April 11, 1805. Henry Houp, Casper Schlater, adms.
OVERLANDER, FRANCONIA. May 6, 1805. Benjamin Campbell, adm.
CHILDS, CEPHAS. May 16, 1805. Robert Kennedy, adms.
CRESSMAN, JOHN GEORGE. May 18, 1805. Samuel Daniels, adm.
VANFOSSEN, ARNOLD. Norriton. May 27, 1805. Leonard Vanfossen, John Vanfossen, adms.
ATKINSON, JOHN. Providence. May 28, 1805. William Fitzwater.
BEARD, PAUL. Norriton. June 3, 1805. Daniel Beard, adm.
FREED, ANNA. Norriton. July 3, 1805. Henry Freed, adm.
WEBER, JOSEPH. Whitpain. July 29, 1805. Jacob Weber, adm.
THOMPSON, WILLIAM. Upper Merion. Aug 13, 1805. Henry Richabough.
ROBERTS, NATHAN. Whitpain. Aug 26, 1805. Amos Roberts, adm.
ALLBRIGHT, JACOB. Gwynedd. Sept 9, 1805. Margaret Allbright.
LUKENS, JOSEPH, JR. Upper Dublin. Sept 17, 1805. Thomas Livezey, adm.
FLETCHER, ROBERT. Sept 20, 1805. Thomas Fletcher, Isaac Hallowell, adm.
BERGEY, ISAAC. Franconia. Oct 4, 1805. Jacob Bergey, Isaac Bergey, adm.
BLETZ, JACOB. Upper Salford. Oct 7, 1805. Isaac Moses, Jacob Levy, Abraham Gumpert, adms.

WEAVER, HENRY. Oct 10, 1805. George Weaver, Enoch Armitage, adms.
ZILLING, GEORGE. Worcester. Oct 15, 1805. Hannah Zilling, Daniel Springer, adms.
RHOADS, PHILIP. Douglass. Oct 31, 1805. John Rhoads, adm.
ARWIN, SARAH. Gwynedd. Nov 1, 1805. John Arwin, adm.
ARWIN, ELIZABETH. Gwynedd. Nov 1, 1805. John Arwin, adm.
COPE, JOHN. Franconia. Nov 2, 1805. George Cope, Samuel Cope, adms.
MURRAY, JESSEE. Horsham. Nov 4, 1805. Stephen Murray, adm.
LEWIS, JOHN. Worcester. Nov 11, 1805. Hester Lewis adm.
HALLOWELL, MATTHEW. Abington. Nov 12, 1805. John Hallowell, Nathan Hallowell, adm.
LEAVER, ERASMUIS. Limerick. Nov 13, 1805. Frederick Leaver, Erasmuis Leaver, adms.
NINE, JOHN. Skippack and Perkiomen. Nov 16, 1805. Elizabeth Nine, John Stroup, adms.
THOMAS, JOHN. Lower Merion. Nov 23, 1805. Mary Thomas, Eleanor Thomas, adms.
PRICE, WILLIAM. Lower Salford. Nov 28, 1805. Catharine Price, Jacob Landis, John Nice, adms.
FOLAND, HUGH. Abington. Nov 30, 1805. Enos Foland, adm.
McDERMOND, JOHN. Lower Merion. Dec 16, 1805. Mary McDermond, Samuel McDermond, adms.
AULD, JACOB. Norristown. Dec 17, 1805. Morris Jones, adm.
BOGER, MARTIN. Lower Salfrod. Jan 25, 1806. Abraham Markley, Michael Wagner, adm.
JOHNSON, JOHN. Moreland. Feb 11, 1806. Isaac Thompkins, adm.
HOOVER, MARGARET. Douglass. Feb 11, 1806. Henry Varley, Jr., adm.
PROTZMAN, CONRAD. Providence. Feb 11, 1806. John Protzman, adm.
FLASHAUKER, GEORGE. Gwynedd. Mar 19, 1806. John Griffin, adm.
MOYER, SUSANNAH. Franconia. April 8, 1806. Samuel Moyer, Abraham Moyer, adms.
HACKMAN, ELIZABETH. Franconia. April 29, 1806. Michael Shoemaker, adm.
BURGER, GEORGE. New Hanover. May 12, 1806. Eve Burger, adm.
SOUDER, ISAAC. May 12, 1806. Joseph Reed, adm.
SNYDER, ADAM. Springfield. June 13, 1806. Henry Snyder, Daniel Snyder, adms.
COULTER, MICHAEL. June 14, 1806. Mary Coulter, adms.
SHOEMAKER, JAMES. Upper Dublin. Aug 4, 1806. Phebe Shoemaker, Daniel Shoemaker, adms.
SHOEMAKER, WILLIAM. Upper Dublin. Aug 4, 1806. Phebe Shoemaker, Daniel Shoemaker, adms.
HAVERSTREIGHT, JONAS. Abington. Aug 12, 1806. Elizabeth

Haverstreight.
STREPER, ANN. Whitemarsh. Aug 13, 1806. William Streper, adm.
PUGH, JOB. Upper Merion. Aug 27, 1806. Ruth Pugh, Benjamin Brooke, adms.
BOILS, JOHN. Gwynedd. Sept 10, 1806. Catharine Boils, John Garner, adms.
MEGAREL, JACOB. Abington. Oct 2, 1806. Hannah Megarel, George Wentz, adms.
WALTERS, JONATHAN. Oct 17, 1806. Jane Walters, adm.
KNIPE, DAVID. Gwynedd. Oct 18, 1806. Mary Knipe, Joseph Knipe, adms.
JENKINS, DAVID. Hatfield. Oct 18, 1806. John Roberts, adm.
SUPPLEE, ANDREW. Upper Merion. Oct 27, 1806. Zimmerman Supplee, Rachel Supplee, adms.
PRIEST, PHEBE. Plymouth. Nov 4, 1806. John Priest, Samuel Priest, adms.
LONG, GEORGE. Douglass. Nov 6, 1806. George Long, Henry Long, adms.
MATHER, MICHAEL. Norristown. Nov 14, 1806. Levi Pawling, adm.
KRIEBLE, ISAAC. Lower Salford. Now 18, 1806. Melchior Shultz, adm.
RAMBO, MOSES. Upper Providence. Nov 18, 1806. Israel Bunghurst, Moses Hobson, adms.
THOMAS, LEVI. Lower Merion. Nov 19, 1806. Thomas Pratt, adm.
THOMAS, ISAAC. Lower Merion. Nov 19, 1806. Thomas Pratt, adm.
THOMAS, BENJAMIN. Montgomery. Nov 21, 1806. Peter Evans, adm.
FREDERICK, GEORGE. Upper Salford. Dec 1, 1806. Henry Frederick, Joseph Hendricks, adms.
GRIFFITH, JOSEPH. Gwynedd. Dec 24, 1806. Rebecca Griffith, Amos Griffith, adms.
GERHARD, CHRISTINA. Franconia. Jan 13, 1807. Isaac Gerhard, Henry Herhard, adms.
WEBB, PAUL. Jan 28, 1807. Levi Pauling, adm.
HAVERSTRITE, JONES. Abington. Feb 17, 1807. Thomas Shoemaker, Elizabeth Haverstrite.
ZELL, JACOB. Lower Merion. Feb 23, 1807. Anthony Zell, Hannah Zell, adms.
FETTER, JOHN. Moreland. Feb 23, 1807. Casper Fetter, George Fetter, adms.
FORCE, HENRY. Feb 23, 1807. John Force, adm.
TOWERS, ARCHIBALD. Upper Providence. March 12, 1807. Elizabeth Towers, Samuel Horning, adms.
LEONARD, GEORGE. Potts Grove. April 13, 1807. George Leaf, John Rinehart, adms.
CLEVER, ANN. April 9, 1807. Joseph Clever, Isaac Clever, adms.
STEM, ALICE. Perkiomen. April 15, 1807. Abraham Ziegler, adm.
EMMERICK, JOHN. New Hanover. April 16, 1807. John Emmerick,

adm.
YAHN, PHILIP. Pottstown. April 27, 1807. George Groff, adm.
CONRAD, JOHN. Upper Dublin. May 18, 1807. Martha Conrad, am.
BOYER, SAMUEL. Frederick. May 19, 1807. Mary Boyer, Jacob Boyer, adms.
STALL, JAMES. Limerick. May 25, 1807. John Stall, Matthew Dill, adms.
KEPLER, WILLIAM. New Hanover. June 10, 1807. Jacob Kepler, Valentine Seiwell, adms.
KROUS, MICHAEL. Frederick. July 6, 1807. Elizabeth Schwenck, Daniel Schwenck, adms.
ELLIS, JUDA. Hatfield. July 9, 1807. Jacob Ford, adm.
LAPP, JOSEPH. Cheltenham. Aug 3, 1807. John Lapp, adm.
ROAD, CASPER. Limerick. Aug 3, 1807. Catharine Road, Jacob Shoemaker, adms.
LONGACRE, JACOB. Lower Providence. Aug 20, 1807. John Longacre, Peter Waggonseller, adms.
JACOB, HENRY. Douglass. Aug 18, 1807. Elizabeth Jacob, Henry Jacob, adms.
BROOKE, THOMAS. Limerick. Aug 19, 1807. Elizabeth B. James, Owen Evans, adms.
LLOYD, JOSEPH. Aug 31, 1807. Philip Lloyd, adm.
CRAWFORD, MATTHEW. Upper Merion. Sept 17, 1807. Samuel Crawford, Hugh Long, adms.
ROBERTS, HUGH. Horsham. Sept 19, 1807. Seneca Lukens, adm.
DAVIS, DAVID. Upper Providence. Oct 6, 1807. Benjamin Brooke, Samuel Henderson, adms.
SHOESTER, JOSEPH. Lower Merion. Nov 12, 1807. Jacob Shoester, adm.
POTTS, JESSEE. Upper Dublin. Nov 12, 1807. Mary Potts, Johan Potts, adms.
DuPORTAIL, LEWIS LEBEUE. Nov 17, 1807. Robert Porter, adm.
JENKINS, JOHN. Nov 17, 1807. Thomas Bower, adm.
LEHMAN, ABRAHAM. Norriton. Nov 25, 1807. George Lehman, Stephen Porter, adms.
MISSIMER, JOHN. Dec 19, 1807. Samuel Missimer, John Bechtel, adms.
HALLOWELL, WILLIAM. Plymouth. Dec 26, 1807. Grace Hallowell, Nathan Hallowell, adms.
BOWMAN, PHILIP. Towamencin. Jan 9, 1808. Matthias Stouffen, Jacob Wampole, adms.
MILLER, MARY. Upper Providence. Jan 22, 1808. John Benjamin, adm.
GRUB, THOMAS. Providence. Feb 18, 1808. Jesse Harper, adm.
HERBLE, JACOB. New Hanover. Mar 12, 1808. Jacob Renninger, Henry Yerger, adms.
OVERHOLTZER, JACOB. Hatfield. March 18, 1808. Jacob

Overholtzer, John Shutt, adms.
SHULER, BENJAMIN. Lancaster County. March 24, 1808. John Shuler, adm.
LANDES, ELIZABETH. Perkiomen. March 25, 1808. Henry Landes, adm.
BURKERT, JOHN. New Hanover. April 2, 1808. George Burkert, Peter Miller, adms.
EDWARDS, JOHN. Towamencin. April 2, 1808. Robert Edwards, adm.
WALT, HENRY. April 14, 1808. Peter Fry, Henry Walt, adms.
LOGAN, WILLIAM. Norriton. April 19, 1808. Mary Logan, adm.
JACKSON, HENRY. April 25, 1808. Daniel Green, adm.
WEBSTER, ANN. Abington. April 28, 1808. William Webster, adm.
WISLER, HENRY. Marlborough. June 16, 1808. George Geiger, adm.
SWARTZ, ESTHER. June 16, 1808. Jacob Swartz, Andrew Swartz, adms.
URFER, BALTZER. Aug 1, 1808. Michael Urfer, John Crouse, adms.
BEAN, GARRET. Worcester. Aug 13, 1808. Catharine Bean, Jacob Bean, adms.
WIERMAN, MICHAEL. Hatfield. Aug 16, 1808. John Wierman, Molly Wierman, adms.
DRAKE, RICHARD. Aug 23, 1808. Mary Drake, adm.
ELLIS, ROLAND. Lower Merion. Sept 10, 1808. Jacob Ford, adm.
ELLIOT, ROBERT. Lower Merion. Sept 15, 1808. William Elliot, John Elliot, adms.
YEXELEY, ANN. Gwynedd. Sept 16, 1808. Esther Johnson, adm.
TUCKER, ELIZABETH. Oct 6, 1808. Isaac Tucker, adm.
SHRIVER, JESSE. Oct 15, 1808. Mary Shriver, Benjamin Shriver, George Dellen, adms.
CLEMMENS, ABRAHAM. Oct 17, 1808. John Clemmens, George Clemmens, adms.
THOMAS, JONATHAN. Upper Dublin. Oct 19, 1808. Allice Thomas, David Thomas, Samuel Maulsby, adms.
GILMORE, MARY. Oct 20, 1808. William Gilmore, adm.
CONARD, THOMAS. Norriton. Oct 26, 1808. Mary Conard, John Conard, adms.
ZEIGLER, BARA. Skippack and Perkiomen. Oct 31, 1808. David Longacre, adm.
LANDES, ISAAC. Perkiomen. Nov 2, 1808. Jacob Landes, adm.
IREDELE, JOHN. Moreland. Nov 9, 1808. John Iredele, Jonathan Thomas, adms.
BITTING, JOHN. Marlborough. Nov 14, 1808. Henry Roshon, adm.
MORRISON, WILLIAM. Providence. Nov 16, 1808. Samuel Daniels, adm.
STEWART, THOMAS. Nov 16, 1808. James Stewart, adm.
SEESHOLTZ, LAWRENCE. Nov 23, 1808. Jacob Seesholtz, John Seesholtz, adms.
ALBERTSON, BENJAMIN. Abington. Nov 29, 1808. Benjamin

Albertson, Jonathan Albertson, adms.
MATHER, ISAAC. Jan 11, 1809. John Collom, William Collom, adms.
MARIS, JANE. Gwynedd. Feb 1, 1809. Levi Foulke, John Wilson, adms.
BEAVEN, JOHN. Feb 3, 1809. Mary Beaven, David Roberts, Joseph Price, adms.
REIFSNYDER, HARMAN. Feb 7, 1809. John Reifsnyder, adm.
REIFSNYDER, HERMAN. Feb 7, 1809. Christian Shiner, John Reifsnyder, adms.
ELEANHOOF, GODFREY. Feb 13, 1809. Josiah Eleanhoof, Ann Mary Eleanhoof, adms.
BURK, JOHN. Upper Dublin. Feb 15, 1809. Edward Burk, Andrew Zilkison, adms.
HERNER, GEORGE. Douglass. Feb 17, 1809. Bernard Gilbert, Peter Herner, adms.
VANDERSLICE, Elizabeth. Providence. March 6, 1809. Peter Custer, adm.
WIRTZ, CHRISTIAN. Montgomery. March 13, 1809. George Weaver, adm.
JONES, JOHN. Montgomery. March 23, 1809. Henry Jones, Evan Jones, William Foulke, adms.
HOOVER, HENRY. Gwynedd. April 17, 1809. Christian Hoover, Jacob Hoover, Philip Hoover, John Rile, adms.
BROWER, DANIEL. Upper Providence. April 18, 1809. Henry Brower, Christian Brower, adms.
SHANNON, MARY. Lower Providence. April 25, 1809. John Shannon, adm.
LOUP, PETER. Frederick. May 15, 1809. Catharine Loup, Henry Loup, adms.
DAGER, JACOB. Whitemarsh. June 22, 1809. George Dager, Peter Dager, Henry Scheetz, adms.
EVERHART, JACOB. June 28, 1809 Abraham Everhart, Frederick Dull, adms.
MILLER, PHILIP. Providence. July 8, 1809. John Benjamin, adm.
MILLER, DAVID. North Carolina. July 8, 1809. John Benjamin, adm.
PRIZER, HENRY. Upper Providence. July 22, 1809. John Prizer, Isaac Prizer, adms.
POTTS, PHILIP B. Pottstown. Aug 4, 1809. Peggy Potts, adm.
VANDYKE, AARON. Aug 9, 1809. Isaac Huddleson, adm.
GABLE, PHILIP. Upper Salford. Aug 14, 1809. Philip Gable, adm.
DOTTS, HENRY. Abington. Aug 21, 1809. Philip Dotts, Henry Dotts, Adam Dotts, adms.
JONES, SAMUEL. Cheltenham. Aug 22, 1809. Hannah Jones, adm.
PARRY, CHARLES. Abington. Sept 13, 1809. John Parry, adm.
CRESSMAN, JACOB. Limerick. Oct 10, 1809. George Cressman, adm.
LIPPEN, JOHN. Lower Merion. Dec 18, 1809. John Evans, adm.
SINSENDERFER, HANNAH. New Hanover. Dec 19, 1809. Michael

341

Sinsenderfer, Christian Specht, adms.
BELLEW, DANIEL. Gwynedd. Dec 26, 1809. Mary Bellew, John Fitzwater, adms.
GUCKER, SUSANNA. Upper Hanover. Dec 29, 1809. Abraham Sell, John Detwiler, adms.
STEM, CONRAD. Lower Providence. Jan 8, 1810. John Stem, adm.
FREIS, GEORGE. Whitemarsh. Jan 13, 1810. George Freis, adm.
REIFSNYDER, JULIANA. Pottstown. Jan 24, 1810. Christian Lassheg, adm.
TOOL, AQUILLA. Whitpain. Jan 30, 1810. Aquilla Tool, Aaron Tool, adms.
LIMING, SARAH. Lower Merion. Feb 20, 1810. Jacob Morris, adm.
SMITH, JACOB. Frederick. Feb 13, 1810. Jacob Hout, adm.
HOLLOWBUSH, PETER. Limerick. Feb 13, 1810. Martha Hollowbush, Amos Evans, adms.
BALL, MARY. Horsham. Feb 14, 1810. Samuel Richards, adm.
HALL, JOHN. Lower Providence. Feb 21, 1810. Michael Alabach, John Detwiler, Henry Fox, Jr., adms.
WENNER, JOHN. Upper Providence. Feb 22, 1810. Samuel Wenner, John Grove, Adms.
BOSSERT, HENRY. Marlborough. Feb 6, 1810. Philip Reed, adm.
SCHROEDER, PHILIP. Upper Providence. Feb 28, 1810. Philip Schroeder.
ROBERTS, EDWARD. Lower Providence. March 3, 1810. John Roberts, Jessee Roberts, adms.
CASTNER, JOHN. Norriton. March 20, 1810. Lydia Castner, Ezekiel Rhoads, Jr., Jesse Castner, adms.
MINNER, JACOB. Frederick. March 30, 1810. Jacob Hunck, adm.
ZIMMERMAN, DAVID. Whitpain. April 2, 1810. Isaac Zimmerman, John Matthias, adms.
REICHSTINE, CONRAD. Potts Grove. April 14, 1810. Elizabeth Reichstine, Catharine Reichstine.
SCHLATER, BARBARA. Whitemarsh. April 30, 1810. Casper Schlater, John Schlater, adms.
WEEK, MARGARET. Horsham. May 26, 1810. John Week, adm.
GERHART, PETER. Worcester. May 29, 1810. Jeremiah Krous, William Gerhart, adms.
PALMER, SARAH. Providence. June 19, 1810. Thomas Pears, adms.
BASETER, ELIZABETH. Abington. May 29, 1810. Edward Rice, adm.
GROVE, JOHN. Upper Providence. July 5, 1810. David Dewees, Isaac Hallman, adms.
PUGH, JOHN. Lower Providence. July 21, 1810. William Smith, Rebecca Pugh, adms.
HAGY, DANIEL. Whitemarsh. July 30, 1810. William Henvis, Mary Hagy, adms.
LOTSHAW, ABRAHAM. Lower Providence. Aug 6, 1810. Jacob Lotshaw, adm.

MUCKELSTON, PETER. Horsham. Aug 21, 1810. Peter Muckelston, Mary Muchelston.
STELLER, ISAAC. Lower Providence. Sept 3, 1810. John Steller, Jacob Keely, adms.
WAGGONER, CONRAD. Upper Providence. Oct 16, 1810. Frederick Alderfer.
HILLEGAS, PETER. Upper Hanover. Oct 24, 1810. Abraham Levy, adm.
WOOD, SAMUEL. Whitpain. Oct 29, 1810. Sophia Wood, adm.
FARMER, EDWARD. Horsham. Oct 29, 1810. Benjamin Lloyd, Sarah Farmer, adm.
BITTING, JOSEPH. Potts Grove. Nov 1, 1810. George Nice, adm.
REED, ANDREW. Marlborough. Nov 12, 1810. Philip Reed, Andrew Reed, adms.
METZ, SAMUEL. Upper Providence. Nov 15, 1810. Jacob Metz, John Boorse, adms.
KEESLER, CHRISTIAN. Springfield. Nov 15, 1810. Jacob Keesler, adm.
SOUDER, JACOB. Franconia. Nov 16, 1810. Benjamin Souder, Christian Souder.
DOTTERER, BARNHART. New Hanover. Nov 26, 1810. Abraham Dotterer.
WIDEMIRE, GEORGE. Marlborough. Dec 3, 1810. Jacob Leister, Jacob Reickstool, adms.
SULLIVAN, ANTHONY. Whitemarsh. Dec 10, 1810. Samuel Thomas, adm.
WAGENER, CHRISTOPHER. Worcester. Dec 22, 1810. Abraham Yeakle, Melchior Shultz, Abraham Heebner, Sr.
CANTWELL, JAMES. Whitemarsh. Dec 22, 1810. Adam Reiller, adm.
ROUSHONG, JOHN. Douglass. Jan 23, 1811. Henry Roushong, Jacob Johnson, adms.
JACOBY, JOHN. Upper Dublin. Feb 9, 1811. Barbara Jacoby, Casper Schlater, adms.
RAMBO, JOHN. Upper Merion. Feb 25, 1811. Matthias Holstein, George Holstein.
TRUMBOWER, George. Lower Salford. March 11, 1811. Susanna Trumbower, Jacob Kulp, adms.
JONES, DAVID. Plymouth. March 29, 1811. Elizabeth Jones, Benjamin Jones, adms.
LYSINGER, MARY. Plymouth. April 16, 1811. John Lysinger, adm.
POTTS, EDWARD B. Moreland. May 13, 1811. Isaac Williams, Thomas Shoemaker, adms.
FUNK, CHRISTIAN. Skippack and Perkiomen. June 6, 1811. Christian Gotwals, Christian Rosenberry.
SPEAR, LEONARD. Upper Providence. July 3, 1811. Catharine Spear, Philip Spear, adms.
DILLON, JACOB. Abington Aug 2, 1811. Mary Dillon, Jesse Dillon,

adms.
DETWILER, SAMUEL. Upper Salford. Aug 20, 1811. John Dillon, John Reiff, adms.
TOMPKINS, JONATHAN. Plymouth. Sept 4, 1811. Lydia Tompkins, adm.
WEBSTER, THOMAS, JR. Abington. Sept 25, 1811. Thomas Webster, adm.
DRASHER, ABRAHAM. Towamencin. Sept 28, 1811. Jacob Drasher, Abraham Anders, adms.
KOLB, HENRY. Skippack. Oct 12, 1811. Jacob Kolb, Dillman Kolb, adms.
JONES, MARY. Lower Merion. Nov 5, 1811. Mordecai Lawrence, Algernon Roberts, adms.
POTTS, FRANCIS R. Pottsgrove. Nov 9, 1811. Lydia Potts, adm.
STYER, HENRY. Whitpain. Nov 12, 1811. John Styer, David Styer, Leonard Styer, adms.
DENGLER, GEORGE. Douglass. Dec 11, 1811. Moses Kehl, John Dengler, adms.
BRINGHURST, ISRAEL. Upper Providence. Jan 4, 1812. Moses Hobson, Mary Bringhurst, adms.
TAYLOR, ELEANOR. Cheltenham. Jan 9, 1812. Robert Taylor, George D. Bennewille.
RANKIN, JANE. Moreland. Jan 22, 1812. George Richards, Henry Puff, adms.
DAVES, DAVID. Moreland. Jan 22, 1812. William Ryman, Rebecca Daves, adms.
HOLLIS, ELIZABETH. Horsham. Feb 3, 1812. William Hollis, adm.
PENNEBECKER, CATHARINE. Providence. Feb 5, 1812. Jacob Pennebecker.
DAVIS, ISAAC. Moreland. Feb 7, 1812. Mary Davis, adm.
GILKEY, MARY. Lower Merion. Feb 20, 1812. Job Davis, adm.
RANDALL, NICHOLAS. Abington. Feb 20, 1812. George Randall, adm.
HUMPHREY, RICHARD. Lower Merion. Feb 25, 1812. William Mendenhall, Morris Humphrey.
SPENCER, JOHN. Upper Dublin. Feb 26, 1812. Jeremiah McLlvain.
WHITE, BENJAMIN. Horsham. Feb 28, 1910(?). Thomas White, William White, adms.
YOCUM, JOHN. Worcester. March 5, 1812. Joseph Tyson, Barbara Yocum, adms.
NEIMAN, CATHARINE. Providence. March 23, 1812. Jacob Neiman, adm.
MINTZER, JOSEPH. Potts Grove. April 3, 1812. William Mintzer, adm.
KLINE, JOHN. Whitpain. April 11, 1812. Elizabeth Kline.
BROADES, WILLIAM. April 18, 1812. William Broades, adm.
GRAVER, LUDWIG. Upper Hanover. April 27, 1812. Elizabeth Graver, Andrew Graver, Jr., John Graver, adms.

BENJAMIN, FREDERICK. Pottsgrove. May 11, 1812. Elizabeth Benjamin, Amos Evans, adms.
EVANS, MARGARET. Gwynedd. May 28, 1812. Robert Edwards, adm.
KIMBLE, JOHN. Montgomery. June 1, 1812. Charlotte Kimble, Jacob Cassel, adms.
MARKLEY, ISAAC. Hatfield. June 15, 1812. Henry Markley, Abraham Markley, adms.
HOXWORTH, ELIZABETH. Hatfield. June 20, 1812. Edward Hoxworth.
CRISMAN, NICHOLAS. Limerick. June 22, 1812. Jacob Crisman, George Crisman, Henry Longacre, adms.
RAWLINS, RUTH. Lower Merion. June 23, 1812. John Rawlins, Nathan Rawlins, adms.
EVANS, OWEN. Lower Providence. July 13, 1812. Eleanor Evans, Edward Evans, adms.
NASH, WILLIAM. Upper Dublin. July 20, 1812. Sarah Nash, Daniel Nash, adms.
RICHARDS, JOHN. Hatfield. July 23, 1812. Mary Richards, adms.
BICKLE, JOHN, JR. Potts Grove. July 12, 1812. Elizabeth Bickle, Ludwig Bickle, Valentine Steltz, adms.
WICKS, WILLIAM. Pottsgrove. July 28, 1812. Samuel Heister, Thomas W. Leonard.
MATTHIAS, DAVID. Whitpain. July 30, 1812. George Martin, Andrew Fetzer, adms.
EVERHART, PHILIP. Upper Dublin. Aug 17, 1812. John Everhart, adm.
CHILD, AGNES. Abington. Aug 22, 1812. Robert Kennedy, adm.
COPE, TOBIAS. Montgomery. Sept 29, 1812. Henry Danehower, adm.
RYNOLD, DANIEL. Lower Providence. Oct 1, 1812. Catharine Rynold, John Hartenstine.
WAGGONER, BARBARA. Marlborough. Oct 2, 1812. Henry Stroman, adm.
ABRAHAMS, JAMES, JR. Upper Merion. Nov 5, 1812. James Abrahams, adm.
HOLLIS, WILLIAM. Horsham. Nov 11, 1812. Casper Schlater, adm.
KRIEBLE, CHRISTIAN. Towamencin. Nov 16, 1812. Andrew Krieble, adm.
SPARE, DANIEL. Worcester. Nov 17, 1812. Rosanna Spare, Jacob Spare, adms.
EVANS, MARY. Lower Merion. Nov 17, 1812. William Thomas, adm.
SELL, ABRAHAM. Upper Hanover. Nov 19, 1812. Abraham Sell, adm.
MESSEMER, JACOB. Pottstown. Dec 8, 1812. Philip Yost, Samuel Rodarmel, adm.
LENTZ, JOHN. Whitemarsh. Dec 16, 1812. Jacob Lentz, Daniel Streper, Catharine Lentz, adm.
HOLT, MORDECAI. Horsham. Dec 19, 1812. Nathan Holt, adm.
SNARE, JACOB. Hatfield. Dec 19, 1812. William Snare, adm.

STITLER, JOHN. Limerick. Jan 4, 1813. Matthew Brooke, Catharine
  Stitler, Samuel Stitler, Michael Stitler, adms.
YEAKLE, ABRAHAM. Towamencin. Jan 8, 1813. Sarah Yeakle, Jacob
  Wampole, adms.
KOPLIN, MATTHIAS. Norristown. Jan 12, 1813. John Markley,
  Nathaniel Koplin, adm.
LINN, JOSEPH. Cheltenham. Jan 17, 1813. Samuel Felty, adm.
LANCASTER, THOMAS. Whitemarsh. Jan 25, 1813. Ann Lancaster,
  Knowles Lancaster.
TYSON, ISAAC. Abington. Jan 27, 1813. Isaac Tyson, Jonathan Tyson,
  Jr., adms.
KIMBLE, WILLIAM. Moreland. Feb 1, 1813. Peter Tyson, adm.
SAHLOR, JOHN. New Hanover. Feb 15, 1813. John Markley, Henry
  Walt, adms.
WILLIAMS, MARY. Whitemarsh. Feb 16, 1813. Joseph Mather, David
  Meredith, adms.
GEHMAN, JOHN. Franconia. Mar 2, 1813. Samuel Gehman, Sarah
  Gehman, adms.
KROUSE, ABRAHAM. Skippack. March 10, 1813. Jacob Server,
  Garret Zeigler, adms.
HURST, ELIAS. Whitpain. March 25, 1813. John Hurst, Henry Hurst,
  adms.
RAMBO, WILLIAM. Limerick. April 5, 1813. John Rambo, Peter
  Tyson, adms.
MOORE, JONATHAN. Upper Merion. April 5, 1813. Richard Moore,
  Catharine Moore, adms.
WIREMAN, MARTIN. Hatfield. April 12, 1813. John Wireman, Daniel
  Rosenberger.
KEELY, GEORGE. New Hanover. April 17, 1813. Michael Dotterer,
  Sebastian Keely, adms.
EGBERT, JOHN. Whitemarsh. May 3, 1813. Lawrence Egbert, Samuel
  Maulsby, adms.
WISLER, ISAAC. Hatfield. May 15, 1813. Abraham Cassel, John
  Wisler, adms.
SCHULTZ, BALTZER. Upper Hanover. May 17, 1813. Matthias
  Schultz, David Schultz, adms.
MISSEMER, FREDERICK. Potts Grove. May 18, 1813. John Missimer,
  adm.
LUKENS, MATTHIAS. Upper Dublin. May 18, 1813. Mary Lukens,
  adm.
DETWILER, JOHN. Lower Providence. May 19, 1813. Jacob Detwiler,
  Abraham Gotwals, adms.
AMBLER, JOSEPH. Montgomery. May 27, 1813. Joseph Ambler, John
  Ambler, David Ambler, adms.
RICHARDS, MATTHIAS. New Hanover. June 5, 1813. Matthias
  Gilbert.
WILEY, THOMAS. Lower Merion. June 5, 1813. Joseph Hayes, adm.

HUGHES, EDWARD. Towamencin. June 29, 1813. Urny Hughes, Cadwallader Foulke, adm.
GOTSHALK, WILLIAM. Skippack. July 5, 1813. Andrew Zeigler, adm.
STILLWAGGON, MICHAEL. Skippack. July 6, 1813. Jacob Hases, Peter Wipler, adms.
HALLOWELL, HANNAH. Cheltenham. July 15, 1813. William Hallowell.
JONES, THOMAS, JR. Cheltenham. July 20, 1813. John Jones, adm.
ROYER, JACOB. Marlborough. July 28, 1813. Adam Miller, Elias Hersh, adms.
MADARY, BARBARA. Montgomery. July 29, 1813. John Madary, adm.
DONELLY, JOHN. Montgomery. Aug 7, 1813. Joseph Donelly, Hugh Donelly, adms.
HORN, GEORGE. Lower Merion. Aug 19, 1813. Sarah Horn, William J. Horn.
KNIPE, CHRISTIAN. Gwynedd. Aug 24, 1813. Mary Knipe, Henry Knipe, John W. Knipe, adms.
BURNSIDE, ALEXANDER. Providence. Aug 24, 1813. William Burnside, Jane Burnside, adm.
BERNT, LUDWICK. New Hanover. Aug 27, 1813. George Zigter, Peter Bernt, adms.
GILINGER, HENRY. Plymouth. Sept 4, 1813. John Gilinger, William Gilinger.
APPLE, SAMUEL. Hatfield. Sept 7, 1813. Margaret Apple, Abraham Root, adms.
BURNSIDE, ALEXANDER. Lower Providence. Sept 13, 1813. William Hamill, adm.
NICKLIN, ELIZABETH. Norristown. Oct 7, 1813. Philip H. Nicklin.
PRINCE, GEORGE. Plymouth. Oct 20, 1813. Jacob Prince, adm.
COLFLESH, HENRY. Lower Merion. Oct 25, 1813. John Priest, David Colflesh, adms.
HALLOWELL, BENJAMIN. Abington. Oct 26, 1813. Abigail Hallowell, Thomas Livezey, adms.
FITZWATER, THOMAS. Upper Dublin. Oct 26, 1813. John Fitzwater, Catharine Fitzwater.
LUKENS, ABNER. Upper Dublin. Nov 8, 1813. Moses Lukens, Charles Thomas, adms.
EVANS, JOHN. Gwynedd. Nov 16, 1813. Eleanor Evans, Cadwallader Foulke, William Foulke, adms.
COLFLESH, BARBARA. Lower Merion. Nov 19, 1813. Thomas Lowry, adm.
KULP, MARTIN. Worcester. Nov 30, 1813. Matthias Kulp, Daniel Kulp, adms.
HOOVER, MARGARET. Gwynedd. Dec 7, 1813. Christian Hoover, Philip Hoover, adms.
THOMAS, BENJAMIN. Whitemarsh. Dec 16, 1813. Justus Schultz, adm.

347

ZEIGLER, ANDREW. Lower Salford. Dec 17, 1813. Michael Zeigler, Abraham Tyson, adms.
EPPRIGHT, JOHN. Upper Merion. Jan 8, 1814. William Eppright, Christian Eppright.
RAMBO, MICHAEL. Upper Merion. Jan 15, 1814. Ebeneza Rambo, Sarah Rambo, adms.
REEFINGER, FREDERICK. Marlborough. Jan 18, 1814. Philip Zepp.
YOCUM, WILLIAM. Lower Salford. Jan 25, 1814. Jonathan Yocum, Israel Yocum, adms.
VANCOURT, DANIEL. Moreland. Jan 27, 1814. William Ayres, adm.
DAVIS, JOB. Whitemarsh. Jan 27, 1814. Frederick Dull, adm.
SERVOR, CATHARINE. Hatfield. Feb 8. Philip Servor, adm.
NORNY, ANDREW. Plymouth. Feb 11, 1814. Solomon Norny, Alan Corson, adms.
AMBLER, JOSEPH. Whitemarsh. Feb 16, 1814. Ann Ambler, adm.
EVANS, ELIZABETH. Gwynedd. Feb 16, 1814. Robert Edwards, adm.
SCHLATER, JACOB. Upper Dublin. Feb 24, 1814. Casper Schlater, adm.
DAVIS, THOMAS. Plymouth. March 10, 1814. William Shepard, adm.
KNOX, ROBERT. Whitpain. March 22, 1814. Margaret Knox, Isaac McGlathery, William M. White, adms.
SHARE, PHILIP. Lower Providence. Mar 30, 1814. Sarah Share, Peter Saylor, John Battlepwee, adms.
CRAFT, JOHN. Abington. April 11, 1814. Esther Craft, Thomas Fletcher, adms.
CROLL, CHRISTIAN. Skippack and Perkiomen. May 2, 1814. Jacob Croll, Michael Croll, Benjamin Reiff, adms.
SCHLOTTERER, GEORGE. Upper Salford. May 6, 1814. William Schlotterer.
BUCKWALTER, CATHARINE. May 13, 1814. Henry Shelby, adm.
GORDON, JOHN. Montgomery. May 17, 1814. Joseph Kenderdine, adm.
DUNGAN, JEREMIAH. Moreland. May 17, 1814. Susanna Dungan, Amos Dungan, adms.
LUKENS, ABRAHAM. Whitpain. May 25, 1814. Esther Lukens, Mahlon Lukens, David Lukens, adms.
YOST, JACOB. Whitpain. June 11, 1814. Abraham Yost, adm.
ZIMMERMAN, JACOB. June 15, 1814. Catharine Zimmerman, Nathan Zimmerman.
MOYER, PETER. Upper Providence. July 20, 1814. Catharine Moyer, Henry Hamiller, adm.
DRAKE, JOHN. Montgomery. July 17, 1814. Evan Jones, adm.
MILLER, CHRISTOPHER. Limerick. July 30, 1814. Samuel Fegley, adm.
LONG, GEORGE. Marlborough. Aug 1, 1814. Jacob Long, George Long, adms.
PAUL, ESTHER. Abington. Aug 15, 1814. Thomas Fletcher.

LEECH, JACOB. Cheltenham. Aug 17, 1814. Charles Leech, Thomas Leech, adms.
SMITH, PHILIP JACOB. New Hanover. Aug 1814. Benjamin Markley, adm.
EGBERT, JAMES. Whitemarsh. Aug 19, 1814. Martha Egbert, William Egbert, adms.
RAMBO, JOHN. Limerick. Sept 2, 1814. Samuel Gross, Eli Rambo, adms.
FRENCH, SAMUEL. Plymouth. Sept 7, 1814. David Lukens, adm.
NERMITH, JOHN. Moreland. Sept 8, 1814. Titus Yerkes, adm.
HALLOWELL, CHARLES. Whitemarsh. Sept 9, 1814. Alexander Crawford.
TURNER, WILLIAM. Lower Merion. Sept 10, 1814. Ann Turner, adm.
BRANDSTALL, JOHANNA CHRISTINE. Oct 6, 1814. Jacob Boller, adm.
MACER, MARIA DOROTHY. Oct 6, 1814. Jacob Boller, adm.
TYSON, CORNELIUS. Providence. Nov 14, 1814. Joseph Tyson, Susanna Tyson, adms.
LUNN, THOMAS. Montgomery. Nov 14, 1814. Joseph Lunn, adm.
OWEN, ISAAC. Upper Merion. Nov 15, 1814. Thomas Lowry, David Brooke, adms.
MOORE, BARBARA. Upper Merion. Nov 15, 1814. Thomas Shepard, James Sloan, adms.
JONES, RICHARD. Lower Merion. Nov 16, 1814. James Jones, adm.
HALLOWELL, ISAAC. Abington. Nov 19, 1814. John Tyson, Sarah Hallowell, adms.
KEYSER, SUSANNAH. Worcester. Nov 19, 1814. John Keyser, adm.
PRINCE, MARY. Plymouth. Nov 29, 1814. Jacob Prince, Henry Prince, adms.
DAVIS, JESSE. Montgomery. Nov 30, 1814. William Collom, adm.
CROLL, SAMUEL HENRY. Montgomery. Dec 3, 1814. Peter Freed, adm.
FREDERICK, GEORGE. Upper Salford. Jan 2, 1815. John Frederick, Henry Frederick adms.
KROUS, DAVID. Upper Hanover. Jan 3, 1815. Jeremiah Krous, John Krous, adms.
CLIME, CONRAD. Upper Dublin. Jan 5, 1815. Rachel Clime, Christopher Dresher, adms.
SHEWECK, MATTHIAS. Marlborough. Jan 14, 1814. Philip Zepp.
WILSON, ELIZABETH. Montgomery. Jan 24, 1815. Joseph Milligan, John King, adms.
YOST, PETER. Frederick. Jan 26, 1815. Michael Dotterer.
GROFF, HENRY. Upper Salford. Jan 30, 1815. Jacob Groff, Conrad Keeler, adms.
WYNKOOF, PHILIP. Moreland. Feb 4, 1815. William Ayres, adm.
YOST, JACOB. Frederick. Feb 13, 1815. Jacob Houch, adm.
DAVIS, DAVID. Hatfield. Feb 20, 1815. Henry Buchamman, John

Davis, Sr., adms.
MILLIGAN, JAMES. Montgomery. Feb 23, 1814. Joseph Milligan, Ann Milligan, adms.
HUMPHREYS, CHARLES. March 4, 1815. Thomas Humphreys, Charles Humphreys.
FITZGERALD, THOMAS. March 8, 1815. William Fitzgerald, John Tyson, adms.
WILSON, SARAH. March 14, 1814. Joshua Wilson, Rachel Wilson, adms.
OSBORN, RANDEL. Whitpain. March 18, 1815. Richard Osborn, Nathan Osborn, Jonah Osborn, adms.
WAMBOLD, DAVID. Upper Salford. March 21, 1815. George Wambold, adm.
WAMBOLD, MARIA. Upper Salford. March 21, 1815. George Wambold, adm.
DEHAVEN, SAMUEL, SR. Upper Merion. March 23, 1815. Isaac Dehaven, adm.
FLECK, ADAM, JR. Gwynedd. March 28, 1815. Benjamin Weber, John Clemens, adms.
DAVIS, THOMAS. Hatfield. March 29, 1815. John Davis, David Davis, adms.
KERBOUCH, SIBELLA. Upper Dublin. April 3, 1815. David Kerbouch, adm.
PATTERSON, SAMUEL. Norristown. April 5, 1815. Mary Patterson, Robert Hammill, adms.
REX, MARGARET. Springfield. April 14, 1815. Catharine Snyder, adm.
DUNNET, CHRISTIAN. Springfield. April 17, 1815. George Dunnet, Charles Dunnet, Christian Dunnet, adms.
LEVEY, ABRAHAM. April 24, 1815. George Hillegass, Adam Levey, adms.
KOLB, SUSANNA. Upper Providence. May 10, 1815. Jacob Landis, Lewis Grater, adms.
CUPP, MARY. Upper Dublin. May 15, 1815. Peter Cupp, adm.
DETWILER, JACOB. Perkiomen. May 22, 1815. Jacob Detwiler, John Detwiler, adms.
CONVEAR, CHRISTIAN. Hatfield. May 26, 1815. Abraham Shipe, adm.
MORGAN, BENJAMIN. Hatfield. June 5, 1815. Daniel Morgan, adm.
SLOANE, JAMES. Upper Merion. June 5, 1815. Samuel Henderson, George W. Holstein.
BARNES, ROBERT. Moreland. June 6, 1815. Rachel Barnes, adm.
SHELLENBERGER, JACOB. Hatfield. June 7, 1815. Conrad Shellenberger, Adam Gerhart, adms.
KOLB, DANIEL. Lower Providence. June 8, 1815. Matthias Kolb, Henry Kolb, adms.
FREED, JOHN. Upper Hanover. June 12, 1815. Susanna Freed, John Garber, adms.

DAVIS, ABIGAIL. Lower Providence. June 16, 1815. Elizabeth David, adm.
KUGLER, JOHN. Lower Merion. July 31, 1815. Harriot Kugler, adm.
MILLER, LOWRENCE. Lower Providence. Aug 12, 1815. Ludwig Miller, Daniel Miller, Lowrence Miller, adms.
BEAN, JOHN. Marlborough. Aug 14, 1815. Christian Gaelman.
WEBER, JOHN. Lower Providence. Sept 2, 1815. George Weber, Christian Weber, William Bean, adms.
REIFF, DANIEL. Lower Salford. Sept 3, 1815. George Reiff, Jacob Reiff, adms.
ROADS, CATHARINE. Moreland. Sept 15, 1815. Jacob Roads, adm.
SWINEHART, JOHN GEORGE. Douglass. Sept 19, 1815. Henry Swinehart, adm.
FRANCIS, JACOB. Lower Providence. Oct 3, 1815. Isaiah Wells, adm.
LANDIS, JOHN. Douglass. Oct 17, 1815. Leonard Miller, adm.
LANDIS, JOHN. Douglass. Oct 18, 1815. Abraham Landis, adm.
ARMSTRONG, JOHN. Plymouth. Oct 24, 1815. James Armstrong.
RENNINGER, CONRAD. New Hanover. Oct 28, 1815. John Gilbert, John Renninger, adms.
HENDRICKS, PAUL. Towamencin. Nov 8, 1815. William Hendricks, Benjamin Hendricks.
ROSS, CLYMER. Norristown. Nov 14, 1815. Caleb Newbold, Jr.
HORLACKER, PETER. Upper Hanover. Nov 23, 1815. Alexander Ahe, Adam Snyder, adms.
WARNER, HANNAH. Lower Merion. Nov 27, 1815. Isaac Roberts, Abel Thomas, adms.
SHARP, ANDREW. Whitemarsh. Nov 30, 1815. Mary Sharp, Israel Hoxworth.
COULSTON, JOHN. Plymouth. Dec 4, 1815. Barnabas Coulston, George Coulston, Daniel Davis, adms.
DEWEES, WILLIAM. Whitemarsh. Dec 8, 1815. Jacob Streeper, Bernard Streeper, adms.
COULSTON, ABIGAIL. Whitpain. Dec 9, 1815. George M. Potts, adm.
PLUCK, GEORGE. Norriton. Dec 11, 1815. Peter Pluck, adm.
YERGER, CHRISTIAN. Douglass. Dec 22, 1815. Frederick Dalaker.
McCLENNAN, JAMES. Abington. Jan 4, 1816. Jeremiah Berrell, adm.
PUFF, BURKETT. Plymouth. Jan 17, 1816. David Egbert, adm.
SHOEMAKER, MATTHIAS. Whitpain. Feb 3, 1816. Thomas Shoemaker, Rachel Shoemaker.
MILLER, JOHN. Lower Providence. Feb 5, 1816. Abraham Shult, adm.
ORTLIP, ISRAEL. Potts Grove. Feb 20, 1816. Mahlon Ortlip, adm.
SISLER, MICHAEL. Upper Merion. Feb 13, 1816. Michael Sisler, John Sisler, adms.
CASSEL, MARGARET. Towamencin. Feb 14, 1816. Yellis Cassel, adm.
REINER, SUSANNA. Providence. Feb 26, 1816. Jacob Graher, John Rittenhouse, adms.
PAUL, WILLIAM. Lower Providence. Feb 26, 1816. Peter Lehman,

351

adm.
SEIP, DAVID. Towamencin. Feb 28, 1816. Abraham Seip, Christopher Krieble.
YOUNG, JOHN. Lower Providence. March 4, 1816. George Zimmerman, adm.
KRICKBAUM, CONRAD. March 7, 1816. Samuel Powell, Seth Snyder, adms.
CHILDS, JOHN. Upper Providence. March 9, 1816. Mary Childs, James Childs, adms.
WIRSHING, PHELIX. Lower Merion. March 11, 1816. Phelix Wirshing, Joseph Wirshing.
LONGACRE, CATHARINE. Providence. March 14, 1816. Peter Longacre, James Miller, adms.
HUNSBERGER, ABRAHAM. Limerick. March 16, 1816. Isaac Hunsberger.
MAJOR, JOSEPH. Upper Dublin. April 3, 1816. Alexander Major, James Rutter, adms.
KLINE, GEORGE. Gwynedd. April 4, 1816. Catharine Kline, Abraham Dannehower.
ORTLIP, GEORGE. Limerick. April 10, 1816. James Evans, adm.
WEASNER, HENRY. Douglass. April 15, 1816. Moses Kehl, Mack Yerger, adms.
KIRK, JESSE. Horsham. April 16, 1816. Rachel Kirk, Jacob Kirk, adms.
RHOADS, JACOB. Douglass. April 24, 1816. Margaret Thoads, Christian Shoner.
RAMSEY, ALEXANDER. Plymouth. May 2, 1816. Benjamin Ramsey, George M. Potts, adms.
JOHNSON, LEONARD. Plymouth. May 2, 1816. Elizabeth Johnson, George M. Potts, adms.
TYSON, ROBERT. Upper Providence. May 3, 1816. Mary Tyson, Daniel Tyson, Moses Hobson, adms.
SCHRACK, JOHN. Upper Providence. May 7, 1816. Samuel Gross, adm.
ESSIG, GEORGE. Upper Providence. May 7, 1816. John Essig, Jacob Essig, adms.
ARMSTRONG, ELEANOR. Norriton. May 10, 1816. Joseph Armstrong.
DANNEHOWER, ABRAHAM. Gwynedd. May 13, 1816. Elizabeth Dannehower, Jacob Dannehower, Henry Dannehower.
HARPER, JONATHAN. Upper Providence. May 19, 1816. Martha Harper, Isaac Whitelock, adms.
DEWEES, ABRAHAM. Lower Merion. May 27, 1816. Samuel Bard.
COULSTON, HENRY. Norriton. May 27, 1816. William Coulston.
GOURLEY, SAMUEL. Moreland. May 28, 1816. Priscilla Gourley, Joseph Gourley, adms.
RINER, HENRY. Abington. June 4, 1816. Nicholas Riner, Daniel Riner.

CUSTER, PETER. Skippack. June 7, 1816. John Custer, John Tyson, adms.
SHLIFER, DANIEL. Upper Hanover. June 7, 1816. John Shlifer, Wendel Wean, adms.
SNYDER, JOHN. Worcester. June 19, 1816. Catharine Snyder, Abraham Snyder, Samuel Snyder, adms.
ROBERTS, JESSE. gwynedd. June 19, 1816. Rachel Roberts.
KEYSER, JOHN. Worcester. June 21, 1816. Sarah Keyser, Isaac Keyser, adms.
SHOSTER, JACOB. Lower Merion. July 5, 1816. Amy Shoster, Joseph Hoskins.
FOSTER, REBECCA. Abington. July 11, 1816. Charles Johnson.
BARTHOLOMEW, ELIZABETH. Providence. July 15, 1816. Valentine Saylor, Henry Fry.
BECHTEL, GEORGE. Pottsgrove. Aug 10, 1816. George Bechtel, Joshua Bechtel.
HILLEGASS, JOHN. Upper Hanover. Aug 30, 1816. Catharine Hillegas, George Hillegass.
STYER, JOHN. Whitpain. Sept 14, 1816. Jacob Styer, John Styer, Stephen Styer, adms.
MOYER, JOHN. Whitemarsh. Sept 21, 1816. Baltzer Moyer, William Moyer.
SHOESTER, SOPHIE. Lower Merion. Sept 25, 1816. Leonard Shoester.
KOHLE, CATHARINE. Moreland. Oct 7, 1816. Nicholas Kohle.
ROBINSON, HANNAH. Upper Providence. Oct 10, 1816. William Robinson.
CAMPBELL, ANDREW. Upper Providence. Oct 23, 1816. Jacob Schwenck, adm.
SHEARER, PETER. Whitemarsh. Nov 1, 1816. George Shearer, John Shearer.
DONNELLY, EDWARD. Montgomery. Nov 8, 1816. George Weaver.
DETWILER, JOSEPH. Upper Providence. Nov 25, 1816. Mary Detwiler, Jacob Lantes, adms.
BRITTON, ALEXANDER. Upper Merion. Nov 26, 1816. John Cotton.
JOHNSON, JACOB. Nov 27, 1816. Philip Reed.
JENKINS, LEWIS. Upper Merion. Dec 3, 1816. William Shepherd.
TYSON, ABRAHAM. Abington. Dec 16, 1816. Jonathan Lukens, Thomas Michener.
OWENS, JOHN. Upper Merion. Dec 28, 1816. Samuel Coats, John Owens, adms.
BENJAMIN, ALEXANDER. Upper Providence. Dec 21, 1816. Lewis Schrack.
GRIFFITH, ELIZABETH. Norristown. Jan 1, 1817. John Coats, Jacob Ramsey.
HOOT, ELIZABETH. Gwynedd. Jan 3, 1817. Peter Hoot, Abraham Weber.

TEANY, HENRY. Lower Providence. Jan 6, 1817. John Teany, Henry Teany.
BARLOW, JOHN. Limerick. Jan 13, 1817. Phebe Barlow, Abner Barlow.
BINGEMAN, ELIZABETH. Pottsgrove. Feb 3, 1817. Benjamin Bingeman.
MOURER, PETER. Upper Hanover. Feb 3, 1817. Samuel Kepler, adm.
MULLEN, ISRAEL. Horsham. Feb 4, 1817. John Simpson, adm.
EVANS, EVAN C. Gwynedd. Feb 10, 1817. Robert I. Evans, Cadwallader Foulke.
CRAFT, JACOB. Abington. Feb 10, 1817. Jonathan Craft, John Craft, adms.
THOMAS, JOHN. New Hanover. Feb 18, 1817. Frederick Dellicker.
SIMPSON, JOB. Pottsgrove. Feb 18, 1817. Thomas Jackson.
SWANKERT, PHILIP. Whitemarsh. March 3, 1817. John Dager.
WEBER, JACOB. Worcester. March 18, 1817. Mordecai Jones, George Shade.
MILLER, HENRY. Montgomery. March 18, 1817. Evan Jones, William Burney.
CONARD, BENJAMIN. Norriton. April 1, 1817. John Earnest, Henry Conard.
YETTER, LEWIS. Plymouth. April 5, 1817. Ann Yetter, Alan W. Corson.
WEIST, GEORGE. Lower Merion. April 7, 1817. Esther Weist, Samuel Stearne.
MARPLE, THOMAS, Upper Dublin. April 12, 1817. Margaret Marple.
STEINBACK, MARTIN. Horsham. April 21, 1817. Thomas Barnes.
JONES, MORDECAI. Whitpain. May 10, 1817. Sophia Jones, Job Roberts.
SHEEN, JOSEPH. Lower Providence. May 14, 1817. Elizabeth Skeen, James Skeen, adms.
STILLWAGGON, HENRY. Lower Merion. May 20, 1817. Frederick Stillwaggon, Joseph Stillwaggon.
WEAVER, PETER. Whitemarsh. May 13, 1817. Samuel Campbell, Henry Schutz, adms.
BEAN, JOHN. Worcester. May 27, 1817. Jacob Bean, Joseph Tyson.
BOTTOM, LEVI. Limerick. June 5, 1817. Elizabeth Bottom, Amos Evans, adms.
WHITBY, ANTHONY. Lower Providence. June 12, 1817. John Whitby, William Hamill.
CARL, BARBARA. Upper Providence. June 14, 1817. Christian Carl.
THOMAS, JOHN. Upper Providence. June 17, 1817. John Thomas, David Thomas, adms.
DUBRE, JACOB. Moreland. July 14, 1817. Hiram McNeill.
AMAN, JESSE. Upper Dublin. July 21, 1817. George Aman.
NEALL, LETETIA. Moreland. Aug 1, 1817. Jesse Harker.
HUMEL, GEORGE. Franconia. Aug 8, 1817. Jacob Humel.

HYSER, ANDREW. Perkiomen. Aug 11, 1817. Jacob Hyser, John Tyson.
CADWALADER, ISAAC. Horsham. Aug 27, 1817. Owen Cadwalader.
MYERS, SAMUEL. Hatfield. Sept 8, 1817. Abraham Myers, Sarah Myers.
FAUST, HENRY. Frederick. Sept 9, 1817. Nicholas Faust, adm.
SCHOLL, GEORGE. Franconia. Sept 20, 1817. Jonathan Scholl, Philip Scholl, adm.
CASSEL, JOHN. Lower Providence. Oct 13, 1817. Jacob Cassel, John Tyson, adms.
STREEPER, JOHN. Springfield. Oct 20, 1817. Thomas Sheppard.
EVANS, JOHN. Lower Merion. Oct 20, 1817. Hannah Evans, George Latch.
EVANS, NATHAN. Upper Merion. Oct 25, 1817. Aaron Evans, George M. Potts.
MARKLEY, ISAAC. Norriton. Oct 27, 1817. Abraham Markley, Jesse Bean.
ZIMMERMAN, JACOB. Upper Dublin. Nov 3, 1817. Abraham Zimmerman, Jacob Zimmerman.
HALLOWELL, MARGARET. Moreland. Nov 17, 1817. Joseph Hallowell.
DETTER, ABRAHAM. Frederick. Nov 18, 1817. Conrad Detter, Jr.
SHOEMAKER, NATHAN. Moreland. Nov 19, 1817. Samuel Shoemaker, Comley Shoemaker.
STOVER, HENRY. Hatfield. Nov 27, 1817. Jacob Stover, Joseph Stover.
MOYER, JACOB. Norriton. Dec 8, 1817. Elizabeth Moyer, Abraham Metz.
TYSON, JACOB. Providence. Dec 23, 1817. Jacob Umstead, Christian Miller.
JONES, ABNER D. Springfield, Dec 24, 1817. Ashel Jones, adm.
MOORE, ELIZABETH. Upper Merion. Jan 7, 1818. Abijah Stevens, adm.
MARSH, DANIEL. New Hanover. Jan 20, 1818. Daniel Marsh.
BERGEY, ABRAHAM. Limerick. Jan 20, 1818. Jacob Pennypacker, Jonah Bergey.
HENDERSON, NATHANIEL J. Merion. Jan 17, 1818. Catharine Henderson, Joshua Jones.
CLINE, MARGARET. Upper Dublin. Jan 23, 1818. Jonathan Deaves.
GRUB, ANDREW. Lower Salford. Jan 26, 1818. George Heekler, Elizabeth Grub, Isaac Grub.
DETTERER, CHRISTIAN. Worcester. Jan 31, 1818. Abraham Detterer, Christian Detterer.
WISLER, JOHN. Hatfield. Feb 13, 1818. Isaac Wisler, Henry Stauffer.
GERHART, BARNARD. Whitpain. Feb 19, 1818. Philip Sheneberger.
SHULTZ, WILLIAM. Upper Hanover. Feb 26, 1818. Isaac Shultz, Abraham Gehman.

DAVIS, JAMES. Whitemarsh. March 2, 1817. Rebecca Davis.
URMY, DAVID. Frederick. March 11, 1818. William Tyson.
CARL, HENRY. Upper Providence. March 14, 1818. Abraham Gerhart, Henry Snyder, Isaiah Carl.
MULLEN, MARTHA. Horsham. March 28, 1818. Rachel Kirk, adm.
KLINE, HENRY. Hatfield. March 13, 1818. John Kline, adm.
WILSON, ROBERT. Moreland. April 13, 1818. Mary Wilson.
EVANS, WILLIAM. Limerick. April 25, 1818. Jacob Lewis, Edward Gallony.
HARTMAN, PHILIP. Potts Grove. April 25, 1818. Jacob Hartman, Frederick Hartman.
WAMBOLD, JACOB. Towamencin. May 1, 1818. Frederick Wambold.
HERB, JOHN. Upper Hanover. May 5, 1818. John Herb, Jr.
BROWN, JOSEPH. Horsham. May 11, 1818. Jacob Kirk, Jr.
OVERHOLTZER, GEORGE. Hatfield. May 18, 1818. Jacob Overholtzer, John Shutt.
WHITE, ABNER. Upper Providence. May 19, 1818. William M. White.
BEYER, JOSEPH. Norriton. May 20, 1818. Jacob Beyer, Jacob Bean.
CHILD, GEORGE. Horsham. May 29, 1818. Joseph Kenderdine.
ZIMMERMAN, WILLIAM. Norriton. June 14, 1818. Arnold Zimmerman, Christian Zimmerman, William Zimmerman.
WAGNER, MARY. Skippack. June 6, 1818. Abraham Ziegler.
SHULTZ, ANDREW. Upper Hanover. June 10, 1818. Matthias Shultz, David Shultz.
KNOX, HUGH. Lower Merion. June 11, 1818. Lewis Knox, Hugh Cooper, adms.
BENEZETT, ANTHONY. Abington. June 11, 1818. Mary Benezett, Jeremiah Barrell, Henry Barrello, adms.
McCOY, WILLIAM. Upper Dublin. June 13, 1818. Amos McCoy, adm.
FISS, JOHN. Lower Merion. June 23, 1818. Mary Fiss, Benjamin Fiss.
GUILKEE, BENJAMIN. Plymouth. July 8, 1818. Thomas Davis
HAGY, JOHN. Whitemarsh. July 30, 1818. Mary Hagy.
HARTEL, JACOB. Montgomery. Sept 2, 1818. John Hartel.
BROWN, JOHN. Montgomery. Sept 8, 1818. George Land.
BURNS, ZACHARIAH. Sept 21, 1818. Margaret Burnes, Jesse Roberts, George M. Potts.
STREEPER, GEORGE. Whitemarsh. Sept 28, 1818. George Surns.
MARSHEL, MATTHEW. Moreland. Sept 29, 1818. Hiram McNeill.
FRETCH, JOHN. Abington. Oct 3, 1818. Andrew Fretch.
GRESSEMER, JOHN. Upper Hanover. Oct 8, 1818. Frederick Gressemer, George Green.
GARBER, BENJAMIN. Upper Providence. Oct 19, 1818. Hannah Garber, Henry Garber.
KNIGHT, JONATHAN. Cheltenham. Oct 20, 1818. David Knight, Ezra Towsand, Robert Paste.
RAZOR, MICHAEL. Limerick. Nov 2, 1818. John Razor, Moses Hobson, adms.

PUGH, HENRY. Lower Merion. Nov 14, 1818. Henry Pugh.
CRESS, WILLIAM. Whitemarsh. Nov 16, 1818. Margaret Cress, Henry Schutz, adms.
SHRIVER, JOHN. Springfield. Nov 17, 1818. Sarah Shriver, John Huston.
GYER, JOHN. Upper Hanover. Nov 18, 1818. John Gyer, Jacob Gyer.
ELLIOT, CHARLES J. Upper Merion. Nov 24, 1818. John Elliot, adm.
DAVIS, JOHN. Gwynedd. Dec 7, 1818. Elizabeth Davis, Mary Jones.
ZICHLER, MORDECAI. Potts Grove. Dec 20, 1818. Jacob Zichler.
LENHART, GEORGE. Cheltenham. Dec 28, 1818. Joseph Lenhart, Casper Schlater.
SHOEMAKER, EZEKIEL. Whitpain. Jan 4, 1819. Joseph Shoemaker, Jacob Weber.
KRIEBEL, ABRAHAM, SR. Lower Salford. Jan 7, 1819. Abraham Kriebel, Jr.
BENNETT, JACOB. Moreland. Jan 23, 1819. Whitman Bennett, Christian Snyder.
CLEMMENS, LEONARD. Worcester. Feb 16, 1819. Jacob Clemmens, Henry Moser.
FITZWATER, MATTHEW. Upper Dublin. Feb 16, 1819. George Fitzwater.
HARLEY, JACOB. Lower Salford. Feb 20, 1819. Henry Harley, Joseph Harley, adms.
EATON, JOSEPH. Horsham. March 5, 1819. Levi Jenkins, adm.
POTTS, WILLIAM. Pottstown. March 9, 1819. Thomas Baird.
KROUSE, SUSANNA. New Hanover. March 18, 1819. Charles Krouse.
CAUFFMAN, ARCHIBLAD. Providence. March 30, 1819. Jacob Cauffman.
BURNS, SAMUEL. Plymouth. April 3, 1819. Eve Burns.
SPEES, CHRISTIAN. Upper Salford. April 15, 1819. Henry Markley.
CUSTER, SARAH. Whitpain. May 4, 1819. Isaac Custer, Paul Custer.
CROUSE, SAMUEL. New Hanover. May 11, 1819. Jacob Crouse.
JONES, JONATHAN, SR. Gwynedd. May 18, 1819. Jonathan Jones.
HARVEY, THOMAS. Whitpain. June 5, 1819. Mary Marvey.
HIGHLEY, JOHN. Lower Providence. June 10, 1819. Jacob Highley, Joseph Crawford.
McLERNON, MAY. Upper Merion. June 10, 1819. Francis McLernon, Francis Lyle.
SPENCER, JARRET. Moreland. June 12, 1819. Charles Spencer, Samuel E. Spencer.
DISMANT, DANIEL. Upper Providence. June 14, 1819. Thomas Helbarn, Moses Hobson.
EVERHART, JOHN, SR. Whitpain. June 19, 1819. Joseph Everhart, Abraham Everhart.
CROLL, JACOB. Whitpain. June 26, 1819. Frederick Conrad.
PLACE, JOSEPH. Upper Providence. June 28, 1819. Margaret Place, John Buttesway, adms.

357

MAJOR, JOHN. Worcester. July 1, 1819. Thomas Major, adm.
BEVENS, WILLIAM. Norristown. June 12, 1819. George Govett.
WISLER, SAMUEL. Towamencin. July 16, 1819. Jacob Kulp, Harman Gotshalk.
WILLS, MICHAEL. Norristown. July 29, 1819. Michael Wills.
YERKES, ELIZABETH. Moreland. Aug 12, 1819. Edward Yerkes, Joseph Yerkes.
MAY, JOHN. Lower Merion. Aug 16, 1819. Fronica May.
WEST, RICHARD. Whitemarsh. Aug 19, 1819. Peter Dager.
SHAFFER, PETER. Limerick. Aug 17, 1819. Peter Shaffer.
TOMPKINS, JOHN. Moreland. Aug 18, 1819. Charles Johnson.
BECHTEL, JACOB. Upper Hanover. Aug 20, 1819. John Bechtel.
POTTS, NATHAN. Norristown. Aug 27, 1819. George M. Potts, Nathan R. Potts.
HENDERSON, WILLIAM. Norristown. Sept 11, 1819. Elizabeth Henderson.
STOUFFER, ELIZABETH. Hatfield. Sept 5, 1819. Joseph Stouffer.
OBERHOLTZER, JOHN. Franconia. Oct 1, 1819. Joseph Alderfer, adm.
GREGER, DAVIS. Moreland. Oct 2, 1819. George Rex, adm.
MILLER, WILLIAM. New Hanover. Oct 7, 1819. George Miller, Henry Troxel, adms.
LONGAIM, HENRY. Limerick. Oct 25, 1819. George Moore, Jr.
THOMAS, JOSEPH. Moreland. Oct 28, 1819. Ann Thomas, late Ann Thaw.
MAY, THOMAS P. Norristown. Oct 30, 1819. Samuel Baird.
FISHER, BARBARA. Upper Hanover. Oct 30, 1819. Jacob Fisher, Wendle Fisher.
MICHENER, WILLIAM. Abington. Oct 30, 1819. Isaac Michener.
YOST, PETER. Frederick. Nov 9, 1819. John Yost.
FETTER, GEORGE. Moreland. Nov 24, 1819. Thomas B. Montange.
CUSTER, ELIZABETH. Worcester. Dec 3, 1819. Peter Custer.
LONG, BARBARA. Douglass. Dec 6, 1819. George Long.
McCANN, JOHN. Norriton. Dec 10, 1819. Nancy McCann, Samuel Markley.
PERCY, WILLIAM. Dec 23, 1819. George M. Potts, Joseph Armstrong.
THOMAS, ABEL. Lower Merion. Jan 19, 1820. Jacob Bealer, Anthony Zell.
THOMAS, ABEL, JR. Lower Merion. Jan 19, 1820. Rachel Thomas, Jacob Bealer, Anthony Zell.
MOYER, ABRAHAM. Hatfield. Jan 29, 1820. Mary Moyer, Jacob Moyer, adms.
YETTER, JOSEPH. Whitpain. Feb 3, 1820. John Yetter, David Marple, adms.
WANAMAKER, PHILIP. Upper Salford. Feb 14, 1820. John Beeber, Sr., John Beeber, Jr.
GARBER, CHARLES. Upper Providence. Feb 15, 1820. Elizabeth

Garber, Joseph Garber, Isaac Garber, adms.
HAINER, JACOB. Upper Dublin. Feb 21, 1820. Sarah Hainer, John D. Steel, Joseph Hainer.
GLAUSE, JACOB. Worcester. Feb 25, 1820. John Hendricks.
DEWEES, JONATHAN. Springfield. March 1, 1820. William Johnson.
CROUSE, JACOB. Limerick. March 14, 1820. Henry Crouse.
HAWKINS, AMOS. Moreland. March 16, 1820. William Ayres.
CLEMMENS, JOHN. Gwynedd. March 22, 1820. Jacob Clemmens, John Zimmerman, Isaac Zimmerman.
McANALL, WILLIAM. Upper Merion. April 1, 1820. Robert McAnall, Andrew Keiger.
RENNINGER, JOHN. Douglass. April 14, 1820. Jacob Boyer.
TRUMBORE, SUSANNAH. Lower Salford. May 8, 1820. George Trumbore, Abraham Trumbore.
RAMBO, JONAS. Upper Merion. May 11, 1820. John Michell.
ZIMMERMAN, CHRISTOPHER. May 17, 1820. Arnold Zimmerman, William Zimmerman.
TROLLINGER, PETER. May 24, 1820. Andrew Trollinger.
LUKENS, MATTHIAS. Upper Dublin. June 1, 1820. Azor Lukens.
FOX, JOHN. Douglass. June 1, 1820. George Erle.
COMMINGS, DAVID. Moreland. June 1, 1820. Solomon Commings, Wiliam Spoone, adms.
PARKER, JOHN EWING. Plymouth. June 2, 1820. Thomas M. Potts.
CARREL, ELIAS. Moreland. June 24, 1820. James Carrel.
ROSHONG, HENRY. June 27, 1820. Philip Reed.
MARPLE, DAVID. Plymouth. Juny 1, 1820. Hannah Marple.
SMILY, WILLIAM. Upper Providence. July 4, 1820. Samuel Mann, Samuel Horning.
BAIRD, SAMUEL. Pottsgrove. July 17, 1820. Thomas Baird, Samuel Baird.
STOUFFER, JOHN. Skippack and Perkiomen. July 22, 1820. Henry Kolb, Abraham Zeigler.
BUTLER, JONATHAN. Upper Dublin. Aug 16, 1820. Priscilla Butler, Charles Thomas.
TERRY, WILLIAM. Abington. Aug 17, 1820. James Paul.
WALTON, ANTHONY. Upper Merion. Aug 18, 1820. William Richardson.
WILLIAMS, DAVID. Norristown. Sept 5, 1820. John Boyer, adm.
MEREDITH, JOSEPH. Gwynedd. Sept 6, 1820. Rachel Meredith, Cadwallader Foulke.
HELLINGS, ROBERT. Whitemarsh. Sept 11, 1820. Jonathan Shoemaker.
BOYERS, ANDREW. Upper Hanover. Sept 14, 1820. John Kolp.
TENNIS, CHRISTIAN, alias HITSELBERG. Skippack and Perkiomen. Sept 27, 1820. Jacob Allaback.
SHAMBOUGH, VALENTINE. Lower Providence. Oct 14, 1820. Mary Shanbough, John Getty.

KRATZ, JOHN. Skippack and Perkiomen. Oct 28, 1820. Abraham Tyson, Garret Hunsicker.
HAWK, ABRAHAM. Lower Providence. Nov 3, 1820. Catharine Hawk, George Hawk.
EVANS, AARON. Montgomery. Nov 7, 1820. Enos Evans, George M. Potts.
CRAWFORD, ALEXANDER. Plymouth. Nov 13, 1820. Isabella Crawford, Andrew Hugh Crawford.
WALKER, DANIEL. Montgomery. Nov 15, 1820. Joseph Lukens.
BISBING, GEORGE. Worcester. Nov 16, 1820. Susannah Bisbing, Peter Bisbing.
BEAN, SIBLELLA. Worchester. Nov 28, 1820. Siblella Knittee.
ROBERTS, ARNOLD. Lower Providence. Nov 29, 1820. John Roberts, Jacob Highley.
JONES, BENJAMIN T. Lower Merion. Nov 30, 1820. Lloyd Jones, John Levering.
HAGEY, JACOB. Franconia. Dec 4, 1820. Catharine Hagey, Henry Hockman, adms.
GILBERT, ADAM. Pottstown. Dec 20, 1820. George Gilbert, Jacob Gilbert.
SHAW, STEPHEN. Worcester. Dec 13, 1820. Ezekiel Rhoades.
ROSEN, JANE. Worcester. Dec 20, 1820. John Rosen.
FRY, JOHN. Limerick. Dec 27, 1820. Jacob Fry, Peter Fry.
KLINE, MARY. Worcester. Dec 28, 1820. Jesse Kline.
SOWER, ELIZABETH. Gwynedd. Dec 28, 1820. Jacob G. Sower.
ROSENBERGER, ABRAHAM. Franconia. Dec 30, 1820. Margaret Rosenberger, Christian Schwartz.
KUGLER, SARAH. Lower Merion. Jan 18, 1821. George Wells.
KRIEBEL, ROSINA. Gwynedd. Jan 20, 1821. Christopher Kriegel, Benjamin Anders.
ADAMS, HENRY. Limerick. Feb 20, 1821. Henry Thomas, Henry Crouse.
FOX, HENRY. Upper Providence. Feb 13, 1821. Philip Fox, George Zimmerman.
BERRY, ISAAC. Lower Merion. Feb 13, 1821. William Holgate.
TRUMP, CATHARINE. Limerick. Feb 15, 1821. Daniel Hause.
GILBERT, BARNARD. Douglass. Feb 19, 1821. Susannah Gilbert, Henry Gilbert.
TOMLINSON, THOMAS. Whitpain. Feb 23, 1821. William Wells, amds.
CRESSMAN, JACOB. Upper Salford. Feb 26, 1821. Isaac Cressman. adm.
KRIEBLE, SUSANNAH. Towamencin. March 6, 1821. Andrew Krieble.
HIPPLE, LAWRENCE. Lower Merion. March 20, 1821. Henry Hipple, George Hartman, adms.
STETLER, CHRISTIAN. Upper Providence. March 23, 1821. Jacob Tyson.

HARRIS, JAMES B. Limerick. March 26, 1821. Amos Evans.
COLFLESH, MATTHIAS. Norristown. March 30, 1821. Matthias Colflesh, John Priest.
BERKEY, ESTHER. Limerick. April 3, 1821. Jones Berkey.
LOCK, EVE. New Hanover. April 11, 1821. Jacob Lock.
SLOANE, CATHARINE. Upper Merion. April 18, 1821. Mary Sloane.
JONES, HANNAH P. Gwynedd. April 20, 1821. Evan Jones.
SPARE, CATHARINE. Upper Providence. April 24, 1821. Nathan Spare, Jonas Spare.
HALLMAN, JOHN. Plymouth. Arpril 23, 1821. Elizabeth Hallman, Jacob Hallman, George Hallman.
HAGY, WILLIAM. Lower Merion April 26, 1821. Sarah Hagy.
COOPER, WILLIAM. Horsham. April 28, 1821. Seneca Lukens, Isaac Parry.
MILLER, MARY. Upper Providence. May 21, 1821. Jacob Miller.
NEWELL, GEORGE. Moreland, May 16, 1821. Esther Newell, John Newell, adms.
WEAND, WENDAL. Upper Hanover. May 21, 1821. Wendal Weand.
ROBINSON, JOHN. Whitpain. June 11, 1821. Sarah Robinson.
SUPPLEE, EDWARD. Norriton. June 11, 1821. John Richards.
POTTS, MARY. Upper Dublin. June 16, 1821. Daniel Potts.
JACKSON, THOMAS. Pottstown. July 7, 1821. Samuel Gartley, William Mintger.
HALLMAN, HENRY. New Hanover. July 17, 1821. Jacob Hallman, Benjamin Hallman.
BRECK, CHARLES. ABINGTON. July 23, 1821. Samuel Breck.
ZIMMERMAN, ARNOLD. Norristown. July 21, 1821. William Zimmerman.
POTTS, DAVID. Upper Dublin. July 23, 1821. Miriam Potts, John Potts.
UPDEGRAVE, ANN. Skippack and Perkiomen. Aug 20, 1821. John Tyson.
ZARLEY, DAVID. Frederick. Aug 20, 1821. Tobias Albright.
WYANT, WENDEL, SR. Sept 13, 1821. Wendel Wyant, Henry Frick, Jr.
JOHNSON, JOHN. Franconia. Sept 27, 1821. Matthias Johnson, Valentine Clemmens.
KOLB, NICHOLAS. Skippack and Perkiomen. Sept 29, 1821. Dillman Kolb, John Kolb.
BOWER, CATHARINE. Whitemarsh. Oct 5, 1821. Leonard Culp, adm.
TOMPKINS, ANN. Whitemarsh. Oct 11, 1821. Samuel Tompkins, Benjamin Marple.
SCHLICHER, HENRY. Upper Hanover. Oct 20, 1821. John Schlicher, Michael Hillegass.
SWARDLEY, SAMUEL. Hatfield. Oct 13, 1821. John Swardley.
CLAY, SLATER (REV.). Upper Providence. Oct 13, 1821. George Clay, Charles H. Clay.

RAMSEY, BENJAMIN. Plymouth. Oct 15, 1821. Ann Ramsey, Alexander Ramsey.
HOCKER, GEROGE. Whitemarsh. Oct 17, 1821. Martin Hocker.
METZ, JOHN. Worcester. Oct 22, 1821. Joseph Metz.
FARINGER, JOHN. Whitemarsh. Oct 22, 1821. Anna Faringer, John Faringer, Joseph Harver.
MILLER, CHRISTIANA. Upper Providence. Oct 22, 1821. Sophia Miller.
NEWMAN, SUSANNA. Gwynedd. Oct 26, 1821. Melchior Newman, Henry Snyder.
BEAN, WILLIAM. Upper Providence. Oct 27, 1821. William Bean, Eleanor Bean.
MILLER, ANN. Montgomery. Oct 27, 1821. Joseph Milligan.
FEADLEY, JONATHAN. Lower Providence. Oct 27, 1821. Michael Feadley, Abraham Spear.
WHITE, SOLOMON. Plymouth. Oct 27, 1821. John White, adm.
WOOLMAN, GEORGE. Lower Providence. Oct 29, 1821. David Woolman.
HOBENSACK, JOHN. Moreland. Oct 30, 1821. George Hobensack.
FAVINGER, JOHN. Upper Providence. Oct 30, 1821. Margaret Favinger, John Hunsicker.
HARNER, CHRISTIAN. Upper Dublin. Oct 31, 1821. Christian Harner.
LEWIS, NATHAN. Lower Merion. Nov 1, 1821. Elizabeth Lewis, John Levering, Silas Jones.
SHOLL, JOHN. Upper Salford. Nov 1, 1821. Jacob Sholl, Peter Blyler.
MILLER, NICHOLAS. Pottsgrove. Nov 6, 1821. John Miller, Henry Miller, Jacob Miller.
GILBERT, HENRY. New Hanover. Nov 7, 1821. Mary Gilbert, Jacob Gilbert, Samuel Gilbert.
SINSINDERFER, GEORGE. New Hanover. Nov 12, 1821. Henry Snyder, Adam Warthman.
SHEPPARD, THOMAS. Whitemarsh. Nov 10, 1821. Sarah Sheppard.
BURKART, ELIZABETH. New Hanover. Nov 12, 1821. George Burkart.
COPE, MAGDALENA. Franconia. Nov 12, 1821. Joel Cope.
CASSEL, YELLIS. Towamencin. Nov 13, 1821. John Cassel, Jacob Cassel.

INDEX

-A-

ABATT, William, 272
ABBETT, Miles, 153; William, 86
ABBIT, Catharine, 37; William, 37
ABEL, Susanna, 220
ABRAHAM, Dinah, 37; Hannah, 85; Isaac, 37; James, 37, 75; Margaret, 37; Miriam, 37
ABRAHAMS, Isaac, 335; James, 344
ABRECHT, Michael, 260
ACHE, Ache, 236; Harman, 188; Harmon, 236; Jacob, 236; John, 236; Ludwig, 236; Maria, 236; Valentine, 236
ACHEY, Barbara, 139; John, 139
ACHUFF, Jacob, 291
ACKER, Elizabeth, 94
ACKLEY, John, 275; Mordecai, 321; Rachel, 133; Rebecca, 321; Thomas, 275, 331
ACOFF, Jacob, 319; Mary, 132
ACUFF, David, 250; Jacob, 234, 250; Mary, 250; William, 250
ACUFT, Christina, 168; Elizabeth, 168; Jacob, 168; Joseph, 168; Mary, 168
ADAM, 321; George, 316; John, 182; Sarah, 316
ADAMS, Catharine, 191, 333; Henry, 359; James, 71, 122, 328; Margaret, 161; Rachel, 122; Simon, 191, 333
ADAMSON, Amos, 201; Ann, 271; Charles, 271; Esther, 271; John, 201; Jonathan, 271; Rebecca, 271; Robert, 201, 270; Sidney, 201; Tabitha, 271; Thomas, 271
ADDIS, Amos, 176
AGALMOSE, Elizabeth, 173; Henry, 173
AGLEVIA, James, 187
AHE, Alexander, 350
AKEHUFF, David, 189; Jacob, 189; Mary, 189
AKINS, James, 90, 116, 134
ALABACH, Michael, 341
ALBERTSON, Benjamin, 339, 340; Jacob, 99, 201, 217, 226, 228, 243; Jonathan, 340; Josiah, 296; William, 228
ALBRECHT, Michael, 101
ALBRIGHT, Jacob, 296; Tobias, 360
ALDEMAN, John, 309

ALDERFER, Abraham, 30, 284, 287, 314; Benjamin, 284, 287, 314; Elizabeth, 286; Frederick, 321, 342; Isaac, 287, 321; Jacob, 321; John, 286; Joseph, 217, 287, 299, 314, 329, 357
ALDERFFER, Joseph, 41
ALHOUSE, Henry, 283; Juliana, 283
ALLABACH, David, 215; Jacob, 307
ALLABACK, Jacob, 358
ALLABOUGH, John, 300
ALLAWAY, Mersena, 198
ALLBRIGHT, Catharine, 192; Conrad, 192; Elizabeth, 192; Jacob, 335; Margaret, 335; Maria, 192; Michael, 192; Tobias, 192
ALLEBACH, Abraham, 251, 321; Catharine, 321; David, 28, 271; Jacob, 305, 310
ALLEBOUGH, Mary, 184
ALLEN, Joseph, 306; Sarah, 302; William, 306
ALLIMUS, Amelia, 213
ALLINGER, Stephen, 321
ALLOWAY, Marsena, 101
ALTEMUS, David, 58; Frederick, 261
ALTERFFER, Elizabeth, 109; John, 109
AMAN, Agnes, 19; Arnold, 281; Barbara, 281; George, 19, 100, 281, 353; Jacob, 271; Jesse, 353; John, 19, 281; Joseph, 281; Magdalena, 281
AMBLER, Andrew, 198, 275; Ann, 184, 198, 347; David, 312, 345; Edward, 148, 198; Gainor, 148; Jesse, 148, 220; John, 75, 148, 216, 345; Joseph, 66, 87, 148, 184, 198, 345, 347; Priscilla, 75; Sarah, 66; Susanna, 148; Tacy, 148; William, 198
AMBLERS, William, 275
AMBROS, Ruth, 321
AMEN, John, 188
AMMERMAN, William, 278
AMOS, Abel, 317; Abraham, 317; Agnes, 317; Amos, 317; Elizabeth, 317; Hannah, 317; John, 317; Margaret, 317; Sophia, 93; Walter, 317
AMRAM, 78
ANDER, Andrew, 263

ANDERS, Abraham, 146, 272, 327, 343; Andrew, 146; Anna Barber, 146; Benjamin, 272, 359; George, 125, 146, 263; James, 205; John, 146, 169; Rosina, 272; Susanna, 146
ANDERSON, Alexander, 59; Andrew, 164; Thomas, 268
ANDICH, William, 226
ANDIG, William, 293
ANDREWS, Abraham, 157, 321
ANITS, Christiana, 5; William, 5
ANTES, Catharine, 29; Frederick, 29
APPLE, Margaret, 346; Samuel, 346
APPLETON, Martha, 67; Mary, 67; Naomi, 67; Rebecca, 67
ARCHABACH, Belinda, 113; Casper, 113; Elizabeth, 113; Molly, 113
ARCHE, Ludwig, 140
ARCHIBALD, Alexander, 321; Robert, 22
ARMITAGE, Elizabeth, 186; Enoch, 186, 336; Mary, 186; Rachel, 186
ARMSTRONG, Ann, 269; Augustus, 266; Benjamin, 329; Eleanor, 351; Elizabeth, 164; Ephraim, 164, 335; Hannah, 164; James, 164, 239, 266, 267, 269, 350; Jane, 239; John, 140, 157, 164, 239, 266, 350; Joseph, 164, 239, 243, 266, 267, 296, 329, 335, 351, 357; Margaret, 164; Mary, 164, 239; Rebecca, 164; Sarah, 164; Simon, 140, 164, 239; William, 74, 157, 164, 202, 239, 266, 335
ARNDT, Elizabeth, 48; Jacob, 48
ART, Mary Elizabeth, 51; Yost, 51
ARWIN, Cadwalder, 200; Cadwallader, 63; Elizabeth, 63, 336; Ellin, 63; Hannah, 200; John, 63, 184, 200, 336; Rebeckah, 63; Sarah, 63, 336; William, 63
ASHBRIDGE, Elizabeth, 80; Tacy, 313; Thomas, 313
ASHENFELDER, John, 48; Solomy, 48
ASHMEAD, Samuel, 213
ASHTON, Sarah, 179
ASTON, Elizabeth, 17; Peter, 17, 18
ATCHINSON, William, 173
ATHERHOLT, Christian, 293; Elizabeth, 293

ATKINS, George, 103
ATKINSON, John, 335
ATOM, Jacob, 264
AUCHY, John, 248, 264, 265, 293
AUKE, Ludwig, 127
AULD, Jacob, 22, 41, 71, 74, 116, 336
AULTHOUSE, Henry, 293; John, 115, 284
AUSTIN, Benjamin, 27, 114; Elizabeth, 253; Jonathan, 114, 116, 150; Martha, 133, 150; Mary, 114, 116, 150; Rebecca, 151; Robert, 114, 116; Susanna, 88, 201, 253; Thomas, 26, 114, 151, 321; William Tennent, 201
AXFORD, Mary, 197
AYRES, Charles, 79, 152; Deborah, 79, 151; Elizabeth, 152; Esther, 79, 151, 152; Hiram, 151, 152, 307; Samuel, 44, 79, 120, 151; William, 133, 151, 152, 201, 278, 310, 347, 348, 358

-B-

BAAR, Sarah, 135
BACHMAN, Henry, 10
BACHTEKERUH, William, 196
BACHTEL, Anna, 16; Christian, 16; Daniel, 16; David, 16; Elisabeth, 16; Jacob, 16; Joseph, 16; Martin, 16; Mary, 16; Samuel, 16
BACHUS, Godfrey, 175
BACKMAN, George, 63; Magdalena, 63
BADMAN, ---, 22
BAHTINGER, B., 101
BAIRD, Samuel, 140, 158, 357, 358; Thomas, 356, 358
BAKER, Catharine, 188; Christian, 188; Daniel, 71, 188; Elisabeth, 26, 97; Elizabeth, 130; Frederick, 220, 221; George, 220; Jacob, 188; John, 22, 97, 106, 221; Mary, 188, 227; Nancy, 220, 221; Sarah, 220, 221; William, 71, 99
BAKEWELL, Ann, 301; Eliza, 301; Rebecca, 301; Srah, 301; Thomas, 301; William, 300, 301
BALDERSON, Mark, 273
BALDWIN, Lydia, 313; Mary, 158
BALKE, Rachel, 238
BALL, Mary, 341
BALLERT, Mary, 76

BALOO, Ann, 246; Daniel, 246; Jeremiah, 246
BALTY, Catherine, 6; Hannah, 6; Jacob, 6; John, 6; Maria, 6
BANES, Eliza, 230; Isaac, 230; Rachel, 175
BANNEBACKER, Frederick, 32
BANTON, Mansfield, 85
BARBOW, Barbara, 159; Christian, 159
BARD, Frncis, 322; Samuel, 319, 351
BARE, Daniel, 164; Elizabeth, 131, 164; Frederick, 114; John, 76, 130, 164; Margaret, 76
BARGERT, Valentine, 325
BARKER, Anna, 14; Barker, 14; Betsey, 14; Catharine, 14; Charles R., 43; Christina, 14; Dorothy, 14; Elizabeth, 14; Frederick, 14; George, 14; Jacob, 14; John, 14; Mary, 14; Mary Sophia, 14; Peter, 14; Philip, 14; Susanna, 14
BARKEY, Christian, 65; Isaac, 119; Jacob, 60; John, 9, 13, 31, 36, 40, 41, 51, 60, 65, 69, 72, 100, 113, 118, 119, 175
BARKLEY, John, 16
BARLEY, Abraham, 191; Henry, 191; Jacob, 191; Mary, 191; Rudolph, 191; Samuel, 191
BARLINGER, Solomy, 151
BARLORT, Dorothy, 10
BARLOW, Abner, 253, 353; John, 187, 253, 353; Phebe, 353
BARND, John, 19
BARNED, ---, 194; Rachel, 194
BARNES, Abigail, 103; Baker, 89, 103; Barker, 175; Elizabeth, 103, 259; James, 57, 189, 267, 268; Jesse, 239; Lydia, 268; Martha, 144; Mary, 103; Rachel, 96, 175, 349; Robert, 42, 103, 349; Samuel, 103; Sarah, 268; Semen, 249; Stephen, 42, 103; Thomas, 353; Timothy, 103
BARNS, Elizabeth, 323; Racheal, 142; Samuel, 142; Thomas, 323
BARNWELL, Henry, 103; Letitia, 254; Mary, 254
BARR, Jacob, 282; Joseph, 231; Margaret, 282; Susanna, 282
BARRED, John, 137; Margaret, 137
BARRELL, Jeremiah, 355
BARRELLO, Henry, 355

BARRET, Casper, 322
BARRETT, Elizabeth, 313
BARRY, Anstis, 73; Isaac, 73; James, 73; Lydia, 73; Mary, 73; Rachel, 73; Richard, 73; Samuel, 73; Tacy, 73
BARTHOLMEW, Rachel, 53
BARTHOLOMEW, Elizabeth, 352
BARTLESOME, Jane, 266; Mary, 266; William, 266
BARTLESON, Abner, 7, 322; Bartle, 7, 175, 321, 322; Catharine, 134, 203; Enos, 28, 322; Ezra, 322; Henry, 7, 28; James, 7, 134, 321; Jane, 7, 322; John, 322; Katharine, 28; Levi, 6, 321, 324; Maria, 134, 203; Mary, 46, 78, 321, 322; Nicholas, 322; Samuel, 7, 134, 203
BARTMAN, Adam, 266; Catharine, 266; Christina, 266; Jacob, 266; John, 266; Margaret, 266; Maria, 266; Michael, 266
BARTOLAT, Samuel, 123
BARTOLET, Abraham, 153; Daniel, 153; Elizabeth, 153; Esther, 153; Jacob, 153; John, 153; Martha, 191; Samuel, 128, 153; Susanna, 153
BARTON, Isaac, 310
BASETER, Elizabeth, 341
BASLER, Elizabeth, 91; Henry, 91; Mary, 91; Ulrick, 91
BASTRES, Peter, 196, 316
BASTRESS, Peter, 138
BATE, Hannah, 99; Jesse, 99; Margaret, 99, 303; Rebecca, 99; Ruth, 99; Sarah, 99; Thomas, 99, 303
BATES, Humphrey, 322; Joseph, 18
BATTLEPWEE, John, 347
BAUER, John, 301
BAUMAN, Peter, 41
BAUSMAN, Lawrence, 152
BAYS, Mary, 53
BEAKLEY, George, 322
BEALER, Jacob, 255, 357; Joseph, 277; Thomas, 255
BEAN, Adam, 333; Benjamin, 163; Catharine, 339; Edward Lane, 111; Eleanor, 361; Elizabeth, 279; Garret, 143, 339; Hannah, 111; Henry, 116, 192; Jacob, 143, 339, 353, 355; James, 81, 111, 214, 226; Jesse, 81, 183, 271, 317, 330, 354; John, 41, 112, 116, 138, 330, 333, 350, 353; Joshua, 213, 214, 322; Mary,

116; Sarah, 47; Siblella, 359; Thomas, 194; William, 308, 350, 361
BEANS, Elizabeth, 78, 247; Evan, 78; Isaac, 78, 100, 279, 289; James, 78; Jane, 78; John, 279; Margaret, 279; Nathan, 78; Phebe, 78; Stephen, 78; Thomas, 78, 100, 279
BEAR, Jacob, 191
BEARD, Daniel, 335; Francis, 302; Paul, 335
BEATON, Stephen, 277
BEAVEN, John, 340; Mary, 340
BEAVER, Barney, 331; Bernard, 79; Rachel, 79; Susanna, 331
BECHER, Elizabeth, 72
BECHHART, Adam, 239; Benjamin, 239; Catharine, 239; Christian, 239; Conrad, 239; Henry, 239; Mary, 239; Susanna, 239
BECHTEL, Abraham, 247, 252, 323; Catharine, 298; David, 263; George, 29, 212, 244, 263, 325, 352; Hannah, 263; Isaac, 16; Jacob, 263, 357; John, 263, 305, 338, 357; Joseph, 298; Joshua, 352; Mary, 235; Peter, 263; Samuel, 263; William, 263
BECHTELL, Abraham, 23, 107; Catharine, 128; Daniel, 23; George, 23, 128, 135, 320; Isaac, 328; Jacob, 15, 23, 99; Magdalena, 23; Martin, 15, 23; Mary, 23; Peter, 101
BECHTELLE, Jacob, 6
BECK, Elizabeth, 174; Philip, 200
BECKER, George, 54; Susanna, 54
BEEBER, John, 357
BEEGNER, John, 94
BEEK, Elizabeth, 174
BEEKLEY, George, 22
BEEM, Enoch, 56
BEEN, Elizabeth, 160; Henry, 139, 160, 333; John, 160, 333; Margaret, 160; Maria, 333; Peter, 160; Susanna, 160
BEESCTSE, Jacob, 91
BEGHTELL, John, 35
BEIDEMAN, Adam, 322; Catharine, 322; George, 322
BEIDLER, Conrad, 21
BEITEMAN, Frederick, 60
BEITENMAN, Frederick, 12
BEITMAN, Frederick, 97
BEKLEY, Elizabeth, 13
BEKLY, Michael, 13

BELINDA, Hannah, 249; Jane, 249; Mary, 249
BELL, Andrew, 321; Ann, 321; Isaiah, 27; James, 27; Mary, 27; Samuel, 334
BELLEW, Daniel, 341; Mary, 341
BELTZ, Christina, 130; George, 129, 130, 274; Jacob, 26, 129, 130; John, 129, 130; Philip, 129, 130
BENDER, Anna Margaret, 202; Anna Maria, 202; Anthony, 34; Catharine, 34, 202; Cathrine, 228; Christina, 202, 227; Elizabeth, 202, 228; Fronica, 202; Jacob, 228; John, 148, 202, 236; Ludwig, 201, 202; Margaret, 202; Mary, 228; Michael, 227
BENER, Joseph, 191
BENEZET, Anthony, 190
BENEZETT, Anthony, 355; Mary, 355
BENGETT, Molly, 331; Sarah, 331
BENJAMIN, Alexander, 352; Elizabeth, 344; Frederick, 344; John, 338, 340
BENNER, Abraham, 282, 292, 300, 323; Barbara, 220; Catharine, 220; Cathrine, 217; Christian, 300; Elizabeth, 5, 157; George, 217, 311; Hannah, 169; Henry, 220; Jacob, 169, 220; John, 202; Ludwig, 157, 159; Mary, 217, 292; Peter, 305; Rosina, 159
BENNETT, Jacob, 356; John, 173; Simon, 78; Whitman, 356
BENNEWILLE, George D., 343
BENSON, Anna, 185, 211
BENTZ, John, 264
BERGA, Abraham, 215; Saloma, 215
BERGER, Andrew, 99; Christian, 90
BERGEY, Abraham, 354; Henry, 258; Isaac, 335; Jacob, 113, 244, 335; Jonah, 354
BERGY, Abraham, 271; Ann, 271; Barbara, 271; Catharine, 271; Christian, 271; Elizabeth, 271; Jacob, 271; John, 271; Margaret, 271; Philip, 271; Sarah, 271
BERKEY, Abraham, 334; Christian, 322; Esther, 360; Jacob, 334; John, 334; Jones, 360; Mary, 322
BERKHAMMER, Rachel, 192
BERKHEIMER, Andrew, 147; Catharine, 147; George, 147;

Henry, 147; Leonard, 147;
Magdeline, 147; Philip, 147;
Solomy, 147; William, 147
BERKHYMER, Rachel, 192
BERKIMER, George, 168; Mary, 173
BERKY, Christian, 18; John, 18
BERNDT, John, 127
BERNETT, Margaret, 81; Philip, 81
BERNHARD, Ann Maria, 46; Betty, 1; Casper, 46; Charlotte, 1; Christiana, 1, 2; Elizabeth, 1; Henry, 1, 2; Jacob, 1, 46; Maria, 46; Marilis, 46; Mary, 46; Philip, 1; Susanna, 1; William, 46
BERNT, Ludwick, 346; Peter, 346
BERREL, Eleanor, 313; Jeremiah, 89; William, 255
BERRELL, Eli, 255; Henry, 190; Jeremiah, 190, 350; Justus, 245
BERRIL, Eli, 221
BERRY, Isaac, 359
BETSEY, 82
BETTY, 59
BETZ, Christian, 8; Christiana, 8; George, 247; Margareth, 6
BEVENS, William, 357
BEWLEY, Ann, 95; George, 322; Hannah, 193, 194; Isaac, 194, 322; John, 193, 194, 253, 322; Mary, 194; Nathan, 193; Rachel, 253
BEYDERMAN, George, 225
BEYER, Abraham, 68; Anthony, 51; Catharine, 51; Elizabeth, 51; George, 50, 51; Henry, 51; Jacob, 51, 319, 355; Joseph, 355; Philip, 41; William, 51
BEYERS, Henry, 301
BICHEL, Henry, 305; Polly, 305
BICKEL, Jacob, 100, 229; John, 156
BICKLE, Barbara, 127; Elizabeth, 344; Henry, 127, 128; Jacob, 66, 128, 292; John, 128, 344; Ludwig, 127, 344
BICKNEY, Francis, 213
BIDDLE, Charles, 209; Isaac, 158; Maria, 158
BIEBER, John, 150; Susanna, 150
BILLEW, Adam, 132; Ann, 124; Daniel, 321; David, 132; Elizabeth, 132; Jacob, 124; Jeremia, 124; Jeremiah, 124, 295; Naomi, 124; Rebecca, 321; Samuel, 124

BILLGER, George, 107, 150
BILLING, John, 147
BINDER, Anna, 139; Anna Mary, 139; Anthony, 139; Catharine, 139; Elizabeth, 241; Frederica, 139; George, 241; Hannah, 139; Henry, 241; Jacob, 139, 241; John, 139, 241; Michael, 241; Moses, 139; Susanna, 241
BINGEMAN, Benjamin, 353; Elizabeth, 353
BIRD, Joseph, 162
BIRNEY, Mary, 68
BISBING, Andrew, 107; Barbara, 107; Bernard, 107; Catharine, 107; Elizabeth, 107; Eve, 107, 157; George, 107, 185, 279, 359; Jacob, 107, 293, 299; John, 107, 185; Margareth, 107; Michael, 185; Peter, 359; Susannah, 359
BISHOF, John, 322
BISHOP, Paul, 149
BISSON, Charles, 265
BITTENBENDER, John, 211; Magdalena, 211
BITTING, Anthony, 194, 204, 236, 264, 325, 331; Archibald, 265; Catharine, 128; Henry, 128; John, 42, 128, 339; Joseph, 128, 213, 342; Jost, 128; Ludwig, 128; Magdalena, 265; Maria, 265; Mary, 42; Molly, 305; Peter, 128; Philip, 128, 305; Rebecca, 128; Sarah, 265; Sophia, 128
BITTLE, Andrew, 317
BLACK, Rachel, 1
BLACKWOOD, Samuel, 331
BLAKE, Jane, 175
BLAKER, Alice, 44
BLANK, Adam, 87; Barbara, 159; George Adam, 159
BLANKLY, Anthony, 106; Martha, 106; Richard, 106
BLARE, Jonathan, 160; Mary, 188
BLEE, John, 133
BLETZ, Jacob, 335
BLIEM, Christian, 16
BLIM, Christian, 244; Jacob, 244, 298; John, 244; Maria, 244; Philip, 244
BLOOM, Daniel, 12; Stephen, 34, 54
BLUMSBERGER, Abraham, 279
BLYBAN, Rebecca, 123
BLYLER, Ann, 166; Peter, 361
BOAZ, Matthias, 196

BOB, 257; Abraham, 15, 53, 54;
  Catharine, 100; Daniel, 100
BOBINSON, Samuel, 335
BOEHM, Betsey, 71; Mary, 71
BOGANER, Eleanor, 5; Tobias, 5
BOGART, Cornelius, 331
BOGER, Martin, 336
BOGGS, Elizabeth, 244; John,
  119
BOHR, George, 256
BOILEAU, Ann, 142; Isaac, 142;
  N. B., 196, 210; Nathan B.,
  103; Nathaneal B., 142;
  Nathaniel B., 187, 269;
  Racheal, 142
BOILS, Catharine, 337; John,
  337
BOLIG, Thomas, 153
BOLIGH, John, 140
BOLIN, Elizabeth, 322; George,
  322
BOLLER, Jacob, 348
BOLTON, Elisabeth, 37
BOND, Eleanor, 197; Mary, 155;
  Robert, 197; Samuel, 197
BONDMOT, Elizabeth, 105
BONES, Elizabeth, 252; Melson,
  252
BOOCHER, George, 333
BOON, George, 18; Margaret, 18;
  Sarah, 60
BOONE, Betsey, 255
BOORS, Arnold, 122, 321;
  Daniedl, 235; Harman, 122;
  Henry, 122, 321; John, 122;
  Jonas, 235; Mary, 322; Peter,
  122, 322; Susanna, 235
BOORSE, Anna, 207; Catharine,
  207; Daniel, 200, 292;
  Elizabeth, 207; Harman, 207;
  Henry, 200; John, 200, 207,
  292, 342; Jonas, 200;
  Margaret, 207; Maria, 109;
  Peter, 109, 207; Sibilla,
  207; susanna, 207
BOOSKIRK, Mahlon, 226; Mahlon
  V., 193, 251
BOOZ, Catharine, 309; Conrad,
  309; Jacob, 309; John, 309;
  Margaret, 309; Mary, 309;
  Matthias, 309; Phoebe, 309;
  Samuel, 309
BORELAN, James, 322
BORGER, Jonas, 312
BORKMAN, Anna, 264; John, 264
BORNAMAN, Henry, 32
BORNEMAN, Henry, 137, 180
BORTMAN, Jacob, 332
BOSERT, Adam, 159; Andrew, 127;
  Gertraude, 139; Henry, 139
BOSLER, Hannah, 313

BOSSERT, Adam, 171, 172;
  Andrew, 36; Catharine, 172;
  Elizabeth, 172; Henry, 172,
  341; John, 172; Margaret,
  172; Philip, 172; Robert, 172
BOSSLER, Christian, 89;
  Margaret, 89
BOSSUM, Godfrey, 231; Maria,
  231
BOSTER, Joseph, 255
BOTERSUAY, Elizabeth, 173;
  John, 173
BOTTGER, Ludowig, 50
BOTTOM, Elizabeth, 353; Levi,
  353
BOUCH, Charenah, 94; John, 94
BOULANGE, Frederick, 59
BOULLONGE, Catharine, 322;
  Frederick, 322
BOULTON, Aaron, 9; Edward, 8;
  John, 8, 9, 105, 129; Levi,
  129; Levy, 9; Mary, 8;
  Nathan, 9, 105; Pheby, 8
BOURDMAN, Moses, 322
BOURQUIN, Henry, 265
BOUTCHER, Ann, 104; Benjamin,
  104; Elisha, 104; Elizabeth,
  104; Enos, 104; John, 104;
  Joseph, 104; Martha, 104;
  Nathaniel, 104; Priscilla,
  104; Rachel, 104; Sarah, 104
BOWER, Andrew, 81, 307; Anna,
  307; Barbara, 15, 307;
  Catharine, 59, 360; Daniel,
  150; Deborah, 307; Elizabeth,
  81, 146, 296, 307; Henry,
  150; Jacob, 243; John, 150,
  307, 310; M., 9; Margaret,
  296; Moses, 15; Nicholas,
  242, 296, 319, 331; Samuel,
  146, 307; Sarah, 296;
  Susanna, 307; Thomas, 338
BOWMAN, Abraham, 34; Casper,
  34; Charles, 203; Esther, 34;
  Hannah, 297; Henry, 197, 297;
  Isaac, 34; Jacob, 34, 35,
  114, 239; John, 34;
  Magdalena, 236; Martin, 34;
  Peter, 145; Philip, 338;
  Roger, 297
BOWYER, Elizabeth, 47; Levi,
  47; Stephen, 47; Thomas, 47
BOYD, Alex, 252; Betsey, 252;
  James, 252; Mary, 252;
  William, 252
BOYER, Abelona, 41; Abraham,
  84; Andrew, 22, 84, 255;
  Barbara, 84; Catharine, 31,
  127, 152, 225, 255; Charles,
  152; Conrad, 102; Daniel,
  123, 299; Elizabeth, 47, 102,

152, 225; Frederick, 176; George, 86, 127, 152, 225, 251; Henry, 41, 84, 111, 171, 225, 255, 322; Jacob, 84, 130, 152, 291, 328, 338, 358; John, 41, 84, 201, 225, 255, 292, 358; Jonah, 225; Joseph, 74; Levi, 47; Margaret, 225, 322; Maria, 255; Mary, 21, 225, 338; Matthias, 171; Michael, 299; Peter, 127, 152, 281; Philip, 21, 52, 55, 225, 260, 273, 299, 309; Philippina, 22; Polly, 255; Sally, 225; Samuel, 31, 60, 334, 338; Sarah, 152, 316; Simon, 194; Sophia, 299; Susanna, 84, 225; William, 41, 225
BOYERS, Andrew, 358
BOYLE, John, 321
BOZA, Magdalena, 196
BRADES, Arthur, 61; Leah, 61
BRADFIELD, Abner, 198; Ann, 265; Isaac, 198; John, 198; Mahlon, 198; Phebe, 198; Rachel, 198; Samuel, 198, 199; William, 198, 199
BRADFORD, Benajah, 169; Mary, 332; Samuel, 169, 332; William, 11
BRADLEY, Thomas, 333
BRADY, Hugh, 322; Patrick, 322
BRAND, Benjamin, 289; Elizabeth, 68, 289; Frederick, 68; George, 289; Hannah, 68; Jacob, 68; John, 68; Magdalena, 68; Michael, 322; Philip, 322; Samuel, 289; Sophia, 68
BRANDSTALL, Johanna Christine, 348
BRANT, Abigail, 147; Adam, 15, 147; Frederick, 329; George, 145; Hannah, 331; Henry, 148; Jacob, 21, 329, 331; John, 290, 331; Samuel, 148
BRECK, Charles, 360; Samuel, 360
BRENDLINGER, Jacob, 173, 227, 241; John, 34; Joseph, 34; Rosina, 34
BRESS, Conrad, 324
BREY, Catharine, 57; Christopher, 57; Conrad, 57, 256; Elizabeth, 57; Eva Martha, 57; George, 36, 57; Jacob, 57; John, 57; Windle, 57
BRIDSON, George, 187; Hannah, 187

BRIGGS, John, 122
BRIGHT, Jacob, 325; John, 273, 304; Jonathan, 249, 313; Samuel, 186
BRILE, Nicholas, 201
BRINGHURST, Israel, 343; Mary, 343
BRINKERHOFF, Philip S., 277
BRITTAIN, Elizabeth, 209; Hannah, 209; Jacob, 209; John, 209; Martha, 209; Peter, 209; Rachel, 209; Sarah, 209; Thomas, 209
BRITTON, Alexander, 352
BROADES, Arthur, 295; Leah, 295; Mary, 295; Peter, 295; William, 6, 103, 343
BROCK, Sarah, 44
BROCKE, Jesse, 215; Lavina, 215
BROCKHOLDER, Elizabeth, 185; Henry, 185
BRODES, Leah, 280
BROOK, Benjamin, 103, 106; Elizabeth, 206; George, 168; John, 168; Martha, 206; Matthew, 21, 168; Sarah, 168; Thomas, 168; William, 168
BROOKE, Ann, 21, 221, 312; Anna, 183; Barnabas, 21; Benjamin, 9, 21, 141, 183, 312, 332, 337, 338; Charles, 141; Charlotte, 119, 221; Clarissa, 141; David, 205, 211, 348; Elizabeth, 21, 62, 183, 221, 322; Hannah, 21, 141; Harriet, 221; James, 21, 38, 141, 221, 312; Jesse, 215, 221, 322; John, 62, 156, 221, 298, 331; Jonathan, 21, 141, 332; Louisa, 183; Mark, 183; Mary, 21, 141, 221; Matthew, 187, 237, 253, 267, 274, 292, 345; Matthias, 59; Nathan, 141, 221, 298; Owen, 21; Rachel, 21, 59, 221; Robert, 221; Ruth, 21; Samuel, 141, 322; Susanne, 332; Thomas, 221, 338; William, 141, 221, 237
BROOKEFIELD, Joseph, 289
BROOKS, George, 151; Michael, 322; Sarah, 75
BROWER, Abraham, 275, 322; Christian, 340; Daniel, 340; Henry, 340; Isaac, 322
BROWN, A., 180; Benjamin, 211; Caeper, 248; David, 248; Elizabeth, 180, 233, 248; Esther, 233; Isaac, 248; Jacob, 248; James, 143; Jane, 233; John, 248, 249, 322,

355; Joseph, 355; Joseph A.,
180; Lydia, 233; Margaret,
233; Mary, 180, 233; Samuel,
248, 322; Sarah, 180, 233,
276; Soloman, 322; Thomas,
233; William, 233;
Williamina, 322
BROWNBOLT, Susannah, 122
BROY, Christopher, 127
BRUCKENMILLER, John, 194;
Sarah, 194
BRUNER, Anna, 145; David, 28,
105, 208; Jacob, 28, 274
BRUNNER, Michael, 222
BRUTZMAN, Hannah, 5; Jacob, 5
BRYANT, Benjamin, 307
BRYDEN, Isaiah, 170
BRYMAN, Christian, 39, 49, 54,
101, 317
BRYSON, James, 198
BUCH, Magdalena, 191; Nicholas,
191
BUCHAMER, Catharine, 108;
Elizabeth, 108; Henry, 108;
Jacob, 108; John, 108; Mary,
108; Peter, 108
BUCHAMMAN, Henry, 348
BUCHER, Albertine, 29; Dieter,
29; George, 29, 165, 313;
George D., 29; Helena, 29;
Mary, 29; Matthias, 29;
Solomy, 29
BUCK, Nicholas, 191
BUCKAMMER, Catharine, 228;
Elizabeth, 228; George, 228;
Henry, 228; Jacob, 228; John,
228
BUCKMAN, Jonathan, 35; Sarah,
35
BUCKWALTER, Barbara, 146;
Catharine, 347; David, 146;
Jacob, 20, 128; John, 220,
235; Mary, 235
BULL, Elisabeth, 22; Mary, 22;
Rebecca, 22; Thomas, 59;
William, 22
BUNGHURST, Israel, 337
BUNN, Harry, 48; Herman, 29;
John, 260; Mary, 140;
Nicholas, 21; Polly, 140
BUNNER, Elizabeth, 211; John,
211; Nancy, 211
BURCKART, David, 329;
Elizabeth, 329
BURD, Elizabeth, 263; James,
263; Jane, 263; Joseph, 263;
Margaret, 263
BURGER, Eve, 336; George, 336
BURGERT, Anna Margaret, 77;
Sigmont, 77

BURK, Anthony, 200; Daniel,
217; Edward, 49, 76, 161,
231, 340; Elizabeth, 76;
James, 1; John, 49, 76, 110,
180, 217, 340; Mary, 49;
William, 249
BURKARD, David, 327
BURKART, Elizabeth, 361;
George, 361
BURKERT, George, 339; John, 339
BURKEY, Abraham, 163;
Elizabeth, 163; John, 163;
Magdalena, 163; Mary, 163;
Sarah, 163; Susanna, 163
BURKHARD, David, 322; John
George, 322
BURKIRK, Andrew, 100;
Cornelius, 100; Lena, 100;
Mahlon, 100; Rebecca, 100
BURNEMAN, Barbara, 187;
Christil, 187; Daniel, 187;
Henry, 187; John, 187; Mary,
187
BURNER, William, 131
BURNES, Margaret, 355
BURNEY, William, 353
BURNS, Christian, 91; Eve, 356;
Michael, 254; Samuel, 356;
Zachariah, 355
BURNSIDE, Alexander, 346;
Francis, 275; Jane, 346;
Thomas, 275; William, 275,
346
BURNSIDES, James, 330; William,
330
BURRAS, Thomas, 323
BURRES, Daniel, 322
BUSH, Peter, 143; Susanna, 143
BUTLER, Henry, 16; John, 291;
Jonathan, 64, 333, 358;
Joseph, 46, 63; Priscilla,
189, 358; Sarah, 64, 291,
333; Thomas, 64, 236, 284,
316, 333
BUTTERWEEK, Joseph, 271; Sarah,
271
BUTTESWAY, John, 356
BUTTETSWA, John, 225
BYDEMAN, Adam, 330; Frederick,
330; Fronica, 330
BYER, Henry, 46; Margaret, 46

-C-

CADWALADER, Isaac, 323, 354;
Owen, 354
CADWALDER, Benjamin, 144, 262;
Elizabeth, 261; Joel, 317;
Joseph, 261
CADWALLADER, Abraham, 61;
Agnes, 61; Christiana, 25;
Isaac, 43; Joel, 61; Joseph,

25, 124; Martha, 61; Martin, 61; Rebeckah, 25; Ruth, 61
CAIN, Ginn, 321; Magdalena, 126
CAKE, May, 211
CALBFLISH, Barbara, 76
CALENDER, Catherine, 8
CALER, John, 178, 186
CALFLESH, Elizabeth, 197; Esther, 197; Henry, 197; Mary, 197
CAMPBELL, Andrew, 352; Ann, 95; Barbara, 102, 164, 331; Benjamin, 95, 335; Elizabeth, 164; Jacob, 164; James, 164; Joseph, 102, 164, 331; Margaret, 164; Mary, 183; Samuel, 353; Thomas, 164
CAMPMAN, Martha, 138
CANE, Barbara, 202; Elizabeth, 202; James, 202; John, 202; Mary, 202; Robert, 202
CANNON, Forgus, 323
CANTWELL, Eve, 125; James, 125, 342
CAPEL, Elizabeth, 212; Henry, 212; Herbert, 212; Jacob, 220; John, 212; Zeller, 212
CARE, Polly, 113
CAREY, Enoch, 186; Hannah, 186
CARL, Abraham, 176; Barbara, 176, 353; Catharine, 40; Christian, 176, 353; Christina, 176; Elizabeth, 40, 176; Hannah, 176; Henry, 40, 176, 355; Isaiah, 40, 176, 355; Jacob, 40, 143, 176; John, 40, 176; Katie, 176; Peter, 176
CARMALT, Isaac, 227; Jonathan, 144
CARNALT, Hannah, 174
CARNEY, Henry, 300
CARPENTER, Joel, 144
CARR, Daniel, 178; Edith, 177; Elizabeth, 178; John, 178; Joseph, 140, 142, 178; Leah, 313; Mary, 178, 279; Michael, 178; Robert, 279; Streeper, 279; William, 177
CARREHER, Sabella, 240
CARREL, Elias, 358; James, 358
CARRELL, James, 195
CARROLL, Daniel, 323
CARTER, Latatia, 4
CARVER, Ann, 245; Elizabeth, 218; Jesse, 218; Mary, 218; Rachel, 108; Silas, 245; William, 211, 218, 283
CASE, Ann, 43
CASEL, Isaac, 33
CASEY, Hannah, 117

CASHO, Catharine, 111; Elizabeth, 111; Gabriel, 111; Jacob, 111; John, 111; Maria, 111; Maria Magdalena, 111; Mary, 111; Rebecca, 111; Sally, 111
CASKY, John, 280; Rebecca, 280
CASSEL, Abraham, 293, 313, 345; Barbara, 169, 276; Catharine, 137, 293; Eve, 94; George, 276; Henry, 10, 93, 137, 138; Herbert, 13; Isaac, 169, 313; Jacob, 137, 138, 257, 260, 276, 291, 301, 313, 344, 354, 361; John, 137, 138, 257, 313, 354, 361; Magdalena, 313; Margaret, 93, 350; Mary, 137, 138; Susanna, 94; Yellis, 75, 93, 94, 137, 138, 350, 361
CASSELBERRY, Ann, 315, 316; Anna, 81; Benjamin, 81, 315; Derick, 31, 97; Jacob, 81, 315; Rebecca, 315; Richard, 81; William, 81, 226, 316
CASSELBURRY, Jacob, 325
CASSELBURY, Ann, 194; Jacob, 194; Richard, 253; William, 214, 215
CASSELL, Jacob, 274
CASTEL, Abraham, 324; Hobert, 323
CASTLE, Yellis, 323
CASTNER, Jane, 198; Jesse, 341; John, 341; Lydia, 341; Samuel, 112
CAUFFMAN, Archibald, 356; Jacob, 356; John, 31
CHAIN, John, 119; Matthew, 119, 123
CHAPIN, Nathan, 322
CHAPMAN, James, 312; Juluan, 312; Seth, 207
CHECK, Magdalena, 253
CHEW, Mary, 32
CHICAN, John, 25
CHILD, Agnes, 344; George, 142, 355; John, 6, 14, 17, 111; Mary, 96; Naylor, 118
CHILDS, Cephas, 335; Elizabeth, 38; George, 80; Henry, 83; James, 351; Jane, 38, 80; John, 75, 83, 351; Mary, 351
CHRISMAN, Catharine, 282; Daniel, 269; Elizabeth, 282; George, 282; Hannah, 282; John, 282; Magdalena, 282; Margaret, 282; Maria, 282; Mary, 282; Rebecca, 282; Susanna, 282

CHRISTIAN, Ann, 292; Christian, 292; Elizabeth, 292; George, 292; Sarah, 292; Thomas, 292
CHRISTINE, Christian, 44; Joanna, 144
CHRISTMAN, Catharine, 127, 145; Daniel, 127, 145; David, 127; Elizabeth, 127, 145, 211; George, 127, 145; Gertraude, 127; Henry, 145; Jacob, 145; John, 127, 145; Joseph, 127; Magdelena, 145; Mary, 127; Philip, 2, 127, 211, 301; Solome, 127; Susanna, 145
CHURCH, Ann, 111
CHUTT, Barbara, 210
CLAIR, Elizabeth, 95
CLARE, Hannah, 126
CLARK, Amy, 155; Israel, 74; William, 323
CLAWSON, Mary, 219
CLAY, Charles, 293; Charles H., 360; George, 360; Jesse Curtis, 304; Slater, 105, 360; Slator, 293
CLAYTON, Abraham, 281; Elisabeth, 38; Hannah, 38; John, 38, 44, 70, 80, 142, 145, 170, 281; Jonathan, 38, 281; Joseph, 281; Margaret, 80, 158; Mary, 70, 281
CLEAVER, Alice, 188; Ann, 97; David, 105; Elizabeth, 8, 192, 297; Ellis, 8, 163, 294; Ezekiel, 7, 8; Hannah, 97, 111, 148; Isaac, 19, 97, 111, 153; Jesse, 64, 148; John, 8, 46, 64, 65, 67, 97, 148, 265; Jonathan, 105, 116, 191, 192, 201, 215, 235, 241, 278, 282, 283, 297, 315; Joseph, 97; Lydia, 97; Martha, 8; Mary, 8, 89, 97, 192, 296; Nathan, 8, 108, 126, 192; Peter, 8, 97; Rebecca, 111, 297; Salathiel, 192; Samuel, 188; Sarah, 8; William, 191
CLEEVER, Isaac, 7
CLEMENS, Ann, 23; Catharine, 27, 281; Elizabeth, 281; Gerhart, 280; Henry, 281, 287; Jacob, 23, 192, 281; John, 280; Sarah, 281
CLEMENTS, Henry, 314; John, 349
CLEMMANS, Jacob, 104
CLEMMENS, Abraham, 339; Elizabeth, 145; George, 339; Hannah, 147; Jacob, 246, 356, 358; John, 147, 339, 358; Leonard, 356; Thomas, 145; Valentine, 360

CLEMMER, Abraham, 96, 164, 323; Ann, 96; Henry, 323, 332; John, 332; Mary, 332
CLEMMONS, Ann, 226; Jacob, 226
CLENNAH, Elizabeth, 238; Mary, 238; Susanna, 238; Thomas, 238; William, 238
CLEVER, Ann, 337; Isaac, 337; Joseph, 337
CLIME, Ann, 123, 124; Conrad, 348; Elizabeth, 123, 124; Henry, 143; Jesse, 123, 124; John, 123, 124; Mary, 143; Rachel, 348; Samuel, 123; Sarah, 123, 124
CLIMER, Henry, 10; Michael, 227
CLINE, Barbara, 77, 175, 184; Catharine, 77; Conrad, 87; Elizabeth, 323; Gabriel, 320; Henry, 175, 184, 323; Jacob, 76; John, 77, 175, 323; Margaret, 354; Matthias, 175; Michael, 175; Peter, 175; Sarah, 87; William, 87
CLOCK, Henry, 147
CLUMBERG, Philip, 3; Susanna, 3
COAL, John, 113
COATES, William, 170
COATS, John, 246, 352; John H., 124; Lindsay, 1, 9, 21, 48, 93, 105, 144; Matthias, 105; Rachel, 105; Samuel, 352; Septimus, 84; Tacy, 262; William, 6
COBLANZ, David, 7; Elizabeth, 7; Jacob, 7; Peter, 7; Philip, 7
COCHRAN, Benjamin, 27; James, 43, 229; Margaret, 229; Mary, 197; Robert, 229; Thomas, 16, 43, 197; William, 197
COCKBURN, Thomas, 255
COGGINS, Jonathan, 323; Mary, 323
COIL, Sarah, 143
COILS, Elizabeth, 62
COLEFLESH, Matthias, 323
COLEMAN, Catharine, 35; Elizabeth, 35; Jacob, 35; John, 35; Mary, 35; Nicholas, 35; William, 35
COLER, Barbara, 250; Casper, 250; Christopher, 109; David, 109; Henry, 82; John, 250
COLFLESH, Barbara, 346; David, 346; Henry, 160, 229, 346; Jacob, 329; John, 323; Mathias, 43; Matthias, 103, 178, 360; Nathan, 43
COLFLISH, Barbara, 12, 13; Catharine, 13; Henry, 12;

Jacob, 13; John, 12, 13;
Mattis, 12; William, 12, 13
COLL, Philip, 51
COLLADAR, Daniel, 291
COLLEY, ---, 14; Abigail, 157;
Alice, 157; Jonathan, 157,
318
COLLINS, Ann, 73
COLLOM, Alice, 96; Benjamin,
96; Clement, 96; Elizabeth,
96; Hannah, 96; Jesse, 96;
John, 96, 233, 331, 340;
Martha, 175; Rachel, 96;
William, 148, 340, 348
COLLON, John, 73, 89
COLLUM, Alice, 175
COLSTON, Barnabas, 161; David,
323
COLTMAN, Ann, 307; Jane, 307;
John, 248; Joseph, 307;
Robert, 248; William, 248
COMALY, Jonathan, 104; Joshua,
104
COMBE, Barnet B., 112; Hannah,
112; John R., 112; Mary, 112;
Sarah, 112; Thomas, 112
COMBS, David, 34; Hannah, 34;
John, 231
COMFORT, Alice, 278; Elizabeth,
278, 323; Ezra, 27, 171, 201,
278; John, 278
COMLEY, John, 329; Joshua, 116,
321
COMLY, Agnes, 261; Agness, 302;
Asa, 261; Franklin, 281;
Hannah, 110, 209; John, 232;
Joshua, 114, 150, 190, 217,
244, 281; Nathan, 249, 261;
Sarah, 29
COMMINGS, David, 358; Solomon,
358
COMMINS, Catharine, 20; Jacob,
20
CONARD, Benjamin, 353; Hannah,
300; Henry, 189, 300, 353;
John, 300, 339; Mary, 339;
Thomas, 339
CONBY, Samuel, 138
CONNARD, Streeper, 132
CONNER, Mary, 112
CONRAD, Ajar, 117; Ann, 55;
Anna, 167; Benjamin, 56, 115,
242; Catharine, 56, 175;
Cornelius, 276; David, 188,
206; Deborah, 44, 117;
Dennis, 44, 167, 277; Edward,
93; Elizabeth, 124, 164, 188,
206; Esther, 281; Fred, 58,
214; Frederick, 48, 100, 102,
112, 114, 132, 143, 150, 155,
164, 166, 177, 192, 216, 221,
222, 223, 224, 228, 231, 257,
258, 265, 266, 273, 281, 304,
310, 313, 315, 323, 280;
Frederick K., 253; Grace,
261, 276; Hannah, 167, 175,
276; Henry, 55, 56, 258, 323;
Henry W., 206, 266; Henry
William, 222; Isaac, 44;
John, 44, 55, 115, 124, 164,
167, 278, 281, 297, 338;
Jonathan, 124, 167, 206;
Joseph, 259; Lydia, 206;
Magdalena, 323; Martha, 338;
Mary, 44, 164, 168; Matthew,
117, 272; Michael, 51; Nancy,
206; Peter, 175; Priscilla,
276, 281; Reese, 206; Robert,
56; Ruth, 276; Samuel, 276;
Sarah, 55, 56, 105, 276, 281;
Susanna, 44, 117, 167
CONROE, Flora, 235
CONVEAR, Christian, 349
CONVER, Peter, 186
CONWARE, Jacob, 70
CONWAY, Neal, 173
CONWELL, Robert, 329; Sophia,
329
COOK, Henry, 323; Jacob, 249;
Nathan, 102, 104, 117; Peggy,
262
COOLY, John, 163; Rebecca, 163
COOMBS, David, 323
COOPER, Amy, 14; Elizabeth, 14;
Hugh, 355; William, 360
COPE, Catharine, 253; George,
336; Henry, 282, 300; Jacob,
59, 253; Joel, 361; John,
336; Magdalena, 361; Samuel,
336; Sarah, 31; Tobias, 344
COPLIN, Maria, 264
COPNER, Thomas, 248
CORASDILL, Martha, 115
CORBIN, Rebecca, 253
CORBITT, Michael, 250
CORNER, John, 169; Salomy, 169
CORNOG, Dinah, 37; Margaret, 47
CORPER, Catharine, 139
CORSEN, Richard, 160
CORSON, Alan, 347; Alan W.,
353; Allan, 272; Allen, 275,
297; Benjamin, 189;
Catharine, 315; John, 315;
Joseph, 133; Mary, 264
COSSLY, Samuel, 187
COTMAN, Benjamin, 26
COTON, Mary, 166
COTTEN, Mary, 116
COTTMAN, Benjamin, 78
COTTON, John, 181, 332, 352;
Mary, 120, 181, 208

COUCH, Abigail, 111; Edward, 111; William, 111
COUF, Charles, 20
COUGHAR, Frederick, 145; Shelah, 145
COULSTON, Abigail, 9, 350; Ann, 280; Barnabas, 37, 140, 350; Barnard, 254; Bulah, 9; Edward, 38, 140; Elizabeth, 9, 37, 140, 323, 330; Eve, 323; George, 350; Henry, 351; Israel, 9, 323; Isreal, 330; James, 140; John, 38, 140, 323, 350; Mary, 140; Samuel, 9, 323; Thomas, 140; William, 9, 140, 323, 351
COULTER, Mary, 336; Michael, 336
COUNT OF VILLEFORT, 59
COURSEN, Daniel, 4; Prudey, 4
COUSTLY, Hugh, 333
COWDEN, Hester, 323; Samuel, 323; Thomas, 289
COX, Alice, 223; Ann, 234; Benjamin, 89, 206, 230, 331; James, 234; John, 234; Jonathan, 89, 220; Joseph, 220; Mary, 220, 234; Rachel, 100, 234; Sarah, 220, 234; Thomas, 100, 234; Thomas Jefferson, 234; William, 220
CRACKER, Abraham, 33
CRAFT, Agnes, 210; Agness, 253; Alice, 210; Ann, 209; Barnet, 331; Elizabeth, 210; Esther, 347; George, 323; Hester, 240; Jacob, 3, 210, 353; John, 14, 210, 323, 331, 347, 353; Jonathan, 210, 353; Mary, 210; Rebecca, 111, 323; Sarah, 14
CRAIG, Anne, 323; Daniel, 312; Hannah, 312; James, 312; Jane, 312; Joanna, 312; John, 335; Lewis, 312; Thomas, 323
CRATOR, Catharine, 305; Jacob, 305; John, 305; Peter, 305
CRAVIN, Ann, 193, 267; Catharine, 193; Christiana, 193; Helena, 193; Isaac, 193; James, 193; Lena, 193; Rose, 193; Thomas, 193; William, 193
CRAWFORD, Alexander, 30, 247, 348, 359; Andrew, 30, 312; Andrew Hugh, 359; Anna, 333; Elizabeth, 30; Isabella, 359; Joseph, 30, 47, 175, 238, 294, 304, 356; Matthew, 333, 338; Samuel, 338; Sarah, 30; William, 30, 333

CRAY, John, 98
CREASAMER, Catharine, 141; Jacob, 141
CREATER, Margaret, 131
CREEBLE, Abraham, 33
CRESS, Margaret, 356; William, 356
CRESSMAN, Anthony, 15; Catharine, 15, 157; Charlotte, 255; Daniel, 323; Elisabeth, 15; George, 340; Hannah, 15; Isaac, 255, 359; Jacob, 15, 328, 340, 359; John, 15; John Adam, 157; John George, 335; Margaret, 136; Mary, 15, 267; Nicholas, 48, 318, 323; Samuel, 238, 280
CRISMAN, George, 344; Hannah, 31; Jacob, 344; Nicholas, 344
CRISPEN, John, 311; Susanna, 155
CRISTY, Dennis, 323
CROASDEL, Martha, 68
CROASDILL, Anna, 115; Jane, 115; Martha, 115; Mary, 115; Molly, 115
CROLL, Christian, 347; Elizabeth, 54; Frederick, 356; Henry, 54, 331; Jacob, 247, 299, 323, 347, 356; John, 299; Jonathan, 315; Mc., 72; Michael, 21, 36, 102, 323, 347; Samuel Henry, 348
CROSS, Jeremiah, 282
CROTHERS, Anthony, 317, 326
CROUS, Catharine, 99; Daniel, 99; Elizabeth, 99; George, 99; Henry, 289; Jacob, 2, 26, 46, 51, 56, 62, 93, 94, 123, 130, 151, 289; Michael, 99; Molly, 99; Salome, 99
CROUSE, Henry, 358, 359; Jacob, 356, 358; John, 339; Samuel, 356
CROW, Frederick, 76
CROWS, Elizabeth, 305; Henry, 305; Jacob, 305; Sophia, 305
CRYELER, Daniel, 68; Magdalena, 68
CUCKER, George, 112
CUFF, 82; Henry, 115
CULP, Elizabeth, 205, 323; Jacob, 205; Leonard, 45, 116, 360; Lewis, 323; Margaret, 205; Mary, 45, 158; Philip, 14, 45; Rachel, 158; Susanna, 158
CULTZ, Jacob, 62
CUMLEY, Hannah, 141

CUMMING, Ashey, 122; David, 2, 122; David Blair, 122; Deborah, 122; George, 122; Gulichma, 122; Martha, 73; Rachel, 122; Rebecca, 122; Samuel, 122; Solomon, 122; Thomas, 122; William, 122
CUMMINS, Jacob, 152
CUMMIUS, Charles, 323
CUMPSTON, Thomas, 174
CUNARD, Samuel, 18
CUNNARD, Catharine, 37; David, 17, 37; Dennis, 37; Elisabeth, 17; Henry, 17, 37; John, 16; Jonathan, 17, 37; Joseph, 16; Lydia, 37; Rachel, 16; Rebeckah, 37; Rebekah, 16, 17; Streeper, 17, 37
CUNNINGHAM, Elizabeth, 278; George, 278
CUNRAD, Benjamin, 87; David, 323; Frederick, 92, 93; Henry, 126; Lydia, 323
CUP, Margaret, 72; Mary, 72
CUPP, Mary, 349; Peter, 349
CUREMEN, Philip, 216
CURRY, Agnes, 91; James, 97; Joseph, 74; Mary, 74; Rebecca, 97; Robert, 22, 41, 68, 74, 84; Samuel, 74
CURTEY, Robert M., 107
CURTIS, Dr., 284
CURTZ, Valentine, 328
CURWIN, John, 258
CUSTARD, John, 323; Jonathan, 217
CUSTER, Abraham, 76; Anna, 153, 250; Benjamin, 76; Catharine, 153, 250; Cornelius, 250; Elizabeth, 76, 152, 153, 357; Eve, 250; Gertraut, 76; Harman, 76, 329; Henry, 231, 250, 329; Isaac, 356; Jacob, 119, 138, 152, 153, 314, 329; John, 76, 206, 330, 352; Jonas, 330; Joseph, 152, 153; Levi, 231, 250; Magdalena, 76; Margaret, 323; Mary, 153, 250; Nathan, 221; Paul, 38, 76, 318, 330, 356; Peter, 76, 138, 152, 153, 340, 352, 357, 323; Rebecca, 138, 153; Samuel, 152, 153; Sarah, 356; Sybilla, 76; William, 2, 48, 211

-D-

DAGEN, Christiana, 109; Daniel, 109; Eve, 109; John, 109; Ludwick, 109

DAGER, Barbara, 6; Catherine, 6; Christiana, 6; Elizabeth, 6; George, 340; Jacob, 6, 7, 220, 340; John, 6, 253, 353; Margaret, 6; Mary, 6; Peter, 6, 340, 357; Rachel, 6; Sarah, 6
DALAKER, Frederick, 350
DALLEN, Hannah Vansant, 90; John Vansant, 90; Simon Vansant, 90
DALLIKER, Frederick, 324
DANCE, Gilbert, 91, 95; John, 95; Joseph, 91, 94, 95; Mary, 67, 95
DANEHAUER, Elizabeth, 31; John, 31
DANEHOWER, Abraham, 34; Catharine, 34; George, 34; Henry, 34, 344
DANIEL, Isaac, 160
DANIELS, Herman, 216; Samuel, 335, 339
DANKEL, Jacob, 33; Susannah, 33
DANNEHOWER, Abraham, 351; Elizabeth, 351; Henry, 351; Jacob, 351
DAR, John, 173; Maria, 173
DARRAH, Agnes, 74; Ann, 231; Archibald, 74, 317, 318, 319, 320, 321, 322, 323, 325, 326, 327, 328, 329, 331; Mary, 74; Rebecca, 74; Robert, 231
DAST, Jacob, 324
DAUB, Catharine, 84; Cathrine, 248; Christiana, 84; Christina, 248; Henry, 84, 248, 273, 281, 306; Jacob, 202; Molly, 248; Peter, 84
DAVES, David, 343; Rebecca, 343
DAVID, Elizabeth, 350; Jane, 85; Margaret, 133; Rebecca, 87
DAVIDSON, Henry, 135
DAVIES, Evan, 20; Hannah, 20; John, 20, 231; Margaret, 20
DAVIS, Abigail, 350; Abner, 109; Abraham, 61; Ann, 24, 230, 315; Catharine, 25, 229; Daniel, 290, 350; David, 38, 61, 215, 324, 338, 348, 349; Edward, 311, 324; Edward M., 311; Elijah, 324; Elisha, 324; Elizabeth, 61, 156, 229, 311, 324, 356; Esther, 315; Ezekiel, 324; Gainor, 324; Hannah, 25, 59, 103; Hugh, 61; Isaac, 61, 141, 311, 318, 343; Isaac R., 311; Isaiah, 70, 86, 105, 145, 315, 326; Israel, 61; James, 20, 25,

41, 133, 324, 355; Jane, 25, 111; Jesse, 284, 324, 348; Job, 343, 347; John, 61, 103, 183, 198, 230, 258, 284, 349, 356; Joseph, 171; Lewellin, 109; Lydia, 324; Margaret, 25, 59; Marmaduke, 324; Martha, 109, 133; Mary, 25, 86, 169, 197, 284, 285, 315, 324, 343; Mordecai, 125, 198, 209, 231, 237; Moses, 25; Nancy, 103; Rachel, 25, 259; Rebecca, 91, 128, 315, 324, 355; Rees, 25; Robert, 60; Roger, 109; Samuel, 101, 290; Sarah, 25, 75, 103; Sarha, 109; Sophia, 40, 315; Susannah, 25; Tacey, 61; Tamer, 103; Thomas, 25, 86, 108, 259, 284, 312, 315, 324, 347, 349, 355; William, 103, 166, 209, 324
DEAL, Daniel, 331
DEAN, Benjamin, 176; Hannah, 96; John, 133, 176; Joseph, 176; Mary, 176; Samuel, 176; Sarah, 176; William, 152, 176
DEAVES, Ann, 104; Elizabeth, 254; Isaac, 104; Isreal, 104; Jacob, 104; Jesse, 104; Jonathan, 104, 354; Joseph, 104; Martha, 104; Samuel, 104; Thomas, 104, 254
DEAVS, Ann, 171; Anna, 171; Elizabeth, 171; Isaac, 171; Isreal, 171; Jesse, 171; John, 171; Jonathan, 171; Joseph, 171; Samuel, 171; Thomas, 171
DEBENNEVILLE, George, 117
DEBRE, Homer, 215; Lydia, 118
DEEN, Adam, 324; Catharine, 324
DEETS, Margaret, 91
DEHAVEN, Abraham, 291; Catharine, 291; David, 17, 134, 158, 216, 239, 291; Elizabeth, 216; Hannah, 93; Hugh, 1; Isaac, 87, 103, 239, 349; John, 37, 47, 93, 216, 239, 311, 324; Jonathan, 311; Magdalena, 126, 239; Margaret, 185; Mary, 252; Moses, 185; Peter, 126, 231, 311; Rachel, 239; Rebecca, 231, 252; Samuel, 86, 124, 291, 349
DEITZ, Henry, 45
DELGARD, Johannes, 20
DELL, Matthew, 173
DELLEN, George, 339
DELLICKER, Frederick, 353

DELP, Abraham, 35, 36, 153; Catharine, 36; Elizabeth, 36; George, 35, 36; Isaac, 36; John, 36, 302; Samuel, 35, 36
DEMAN, Cornelia, 90
DENGLER, Catharine, 12; Elizabeth, 12; George, 1, 12, 54, 156, 343; Henry, 12; Jacob, 12, 225; John, 12, 165, 239, 343; Magdalena, 165; Susanna, 239
DENNEHOWER, Abraham, 101; Catharine, 101; Elizabeth, 101; Henry, 101; John, 101; Sarah, 101
DENNER, Jacob, 303
DENNIS, James, 119
DERDINGER, Catharine, 152
DERRICK, Jacob, 221
DERRINGER, Adam, 20; Anna Elisabeth, 20; Catharine, 20; John, 20; Thomas, 20
DESHLER, Charles, 62
DETTER, Abraham, 354; Conrad, 354
DETTERER, Abraham, 354; Christian, 354
DETTRA, Isaac, 194
DETWEILER, Abraham, 92; Barbara, 32; Catharine, 57; Elizabeth, 92; Felix, 51, 65, 324; Frederick, 324; Jacob, 28, 32, 57; John, 28, 32, 112; Joseph, 28; Magdalena, 112; Margareth, 32; Mary, 28; Philip, 65
DETWELLER, Joseph, 329
DETWILER, Abraham, 169, 276, 311; Anna, 244; Barbara, 169, 276; Benjamin, 276; Catharine, 169; Christian, 179, 276; Elisabeth, 16, 17; Elizabeth, 123, 169, 179; Felix, 123; Hannah, 169, 276; Henry, 192, 193; Hester, 169; Isaac, 192, 193; Jacob, 16, 169, 170, 192, 246, 276, 324, 345, 349; John, 16, 106, 123, 136, 169, 180, 192, 246, 341, 345, 349; Joseph, 16, 250, 276, 352; Magdalena, 169; Maria, 276; Martin, 20, 276; Mary, 16, 169, 276, 352; Molly, 246; Salomy, 169; Samuel, 276, 293, 343; Sarah, 169, 276; Susanna, 16, 169, 276
DEUGLER, George, 156; Mary Margaret, 156
DEVAN, David, 324

DEWEES, Abraham, 69, 351;
  Agnes, 69; Benjamin, 117;
  Charles, 124, 272; Christian,
  69; David, 200, 341;
  Elizabeth, 69; Henry, 124,
  332; Jacob, 124, 168, 276;
  John, 69, 124, 332; Jonathan,
  124, 332, 358; Mary, 124;
  Rachel, 124; William, 69,
  124, 240, 324, 350
DICKENSHEED, Christopher, 26;
  Dillman, 26; Margaret, 26;
  Susanna, 26; Valentine, 26;
  William, 26
DICKENSON, Jonathan, 35
DICKHOWKE, Henry, 335
DICKINSON, Caroline, 155; Eli,
  155; Mary, 124, 155
DICKSON, Hugh, 252, 269, 273
DIEHL, George, 22
DIEM, John, 216
DIEMER, Catharine, 70; Daniel,
  70; Eve, 70; George, 70;
  Michael, 70
DIENER, Anna Margaret, 1;
  Peter, 1
DIFFENDEFFER, Abraham, 324
DILCART, Eve, 11; John, 11
DILL, Frederick, 191; Margaret,
  324; Matthew, 195, 225, 230,
  295, 338; Robert, 324
DILLER, Frederick, 42
DILLON, Jacob, 342; Jesse, 342;
  John, 343; Mary, 342
DILLS, Anna Margaret, 7;
  Hartman, 7
DILWORTH, Jacob, 329
DINNIGH, Elizabeth, 139; Peter,
  139
DIRSTINE, Isaac, 36
DISMANT, B., 88; Benjamin, 7,
  8, 17, 29, 40, 44, 47, 64,
  71, 81, 99, 101, 130, 152,
  167; Christian, 167; Daniel,
  130, 356; Elizabeth, 8, 130;
  Esther, 40; Henry, 40, 43,
  167; Jacob, 61; John, 8, 44,
  130, 167; Maria, 167;
  William, 130, 152, 167, 294,
  308
DODDER, Berni, 29
DOLLY, 72
DONALD, Elizabeth, 255
DONALDSON, Joseph, 174
DONELLY, Hugh, 346; John, 346;
  Joseph, 346
DONNELLY, Edward, 352
DORGERS, William, 277
DORSTONE, Isaac, 20
DOTERO, Abraham, 273

DOTOROW, Barney, 265; Maria,
  265
DOTTERA, Catharine, 285, 286;
  Conrad, 286; John, 286;
  Maria, 286
DOTTERER, Abraham, 123, 223,
  342; Barnhart, 342;
  Catharine, 123, 204;
  Christian, 123; Conrad, 16,
  123, 204; Elizabeth, 123,
  223; Jacob, 123; Jacob
  Conrad, 123; John, 123, 204,
  324; Magdalena, 123;
  Margaret, 16; Maria, 204;
  Michael, 16, 27, 204, 221,
  324, 345, 348; Nathan, 254;
  Peter, 204; Philibina, 204;
  Philip, 204; Susanna, 123
DOTTS, Adam, 340; Henry, 340;
  Philip, 340
DOUB, Jacob, 129
DOUGHERTY, Hannah, 86; Philip,
  86; Thomas, 294
DOUL, Henry, 8
DOWERS, Mary Ann, 303
DOWILLAN, Ann, 30; Anne, 30
DOWLIN, David, 119, 302; John,
  119; Josiah, 119; Margaret,
  119; Paul, 119, 146, 291
DOWNES, Elizabeth, 183; Mary,
  183; Matthew, 183; Robert,
  183
DOWNING, Jane, 313
DOYLE, Mary, 146; Stephen, 146
DRAKE, Andrew, 105, 205, 257;
  Benjamin, 105; Elizabeth,
  257; George, 105; Hannah,
  105, 205, 250, 257; James,
  205; John, 32, 46, 105, 205,
  347; Jonathan, 105, 257;
  Levi, 205, 249; Mary, 257,
  339; Michael, 249; Rachel,
  46, 205, 249; Richard, 339;
  Sarah, 257; Thomas, 105, 205,
  257; William, 105, 257
DRASHER, Abraham, 343; Jacob,
  343
DRESHER, Abraham, 84, 121, 163,
  324; Christopher, 272, 348;
  Eve, 84, 324; George, 73;
  Samuel, 273
DRESSHER, Christopher, 304;
  George, 304; Mary, 304;
  Samuel, 304
DRIECHLER, Mary, 231
DRIESBAUCH, John, 226
DRINKHOUSE, Adam, 262; Jacob,
  99, 209, 224, 228, 262, 263,
  275, 295, 315
DROLLINGER, Peter, 19; Sophia,
  19

DROSS, Michael, 309
DRUMBORE, Andrew, 19;
  Catharine, 19; George, 19;
  Henry, 19; Jacob, 19; John,
  19; Louisa, 19; Sophia, 19
DUBOIS, Joseph, 36
DUBRE, Elizabeth, 215; Hannah,
  190; Jacob, 10, 190; Lydia,
  118; Margaret, 10, 190;
  Martha, 190; Rebecca, 190;
  Rebekah, 10; Sarah, 190;
  Thomas, 10; William, 324
DUFF, Margaret, 119
DUFFIELD, Elizabeth, 213
DULL, Ann, 85, 275; Barbara,
  66; Catharine, 66; Christian,
  284, 320; Elizabeth, 66, 284;
  Frederick, 66, 168, 340, 347;
  John, 66, 275, 284; Margaret,
  66; Mary, 66; Susanna, 66
DUNBAR, Andrew, 56; Martha, 56;
  Sarah, 56, 57
DUNGAN, Amos, 244, 347;
  Jeremiah, 347; Joseph, 324;
  Lydia, 74; Rachel, 324;
  Susanna, 244, 347
DUNGAS, James, 79
DUNKNOUSE, Jacob, 138
DUNLAP, Ann, 269; Eleanor, 231;
  Elizabeth, 269; Robert, 140,
  142; William, 269
DUNN, Elizabeth, 161; James,
  161; Margaret, 161; William,
  161
DUNNET, Charles, 228, 349;
  Christian, 349; George, 277,
  349
DUNNETT, Charles, 228; George,
  228, 281
DUPORTAIE, Lewis Libeque, 334
DUPORTAIL, Lewis L., 332; Lewis
  Lebeue, 338; Lewis Libeque,
  334
DUPUE, Elizabeth, 232
DURBRE, Jacob, 353
DUTTEREO, Michael, 274
DUTWEILER, Jacob, 199
DUY, John, 254; John K., 199
DYER, Deborah, 210; Edward,
  232; Elizabeth, 210; James,
  210, 232; John, 210; Joseph,
  210, 232; Mary, 232; Mary
  Ann, 232; Phebe, 232; Philip,
  232; Samuel, 232; Sarah, 45,
  232; Susanna, 232; Thomas,
  275

-E-
EARNEST, Baltzer, 174;
  Catharine, 324; Henry, 174,
  324; John, 324, 353

EASTBORN, Benjamin, 9
EASTBURN, Abigail, 75; Amos,
  164; Benjamin, 37, 75, 164;
  David, 164; Hannah, 75;
  James, 164; John, 37, 75,
  164; Joseph, 164, 174;
  Margaret, 37, 75; Mary, 164;
  Miriam, 37; Rebecca, 164;
  Samuel, 75, 164
EATON, Joseph, 267, 356;
  Rebecca, 267
EBERHARD, Adam, 212; Margaret,
  211
ECHEL, John, 203
ECHTLE, Jacob, 166; Susanna,
  166
ECKEL, John, 87; Mary, 87
EDER, John, 311
EDGE, Ann, 3; Jacob, 3;
  Margaret, 3; Mary, 3, 178;
  Rachel, 3; Susanna, 3
EDMINSTON, James, 100; Nancy,
  100
EDWARDS, Ann, 158; David, 158;
  Edward, 30, 57, 111, 158,
  161, 253; Elizabeth, 47, 158,
  189, 325; Jane, 133; John,
  23, 47, 53, 123, 135, 136,
  158, 173, 322, 339; Margaret,
  104; Martha, 133; Mary, 133;
  Nathan, 325, 330; Rebecca,
  253; Robert, 158, 339, 347;
  Samuel, 133, 325; Thomas,
  133, 325
EGBERT, David, 289, 350;
  Elizabeth, 290; George, 289;
  James, 348; John, 345;
  Lawrence, 156, 289, 331, 345;
  Martha, 348; Sarah, 289;
  Susanna, 289; Thomas, 289;
  William, 348
EGELMAN, Henry, 329
EGG, Anna, 191; Catharine, 191;
  Conard, 191; Darius, 191;
  Dorothy, 191; Fanny, 191;
  John, 175, 190, 191;
  Magdalena, 191; Margaret,
  191; Sabella, 191; Theodore,
  333; Theresa, 191
EGNER, Peter, 12
EGOLF, Adam, 77, 296; Anna
  Margaret, 77; Catharine, 77,
  194; Elizabeth, 77, 194;
  George Adam, 77; Henry, 77;
  Jacob, 77, 194; John, 77,
  296; Maria Elizabeth, 194;
  Mary, 77; Michael, 77, 194
EHMAN, Agnes, 8; George, 8;
  John, 8

EIDEMILLER, Catharine, 21; Jacob, 21; Michael, 21; Nicholas, 21; Philip, 21
EINGHURST, Isreal, 174
ELDNY, Elizabeth, 112
ELEANHOOF, Ann Mary, 340; Godfrey, 340; Josiah, 340
ELLIOT, Charles J. 356; J., 106; John, 86, 339, 356; Robert, 339; William, 339
ELLIOTT, Daniel, 306; John, 240, 252, 259; Thomas, 263; William H., 268
ELLIS, Amos, 25, 37, 108, 189, 207, 325; Elizabeth, 25; Hannah, 207; Humphrey, 25; Isaac, 7, 25, 108; Juda, 338; Lydia, 108; Mary, 75, 98, 108, 325; Rachel, 25, 325; Robert, 75; Roland, 339; William, 25, 85, 108, 260, 272, 316
ELMS, George, 274; Mary, 274
ELWELL, Elijah, 283
ELY, Hugh, 179; Joseph, 179
EMERICH, Catharine, 227; Dorothy, 227; Elizabeth, 227; George, 227; John, 227; Philip, 227; Valentine, 227
EMERSON, Christiani, 11
EMERT, George, 251
EMLEN, Samuel, 306
EMMERICK, John, 337
EMRICH, ---, 316; Rebecca, 316
ENGARD, Catharine, 124, 230, 231; Dorothy, 124; Elizabeth, 124, 230; Jacob, 124; Margaret, 124; Mary, 124; Susanna, 124; William, 230, 231
ENGART, Adam, 18; Anne, 18; Catharine, 18, 72, 324; John, 18, 72; Mary, 18; Peter, 236; Philip, 324
ENGEL, Henry, 1; Jacob, 332
ENGLAND, Mary, 17
ENGLE, Ann, 208; Catharine, 208, 324; John, 38
ENGLES, Agnes, 116; Benjamin, 116; Catharine, 116; Hannah, 116; Jacob, 116; Jonathan, 116; Joseph, 116; Moses, 116; Rachel, 116; Susannah, 116; Thomas, 116
ENRICK, Valentine, 54
ENYARD, Abraham, 335; Charles, 335
ENZEST, Dorothy, 219; Elizabeth, 219; Nicholas, 218; Peter, 219; Philip, 218

EPPRIGHT, Christian, 347; John, 347; William, 347
EPTING, Catharine, 282
ERB, Casper, 331; Elizabeth, 231; George, 173, 241, 244, 331; Henry, 331; John, 231; Susanna, 241
ERHARD, Catharine, 100; Christopher, 100; Elizabeth, 100; Jacob, 100; John, 100; Peter, 100; Sarah, 100
ERLE, George, 358
ERNST, Baltzer, 107
ERWIN, Rebecca, 11, 151; Samuel, 3, 13, 56
ESBESHIP, Henry, 333
ESHBACH, Abraham, 192, 310; Catharine, 310; Elizabeth, 310; Henry, 301; Jacob, 310; Margaret, 325; Susanna, 310
ESSIG, George, 14, 351; Jacob, 128, 351; John, 139, 351; Margaret, 325
ESTENMILLER, Christian, 225; Jacob, 225
ESTERLINE, Peter, 227, 233
EVANS, Aaron, 149, 354, 359; Adna, 11, 70, 332; Amos, 11, 119, 126, 250, 292, 303, 341, 344, 353, 360; Ann, 111, 198, 333; Athanar, 332; Benjamin, 243, 267, 305; Cadwalader, 87, 140, 141; Cadwalder, 152, 154, 177, 188, 198, 204, 222; Cadwallader, 71, 79, 104, 125, 126, 133, 329, 333; Caleb, 126, 300; Charlotte, 221; Curtis, 198, 259, 294; David, 104, 119, 243, 255, 308, 324, 330; Edward, 111, 251, 344; Eleanor, 111, 149, 258, 311, 344, 346; Elisha, 324; Elizabeth, 21, 126, 149, 154, 177, 308, 330, 347; Ellen, 188; Emmeline, 311; Enoch, 21, 148, 149; Enos, 311, 359; Esther, 188; Evan, 158, 333; Evan C., 353; Ezekiel, 324; George, 11, 149, 196, 311, 331; Hannah, 126, 148, 149, 311, 354; Hugh, 324; Jacob, 14, 110, 119, 148, 290; James, 21, 59, 221, 308, 309, 333, 351; Jane, 126; Jehu, 326; Jesse, 140; Job, 126; John, 1, 2, 3, 5, 7, 8, 17, 20, 28, 55, 79, 108, 112, 119, 126, 140, 141, 148, 154, 177, 192, 215, 250, 251, 275, 308, 319, 340, 346, 354; Jonathan, 126, 149, 311,

324; Joseph, 12, 158, 198, 288; Josiah, 2; Levi, 223, 334; Lydia, 42, 308, 333; Margaret, 344; Mark, 308, 309; Mary, 11, 21, 119, 158, 198, 243, 251, 255, 259, 303, 308, 334, 344; Matilda, 246; Matthew, 243; Miles, 5, 126; Monroe, 255; Mordecai, 70; Nathan, 126, 174, 255, 266, 311, 354; Nehemiah, 325; Owen, 119, 176, 198, 221, 251, 259, 283, 303, 333, 338, 344; Peter, 308, 334, 337; Phebe, 11; Rachel, 221, 222, 311; Rebecca, 198, 259, 284; Reese, 198; Robert, 177, 344; Robert I., 152, 353; Roberts, 12; Rowland, 140; Ruth, 198, 259, 332; Samuel, 21, 59, 119, 149, 154, 156, 158, 176, 185, 213, 220, 223, 235, 303, 304, 308; Sarah, 119, 255, 303, 308; Septimus, 308; Susannah, 325; Tacy, 126, 266; Thomas, 140, 158, 255, 265, 303; Walter, 308; William, 11, 21, 59, 324, 355

EVE, Abraham, 295; Adam, 295; Daniel, 295
EVERHART, Abraham, 340, 356; Jacob, 124, 340; John, 344, 356; Joseph, 243, 356; Philip, 344
EVNAS, Calip, 266
EWALT, George, 149
EWING, Washington, 271

-F-

FABER, Barbara, 325; Theobald, 325
FABRICIUS, Frederick, 325; Margaret, 325
FAIRBANKS, Susanna, 313
FAIRBEE, Elizabeth, 120
FAIRES, John, 260; William, 260
FAIRLAMB, Mary, 118, 198
FALLOUS, William, 262
FAMOUS, Andrew, 165; Catharine, 165; George, 165; Jacob, 165; John, 165, 171; Maria, 165; Mary, 165; William, 165
FARIBEE, Elizabeth, 172
FARINGER, Anna, 361; John, 361
FARMER, Edward, 2, 108, 342; Jonathan, 310; Sarah, 342
FARRA, Atkinson, 117, 289; Samuel, 289
FARRINGER, Catharine, 286; Christina, 286; Elizabeth, 286; Frederick, 286; George,

62; Henry, 62; John, 62, 286; Margareth, 62; Martin, 62; Mary, 286
FAUS, Margaret, 247; Philip, 247
FAUST, Henry, 354; Nicholas, 354
FAVINGER, John, 239, 361; Margaret, 361
FEADLEY, Adam, 325; Jonathan, 141, 324, 361; Mary Magdelena, 141; Michael, 361
FEAGLEY, Barnt, 135; Conrad, 135; George, 135; John, 135; Mary, 135; Nicholas, 135; Philipbina, 135; Rosana, 135
FEATHER, Isaac, 292
FEDLEY, Adam, 94; Catharine, 94; David, 94; Elizabeth, 94; John, 94; Jonathan, 94; Maria, 94; Michael, 94
FEGALLY, George, 325; Henry, 325; John, 325
FEGELY, Catharine, 49; Christian, 305; Conrad, 49; Elizabeth, 305; John, 305; Peter, 305; Polly, 305
FEGLE, Peter, 313
FEGLEY, Barney, 195; Conrad, 132; George, 132; Samuel, 347; Sarah, 132
FEGOLY, Conrad, 130
FELL, Grace, 144; Mary, 17
FELTER, Matthias, 286
FELTY, Samuel, 345
FENNELL, James, 21; Mary, 263
FENNELLS, Robert, 263
FENNELS, Elizabeth, 263
FENTON, Ephraim, 248; John, 34
FERGUSON, Elizabeth, 19
FERIES, John, 247
FERRY, Charles, 288
FERYE, Paul, 246
FETTER, Ann, 217; Anna, 217; Casper, 337; Catharine, 217; George, 217, 272, 337, 357; John, 337; Matthias, 262; Michael, 217, 309; Rachel, 217; William, 217
FETTY, Jacob, 166
FETZER, Andrew, 157, 185, 259, 344; Frederick, 157; Isaac, 157, 307; John, 157; Susanna, 185
FIE, Andrew, 107; Philip, 186, 292
FIFER, Jesse, 75
FILLMAN, Abraham, 291, 292; Catharine, 291; Christina, 291; Frederick, 291; Hannah, 291; Henry, 291, 294; Jacob,

10, 129, 291, 292; John, 291;
    Philip, 291
FINK, Jacob, 81
FISHER, Andrew, 116; Ann, 116;
    Anne Margaretha, 29; Barbara,
    67, 357; Catharine, 116, 215,
    325; Christian, 51, 170;
    Christina, 142, 145;
    Christine, 145; Conrad, 29,
    325; Elizabeth, 67; Esther,
    211; George, 6, 44, 116, 142,
    145, 325; Henry, 123, 234;
    Jacob, 50, 116, 211, 357;
    John, 51, 115, 116, 143, 145,
    161, 325; Joseph, 66, 145,
    325; Lewis, 116; Malachi,
    145; Maria, 130; Mary, 51,
    170; Peter, 325; Philip, 215;
    Rachel, 170; Rebecca, 170;
    Sabina, 234; Sarah, 234;
    Susanna, 170; Susannah, 51;
    Thomas, 16; Wendle, 357;
    William, 116
FISS, Benjamin, 355; John, 355;
    Mary, 355
FITTELS, David, 242; Elizabeth,
    242
FITZGERALD, Barbara, 196;
    Elizabeth, 196; James, 92,
    196; John, 196; Matthias,
    196; Peter, 196; Rosanna,
    196; Sophia, 196; Thomas,
    349; William, 249, 349
FITZWATER, ---, 24, 238;
    Amelia, 176; Catharine, 346;
    Cathrine, 238; David, 97;
    Esther, 176; George, 97, 174,
    194, 214, 238, 268, 307, 332,
    356; Hannah, 238, 325; Jacob,
    238, 268, 270, 316; Jane,
    229; John, 67, 97, 179, 199,
    238, 253, 298, 307, 325, 341,
    346; Joseph, 47, 249; Mary,
    97, 307; Matthew, 67, 332,
    356; Rachel, 97, 307; Rynear,
    219, 238; Sarah, 97, 238,
    307; Thomas, 47, 97, 238,
    307, 346; William, 97, 307,
    335
FLASHAUKER, George, 336
FLECH, Adam, 243; Hannah, 243
FLECK, Adam, 280, 349;
    Catharine, 280; Daniel, 280;
    Jacob, 280; Margaret, 280;
    Maria Margaret, 280; Mary,
    280; Susanna, 280; Thomas,
    280
FLEEK, John, 321
FLEMMING, Charles, 325
FLESHOCER, Samuel, 290

FLETCHER, Agnes, 249; Daniel,
    255, 283, 314; Elizabeth, 80,
    121; Hannah, 80, 121; Jane,
    121; Mary, 313; Priscilla,
    121; Robert, 80, 121, 332,
    335; Susanna, 80, 121; Tacy,
    121; Thomas, 80, 96, 121,
    190, 202, 249, 256, 298, 332,
    334, 335, 347
FLING, Edward, 114; Elizabeth,
    114
FLINN, Edmund, 249
FLITCHER, Elizabeth, 88;
    Priscilla, 88; Rachel, 88;
    Robert, 88
FLUCK, John, 69
FOGEL, Frederick, 84; Margaret,
    84
FOLAND, Enos, 336; Hugh, 336
FOLK, Barbara, 34; George, 34
FOLLOWS, William, 302
FOLLWELLO, Ann, 142
FOLTZ, Mary, 76; Matthias, 76
FORCE, Henry, 337; Jacob, 271;
    John, 315, 337
FORD, Jacob, 338, 339
FOREST, Thomas, 248
FORMAN, Alexander, 148
FORST, Henry, 131
FOSSETT, Hannah, 102
FOSTER, Ann, 176; Benjamin,
    172, 176; George, 176;
    Rebecca, 176, 352
FOULK, Jesse, 329, 332; Levi,
    158; Owen, 329
FOULKE, Anna, 237; Cadwalder,
    158, 170, 176, 191, 214, 223,
    239, 240, 275, 297, 307, 312,
    316; Cadwallader, 346, 353,
    358; Caleb, 167, 203, 204;
    Charles, 203, 204; Edward,
    288; Franklin, 316; George,
    288; Hannah, 169; Hugh, 158,
    176, 192, 200, 201, 222;
    Jesse, 87, 94, 140, 141, 152,
    154, 170, 174, 177, 204, 288,
    324; John, 237; Joseph, 228,
    271, 290; Joshua, 158; Levi,
    140, 141, 152, 170, 174, 177,
    237, 324, 333, 340; Margaret,
    214; Priscilla, 167, 170,
    288; Susanna, 288; Thomas,
    158; William, 140, 141, 152,
    154, 237, 288, 295, 312, 340,
    346
FOUST, Abelona, 55; Anna, 325;
    Elizabeth, 55; Henry, 325;
    John, 55; Peter, 55
FOUT, Barbara, 71; Catharine,
    71; Henry, 71; Martin, 71;
    Mary, 71; Susannah, 71

FOX, Charles, 51; George, 183; Henry, 341, 359; John, 358; Margaret, 183, 205; Philip, 359; Rebecca, 183; Sarah, 183
FOY, Andrew, 317; Hannah, 317
FRACK, Catharine, 104; Michael, 104
FRAME, Elizabeth, 71
FRANCE, Elizabeth, 243; Jacob, 243; John, 243; Lydia, 243; Mary, 243; Nancy, 243; Nicholas, 243; Paul, 243; Simon, 243; Tobias, 243
FRANCIS, Arnold, 47, 136; Catharine, 136; Elizabeth, 136; Griffith, 40, 325; Jacob, 350; John, 136, 238; Joseph, 40; Rachael, 325; Sarah, 40; Thomas, 136, 275, 313, 325; William, 40, 119, 325
FRANKENBERG, John, 325
FRANTZ, Aaron, 286; Enos, 286; Jesse, 286; Sarah, 286; Tobias, 286
FRASHER, Catharine, 309; Peter, 309
FRAT, William, 219
FRAZER, Joshua, 268
FREADLEY, Susannah, 48
FREAS, Catharine, 189; Elizabeth, 189; George, 189; Jacob, 189, 247; Mary, 189; Philip, 189; Samuel, 53, 189; Sarah, 189; Simon, 189
FREATZ, Christian, 199
FREDERICK, Anna Mary, 15; Barbara, 15; Catharine, 297; Charles, 297; Elizabeth, 325; Esther, 15; George, 297, 337, 348; George Michael, 14; Henry, 297, 337, 348; Jacob, 297; John, 14, 15, 298, 325, 348; Joseph, 297; Margaret, 72; Michael, 14, 15, 325; Peter, 14, 15, 72; Rosina, 15
FREE, Benjamin, 295
FREED, Anna, 335; Henry, 74, 335; John, 349; Peter, 348; Samuel, 246; Susanna, 349
FREEDLEY, Catharine, 316; Elizabeth, 316; Harriet, 316; Henry, 262, 316; Jacob, 316; John, 316; Samuel, 316
FREES, Simon, 125
FREEZ, Casper, 81; Catharine, 81; Eve, 81; George, 81; Hannah, 81; Mary, 81
FREGELE, Amelia, 288; Daniel, 288; George, 288; Jesse, 288
FREIDMIRCH, Michael, 101

FREIND, John, 31
FREIS, George, 341; Solomon, 328
FREISE, George, 118
FREITZ, Elizabeth, 143; John, 143
FRENCH, Samuel, 348
FRETCH, Andrew, 355; John, 355
FRETZ, Philip, 283
FREY, Joseph, 17
FRICH, John, 307
FRICK, Ann, 212; Catharine, 212; Eleanor, 303; Henry, 22, 212, 360; Jacob, 212, 248; John, 212, 279, 285; Michael, 212; Peggy, 212; Peter, 212; Philippina, 22; Samuel, 212
FRIED, Abraham, 41; Catharine, 54; Henry, 54, 91; Jacob, 101; John, 242; Mary, 242; Peter, 41; Veronica, 91
FRIEDER, Benjamin, 242; Hannah, 242
FRIEN, Bernard, 244
FRIET, Abraham, 30; Mary, 30
FRIS, Solomon, 256
FRISK, Benjamin, 303
FRITMER, John, 224
FRITZ, Catharine, 183; Elizabeth, 183, 199; George, 325; Jacob, 183; John, 140, 183; Magdalena, 183; Martin, 183; Mary, 183; Peter, 183, 306, 316; Philip, 144
FRONEFIELD, John, 325; Mary, 325
FRONFIELD, Jacob, 226
FRONHEUSER, Christina, 31; Jacob, 31
FRONTFIELD, Elizabeth, 141; Jacob, 141
FRY, Anna, 287; Barbara, 287; Catharine, 251, 287; Cremona, 325; Elizabeth, 107, 172, 333; Enoch, 251; George, 4, 241; Henry, 4, 144, 352; Isaac, 287; Jacob, 4, 60, 171, 175, 213, 251, 287, 359; John, 40, 58, 251, 287, 333, 359; Joseph, 4, 60, 107, 213; Margaret, 4, 60; Michael, 233; Nanny, 58; Paul, 256; Peter, 240, 339, 359; Susanna, 60, 153, 233; Susannah, 335; William, 4, 251, 303
FRYER, Christian, 265; Dinah, 233; Henry, 326; Jacob, 233
FUCHS, Anna Mary, 1, 49; Anthony, 1, 49, 195; Catharine, 49; Jacob, 49;

John, 49; Margareth, 49;
Matthias, 1, 49
FULLER, William, 264
FULMORE, Elizabeth, 313;
George, 313; Jacob, 313;
Mary, 313
FULTON, Andrew, 325; Elizabeth,
44; James, 44, 331; Jane,
133; John, 74, 133; Joseph,
93; Sarah, 296
FUNCK, Abraham, 325; Catharine,
279; Elizabeth, 325; Henry,
279; John, 24, 57, 88, 279,
325, 331; John Delp, 279;
Margaret, 279; Martin, 279;
Mary, 27, 88, 279; Mary
Elizabeth, 279; Samuel, 131,
279
FUNK, Anna, 244, 245; Barbara,
245; Christian, 342;
Elizabeth, 245, 199; Jacob,
51, 244; John, 51, 143, 212,
214, 244, 245, 307; Martin,
143, 212, 305; Mary, 245;
Samuel, 190, 245; SJohn, 199
FURGUSON, Samuel, 325
FURMAN, Henry, 163, 325; John,
325
FUSH, Anthony, 241; Elizabeth,
241
FYCHIR, Johannes, 81
FYE, Catharine, 189; Philip,
189

-G-

GABB, Rebecca, 156; William,
156
GABEL, Catharine, 294; Henry,
322; Philip, 294, 325
GABLE, Jacob, 150, 226; Philip,
40, 90, 102, 129, 137, 147,
170, 291, 340
GABREL, Philip, 72
GACE, Gilbert, 275
GAELMAN, Christian, 350
GALLMAN, Catharine, 109;
Cathrine, 326; John, 109, 326
GALLONY, Edward, 355
GALONY, Edward, 303
GAMBLE, Elizabeth, 38; Hannah,
38; Joseph, 38; Katharine,
38; Mary, 38; Samuel, 38;
Susannah, 38
GAMPLE, Andrew, 181; Mary
Magdalena, 181
GARBER, Andrew, 256; Benedict,
14, 39, 44, 88, 113, 128,
139, 175, 176, 200, 256;
Benjamin, 256, 355; Charles,
88, 256, 309, 357; Elizabeth,
243, 358; Hannah, 243, 355;
Henry, 355; Isaac, 358;
Jacob, 88, 139, 146, 172,
176, 243, 256; Jacon, 113;
John, 172, 349; Joseph, 358;
William, 243
GARDNER, Hephzibah, 225;
Keziah, 225
GARNALT, Isaac, 174; Jonathan,
174; Philip, 174
GARNER, John, 53, 337
GARRET, Christopher, 62;
Susanna, 102
GARRETT, Christopher, 156;
Elizabeth, 156; Hannah, 156;
James, 119, 156; Ruth, 156;
Sarah, 119; Thomas, 156
GARTLEY, Samuel, 257, 360
GARVER, Owen, 179
GASSINGER, George, 41
GEARHART, Conrad, 100
GEARHERD, Conrad, 35
GEARY, Sarah, 158
GEBHARD, Barbara, 39;
Catharine, 38; Mary
Magdalena, 38; Michael, 38
GEER, William, 121
GEHMAN, Abraham, 273, 354;
Esther, 20; John, 345;
Samuel, 227, 279, 345; Sarah,
345
GEHRY, Ann Maria, 182;
Catharine, 182; Elizabeth,
182; Gertrude, 182; Jacob,
182; John, 182; Michael, 182;
Peter, 182; Rebecca, 182
GEIGER, George, 14, 137, 339
GEISENHAINER, H., 286
GEISENHEIMER, Frederick
Wilhalm, 159; Mary, 159
GEISINGER, Philip, 38
GEIST, Conrad, 225
GEIZER, Conrad, 211; Margaret,
211
GENTLE, James, 285
GEORGE, 49; Ann, 169;
Catharine, 307; Claura, 87;
David, 85, 86, 165; Eliza,
307; Elizabeth, 168, 169,
307; George, 2, 25, 85, 307;
Hannah, 86, 169; Jane, 86,
169; Magdalene, 2; Margaret,
307; Mary, 86, 307; Rebecca,
169, 197; Samuel, 165; Sarah,
169; Thomas, 95, 102, 181;
William, 85, 86, 90
GEORGES, Abraham, 65; Jacob,
65; Jacobina, 65; John, 65;
William, 65
GEORGIN, Magdalena, 78
GERBER, Ludwick, 7

GERGES, Abraham, 215; Andrew, 215; Conrad, 215; Elizabeth, 215; George, 215; Henry, 215; John, 215; Mark, 215; Philip, 215; William, 215
GERHARD, Abraham, 86; Anna, 46, 47; Catharine, 86; Christina, 337; Daniel, 86; Isaac, 337; Jacob, 46, 47; John, 81, 82; Magdalena, 46, 47; Margaret, 86; Matthias, 46, 47; Molly, 81; Peter, 46, 86; Susannah, 46, 47
GERHART, Abraham, 355; Adam, 349; Barnabas, 284, 285; Barnard, 354; George, 259; Isaac, 293; Jacob, 208, 284, 285, 297; John, 208, 220; Matthias, 269, 308; Nicholas, 269, 284; Peter, 282, 285, 341; Philip, 284, 285; William, 341
GERRET, Michael, 10
GETTY, John, 358
GETZ, Barnd, 188
GEYER, Andrew, 76; Anna Mary, 180; Caterine, 6; Catharine, 180; Conrad, 180; Henry, 5, 6, 156, 180, 326; Jacob, 47, 248; John, 180; Mary, 47; Michael, 180; William, 180
GEYSER, Andrew, 248
GEYSINGHEIMER, Henry, 192; Maria, 192
GIBSON, John, 52; Lydia, 198; Mary, 52
GILBERT, Adam, 100, 101, 359; Anthony, 128, 229; Barbara, 229; Barnard, 359; Barney, 80, 192, 335; Benjamin, 326; Bernard, 1, 100, 101, 128, 340; Bernhard, 2, 33, 67; Bernhart, 139; Catharine, 100, 101; Charles, 190; David, 128; Dedemiah, 189; Elizabeth, 19, 80, 101, 159; Frederick, 271, 309; George, 2, 80, 100, 101, 359; Henry, 66, 98, 128, 229, 359, 361; Israel, 190; Jacob, 18, 101, 139, 186, 234, 359, 361; Jane, 68, 115; Jesse, 68, 190; John, 67, 101, 112, 115, 159, 190, 196, 350; Jonathan, 68, 189, 190; Magdalena, 101; Mary, 48, 67, 101, 128, 361; Mary Elizabeth, 100; Matthias, 316, 345; Myra, 155; Nicholas, 48; Samuel, 361; Susanna, 80; Susannah, 359; William, 190

GILBERTS, Mary, 132
GILDERGER, Benjamin, 271
GILINGER, Henry, 346; John, 346; William, 346
GILKESON, Andrew, 229, 230; Edith, 229, 230; Elias, 229; Esther, 229, 230; Harriet, 229, 230; James, 229, 230; Joseph, 229, 230; Samuel, 229, 230
GILKEY, Mary, 343
GILLER, Conrad, 185; John, 185; Susanna, 185
GILLINGHAMN, Grace, 278
GILMORE, Mary, 339; William, 339
GINKINER, John, 150; Nancy, 150
GISH, John, 328
GIVEN, John, 271
GLAUSE, Jacob, 358
GLOESS, Daniel, 310; Jacob, 310; Sarah, 310
GLOSS, Samuel, 76
GLUCK, John Albrecht, 19; John Ludowig, 19; Mary, 19; Peter, 19
GODSHALK, Catharine, 132; Edy, 122; Elizabeth, 271; Garret, 55, 132, 326; Garrett, 122; Gerred, 101; Gerret, 55; Godshalk, 28, 114, 132, 326; Godshall, 271; Hebena, 271; Helena, 101; Jacob, 101, 132, 271, 311; Jane, 132; Jarret, 47; John, 132; Magdalena, 132; Margaret, 311; Mary, 132; Peter, 55, 132; Sarah, 271; William, 132, 311
GODSHALKS, Gerred, 4
GODSHALL, Jacob, 166, 264
GODWALS, Abraham, 60
GODWALT, Abraham, 74, 75; Adam, 74; Anna, 75; Catharine, 74; Elizabeth, 74; Fronica, 74, 75; Genio, 74; Henry, 74, 75; Maria, 74; Susannah, 74
GOETTGE, Ludowick, 61
GOLDY, Casper, 188; David, 188; Henry, 188; Jacob, 188
GOME, Mary, 148
GOOD, Jacob, 20
GOODMAN, Conrad, 335; Elizabeth, 326, 335; John, 326
GOODNIGHT, Magdeline, 147; Samuel, 147
GOODWIN, John, 119
GOR, Hannah, 108
GORDON, Elizabeth, 214; George, 214; John, 214, 251, 347;

Jonathan, 214; Samuel, 113, 195; Sarah, 214
GOSINGER, Catharine, 71; George, 71; Magdalena, 71; Susannah, 71
GOSSINGER, George, 23, 56
GOSSLY, Mary, 187
GOTSHALK, Harman, 357; Sarah, 27; William, 213, 346
GOTTSHALK, Gottshalk, 23
GOTWALS, Abraham, 169, 345; Christian, 342; Magdalena, 169
GOTWALTS, Fronica, 326; Henry, 326
GOTZ, Sebstian, 40
GOUGLER, Anna Mary, 84; Nicholas, 84
GOULDY, Anna, 243; Jacob, 125; Jonathan, 243
GOULSTON, William, 192
GOURLEY, Joseph, 351; Priscilla, 108, 351; Samuel, 36, 63, 351
GOVETT, George, 357; Sarah, 313
GRABER, Andrew, 95; Ann Maria, 95; Christiana, 95; Eve, 95; Ludowig, 95; Margaret, 95; Michael, 95; Ulrich, 95
GRAHAM, John, 184; Mary, 315
GRAHER, Jacob, 350
GRANT, Robert, 43; Sarah, 43, 44; William, 170, 317
GRATER, Abraham, 147, 261; Catharine, 261; Elizabeth, 260, 261; John, 260, 261; Lewis, 224, 260, 261, 349; Margaret, 260; Mary, 260
GRAUER, Johann Jacob, 43
GRAVER, Andrew, 343; Elizabeth, 343; John, 343; Ludwig, 343
GRAY, John, 184; Mary, 184
GREBER, Andrew, 171, 172; Anna Margaret, 172; Eve, 172; Henry, 172, 211; John, 172; Ludowig, 172; Mary Lizabeth, 172
GREEBER, Ulrick, 109
GREEN, Daniel, 339; George, 355
GREENWALT, Henry, 286
GREENWOLT, Ann, 82; Christian, 82
GREGER, Abraham, 266; Catharine, 266; Davis, 357; Elizabeth, 266; George, 266; Margaret, 266
GRENWALT, Christian, 95; Henry, 95; John, 95; Susanna, 95
GRESINGER, George Leonard, 8
GRESMER, Catharine, 179; Frederick, 179; John, 179

GRESNER, William, 326
GRESSEMER, Frederick, 355; John, 355
GRIER, Matthew, 118
GRIESINGER, Anna Catherine, 8; George, 8; Jacob, 8; Leonard, 8; Leonh, 11
GRIFFIN, John, 303, 336
GRIFFITH, Alice, 275; Amos, 192, 273, 326, 337; Eleanor, 61; Elizabeth, 203, 352; Evan, 113; Howell, 275; James, 268; James B., 268; Jane, 113; Jesse, 310; Joseph, 326, 337; Mary, 144; Rebecca, 337
GRIFFITHS, Anos, 18; Elizabeth, 2; Hugh, 2
GRIM, Adam, 239; Conrad, 72; Daniel, 72; Elizabeth, 239; George, 72, 239; Maria, 72; Maria Barbara, 72; Mary, 239; Philip, 72
GRIMES, Elizabeth, 57
GRIMLEY, Frederick, 302, 334; John, 334
GRIMLING, Elizabeth, 139; Solmon, 139
GROB, Henry, 58, 60
GROFF, George, 338; Henry, 348; Jacob, 348; John, 239; Joseph, 269; Samuel, 313
GROP, John, 249; Samuel, 206, 212, 223, 227, 249
GROSS, Christian, 25, 329; Jacob, 38, 54; Joseph, 51; Samuel, 308, 348, 351; Susannah, 54
GROSSCUP, Christopher, 130; Jacob, 130; Paul, 130
GROVE, Jacob, 242; John, 341; Sarah, 242
GROVER, Christian, 43; Christiana, 43; Christina, 43; George, 326; Jacob, 326; John, 43, 326; Joseph, 43; Mary, 43
GROVES, John, 141; Susanna, 141
GROW, Adam, 335; George, 335
GRUB, Abraham, 98, 102, 186, 305; Andrew, 329, 354; Anna, 102; Barbara, 98; Catharine, 102; Conrad, 102; Daniel, 102; David, 102; Elizabeth, 102, 186, 354; George, 102, 186; Hannah, 98; Henry, 102; Isaac, 354; Isaiah, 98; Jacob, 98, 102; John, 102; Margaret, 305; Ruth, 98; Samuel, 329; Susanna, 186; Thomas, 338

GRUBB, Jacob, 100
GUARDNER, John, 143
GUCKER, Barbara, 112;
    Christiana, 156; Elizabeth,
    112; George, 112, 156;
    Magdalena, 112; Peter, 112;
    Susanna, 112, 341; Susannah,
    112
GUDLLER, Ludwig, 123
GUIGER, Charles, 147
GUILKEE, Benjamin, 355
GUILLINGER, Rebecca, 247
GUIST, Matthias, 319
GULDY, Casper, 114; David, 114;
    Gallus, 114
GUMMERE, John, 134; Lydia, 134;
    Samuel, 36, 49, 57, 74, 83,
    86, 108, 134, 137, 155, 321,
    327, 331
GUMPERT, Abraham, 335
GUY, Barbara, 314; Jonathan,
    314
GWINER, John, 5
GYER, Conrad, 173; Elizabeth,
    173; Henry, 173; Jacob, 356;
    John, 356; Mary, 173

-H-
HAAF, Charles, 155; Jonah, 156
HAAG, George, 168
HAAS, Ann, 166; Frederick, 289;
    George, 166; Jemima, 166
HACKER, Hannah, 197
HACKETT, John, 311
HACKMAN, Elizabeth, 336
HAGA, Daniel, 200
HAGAY, William, 334
HAGEY, Catharine, 359; Jacob,
    359; John, 116; William, 181
HAGLER, Abraham, 249; Barbara,
    249; Catharine, 249;
    Christina, 249; David, 249;
    Elizabeth, 249; George, 249;
    Hannah, 249; Jacob, 249;
    Peter, 249
HAGY, Ann, 254; Daniel, 53, 58,
    64, 149, 341; Jacob, 53;
    John, 53, 355; Joseph, 254;
    Mary, 341, 355; Sarah, 360;
    Susanna, 53; William, 53, 64,
    144, 254, 360
HAHN, Catharine, 174, 310;
    Henry, 123, 145, 199; John,
    310; Joseph, 243, 310;
    Philip, 48, 327, 330;
    Susanna, 243; William, 310
HAIN, Catharine, 292; John,
    292; Margaret, 292; Philip,
    292; Susanna, 292
HAINER, Jacob, 358; Joseph,
    358; Sarah, 358

HAINS, Barney, 88; Sarah, 88
HAIR, Benjamin, 146; Elizabeth,
    146; John, 146; Mary, 146;
    Matthew, 146
HALAFFER, Peter, 179
HALEY, Ann, 200; Sarah Ann, 200
HALL, Barbara, 131, 326;
    Ceaser, 326; Hannah, 184;
    Henry, 326; Jacob, 247;
    Jervice, 184; John, 341;
    Joseph, 117
HALLMAN, Abraham, 141, 206;
    Anthony, 141, 232, 326;
    Benjamin, 141, 360;
    Catharine, 141; Christiana,
    141; Daniel, 141; Elizabeth,
    71, 141, 258, 261, 360;
    George, 232, 360; Henry, 71,
    141, 145, 205, 232, 248, 258,
    261, 360; Isaac, 141, 239,
    341; Jacob, 141, 144, 194,
    360; John, 71, 75, 106, 137,
    141, 222, 290, 360; Margaret,
    141; Maria, 74; Mary, 141,
    232, 257, 258; Samuel, 232;
    Sarah, 141, 232, 257, 258;
    Susanna, 141; Weikle, 232;
    William, 232, 257, 326
HALLOW, Anna, 193; Charles, 193
HALLOWELL, Abigail, 96, 346;
    Agnes, 70; Amos, 176; Amy,
    205, 261; Anna, 70; Benjamin,
    18, 30, 31, 43, 96, 182, 346;
    C. F., 202; Caleb, 39, 70;
    Chalkey, 70; Charles, 348;
    Daniel, 70; Dorothy, 38, 80,
    273; Elisabeth, 30;
    Elizabeth, 30, 63, 86, 121;
    Ezra, 296; Grace, 338;
    Hannah, 334, 346; Isaac, 70,
    121, 182, 335, 348; Israel,
    313; Jane, 204, 205, 313;
    Jesse, 30, 57, 215; Job, 126,
    334; John, 30, 70, 122, 171,
    326, 336; Jonas, 261;
    Jonathan, 63; Joseph, 30, 57,
    70, 215, 273, 354; Josiah,
    70; Margaret, 30, 273, 354;
    Martha, 63, 182, 296, 326;
    Mary, 30, 70, 126, 160, 182,
    253; Matthew, 70, 336;
    Nathan, 336, 338; Peter, 182;
    Priscilla, 30; Rynear, 70;
    Samuel, 63; Sarah, 126, 133,
    182, 203, 348; Susanna, 253;
    Tacy, 182; Thomas, 18, 30,
    70, 155, 296; Walter, 40;
    William, 63, 70, 126, 215,
    274, 326, 334, 338, 346
HALTEMAN, John, 279
HALTMAN, Christian, 60

HAMER, Elizabeth, 206; James, 20, 206, 322; Martha, 20, 206; Mary, 206; Rachel, 71; Sarah, 20, 206
HAMILL, William, 271, 308, 346, 353
HAMILLER, Henry, 347
HAMILTON, Gavin, 106; Hugh, 326
HAMLET, Elizabeth, 192; Godfrey, 192
HAMMER, James, 18
HAMMIL, John, 314
HAMMILL, Robert, 349
HAMSHER, John, 224
HANAS, Nathan, 251
HANCOCK, Benjamin, 312
HANGEN, Barbara, 253; Catharine, 253; Elizabeth, 253; George, 253; Jacob, 253; John, 253
HANIS, Benjamin, 161; Elizabeth, 161; Isaac, 161; Jacob, 161; John, 161; Samuel, 161
HANK, Mary, 281
HANNA, William, 324
HANNAH, Ann, 180; James, 125; Jane, 125, 180; John, 125, 180
HANWAY, Daniel, 114; Jacob, 114; Susanna, 114
HAPPERSET, Samuel, 269
HARANY, Thomas, 262
HARBOE, John, 158
HARDY, George, 326
HARG, Matthew, 327
HARKER, James, 43; Jesse, 43, 152, 353; John, 43
HARKIN, Alexander, 326
HARLEY, Abraham, 227; Henry, 107, 356; Jacob, 356; Joseph, 356; Samuel, 159, 181
HARMAN, Abraham, 307; Jaccb, 334; John, 143; King, 307; Philip, 334
HARMER, Amos, 134
HARMON, Abraham, 199; David, 199; Peter, 199
HARNER, Amos, 134, 261; Chalkey, 134; Christian, 361; James, 287; Mary, 261; Michael, 301
HARPEL, David, 234; Magdalena, 234
HARPER, Eleanor, 311; Elizabeth, 276; Jesse, 179, 338; Jonathan, 351; Martha, 351; Nathan, 122
HARPLE, Anna Maria, 227; Barbara, 227; Catharine, 227; Christina, 227; Jacob, 227; John, 333; Ludwick, 333
HARRAR, Nathan, 303
HARRIS, Henry, 257; James, 199, 221; James B., 360; John, 185, 245; Robert McClintuck, 285; T. B., 268
HARRISON, Isabella, 200; Jada, 200
HARRY, Ann, 23, 24, 42, 127, 198, 259; Benjamin, 23, 24, 42, 49, 73, 137, 198; David, 24, 42, 118, 198; Elizabeth, 73; Jane, 23, 24, 42, 127; John, 2, 24, 42, 73, 118; Latitia, 118; Lydia, 24, 198; Mary, 118; Rees, 23, 118, 198; Sarah, 24, 118; Thomas, 73
HARSH, Sarah, 228
HARST, John, 130
HART, Andrew, 116, 326; Barny, 327; Deborah, 117; Elizabeth, 116; John, 117, 311, 326; Joseph, 155, 187; Mary, 196; Samuel, 187, 196; Silas, 155
HARTEL, Jacob, 355; John, 355
HARTENSTINE, John, 344
HARTING, William, 211
HARTINSTAIN, Jacob, 247
HARTLE, John, 231
HARTLEY, James, 315
HARTMAN, Catharine, 91, 92; Elisabeth, 15; Elizabeth, 301; Frederick, 301, 355; George, 91, 359; Henry, 15, 220; Jacob, 355; John, 171, 290; Margaret, 91, 301; Mary, 91; Michael, 301; Philip, 355
HARTRANFT, Leonhard, 15
HARTZEL, Catharine, 157; George, 170; Philip, 301
HARTZELL, Catharine, 81, 82; Elizabeth, 290; George, 81, 82, 183, 247, 255, 302; Jacob, 251; Margaret, 81, 82; Molly, 81, 82; Ulrich, 251
HARVER, Joseph, 361
HARVEY, James, 213, 275; John, 213; Rebecca, 275; Samuel, 213; Thomas, 213, 356; William, 213
HARWOOD, John, 200; Margaret, 200
HASES, Jacob, 346
HASS, John, 45
HATFIELD, Catharine, 147; Christian, 315; Samuel, 138, 139, 147
HATTERBACHEN, Catherine, 2

HAUBERGER, Daniel, 77; John, 77; Mary Margaret, 77; Nicholas, 77; Peter, 77
HAUCK, Catharine, 224; Charles, 224; Daniel, 224; Elizabeth, 224; George, 224; Henry, 224; Jacob, 224; John, 224; Margaret, 224; Molly, 224; Sarah, 224
HAUGHTER, Casper, 250
HAULEY, Peter, 112
HAUS, Benjamn, 326; Daniel, 326; Elizabeth, 326; Mary B., 326
HAUSE, Daniel, 359
HAUSER, Elizabeth, 203; Michael, 203; Rachel, 203
HAVERSTREIGHT, Elizabeth, 337; Jonas, 336
HAVERSTRITE, Elizabeth, 337; Jones, 337
HAVNER, Barbara, 13; John, 13; Rosina, 13
HAWK, Abraham, 195, 359; Catharine, 359; David, 195; George, 195, 359; Isaac, 21, 195; Jacob, 152, 195; John, 195; Joseph, 195
HAWKINS, Amos, 238, 239; Amosf, 358; Elizabeth, 238; Isaac, 238, 239; James, 238, 239, 242, 309; Jesse, 238, 239; Keziah, 238; Mary, 238; Rebecca, 238; William, 238, 239
HAWS, Ann, 289; Benjamin, 39; Catharine, 39, 289; Daniel, 39; Elizabeth, 289; Frederick, 289; Hannah, 289; Hartman, 39; John, 39, 289; Margaret, 289; Mary, 39; Rachel, 289; Samuel, 289
HAYCOCK, Race, 185; Rachel, 185; Tacie, 39
HAYDRICK, Balzer, 30
HAYES, Joseph, 345
HAYS, Elizabeth, 105; Mary, 197
HEARING, Nicholas, 110
HEARSH, Sarah, 189
HEART, Rhoda, 2
HEATON, Joseph, 268
HECE, William, 190
HEDRICK, Abraham, 226; Catharine, 226; Christian, 226; Henry, 226; Jacob, 226; John, 226; Michael, 226; Nicholas, 327; Peter, 226, 327
HEEBNER, Abraham, 256, 257, 334, 342; Anna, 326; Balser, 272; Bolser, 138; Catharine, 81; Christopher, 256; Eve, 159; George, 52, 81; John, 52, 256, 324; John Christopher, 334; Margarta, 52; Mary, 52; Michael, 52; Peter, 159; Philip, 52; Sarah, 256, 257; Sophia, 52; Susanna, 256
HEEKLER, George, 354
HEESTON, John, 82
HEFENTRAGER, Cunrad, 19; Margareth, 19
HEFFILFINGER, Elizabeth, 131
HEFNERS, Mary, 16
HEGHT, Anthony, 41
HEIGHLICK, George, 109
HEIL, Abraham, 176
HEILEY, John, 327; Susanna, 327
HEILICH, Adam, 87; Anna, 87; Barbara, 87; Elizabeth, 87; Eve, 87; George, 87; George Michael, 87; Henry, 87; Jacob, 87; John George, 87; Mary, 87; Peter, 87
HEILIG, Peter, 172
HEINNEMAN, Barbara, 170; John, 170
HEIS, John, 23
HEISER, Baltzer, 326; Jacob, 333; John, 333; Margaret, 326
HEISLER, Jacob, 145, 228
HEIST, Anna, 308; Christina, 308; Conrad, 308; Elizabeth, 308; George, 11, 12, 149, 308, 309; Henry, 308; John, 109, 262, 308, 309; Jonathan, 236; Magdalena, 308; Maria, 308; Mary, 308; Peter, 308
HEISTER, Catharine, 295; Elizabeth, 295; Hannah, 47, 50; Jacob, 41, 228; John, 50, 289, 295, 318; Jonathan, 295; Rachel, 295; Samuel, 295, 344; Thomas, 295
HEISTLER, Catharine, 293; Daniel, 293; Elizabeth, 293; Jacob, 293; John, 293; Nancy, 293; Susanna, 293
HELBARN, Thomas, 356
HELLINGS, Robert, 358
HELMBOLD, Charles, 184; Conrad, 184; Elizabeth, 184; George, 16, 88, 184; Henry, 184; Jacob, 184; Joseph, 184; Mary, 184
HELPER, George, 64
HEMBOLD, Elisabeth, 16
HENDERSON, Alexander, 330; Catharine, 354; Elizabeth, 357; Matthew, 326; Nathaniel J., 354; Samuel, 113, 218,

278, 331, 338, 349; William, 319, 321, 326, 357
HENDRICKS, Abraham, 53, 54, 55, 207, 246; Alice, 54, 55; Anna, 10, 75, 207; Anna Maria, 237; Barbara, 54, 55; Benjamin, 10, 54, 55, 246, 292, 350; Catharina, 10; Catharine, 13, 54, 55, 117, 122; Charles, 257, 287; Christiana, 90; Dorothe, 10; Elizabeth, 13, 54, 117; Eve, 78; Hannah, 13, 117; Ida, 55; Jacob, 90, 122, 141; John, 13, 78, 117, 141, 168, 257, 358; Joseph, 10, 55, 207, 298, 330, 337; Leonard, 117, 122; Magdalena, 78; Margaret, 10, 13, 141; Margareth, 55; Maria, 10; Mary, 13, 117; Mary Magdelena, 141; Matthias, 55, 132; Paul, 55, 200, 350; Peter, 10, 141; Rachel, 117; Samuel, 75, 117; Sarah, 117; Susanna, 13, 54; Thomas, 237; William, 117, 228, 253, 350
HENRICK, Catharine, 94; Cathrine, 94; Hannah, 94; John, 94; Peter, 94; Sarah, 94
HENRY, Daniel, 25, 254; Elizabeth, 266; George, 264; High, 101; John George, 87; Joseph, 111, 149, 215, 243, 244, 293; Robert, 88
HENTZ, Andrew, 9
HENVIS, William, 341
HEPP, Sebastian, 327
HEPPLER, Barbara, 139; Catharine, 200; George, 200; Hannah, 200; Margaret, 200; Mary, 200; Susanna, 200; Tobias, 139
HERB, Anthony, 40; Eva, 40; John, 355
HERBERGER, Andrew, 326; Christian, 326
HERBLE, Jacob, 338
HERCHER, John, 326
HERHARD, Henry, 337
HERITAGE, John, 217
HERLEY, Rudolph, 60
HERNAR, Christina, 234
HERNER, Barbara, 79; Christian, 79; George, 340; Henry, 79; Jacob, 79; John, 79; Joseph, 79; Magdalena, 79; Michael, 79; Peter, 340; Sarah, 79
HERRING, Jacob, 207

HERSH, Catharine, 110; Elias, 346; Ludwig, 110
HERSTEIN, John, 18
HERSTINE, John, 240, 332
HERTON, Jane, 233; Maria, 233
HERTZEL, Michael, 4
HERTZOG, Peter, 306
HESSER, John, 217
HESTON, Catharine, 199; Mary, 125; Rebecca, 174; Susanna, 174
HEYDIRCK, Abraham, 226, 227; Susanna, 226
HEYDRICK, Abraham, 226, 227, 304, 326; George, 30; Susanna, 226, 304
HEYSER, A., 180; William, 180
HEYSLER, Peter, 129
HIBBLEHOUSE, William, 303
HICKS, Barbara, 136, 265; Catharine, 136; Elizabeth, 125; Mary, 136, 265; Nicholas, 136; Sarah, 136, 265; William, 136, 265
HIGH, Elizabeth, 325; Frederick, 325; George, 70; Hannah, 70
HIGHLEY, Elizabeth, 293, 294; Hannah, 173; Henry, 294; Jacob, 294, 356, 359; John, 293, 294, 356; Mary, 293, 294
HIGHMAN, Barbara, 260; John, 260; Mary, 260; Peter, 260
HILBART, George Adam, 326
HILBELITEL, John, 147
HILBERT, Michael, 233
HILDABIALE, John, 215; Mary, 215
HILDEBITLE, John, 41, 51
HILEGASS, George, 145
HILL, Ezekiel, 132
HILLEGAS, George, 179; John, 179; Michael, 179, 182; Peter, 342
HILLEGASS, Adam, 283; Ann Maria, 182; Catharine, 352; Conrad, 159; George, 212, 246, 287, 349, 352; Jacob, 298; John, 182, 352; Michael, 360; Peter, 301
HILLIGAS, Peter, 329
HILLIS, Ann, 158; David, 158; William, 158
HILTEBRITEL, John, 176
HILTENBEITEL, John, 65
HILTNER, Agnes, 186; Charles, 292; Christian, 292; Elizabeth, 186; George, 292; Hannah, 186; Jacob, 186; John, 109, 186, 292; Jonathan, 292; Margaret, 186;

Mary, 186, 292; Michael, 109, 186; William, 109, 186
HIMER, Magdalena, 326
HINDERLIGHTER, John, 266; Margaret, 266
HINES, Ann, 139; Eleanor, 139; Elizabeth, 139; Hannah, 139; Margaret, 139; Mary, 139; Matthew, 139, 335; Matthias, 32; Samuel, 139; William, 335
HINKLE, Peter, 187
HIPPLE, Henry, 359; Lawrence, 359
HIST, Frederick, 329; George, 330
HISTLER, Jacob, 7
HITLEBIDLE, Adam, 54; Salome, 54
HITNER, Daniel, 118; George, 118, 319, 330; Hannah, 330; Mary, 118
HITSELBERG, Christian, 358
HITTLE, Adam, 212
HOBART, R. E., 316; Robert, 77, 262; Robert E., 138; Sarah, 59, 138, 262
HOBENSACK, George, 361; John, 361
HOBER, Henry, 208; Margaret, 208
HOBSON, Francis, 9, 11, 21, 48, 326; Moses, 324, 326, 337, 343, 351, 355, 356; Phebe, 89; Susanna, 21
HOCKAMILLER, Jacob, 172; Mary, 172; Nancy, 172
HOCKER, Catharine, 219; Cathrine, 248; Christopher, 248; George, 326, 361; Martin, 361
HOCKLEY, Sarah, 138
HOCKMAN, Henry, 359; John, 58
HOERING, John, 293
HOFF, Eleanor, 201; Michael, 201
HOFFACRE, Elizabeth, 272; John, 272; Mary, 272; Michael, 272; Philip, 272; Susanna, 272
HOFFMAN, Abraham, 22; Catharine, 211; Christopher, 33; Daniel, 22, 248, 264; Elizabeth, 203; Henry, 203, 211; Jesse, 248; John, 22, 76, 107, 306; Katharine, 22; Mary, 22; Michael, 22; Peter, 22; Philip, 45, 76; Rebecca, 76; Sarah, 248; William, 22, 158, 240
HOFMAN, Adam, 92, 93; Baltzer, 92; Barbara, 92; Christiana, 92; Christopher, 149; Elizabeth, 92; Jacob, 92, 93; John, 92; Maria, 92; Paul, 92; Peter, 92; Philip, 92
HOFNER, Jacob, 61
HOGELAND, Adrianna, 90; Andriana, 90; Cornelia, 90; Deborah, 210; Derick, 4, 90; Jane, 90; John, 4, 90, 210, 272
HOGLAND, John, 326
HOLDERMAN, Abraham, 271, 285; Ann, 271; Catharine, 271, 285; Christian, 271, 285; Elizabeth, 169, 285; Hannah, 285; Henry, 285; Jacob, 285; John, 285; Margaret, 285; Nicholas, 169
HOLGATE, Jacob, 248; William, 359
HOLGET, Cornelius, 107
HOLLABACK, Matthias, 128
HOLLABURK, Catharine, 239; Daniel, 239
HOLLABUSH, John, 156
HOLLAND, Benjamin, 129, 143, 160, 187, 320; James, 143; Jane, 52; Joanna, 138; Mary, 138; Nathaniel, 138; Robert, 45, 52; Samuel, 138; Sarah, 138; Thomas, 138
HOLLAS, Abraham, 106; Edwardd, 106
HOLLIS, Elizabeth, 343; William, 343, 344
HOLLMAN, Henry, 23
HOLLOBUSH, Adam, 40; Henry, 94
HOLLONBUSH, William, 305
HOLLOWBUSH, Henry, 303, 304; Jacob, 304; John, 304; Martha, 341; Mary, 304; Peter, 304, 341; Susanna, 304
HOLLOWELL, Thomas, 10
HOLMAN, Daniel, 330; Jacob, 330; Mary, 69
HOLSTEIN, George, 295, 305, 332, 342; George B., 171; George W., 349; Matthias, 202, 236, 332, 342; Samuel, 332; W. H., 204; William, 295
HOLSTEN, Catharine, 9; Mary, 9; Peter, 9
HOLSTON, Samuel, 9
HOLT, Abner, 144; Benjamin, 44, 144; Charles, 144, 190; Jesse, 144; Margaret, 144; Mordecai, 344; Nathan, 144, 344; Rachel, 251; Sarah, 327, 334; Thomas, 144, 327
HOLTZHOUSEN, Andrew, 7; Anna Margaret, 7; Casper, 7;

Catharine, 7; Jacob, 7; Michael, 7
HOMER, Elizabeth, 214, 215; Jona, 215; Mary, 214; William, 214, 215
HOMSHER, Anthony, 93; John, 93
HOMSHIRE, Adam, 188
HOOKY, Anthony, 286
HOOT, Barbara, 266; Catharine, 40, 41, 266; Christopher, 100; Conrad, 40; Elizabeth, 266, 352; Eve Elizabeth, 100; Henry, 40; John Erhard, 150; Magdelena, 150; Mary, 40; Peter, 100, 352; Philip, 100; Philip George, 266; Rebecca, 266
HOOVEN, Margaret, 104, 105; Matthew, 105; Rebecca, 105
HOOVER, Catharine, 280; Christian, 340, 346; Henry, 340; Jacob, 33, 62, 280, 340; Margaret, 336, 346; Mary, 172; Matthew, 320; Michael, 120; Philip, 280, 340, 346
HOPKINS, Richard, 122
HOPSON, John, 162
HORLACKER, Eve, 179; George, 179, 326, 327; Peter, 350
HORN, Andrew, 27; Frederick, 27; George, 6, 27, 76, 346; George William, 27; John, 27, 229; Margaret, 27; Sarah, 346; Susannah, 27; William, 197, 238; William J., 346
HORNATER, Valentine, 328
HORNER, George, 335
HORNING, Barbara, 132; Catharine, 131; Eli, 132; Elizabeth, 132, 144; Hannah, 97; Jacob, 132, 144, 261, 300; John, 131, 132, 143; Ludwick, 131, 144; Margaret, 132; Michael, 97, 132; Nancy, 300; Peter, 131; Samuel, 267, 337, 358
HORTENSTINE, Catharine, 304; Eli, 304; George, 304; Henry, 304; John, 304; Joseph, 304; Mary, 304; Rachel, 304; Susanna, 304
HORTLER, George, 201
HORTON, Samuel, 324
HOSKINS, Joseph, 352
HOUCH, Jacob, 348
HOUCK, Jacob, 204
HOUF, Andrew, 36; Anna Mary, 36; Peter, 36
HOUGH, Benjamin, 334; Charlotte, 155; Edith, 155; Elizabeth, 311; John, 155; Nancy, 155; Sarah, 155; Silas, 155, 257, 311, 324; Thomas, 155
HOUP, Anthony, 73; Barbara, 73; Betsey, 73; Catharine, 73; Henry, 73, 335; Jacob, 19, 73; Lissey, 73; Margaret, 73; Samuel, 73, 335
HOUPT, Catharine, 218; Jacob, 218; Margaret, 73; Mary, 327
HOURST, Elias, 46; Elizabeth, 46; Margaret, 46; Philip, 46
HOUSER, Abraham, 8; Albert, 178; Allbright, 178; Christina, 178; Jacob, 332; Mary, 178, 218; Matthias, 178
HOUT, Jacob, 341
HOVAN, Francis, 206
HOVEN, John, 21; Sarah, 21
HOWELL, Daniel, 3, 79; Elizabeth, 79, 330; George, 330; John, 26; Walter, 56, 330
HOXWORTH, Ann, 71, 241; Anna, 241; Edward, 71, 223, 344; Eleanor, 241; Elizabeth, 71, 243, 344; Israel, 241, 333, 350; Jesse, 241; John, 71, 223; Margaret, 241; Mary, 71, 241; Peter, 71, 241, 312, 333; Rachel, 241; Sarah, 71, 241; William, 241
HUBBS, Joseph, 124, 134; Margaret, 154; Mary, 123, 154, 294; Sarah, 131
HUBER, Betsey, 282; Charles, 282; George, 202; Jacob, 67; John, 282; T., 130
HUBLER, Elizabeth, 279; George, 261; Henry, 279; Isaac, 279; John, 279; Mary, 260
HUBLEY, Edward, 263; Jacob, 263, 295, 309; Sarah, 263
HUBNER, Abraham, 58; Catharine, 58
HUBRAND, Christopher, 326
HUDDLESOME, Isaac, 244
HUDDLESON, Isaac, 332, 340
HUFTY, Jan, 69; Jane, 69; John, 69; Joseph, 69; Mary, 69; Sarah, 69
HUGH, Atkinson, 14; Elizabeth, 315; Siles, 105; Thomas, 315
HUGHES, Abner, 218, 283; Ann, 159; Atkinson, 221, 222; Catharine, 159; Edward, 159, 346; Elizabeth, 159, 222; Evan, 4, 15; Humphrey, 136; Isaac, 159; Jane, 221, 222; John, 5, 15, 105, 159, 188, 202, 333; Levi, 159, 334; Martha, 4, 221; Michael, 5,

15; Owen, 20, 159; Rebecca, 334; Ruth, 221; Samuel William, 136; Sarah, 159; Susanna, 15, 221; Thomas, 221, 222; Urny, 346
HUGHS, Atkinson, 269
HUGLER, Charles, 185; John, 185; Mary, 185
HULLS, Isaiah, 285; Sarah, 285
HUMEL, George, 353; Jacob, 353
HUMPHREY, Charles, 155; Euphemia, 304; Hannah, 101; Morris, 343; Rebecca, 304; Richard, 343; Thomas, 258, 262, 304
HUMPHREYS, Benjamin, 326; Charles, 349; Samuel, 312; Thomas, 349
HUNCK, Jacob, 341
HUNSBERGER, Abraham, 212, 351; Anna, 300; Christian, 300; Dorothea, 300; Hannah, 300; Isaacd, 351; John, 300; Peter, 300; Samuel, 300; Susanna, 300
HUNSBERRY, John, 220
HUNSICKER, Abraham, 281; Catharine, 27; Elizabeth, 27; Garnet, 218; Garret, 359; Garrett, 271; Henry, 24, 27, 28, 50, 62, 76, 93, 127, 132, 135, 139, 141, 144, 152, 155, 169, 170, 177, 179, 194, 200, 207, 212, 218, 231, 281, 302, 309, 326; Hester, 169; Isaac, 24, 27, 132, 170; Jacob, 27; Joel, 309; John, 155, 203, 226, 361; Samuel, 27; Sarah, 27; Valentine, 27, 210
HUNSPERGER, Abraham, 163; Anna, 163; Catharine, 163, 164; Christian, 163; Frederick, 163, 164; Jacob, 163
HUNTER, Ann, 43; Jane, 31, 226
HUNTSBERGER, Frederick, 300
HUNTSPERGER, Abraham, 194; Catharine, 194
HURST, Elias, 345; Henry, 261, 345; Jacob, 261, 262; John, 262, 345
HUSTARD, Abraham, 91
HUSTEN, Jacob, 220; John, 220
HUSTON, John, 11, 85, 124, 125, 129, 133, 136, 185, 187, 227, 245, 356; Margaret, 265; William, 136, 187
HUZZARD, Elizabeth, 90
HYNDERLEYNE, Catharine, 86; Matthias, 86
HYSER, Andrew, 354; Jacob, 354

-I-

ICHES, Magdelena, 145; Nicholas, 145
INGHART, Adam, 217; Anna, 217; Catharine, 217; John, 217; Mary, 217
IREDEL, John, 259
IREDELE, John, 339
IREDELL, Abraham, 110, 209; Charles, 110, 209; Gainor, 209; Hannah, 110, 209; Hester, 209; John, 110, 209; Jonathan, 110, 137, 209; Joseph, 110, 202, 242; Mary, 186, 196; Rebecca, 209; Robert, 110, 204, 209, 316; Seth, 110, 209; Susanna, 204, 316
IRWIN, John, 68; Michael, 77; Nathaniel, 30
ISAAC, Frederick, 5; Rebecca, 29; Rebekah, 5
ISCK, Frederick, 37
ISET, Barbara, 139; Elizabeth, 139; Frederick, 139; Hannah, 139; Jacob, 139, 141; Margaret, 141; Rebecca, 139
ISETT, Frederick, 64
ISRAEL, 78
ITOLE, Nathal, 291
IVES, James, 289; Jesse, 158, 289; Mary, 158; Rachel, 158, 289; Rebecca, 158; Thomas, 289; William, 158, 289

-J-

JACK, 142; Andrew, 195
JACKSON, Deborah, 125; Henry, 339; Thomas, 262, 353, 360
JACOB, Barent, 26; Elizabeth, 338; Henry, 338; Israel, 27
JACOBS, Anthony, 25; Barbara, 25; Catharine, 174, 300; Christiana, 25, 95; Elizabeth, 174, 300; George, 95; Hannah, 26, 89; Isaac, 98; Israel, 20, 25, 26, 33, 36, 50, 58, 71, 83, 89; Isreal, 116; Jeremiah, 174, 300; Jesse, 36, 58, 89, 116, 174, 206, 300; John, 25, 26, 36, 58, 89, 98, 174, 206, 220, 244, 300; Lydia, 26, 89; Mary, 25; Nancy, 300; Nathan, 300; Phebe, 116; Rebeckah, 25; Richard, 25, 174, 300, 310; Samuel, 25, 174, 326; Thomas, 26, 89
JACOBY, Barbara, 342; Daniel, 309; Elizabeth, 211; Henry,

203; John, 211, 342; Richell, 203
JAG, David, 327
JAGO, Samuel, 18
JAMES, Christina, 280; Elizabeth, 46, 280; Elizabeth B., 338; Howell, 280; Isaac, 45; Mary, 10, 280; Rachel, 45; Sarah, 45; Seth, 280
JAMISON, Alexander, 54; Catharine, 54
JANNEY, Hannah, 29
JARRET, Ann, 332; Daniel, 75, 332; David, 124, 331; John, 18, 72, 75, 318; Jonathan, 44, 124, 331; Joseph, 259, 331; Levi, 75, 332; Priscilla, 75; Rachel, 331
JARRETT, Chalkey, 274; Charles, 178; Daniel, 274; David, 274; George, 193; Jacob E., 178, 179; Jesse, 257; John, 182, 209, 274, 280, 303; Joseph, 274; Levi, 182, 189, 274; Martha, 274; Mary, 178; Priscilla, 274; Rachel, 274; Sarah, 178; Susanna, 178; William, 178, 274
JEANES, Jacob, 52; William, 281
JEANS, Amos, 210, 211; Ann, 210; Anna, 210; Elizabeth, 210, 229; Esther, 229; Hannah, 229; Isaac, 229, 314; Isaiah, 210, 211; Jacob, 210; Jane, 210; Jesse, 228; Leah, 210, 211; Margaret, 229; Mary, 229; Rachel, 210; Rebecca, 229; Sarah, 229; William, 210, 211, 229
JENDERDINE, Enoch, 334
JENKINS, Charles, 222; Charles F., 233; David, 337; Edward, 152, 154, 158, 171, 177, 248, 312, 322, 333; Elizabeth, 44, 158; Hannah, 238; Isaac, 239; Israel, 44; Jesse, 44, 158, 239, 333; John, 158, 248, 333, 338; Levi, 333, 356; Lewiss, 352; Mary, 44; Owen, 158, 247, 308; Phineas, 44; Priscilla, 44; Sarah, 158; Stephen, 44; Willey, 44; William, 44
JENNINGS, William, 176
JENNY, 132
JERGER, Dewalt, 39
JODON, Martha, 176
JOHN, Evan, 240; John, 140; Jonathan, 311
JOHNS, Elizabeth, 17; Richard, 17

JOHNSON, Abraham, 65, 224; Ann, 188; Anna, 309; Barbara, 56, 302, 309; Benjamin, 46, 76, 127, 140, 155, 282, 299, 309, 327; Catharine, 127, 155, 309; Charles, 288, 352, 357; Christopher, 127; David, 274; Edward, 274; Elizabeth, 56, 155, 274, 351; Ellen, 188; Esther, 188, 339; Genio, 74; Gertraude, 127; Hannah, 274; Henry, 56, 274; Isaac, 155; Jacob, 40, 108, 247, 302, 309, 342, 352; Jesse, 274; John, 56, 124, 140, 155, 177, 258, 274, 309, 327, 336, 360; Joseph, 74, 155, 326; Leonard, 85, 351; Magdalena, 88, 309; Mally, 40; Margaret, 56, 127, 274; Martha, 274; Mary, 88, 137, 188, 218, 274; Matthias, 106, 360; Peter, 39, 88, 116, 127, 137, 138, 155, 160; Philipbena, 247; Racheal, 155; Rebecca, 176, 193; Samuel, 75, 188, 280; Sarah, 88, 288; Sarha, 85; Scyshy, 88; Susanna, 155, 224, 274; Susannah, 56; Walter, 88; William, 88, 115, 119, 140, 155, 184, 288, 302, 358
JOHNSTON, John, 13, 43; Sarah, 19; Thomas, 6; William, 19
JOLLY, Charles, 17, 18; John, 18
JONES, Abigail, 66; Abner D., 354; Abraham, 113, 184, 268; Amos, 29, 70, 78, 108, 321, 327; Ann, 75, 96, 97, 124, 224, 228, 246, 274; Ashel, 354; Benjamin, 65, 97, 116, 124, 166, 209, 246, 342; Benjamin T., 359; Cadwalder, 240; Catharine, 9, 78, 224, 290; Charles, 78, 188, 240, 278, 305; Clement, 240; Daniel, 67, 108, 134; David, 65, 66, 67, 98, 327, 342; Ebenezer, 14; Eleanor, 213, 268, 283; Elijah, 124; Elizabeth, 7, 18, 67, 98, 108, 109, 184, 188, 264, 327, 342; Ellen, 305; Enoch, 109, 134, 305; Evan, 5, 18, 23, 28, 32, 38, 63, 71, 77, 87, 99, 104, 112, 126, 167, 185, 205, 250, 260, 275, 284, 291, 293, 303, 308, 311, 327, 340, 347, 353, 360; George, 224, 327; Grace, 184; Griffith,

78, 109; Hannah, 7, 80, 126, 140, 167, 184, 213, 215, 228, 340; Hannah P., 360; Henry, 104, 126, 167, 185, 240, 340; Hugh, 6, 327; Isaac, 29, 108, 192, 331; Isaiah, 167; Israel, 78, 136, 215; Isreal, 184; Jacob, 75, 97, 124, 149, 169, 196, 246; James, 9, 78, 154, 348; Jane, 108, 240, 294, 305; Jehu, 9; Jesse, 264; John, 1, 9, 11, 13, 28, 29, 43, 65, 98, 99, 106, 126, 141, 154, 162, 167, 177, 183, 185, 188, 228, 240, 246, 275, 295, 296, 297, 327, 340, 346; Jonathan, 29, 65, 66, 98, 99, 117, 164, 181, 188, 196, 197, 228, 245, 247, 264, 275, 276, 289, 290, 315, 327, 331, 332, 356; Joseph, 98, 117, 224, 268; Joshua, 134, 184, 213, 354; Josiah, 67; Lewis, 240; Lloyd, 93, 164, 197, 305, 359; Margaret, 125, 140, 170; Margareth, 9; Martha, 109, 188, 228; Mary, 7, 18, 97, 98, 99, 169, 196, 197, 224, 258, 275, 289, 315, 327, 343, 356; Mordecai, 160, 188, 264, 320, 324, 353; Mordecia, 327; Morris, 336; Naomi, 97; Nathaniel, 134; Norris, 9, 97; Owen, 164, 196, 245, 258, 289; Paul, 25, 93, 165, 184, 242, 305; Peter, 290; Phebe, 67, 305; Priscilla B., 327; Rachel, 246, 38, 327; Rebecca, 9, 29, 209; 228; Rebeckah, 14; Rees, 305; Richard, 348; Robert, 78, 184, 312; Rosanna, 268; Ruth, 108; Samuel, 78, 97, 109, 124, 246, 340; Sarah, 66, 98, 109, 224, 246, 305; Sidney, 181; Silas, 165, 240, 305, 361; Sophia, 353; Susanna, 169, 228, 305, 331; Susannah, 78; Tacy, 116, 120, 166, 209; Thomas, 29, 67, 98, 99, 109, 134, 346; William, 184, 224, 312
JORDAN, Sarah, 8
JORDON, Ann, 200; Thomas, 200
JOST, Johannes, 80
JUDGE, Hugh, 138
JUNKIN, Anna Barbara, 226
JUSTICE, Abraham, 260

-K-
KALBFLEISH, Henry, 12; Mattis, 13
KARR, Robert, 297; Streeper, 297
KARVER, Catharine, 149; Elizabeth, 149; Jacob, 21, 144, 149; John Adam, 149
KASSEL, Henry, 47, 132; Margaret, 132
KASTNER, Andrew, 73, 91, 329; Elizabeth, 68, 73, 114; George, 68, 73; Magdalena, 126; Margaret, 91; Mary, 73, 327; Samuel, 73, 163; Sarah, 73; Thomas, 91
KATCH, Bartholomy, 193
KATES, Andrew, 129, 193; Catharine, 193; Elizabeth, 193; Jacob, 193; Margaret, 193; Philip, 193; Sarah, 193
KATZ, Catharine, 64; Conrad, 64; Elizabeth, 64; George, 64, 189; Henry, 64, 129, 168; Magdalena, 64; Margaret, 129; Maria, 64
KAWLER, Margaret, 127; Martin, 127
KEAN, Elizabeth, 171; Samuel, 171
KEARN, Adam, 208; Catharine, 208; Christian, 208; John, 208; Margaret, 208; Mary, 208; Philip, 208
KEECH, Aaron, 209
KEEL, Anthony, 147
KEELER, Anna, 51; Catharine, 51; Conrad, 348; Hannah, 51; Henry, 51; John, 51; Martin, 51; Michael, 51; Susanna, 51
KEELY, Catharine, 107; Conrad, 106; Daniel, 107; Elizabeth, 107; George, 345; Henry, 106; Jacob, 107; John, 107; Magdalena, 107; Mary, 107; Sebastian, 345; Valentine, 106, 107; William, 107
KEEN, Peter, 330
KEEPAR, Bernd., 147; Catharine, 147; Elizabeth, 147; John, 147; Margaret, 147; Samuel, 147
KEEPLER, Martin, 170
KEEPNER, Elizabeth, 148; Samuel, 147
KEER, George, 166, 221; Hannah, 166; Margaret, 166; Rachel, 166, 221
KEESEY, Elizabeth, 51; Joseph, 51; Philip, 51

395

KEESLER, Christian, 342; Jacob, 342
KEHL, Anna, 298; Barbara, 298; Catharine, 156; Eve, 298; Jacob, 53, 298; John, 53; Moses, 53, 54, 156, 343, 351; Mosi, 27
KEHR, Anna, 187; Catharine, 187; Frederick, 187; John, 187
KEIBER, Peter, 308
KEIGER, Andrew, 358; Peter, 273
KEIM, Elizabeth, 89; Samuel, 89
KEISEL, Christian, 299; Enoch, 299; Hannah, 299; Jacob, 299; Susanna, 299
KELLER, Anna, 18; Bally, 18; Catharine, 18; Elizabeth, 166; Jacob, 293; John, 18, 248; Magdalena, 293; Martin, 18; Mary, 252; Packey, 18; Reinhard, 18; Susanna, 18; William, 252
KEMMERER, Catharine, 16
KEMPER, Abraham, 63; Gertrude, 63; Hannah, 63; John, 63; Mary, 63; Susannah, 63
KENDALL, Henry, 86, 313; Joseph, 313; Mary, 313
KENDELL, Christopher, 206; Elizabeth, 206; Henry, 206; John, 205, 206; Joseph, 196, 205, 206; Mary, 111, 206; Philip, 206; Samuel, 205, 206
KENDERDINE, Anna, 286; Armitage, 186; Benjamin, 121; Charles, 303; David, 286; Eli, 186; Elizabeth, 286, 303; Enoch, 121, 177, 290; Hannah, 121, 302, 303; John, 302, 303; Joseph, 39, 121, 222, 273, 276, 286, 290, 296, 302, 303, 307, 347, 355; Justinian, 303; Mary, 121, 290, 303; Rachel, 121, 186, 290; Rchel, 286; Rebecca, 303; Richard, 121, 286; Robert, 296, 307; Sarah, 121, 286, 290, 303; Tacy, 121, 290; Thomas, 177, 186
KENDIG, Abraham, 165, 166; Fronica, 166; John, 165, 166; Joseph, 166; Magdalena, 166; Susanna, 165, 166
KENNEDY, David, 327; Francis, 327; Robert, 327, 335, 344
KENSERT, Andrew, 19; Michael, 19; Valentine, 19
KEPELER, Elizabeth, 7; Hannah, 7; John, 7

KEPHART, Adam, 221; Andrew, 221; Christian, 221; Elizabeth, 221; Eve, 221; John, 221
KEPLER, George, 152; Jacob, 338; John, 237, 334; Rebecca, 334; Samuel, 353; William, 338
KEPNER, Catharine, 147; Elizabeth, 233; Henry, 327; John, 233, 256; Mary, 327; Michael, 90; William, 147
KEPPLE, Catharine, 129; Christina, 129; Elizabeth, 129; Henry, 128; Margaret, 129; Martin, 129; Peter, 129
KERBOUCH, David, 349; Sibella, 349
KERN, Elizabeth, 211; Eve, 172, 211; Henry, 211; John, 211; Leity, 211; Lorentz, 211; Lorenz, 172; Magdalena, 211; Margaret, 211; Mary, 211; Philip, 99
KERR, Annaotile, 172; Henry, 301; Hetty, 309
KERRDIG, John, 262
KERTEL, Anna Maria, 130; Margaret, 130
KEYSER, A., 232, 238; Aaron, 131, 199, 248, 256, 262, 285, 298, 329; Andrew, 32, 194, 327; Benjamin, 32; Catharine, 19, 62, 199, 329; Christian, 238; Christopher, 131, 199, 327, 329; Derick, 32, 199; Derrick, 256; Elizabeth, 194, 329; George, 160, 329; Henry, 19, 329; Isaac, 352; Jacob, 32, 62, 194; John, 32, 62, 112, 116, 194, 348, 352; Joseph, 32, 295; Mary, 131, 199, 256, 327; Molly, 194; Nathan, 131, 199, 256; Paul, 32; Peter, 32, 252; Rachel, 131, 194, 199; Rchel, 199; Regina, 32; Samuel, 62, 194; Sarah, 131, 194, 199, 352; Susanna, 194; Susannah, 32, 348; William, 131, 199, 248, 256, 262
KIDD, William, 106
KIDNEY, John, 104
KIELER, Hannah, 34; Martin, 34
KIHL, Henry, 206
KILE, Abraham, 215
KILI, William, 285
KIMBLE, Charlotte, 344; John, 344; William, 345
KINCKLE, Mary, 166

KINDERDINE, Eli, 187; Enoch, 187; Jane, 187
KINDIG, Martin, 9; Susanna, 9
KING, Abraham, 307; Ann, 57, 103; Barbara, 57; Catharine, 301; Elizabeth, 57; George, 103; John, 330, 348; Jonathan, 103; Katharine, 57; Margaret, 57; Martha, 103; Martin, 57, 301; Mary, 57, 103; Peter, 24, 57; Samuel, 103; Sarah, 307; Thomas, 103
KINMAN, Jane, 160; Nathan, 160
KINNARD, Emanuel, 327; Esther, 327
KINNEY, John, 250
KINSEY, David, 262
KINZIE, John, 225
KIRK, Elizabeth, 111; Isaac, 142, 253; Jacob, 111, 351, 355; Jesse, 351; John, 111, 253, 288; Joseph, 40, 253, 262, 263; Mary, 253; Rachel, 351, 355; Rebecca, 209; Rynear, 110; Sarah, 191
KIRKBRIDE, Hannah, 193; Joseph, 35, 186; Prudence, 35; Sarah, 35; Stacy, 35
KIRKNER, Joseph, 279
KIRKPATRICK, Elizabeth, 252; Mary, 241, 252
KIRPER, Catharine, 82; Elizabeth, 82; Jacob, 82; John, 82
KIRSHNER, Jeremiah, 84; Margareth, 84
KISSELLER, Magdalena, 174
KITE, John, 162
KITSELMAN, Casper, 90; Jacob, 90; Margaret, 90
KITTLER, Adam, 125; Andrew, 125; David, 125; Elizabeth, 125; Eve, 125; Hannah, 125; John, 125; Mary, 125; Sarah, 125; Susanna, 125
KIZAR, Casper, 284
KLAIRE, Abraham, 126
KLEIN, Elizabeth, 5, 87; Gabriel, 83; Jacob, 87
KLEMMER, Jacob, 273
KLINE, Abraham, 287, 299; Catharine, 54, 157, 287, 351; Conard, 304; Elizabeth, 54, 159, 287, 327, 343; Gabriel, 60, 159; George, 351; Henry, 327, 355; Isaac, 159, 181, 299; Jacob, 54, 80, 157, 159, 299; Jesse, 359; John, 54, 159, 307, 327, 343, 355; Magdalena, 157; Margaret, 122; Margareth, 54; Mary, 54, 199, 287, 299, 307, 359; Mary Elizabeth, 159; Nicholas, 150; Peter, 122, 159; Salome, 54; Susannah, 54
KLOTZ, Jacob, 22; Sophia, 22
KNEEDLER, Adam, 216, 217; Daniel, 216, 217, 284; Elizabeth, 216, 217; George, 216, 217; Jacob, 216, 217; John, 216, 217; Joseph, 216, 217; Samuel, 216, 217; Thomas, 276; William, 216, 217
KNEELEY, Conrad, 321; Michael, 321
KNIGHT, David, 355; Isaac, 45, 51, 52, 67, 117, 235; John, 45; Jonathan, 86, 235, 355; Joseph, 283; Joshua, 52, 235; Mahlon, 52, 235; Mary, 52, 235, 281; Nicholas, 327; Rebecca, 190, 235; Rebeckah, 52; Sarah, 52, 235
KNIPE, Barbara, 54; Catharine, 150; Christian, 54, 346; Daniel, 54; David, 54, 337; Henry, 54, 346; John, 54, 150; John W., 346; Joseph, 54, 250, 337; Mary, 54, 337, 346
KNITTEE, Siblella, 359
KNOEDLER, John Jacob, 15
KNORR, Christian, 124; George, 95; Jacob, 61, 95; Mary, 124
KNOUP, Henry, 203
KNOX, Abner, 177; Andrew, 33, 97, 177; Daniel, 232; David, 177; George, 232; Hugh, 62, 355; Isabella, 33, 177, 232; Jacob, 245; James, 177; John, 177, 232; Lewis, 355; Margaret, 347; Martha, 177; Mary, 33, 177; Matthew, 108, 231; Robert, 33, 177, 321, 347; William, 31, 33, 232
KOHLE, Catharine, 352; Nicholas, 352
KOLB, Abraham, 122, 202; Anna, 284; Barbara, 233; Catharine, 147, 233; Christian, 233; Daniel, 112, 349; Deilman, 38; Dielman, 112; Dillman, 327, 343, 360; Elizabeth, 147, 233, 302; Esther, 112; George, 147, 233, 298; George Michael, 233; Henry, 32, 112, 147, 299, 302, 327, 343, 349, 358; Isaac, 38, 40, 54, 112; Jacob, 10, 13, 33, 55, 94, 109, 122, 125, 147, 217, 219, 284, 321, 343; John, 233,

302, 360; John George, 147;
Joseph, 233; Lydia, 327;
Magdalena, 112, 233;
Magdelena, 147; Margaret,
233; Maria, 147; Martin, 112,
302; Mary, 233; Matthias,
112, 349; Moses, 147;
Nicholas, 360; Peter, 147,
233, 287; Samuel, 147; Sarah,
233; Susanna, 349;
Whilhelmina, 112
KOLP, Henry, 169; Jacob, 193;
John, 358; Susanna, 169
KOONCE, Anna, 65; Barbara, 65;
Henry, 65; Jacob, 65
KOONS, Margaret, 233; Peter,
233
KOP, Catharine, 157; Daniel,
157; Jacob, 165; Maria Eve,
157
KOPLIN, Hannah, 116; Matthias,
116, 345; Nathaniel, 345
KOPP, Daniel, 205
KORL, Phebe, 294
KORNDERFER, Mary, 120; Mary
Margaret, 120; Nicholas, 120;
Philip, 120
KRATZ, Isaac, 314; John, 359;
Maria, 314; Michael, 173
KRAUSS, Anna Mary, 69; Baltzer,
72; Barbara, 69; Daniel, 15,
69, 72, 267; Elizabeth, 15;
Eva, 69; Henry, 15, 69, 72;
Jacob, 15; Jeremiah, 265,
327; John, 15, 69; John
Valentine, 69; Margaret, 69;
Michael, 69; Molley, 69, 72;
Polly, 265; Regina, 69;
Sarah, 265; Valentine, 15, 69
KRAUZ, Vallentin, 6
KREBLE, Abraham, 33
KREBS, Henry, 89, 233, 278
KREEBLE, Abraham, 3
KREEGER, George, 10
KREER, Andrew, 89; David, 89;
George, 89; Henry, 89; John,
89; Peter, 89
KREIBEL, Andrew, 204
KREIBLE, Abraham, 84; Andrew,
327; George, 327; Hester,
327; Melchior, 327; Susannah,
84
KREPS, Catharine, 327; Michael,
327
KRETER, Elisabeth, 30; Jacob,
30
KRETZ, Henry, 46; Marilis, 46
KREWSON, Clarissa, 213; Joshua,
213
KRIBS, Henry, 203
KRICKBAUM, Conrad, 351

KRICKPAUMB, Barbara, 164;
Conrad, 164; Elizabeth, 164;
Nancy, 164; Philip, 164
KRIEBEL, Abraham, 149, 150,
356; Andrew, 216; Christian,
149; Christopher, 149, 150;
Isaac, 149; Mary, 149;
Melchior, 150; Rosina, 359;
Susanna, 150
KRIEBLE, Abraham, 92, 121, 125;
Andrew, 92, 121, 125, 146,
344, 359; Christian, 121,
344; Christopher, 351; Isaac,
337; Jeremiah, 92; Melchior,
92, 121, 326; Susanna, 121;
Susannah, 359
KRIEGEL, Christopher, 359
KRIER, Elizabeth, 253;
Magdalena, 172; Peter, 172
KRIESEMER, Catharine, 326;
Cathrine, 327; William, 327
KROB, Abraham, 13; Andrew, 13;
Catharine, 13; Elizabeth, 13;
Isaac, 13; Jacob, 13; Mary,
13; Samuel, 13; Sarah, 13;
Susannah, 13
KROESEN, Francis, 327; Mary,
327
KROLTZ, Daniel, 256
KROTZ, Abraham, 20; John, 20
KROUS, Daniel, 292; David, 348;
Jeremiah, 341, 348; John,
348; Michael, 338
KROUSE, Abraham, 345; Charles,
356; Daniel, 316; George,
297; Jacob, 316; Jeremiah,
297; John, 316; Magdalena,
297; Margaret, 316; Molly,
316; Nathan, 297; Rebecca,
316; Sarah, 316; Susanna, 356
KROUSSIN, Susannah, 72
KRUP, Jacob, 332; Mary, 332
KRUSON, John, 288
KUGLAR, John, 330; Paul, 330;
Sarah, 330
KUGLER, Catharine, 30; Charles,
185, 203; Elizabeth, 17;
Harriot, 350; John, 350;
Matthias, 17; Peter, 30;
Sarah, 359
KULP, Abraham, 264; Andrew, 81;
Benjamin, 250; Catharine, 81,
264; Daniel, 81, 346; David,
219, 237, 264, 302; David C.,
235; Dilman, 152; Elizabeth,
81, 264, 282; George, 81;
Hannah, 152, 282; Henry, 152;
Jacob, 47, 152, 235, 264,
282, 299, 342, 357; John, 81,
231; Leonard, 81; Margaret,
152; Martin, 346; Mary, 81,

264, 282; Matthias, 299, 346; Nancy, 264; Peter, 47; Sarah, 152; Susanna, 152, 264; William, 282
KUNTZ, Michael, 326
KURKIRK, Andrew, 100
KURR, Anna, 91; Jacob, 91; Magdalena, 91; Susannah, 91
KURTZ, Barbara, 281; Eleanor, 274; Elizabeth, 274; John, 281; Maria, 306; Mary, 274; Samuel, 306; Sarah, 274, 306; Susanna, 274; Valentine, 274
KUSER, Catharine, 31; Christina, 31; Elizabeth, 31; Eva, 30; Jacob, 31; John, 31; Michael, 31; Mira, 31; Peter, 31
KUSTER, Peter, 24
KUTER, Hannah, 63; Henry, 63

-L-

LAASH, Christopher, 50
LABOLD, Christina, 268; Jacob, 268
LADACK, Anna Margareth, 34; George, 34
LAHR, Philip, 83
LAKE, Richard, 162
LALLY, Martha, 226
LANCASTER, Ann, 345; Knowles, 345; Thomas, 86, 193, 345
LAND, Ann, 187; Catharine, 187; Christiana, 187; Eve, 187; George, 157, 187, 355; Jacob, 187; John, 187; Michael, 187
LANDER, Anna, 300; Michael, 300
LANDERS, Jacob, 265
LANDES, Abraham, 311; Anna, 227; Barbara, 60; Catharine, 60, 227; Elizabeth, 60, 227, 339; Hannah, 300; Henry, 60, 227, 339; Isaac, 59, 60, 227, 339; Jacob, 59, 60, 183, 227, 311, 339; John, 60, 169, 227, 300, 311; Mary, 169, 227, 311; Susanna, 60; Yellis, 60
LANDIS, Abraham, 350; Benjamin, 85; Catharine, 82; Hannah, 146; Henry, 191; Isaac, 191, 334; Jacob, 118, 334, 336, 349; John, 114, 350; Margaret, 82; Martin, 146; Yellis, 334
LANE, Abigail, 111; Ann, 111; Edward, 111; Eleanor, 111; Hannah, 111; Jane, 111; Mary, 111; Robert, 183; William, 111, 322
LANG, George, 57; Jacob, 57

LANGBINE, Godfreed, 58; Margaret, 58
LANGDALE, Margaret, 18; Samuel, 18
LANTES, Benjamin, 109; Gertrude, 109; Jacob, 109, 352
LANTIS, John, 328; Martin, 328
LANTZ, Isaac, 323
LAPP, John, 338; Joseph, 338
LARGE, Zenas, 194
LARKIN, Sarah, 187; William, 187
LASSHEG, Christian, 341
LASSLY, Catharine, 125; Samuel, 125
LATCH, Anna, 10; David, 10, 11; George, 10, 354; Hannah, 10; Jacob, 10; John, 10, 11; Mary, 10, 11; Rudolph, 10
LATES, Leonard, 55
LATSHAW, David, 244; Maria, 244
LAUER, Eve, 107; Harman, 107
LAUTERBACH, Philip, 19
LAW, James, 231; Joseph, 231; Rebecca, 231
LAWLER, Dorothy, 328
LAWRENCE, Mary, 56, 57; Mordecai, 343; Thomas, 117
LAYMAN, Andrew, 236, 303; Casper, 303; Catharine, 303; Elizabeth, 303; Mary, 303; Sarah, 303; Thomas, 303
LEA, Sarah, 313
LEAF, George, 224, 262, 286, 337
LEAFF, George, 306
LEAR, Adam, 327; Leonard, 193; Margaret, 327; Matthias, 234
LEAVER, Erasmuis, 336; Frederick, 336
LEDERACH, Anna, 114; Catharine, 114; Elizabeth, 114; Henry, 114; John, 114; Magdalena, 114; Molly, 114
LEDERMAN, Magdalena, 27
LEDOM, Ann, 169; Isaac, 169
LEDYERT, Elisabeth, 26; John, 26; Thomas, 26
LEECH, Ann, 301; Charles, 348; Hannah, 151, 206; Isaac, 11, 150, 151, 205; Jacob, 348; John, 272; Jonathan, 96, 175; Joseph, 11, 150, 151; Margaret, 11; Mary, 150; Rebecca, 11, 151; Richard, 210, 301; Richard T., 151; Samuel, 11, 89, 150, 151, 210, 269, 301; Thomas, 11, 18, 150, 348
LEECK, Thomas, 111

LEEDOM, Ann, 240; George, 240;
  Isaac, 240; Jesse, 240; John,
  240; Joseph, 173, 252;
  Richard, 34; Silas, 240;
  Thomas, 285; William, 34
LEEDY, Richard P., 58
LEFEVER, Minor, 35
LEHMAN, Abraham, 196, 338;
  Andrew, 284; Elizabeth, 196;
  George, 196, 338; John, 196;
  Magdalena, 196; Peter, 91,
  196, 239, 286, 350
LEIBENGUTH, Ann, 160;
  Elizabeth, 160; Henry, 289;
  John, 160; Peter, 289;
  Rachel, 160; Samuel, 160;
  Solomon, 160; Thomas, 160
LEIDER, George, 228
LEIDICH, Catharine, 299;
  Christian, 19, 299;
  Elizabeth, 299; Henry, 299;
  John, 299; Mary, 299; Philip,
  299
LEIDIG, Francis, 128, 153;
  Jacob, 164
LEIDY, Barbara, 69; Catharine,
  69; Conrad, 23; Jacob, 69,
  70; John, 69
LEISTER, Jacob, 342
LEITIG, Philip, 29
LEITY, Catharine, 48; Leonard,
  48
LENDERMAN, Aaron, 220
LENHART, George, 356; Joseph,
  356
LENSINBEGLER, Ludwig, 305
LENTZ, Barbara, 327; Catharine,
  344; Christopher, 327;
  Elizabeth, 216; Jacob, 207,
  327, 344; John, 327, 344;
  Lydia, 205; Mary, 129;
  Nicholas, 216; William, 129,
  263
LEONARD, Anna, 70; Anna Walker,
  70; Elizabeth, 70; George,
  120, 121, 135, 148, 154, 199,
  337; Thomas W., 344
LEONHART, George, 299
LEOSER, Christian, 328;
  Christopher, 328; Elizabeth,
  328; Peter, 328
LESHER, Catharine, 306; James,
  306; Rachel, 306; William,
  306
LESTER, Jacob, 236
LEVER, George, 169; Philip, 169
LEVERGOOD, Elizabeth, 42;
  Jacob, 42; John, 42; Mary, 42
LEVERING, Abigial, 24; Able, 6;
  Abraham, 11; Agness, 24, 25;
  Alice, 223; Anthony, 11, 24,
  25, 102, 169, 197, 305;
  Benjamin, 6, 247; Daniel, 59,
  262; Elisabeth, 24;
  Elizabeth, 161, 223; Hannah,
  24, 171; Henry, 59; Jacob,
  59; John, 242, 305, 359, 361;
  Joseph, 6, 223, 247;
  Magdalena, 223; Margaret, 11,
  161; Margrate, 24; Mary, 223;
  Nathan, 85; Peter, 171, 223;
  Sarah, 24, 247; Susanna, 262;
  Wickard, 6; William, 11, 103,
  223
LEVEY, Abraham, 349; Adam, 349
LEVI, David, 327; Margaret, 327
LEVINA, Abraham, 136
LEVIZEY, Thomas, 6
LEVY, Abraham, 342; Jacob, 335
LEWELLYN, John, 328; Morris,
  328
LEWIS, Abraham, 93; Amos, 110,
  163, 203, 251, 294, 329;
  Anna, 62; Azariah, 28; David,
  110; Eliner, 62; Elizabeth,
  110, 158, 361; Elsie, 62;
  Enos, 28, 205; Evan, 188;
  Hester, 336; Isaac, 20, 28,
  62; Isaiah, 261; Issachar,
  62; Jacob, 62, 303, 355;
  Jane, 110; Jesse, 207, 292;
  John, 167, 336; Joseph, 24,
  49, 110, 127, 133, 137, 157,
  158, 188, 222, 314, 328, 330;
  Mary, 110; Molley, 62;
  Mordecai, 307; Nathan, 361;
  Peggy, 244; Rachel, 110, 158,
  314; Robert, 110, 325; Sarah,
  110; Seplithah, 328; Sibilla,
  207; Susanna, 110; Tamer,
  110; Thomas, 133; William,
  288
LEYDICH, Catharine, 206;
  Christina, 206; Elizabeth,
  206; Frantz, 206; Henry, 206;
  Jacob, 206; John, 206;
  Magdalena, 206; Philip, 206,
  225
LIBEGUD, Elizabeth, 99
LIBLEY, Jacob, 62
LICK, Catharine, 271; William,
  271
LIDYARD, Esther, 56; Thomas, 56
LIEBENUGH, Adam, 146;
  Catharine, 147; Christina,
  146; Elizabeth, 146; Jacob,
  146; John, 146; Matthias,
  146, 147; Peter, 146, 147
LIGHTCAP, George, 290
LILLING, George, 324
LIMING, Sarah, 341

LIN, John, 196; Maria, 196; William, 196
LINDEBERGER, John, 238; Mary, 238
LINDEL, Ludowig, 34
LINDERMAN, Catharine, 183
LINDSAY, Jane, 229; John, 229
LINENBOCH, Esther, 290; Hannah, 290; Jacob, 290; Joseph, 290
LINN, Jacob, 107; John, 107; Joseph, 345
LINSENBIGLER, Abraham, 195; Anna Maria, 195; Henry, 266; John, 195; Maria Margaret, 195; Paul, 39, 195; Samuel, 195
LINSEPEGLER, Ludwig, 128
LINSEY, Jane, 197
LINTZ, Jacob, 183; Margaret, 183
LIPPEN, John, 340
LIPPINCOT, Jacob, 121
LIPPINCOTT, Elizabeth, 88; Hannah, 88; Jacob, 88; Samuel, 88; William, 88
LISMANT, Benjamin, 44; Daniel, 43, 44; Elizabeth, 43, 44; Henry, 43; John, 43, 44
LITSINGER, Mary, 278
LIVEZEY, Ann, 299, 313; Benjamin, 63, 298; Daniel, 298, 299; Deborah, 299; Esther, 298, 299; Ezra, 299; Hannah, 63; Isaac, 299; John, 63, 298; Jonathan, 63, 299; Lydia, 261; Mary, 63, 298; Robert, 298, 299; Samuel, 66, 118, 165, 217, 295, 296; Sarah, 299; Susanna, 298, 299; Thomas, 39, 44, 52, 70, 80, 88, 89, 96, 110, 119, 120, 136, 142, 145, 151, 160, 174, 176, 179, 182, 190, 199, 206, 208, 219, 230, 231, 232, 235, 238, 249, 253, 265, 268, 274, 282, 298, 299, 334, 335, 346
LLEWELYN, Martha, 144; Morris, 144
LLOYD, Abraham, 285; Ann, 285; Benjamin, 49, 63, 86, 229, 263, 272, 273, 309, 328, 334, 342; Cadwalder, 285, 291; David, 88; Davis, 291; Deborah, 29; Edward, 46; Elizabeth, 273, 283, 309, 334; Hannah, 285; James, 328; Jesse, 273, 283; John, 49, 273, 283, 285, 328; Jonathan, 331; Joseph, 124, 285, 338; Lydia, 285; Mary, 285, 328; Philip, 328, 338; Rachel, 273; Rebecca, 328; Samuel, 74, 86, 246, 328; Sarah, 283, 285, 291, 334
LOAZER, Margaretta, 189
LOBACK, Magdalena, 96; Samuel, 96
LOBER, Anna Maria, 34; Barbara, 34; Catharine, 34; Dorothy, 34; Peter, 34; Rosina, 34
LOCHMAN, Nicholas, 328
LOCK, Eva Mary, 31; Eve, 335, 360; Jacob, 360; John, 335; Magdalena, 233; Peter, 31, 335
LOCKART, David, 6
LODER, Sarah, 90
LOESER, Catharine, 151; Chistopher, 151; Christian, 151, 249; Christopher, 73, 146, 153, 235, 249, 265; Elizabeth, 76, 151, 249; John, 151; Margaret, 151; Mary, 151; Peter, 61; Racheal, 151; Sarah, 151
LOEZER, Christopher, 64
LOGAN, Albanus, 225; Joseph, 170; Mary, 170, 339; William, 339
LOLLER, Alexander, 12, 186; James, 186, 187; Mary, 48, 94, 186, 196; Robert, 48, 50, 57, 59, 60, 68, 76, 79, 92, 94, 107, 110, 121, 124, 131, 135, 142, 186, 187, 234; William, 186
LONG, Alexander, 312; Ann Maria, 95; Anne Catharine, 10; Barbara, 357; Catharine, 129; Elias, 10, 36; Elizabeth, 129, 312; George, 95, 328, 337, 347, 357; George Philip, 10; Henry, 129, 337; Hugh, 245, 312, 338; Isabella, 312; Jacob, 36, 50, 61, 129, 328, 347; Jane, 177; John George, 10; John Jacob, 10, 36; John Peter, 10; Joseph, 10; Lewis, 312; Margaret, 129, 328; Margaret Barbara, 36; Mary, 219, 245, 267; Mary Catharine, 10, 328; William, 260, 312
LONGACKER, Catharine, 264; Isaac, 264
LONGACRE, Catharine, 169, 351; Daniel, 20; David, 339; Henry, 344; Jacob, 20, 33, 146, 169, 321, 332, 338; John, 338; Peter, 351

LONGAIM, Henry, 357
LONGAKER, Peter, 307
LONGBIEN, Catharine, 113;
  Elizabeth, 113; George, 113;
  Godfrey, 113; Henry, 113;
  John, 113; Margaret, 113;
  Mary Barbara, 113
LONGDEIN, Gottfried, 2
LONGENACRE, David, 328;
  Elizabeth, 328; Henry, 328
LONGENECKER, Daniel, 41; David,
  146; Deborah, 146
LONGSTRETH, Benjamin, 263;
  Charles, 263; Daniel, 38, 75,
  323; Isaac, 94, 263, 277,
  286, 303; John, 75, 323;
  Joseph, 118; Sarah, 98
LONGSTROTH, Catharine, 329;
  John, 329; Thomas, 329
LOT, Henry, 4; Leonard, 4;
  Mary, 4; Peter, 4; Stephen,
  4; Zepheniah, 4
LOTSHAW, Abraham, 341; Jacob,
  341
LOUP, Catharine, 340; Henry,
  340; Peter, 340
LOURY, Thomas, 211
LOVE, Andrew, 302; John, 302;
  Sarah, 302; Stephen, 302;
  Thomas, 302; William, 302
LOWDERBACK, John, 328
LOWRY, James, 127; John, 42;
  Thomas, 346, 348
LUDWIG, Samuel, 201
LUKENS, Abner, 346; Abraham,
  24, 43, 80, 118, 203, 215,
  219, 261, 270, 347; Agnes,
  118, 261; Alice, 279, 280;
  Ann, 44; Azor, 24, 44, 358;
  Benjamin, 137; Catharine,
  215; Cathrine, 203; Charles,
  249, 270, 295; Daniel, 137,
  163; David, 137, 165, 203,
  216, 222, 274, 347, 348;
  Deborah, 24; Derrick, 56;
  Dorothy, 24; Edith, 204;
  Elanora, 94; Elijah, 249;
  Elizabeth, 17, 118, 137, 142,
  179, 203, 279; Ellen, 294;
  Esther, 347; Francis, 136;
  Francis Gurney, 215; Gayner,
  118; George, 222, 335;
  Hannah, 17, 24; Isaac, 163,
  206; Isaiah, 142; Jacob, 17;
  Jane, 73, 261; Jesse, 142,
  203, 204, 251, 294; Job, 230;
  Joel, 222; John, 23, 24, 163,
  215, 222; Jonathan, 44, 137,
  203, 204, 279, 282, 352;
  Joseph, 17, 43, 110, 137,
  160, 203, 209, 230, 235, 249,
  259, 270, 277, 335, 359;
  Lavina, 215; Levi, 163;
  Lukens, 230; Lydia, 118;
  Mahlon, 347; Maria, 215;
  Martha, 104, 137, 163, 171,
  203, 204, 261, 270; Mary, 17,
  44, 65, 103, 137, 198, 215,
  230, 279, 280, 295, 345;
  Matthias, 345, 358; Moses,
  190, 346; Nathan, 118, 222,
  302; Peter, 103, 204, 245;
  Rachel, 118, 137; Rebecca,
  111, 151, 206, 249; Rebeckah,
  17; Robert, 80, 118; Rynear,
  17, 104, 120, 249; Ryner,
  182; Samuel, 136, 215; Sarah,
  17, 67, 118, 137, 198, 249;
  Seneca, 118, 279, 292, 338,
  360; Senica, 110; Susanna,
  36, 204; Susannah, 24; Tacy,
  182, 203, 249; Thomas, 137,
  188, 270, 273; William, 137,
  249, 280
LUKINS, John, 30
LUMBACKS, ---, 176
LUNN, Joseph, 134, 348; Thomas,
  348
LUSHE, Amy, 101
LUTHER, John, 328
LUTZ, Adam, 132; Anna Maria,
  132; George, 132; Jacob, 132;
  Katharine, 132; Peter, 132;
  Philip, 132
LYLE, Abi, 241; B. Rush, 252;
  Benjamin, 241, 259; Charles,
  241; Elizabeth, 241, 243;
  Francis, 241, 252, 259, 269,
  356; Henry, 243; John, 86,
  241; Margaret, 241; Martha,
  241, 252; Mary, 241, 252;
  Walter, 241, 252
LYNCH, Christopher, 183;
  Margaret, 183; Rebecca, 47;
  Rebeckah, 50
LYND, Thomas, 307
LYNIGAR, Henry, 173
LYNN, Esther, 197; Franklin,
  197; Jeremiah, 197; John,
  197; Joseph, 197; Mary, 197;
  Sarah, 197; William, 197
LYSINGER, Andrew, 106; John,
  106, 342; Joseph, 106; Mary,
  106, 342

-M-

MCANALL, Robert, 358; William,
  358
MCBEATH, James, 195; William,
  195
MCCACHAN, Sarah, 335

MCCAFEE, Elizabeth, 62; Isaac, 62; Jane, 62; John, 62; Mary, 62; Robert, 62; Thomas, 62; William, 62
MCCAHRON, John, 309; Mary, 309; William, 309
MCCALLA, Dorothy, 131; Jane, 156; Jesse, 285
MCCALLEY, Alex, 285
MCCALLISTER, David, 113; Tamer, 113
MCCALMONT, Ann, 119; Margaret, 119; Mary, 119; Matthew, 119
MCCAMMAN, William, 317
MCCANN, John, 357; Nancy, 357
MCCASIN, Mary, 139; William, 139
MCCHREA, Catharine, 231; John, 231; John Christy, 231
MCCLAINE, Ann, 328
MCCLANE, William, 328
MCCLAY, Hannah, 125; William, 125
MCCLEAN, Alexander, 309; Ann, 45; Archibald, 45; Edith, 45; Elizabeth, 187; Esther, 151; Jane, 296; John, 296; Joseph, 45, 48, 187; Lydia, 309; Margaret, 309; Mary, 296; Moses, 269, 296; Rachel, 48, 269, 295, 296; Rebecca, 296; Samuel, 45, 334; William, 45, 269, 334
MCCLEARY, Thomas, 317
MCCLENNAN, James, 350
MCCLINTICK, Alexander, 317; Francis, 62; James, 62; Robert, 62, 77, 156; Sarah, 156, 317; Thomas, 62
MCCLINTOCK, Alexander, 328; Robert, 317; Thomas, 317
MCCLINTUCK, Robert, 209, 285
MCCOLL, Catharine, 86; Elizabeth, 86; Laura, 86; Mary, 86; Samuel, 86; Walter, 86
MCCOLLESTER, Jesse, 244
MCCOLOUGH, James, 160; John, 160; William, 160
MCCOOL, Alevia, 240; Barbara, 240; Elizabeth, 240; Jonathan, 240; Mary, 240; Rachel, 240; Samuel, 240; Walter, 240
MCCOWN, ---, 139
MCCOY, Amos, 355; Mary, 243; William, 128, 355
MCCRAIG, Alexander, 315
MCCREA, Catharine, 300; David, 310; Hannah, 155; Jane, 155; John, 155, 180, 200, 300, 330; Joseph, 155; Margaret, 155; Mary, 155, 180; Rebecca, 155
MCCRORY, Jacob, 200; John, 200; Jonathan, 200; Joseph, 200
MCCURDY, Robert, 232
MCDARNET, James, 329
MCDERMOND, John, 336; Mary, 336; Samuel, 336
MCDOLE, Alexander, 331; Elizabeth, 331; John, 331
MCDONALD, Elizabeth, 313
MCDOUGAL, Anna, 146
MCDOWELL, Alexander, 68, 82, 235; Ebenezer, 194; James, 329; John, 30; Major, 236; Margaret, 236; Mary, 329; Nancy, 236; Robert, 30, 325; William, 30, 329
MCELHNEY, Esther, 315; George, 315
MACER, Maria Dorothy, 348
MCEWEN, ---, 139
MCFARLAND, Arthur, 41, 328; Elizabeth, 41, 328; James, 41; John, 41, 131, 171, 266, 328; Margaret, 41; Mary, 41; Rebecca, 183, 266
MCGLATHERY, Charles, 31, 232; Elizabeth, 110; Henry, 110; Isaac, 31, 35, 97, 108, 125, 206, 232, 335, 347; Jean, 110; John, 31, 335; Margaret, 110; Mary, 31; Matthew, 31; Mordicai, 110; Rachel, 110; Sarah, 110; William, 31
MACK, Catharine, 205; Elizabeth, 205; Jacob, 205; Mary, 205; Mary A., 72; William, 205
MCKEAN, Hannah, 162; Joseph B., 162, 163
MCKENNEY, James, 329; Morris, 329
MCKENSIE, Dorothy, 17; Robert, 17
MCKINNEY, James, 251
MACKLEIN, Anna Margareth, 11; Jacob, 11; John, 11
MCKNIGHT, David, 334; Robert, 106
MCLEMON, Abi, 252; Francis, 252
MCLERNON, Aby, 269; Charles, 269; Francis, 356; Mary, 269; May, 356
MCLLVAIN, Jeremiah, 343
MCMAIR, Ann, 245; James, 245, 267; John, 245, 267; Mary, 245, 267; Rebecca, 245, 267; Samuel, 245, 267
MCMANNAMAY, Mary, 113

MCNALLEY, Samuel, 80
MCNEAL, Anthony, 42; Elizabeth, 42, 289; Hiram, 42, 152, 186; John, 289; Margaret, 42; Mary, 42; Rebecca, 289; Samuel, 42; Thomas, 289
MCNEALLE, Hiram, 120
MCNEELEY, David, 155
MCNEELY, Daniel, 180; Mary, 180
MCNEIL, Hiram, 201
MCNEILL, Hiram, 161, 167, 176, 195, 201, 222, 232, 258, 260, 269, 277, 279, 280, 288, 291, 292, 298, 301, 302, 309, 310, 353, 355; Hogland, 298; Maria, 201; Mary, 280, 285
MCNEILLE, Hiram, 120
MCNEILY, David, 177; Mary, 177
MCNIEL, Hiram, 63
MCNIELL, Hiram, 235, 285
MCSELAND, John, 135
MADARY, Barbara, 346; John, 346
MADDON, Bernard, 332
MAGARGEL, Eleanor, 50; James, 50; Martha, 50; William, 50
MAGILL, Elizabeth, 142; Hannah, 142; James, 142; Mary, 142; Sarah, 142; William, 142
MAINCE, John, 95
ALEXANDER, Ebenezer, 48; Elizabeth, 48; Hannah, 48; James, 48; Jane, 48; John, 48; Major, 48; Margaret, 48; Mary, 48; Peacock, 48
MAJOR, Alexander, 48, 351; Alice, 246; Ebenezer, 48, 68; Elizabeth, 48, 68; Hannah, 48, 68; Jacob, 114; James, 48, 68; Jane, 48, 68; John, 48, 68, 123, 357; Joseph, 351; Margaret, 48, 68; Mary, 48; Peacock, 48; Thomas, 357
MAKCLINE, Jacob, 196
MALIN, Benedict, 297; Gideon, 297
MALLHARUS, Beonhard, 61
MALSBERGER, Catharine, 154, 286; Edward, 154; Elizabeth, 154; Jacob, 154, 286; Joseph, 154, 286; Mary, 154, 286; Peggy, 154; Susanna, 154, 286
MANDEVILLE, William, 277
MANGOLD, Catharine, 144; Christopher, 144; George Adam, 144; Joseph, 144
MANN, Elizabeth, 276; Isaac, 146, 267, 276; James, 276; Joel, 248; Joel K., 146, 276; John, 3, 56, 63, 66, 72, 98, 121, 210, 235, 236, 276; Joseph, 276; Martha, 276;

403

Mary, 276; Samuel, 57, 98, 121, 146, 178, 245, 267, 276, 307, 329, 358; Sarah, 276; William, 276
MARCH, Daniel, 330; Samuel, 287
MAREWINE, Mary, 11
MARGARGEL, Eleanor, 50; Jacob, 329; James, 50; Joseph, 329; Martha, 50; William, 50
MARGERUM, Thomas, 232
MARIS, Ann, 140, 170, 233; George, 55, 108, 126, 140, 141, 324, 329; Hannah, 140, 170; Jane, 140, 170, 313, 340; Jesse, 140, 170, 233, 329; John, 167; Jonathan, 329; Judith, 140; Nancy, 197; Rebecca, 140, 170; Richard, 304; Susanna, 170; Susannah, 140; William, 7, 140, 141
MARKLEY, Abraham, 181, 281, 330, 336, 344, 354; Andrew, 281; Barbara, 281; Benjamin, 60, 77, 80, 83, 130, 141, 153, 202, 203, 204, 206, 219, 221, 222, 224, 225, 227, 233, 273, 281, 286, 299, 316, 330, 348; Daniel, 116; Elizabeth, 116, 181, 194, 273, 281; Frederick, 304; George, 281; Hannah, 116, 273; Henry, 63, 356; Heny, 344; Isaac, 187, 194, 220, 344, 354; Jacob, 5, 63, 93, 116, 333; John, 95, 116, 156, 173, 194, 273, 281, 330, 345; Jonah, 273; Joshua, 273; Margaret, 95; Maria, 281; Mary, 116, 273; Molly, 194; Philip, 116; Rebecca, 273; Samuel, 357; Sarah, 273; Susanna, 281
MARKLY, Abraham, 5; Barbara, 5; Barbarah, 5; Caterine, 5; Christiana, 5; Eleanor, 5; Elizabeth, 5; Hannah, 5; Isaac, 5; John, 5; Philip, 5; Rebekah, 5; Zornica, 5
MARKS, Catharine, 113; Eve Catharine, 113, 114; George, 113, 114; George Adam, 113; Philip, 113
MAROWINE, Andrew, 175
MARPEL, Enoch, 46; Mary, 46
MARPLE, Abel, 230; Able, 2; Amy, 2; Benjamin, 2, 360; Daniel, 67; David, 103, 230, 357, 358; Eleanor, 230; Eliza, 230; Elizabeth, 2; Enoch, 2, 160; Hannah, 358; Isaac, 67; Jacob, 2; John, 189; Jones, 67; Margaret,

353; Martha, 67; Mary, 160,
253; Nathan, 2, 3, 67; Pheby,
2; Thomas, 353
MARQUEDANT, Mary, 240
MARSH, Ann, 86; Catharine, 12;
Daniel, 12, 354; David, 12;
Elizabeth, 12, 86; Jacob, 12
MARSHA, Ann, 87
MARSHALL, Agnes, 70; Elizabeth,
103; George, 103; John, 280;
Joseph, 70
MARSHEL, Matthew, 355
MARSTELLAR, Frederick, 83;
Susannah, 83
MARSTELLER, George, 70; John,
135; Margaret, 70; Rachel,
135
MARTIN, Anna, 250; Charles,
250; Elizabeth, 107, 250,
332; Frederick, 54; George,
250, 257, 259, 276, 279, 290,
344; Hannah, 250; Henry, 212;
Hetty, 250; Isaac, 257;
Jacob, 250; John, 11, 107,
250; Lydia, 250; Martha, 257;
Mary, 54, 195, 250; Matthias,
107; Nicholas, 144, 150;
Rachel, 158, 245, 257;
Rebecca, 245, 257; Richard,
245; Samuel, 248
MARTSLOFF, Eve, 329; Philip,
329
MARVEY, Mary, 356
MARVIL, Hannah, 201
MASON, Mary, 150; Peter, 150;
Richard, 258
MASTERSON, Elizabeth, 273;
Henry, 273; John, 273; Sarah,
273
MATHER, Bartholomew, 7, 210;
Benjamin, 111, 161; Charles,
217, 230, 266, 297;
Elizabeth, 156; Isaac, 340;
Isaac L., 210; Joseph, 198,
345; Michael, 156, 335, 337;
Racheal, 150; Rebecca, 156;
Richard, 254; Sarah, 73;
Williamsaac, 62
MATHERS, Susanna, 205
MATHIAS, Joseph, 311
MATSON, Abigail, 205; Ann, 86,
87, 205, 216; Catharine, 216;
Elijah, 205; Elizabeth, 87,
216; Esther, 87; Hannah, 86,
87, 216; Isaac, 55, 86, 216;
Job, 216; John, 216;
Jonathan, 216; Mary, 86;
Peter, 13, 21, 48, 55, 87,
205; Robert, 216; Samuel,
216; Susanna, 87; William,
216

MATTES, Catharine, 168;
Christopher, 168; David, 168;
Hannah, 168; John, 168; John
Jacob, 168; Maria, 168;
Philip, 168
MATTHEW, Frederick, 322
MATTHEWS, John, 98, 330; Mary,
330
MATTHIAS, Catharine, 277, 278;
David, 344; Elizabeth, 277;
Jacob, 277; John, 341; Mary,
277
MATTIS, Catharine, 107;
Christian, 141, 268;
Elizabeth, 120; Jacob, 120;
Mary, 120; Peter, 120; Sarah,
141
MATTSON, Ann, 178; Catharine,
178; Elizabeth, 178; Hannah,
178; Isaac, 178; Job, 178;
John, 178; Jonathan, 178;
Peter, 178; Robert, 178;
Samuel, 178; Susanna, 178;
William, 178
MAUCK, Catharine, 305; Conrad,
305
MAUL, Ann, 255
MAULSBY, Hannah, 38; Samuel,
201, 246, 254, 274, 285, 339,
345
MAURER, George, 287; Jacob,
287; Margaret, 287; Mary,
287; Peter, 287
MAUS, Charlotte, 22; Frederick,
22; Frederick Gustavus, 22;
Gustavus, 22; John Nicholas,
22; Louisa, 22; Matthew, 22
MAUSER, Michael, 112
MAXFIELD, Henry, 328
MAY, Christian, 10, 175, 207;
Frederick, 175; Fronica, 357;
James, 138; John, 357;
Lutina, 175; Sarah, 138;
Thomas, 62, 138; Thomas P.,
357
MAYBERRY, Magdalena, 45;
William, 45
MAYBURRY, Charles, 17; Joseph,
328; Rebecca, 317; Silvanas,
332; Thomas, 18, 317
MAYBURY, Anna, 283; Elizabeth,
283; Rebecca, 283; Thomas,
283; William, 283
MAYER, Anna, 118; Barbara, 118;
Benjamin, 146; Catharine,
146; Christian, 19, 20, 118;
Elizabeth, 118; Henry, 91,
118; Isaac, 118; Jacob, 118,
166; John, 118; Magdalena,
19; Margaret, 20; Mary, 91,
118; Samuel, 19, 20, 118

405

MAYOR, Henry, 95
MECHLIN, Samuel, 128
MECKLER, Catharine, 309; Jacob, 309
MECKLIN, Jacob, 188
MEDERA, Jacob, 161
MEETH, Anna Margaret, 172; John Nicholas, 172
MEGAREL, Hannah, 337; Jacob, 337
MEGARER, Allen, 280; Isaac, 280; Jesse, 280; John, 280; Jonathan, 280; Joseph, 280; Rebecca, 280
MEHARD, John, 328
MEISHTER, Baltzer, 133
MELLER, Frederick, 14
MELLINGER, William, 15
MELONE, John, 273
MENAN, Elizabeth, 46; Mary, 46; Pat, 73; Patrick, 46; Sarah, 46
MENDENHALL, William, 343
MENZUS, Archibald, 143
MEREDITH, Aaron, 272; Davd, 272; David, 272, 345; Elizabeth, 113; Hannah, 184; James, 113; Jane, 113; Jesse, 113; John, 15, 85, 113, 191, 232, 272; Joseph, 113, 133, 141, 184, 272, 358; Rachel, 358; Sarah, 66; Susanna, 113
MERKLE, Maria, 38; William, 38
MERSHON, Rebecca, 170; Stephen, 6
MESER, Catharine, 172; Conrad, 172; Henry, 172
MESHTER, Jeremiah, 308
MESSAMER, Magdelena, 151
MESSEMER, Benjamin, 173; Jacob, 344
MESTER, Christopher, 125; George, 125; Susanna, 125
METZ, Abraham, 93, 354; Ann, 93; Barbara, 93; Catharine, 93, 207; Elizabeth, 93; Esther, 93; Jacob, 58, 93, 311, 328, 342; John, 93, 119, 328, 361; Joseph, 361; Leonard, 93; Leonhard, 46; Mary, 93; Muney, 58; Samuel, 207, 342
METZGER, Anna, 91; Frederick, 91
MEWMAN, Leonhard, 46
MEYER, Abraham, 4; Anna Barbara, 1; Anna Catherine, 1; Anna Margaret, 1; Anna Mary, 1; Barbara, 4, 301; Benjamin, 2, 301; Catharine, 113; Catherine, 4; Christian, 36; George, 3, 4, 51; Henry, 4; Isaac, 200; Jacob, 3, 4, 298; John, 1; Margaret, 1, 4; Mary, 4; Ralph, 200; Samuel, 4; Sarah, 4
MEYERS, Joseph, 53; Samuel, 268
MICHAEL, George, 31, 40, 51, 69; Hannah, 130
MICHELL, John, 358
MICHENER, Christina, 295; Isaac, 242, 357; John, 182, 295; Jonathan, 83, 229; Martha, 182; Mary Bean, 279; Priscilla, 253; Thomas, 296, 352; William, 83, 357
MIERS, Ann, 58; Barbara, 58; Elizabeth, 58; Frederick, 58; Jacob, 58; John, 58
MIFFLIN, Elizabeth, 66
MILES, Abigail, 162; Charles, 162; Hannah, 162; James, 162; Jane, 78; John, 162; Joseph, 162, 163; K., 162; Lowry, 162; Mary, 162; Rebecca, 162; Richard, 9, 162; Samuel, 162; Vister, 162; William, 162
MILHOOF, Catharine, 292
MILLER, Abijah, 145, 158; Adam, 61, 256, 346; Andrew, 22, 54; Ann, 328, 361; Ann Elizabeth, 23; Anna, 191; Anna Elizabeth, 23; Anna Margaret, 50; Anna Maria, 188; Anna Mary, 90; Anne Margareth, 23; Anthony, 13; Barbara, 50, 88, 119, 230; Benjamin, 54, 315; Catharine, 23, 88, 108, 109, 149, 251, 315; Charles, 251; Christian, 354; Christiana, 50, 23, 361; Christopher, 87, 347; Daniel, 109, 310, 350; David, 54, 340; Dillilah, 14; Elizabeth, 120, 163, 23, 88, 91, 108, 251, 314, 315; Enoch, 324; Eva, 50; Eva Elizabeth, 23; Eve, 192; Frederick, 50, 61, 192, 251, 256; Fridrick, 10; Fronica, 119; George, 23, 54, 328, 357; Henrietta, 166, 167; Henry, 251, 328, 353, 361; Isaiah, 87; Jacob, 23, 54, 65, 78, 87, 88, 91, 109, 185, 235, 273, 308, 327, 328, 360, 361; James, 351; John, 50, 23, 54, 65, 109, 160, 166, 235, 245, 315, 350, 361; John Adam, 50; John Daniel, 109; Jonah, 98, 317; Joseph, 54, 238, 306; Josiah, 251; Leonard, 251, 350; Leonhard,

23; Lowrence, 350; Ludwig, 350; Lydia, 251; Magdalena, 108; Margaret, 37, 166, 167, 251, 309; Margareth, 23; Maria, 34, 166; Martin, 166, 191; Mary, 14, 54, 62, 87, 122, 166, 230, 315, 338, 360; Mary Catharine, 109; Nancy, 235; Nicholas, 90, 144, 149, 199, 244, 361; Peter, 54, 234, 308, 329, 339; Philip, 54, 329, 340; Rosanna, 188; Samuel, 119, 251, 315; Sarah, 251; Sophia, 361; Susanna, 166, 167, 245; Thomas, 271, 305; William, 23, 251, 357
MILLIGAN, Ann, 349; James, 349; Joseph, 348, 349, 361
MILNE, Robert, 216
MILNOR, James, 310
MINNER, Jacob, 341
MINNET, James, 329; Priscilla, 329
MINNEY, 183
MINNICH, John, 245
MINNIGH, John, 131
MINTGER, William, 360
MINTZER, Ann, 224; Englebert, 328; Joseph, 224, 343; Mary, 328; William, 224, 282, 285, 295, 343
MISSAMER, Elizabeth, 151
MISSEMER, Cassimer, 213; Catharine, 213; Elizabeth, 213; Frederick, 213, 345; George, 213; Hannah, 213; Henry, 213; Jacob, 213; Margaret, 213
MISSIMER, John, 338, 345; John S., 267; Ruth, 308; Samuel, 338
MITCHEL, Hannah, 174
MITCHELL, George, 27; Grove, 296; Jacob, 278; Joshua, 278; Rebecca, 278; Sarah, 283; Thomas, 278; Thomas D., 278; William, 269, 278
MITCHENER, Ann, 133
MOCK, Catharine, 19, 211; Conrad, 199; Elizabeth, 211; Esther, 211; George, 2, 211, 212, 245; John, 71, 211, 212; Margaret, 211; Mary, 71; Veronica, 212; William, 71
MOHR, George, 58, 113
MOIER, John Christopher, 46
MOLAND, William, 19
MOLHERD, Johannes, 102
MOLL, Benedict, 32; Christopher, 33; George, 33;
Henry, 32; Mary Barbara, 32; Michael, 32
MOLSBERGER, John, 298
MONAHON, Catharine, 275; James, 276
MONAN, Patrick, 69
MONTANGE, Thomas B., 357
MONTANY, Thomas, 272
MONTANYE, Thomas B., 230, 311
MONTIER, George, 110; John, 110; Joseph, 110; Robert, 110
MONTULLE, John H., 59
MOODY, Ann, 187
MOORE, Abigail, 315; Ann, 297; Anna Maria, 191; Barbara, 69, 172, 348; Catharine, 255, 313, 345; Cato, 331; Charles, 125; David, 120; Edwin, 315; Eliza, 315; Elizabeth, 31, 201, 277, 354; George, 357; Hannah, 125, 277; Henry, 125; Jane, 215; Jesse, 182, 277; John, 56, 69, 119, 120, 121, 163, 215, 255; Jonathan, 215, 345; Margaret, 120, 201; Mary, 119, 120; Milcah Martha, 125; Mordecai, 125, 191, 269; Richard, 125, 192, 215, 315, 345; Robert, 269, 315; Roberts, 191; Samuel, 315; Samuel Preston, 125; Sarah, 315; Stephen West, 125; Thomas, 172, 215; Walter, 120; William, 31
MOREHAM, Elizabeth, 157; John, 157; Joseph, 157; Rachel, 157
MORGAN, Abraham, 321; Andrew, 99, 246; Anna, 250; Benjamin, 284, 349; Christiana, 5; Daniel, 5, 214, 246, 247, 349; Edward, 5; Eli, 208; Elizabeth, 208; Emma, 208; Enoch, 5; Hannah, 5; John, 106; Mary, 5, 208; Meriam, 5; Morgan, 151, 216, 240, 275; Rebecca, 246, 247; Richard, 250; Sarah, 5; Thomas, 99, 208, 247, 251, 303, 320, 321; William, 123, 124, 317
MORISON, William, 277
MORRIS, Abner, 290; Ann, 290; Anna, 152, 229; Anthony, 66; Catharine, 104, 189; Christina, 189; Elizabeth, 66, 189; George, 152; Hannah, 66; Isaac, 199, 214, 290, 305; Jacob, 169, 341; James, 24, 66, 104; Jane, 152, 229; Jeshua, 29; Jesse, 152, 174; John, 189; Jonathan, 104; Joseph, 66; Joshua, 332; Luke

W., 117; Lydia, 229;
Margaret, 189; Mary, 189;
Morris, 104; Owen, 17; Phebe,
66; Rachel, 125; Sarah, 193,
332; Susanna, 152, 189, 193;
Thomas, 80, 253; William,
152, 154, 290
MORRISON, John, 201, 210, 269;
William, 3, 339
MOSER, Christian, 169, 184;
George, 169; Henry, 356;
Margaret, 169; Peter, 169,
306
MOSES, Isaac, 335
MOSTELLER, Michael, 217; Peter,
217
MOTT, Richard, 255
MOUNT, Hannah, 280
MOURER, Hannah, 233; Mary, 233;
Peter, 353
MOWER, Henry, 204; Philibina,
204
MOWRER, Andrew, 328; Henry, 27;
Jacob, 328; John, 328;
Michael, 27; Philipbina, 27
MOYER, Abraham, 30, 70, 182,
217, 328, 336, 357; Ann, 259;
Baltzer, 352; Barbara, 30,
246; Benjamin, 240; Casper,
47; Catharine, 30, 107, 240,
328, 347; Christian, 182,
217, 311; Deborah, 246;
Dorothy, 135; Elisabeth, 30;
Elizabeth, 70, 246, 264, 354;
George, 240, 328; Hannah, 70,
328; Henry, 182; Jacob, 30,
47, 48, 170, 217, 264, 269,
328, 329, 354, 357; John, 30,
70, 71, 169, 352; Joseph,
217; Magdalena, 182;
Margaret, 70, 246, 328;
Margaretha Barbary, 47;
Maria, 217; Mary, 30, 70,
311, 357; Matthias, 135;
Michael, 130, 246; Molly,
182; Nanny, 182; Peter, 107,
246, 269, 347; Polly, 246;
Samuel, 159, 182, 264, 336;
Sarah, 47, 169, 217; Susanna,
182, 217, 329; Susannah, 70,
336; William, 352
MUCHELSTON, Mary, 342
MUCKELHOES, Agness, 56; Thomas,
56
MUCKELSTON, Peter, 342
MUHLENBERG, Ann Mary, 21, 22;
Ernest Henry, 22; Frederick
A., 22, 152; Henry, 54; Henry
Melchior, 21; Solome, 22
MULBNER, Nicoland, 80

MULL, Elizabeth, 137; Michael,
137
MULLEN, Israel, 353; John, 312;
Martha, 355; William, 201
MULLER, Jacob, 87
MULLIN, Agnes, 39; Isreal, 119;
Mary, 252; Sarah, 252;
William, 39, 73, 243, 252,
271
MULVENY, Patrick, 322
MUMBOWER, George, 172
MUNGESSER, Solomy, 147;
Valentine, 147
MUNNER, Peter, 8, 80
MURFEY, Edward, 328
MURPHY, Frances, 184; Francis,
317
MURRAY, Jessee, 336; Stephen,
336
MURREY, Jermina, 277; Stephen,
276; Thomas, 277
MYER, Samuel, 244; Susanna, 244
MYERS, Abraham, 354; Jacob,
197; Samuel, 354; Sarah, 354;
Susann, 117

-N-

NACE, Jacob, 220; Mary, 220
NAGLE, Grace, 235; John, 173
NAIR, Samuel M., 56
NAN, 20
NANNA, Abraham, 188; Elizabeth,
188; Hannah, 188; Reese, 188,
318; Sarah, 153; Susanna,
188; Tacy, 153; William, 153,
319
NARACKER, Anna, 136; Jacob, 136
NASE, William, 10
NASH, Daniel, 131, 344; John,
131; Joseph, 131, 258; Sarah,
131, 344; Susanna, 258;
William, 131, 258, 344
NAUGLE, Grace, 220; Jacob, 220
NAYLOR, Elizabeth, 94; John,
75, 94; Joseph, 75, 94
NEAL, Letitia, 43
NEALL, Letetia, 353
NEALY, Jane, 42; John, 42;
William, 42
NEATSMITH, John, 153; Margaret,
153
NEELIN, William, 146
NEICE, Elizabeth, 281; George,
281; Jacob, 281; Susanna, 281
NEIDIGH, John, 317
NEIMAN, Barbara, 140;
Catharine, 343; Charles, 146;
Elizabeth, 146; George, 140;
Henry, 317; Jacob, 317, 343;
John, 140; Mary, 140, 317;
Peter, 140; Philip, 140

NEISE, Abraham, 233; Catharine, 233; Dinah, 233; Elizabeth, 233; Eve, 233; Henry, 233; Jacob, 233; John, 233; Margaret, 233; Mary, 233; Michael, 233
NEISS, Abraham, 265; John, 265; Magdalena, 265; Philip, 265
NELSON, Catharine, 97; William, 97
NERMITH, John, 348
NERO, 85
NESS, Dewalt, 127
NESWANGER, Mary, 69; Sarah, 69
NEUMAN, Barbara, 169; Catharine Defrain, 93; Henry, 93; L., 47; Martha Elizabeth, 93
NEVIL, Adam, 145; Agness, 145; Catharine, 165; Elizabeth, 145; Frederick, 165; Henry, 56, 145; Jacob, 145; Peter, 145; Shelah, 145
NEWBERRY, Ann, 33, 317; Elizabeth, 33; George, 214; Henry, 33; Israel, 33; Isreal, 177; Jemima, 33; John, 33, 86, 214; Mary, 33; Rebeccah, 33; Sarah, 214; Sibilla, 177; Thomas, 33
NEWBOLD, Caleb, 304, 350; Margaret, 254; Michael, 254
NEWELL, Esther, 360; George, 90, 360; John, 360
NEWMAN, Henry, 68; Jacob, 165; John, 165, 221; Melchior, 361; Michael, 29; Susanna, 361
NICE, Abraham, 118; Barbara, 170; Charles, 333; Elizabeth, 170; Francoia, 170; Frederick, 170; George, 170, 278, 325, 342; Jacob, 269; John, 130, 145, 170, 336; Maria Elizabeth, 170
NICHOLAS, Elizabeth, 57; Jacob, 57
NICHOLASON, John, 317
NICHOLS, Anna Maria, 209; Arthur, 209; Arthur St., 209; Francis, 209; Harriet, 209; Martha, 209; Michael, 209; William Francis, 209
NICKLIN, Elizabeth, 346; Philip H., 346
NIESS, ---, 45; Catharine, 45
NILE, Hannah, 200
NIMAN, Conrad, 185
NINE, Elizabeth, 336; John, 336
NINES, John, 304
NINETUNHELSER, Elizabeth, 58; Michael, 58

NIPPES, Daniel, 254; Jacob, 67
NISE, John, 231
NIWMAN, Christopher, 34
NODDS, John, 195
NORMAN, David, 25, 84; Elizabeth, 85; Esther, 85, 316; Ezekiel, 85, 316; George, 85; Jonathan, 85, 316; Joseph, 327; Mary, 85, 316; Samuel, 85, 316; Sarah, 85, 316
NORMY, Andrew, 106
NORNEY, Andrew, 98, 189
NORNY, Andrew, 39, 118, 157, 160, 347; Hilary, 157; Solomon, 347
NORRIS, Charles, 225; Deborah, 225; Elizabeth, 218; Hephzibah, 225; Isaac, 85; Magdalena, 242; Mary, 225
NORTH, Ann, 8, 101; Anna, 8; Caleb, 8, 101; Elizabeth, 8, 101; George, 8; John, 8, 101; Joshua, 101; Jossua, 8; Roger, 8; Samuel, 8; Sarah, 8, 101; Sophia, 8, 101; Thomas, 8, 101; William, 8, 101
NOSSES, Mary, 10
NUSGROVE, Esther, 148; Joseph P., 148
NUSS, Ann Mary, 33; Catharine, 33; Conrad, 34; Jacob, 33; Margaret, 34; Michael, 33
NYCE, Catharine, 48; Elizabeth, 48; George, 219, 317; Jacob, 48; John, 48, 317; Margaret, 48; Mary, 48; Susannah, 48; Zachariah, 48
NYER, Daniel, 32; Godfrey, 32; Rosina, 32

-O-

OBERHOLSER, Jacob, 9
OBERHOLTZER, Abraham, 236; Azor, 245; Barbara, 65, 318; Catharine, 65; Elizabeth, 227; Henry, 65; Isaac, 65, 242; Jacob, 36, 65, 199, 227, 293; John, 65, 227, 357; Joseph, 65; Rachel, 242; Samuel, 13, 318
OBERTIER, Elizabeth, 317; Philip, 317
OGLEVIA, James, 196
OGLEVIE, James, 142
OHL, Andrew, 196; Maria, 196
OMENGETTER, Jacob, 314
OMENSETTER, Jacob, 283
O'NEIL, Arthur, 86; Hannah, 86; Mary, 86

409

ORTLIP, George, 351; Israel, 350; Isreal, 151; Mahlon, 350; Racheal, 151
OSBORN, Jonah, 349; Mary, 188; Nathan, 349; Randal, 214; Randel, 349; Richard, 349
OSBORNE, David, 222; Evan, 222; Jane, 222; John, 222; Joseph, 222; Margaret, 222; Robert, 222
OT, Barbara, 181; John, 181
OTT, Andrew, 117; Peter, 81, 102
OTTINGER, Alexander, 131; Ann, 180; Anna, 262; Catharine, 180; Charles, 131; Christopher, 12, 131, 189; Dorothy, 131, 180; Elizabeth, 180; Hester, 248; Isaiah, 131; John, 131, 179, 180, 199, 248, 262; Margaret, 180, 262; Mary, 131, 265; Rachel, 131; Rebecca, 180, 262; Sarah, 180; William, 131
OTTO, Catharine, 118; Dr., 118; Mary, 118
OVERDORF, Jacob, 294
OVERDORFF, George, 273; Jacob, 273; John, 273; Regina, 273
OVERHOLTZER, George, 355; Isaac, 78; Jacob, 338, 339, 355; Joseph, 78
OVERLANDER, Ann, 95; Christiana, 95; Franconia, 335; Fronica, 95; Henry, 95
OWEN, Humphrey, 197; Isaac, 348; Joshua, 197
OWENS, John, 352
OX, Ann, 123
OXFORD, Mary, 143, 169

-P-

PAGE, Deborah, 321
PAINER, George, 295
PAINTER, Catharine, 333; Jacob, 333; Mary, 120
PALMER, Charles, 143, 222; George, 143, 222; John, 222, 318; Joseph, 143; Linda, 10; Lydia, 222; Sarah, 341; Susanna, 222; Tacy, 143, 222; Thomas, 222, 318; William, 143, 222
PANNEBACKER, Henry, 75
PARISH, Robert Austin, 114
PARK, William, 167
PARKER, Elizabeth, 41, 209; John Ewing, 358; Robert, 41
PARRY, Benjamin, 36, 133; Charles, 36, 134, 340; Daniel, 36; David, 10, 36, 73, 74, 242; Elizabeth, 134, 261; Grace, 134; Isaac, 56, 57, 74, 134, 284, 360; John, 36, 134, 340; Margaret, 36; Martha, 73, 74; Samuel, 134; Stephen, 73; Thomas, 36, 49, 133
PARVER, Mary, 289
PASTE, Robert, 355
PATERSON, Stephen, 180
PATRICK, Rebecca, 138
PATTERSON, Elizabeth, 269; Joseph, 301; Mary, 293, 349; Rebecca, 301; Robert, 293, 326; Samuel, 195, 349
PATTON, Elizabeth, 156
PAUL, Andrew, 38; Ann, 190, 283; Anna, 154; Catharine, 318; Daniel, 38, 116, 190, 318, 331, 333; David, 38, 216, 318; Elizabeth, 6, 38, 190, 202, 283, 286; Esther, 190, 318, 347; Hannah, 38; Henry, 38; Jacob, 3, 89, 116, 124, 138, 153, 154, 190, 333, 334; James, 202, 215, 358; Jane, 190, 202, 283; John, 38, 138, 154, 283; Jonathan, 154, 190, 202, 283; Joseph, 153, 154, 318; Joshua, 232; Lillie, 202; Margaret, 333; Martha, 216; Mary, 190, 283; Mary Ann, 190; Samuel, 38, 154; Sarah, 283; Susanna, 190, 202; Susannah, 38; Sutton, 190, 202; Thomas, 154, 190; William, 38, 350
PAULING, Levi, 337
PAWLING, Barney, 53; Benjamin, 52, 53, 93, 330; Catharine, 53; Eleanor, 237; Elizabeth, 47, 49, 50, 93, 237, 318, 332; Fanny, 237; George, 281; Hannah, 93; Henry, 22, 52, 53, 237, 291, 301, 310; Jesse, 52, 53; John, 49, 52, 53, 163, 237, 318; Joseph, 93, 330; Levi, 53, 195, 257, 270, 304, 310, 337; Margaret, 237; Nathan, 52, 53, 318; Rachel, 93, 237; Rebecca, 22, 183, 330; William, 52, 53, 237, 291, 310; Willimina, 318
PAXON, Joshua, 205, 228
PAXSON, Isaac, 245; Mercy, 278
PAXTON, Elizabeth, 49
PEARS, Thomas, 207, 341
PECHIN, Nicholas, 167
PEEK, John, 51
PEGGY, 59

PEIRCE, George, 171, 173, 192, 217, 226, 246, 247, 257, 273, 274; Isaac B., 246; Mary, 274; Rebecca, 274
PENENGTON, Ann, 108
PENEVACER, William, 5
PENINGTON, Edmund, 46, 95; Jacob, 10; Jesse, 95; Will, 10
PENNEBACKER, Adam, 50; Adolph, 20; Ann, 172; Catharine, 172; Derich, 172; Elizabeth, 21, 172; Eve, 21; Frederick, 50; Hannah, 172; Henry, 21, 24, 28, 33, 47, 50; Jacob, 50, 172; John, 21, 50, 212; Ledia, 21; Magdalena, 50; Margaret, 172; Martha, 21; Mary, 212; Rebecca, 50; Samuel, 28, 37, 54, 107, 172; Sebilla, 50; William, 28, 37, 107
PENNEBCKER, Adolf, 212; Catharine, 212; John, 212
PENNEBECKER, Amos, 211; Benjamin, 177; Catharine, 343; Dorothy, 185; Henry, 101, 127, 143, 177, 246, 318; Jacob, 177, 267, 343; John, 185, 318; Magdalena, 177; Nathan, 237; Rebecca, 177; Samuel, 93, 185, 196; Sibilla, 177
PENNEPACKER, Adolph, 138; Henry, 318; Samuel, 318; Wyand, 318
PENNIBECKER, Elizabeth, 50; Jacob, 50; Nathan, 50
PENNINGTON, Abigail, 157; Edmund, 143, 184; Esther, 63; Rebecca, 157
PENNYBACKER, Jacob, 31
PENNYBECKER, Henry, 163
PENNYPACKER, Jacob, 354
PENROSE, Benjamin, 17; Jesse, 17; John, 17; Jonathan, 17; Joseph, 17; Mary, 17; Robert, 17; Samuel, 17; William, 17
PERCY, Mary, 266, 267; William, 357
PERFIRM, Thomas, 238
PERKINS, William Boyd, 278
PERRY, Isaac, 273, 274; Joseph, 277
PETERMAN, Ann, 230; Catharine, 64; Elizabeth, 64; George, 64; Hannah, 64, 230; Jacob, 56, 64, 207, 230; James, 230; John, 56, 64; Joseph, 230; Maria, 56; Mary, 56, 64;
Michael, 56; Priscilla, 230; Sarah, 64; Susannah, 64
PETERS, Edith, 16, 39; Elizabeth, 194; Henry, 194; Jane, 16, 39; Jonathan, 15, 39; Margaret, 16, 39; Rebeccah, 39; Samuel, 318; William, 16, 39, 188
PETERSON, Jacob, 6
PETTINGER, Amos, 102; Margaret, 102
PFLEAGER, George, 320
PHILIPS, Abner, 35; Abraham, 35; Elizabeth, 35; Hannah, 35; Jonathan, 315; Rebekah, 35
PHILLES, 22
PHILLIPS, Abraham, 128, 214; Alice, 128; Catharine, 41; James, 128; Jamima, 20; John, 20; Jonathan, 20, 41, 73, 128, 191, 192, 297; Joshua, 20, 41; Keziah, 41; Leah, 41; Mary, 20, 164; Phineas, 20, 41, 191; Phinehas, 297; Rachel, 41; Rebecca, 128; Samuel, 20, 41; Sarah, 20
PHIPPS, Abigail, 256; Abraham, 208; Agnes, 87; Ann, 208, 318; Catharine, 207, 208; Charlotte, 142, 145; Daniel, 207; Elizabeth, 87, 208; George, 207, 208; James, 256; John, 6, 87, 318; Jonathan, 87, 208; Joseph, 6, 96, 261; Joshua, 261; Margaret, 208; Maria, 208; Mary, 96, 193; Peter, 96; Priscilla, 208; Racheal; Rachel, 145, 208, 261; Rebecca, 87; Samuel, 87, 318; Sarah, 256; Squire, 87; Susanna, 6; Thomas, 96
PICHEON, Peter, 254
PICKERING, Jonathan, 105
PIERCE, George, 89, 102, 104, 116, 186
PILGER, Charlotte, 259; George, 259; Henry, 259; Ludwig, 19; Ludwig, 259; Magdalena, 19, 259
PIPER, Catharine, 51; Hannah, 69; John, 51, 311
PITT, Elizabeth, 318; John, 318
PITTING, John, 99
PLACE, Ann, 267; Benjamin, 267; Frederick, 267; Henry, 267; Jacob, 267; John, 267; Joseph, 356; Margaret, 267, 356; Peter, 267
PLAYTER, Mary, 96; Watson, 96
PLEAS, George, 270

PLIEM, Christian, 199;
  Elizabeth, 199; Esther, 199;
  Eve, 199; Mary, 199
PLUCK, George, 350; Peter, 350
PLUNKET, Sarah, 166
PLURNER, Carolina, 255
POLAND, Elizabeth, 318; George, 318
POLIZ, Catharine, 218; David, 218; Elizabeth, 218; Henry, 218; Jacob, 218; Valentine, 217
PORTER, Andrew, 41, 131; Benjamin, 308; Charlotte, 41; Elizabeth, 41, 131, 289; Harriet, 289; John, 307, 308; Joseph, 308; Margaret, 41, 308; Mary, 91, 308; Robert, 308, 332, 338; Stephen, 41, 46, 131, 173, 271, 308, 328, 338
POTTS, Abigail, 162; Alice, 121; Ann, 121; Anna, 77; Anthony, 12; Benedict, 168; Benedict D., 178; Charles, 121; Daniel, 122, 360; David, 59, 138, 214, 262, 318, 360; Davie, 214; Deborah, 138; Edward, 138, 186; Edward B., 150, 318, 342; Elizabeth, 180, 214; Esther, 121; Francis, 138; Francis R., 318, 343; George, 229, 237, 259, 285, 290, 292; George M., 126, 195, 322, 350, 351, 354, 355, 357, 359; George N., 267; Hannah, 180; Harriet, 315; Hartley, 121; Henry, 7; Herrcretta, 138; Isaac, 138, 154, 190; Isaiah, 121; James, 214; Jane, 121, 214; Jesse, 180, 184; Jessee, 338; Joanna, 59, 138, 262; Johan, 338; John, 59, 64, 138, 180, 230, 262, 331, 360; Jonathan, 180, 244; Joseph, 35, 59, 121, 122, 138, 262, 315, 318, 332; Lydia, 343; Margaret, 121; Martha, 121, 122, 138, 332; Mary, 35, 184, 315, 338, 360; Miriam, 360; Natha, 87; Nathan, 5, 9, 14, 15, 17, 26, 27, 35, 37, 38, 46, 53, 68, 87, 93, 109, 121, 122, 126, 149, 157, 168, 171, 176, 178, 193, 195, 202, 204, 205, 207, 229, 230, 236, 240, 241, 259, 264, 267, 268, 357; Nathan R., 357; Peggy, 340; Philip B., 340; Priscilla, 87, 180, 230, 268; Rebecca,

138; Ruth, 138; Samuel, 58, 138; Sarah, 59, 262, 315, 333; Stephen, 121; Thomas, 17, 59, 77, 138, 162, 180, 214, 262; Thomas M., 358; William, 77, 85, 356; William Robert, 122; Zebulon, 122
POWEL, Elizabeth, 187
POWELL, Edith, 196; Isaac, 334; Samuel, 106, 351; William, 278, 287
POWERS, William, 115
PRACHTHISER, Elizabeth, 28; Henry, 28
PRATT, Matthew, 26; Thomas, 337
PRAYOR, Thomas, 98
PREAST, Andrew, 242; Jacob, 242
PRETZMAN, Henry, 331
PRICE, Catharine, 336; Charles, 247, 297; Edward, 45, 52, 88, 247, 297, 326; Enoch, 247, 297; Hannah, 52, 181, 247, 297; Isaac, 247, 297; Jane, 52, 331; John, 52, 162, 276, 331, 334; Joseph, 52, 129, 143, 197, 228, 240, 297, 319, 326, 331, 340; Mary, 45, 52, 247, 276; Rebecca, 52; Rees, 88; Reese, 45, 247; Sarah, 240, 247, 297; Thomas, 247, 297; William, 336
PRICERER, Maria, 215; Peter, 215
PRICHARD, Anthony, 184; Joseph, 213; Mary, 213
PRICKART, John, 331
PRIEST, George, 330; Henry, 330; John, 337, 346, 360; Levi, 9; Matthias, 330; Phebe, 337; Samuel, 337
PRINCE, George, 346; Henry, 348; Jacob, 346, 348; Mary, 348
PRIOR, Joseph, 229
PRISE, Daniel, 147; Elizabeth, 147; George, 147; Hannah, 147; Henry, 289; John, 147; William, 147
PRITNER, Anthony, 106; Anthony Philip, 106; Hannah, 106; Isaac, 106; John, 106
PRIZER, Henry, 340; Isaac, 340; John, 175, 340; Peter, 300
PROCKDEN, Charles, 17; Elizabeth, 17
PROTZMAN, Barbara, 318; Conrad, 318, 336; John, 336
PRUNER, Jacob, 331
PRUTZMAN, Adam, 236, 237; Catharine, 236; David, 236, 237; Frederick, 237; Hannah,

236, 237, 318; Jacob, 237, 318; Mary, 237
PRYER, Thomas W., 182
PRYOR, Thomas W., 86
PUCHE, Elizabeth, 94; Magdalena, 94; Nicholas, 94
PUFF, Burkett, 350; Henry, 19, 343
PUG, Ann, 158
PUGH, Ann, 158; Henry, 356; James, 239; Job, 59, 141, 188, 337; John, 20, 37, 322, 341; Jonathan, 56, 121; Rachel, 20; Rebecca, 341; Ruth, 337; Samuel, 247; Thomas, 56, 267
PUHL, Thomas, 37
PURDY, William, 122
PYEWELL, John, 77

-Q-

QUEE, Seth, 318
QUICKLEY, Phebe, 67
QUILLMAN, Charles, 283; George, 283
QUINN, George, 246; Joseph, 245

-R-

RACOB, Catharine, 213; Christian, 212; Daniel, 212; Elizabeth, 212; Frederick, 212, 213; John, 212, 213; Joseph, 212; Mary, 212; Nicholas, 212; Susanna, 213
RADCLIFF, John, 261; Joseph, 261; Robert, 261
RAHN, John, 227
RALLWAGON, J. Frederick, 318
RAMBO, Aaron, 9, 44, 129, 143, 171; Abraham, 129, 171; Ann, 47, 171; Anna, 8; Benjamin, 156, 168, 195, 204; Catharine, 202; Charles, 171, 204, 240; Ebeneza, 347; Ebenezer, 83, 232, 240; Eleanor, 171; Eli, 129, 348; Elizabeth, 83, 86, 143, 204, 240, 318; George, 318; Gunne, 9; Gunner, 129; Hannah, 236; Harriet, 171; Jane, 204, 240; Jeremiah, 236, 318; John, 30, 129, 143, 223, 236, 318, 342, 345, 348, 358; Jonas, 39, 318, 358; Jonathan, 178, 202; Levi, 143; Magdalena, 171; Margaret, 83, 84, 202; Martha, 204, 239; Mary, 297, 318; Mary Ann, 294; Michael, 236, 347; Moses, 83, 129, 337; Nathan, 204; Peter, 9, 47, 84, 202, 312; Rachel, 83, 202; Samuel, 83; Sarah, 236, 318, 347; Tobias, 83; William, 83, 143, 345
RAMSEY, Alexander, 56, 230, 351, 361; Andrew, 56; Ann, 21, 361; Barbara, 218; Benjamin, 21, 55, 202, 351, 361; Charles, 156; Jacob, 205, 352; James, 318; John, 56; Joseph, 218; Lawrence, 205, 311; Margaret, 56; Martha, 56, 57; Mary, 56, 57; Sarah, 57
RAMSON, David, 245
RANDALL, George, 343; Nicholas, 343
RANDOLPH, Edward, 66
RANKIN, Jane, 343
RAPINE, Anna, 238; Elizabeth, 238; Jacob, 53; Reuben, 238
RAPP, Margaret, 208
RASOR, John, 161
RATCLIFF, Gayner, 118
RATTIFF, Joseph, 178
RATZEL, Frederick, 199
RATZELL, Frederick, 262
RAWLINS, Anna, 181; John, 181, 198, 344; Margaret, 198; Mary, 198; Nathan, 181, 198, 344; Ruth, 181, 198, 344
RAWN, John, 147
RAY, Margaret, 113
RAZER, Michael, 223
RAZOR, Abraham, 61; Agnes, 317; George, 317; Hannah, 61; Isaac, 61; Jacob, 61; John, 355; Margaret, 61; Melker, 61; Michael, 61, 355
REA, David, 50; Hugh, 11; Martha, 50
READ, Hester, 84
REALL, Samuel, 73; Sarah, 73
REDDING, William, 208, 278
REDHEFFER, Andrew, 15
REDHEIFER, Andrew, 131
REDLEY, Michael, 94
REED, Abraham, 74; Andrew, 37, 127, 207, 301, 322, 342; Baltsar, 102; Barbara, 74; Catharine, 102; Christiana, 102; Esther, 74; Hester, 226; Jacob, 23; John, 74; Joseph, 336; Mary, 74; Philip, 80, 102, 110, 127, 159, 172, 247, 251, 256, 264, 283, 294, 301, 341, 342, 352, 358; Susannah, 74
REEFINGER, Frederick, 347
REES, Abigail, 211; Ann, 290; Benjamin, 58, 207; Daniel, 58, 324; Eleva, 290; Eli, 86;

413

Elizabeth, 1; Esther, 86, 87;
Evan, 58; George, 134;
Hannah, 1, 58; Isaac, 282;
Jesse, 285; John, 1, 211;
Mary, 25, 282; Philip, 113,
211, 282; Rachel, 282;
Samuel, 58; Sarah, 87;
Susanna, 1, 282
REESE, Alexander, 134; Ann,
134; Benjamin, 271;
Christopher, 265; Elizabeth,
271; Enos, 319; George, 134;
Griffith, 134; Hannah, 134;
John, 247; Margaret, 134;
Mary, 247; Philip, 134, 319;
William, 265
REIBER, Catharine, 133; Jacob,
133
REICHSTINE, Catharine, 341;
Conrad, 341; Elizabeth, 341
REICKSTOOL, Jacob, 342
REIER, Jacob, 36
REIF, Frederick, 234; Jacob,
17, 234, 235; Jane, 234;
John, 234; Joseph, 234; Mary,
234; Samuel, 234
REIFF, Abraham, 179, 295; Anna,
244; Benjamin, 244, 247, 259,
299, 347; Catharine, 244;
Daniel, 179, 350; David, 120;
Elizabeth, 179, 244, 281;
George, 179, 244, 281, 302,
350; Jacob, 179, 244, 281,
350; John, 244, 343; Joseph,
179; Michael, 120; Rachel,
47, 49; Sarah, 281
REIFSCHNEIDER, Abraham, 223;
Catharine, 223; David, 223;
Dotterer, 223; Elizabeth,
223; Hannah, 223; Isaac, 223;
Jacob, 223; John, 223; Lidia,
223; Magdalena, 223; Sarah,
223; Sebastian, 223; Susanna,
223
REIFSNIDER, Elizabeth, 135;
Harman, 131; Peter, 135;
William, 135
REIFSNYDER, Andrew, 151;
Benjamin, 270; Catharine,
151; Elizabeth, 151; Hannah,
224; Harman, 166, 340;
Herman, 340; Jacob, 221, 267;
John, 166, 234, 270, 296,
306, 330, 340; Juliana, 341;
Margaret, 234; Mary, 151;
Michael, 330; Philip, 151;
Sebastian, 84; Veronica, 151;
William, 122
REIGHTER, George, 270
REIGNER, John, 223
REILEY, William, 290, 319

REILLER, Adam, 342
REIMER, Elizabeth, 267; Haines,
138; John, 267; Ludwick, 267;
Ludwig, 138, 139; Magdalena,
267; Peter, 138; Philip, 139,
147, 267, 334; Rachel, 333;
Susanna, 267
REINEOR, Melchior, 92; Rosina,
92
REINER, Abraham, 243;
Christian, 306; Elizabeth,
243; Hannah, 243; Henry, 243;
Isaac, 60; John, 243; Mary,
243; Philip, 243; Susanna,
243, 350
REINEWALT, Jonas, 216; Lydia,
216; Melchior, 216; Rosanna,
216
REINHART, Lawrence, 319
REINWALD, Balthaser, 263;
Regina, 263; Sarah, 263
REINWALT, Christopher, 125;
Jonas, 299; Mary, 125
REITER, Catharine, 159;
Catharine, 159; Christiana,
50; Elizabeth, 159; Eve, 159;
George, 50, 159; George
Micheal, 159; John, 159;
Margaret, 159; Martha, 159;
Mary, 159; Mary Elizabeth,
159; Micheal, 159; Peter, 159
RELLER, Catharine, 318;
Catharine, 159; Conrad, 318;
George, 318; John Conrad, 159
RENDELL, Joseph, 196
RENNINGER, Conard, 195, 196;
Conrad, 350; Elizabeth, 195,
236, 312; Frederick, 38;
George, 195, 313; Henry, 236;
Jacob, 195, 196, 236, 338;
John, 195, 236, 350, 358;
Magdalena, 236, 311;
Margeretha, 195; Maria, 236;
Mary Magdalena, 38; Peter,
144, 195; Susanna, 236;
Wendell, 195
RESE, Christiana, 23;
Elisabeth, 23; Harry, 23;
Jacob, 23; Magdalena, 23
RESH, Barbara, 153; Catharine,
153; Elizabeth, 153
RETHERFORD, John, 165
REUBEN, Jesse, 252
REUMOST, Anna, 3
REX, Ann, 136, 227; Anna, 228;
Catharine, 227; Christian,
227; Christopher, 136, 228;
Elizabeth, 330; George, 122,
260, 331, 357; Jacob, 86,
330; Jesse, 27, 189, 227,
228, 319; Margaret, 131, 136,

227, 228, 319, 349; Mary, 189, 228; William, 136, 189, 227, 228, 319, 320
REYMY, Mary, 158
RHOADES, Ezekiel, 359
RHOADS, Abraham, 218, 268; Ann, 158; Anna, 218; Barbara, 218; Eleanor, 218; Elizabeth, 218, 251; Ezekiel, 218, 341; Hannah, 218; Issacher, 268; Jacob, 204, 351; John, 193, 251, 336; Joseph, 218; Lydia Barbara, 218; Margaret, 218; Mary, 251; Peter, 275; Philip, 336; Rachel, 251; Rosanna, 268; Rosannah, 154; Sophia, 251; Susanna, 251; William, 251; Zebedee, 268
RHODES, Ezekiel, 91, 106, 323
RHODS, Ezekiel, 119, 317, 323
RIAL, Margaret, 29; Nicholas, 29
RIBERCOM, Ann, 132
RICE, Edward, 341; Lewis, 335
RICHABOUGH, Henry, 335
RICHARD, Catharine, 129; George, 315; Jacob, 129; John, 129, 302; Leonard, 129; Margaret, 129; Mary, 129; Matthias, 5; Peter, 302; Sarah, 302
RICHARDS, Caleb, 25; Charles, 149; George, 18, 149, 316, 343; Henry, 178; Hosiah, 25; Hugh, 1; Isaac, 1; Joel, 319; John, 1, 12, 25, 27, 29, 34, 48, 84, 112, 122, 128, 150, 165, 229, 233, 269, 329, 344, 360; Jonathan, 195, 292, 305; Joseph, 158; Margaret, 319; Maria, 225; Mary, 149, 233, 344; Matthew, 266, 327; Matthias, 22, 178, 345; Mths., 31; Patrick, 319; Peter, 1, 12, 90, 135, 147, 156, 160, 166, 196, 244, 248, 263, 324, 326, 332; Philip, 248; Rachel, 25; Richard, 1; Sally, 226; Samuel, 341; Solome, 22; Thomas, 66, 68, 77, 97
RICHARDSON, Eleanor, 169; George, 306; Joel, 169; John, 306; Jonathan, 169, 319; Mark, 306; Nancy, 306; Salome, 306; Sarah, 169; William, 169, 358
RICHS, Peter, 286
RICKER, Henry, 92, 166
RIDDLE, George, 318; John, 132; Mary, 132; Thomas, 318

RIDERPOGH, Barbara, 13
RIEFF, Ann, 314; George, 314; Israel, 314; Jacob, 314; Mary, 314; Rebecca, 314; Samuel, 314
RIEL, Nicholas, 112
RIETER, Michael, 251
RIFE, Jacob, 181; Mary, 16
RIGHTER, Anthony, 16; Bartle, 62, 193; Catharine, 193; Charlotte, 193; Elisabeth, 96; Elizabeth, 173, 174, 193; Hannah, 193; John, 62, 96, 181, 290; Joseph, 193; Mary, 193; Rebecca, 193; Rudolph, 193; William, 193
RILE, John, 340; William, 279
RIMBEY, Elizabeth, 128; Margaret, 128; Peter, 128
RINARD, Abraham, 76
RINEHART, John, 337
RINER, Daniel, 351; Henry, 351; Nicholas, 351; Philip, 286, 315
RINERD, David, 156
RINGFIELD, Catharine, 203; Margaret, 203; Maria, 203; Mary, 203; Wendle, 203
RITENHOUSE, Barbara, 58; Magdalena, 58; Matthias, 58; Sarah, 58
RITTENHOUSE, Benjamin, 155; Catharine, 58; Christopher, 68, 74, 84, 271; David, 38; Elizabeth, 293; Gertraude, 127; Henry, 68, 83; Jacob, 58, 243, 307; John, 68, 350; Joseph, 58, 293; Margaret, 319; Mary, 243, 252; Matthias, 58, 135; Muney, 58; Nanny, 58; Sophia, 68, 83; William, 58, 127, 319, 320; Zacharias, 185
RITTER, Jacob, 289; Mary, 141; Matthias, 141
ROAD, Casper, 338; Catharine, 338; Elizabeth, 13; Sophia, 13
ROADES, Ezekiel, 68
ROADS, Catharine, 350; Jacob, 350
ROAT, Abraham, 57; David, 57
ROBB, David, 119
ROBER, Abraham, 255; Christiana, 255
ROBERS, Algernon, 181
ROBERT, Benjamin, 143; Job, 128; John, 143
ROBERTS, Abraham, 184; Agnes, 243; Algernon, 11, 25, 81, 129, 143, 164, 169, 181, 184,

193, 196, 197, 242, 343;
Algernon S., 242; Algernor,
242; Amos, 28, 55, 258, 335;
Ann, 55, 67, 126, 184; Anna,
143, 146, 169, 242; Arnold,
97, 333, 359; Barbara, 134;
Cadwalder, 174, 200, 242,
243, 266, 303; Cadwallader,
39, 63, 73, 105; Catharine,
94, 97, 333; Charles, 55,
105, 162; David, 181, 197,
340; Edith, 28; Edward, 74,
97, 143, 197, 242, 243, 258,
333, 341; Eldad, 32; Eleanor,
211; Eli, 334; Elisabeth, 97;
Elizabeth, 10, 32, 88, 94,
126, 143, 162, 242; Ellend,
201; Ellin, 28, 126; Enoch,
99; Enos, 28, 258; Evan, 94;
Ezekiel, 73, 146, 243;
Gainor, 197, 242; George, 55,
105, 141, 143, 198, 241, 243,
273, 295, 312, 330, 334;
George W., 242; Hannah, 67,
97, 125, 162, 181, 237, 305;
Hannah Bartholomew, 191;
Hugh, 105, 181, 338; Isaac,
11, 28, 69, 105, 134, 143,
160, 197, 207, 237, 242, 254,
319, 350; Isaac Warner, 242;
Isreal, 162; Jacob, 66, 188;
James, 241; Jane, 32, 55, 67,
94, 126, 162, 330; Jeshu,
181; Jesse, 9, 12, 96, 111,
134, 239, 241, 290, 305, 319,
341, 352, 355; Job, 10, 28,
36, 75, 91, 95, 115, 126,
134, 153, 157, 158, 163, 201,
208, 213, 217, 230, 239, 240,
243, 259, 265, 266, 272, 273,
278, 285, 288, 297, 322, 353;
John, 3, 10, 21, 32, 36, 67,
97, 105, 116, 120, 126, 134,
143, 150, 162, 166, 169, 181,
191, 193, 197, 207, 211, 218,
220, 242, 260, 267, 312, 318,
330, 332, 337, 341, 359;
Jonathan, 37, 42, 73, 93,
105, 111, 113, 134, 165, 183,
184, 191, 197, 241, 291, 312,
315; Joseph, 1, 12, 17, 32,
64, 85, 105, 116, 207, 243,
318; Levi, 12; Lewis, 67;
Lydia, 143, 196, 242, 333;
Martha, 111; Mary, 12, 32,
39, 55, 67, 75, 97, 99, 162,
191, 197, 207, 229, 237, 241,
243, 315, 319; Matthew, 183,
191, 241, 252, 315; Mercy,
105; Mordecai, 32, 241, 312;
Nathan, 28, 214, 233, 335;

Nehamiah, 126; Owen, 120,
198; Peter, 105; Phebe, 162;
Phineas, 11, 181; Rachel, 67,
207, 249, 305, 352; Rebecca,
97, 181, 197, 208, 238, 290;
Rees, 55, 330; Richard, 39,
183, 237, 240, 243, 252, 273,
290, 319; Robert, 55, 162,
198, 295; Ruth, 12, 126, 237;
Samuel, 97, 134, 241, 333;
Sarah, 39, 42, 55, 94, 126,
237, 305; Septemus, 105;
Sidnah, 198; Sidney, 295;
Susanna, 111, 162; Sydney,
55; Tacy, 237, 242; Thaman,
181; Washington, 143;
William, 67, 94, 133, 237,
238, 241, 319
ROBESON, Abigail, 52; Ann, 129,
181; Conrad, 181; Eleanor,
88; Elizabeth, 88, 179, 181,
254, 313; John, 52; Jonathan,
16, 52, 88, 181; Joseph, 181;
Mary, 181, 257; Peter, 179,
254, 314; Rachel, 205;
Thomas, 52, 88, 129, 181
ROBIN, 49
ROBINSON, Ann, 133; Elizabeth,
175; Hannah, 352; Isaac, 284;
Israel, 103, 201, 307, 322;
James, 318; Jane, 284; John,
307, 318, 335, 360; Jonathan,
103, 133; Mary, 318; Peter,
112; Robert, 133; Samuel,
257; Sarah, 284, 360;
William, 97, 133, 209, 352
ROCKLEY, Richard, 188
RODARMEL, Samuel, 344
RODGERS, Joanna, 277; John,
277; John R., 277
ROEDER, Adam, 34; Anna
Margareth, 34; Barbara, 34;
Catharine, 33, 34; Eva, 34;
Hannah, 34; Henry, 34; John,
33, 34; Magdalena, 34;
Margaret, 34; Michael, 33;
Peter, 34; Susannah, 33
ROFF, Elizabeth, 266; Margaret,
266; Mary, 266; Samuel, 271;
William, 266
ROGERS, Grace, 137, 184; Ravard
Rarney, 201; William, 201;
William Tennent, 201
ROHR, Christian, 249; Hannah,
249
ROHT, Elizabeth, 27; Henry, 27;
Jacob, 27
ROLLER, John, 191
ROMCICH, Christian, 178
ROMFELD, Elizabeth, 196; Jacob,
196; Margaret, 196

RONEY, Mary, 288; Silas, 251
ROOP, Jacob, 219
ROOSEN, Henry, 135, 333; Jane, 333; John, 135, 149, 333
ROOT, Abraham, 346; Peter, 286
ROSEN, Jane, 359; John, 359
ROSENBERGER, Abraham, 186, 359; Barbara, 184, 293; Benjamin, 186; Catharine, 186; Christina, 186; Daniel, 186, 254, 345; David, 293; Deborah, 293; Dorothea, 254; Elizabeth, 109, 186; Frederick, 293; Froney, 293; Gertrude, 109; Hannah, 291; Hellena, 108, 109; Henry, 109, 186, 254, 293; Jacob, 227, 293; John, 186, 291, 293; Margaret, 359; Martin, 186; Mary, 186, 293; Samuel, 254; Susanna, 293; Yellis, 109
ROSENBERRY, Christian, 342; Hannah, 276; Henry, 276; Isaac, 276; Susanna, 276
ROSHON, Catharine, 225; Christian, 225; Christina, 225; Elizabeth, 173, 225, 268; Henry, 173, 225, 339; Jacob, 123, 173, 268; John, 225, 268; Maria, 123, 173; Molly, 225; Peter, 173, 225, 268; Philip, 173; Samuel, 268
ROSHONG, Henry, 40, 283, 358
ROSS, Clymer, 350; Elizabeth, 304; Rebecca, 261; Thomas, 304
ROSSEN, Henry, 135; Jenny, 135
ROSSENBRGER, Henry, 9
ROSSETTER, Samuel, 270
ROTH, George, 324; Henry, 273; John, 243
ROUDEBUSH, John, 139
ROUDENBAUGH, Ann, 254
ROUDENBUSH, John, 256; Michael, 246; Peter, 280
ROUSHONG, Henry, 342; John, 342
ROUTEBUCH, Jonathan, 302
ROUTEBUSH, Anna Mary, 137; Annamaria, 105; Catharine, 105; Henry, 105; John, 105; Michael, 105, 137
ROW, Elizabeth, 292; George, 318; Sarah, 292
ROWEN, Patrick, 319
ROWLAND, Benjamin, 58, 99, 138, 163, 197; John, 126; Mary, 85; Samuel, 276
ROWRY, Job Thomas, 184
ROYER, Catharine, 29; Dieter, 172; Elizabeth, 7; Elizabeth Catherine, 7; Jacob, 346; John, 7, 29; Joseph, 29; Mary Lizabeth, 172; Michael, 7, 29
RUBEN, Susanna, 189
RUCHON, Pierre, 225
RUCKSTOOL, Margaret, 90; Ulrick, 90
RUDDERTON, Jacob, 78
RUDOLPH, Anna Mary, 83; Christian, 83
RUDY, Catharine, 255; Charlotte, 255; Christiana, 255; Frederick, 19, 255; Jacob, 255; Maria, 255; Philip, 255; Polly, 255
RUE, Ann, 331
RUMER, Ann, 82; Catharine, 82; Dorothy, 82; Elizabeth, 82; Frederick, 82; Henry, 82; Jacob, 82; John, 82
RUMFIELD, Christina, 266; Henry, 266
RUMOR, Frederick, 280; Mary, 280
RUNTZ, Frederick, 38
RUPLE, Conrad, 334
RUSH, Barbara, 53; David, 53; Elizabeth, 53, 191; George, 53; Hannah, 191; Henry, 80; Jacob, 19; Katharine, 53; Lewis, 103; Louisa, 191; Mary, 103, 191; Peter, 191; Susanna, 174
RUSHER, John, 91; Magdalena, 91
RUSSEL, James, 101, 319; Mary, 101
RUTH, Abraham, 24, 38, 214, 331; Alana, 228; Catharine, 293; Charles, 204; David, 241; Elizabeth, 204, 293; Hannah, 204; Isaac, 293; Jacob, 262, 284, 293, 319, 292; John, 204, 228, 293, 335; Magdalena, 185, 293; Mary, 204, 293, 292; Nathaniel, 204; Philip, 204; Samuel, 335; Sarah, 293; Sinson, 185; Stinson, 255
RUTHERFORD, George, 288
RUTTER, Anna, 77; David, 59, 70, 77; James, 351; John, 59; Katharine, 77; Martha, 77; Mary, 77; Ruth, 77; Samuel, 77; Thomas, 77, 112
RYMAN, Christiana, 94; Daniel, 335; Henry, 335; William, 343
RYMER, David, 335; Lewis, 335
RYMEWALT, Abraham, 231; Catharine, 231; Christopher, 231; David, 231; Elizabeth, 231; Magdalena, 231; Maria,

231; Nancy, 231; Rachel, 231; Rosanna, 231; Susanna, 231
RYNEAR, Barbara, 86; Daniel, 7; John, 7, 86
RYNOLD, Catharine, 344; Daniel, 344
RYON, Hannah, 144; Mary, 215

-S-

SADLER, Philip Reed, 110
SAHLER, Catharine, 219; Elizabeth, 219; John, 219; Perter, 219; Sarah, 219; Susanna, 219
SAHLOR, John, 345
ST. CLAIR, Arthur, 117; Daniel, 117, 235; Rachel, 117
SAINTMAN, Mary, 13
SAKLOR, Gottfried, 322
SAL, 52
SALER, Peter, 252
SALOR, Godfrey, 113
SAMES, Jesse, 262; Sophia, 262
SAMMS, Ann, 309; John, 309; Mary, 309; Sarah, 309; Thomas, 309
SAMPEY, Ann, 237; William, 237
SANCE, Daniel, 130; Elizabeth, 130
SANCEY, Martha, 169
SANDMAN, Charles, 195; Christian, 195; Elizabeth, 195; George, 195; Henry, 195; Jacob, 195; John, 195; Lawrence, 195; Mary, 195; Michael, 195; William, 195
SANDS, Aaron, 157; Elizabeth, 157; Esther, 117, 157; Ezra, 157; Isaac, 157; Jacob, 157; James, 97; Joseph, 117, 157; Mary, 97, 200; Richard, 117, 157; William, 157, 200
SANKEY, Martha, 197
SANO, Eve, 159; Frederick, 159
SANSOM, Susan, 314
SASSAMAN, Jenry, 294
SASSEMAN, Henry, 41, 80, 99, 113, 115
SASSMAN, Henry, 288
SATZELER, Elizabeth, 174; Frederick, 174; Hannah, 174; John, 174, 175; Margaret, 174; Philip, 174, 175
SAUDER, Barbara, 300; Christian, 300; Elizabeth, 300; Henry, 300
SAUR, Frederick, 17
SAUREMAN, Peter, 201
SAUSIMAN, Henry, 52
SAUTER, Jabob, 38

SAVAGE, George, 331; Jeremiah, 331
SAVERY, William, 138
SAXON, John, 313
SAYBOLD, Ann, 298; Peter, 298
SAYLOR, Ann, 98, 265; Arnold, 274; Catharine, 173; Elizabeth, 98; Henry, 223; Isaac, 98; Jacob, 98; John, 173; Joseph, 98, 173; Mary, 98; Peter, 173, 185, 211, 265, 274, 347; Susanna, 223; Valentine, 173, 352
SCARLET, Mary, 188
SCHAFFER, John, 138
SCHANER, Christopher, 99
SCHANTZ, Jacob, 228
SCHARER, John, 64
SCHEDER, Catharine, 247; John, 247
SCHEETZ, Ann, 61; Catharine, 61; Elizabeth, 61; Frances, 187; George, 61; Henry, 8, 61, 118, 132, 208, 219, 340; Justus, 61, 240, 334; Mary, 61
SCHEIDE, John, 244
SCHEIFFLE, Christina, 40; George, 40; Jacob, 40; John, 40; Matthias, 40
SCHEIFLY, Catharine, 225; Jacob, 225
SCHEIVE, Catharine, 60; Elizabeth, 60; George, 60; John, 60; Margaret, 60; Martin, 60; Susannah, 60
SCHELEOP, Abraham, 306; Catharine, 306; Daniel, 306; Feronica, 306; Valentine, 306
SCHELL, John, 96
SCHELLE, Samuel, 300
SCHELLINGER, George, 320
SCHELOFF, Abraham, 186
SCHICK, Anna Mary, 15; Ludwick, 15
SCHIEVE, George, 77
SCHLATER, Barbara, 82, 341; Casper, 79, 82, 123, 168, 178, 189, 217, 234, 249, 335, 341, 342, 344, 347, 356; Catharine, 82; Elizabeth, 82; Hans Casper, 82; Jacob, 82, 347; John, 82, 186, 341; Ulrich, 250; Ulrick, 82
SCHLATTER, Casper, 65
SCHLEIFFER, Abraham, 91; Anna, 91; Elizabeth, 91; Henry, 91; Jacob, 91; John, 91, 96; Veronica, 91

SCHLICHER, Christopher, 83;
    George, 83; Henry, 83, 360;
    John, 360; Jost, 83
SCHLICHTER, John, 253
SCHLIEFFER, John, 83, 91; Mary,
    91
SCHLIVER, John, 34
SCHLOTTERER, George, 347;
    William, 347
SCHMIDT, John, 6
SCHMIT, Conrad, 188; John, 188;
    Thomas, 188
SCHNEIDER, Adam, 149;
    Christian, 199, 231, 232;
    Christiana, 2, 167;
    Christopher, 92; Elizabeth,
    2; George, 2, 92, 199; H.,
    234; Henry, 92, 167, 168,
    176, 199, 259, 278, 290;
    Jacob, 77, 83, 92, 211, 296,
    319; John, 92, 168, 196, 223;
    Juliana, 2; Margretha, 2;
    Mary, 199; Peter, 167;
    Rosina, 92; Samuel, 167;
    Seth, 167, 168; Sophia, 167;
    Susanna, 2, 196, 231;
    Susannah, 92
SCHNELL, Anna Dorday, 244;
    Christina, 244; Elizabeth,
    12, 244; George, 244; Hannah,
    244; Jacob, 244; John, 12,
    128; Mary, 244; Salome, 244;
    Samuel, 244
SCHNEYDER, Abraham, 250
SCHNIDER, Benjamin, 319; Henry,
    332; Jacob, 102; John, 332;
    Nicholas, 319; Seth, 164
SCHOENER, Elizabeth, 295; John,
    295; Maria, 295; Susanna, 295
SCHOENLY, Frederick, 310
SCHOLFIELD, Rebecca, 231;
    Samuel, 231, 237
SCHOLL, Abraham, 255; George,
    354; Jonathan, 354; Michael,
    4; Philip, 354
SCHOLTZ, Christopher, 133;
    Maria, 133; Rosina, 133
SCHOOL, George, 191
SCHRACH, Daniel, 147;
    Elizabeth, 147
SCHRACK, Catharine, 37; David,
    225; Gertrout, 37; John, 351;
    Lewis, 352; Martha, 206
SCHRAUDER, Frederick, 308
SCHREDER, Philip, 152
SCHREIVER, Catharine, 131;
    George, 131
SCHRIEVER, Ann, 319; Philip,
    319
SCHROEDER, Philip, 341

SCHULTZ, Abraham, 71, 308;
    Abrham, 84; Adam, 308; Anna,
    84, 283; Balthaser, 84, 150;
    Baltzer, 92, 182, 319, 345;
    Barbara, 327; Casper, 283;
    Christine, 194; Christopher,
    84; David, 83, 84, 194, 265,
    297, 345; Gabriel, 194, 283;
    George, 71, 84, 92, 194, 283,
    319; Gregory, 92, 319; Isaac,
    194, 265, 283, 308; Jeremiah,
    194; Joseph, 308; Juliana,
    194; Justus, 346; Ludwig,
    224; Matthias, 283, 345;
    Melchior, 146, 150, 169, 263;
    Melechior, 272; Regina, 308;
    Rosiana, 283; Susannah, 84;
    William, 194
SCHULTZE, Ann, 96; David, 95;
    Elisabeth, 96; Magdalena, 96;
    Mary, 96; Rosina, 96
SCHUNK, Barbara, 48; Christian,
    48; Elizabeth, 48; Francis,
    48; John, 48; Peter, 48
SCHUTZ, Henry, 353, 356
SCHWARTZ, Christian, 359;
    Esther, 114; Jacob, 114
SCHWEINHART, Michael, 316
SCHWEITSER, Catharine, 94
SCHWENCK, Andrew, 97;
    Catharine, 97; Daniel, 338;
    Elizabeth, 338; Jacob, 61,
    352; Maria Magdalena, 97;
    Matthias, 97
SCHWENK, George, 218, 228;
    Jacob, 41, 54, 200
SCHWISEFORT, Peter, 94
SCIPIO, 52
SCOTHRON, Lewis, 45
SCOTT, Agness, 56; Alexander,
    273; Andrew, 115; Edith, 204;
    Esther, 56; George, 56;
    Israel, 273; Jane, 273;
    Margaret, 56; Mary, 56;
    Susanna, 310; Susannah, 56
SCOUT, Elizabeth, 140;
    Jonathan, 110, 161, 231;
    Sarah, 67
SEAM, Elizabeth, 15; Philip, 15
SEAMS, Philip, 40
SEARFOSS, Catharine, 243;
    Frederick, 243
SEASHOLTZ, David, 264; Jacob,
    264
SEBOLT, John, 166
SECHLAR, Abraham, 33; Barbara,
    33
SECHLER, Abraham, 236;
    Elizabeth, 112; Henry, 112;
    Jacob, 246; John, 227;
    Susanna, 112

SEENKY, Thomas, 91
SEESHOLTZ, David, 312; Jacob, 339; John, 339; Lawrence, 339
SEIDLE, Anna, 146
SEIGLER, Catharine, 261; Dillman, 261
SEIP, Abraham, 351; David, 351
SEIPLE, George, 60
SEIVER, Catharine, 48; Frederick, 48
SEIWELL, Anthony, 199, 256; Catharine, 256; Elizabeth, 256; Henry, 256; John, 256; Maria, 256; Mary, 199; Valentine, 256, 338
SELAH, 69
SELEER, Abraham, 220; Ellis, 220; Jacob, 220; John, 220; Mary, 220
SELL, Abraham, 112, 341, 344; Anna Mary, 136, 137; Barbara, 112, 137; Benjamin, 32; Catharine, 137; Elizabeth, 137; Henry, 136, 137; John, 136, 137; Magdalena, 137; Margaret, 137; Margareth, 32; Philip, 137
SELLERS, Barbara, 71; David, 293; James, 203; Leonard, 71; Philip, 270; Sarah, 293; Tobias, 283
SELLS, Benjamin, 246
SELTZER, Frederick, 37; Henry, 79; John, 79; Mary, 79; Nicholas, 79
SENSENDEFFER, George, 265; Magdalena, 265; Sarah, 265
SENSENDERFER, Marin, 11
SENTMAN, Lavance, 13
SEPPERT, Michael, 245
SERVER, Jacob, 345
SERVOR, Catharine, 347; Philip, 347
SEYFREED, Anna Maria, 34; George, 34
SEYPEL, Catharine, 21; Valentine, 21
SHADE, Christian, 37, 176; George, 143, 243, 353; Henry, 142; Jacob, 142; John, 142, 220; Margaret, 142; Mary, 243; Nancy, 220; Susanna, 143
SHAEFFER, Elizabeth, 264
SHAFER, Samuel, 285
SHAFFER, Andrew, 137; Catharine, 137; Elizabeth, 137; George, 137; Henry, 137; Jacob, 137; Peter, 357; Susanna, 137; William, 137
SHAFOR, Barbara, 173
SHAIN, John, 272

SHAINLINE, Andrew, 319; Jacob, 171; Magdalena, 319
SHAMBACH, Daniel, 10
SHAMBACK, Dorothy, 185; Elizabeth, 185; Mary, 185; Philip, 185; Valentine, 185
SHAMBOUGH, Mary, 358; Philip, 97; Valentine, 358
SHANE, William, 238
SHANER, Andrew, 154; Christopher, 42
SHANNON, Amelia, 267; Amos, 267; Benjamin, 267; Elizabeth, 164, 183; Emelia, 117; Hannah, 21; James, 91, 117; Jane, 91, 267; John, 266, 267, 340; Lily, 90; Martha, 267; Mary, 91, 183, 267, 340; Rachel, 117; Rebecca, 91, 266; Robert, 21, 25, 39, 91, 238, 267, 324; Samuel, 266; Thomas, 117, 183, 266; William, 91, 164, 266, 332; William L., 231
SHANTZ, Abraham, 332; Barbara, 332; Isaac, 325, 332; Jacob, 148; John, 218
SHANZ, Jacob, 15
SHARE, Philip, 347; Sarah, 347
SHARER, Adam, 19; John, 56; Mary, 56; Valentine, 29
SHARP, Andrew, 350; Elizabeth, 125; Jacob, 125; John, 125; Mary, 350; Susanna, 125
SHAT, Henry, 63; Susannah, 63
SHATZ, Catharine, 102; Yost, 102
SHAUL, Adam, 145; Conrad John, 146; Elizabeth, 145; Jacob, 145; John, 145
SHAW, Charles, 123; Elizabeth, 160, 231; Joseph, 123; Martha, 123; Mary, 123; Moses, 80; Samuel, 123; Stephen, 359
SHAY, Jesse, 252, 277, 290; John, 233, 277, 290; Jonathan, 277; Mary, 277; Thomas, 277; William, 277
SHEAF, Margaret, 245
SHEAFF, Philip, 167
SHEARER, Elizabeth, 243; George, 352; Jane, 195; John, 157, 243, 313, 352; Jonathan, 304; Ludwick, 192; Margaretta, 192; Maria, 192; Peter, 352; Valentine, 192
SHEEN, Joseph, 353
SHEERMAN, John, 3; Margerat, 3; Robert, 3

SHEETZ, Ann, 16; Benjamin, 16; Catharine, 16; Conrad, 16; Elisabeth, 16; Ellis, 16; Francis, 16, 53; Frederick, 16; Henry, 15, 16, 19; Hester, 16; Sarah, 124; William, 16
SHEFFE, Christopher, 326
SHEID, Christian, 21, 40, 84, 309; Daniel, 130; Elizabeth, 130; George, 130, 309; Henry, 130; Jacob, 130, 294, 309; John, 130; Joseph, 130; Mally, 130; Susanna, 309
SHEIP, George, 78
SHEIRER, George, 290
SHEIVE, George, 266
SHEIVELY, Matthias, 321
SHELBY, Henry, 347
SHELLENBER, Philip, 184
SHELLENBERGER, Barbara, 196; Catharine, 78; Charles, 70, 78; Conrad, 78, 349; Elizabeth, 78; Eve, 78; Henry, 70, 78, 196, 307; Jacob, 78, 349; John, 77; Margaret, 78; Philip, 78
SHELLER, Barbara, 87; Ludowig, 87
SHELLY, Henry, 175; Joseph, 70; Mary, 70
SHELMIRE, Abraham, 288; Ann, 288; Benjamin, 288; Catharine, 288; Daniel, 288; George, 60, 92, 94, 123, 165, 189, 208; Jacob, 123, 165; John, 57, 94, 123, 165, 193; Lewis, 165; Martha, 165, 190; Mary, 288; Rachel, 189; Samuel, 165
SHENBERGER, Philip, 285
SHENEBERGER, Philip, 91, 172, 354
SHENLINE, Jacob, 236
SHEPARD, James, 133; Martha, 133; Mary, 133; Robert, 133; Thomas, 133, 247, 348; William, 133, 347
SHEPER, Daniel, 333; Elizabeth, 333
SHEPERD, Catharine, 165; Eleanor, 168; James, 168, 171; Jane, 171; John, 165, 168; Martha, 171; Mary, 168, 171; Robert, 171; Thomas, 171; William, 165, 171
SHEPHARD, Jane, 74; Martha, 74; Robert, 74
SHEPHERD, William, 118, 223, 352

SHEPPARD, Clement, 80, 245; John, 53; Morris Fletcher, 80; Moses, 52, 324; Sarah, 361; Thomas, 354, 361
SHERER, Barbara, 37; Catharine, 37; John, 37; Magdalena, 37; Mary, 37; Susanna, 37; Valentine, 37
SHERFF, George, 318
SHERMAN, Margaret, 210
SHERMER, John, 330
SHEWECK, Matthias, 348
SHIBLEY, Jacob, 164
SHICK, Barbara, 159; Elizabeth, 159; Frederick, 159; Henry, 159; John, 159; Ludwick, 318; Ludwig, 158; Rosina, 159
SHIENLIN, Frederick, 15
SHILLIG, Matthias, 81; Philip, 81; William, 81
SHILLIGH, Elizabeth, 37; Michael, 36; Susanna, 37
SHIMER, Mary Magdalena, 26
SHINER, Andrew, 122, 166; Christian, 340; Henry, 166; Juliana, 166
SHINLINE, Catharine, 242; Dolly, 242; Magdalena, 242; Susanna, 242
SHIPE, Abraham, 262, 293, 349; Elizabeth, 262; Henry, 262; Mary, 262
SHITTLER, Ludowig, 100
SHIVE, Catharine, 208; George, 208
SHIVER, Andrew, 135
SHLEIFFER, Daniel, 252; John, 47
SHLEISSER, John, 30
SHLETORA, William, 147
SHLIFER, Daniel, 352; John, 352
SHLONECKER, John, 241
SHOEMAKER, Abigail, 66, 313; Abraham, 110, 148, 184, 314; Agnes, 261, 301; Agness, 262; Ann, 201, 252, 255, 261, 297; Barbara, 254; Benjamin, 204, 205, 261, 301, 319; Catharine, 188, 281; Charles, 179, 221, 254, 255, 261, 283, 314; Comley, 354; Comly, 205, 261, 262, 302; Daniel, 64, 65, 107, 148, 155, 160, 188, 294, 336; David, 26, 64, 171, 201, 255, 260, 297; Dennis, 260; Eli, 205, 319; Elizabeth, 148, 179, 188, 219, 254; Ellen, 201, 297; Ellin, 5; Ezekiel, 39, 252, 261, 356; Frederick Michael, 106; Geoirge, 184; George,

40, 58, 162, 184, 254, 255, 261, 296, 314, 319, 329; Hannah, 64, 148, 252; Henry Michael, 82; Isaac, 7, 17, 25, 26, 37, 64, 108, 162, 254, 255, 260, 277, 296; Jacob, 58, 115, 128, 147, 184, 194, 261, 281, 338; James, 64, 65, 167, 319, 336; Jane, 201, 252, 254, 255, 261, 283, 297, 313; Jesse, 148, 314; John, 78, 122, 166, 170, 179, 221, 254, 255, 261, 332; Jonathan, 254, 255, 358; Joseph, 5, 66, 148, 158, 179, 184, 185, 252, 261, 314, 356; Lydia, 148, 261, 314; Malachi, 148; Margaret, 64, 201, 254, 260, 297; Martha, 64, 151, 179, 204, 245, 255, 261, 314, 334; Mary, 64, 148, 184, 188, 194, 201, 205, 254, 297, 302; Mathias, 9; Matthias, 350; Michael, 58, 115, 147, 157, 163, 181, 186, 200, 208, 220, 227, 249, 253, 254, 258, 265, 280, 284, 311, 336; Micheal, 164, 166; Nathan, 205, 255, 261, 262, 354; Nicholas, 269; Peter, 64, 65; Phebe, 336; Phoebe, 155; Rachel, 37, 205, 260, 261, 350; Rebecca, 64, 205, 245, 261; Richard, 39, 177, 245, 252, 261, 275, 276, 286, 314; Richard M., 194; Robert, 205, 261; Samuel, 39, 230, 261, 262, 288, 296, 302, 354; Samuel Charles, 314; Sarah, 115, 148, 162, 261, 301; Susanna, 148; Susannah, 58; Thomas, 23, 28, 64, 65, 121, 126, 138, 148, 162, 167, 182, 184, 185, 191, 194, 205, 237, 240, 245, 254, 255, 257, 261, 262, 276, 296, 298, 302, 307, 314, 316, 328, 337, 342, 350; William, 148, 255, 336
SHOENER, Jacob, 93
SHOESTER, Jacob, 338; Joseph, 338; Leonard, 352; Sophie, 352
SHOLL, Elizabeth, 253; George, 9; Hannah, 273; Jacob, 361; John, 361; Michael, 259; Philip, 253
SHOLTZ, Christopher, 133
SHONER, Christian, 351
SHOP, Elizabeth, 172
SHOSTER, Amy, 352; Jacob, 352
SHOT, Abraham, 114

SHOUP, John, 66
SHRACK, Elizabeth, 271; Hannah, 271; Mary, 271
SHRIVER, Benjamin, 333, 339; George, 333; Jesse, 339; John, 45, 333, 356; Mary, 339; Sarah, 356
SHUCK, Maria, 264; Peter, 264
SHULER, Benjamin, 339; Catharine, 21, 29, 269; Daniel, 269; Elisabeth, 29; Elizabeth, 90, 269; Gabriel, 26, 29, 41; Henry, 29, 30, 264; Hester, 269; Jacob, 90, 269; John, 21, 26, 29, 269, 339; Magdalena, 90, 269; Margaret, 29, 269; Maria, 269; Polly, 264; Samuel, 90, 269; Sarah, 269
SHULT, Abraham, 350
SHULTZ, Abraham, 22; Andrew, 355; Baltzer, 47; Balzer, 30; Christopher, 35, 265; David, 355; Isaac, 354; Matthias, 355; Melchior, 32, 33, 326, 337, 342; William, 354
SHULTZE, Melchior, 121
SHUNK, Abraham, 308; Christian, 308; Conrad, 108, 132; Francis, 175; John, 139; Martha, 206; Rebecca, 139
SHUPERD, Christian, 149; Christina, 149; Christopher, 149; Elizabeth, 149; Eve, 149; John, 149; Margaret, 149; Mary, 149; Philip, 149
SHUPPING, Catharine, 7; Nicholas, 7
SHUT, Barbara, 24; Elizabeth, 24; George, 24; Henry, 24; John, 24; Magdalena, 24; Margaret, 24; Rebeckah, 24
SHUTT, Abraham, 211; Barbara, 119; John, 119, 339, 355
SHWENCK, Abraham, 119; Fronica, 119
SHWINK, Abraham, 141; George, 153
SIBERT, Simon Felix, 59; Therese Sophia, 59
SIBLEY, Rachel, 164; Rudolph, 334
SIDDONS, Anthony, 7, 157
SIDEL, Dorothy, 102; Elizabeth, 102; Immanuel, 102; Michael, 102; Nicholas, 102
SIEBER, Elizabeth, 116; John, 116
SIEGFRIED, Joseph, 7, 22
SIESHOLTZ, Lawrence, 8

SIMPSON, Amos, 334; Job, 353; John, 57, 146, 334, 353; Martha, 65; Samuel, 114; Sarah, 146; William, 334
SIMSON, Samuel, 270
SINES, Conrad, 78
SINGER, Christina, 268; Elizabeth, 92, 268; Jacob, 235, 242, 268; John, 217, 268, 290; Margaret, 268; Peter, 92, 268
SININGER, Henry, 113
SINKET, John, 317
SINSENDERFER, Hannah, 340; Michael, 341
SINSINDERFER, George, 361
SIPLE, Cunrad, 15; Hannah, 15
SIREDELL, Hannah, 111
SISLER, Catharine, 236; Elizabeth, 236; Isaac, 236; Jesse, 236; John, 236, 350; Mary, 236; Michael, 350; Rachel, 236
SKEEN, Abraham, 33; Elizabeth, 353; Elmer, 223; James, 353; Jamima, 223; Jemima, 33; Mary, 223; Peter, 223; Rebeccah, 33; Samuel, 33, 223; William, 223
SKENN, Joseph, 250
SKERN, Mary, 211
SKIPPEN, Edward, 323
SLANECKER, Michael, 48; Susannah, 48
SLATTER, John, 61; Ulley, 61
SLAUGH, Kitty, 271
SLAUTER, Casper, 79
SLIFER, Abraham, 74; Daniel, 247; Davidf, 74; Elizabeth, 247; Esther, 247; John, 247; Susannah, 74
SLIGHTER, John, 187
SLINGLOOF, Hannah, 12; Henry, 12; Jesse, 12; John, 12; Joseph, 12; Samuel, 12, 216
SLINGLUFF, Hannah, 213; John, 232, 234; Mary, 213
SLINGOFFLIN, John, 180
SLOAN, Barbara, 102; Jacob, 102; James, 348
SLOANE, Catharine, 360; James, 332, 349; Mary, 360
SLOANECKER, John, 195
SLOTTERAR, William, 309
SLOUGH, Maria, 92; Nicholas, 92, 114, 296, 310
SMECK, Anna Mary, 165; John, 165
SMILY, William, 358
SMITH, Abraham, 80; Andrew, 165; Anna Mary, 90, 165; Barbara, 196; Barbarah, 5; Benjamin H., 167, 169; Benjamin Hays, 196, 197; Catharine, 165, 196, 224, 243, 306; Christian, 15, 176; Christina, 219; Christopher, 39, 229; Conrad, 6, 89, 90; Cornelius, 245; Daniel, 301; Elizabeth, 12, 58, 89, 108, 165, 196, 234, 294; Esther, 131; Frederick, 224; George, 58, 196, 306; Hannah, 229, 263; Henry, 57, 136, 145, 163, 165, 172, 219, 246, 301, 320; Isaac, 80; Isaiah, 263; Jacob, 12, 55, 79, 80, 89, 196, 224, 255, 286, 294, 302, 341; James, 102, 243; Jane, 330; John, 5, 43, 80, 89, 108, 131, 165, 196, 198, 219, 234, 301; Joseph, 219; Liss, 89, 90; Magdalena, 165; Margaret, 89, 90, 196, 294; Margareta, 79; Maria, 196, 286; Mary, 108, 131, 219, 319; Mary P., 315; Mary Susannah, 15; Michael, 319; Peter, 196, 301; Phebe, 305; Philip, 230; Philip Jacob, 348; Price, 243; Rachel, 131; Rebecca, 131, 155, 180; Resolve, 2; Richard, 306; Robert, 131, 160, 203; Samuel, 263, 282; Sarah, 294; Sophia, 294; Susanna, 196, 233; William, 112, 138, 206, 219, 237, 243, 319, 341; William Moore, 18
SMOYER, Henry, 130
SMYNERS, Mary, 187
SNARE, Jacob, 344; William, 344
SNEIDER, Conrad, 78; Jacob, 78; John, 78; Mary, 78
SNELL, George, 56; John, 77, 321
SNIDER, Ann, 10; Benjamin, 123; Henry, 130, 137; Jacob, 29; John, 324
SNOBLE, Catharine, 85; John, 85
SNOWDEN, Leonard, 174; thomas, 120
SNYDER, Abraham, 352; Adam, 50, 336, 350; Ann, 331; Anna Maria, 90, 278; Barbara, 90; Benjamin, 334; Catharine, 100, 166, 294, 333, 349, 352; Christian, 217, 298, 356; Christiana, 50, 90, 141, 294; Christina, 166, 294; Daniel, 189, 299, 336; Elizabeth, 90, 127, 166, 189, 247, 277, 294,

334; George, 50, 164, 247,
294; George Adam, 50; Henry,
21, 45, 90, 159, 189, 216,
263, 277, 294, 336, 355, 361;
Jacob, 50, 141, 166, 216,
243, 278, 294; John, 50, 100,
127, 166, 334, 352; Joseph,
299; Leonard, 90; Magdalena,
90; Margaret, 90, 166, 294;
Maria Elizabeth, 90; Michael,
110, 282; Nancy, 48;
Nicholas, 331; Phebe, 334;
Samuel, 189, 352; Seth, 351;
Thomas, 291; Valentine, 278
SOCKRITTER, Elizabeth, 209
SOLIDAY, Emanuel, 233; Eve, 233
SOLLADA, Frederick, 285
SOLLADY, Frederick, 298
SOPLATER, Casper, 79
SORBER, Catharine, 223;
Christiana, 185; David, 223;
Elizabeth, 185, 223, 245;
Jacob, 185, 222, 223, 245;
John, 185, 223, 245; Joseph,
245; Margaret, 185, 245;
Philip, 223
SORVER, John, 312; Margaret,
312; Philip, 312
SOUDER, Benjamin, 342;
Christian, 239, 342; Isaac,
336; Jacob, 342
SOUR, Catharine, 107;
Elizabeth, 107; Frederick,
107; John, 107; Margaret, 107
SOWER, Christian, 274;
Christopher, 319; Elizabeth,
8, 359; Frederick, 39; Jacob
G., 359; John, 39
SOWERS, Catharine, 173; Mary,
173; William, 228
SPAID, Barbara, 291; Christian,
291; Jacob, 291
SPARE, Benjamin, 319;
Catharine, 360; Daniel, 319,
344; Hannah, 310; Henry, 102,
310; Jacob, 344; Jonas, 360;
Mary, 319; Nathan, 360;
Philip, 301; Rosanna, 344;
William, 310
SPARY, Henry, 290; John, 290
SPATZ, Andrew, 270; Elizabeth,
270; John, 270; Maria, 270;
Rachel, 270; Sarah, 270;
Susanna, 270
SPEAK, Sarah, 173
SPEAR, Abraham, 361; Barbara,
113; Benjamin, 113;
Catharine, 113, 342;
Christina, 113; Daniel, 113;
Henry, 113; Jacob, 113;
Leonard, 113, 342; Mary, 113;
Philip, 113, 342
SPECHT, Adam, 66; Barbara, 66;
Catharine, 316; Christian,
341; Conrad, 66; Elizabeth,
66; Jacob, 66, 315; John, 66;
Magdalena, 66; Margaret, 66;
Peter, 66
SPEER, Catharine, 218; Jacob,
218
SPEES, Anthony, 1, 156;
Catharine, 156; Christian,
356; Christiana, 156; Daniel,
156; Margaret, 1, 156; Mary
Margaret, 156
SPEITLE, Barbara, 178; Joseph,
178
SPENCER, Abner, 219; Charles,
258, 263, 356; Elizabeth,
219; Enos, 18; George, 263;
Hannah, 158, 263; James, 18,
24, 219, 263, 268; Jarret,
86, 103, 329, 356; Jarrett,
258; Jesse, 265, 288; Job, 5;
John, 57, 86, 329, 343;
Josiah, 219; Lydia, 167, 170,
288; Mariam, 219; Mary, 67,
219, 247; Morgan, 219;
Priscilla, 288; Samuel, 98,
247, 298; Samuel E., 356;
Sarah, 18, 268; William, 219
SPENGLER, Elizabeth, 165; John,
165
SPERRY, Elizabeth, 176; George,
176; Jacob, 176; John, 176,
304; Margaret, 176; Peter,
176
SPIDLE, Joseph, 306
SPIKLE, Joseph, 326
SPOONE, William, 358
SPOTTS, Nathan, 180
SPRINGER, Barbara, 47; Daniel,
47, 336; Elizabeth, 257; Eve,
94; Gertrude, 257; Henry, 47;
Jacob, 47, 246, 257; John,
47, 94, 257; Joseph, 47;
Margaret, 257; Mary, 47;
Morris, 246; Susanna, 246;
William, 47
STACHLER, Christina, 172;
Peter, 172
STADDLEMAN, William, 6
STADELMAN, Mary, 6; Thomas, 6;
William, 6
STAFF, Frederick, 235
STAGER, Adam, 104; Hannah, 104;
Jacob, 105; Peter, 104, 105;
Philip, 104
STAGNER, Ludwig, 291
STAHL, Christina, 38;
Elizabeth, 196; Eva Martha,

57; John, 38, 196; Melchior, 57
STALFORD, Elizabeth, 284
STALL, Christian, 319; Daniel, 44, 130, 294, 319; Esther, 294; James, 70, 338; John, 35, 338; Ulrich, 135
STALNFORD, Catharine, 53
STAM, John, 62
STANBERGER, John, 227
STANERT, Catharine, 76; Hannah, 76; Jacob, 76; John, 8, 18, 19, 76; Lewis, 50, 75, 76, 92; Nancy, 76; William, 76
STARE, Deborah, 222; Rosanna, 222
STARK, Ludwig, 305; Maria, 305
STAUFFER, Abraham, 242; Catharine, 135, 242; Christian, 135, 237, 242; Dorothy, 135; Elizabeth, 242; Garret, 135; Hannah, 242; Henry, 242, 354; Jenny, 135; John, 242, 314; John Ulrich, 135; Mary, 242; Rachel, 242; Rudolph, 242; Sarah, 242; Ulrich, 242
STAUT, Lydia, 8
STEALY, John, 98
STEARNE, Samuel, 268, 353
STEDGOON, Mary, 16
STEEL, Ephraim, 131; Esther, 131; John D., 358; Robert Smith, 131
STEELEY, William, 189
STEER, Catharine, 118; Christian, 318, 319; Daniel, 118; Frederick, 118; George, 118; John, 124; Joseph, 124; Mary, 118, 319
STEEVER, Michael, 301
STEGNOR, Christian, 305
STEIN, Barbara, 37
STEINBACK, Martin, 353
STEINROOK, Anna, 306; Christian, 306; John, 306; Margaret, 306; Samuel, 306
STEITEL, Emanuel, 293
STELER, Henry, 211; Margaret, 211
STELL, John, 248
STELLER, Isaac, 342; John, 342
STELTZ, John, 321; Valentine, 344
STELY, Jacob, 64
STEM, Alice, 337; Conrad, 341; Frederick, 83; Hannah, 83; John, 341; Peter, 12
STEMPLE, John, 285; Lydia, 332; Rachel, 275; Thomas, 216; William, 285

STEPHENS, Abijah, 215; David, 215, 280; John, 333; Mary, 186; Morris, 215; Robert, 186; Sarah, 280
STERIGER, David, 161; Elizabeth, 161; John, 65, 161; Margaret, 161; Martha, 161; Mary, 161; Peter, 72, 107, 161; Sarah, 161; William, 161
STERN, Henry, 303; John, 253; Salomi, 253
STETLER, Abraham, 89, 225, 305; Adam, 225; Catharine, 225; Christian, 225, 359; Elizabeth, 305; Henry, 225; Liss, 89; Salomi, 225
STEVENS, Abijah, 354; John, 327
STEWART, Ann, 201, 311; Ann T., 277; Christopher, 319; Elizabeth, 319; Francis, 164; Hannah, 173, 180, 231; James, 328, 339; Jane, 164, 183; John, 173, 231; Joseph, 173; Maria, 311; Maria Eleanor, 201; Mary E., 277; Robert, 173; Sarah, 236; Solomon, 117, 125, 173; Thomas, 173, 339; William, 183
STEYER, Barbara, 32; Leonard, 229; Nicholas, 32
STICHTER, George, 101; Magdalena, 101
STIER, Henry, 298
STILES, Edward, 306
STILLWAGGON, Frederick, 353; Henry, 353; Joseph, 353; Michael, 346
STIMPLE, Ann, 57; Benjamin, 57; John, 57; Thomas, 57
STINSON, James, 243
STIRKE, George, 14; Henry, 14; James, 14; Rebeckah, 14
STITLER, Catharine, 345; John, 345; Michael, 345; Samuel, 345
STOCKER, John C., 59; John Clemens, 77
STOFFER, Garret, 144; Jacob, 38
STOKES, Joshua, 245; Mary, 245
STONEBURNER, Margaret, 104
STONG, Barbara, 150, 224; Conrad, 224; Frederick, 224; Henry, 224; Jacob, 224; Philip, 150, 224
STORM, Joseph, 191; Margaret, 191
STOTT, John, 150
STOUCH, George, 114
STOUFFEN, Matthias, 338

425

STOUFFER, Abraham, 35;
  Catharine, 218; Dillman, 218;
  Elizabeth, 357; Garnet, 218;
  Jacob, 195, 213; John, 218,
  358; Joseph, 357; Margaret,
  218; Matthias, 132; Susannah,
  34
STOUT, Abraham, 4, 19, 20, 36;
  Catharine, 189; Elizabeth,
  232; Frederick, 232; George,
  232, 321; Henry, 180, 232;
  Jacob, 232; John, 232;
  Jonathan, 100; Peter, 232,
  273; William, 232
STOUVER, Catharine, 83;
  Christian, 62, 83; Matthias,
  322
STOVER, Abraham, 246, 264;
  Henry, 354; Jacob, 354;
  Joseph, 354
STRAFFORD, Thomas, 267
STREEPER, Barnabas, 279;
  Bernard, 350; Catharine, 85,
  279; Christiana, 279; Daniel,
  85, 279; Deborah, 85; Dennis,
  85; Elizabeth, 279; George,
  69, 85, 355; Jacob, 85, 350;
  John, 11, 69, 85, 279, 354;
  Leonard, 11, 85, 279; Lydia,
  69; Magdalena, 69; Margaret,
  85; Mary, 85; Peter, 85, 161,
  279; Rebecca, 85, 279;
  Samuel, 279; Sarah, 69, 279;
  Susanna, 85; William, 69, 85
STREIGHT, Christian, 22
STREIT, Emeline, 282
STREPER, Abraham, 319; Ann,
  337; Daniel, 344; George,
  258; John, 45; Mary, 319;
  William, 337
STREPERS, Ann, 275; Catharine,
  275; Deborah, 275; George,
  275, 276; Margaret, 275;
  Mary, 275; Rebecca, 275;
  Susanna, 275, 276
STRICKLAND, Miles, 103
STRINGER, Sarah, 153
STROMAN, Anna, 264; Barbara,
  90; Charles, 264; Christina,
  264; Elizabeth, 264; Henry,
  264, 344; Jacob, 264; John,
  90, 264; Joseph, 264; Maria,
  264; Polly, 264
STROUD, Edward, 27; Elisabeth,
  27; James, 27, 38; Joshua,
  27; Joshua Josiah, 27; Mary,
  27, 125; Samuel, 27; Thomas,
  27, 35; William, 38
STROUP, John, 336
STROWMAN, John, 280; Rebecca,
  278

STRUKER, Christian, 199;
  Elizabeth, 200; Jacob, 200
STUART, Christopher, 22, 106;
  Elisabeth, 22; Jane, 42;
  John, 42; Lawrence, 42;
  Robert, 84; William, 42
STUBERT, Elizabeth, 107
STURGES, Mary, 161
STYER, David, 266, 284, 343;
  Elizabeth, 319; Henry, 319,
  343; Jacob, 319, 352; John,
  175, 343, 352; Leonard, 343;
  Stephen, 352; Tacey, 175;
  Tacy, 149
SUCH, Mary, 331
SUE, 78
SULLIVAN, Anthony, 342
SUPLEE, Mary, 55
SUPPLEE, Abraham, 126; Andrew,
  39, 83, 126, 170, 337; Ann,
  39; David, 110, 170; Deborah,
  126; Edward, 360; Eleanor,
  169; Elizabeth, 39; Enoch,
  110, 117, 149, 170, 173, 196;
  Hannah, 126, 218, 240; Isaac,
  39, 55; Jacob, 55, 126; John,
  5, 39, 126, 240; Jonathan,
  169; Magdalena, 39, 126;
  Margaret, 21; Martha, 39;
  Mary, 55, 83, 126; Nathan,
  126; Peter, 75, 315; Phebe,
  126; Rachel, 126, 337;
  Randolph, 311; Rebecca, 126;
  Samuel, 126; Sarah, 126;
  Susanna, 170; Zimmerman, 337
SURBER, Ann Mary, 136; Barbar,
  117; Elizabeth, 136; Jacob,
  136; John, 136; Joseph, 136;
  Margaret, 136
SURNS, George, 355
SUSANNAH, 22, 53
SUTCH, Benjamin, 319; Mary,
  319; William, 319
SUTTON, Robert, 222
SWAINE, Francis, 22, 111, 152
SWANER, Anna, 332; Peter, 332
SWANKERT, Philip, 353
SWANNER, Margaret, 319
SWARDLEY, John, 360; Samuel,
  360
SWARTZ, Abraham, 258, 259;
  Andrew, 153, 259, 339; Anna,
  258; Catharine, 259;
  Elizabeth, 258; Esther, 339;
  Eve, 132; Henry, 258; Isaac,
  259; Jacob, 65, 132, 258,
  259, 339; John, 132, 258;
  Joseph, 258; Mary, 258;
  Philip, 258; Samuel, 258
SWEITZER, Barbara, 48; Henry,
  26, 27, 43, 60, 63, 81, 88,

92, 93, 104, 107, 139, 147, 163, 210, 300; Simon, 48, 107
SWEIZER, Henry, 28
SWENCK, Abraham, 333; Eva, 72; George, 72, 123, 333; Henry, 72; Jacob, 72; John, 72, 332, 333; Mary, 72; Regina, 72
SWENK, Abraham, 99; Anna Barber, 181; Barbara, 181; Catharine, 105; Daniel, 105; Elizabeth, 181; George, 181, 332; Jacob, 34, 181, 322; John, 15, 34; Martin, 181; Mary, 54, 181; Mary Magdalena, 181; Nicholas, 180; William, 54
SWINEHART, Anna Maria, 227; Daniel, 227; Henry, 150, 314, 350; John George, 350; Michael, 229
SWINFORD, Mary, 239; Peter, 239
SWINK, Catharine, 240; George, 240; Jacob, 318
SWISEFORT, John, 319; Mary, 319; Peter, 319
SWISHER, Mary, 196
SWITZER, Henry, 30
SWOYER, Magdalena, 223; Nicholas, 223
SYBRANA, Samuel, 334
SYFRET, Bolster, 9; Boltser, 9; Catharine, 9; George, 9; Margaret, 9; Michael, 9
SYKEN, 132

-T-

TARRANCE, Mary, 330
TATNAL, Joseph, 138
TATT, Michael, 145
TAYLOR, Agness, 115; Catharine, 173; David, 115; Eleanor, 50, 200, 343; Elizabeth, 99, 115; Hannah, 36, 103; Isaac, 36; Jacob, 103; Jane, 146; John, 70, 139, 174, 201, 204, 238, 306; Jonathan, 115; Joseph, 99, 115, 332; Lewellyn Joe, 174; Lydia, 115; Magdalena, 126; Mary, 115; Morris, 17, 115; Rebecca, 115; Robert, 50, 343; Susanna, 332; Susannah, 70; Thomas, 200
TEA, Ann, 17
TEANY, Christiana, 296; Henry, 135, 353; John, 353; Joseph, 294
TELP, Abraham, 53; George, 53
TENANY, John, 188
TENNENT, Christopher, 273; Susanna, 201, 277; William, 120; William M., 201

TENNIS, Christian, 358; Hannah, 136; Israel, 136, 320; Jane, 320; Levina, 136; Magdalena, 136; Mary, 136; Rachel, 136; Samuel, 136; William, 136
TERRY, William, 358
TETEMENT, Susanna, 175; William M., 175
THAW, Ann, 357; Benjamin, 320; Charles, 190; Jacob, 160; John, 320; Mary, 190
THOADS, Margaret, 351
THOMAS, A., 298; Abel, 98, 160, 181, 350, 357; Alice, 339; Ann, 242, 312, 320, 357; Anna, 98; Aubrey, 154; Benjamin, 337, 346; Charles, 346, 358; Christiana, 277; Daniel, 226; David, 33, 91, 98, 137, 154, 157, 184, 286, 339, 353; Eleanor, 154, 336; Elijah, 287; Elizabeth, 33, 85, 91, 242, 287; Ellen, 181; Enoch, 261, 287; Evan, 42, 137, 157; George, 114, 272, 284; Grace, 137, 184, 226; Hannah, 160, 242; Henry, 359; Howell, 277; Isaac, 198, 332, 337; Isaiah, 139; Jacob, 190, 242, 272; Jane, 137, 177; Jerusha, 133; Jesse, 272; Job, 137, 222; John, 52, 115, 137, 157, 163, 177, 220, 226, 235, 242, 268, 272, 327, 336, 353; Jonathan, 3, 64, 88, 94, 97, 242, 245, 260, 339; Joseph, 137, 157, 171, 235, 245, 259, 268, 304, 310, 312, 332, 334, 357; Levi, 337; Lydia, 154; Margaret, 91, 137, 157, 190, 222; Martha, 154, 242; Mary, 98, 105, 134, 226, 261, 287, 336; Mordecai, 242; Mordecia, 122; Nathan, 245, 272; Owen, 3, 24, 42, 49, 137; Rachel, 137, 157, 222, 242, 357; Reuben, 242; Richard, 320; Robert, 137, 157; Samuel, 137, 157, 184, 198, 222, 226, 242, 248, 259, 285, 287, 342; Sarah, 91, 181, 222, 226, 272; Stacy, 310; Susanna, 137, 157, 222; Tacy, 242; Thomas, 154; William, 67, 154, 184, 200, 224, 225, 287, 320, 344
THOMASON, James, 22; Rachel, 170; William, 6
THOMPKINS, Isaac, 336
THOMPSON, Benjamin, 331; Hannah, 320; James, 143;

John, 121, 326; Mark, 331;
Robert, 320, 331; Ruth, 45;
William, 335
THOMSEN, John, 191
THOMSON, Archibald, 74; Daniel,
320; Ganor, 39, 40; Geanor,
185; James, 331; John, 39,
40, 70, 76, 185, 261, 296;
Jonah, 39, 40, 185; Margaret,
39, 40, 185; Mark, 74;
Martin, 74; Mary, 74; Peter,
35, 66; Rachel, 40, 185;
Robert, 74; Robert Curry, 74;
Tacie, 40; William, 70, 331
THORNTON, Ann, 190; Joseph, 90
THORP, Jacob, 193
THURNINGER, Benjamin, 320
TIMANUS, Catharine, 63, 120,
121; Conrad, 120; Henry, 320,
329; Rosanna, 120
TINTSHMAN, Elisabeth, 27
TOBY, 78
TODD, Andrew, 47, 183, 227,
287, 334; John, 139;
Margaret, 213; Martha, 320;
William, 320
TOLAN, Hannah, 255
TOLBERT, Amos, 146
TOLEY, 69
TOM, 52
TOMKIN, Jacob, 178
TOMKINS, Abigail, 19; Ann, 277;
Anna, 232; Benjamin, 232;
Benjamin D., 232; Elizabeth,
19; Isaac, 140, 242, 277,
289; Jacob, 232; Jacob E.,
232; John, 19; Joseph, 179;
Samuel, 177
TOMLINSON, Thomas, 359
TOMPKIN, Jacob, 94
TOMPKINS, Ann, 87, 320, 360;
John, 357; Jonathan, 320,
343; Lydia, 343; Samuel, 360
TOOL, Aaron, 341; Aquilla, 341
TORBET, Elizabeth, 175; James,
175; Samuel, 175; Thomas, 175
TORBIT, Andrew, 30; Samuel, 30
TORRENCE, Mary, 98; Samuel, 98
TOWER, William, 304
TOWERS, Archibald, 337;
Elizabeth, 337; William, 303,
308, 313
TOWMILLER, Christopher, 197,
198; John, 198; Mary, 198
TOWNSAND, Grace, 186
TOWNSEND, Mary, 96
TOWSAND, Ezra, 355
TOY, Mary, 330
TRAYXLER, Elisabeth, 27; Mary,
27
TREAT, Rebecca, 11

TREDAL, Mary, 190
TREXLER, Catharine, 234, 320;
Elizabeth, 107; Peter, 320
TREXLEY, David, 254
TRIMBLE, Ann, 181; Mary, 193;
William, 193
TROLLINGER, Andrew, 358; Peter,
358
TROXEL, Henry, 357; John, 140;
Suffia, 16
TRUCKEMILLER, Lewis, 93;
Rachel, 93
TRUMBORE, Abraham, 358; George,
94, 358; Susanna, 94;
Susannah, 358
TRUMBOWER, George, 342;
Susanna, 342
TRUMP, Abraham, 75, 182; Anna,
182; Catharine, 359; Daniel,
75; Elizabeth, 46, 182, 327;
Eva, 34; Grace, 182; Hannah,
75, 182; Jesse, 31, 98, 182,
274; John, 46, 76, 182, 209;
Levi, 69; Lydia, 182;
Margaret, 46; Michael, 182,
242; Peter, 34; Rachel, 133;
Sarah, 46, 182
TRUNER, Abraham, 303; David,
303; Jacob, 303; John, 303;
Joseph, 303; Margaret, 303
TUCHS, Jacob, 223
TUCKER, Elizabeth, 339; Isaac,
339; Jonathan, 41
TUNIS, Jane, 181; Richard, 52,
326
TURNER, Abraham, 145; Ann, 348;
Peter, 71; Susanna, 145;
William, 348
TWADDLE, Charles, 47; Deborah,
47, 49; James, 47; John
Pawling, 47; Rachel, 47;
William, 47, 50
TYSON, Abraham, 18, 31, 320,
347, 352, 359; Agnes, 111;
Agness, 18; Ann, 194, 210;
Barbara, 194, 294; Benjamin,
83, 111, 160, 231; Catharine,
194, 234; Christina, 264;
Cornelius, 153, 196, 242,
270, 348; Daniel, 351;
Eleanor, 42, 287; Elijah,
231; Elizabeth, 83, 194, 231,
234, 271, 287; Grace, 189;
Hannah, 83, 111, 151, 206,
210, 231, 287; Isaac, 18, 75,
76, 111, 150, 151, 163, 174,
194, 206, 253, 345; Jacob,
83, 163, 271, 354, 359; Jacob
Sorver, 215; Jane, 158, 238;
Jesse, 83, 111; John, 18, 75,
111, 141, 144, 151, 155, 170,

182, 193, 194, 206, 253, 261, 282, 288, 311, 320, 323, 348, 349, 352, 354, 360; Jona, 163; Jonas, 264; Jonathan, 52, 136, 231, 234, 345; Joseph, 18, 43, 150, 153, 159, 163, 194, 213, 218, 242, 250, 270, 294, 320, 334, 343, 348, 353; Joshua, 163, 297, 332; Leech, 151; Magdalena, 126; Magdelane, 194; Mahlon, 282; Margaret, 42, 43; Mary, 31, 63, 75, 83, 111, 163, 194, 287, 288, 294, 351; Matthew, 67, 110, 136, 151, 234; Matthias, 194; Peter, 42, 43, 83, 111, 160, 163, 294, 345; Rebecca, 18, 151, 231, 282; Robert, 351; Rynear, 18, 31, 42, 43, 83, 88, 111, 159, 160, 234, 265, 281, 331; Ryner, 151; Samuel, 31, 235; Sarah, 18, 111, 234, 253, 287; Seth, 75, 151, 206; Susanna, 287, 348; Thomas, 18, 42, 43, 75, 83, 189, 253, 287, 288, 301, 320; William, 18, 31, 63, 76, 194, 282, 355

-U-
ULMER, John, 51
ULRICH, Jacob, 132, 250
ULTZFESSER, George, 23; Margareth, 23
ULYCH, Adam, 168; Jacob, 168; Joseph, 168; Margaret, 168; Mary, 168; William, 168
UMSTAD, Anna, 231; John, 230, 275; Jonas, 275; Mary, 231
UMSTATE, Harman, 76
UMSTEAD, Alice, 250; Hannah, 250; Henry, 320, 331; Herman, 320; Jacob, 115, 250, 354; John, 122, 138, 320, 323, 331; Richard, 250
UMSTED, Arnold, 307; Barbara, 252; David, 307; Harman, 307; Jacob, 307; Joseph, 307; Magdelane, 194; Mary, 307; Richard, 194; Thomas, 307
UNDERKOFFLER, Anna Mary, 31; David, 31; Elizabeth, 31; Eva Mary, 31; Jacob, 31; Mary Eva, 31; Regina, 31
UNTERGOFFLER, Annmercy, 115; David, 115; Efamary, 115; Elizabeth, 115; Jacob, 115; Mary Efa, 115
UPDEGRAFF, Abraham, 9
UPDEGRAVE, Ann, 23, 360; Edward, 23; Joseph, 23

UPDEGROVE, Abraham, 320; Ann, 226; Edward, 331; Elizabeth, 214, 331; Henry, 193, 320
UPTECRAVE, Abraham, 158
URFER, Baltzer, 72, 339; Barbara, 72; Catharine, 72; David, 72; George, 72; Gertrude, 72; Mary, 72; Michael, 72, 339; Susannah, 72
URMY, Barbara, 135; David, 135, 355; Henry, 3, 135; Isaac, 135; John, 135; Joseph, 62; Magdalena, 135

-V-
VAN BURKIRK, Jacob, 330; Mary, 330
VAN COURT, Charles, 310; Cornelius, 310; Elizabeth, 310; Hannah, 310; John, 310; Jonathan, 310; Maria, 310; Sarah, 310; William, 310
VAN DIKE, Jacob, 165; John, 165
VAN FOSSEN, Benjamin, 159; Leonard, 171
VAN HORN, Dorothy, 134
VAN HORNE, William, 68
VAN WINKLE, Peter, 256
VANCOURT, Daniel, 347; Jane, 114, 116
VANDERSLICE, Anthony, 138; Augustus, 257, 298; Edward, 257, 298; Elizabeth, 138, 340; Jacob, 257, 298, 320; John, 138, 257, 298; Joseph, 200, 257, 298; Marcus, 298; Mark, 257; Mary, 257; Rebecca, 138, 175; Thomas, 257, 320
VANDYKE, Aaron, 340
VANFOSSEN, Anna, 299; Arnold, 335; Barbara, 299; Benjamin, 299; Eleanor, 299; Frania, 299; Jacob, 325; John, 299, 335; Joseph, 119; Leonard, 335; Margaret, 299; Matthias, 299
VANHORNE, Ann, 103
VANPELT, Samuel, 25
VANSANT, Catharine, 90; Cornelia, 213; Hannah, 90; Henry, 213; Rebecca, 213; Thomas, 302
VANWINKLE, Elizabeth, 185; Peter, 185
VARLEY, Henry, 336
VAX, James, 53
VELVET, Elizabeth, 334
VERNER, Elizabeth, 63, 320; George, 63

VOEGELY, Conrad, 127; Solome, 127
VOGELL, Anna Maria, 2; Conrad, 2; George, 2; John, 2; Nicholas, 2; Philippina, 2
VOGLE, George, 148

-W-

WACK, George, 275
WAEF, George, 91
WAGENER, Anna, 3; Christopher, 342; David, 3; Gertraut, 3; Jacob, 3; Melchior, 3, 4, 12; Susanna, 3
WAGENOR, Grace, 46
WAGER, Abigail, 157; Benjamin, 14, 55, 120, 157; Cartry, 14; Gartry, 14; Hannah, 14; Jacob, 14; Jesse, 14, 156; Mary, 157
WAGGONER, Barbara, 344; Catharine, 321; Conrad, 342; David, 322; Margaret, 95; Peter, 321
WAGGONSELLER, Peter, 338
WAGNER, Anna Mary, 37; Balter, 224; Catharine, 37, 182, 224; Dorothy, 224; Elizabeth, 224, 270; Frederick, 224, 269; George, 224; Hannah, 37; Henry, 333; Isabella, 269; Jacob, 270; John, 37, 182, 224; John D., 37; Mary, 37, 181, 224, 355; Michael, 181, 336; Peter, 224; Susannah, 333
WAGONER, Eve, 187; George, 187; Sarah, 187
WAGONSAIL, Elizabeth, 71; John, 71
WAGONSELLER, John, 53, 329; Peter, 329
WALD, Frederick, 316; Molly, 316
WALDON, John, 331; Magdalena, 331
WALKER, Anna, 70; Daniel, 359; David, 70; Joseph, 67, 192; Lewis, 70; Mary, 120, 244, 332; Michael, 332; Thomas, 70
WALLACE, Elizabeth, 321; William, 321
WALN, Nicholas, 63
WALT, Barbara, 329; Casper, 329; George, 332; Henry, 219, 339, 345; Jacob, 329
WALTER, Abraham, 93; Catharine, 203; Charles, 172; George, 130, 203; John, 203; Joseph, 262; Mary, 203; Samuel, 259;

429

Walter, 93; William, 203, 259, 284
WALTEREN, Philipbeana Elisabeth, 26
WALTERS, Abraham, 76; Jane, 337; Jonathan, 337
WALTON, Abigail, 158; Amos, 49, 270; Ann, 270; Anna, 82; Anthony, 358; Charles, 107, 108; Elizabeth, 18, 64, 82, 108, 155, 167, 270; Hannah, 65; Isaac, 49, 133, 237, 256, 263, 270, 273, 285, 331; Isaiah, 107, 108, 258, 270; Jacob, 107, 108, 258, 270; James, 133; Jeremiah, 49, 82, 83, 132, 155, 229, 270; Jesse, 49, 270; John, 155; Jonathan, 49, 270; Joseph, 49, 270; Lydia, 270; Margaret, 132; Mary, 49, 82, 107, 108, 154, 270; Phebe, 36, 82; Rachel, 203; Samuel, 133; Sarah, 82, 134; Silas, 49, 82, 83, 155, 321; Thomas, 30, 49, 82, 83, 321; William, 125
WAMBACH, Bartholomew, 183; John, 183
WAMBACK, Bartholemew, 108; Bartholomew, 255; Barthw., 112; Gerdraude, 108; John, 255
WAMBOLD, Barbara, 202, 220; Catharine, 202, 220; Daniel, 15, 202; David, 15, 202, 349; Elizabeth, 202; Frederick, 355; George, 202, 220, 349; Henry, 202; Isaac, 224; Jacob, 202, 220, 355; John, 202; Margaret, 202; Maria, 349; Mary, 202
WAMPOLE, Abraham, 115, 157; Catharine, 115, 157; Elizabeth, 115; Eve, 115; Frederick, 115, 157; Isaac, 115; Jacob, 115, 157, 246, 338, 345; Magdalena, 115; Maria, 115; Mary, 115
WAMPOLT, David, 102; Elizabeth, 102
WANAMAKER, Philip, 357
WANNAMAKER, Christian, 225; Elizabeth, 225; Frederick, 255
WANOMAKER, Nicholas, 304
WARD, Dennis, 320; Hugh, 181; Joseph, 207; Joshua, 313; Mary, 207; Rebecca, 116, 120, 166, 181, 208; William, 181
WARDER, John, 317; Thomas, 317

WARE, David, 295; Rachel, 295
WARING, Edward, 306; Elijah, 306; Sarah, 306
WARLEY, Henry, 6, 42, 99, 204, 295; Lewis, 295
WARNER, Anthony, 320; Catharine, 258; Christian, 258; Dewalt, 258; Hannah, 160, 258, 350; Isaac, 93, 116, 120, 160, 166, 181, 206, 209, 226, 249; Israel, 333; Jacob, 298; John, 258; Joseph, 289; Peter, 194, 258, 287, 316; Rachel, 320; Susanna, 194; Thomas, 249; William, 160
WARREN, George, 205
WARTHAN, Adam, 194
WARTHMAN, Adam, 361; Matthias, 60
WARTMAN, Caterine, 5
WASHEN, Margaret, 90
WATER, Mary, 96
WATERMAN, Abigail, 96; Charles, 96, 194; Hannah, 19, 96, 317; Humphrey, 19, 45; Isaac, 39, 96, 194; Isaiah, 96, 169, 317; James, 194; John, 194; Joseph, 96, 169, 194, 317; Phineas, 16, 194; Priscilla, 317; Rebecca, 194
WATKIN, Isaac, 319
WATKINS, Catharine, 140; Sarah, 144
WATSON, Mark, 280
WATTS, Arthur, 68; John, 69, 79, 103, 117, 133, 152; Silas, 50, 60, 67; Siles, 18
WAULT, Barbara, 280; Catharine, 280; Christiana, 280; Elizabeth, 280; Jacob, 280; Margaret, 280; Mary, 280; Sophia, 280; Susanna, 280
WAXELLER, Letitia, 240; Matthias, 240
WAYNE, Charles, 202
WEAN, Appollo, 33; John, 33; Wendel, 352
WEAND, Wendal, 360; Wendel, 247
WEASNER, Anna Mary, 83; George, 83, 320; Gertrude, 83; Henry, 83, 351; John, 329; Leonard, 329; Martin, 83; Morton, 320
WEAVER, Abraham, 253; Adam, 205; Elizabeth, 253, 264; Eve, 11; George, 73, 125, 250, 336, 340, 352; Hannah, 205; Henry, 155, 264, 336; Hiltner, 253; Jacob, 268; John, 250, 260; Peter, 353; William, 205, 253

WEBB, A., 123; Paul, 174, 337; Thomas, 166
WEBER, Abraham, 100, 224, 320, 352; Amos, 265; Ann, 32; Anna, 243; Benjamin, 243, 320, 349; Catharine, 243; Christian, 320, 330, 350; Elizabeth, 100, 243, 244, 268; Eve, 320; George, 32, 350; Hannah, 32, 243; Jacob, 61, 186, 230, 243, 268, 280, 320, 335, 353, 356; John, 32, 350; Joseph, 335; Mary, 31, 32, 243; Rebecca, 243; Sarah, 32; Susanna, 243, 280; Tacy, 230
WEBSTER, Ann, 339; George, 34, 323; Joseph, 34, 142, 145, 272; Margaret, 213; Mary, 175; Oliver, 213; Sarah, 34; Thomas, 175, 241, 343; William, 339
WEEGENER, Ann, 3; Christopher, 3; Rosina, 3
WEEK, George, 320; John, 341; Margaret, 320, 341
WEEPERT, William, 280
WEEST, Casper, 268; Elizabeth, 268; Francis, 268; Mary, 268
WEIDEMOYER, Jacob, 309
WEIDMAN, Anna Mary, 31; George, 31; Regina, 31
WEIDNER, Elizabeth, 147; Jacob, 147
WEIGNER, Catharine, 320
WEIKLE, Samuel, 232
WEIL, Elizabeth, 54; Peter, 54
WEINE, Jacob, 62; Mary, 62
WEINLAND, Benjamin F., 84
WEIREMAN, Abraham, 302; Barbara, 302; John, 60; Jonathan, 302; Mary, 60, 302; Michael, 302; Nancy, 302; Sophia, 302
WEIRMAN, John, 78
WEIS, Christina, 26; Christopher, 26; Elizabeth, 26; Frederick, 26; Hannah, 26; John, 26
WEISE, John, 325
WEISEL, George, 301
WEISER, Conrad, 22; Benjamin, 54
WEISNER, Catharine, 314; David, 314; Elizabeth, 314; George, 314; Henry, 314; John, 314; Martin, 314
WEISS, ---, 258; Jacob, 146; Johannes, 80; John, 54; Susanna, 146; William, 307, 328

WEIST, Esther, 353; George, 353
WEITNER, Abigail, 71; Abraham, 71; David, 71; Deborah, 71; Elizabeth, 71; George, 71; Margaret, 71; Rachel, 71
WELKER, Dietrick, 320; George, 212; Jacob, 91, 137, 212; John, 91, 212; Margaret, 212; Susannah, 91; Veronica, 120
WELLS, Abel, 19; Edward, 331; Elizabeth, 209; George, 359; Henry, 116, 120, 166, 181, 208; Isaiah, 195, 350; Jacob, 181; James, 111; Joseph, 116, 120, 166, 208; Levi, 331; Lydia, 93, 315; Miriam, 93; Peter, 93; Sarah, 179; William, 132, 331, 359
WELTZ, George, 207; Michael, 207; Susanna, 207
WENNER, John, 341; Samuel, 341
WENSLEY, Daniel, 275; Mary, 275
WENTS, Jacob, 216; Jonathan, 216; Levi, 216; Lydia, 216; Samuel, 216
WENTZ, Abraham, 150, 188, 203, 261, 264; Albert, 261; Appellonia, 150; Barbara, 150; Benjamin, 264; Catharine, 139, 150, 207; Christopher, 272; Daniel, 261; Elizabeth, 35, 36, 139, 207, 331; Frederick, 150; George, 261, 337; Hannah, 188, 261; Jacob, 10, 207; John, 26, 91, 132, 143, 150, 172, 188, 203, 207, 208, 243, 261, 285; John P., 207; Magdalena, 10; Magdelena, 150; Mary Magdalena, 207; Mordecai, 264; Nancy, 150; Peter, 10, 150, 320, 333; Philip, 4, 10, 139, 150, 331; Rebecca, 261; Samuel, 258, 261, 304; Sophia, 262, 264; Susanna, 150; Susannah, 261; Valentin, 10; Wendel, 10; William, 35
WERTSNER, Adam, 115
WEST, James, 122; Richard, 357; William, 321
WETZEL, Elizabeth, 159; John, 159
WEYANT, Wendal, 7
WEYERMAN, John, 38; Martin, 38
WEYERMEM, Martin, 57
WEYMAN, Christian, 54
WHEELER, Enoch, 117; Samuel, 174
WHITBY, Anthony, 301, 353; John, 353

WHITCOMB, Ann, 330; John, 330; Joseph, 330
WHITE, Abner, 33, 180, 355; Ayres, 177; Benjamin, 255, 343; David, 100; Elizabeth, 334; Hannah, 176, 180; Henry, 144; Isaac, 120; Isaiah, 100; Jabez, 176; James, 20, 100, 228, 253; Jane, 69, 100, 180, 334; John, 9, 139, 155, 177, 254, 321, 361; Joseph, 155, 177; Josiah, 100; Lydia, 176; Marcey, 68; Mary, 9, 33, 120, 176, 254; Nancy, 100; Priscilla, 9; Rachel, 100; Robert, 33, 180; Sarah, 44; Solomon, 254, 361; Thomas, 33, 98, 100, 248, 253, 254, 343; William, 33, 180, 310, 315, 321, 343; William M., 347, 355
WHITEHEAD, Bob, 211; Hannah, 304; R., 211, 295
WHITELOCK, Isaac, 351
WHITEMAN, Hannah, 230; John, 230; Mary, 156
WHITESIDE, James, 136
WHITMAN, Elizabeth, 60; Jacob, 60; John, 60, 320; Maria, 60; Michael, 320
WHITTEN, Abednego J., 209
WHITTON, Amy, 133; Martha, 133; Mary, 133; Richard, 78
WIAND, Andrew, 176; Daniel, 282; David, 176; Elias, 176; Henry, 282; Scharlota, 176; Sibilla, 176
WIANT, Catharine, 286; Wendel, 286
WICK, Balthazar, 320
WICKS, William, 344
WIDEMIRE, George, 342
WIDENER, Peter, 107
WIEANT, Barbara, 251; Catharine, 252; Daniel, 251, 252; Elizabeth, 252; Henry, 252; John, 252; Maria, 252; Michael, 252; Samuel, 252; Susanna, 252; Wendel, 251; Yost, 251
WIEN, John, 159
WIERMAN, Anna, 109; Hellena, 109; John, 339; Michael, 109, 339; Molly, 339
WIESS, George, 328, 329
WILBARHAM, Thomas, 43, 44
WILBERHAM, Margaret, 99, 130; Thomas, 99
WILDBAHN, Charles Frederick, 334
WILEY, Thomas, 345

WILFONG, Andrew, 164; John, 164
WILGUS, John, 235
WILLARD, David, 278; Duffield, 278; Esther, 278; Isaac, 278; Jesse, 208, 278; Margaret, 278; Thomas, 278
WILLAUER, Christian, 187, 255; Elizabeth, 255; Jonathan, 255, 256; Mary, 187, 255; Samuel, 255
WILLHELMS, Elizabeth, 218
WILLIAM, George, 276; John L., 276; Thomas, 276
WILLIAMS, Ann, 112, 259; Anthony, 111, 161, 253; Benjamin, 185; Charity, 125; David, 358; Eleanor, 251; Elizabeth, 112, 120, 251, 253, 259; Ellin, 112; Enoch, 112; George, 67, 96, 121, 134, 170, 261, 276; Hannah, 169, 197, 276; Isaac, 112, 192, 261, 342; Jesse, 228; John, 112, 134, 161, 251, 276; John L., 170; Joseph, 21, 48, 65, 161, 259; Margaret, 185; Mary, 36, 189, 243, 259, 345; Rachel, 161; Richard, 228; Samuel, 265; Sarah, 105, 112, 259; Theophilus, 28, 71, 99, 251; Thomas, 112, 276; William, 112, 120
WILLIAMSON, James, 302; Sarah, 302
WILLS, Ann, 53; Elizabeth, 156; Jane, 73, 156; Jeremiah, 73, 156, 330; John, 73, 156; Mary, 73, 156, 270, 330; Michael, 73, 156, 270, 274, 330, 357; Rebecca, 73, 156; Sarah, 156
WILLSON, James, 18
WILSON, Amos, 296; Ann, 106, 198, 200, 333; Bird, 209; Catharine, 321; David, 193, 296; Eleanor, 317; Elizabeth, 193, 260, 296, 348; Enos, 317; George, 152; Hannah, 174, 233, 260; Henry, 106; Isaac, 193; Isabella, 200, 314; James, 161, 200, 260; Jane, 106; John, 42, 86, 106, 164, 177, 184, 193, 200, 233, 296, 314, 340; Joseph, 106, 184, 296, 333; Joshua, 349; Margaret, 106, 260; Mary, 106, 200, 355; Matthew, 200; Oliver, 164, 193, 332; Peter, 281; Rachel, 193, 349; Rebecca, 193, 296; Robert, 355; Samuel, 193; Sarah, 142, 184, 197, 220, 296, 349; Stephen, 193; Tacy, 106; Thomas, 73, 124, 125, 156, 161, 200, 260, 321; William, 106, 260, 317
WINCHINGER, Rosina, 15; Yost, 15
WINDARD, John F., 97
WINTER, James, 129; John, 212, 314; Peter, 320
WINTEROTH, Adam, 16
WINTERS, James, 143
WIPLER, Peter, 346
WIREMAN, Abraham, 214; Barbara, 24; Catharine, 24, 156; Charles, 156; Henry, 24; Hester, 24; Jacob, 156; John, 24, 214, 345; Margaret, 24; Marharet, 24; Martin, 24, 345; Mary, 24; Michael, 24; Sarah, 156; Sophia, 24, 214
WIRL, Barbara, 253; William, 253
WIRSHING, Joseph, 351; Phelix, 351
WIRTZ, Christian, 340
WISE, Elizabeth, 56; John, 332; Peter, 332
WISEMER, Jacob, 320
WISHLER, Jacob, 228
WISLER, Casper, 320; Catharine, 242; David, 302; Elizabeth, 171; Esther, 171; Henry, 339; Isaac, 345, 354; Jacob, 171; John, 171, 242, 345, 354; John Wolf, 320; Mary, 292; Samuel, 357; Wolf, 213
WISMER, Barbara, 284; Esther, 284; Henry, 195, 312; Jacob, 5, 38, 143, 284, 335; Joseph, 284; Mary, 313
WISSEL, George, 15; Mary, 15
WISSEMER, Jacob, 60
WISSLER, Peter, 313
WISTLER, Jacob, 23
WITCOMB, Ann, 208; John, 208; Joseph, 208
WITHE, Matthias, 332
WITMAN, Barbara, 80; Elizabeth, 80; Jacob, 80; John, 31, 80; Maria, 31; Michael, 80; Mira, 31; Polly, 80; Samuel, 80, 335; Susanna, 80; Susannah, 80
WITZ, Charles, 99; Jacob, 22, 99, 125; Mary, 99, 125
WOELPER, Barbara, 105; Hannah, 104, 320; Margaret, 105; Peter, 105
WOHLSATH, W., 102

WOLF, Barbara, 98; Benjamin, 98; Bottis, 51; Casper, 50; Catharine, 98; Christiana, 98; Cornelius, 76; Frederick, 98; George, 98; John, 98; Magdalena, 51; Mary, 98
WOLFARTH, Abraham, 84; Anna Mary, 84; Catharine, 84; Christiana, 84; John, 84; Margareth, 84; Nicholas, 84
WOLFINGER, Ann, 123; Catharine, 123; Christiana, 74; Eve Maria, 123; Jacob, 74, 123; John, 74; Maria, 123; Mary, 74; Rebecca, 123
WOLLARD, Martha, 114, 116
WOLMER, D., 312; Jacob, 86, 320
WOMBOLT, Casper, 13; Elisabeth, 14; Frederick, 14; Hannah, 13, 14; Magdalena, 14; Margaret, 13
WOOD, Allen, 226; Ann, 284; Catharine, 226; E., 311; Elizabeth, 241; Ezekiel, 277, 278; Isaac, 109; James, 226, 324; John, 109, 284, 309; Jonathan, 284; Joseph, 262, 263, 284, 320; Joshua, 161; Josiah, 109, 110, 194, 214, 231; Margaret, 109; Mary, 226, 284; Phebe, 158; Rachel, 39; Rebecca, 60; Robert, 241; Samuel, 342; Sarah, 109, 226, 284; Sephimers, 102; Septimus, 201; Sophia, 277, 342; Thomas, 61, 226
WOOLLIN, Joseph, 148; Rebecca, 148
WOOLMAN, David, 361; George, 361; John, 334; Lewis, 334
WOOLSEY, Ann, 140; Ephraim, 140
WORKEISER, Adam, 185; Rosannah, 185
WORNER, Frederick, 248; Sarah, 248
WORREL, Alice, 88, 175; Demas, 88; Elizabeth, 88; Isaac, 88; Jane, 88; Martha, 88; Tacy, 88
WORSHELER, Henry, 16
WORTH, Elizabeth, 253; James, 235; Mary Elizabeth, 235; Susanna, 253
WORTHINGTON, John, 217
WORTHMAN, Adam, 281, 306
WORTON, Thomas, 122
WRAY, James, 98
WRIGHT, Jacob, 56, 57, 291; Jane, 57; Jesse, 272; John, 57, 69, 160, 239; Joseph, 14, 57; Mary, 57; Samuel, 57; Stephen John, 14; Tacey, 321; William, 15, 117, 321
WUNDERLICH, Eva Margaret, 208; George, 208; Jacob, 208
WYANT, Barbara, 34; Christiana, 22; Jacob, 22, 320; Mgdalena, 22; Philippina, 22; Sophia, 22; Wendel, 22, 360; Wyndle, 325; Yost, 22, 34
WYCE, Edith, 229; Jacob, 229
WYLAND, Charlotte, 189
WYNKOOF, Ann, 298; Belinda, 206; Cornelius, 206; Cuffee, 206; Garrett, 298; Hannah, 206; Mary, 206; Philip, 348; Thomas, 206
WYNKOOP, Abraham, 226; Catharine, 226; Cornelius, 226; Isaac, 226; Philip, 44; Rebecca, 226

-Y-

YAGER, Bernhard, 86
YAHN, Philip, 338
YARNALL, Benjamin, 26; Elizabeth, 63
YEAGER, Bernard, 127
YEAKEL, Casper, 182
YEAKLE, Abraham, 33, 321, 342, 345; Baltzer, 33, 321; Catharine, 33; Christain, 283; Christopher, 207; Hester, 33; Jacob, 47, 72, 150, 228; Jeremiah, 324; Rosina, 33; Sarah, 345; Susanna, 146
YEALOUS, Henry, 127; Margaret, 127
YEARNHART, Ann, 46; Elizabeth, 46; Henry, 46; Jacob, 46; Jesse, 46
YEGAR, Christian, 99; Elizabeth, 99
YELTER, Nancy, 203
YERBER, Catharine, 196; Jacob, 196
YERGER, Abraham, 101, 104, 260; Andrew, 260; Barbara, 89; Catharine, 89, 234, 260; Christian, 350; Conrad, 260; Daniel, 260; David, 89, 260; Dewalt, 130; Dewart, 49; Elizabeth, 89, 234; George, 89, 265; Henry, 338; John, 260; Joseph, 260; Mack, 351; Magdalena, 234; Margaret, 234, 260; Maria Margaret, 130; Matthias, 260; Peter, 89; Philipina, 260; Samuel, 89, 234, 260; Solomon, 89; Tobias, 89, 223, 234, 322

YERKER, Harmon, 201; Silas, 201
YERKERS, Elizabeth, 208;
  Joseph, 208; Rachel, 208;
  Rebecca, 208; Samuel, 208;
  Stephen, 208
YERKES, Abraham, 331; Anthony,
  43, 44, 179, 206, 278, 307,
  334; Arthur, 296; Benjamin,
  79, 151, 213, 278; Catharine,
  247; Conrad, 247; Daniel, 79,
  88, 201; David, 44, 296;
  Deborah, 79, 275; Edward,
  357; Elias, 44, 79, 296, 321;
  Elizabeth, 3, 79, 247, 291,
  357; Esther, 79, 88;
  Franklin, 290; George, 79,
  291; Hannah, 79, 213; Harman,
  56, 89, 173, 333; Herman, 44,
  323, 326; Hester, 291; Isaac,
  296, 321; Jacob, 44, 206,
  271; James, 213; John, 291,
  333; Joseph, 44, 179, 272,
  334, 357; Joshua, 60; Josiah,
  60; Margaret, 56, 60, 213,
  247, 291; Mary, 60, 181, 247,
  291, 296, 297, 334;
  Nathaniel, 60; Obadiah, 44;
  Rebecca, 296; Rebekah, 3;
  Robert, 334; Sarah, 272, 296;
  Silas, 79, 150, 162, 206,
  210, 291; Susanna, 179, 291,
  296; Titus, 143, 181, 228,
  297, 348; William, 275
YETTER, Amy, 101; Ann, 101,
  353; Baltzer, 10; Catharine,
  101; John, 35, 101, 357;
  Joseph, 357; Lewis, 353;
  Ludwick, 101, 102; Mary, 101;
  Samuel, 101
YEXELEY, Ann, 339
YEXLEY, Ann, 188
YOANY, Thomas, 249
YOCUM, Aloses, 255; Barbara,
  343; Hannah, 154; Israel,
  347; Jacob, 183; James, 293;
  John, 263, 343; Jonathan,
  347; Martha, 21, 48; Mary,
  293; Moses, 21; Reuben, 48;
  Samuel, 48; Thomas, 21;
  William, 21, 154, 290, 347
YODER, Anna, 132; Melchior, 132
YOHN, George, 72; Henry, 160
YORGEY, Matthias, 288
YORGY, Ann, 313; Catharine,
  313; Henry, 313; John, 313;
  Mary, 313; Mathias, 313;
  Peter, 313
YOST, Abraham, 35, 177, 214,
  347; Adam, 144; Andrew, 105;
  177; Danel, 140; Daniel, 17,
  31, 35, 105, 137, 147, 153,
  214; Harmon, 151; Isaac, 214;
  Jacob, 31, 177, 214, 275,
  347, 348; John, 151, 256,
  274, 275, 357; Mary, 214,
  274, 275; Peter, 123, 214,
  220, 348, 357; Philip, 123,
  148, 151, 275, 344; Rchel,
  274; Sarah, 214, 275;
  Veronica, 151
YOUNG, Abraham, 139; Andrew, 1,
  139, 140, 148, 202; Anna,
  139; Anna Catherine, 1;
  Ariadna, 144; Aridena, 144;
  Barbara, 139; Catharine, 45,
  148; Christina, 148;
  Elizabeth, 139, 144;
  Gertraude, 139; Henry, 139,
  145, 148; Jacob, 45; John,
  116, 120, 144, 148, 166, 169,
  209, 351; Lewellyn, 328;
  Llewelwyn, 324; Llewelyn,
  143, 144; Llwellyn, 183;
  Magdalena, 45; Magdalena,
  148; Margaret, 139, 148, 169;
  Maria, 139; Maria Adelhert,
  45; Martha, 144; Martin, 45;
  Mary, 19; Michael, 45, 139,
  140, 145; Nicholas, 8, 145;
  Peter, 45; Rebecca, 91;
  Rosanna, 148; Rowland, 34,
  148; Sophia, 45; Susanna,
  139, 140; William, 19

-Z-

ZAN, John, 294
ZARLEY, David, 130, 360
ZEARFOS, Benjamin, 332;
  Frederick, 332
ZEBER, Jacob, 327
ZEHMAN, Jacob, 258
ZEIBER, Philip, 299
ZEIGLER, Abraham, 88, 210, 300,
  358; Andrew, 279, 300, 346,
  347; Bara, 339; Barbara, 194;
  Catharine, 300; Dillman, 271,
  300; Ditman, 65; Elizabeth,
  181, 300; Garret, 302, 345;
  Garrett, 300; George, 273;
  Gerret, 88; Henry, 215;
  Isaac, 300; Jacob, 71, 300;
  John, 181; Magdalena, 88;
  Mark, 191; Michael, 88, 179,
  194, 300, 347; Rebecca, 205;
  Sabella, 191; Samuel, 294;
  Susanna, 300; Susannah, 58
ZELL, Amy, 95; Anthony, 337,
  357; David, 95; Hannah, 337;
  Jacob, 95, 337; John, 95
ZELLER, George, 35; Mary, 35
ZENTMAN, George, 245

ZEPP, Anna Maria, 90; Hannes, 37; Jacob, 90; Philip, 37, 269, 286, 347, 348
ZERLEY, David, 132; Mary, 32, 33
ZERLY, David, 86; Elizabeth, 86; John, 86; Ludowick, 86
ZERN, Frederick, 321; Jacob, 321; John, 321
ZICHLER, Jacob, 356; Mordecai, 356
ZIEBER, John, 100
ZIEGLER, Abraham, 92, 337, 355; Andrew, 92, 127, 146, 321, 326; Barbara, 146; Catharine, 104, 127, 146; Christopher, 30, 146; Deborah, 146; Dillman, 92, 321; Elizabeth, 92, 104, 127, 146; Garret, 104; George, 127; Hannah, 146; Henry, 127; Hester, 104; Jacob, 104, 114, 321; John, 127, 146; Mark, 127; Michael, 43, 92, 104, 146; Philip, 127; Susanna, 146
ZIGLER, Christopher, 7; Dillman, 321
ZIGTER, George, 346
ZILKISON, Andrew, 340
ZILLING, George, 336; Hannah, 336
ZIMERMAN, Conrad, 10
ZIMMERMAN, Abraham, 186, 354; Arnold, 83, 135, 270, 355, 358, 360; C., 319; Catharine, 83, 347; Chistopher, 358; Christian, 355; Christopher, 58, 62, 71, 74, 83, 135, 149, 226, 253; Conrad, 321; David, 341; Elizabeth, 270; George, 351, 359; Hannah, 83; Isaac, 239, 341, 358; Jacob, 83, 119, 126, 135, 250, 270, 321, 347, 354; John, 83, 270, 358; Magdalena, 126, 270; Mary, 83, 135, 270; Matthias, 83; Nathan, 347; Rachel, 135; Susanna, 83; Susannah, 83; William, 135, 218, 312, 355, 358, 360
ZIMMERS, Lydia, 190; Samuel, 190
ZINCH, Cathrine, 283
ZINGLA, Philip, 45
ZINSENDENFER, Martin, 321
ZIRGLER, Philip, 175
ZOLIG, Frederick, 144
ZOLLER, Catharine, 123, 203, 305; Christian, 203; Elizabeth, 203, 305; Francis, 203, 305; George, 203, 305; Jacob, 203, 206, 305; John, 287; Margaret, 203, 305; Maria, 203, 305; Mary, 203; Molly, 305; Sophia, 203, 305
ZORN, George, 281
ZUBER, Henry, 310
ZUCHT, Thomas, 285

www.ingramcontent.com/pod-product-compliance
Lightning Source LLC
Chambersburg PA
CBHW050830230426
43667CB00012B/1941